CAMBRIDGE GREEK AND LATIN CLASSICS

GENERAL EDITORS

P. E. EASTERLING
Regius Professor Emeritus of Greek, University of Cambridge

PHILIP HARDIE
Senior Research Fellow, Trinity College, and Honorary Professor of Latin, University of Cambridge

NEIL HOPKINSON
Fellow, Trinity College, University of Cambridge

RICHARD HUNTER
Regius Professor of Greek, University of Cambridge

E. J. KENNEY
Kennedy Professor Emeritus of Latin, University of Cambridge

S. P. OAKLEY
Kennedy Professor of Latin, University of Cambridge

EURIPIDES

HECUBA

EDITED BY

LUIGI BATTEZZATO

*Professor of Greek Literature, Dipartimento di Studi Umanistici,
Università del Piemonte Orientale, Vercelli, Italy*

CAMBRIDGE
UNIVERSITY PRESS

CAMBRIDGE
UNIVERSITY PRESS

University Printing House, Cambridge CB2 8BS, United Kingdom

One Liberty Plaza, 20th Floor, New York, NY 10006, USA

477 Williamstown Road, Port Melbourne, VIC 3207, Australia

314–321, 3rd Floor, Plot 3, Splendor Forum, Jasola District Centre, New Delhi – 110025, India

79 Anson Road, #06–04/06, Singapore 079906

Cambridge University Press is part of the University of Cambridge.

It furthers the University's mission by disseminating knowledge in the pursuit of education, learning, and research at the highest international levels of excellence.

www.cambridge.org
Information on this title: www.cambridge.org/9780521191258
DOI: 10.1017/9780511978746

© Cambridge University Press 2018

This publication is in copyright. Subject to statutory exception and to the provisions of relevant collective licensing agreements, no reproduction of any part may take place without the written permission of Cambridge University Press.

First published 2018

Printed in the United Kingdom by Clays, St Ives plc

A catalogue record for this publication is available from the British Library.

Library of Congress Cataloging-in-Publication Data
NAMES: Euripides, author. | Battezzato, Luigi, editor.
TITLE: Hecuba / Euripides ; edited by Luigi Battezzato.
OTHER TITLES: Cambridge Greek and Latin classics.
DESCRIPTION: Cambridge : Cambridge University Press, 2018. | Series: Cambridge Greek and Latin classics
IDENTIFIERS: LCCN 2017040745 | ISBN 9780521191258
SUBJECTS: LCSH: Euripides. Hecuba.
CLASSIFICATION: LCC PA3973.H3 B38 2018 | DDC 882/.01–dc23
LC record available at https://lccn.loc.gov/2017040745

ISBN 978-0-521-19125-8 Hardback
ISBN 978-0-521-13864-2 Paperback

Cambridge University Press has no responsibility for the persistence or accuracy of URLs for external or third-party internet websites referred to in this publication and does not guarantee that any content on such websites is, or will remain, accurate or appropriate.

CONTENTS

Acknowledgements	*page* vi
Abbreviations	vii
Key to Metrical Symbols	viii

Introduction	1
1 *Euripides: Life and Works*	1
2 *The Date of* Hecuba	2
3 *Production*	4
3.1 Casting the Play	4
3.2 Stage Movements	5
4 *Myth*	8
5 *Characters and Reciprocity:* charis, xenia, philia	9
6 *Hecuba's Revenge*	14
7 *Reception*	18
8 *Transmission of the Text*	22
9 *Presentation of Textual Evidence in This Edition*	25
10 *Metre and Language*	25

Symbols, Sigla and Abbreviations Used in the Edition of the Greek Text	29
ΕΥΡΙΠΙΔΟΥ ΕΚΑΒΗ	31
Commentary	71
Works cited	257
Subject Index	279
Greek Index	286

ACKNOWLEDGEMENTS

Many people have assisted me during this project. Donald J. Mastronarde commented on several versions of the commentary, and also read the whole final manuscript. Benjamin Acosta-Hughes, Ettore Cingano, Gian Biagio Conte, Martin Cropp, Giambattista D'Alessio, Vincenzo Di Benedetto, Franco Ferrari, Barbara Graziosi, Chiara Martinelli, Lucia Prauscello, Mario Telò and Vittorio Citti made very useful comments and suggestions on several sections and interpretive problems. Richard Hunter and Pat Easterling painstakingly revised many drafts of the present book; their care is only matched by their ability to find the *mot juste* and to spot what students and scholars need (and do not need). The Università del Piemonte Orientale supported this research, providing a very lively and stimulating academic environment; I am grateful in particular to my head of department, Raffaella Tabacco, and to my colleagues Gabriella Vanotti and Maria Napoli for their support. I also thank my students at the Scuola Normale Superiore, Pisa for discussing a draft of the commentary in a seminar, and Glenn W. Most for inviting me and for commenting on the main issues of the interpretation of the play. Christophe Cusset invited me to give a series of seminars at the Lyon ENS, which enabled me to make great progress in writing the introduction. In the past, the Arnaldo Momigliano Studentship in Arts at University College London provided support at a crucial stage. I must thank Anna Laura and Giulio Lepschy for their generosity in establishing this scholarship. For help at the copy-editing and proof-checking stage, I thank Benjamin Acosta-Hughes, Marco Catrambone, Stefano Fanucchi, Federico Favi, Ruggiero Lionetti, Martina Loberti, Lucia Mariani, Laura Marshall, Leyla Ozbek and Nadia Rosso. Many thanks are due to my copy-editor, Iveta Adams. I alone am responsible for any remaining errors.

My father Leopoldo turned 100 on 12 November 2016, and it was a special pleasure for me to celebrate this with my wife Paola, our son Marcello, my mother Rosa, my sister Laura and her husband Massimo. Sadly, my father passed away before the publication of this work. My family has been a source of strength and joy throughout this very long process. I dedicate this book to my son Marcello.

ABBREVIATIONS

D–K	*Die Fragmente der Vorsokratiker*, ed. H. Diels and W. Kranz, 10th edn (Berlin 1961)
Denniston	J. D. Denniston, *The Greek particles*, 2nd edn (Oxford 1954)
FGrHist	*Die Fragmente der griechischen Historiker*, ed. F. Jacoby (Berlin, then Leiden 1923–58)
K–A	*Poetae comici Graeci*, ed. R. Kassel and C. Austin (Berlin 1983–2001)
K–B	R. Kühner, *Ausführliche Grammatik der griechischen Sprache*, part I: *Elementar- und Formenlehre*, 3rd edn, rev. F. Blass (Hannover 1890–2) (references are to volume and page number)
K–G	R. Kühner, *Ausführliche Grammatik der griechischen Sprache*, part II: *Satzlehre*, 3rd edn, rev. B. Gerth (Hannover 1898–1904) (references are to volume and page number)
LfgrE	*Lexikon des frühgriechischen Epos* (Göttingen 1955–2010)
LIMC	*Lexicon iconographicum mythologiae classicae* (Zurich and Munich 1981–2009)
LSJ	H. G. Liddell and R. Scott, *Greek–English lexicon*, rev. H. S. Jones (Oxford 1925–40) with *Revised supplement*, ed. P. G. W. Glare and A. A. Thompson (Oxford 1996)
OCD	*The Oxford classical dictionary*, ed. S. Hornblower, A. Spawforth and E. Eidinow, 4th edn (Oxford 2012)
PMG	*Poetae melici Graeci*, ed. D. L. Page (Oxford 1962)
Smyth	H. W. Smyth, *Greek Grammar*, rev. G. M. Messing (Cambridge, Mass. 1956) (references are to numbered paragraphs)
TrGF	*Tragicorum Graecorum fragmenta*, ed. B. Snell, R. Kannicht and S. Radt (Göttingen 1971–2004)
West	*Iambi et elegi Graeci ante Alexandrum cantati*, ed. M. L. West (Oxford, vol. I 1971, 1989^2, vol. II 1972, 1992^2)

Abbreviations of ancient authors and works follow *OCD* and LSJ. The siglum 'Eur.' has been left out, except where the omission could create ambiguity. Classics journals are cited according to the abbreviations of *L'Année philologique* (see http://www.annee-philologique.com/files/sigles_fr.pdf, consulted November 2016).

KEY TO METRICAL SYMBOLS

⌣	short syllable
–	long syllable
⌣̱	short syllable in the strophe, matched by a long syllable in the antistrophe
⌐	long syllable in the strophe, matched by a short syllable in the antistrophe
⌢	syllable preceding metrical pause; its length does not matter (*indifferens*)
⌣⌣̱	a long syllable or two short ones
⌣⌣̄	two short syllables or a long one
×	anceps: an element that can be implemented by either a short or a long syllable
⚪⚪	corresponds to – –, – ⌣ –, ⌣ ⌣ ⌣ (occasionally) or – ⌣ ⌣ (even more rarely) (cf. Itsumi 1982 and 1984)
∧	before a metrical unit or colon indicates that the unit is acephalous, i.e. is one syllable shorter at the beginning (e.g. ia = × – ⌣ –, ∧ia = – ⌣ –)
∧	after a metrical unit or colon indicates that the unit is catalectic, i.e. the last two elements of the metrical unit are substituted by a long element (cf. Parker 1976)
∧∧	after a metrical unit or colon indicates that the last three elements of the metrical unit are substituted by a long element: e.g. 4da∧∧ = 3da followed by a long element
:	a place in the line where word-end occurs frequently
⁞	a place in the line where word-end occurs very frequently
‖	metrical pause: elision is impossible across ‖. It indicates the end of a metrical line.
‖^b	metrical pause detected by the presence of a *breuis in longo* (‖^{b1}: in the strophe; ‖^{b2}: in the antistrophe)
‖^h	metrical pause detected by the presence of hiatus (‖^{h1}: in the strophe; ‖^{h2}: in the antistrophe)
‖^c	metrical pause detected thanks to the knowledge of ancient Greek metrical practice
⦀	end of sung metrical structure, accompanied by metrical pause

Aeolic hexasyllable	× × – ⌣ ⌣ – (Lourenço 2011: 111)
an (anapaest)	⌣⌣̄ ⌣⌣̱ ⌣⌣̄ ⌣⌣̱
aristophanean	– ⌣ ⌣ – ⌣ – –
ba (baccheus)	⌣ – –
cho (choriamb)	– ⌣ ⌣ –

KEY TO METRICAL SYMBOLS

cr (cretic)	− ⏑ −
D (dactylic hemiepes)	− ⏑ ⏑ − ⏑ ⏑ −
da (dactyl)	− ⏑ ⏑
dodrans	− ⏑ ⏑ − ⏑ −
δ (dochmius or dochmiac)	× ⏕ ⏕ × ⏕
glyconic	○ ○ − ⏑ ⏑ − ⏑ −
hδ (hypodochmius)	⏕ ⏑ ⏕ ⏑ ⏕
hipponactean	○ ○ − ⏑ ⏑ − ⏑ − −
ia (iambus)	× − ⏑ −
ia trim (iambic trimeter)	‖ × − ⏑ − × − ⏑ − × − ⏑ ⌒ ‖
kδ (dochmius kaibelianus)	× − ⏑ − ⏑ −
paroemiac	⏓⏓ − ⏓⏓ − ⏑⏑ − ⌒ ‖ (or, occasionally, in sung contexts, ⏓⏓ − ⏓⏓ − ⏓⏓ − −)
penth (iambic penthemimer)	× − ⏑ − ×
pherecratean	○ ○ − ⏑ ⏑ − −
sp (spondee)	− −
telesillean (also called ^glyconic)	× − ⏑ ⏑ − ⏑ − (note that ⏑ ⏑ − ⏑ ⏑ − ⏑ − is a possible implementation of the pattern, which some scholars call T: cf. 635, 644, 653–4, 655, 905, 927, Parker 1997: 73, Lourenço 2011: 97–8)
tro (a trochaic metron)	− ⏑ − ×
wilamowitzian (often called 'choriambic dimeter')	○ ○ − × − ⏑ ⏑ − (cf. Itsumi 1982)

INTRODUCTION

1 EURIPIDES: LIFE AND WORKS

Euripides was born of Athenian parents around 480 BCE. According to the ancient sources, he wrote ninety-two plays, seventy-eight of which survived until the Hellenistic age.[1]

Scholars are sometimes able to establish the exact date when an extant or fragmentary play was first staged in Athens, on the basis of evidence ultimately deriving from epigraphic records made in Athens, which list all plays staged at the Dionysia festival.[2] In addition, in the case of Euripides, the iambic trimeter provides robust evidence for a relative dating of the plays, as the rate of resolutions increases regularly over the years.[3]

On these criteria, the main dates of Euripides' career can be reconstructed as follows:[4] 455 first tragic tetralogy presented at the Athenian Dionysia; 441 first victory at the tragic context at the Athenian Dionysia; 438 *Alcestis*; 431 *Medea*; 430–427 *Children of Heracles*; 428 (?) *Hippolytus*; 425–421 *Andromache*; 423–418 *Hecuba* (see however the discussion below); 424–420 *Suppliant Women*; 422–417 *Electra*; 421–416 *Heracles*; 415 *Trojan Women*; 418–413 *Ion*; 417–412 *Iphigenia among the Taurians*; 412 *Helen*; 414–408 *Phoenician Women*; 408 *Orestes*; 407–406 *Bacchae, Iphigenia at Aulis* (composition; 405–400: posthumous staging).[5] Euripides is also the author of the only complete extant satyr drama, *Cyclops*, of uncertain date.[6] He produced almost all his plays in Athens, but it is likely that at least some of them were first staged in festivals other than the Dionysia,[7] and

---

[1] Cf. Kannicht 2004: 45–7, 57–67, Collard and Cropp 2008a: xi–xxii, with bibliography. On the life of Euripides see Mastronarde 2002: 1–7, Scullion 2003: 391.

[2] Cf. Snell 1966, Sommerstein 2010b: 11–29.

[3] The list printed in the text gives the secure dates registered in Kannicht 2004: esp. 77–80; when we lack secure non-metrical evidence, the list gives the date ranges registered in Cropp and Fick 1985: 23 (column for the 10% Relative Likelihood Interval), rounded to the nearest whole number. Cf. also Cropp 2000: 61.

[4] For a survey of Euripides' plays, with discussions of dating, see Mastronarde 2010: 28–43. More detailed discussion can be found in the commentaries listed on pp. 257–8.

[5] The tragedy *Rhesus*, transmitted as part of the corpus of Euripides in ancient and medieval manuscripts, is now generally considered a fourth-century play, not by Euripides: Fantuzzi 2007: esp. 195, Liapis 2012: lxvii–lxxv, Fries 2014: 22–47.

[6] It is not clear how the criterion of the resolution rates can be applied to satyr drama, a genre which used iambic trimeters much more freely than tragedy. Seaford 1982 and Marshall 2001 favour 408 as a date for the play, but it can be earlier: Battezzato 1995: 134–5.

[7] Ael. *VH* 2.13 (= Kannicht 2004: 73 (T 47a)) attests that Euripides competed at a theatrical festival at the Piraeus with a new play.

outside Athens.[8] Some scholars have suggested that Euripides wrote *Bacchae* while in Macedonia,[9] or that he envisaged the possibility of performing (or reperforming) the play in Macedonia, after a first performance in Athens.[10]

2 THE DATE OF *HECUBA*

On the basis of metrical evidence, Cropp and Fick judge that *Hecuba* was probably composed between 423 and 419. They also note that the number of resolutions in this play may suggest a later date than was actually the case, because of 'an excessive incidence of proper-name resolutions': names such as Ἑκάβη, Ἀγαμέμνων, Πολύδωρος and Πολύμηστωρ occur very frequently in the play.[11]

Scholars have also tried to date the play by discovering allusions to historical events, but such arguments are very fragile. Matthiae, for example, suggested that *Hec.* 454–65 alludes to the reorganisation of the festival at Delos that took place in 426/425 (see Thuc. 3.104); if so, the play must be dated after 425.[12] The text however simply mentions the existence of festivals in Delos, and such festivals are attested from the Archaic age onwards.[13] Müller suggested that *Hec.* 650–6 'seems to refer to the misfortunes of the Spartans at Pylos in BC 425'.[14] Mentioning the suffering of the enemies is however a *topos*, often employed as a self-consolation in misery (*Il.* 24.736–9, Eur. *Andr.* 1028–46, *Tro.* 374–82); the audience may have interpreted this passage as an allusion to contemporary events, but Euripides was well capable of writing it before the events of 425 at Pylos.

The study of literary allusions in and to *Hecuba* does not change the date range established on the basis of metrical criteria. Ar. *Nub.* 1165–6 is a parody of *Hec.* 172–4;[15] it is also possible, but less certain, that Ar. *Nub.*

---

[8] Cf. Easterling 1994: 89, Taplin 1999: 44–8, W. Allan 2000: 159–60. For other possible productions of Euripides' plays outside Athens, in Euripides' lifetime or shortly afterwards, see Taplin 1992: 3 and 98–9, Dearden 1999, W. Allan 2001, Scullion 2003: 394.

[9] Dodds 1960: xlvii.

[10] Easterling 1994: 75–8, Csapo 1999: 414, Revermann 1999: 460–1, Scullion 2003: 393–4.

[11] Cropp and Fick 1985: 6–7, 23. The date is approximated to the nearest integer (their figures are 422.6–418.6).

[12] Matthiae 1821: 53 (note on line 451 in his edition = 455 in modern editions). Cf. the commentary *ad loc.*

[13] Wilamowitz-Moellendorff 1895: 1.140–2, Zuntz 1955: 58, Ley 1987, Matthiessen on 462–5.

[14] Müller 1840: 369 n. *.

[15] As noted in the scholia to *Clouds*: see Koster 1974: 165 on 1165–6. On philological problems in Ar. *Nub.* 1165–6 see Ley 1987, Dover 1968 and Sommerstein 1982 *ad loc.*

718–19 parodies *Hec.* 159–61. *Clouds* was put onstage in 423, but the text we have is a revised version, written before the ostracism of Hyperbolus (an event variously dated to the year 417, 416 or 415).[16] It is probable, but not certain, that the passages alluding to *Hecuba* belong to the original version. Other possible allusions to *Hecuba* in Aristophanes are less conclusive.[17] Scholars have also noted several points of contact with Euripides' own satyr drama *Cyclops*: both the Cyclops and Polymestor are blinded, and both appear onstage lamenting their fate.[18] Some scholars argue that *Cyclops* was presented in the same dramatic festival as *Hecuba*,[19] but this must remain an intriguing, yet ultimately unverifiable, hypothesis; it would be unusual for serious drama to allude to a comic or humorous treatment of similar narrative material.[20] *Cyclops* is in fact generally thought to be considerably later than *Hecuba*.[21]

Another possible intertextual relationship concerns Sophocles' play *Polyxena*. The subject matter of *Polyxena* clearly coincided with the events narrated in the first half of Euripides' *Hecuba*.[22] In Sophocles' play the ghost of Achilles appears onstage, probably at the beginning of the play, like Polydorus' ghost at the beginning of *Hecuba* (Soph. fr. 523: cf. 1–2 n.). In Sophocles, a messenger narrates Achilles' apparition to the Greek fleet departing towards Greece, as do the chorus in *Hecuba*.[23] Many scholars claim that Sophocles' play was the earlier one, since it presented the traditional version, involving Achilles' ghost, whereas Euripides innovated by inventing the ghost of Polydorus.[24] However, Sophocles' treatment is equally innovative, implying two apparitions of Achilles' ghost[25] (did Sophocles match Polydorus' and Achilles' apparitions in *Hecuba*? Or did Euripides split into two characters Achilles' double apparition in Sophocles' play?). Clearly there are intertextual links between the two plays; it is probable, but not certain, that Euripides' is the later. We have no information about the date of Sophocles' *Polyxena*.

In conclusion: the metrical evidence demonstrates that *Hecuba* was certainly written after *Hippolytus* (428),[26] and that the period 424–418 is

---

[16] Dover 1968: lxxx–xcviii and on line 551, Kopff 1990, Storey 1993, Hornblower 2008: 968–72 on Thuc. 8.73.3.
[17] Ar. *Eq.* 725–8 is similar to *Hec.* 172–4: Battezzato 2010: 115–17. Cf. also Sommerstein 1982 on *Clouds* 1154.
[18] Compare *Cycl.* 663~*Hec.* 1035, *Cycl.* 666–8~*Hec.* 1039–41; Ussher 1978: 196–7.
[19] Sutton 1980: 114–20. Zeitlin 1996: 197 considers the idea attractive.
[20] Marshall 2001: 230.   [21] Cf. above, n. 6.
[22] Mossman 1995: 42–7, and below, nn. 23–5.
[23] Cf. 109–10n., [Longinus], *Subl.* 15.7, Sommerstein, Fitzpatrick and Talboy 2006: 52–3 and 68–9.
[24] Sommerstein, Fitzpatrick and Talboy 2006: 65.
[25] Sommerstein, Fitzpatrick and Talboy 2006: 52–65.
[26] Cf. Cropp and Fick 2005.

a plausible range. *Hecuba* is, however, also probably earlier than the first version of Aristophanes' *Clouds* (423). Possible allusions to contemporary events would work well if the play was staged in 424 and it seems, therefore, that 424 BCE is a very likely, but not certain, date.

3 PRODUCTION

3.1 Casting the Play

The original production involved three actors, fifteen chorus members and a few mute extras. The first actor (protagonist) played Hecuba. The distribution of the other roles is less certain. The second and third actor played Polyxena and Odysseus in the first episode, and Polydorus and Talthybius might have been played by either the second or the third actor. The actor who played Agamemnon (onstage 726–904 and 1109–1295) could not play the Servant (onstage, with a speaking part, at 658–894) or Polymestor (onstage 953–1022 and 1055–1286). The Servant is present onstage, as a mute extra, at 609–18[27] and again at 953–81 (see 966n.). One can envisage the following distribution of parts:

1. Hecuba
2. Polydorus; Polyxena; Servant; Polymestor
3. Odysseus; Talthybius; Agamemnon

This arrangement has the advantage of requiring only one singing actor besides Hecuba for delivering the monodies of Polyxena and Polymestor.[28] It also ironically has one single actor playing Polydorus, Polyxena and Polydorus' killer Polymestor. The third actor would be playing all the Greek characters: Odysseus, Talthybius and Agamemnon.[29] Talthybius could be assigned to the second actor as well, but this combination of roles would be a very demanding one; the distribution of roles suggested above is more balanced.[30] These are however only tentative suggestions. Euripides may, for example, have had two very good actors, and decided to leave a very lightweight part for the third actor. We have no means of knowing what the usual practice was in

---

[27] She must have arrived onstage with Hecuba at 59.
[28] So Collard 1991: 37. The scholiast on *Pho.* 93 suggested a complex arrangement for *Phoenician Women*, so that a single actor would play the demanding monodies of Jocasta and Antigone. The fact that this 'principle of lyric assignment' (Marshall 2003: 264 for other references) was formulated already in antiquity suggests a possible echo of actual ancient (probably Hellenistic, possibly already Classical) theatrical practices.
[29] This is the 'principle of thematic significance': Marshall 1994: 53, Damen 1989.
[30] 'Principle of equal stage time': Marshall 1994: 53.

general, and other arrangements are also possible, apart from the two outlined above (e.g. the second actor playing Polyxena, Talthybius and Agamemnon; the third actor playing Odysseus, the Servant and Polymestor).[31]

3.2 Stage Movements

The play is set on the Thracian Chersonese (Gallipoli peninsula); the *skēnē* represents Agamemnon's tent, where Hecuba is also lodged (1–58n. 'Staging'). This is a reconstruction of the stage movements:[32]

1	Polydorus enters above the *skēnē* (1–58n. 'Staging').
53	Hecuba opens the *skēnē* door(53–4n.).
58	Polydorus leaves the space above the *skēnē* (52–3n.).
59	Hecuba arrives onstage, accompanied by mute female attendants (fellow Trojan slave women). The attendants include the (female) Servant who will have a speaking part at 658–894.
98	The chorus arrive onstage through *eisodos* A.
177	Polyxena enters onstage through the *skēnē* door(cf. 174).
218	Odysseus enters onstage through *eisodos* A, accompanied by male attendants (soldiers: cf. 405–8).
275	Hecuba touches Odysseus' knee, hand and chin in supplication (245n., 274–5n.). Physical contact is interrupted at 334 at the latest.
342–5	Odysseus hides his hand in his mantle, and turns his face away from Polyxena, avoiding supplication.
409–31	Polyxena and Hecuba embrace.
432	Polyxena asks Odysseus to veil her head (432n.).
437	Polyxena and Odysseus (with male attendants) leave through *eisodos* A.
438–40	Hecuba falls to the ground, veiling herself (438n., 486–7n.).
484	Talthybius enters onstage from *eisodos* A.
499–505	Hecuba stands up (499–500n., 501–2n.).
608–9	Talthybius leaves through *eisodos* A (609n.).
618	The Servant leaves through *eisodos* B, probably with female attendants.[33]

---

[31] Pickard-Cambridge 1968: 145 suggests the following distribution: '(a) Hecuba; (b) Polyxena, Agamemnon; (c) Odysseus, Serving woman, Polymestor: Talthybios and Polydoros could be (b) or (c)'. Di Benedetto and Medda 1997: 224–5 suggest the distribution: (a) Hecuba; (b) Polyxena, Talthybius, Servant, Polymestor; (c) Polydorus, Odysseus, Agamemnon.
[32] Cf. also Mossman 1995: 50–68, Matthiessen 2010: 10–13.
[33] Matthiessen 2010: 11 argues that 609 λαβοῦσα τεῦχος implies that the water jar is onstage at that moment. If so, it must have been onstage from the beginning of

628	Hecuba leaves the stage, exiting through the *skēnē* door, with her female attendants.
658	The Servant (now played by an actor) arrives onstage from *eisodos* B, probably with female attendants who help her carry the veiled body of Polydorus.
665	Hecuba arrives onstage through the *skēnē* door, with her female attendants.
679–80	The Servant unveils the body of Polydorus.
724–6	Agamemnon arrives onstage from *eisodos* A, accompanied by male attendants (soldiers).
752	Hecuba touches Agamemnon in supplication (736–51n.).
812	Agamemnon moves away from Hecuba (812n.).
894	The Servant leaves along *eisodos* A (cf. 889–90).
904	Agamemnon leaves along *eisodos* A, accompanied by his male attendants. The attendants carry away the body of Polydorus (904n.).[34]
953	Polymestor arrives onstage from *eisodos* A, accompanied by the Servant, male attendants (soldiers) and his two sons (played by mute extras). He carries two spears (cf. 1155–6).
981	Polymestor's attendants leave along *eisodos* A.[35] The Servant probably leaves at this point, too.
1019–22	Polymestor leaves the stage, exiting through the *skēnē* door, accompanied by his sons.
1022	Hecuba leaves the stage, exiting through the *skēnē* door, with her female attendants (1019–22n.).
1035, 1037, 1039–41	Polymestor cries from inside the *skēnē* (1035–41n.).
1044	Hecuba arrives onstage through the *skēnē* door.
1053–5	Polymestor enters onstage on all fours through the *skēnē* door. His mask has changed (he is blind). He does not have his spears with him any more (cf. 1155–6). The *skēnē* door is opened (1051–3n.). Hecuba's female attendants arrive onstage too, running away from Polymestor (Polymestor mentions them at 1063–5, 1069–74). Hecuba moves aside (1054–5n.).
1109	Agamemnon arrives onstage from *eisodos* A, accompanied by male attendants (soldiers).

the play, incongruously, or must have been brought onstage by the attendants at 58. However, the wording of Hecuba's order does not imply that the jar must be onstage: cf. *Med.* 393 ξίφος λαβοῦσα, *Hec.* 876–7 φάσγανον χερί | λαβοῦσα (in neither passage is the sword onstage); *Tro.* 92–3 (the thunderbolts are clearly not onstage), *Ion* 423 (no branches onstage: see Wilamowitz-Moellendorff 1926 *ad loc.*).

[34] Hecuba may go inside the tent at 904 and enter onstage again at 953 (so Matthiessen 2010: 10); the text does not prove nor disprove this possibility.

[35] Polymestor will call them for help, without success, at 1088–90.

1124–31	Polymestor attempts to lay hands on Hecuba; Agamemnon's attendants possibly restrain him (1127n.).
1282–5	Some of Agamemnon's attendants gag Polymestor (1283) and take him away, leaving the stage along *eisodos* A (1284–5n.).
1287	Hecuba leaves the stage along *eisodos* A; alternatively, but less likely, she leaves with the chorus, a few lines later.
1295	Agamemnon leaves the stage, accompanied by his attendants and the chorus, along *eisodos* A.

Eisodos A leads to the Greek camp, *eisodos* B to the seashore. *Eisodos* B is used only at 618 and 658, when the Servant goes to the seashore to fetch water and returns carrying the body of Polydorus. It would be possible to imagine that the Servant is using *eisodos* A, since the Greek camp must have been close to the seashore. However, it would be unusual if only one *eisodos* was used in the play. Moreover, when the Servant must go through the Greek camp to call Polymestor, Hecuba feels the need to ask Agamemnon to guarantee her safety (889–90). It is thus unlikely that the Servant left through *eisodos* A at 618 when no such guarantee was granted.

The focus on a single *eisodos* has thematic significance: it symbolises Greek domination. *Eisodos* A is the only possible space through which Trojan characters can communicate with the external world, and it is firmly under the control of the Greek army. The sacrifice of Polyxena, the revenge on Polymestor and the final departure to slavery all depend on the benevolence or malevolence of the Greeks. Even the burial of Hecuba's children is controlled by the Greeks, and requires an exit through *eisodos* A (894–7, 904n.). By allowing the Servant to cross the Greek encampment (889–90), Agamemnon becomes complicit with Hecuba. Agamemnon also allows Hecuba to exercise complete control over the tent and the *skēnē* space in the second half of the play. Hecuba makes the most of the *skēnē* space in order to accomplish her revenge scheme (see esp. 1013–55, 1145–75). However, the main significance of this *eisodos* is stressed again at the end of the play. Polymestor is dragged away through it towards a lonely place of punishment (1284–6), and the Trojan women exit this way at the end of the play, when they go into slavery (1293–5). Ironically, Agamemnon offers a completely plausible, but wrong, interpretation of his own departure through the same *eisodos*. He thinks that, by taking this route, he will find 'freedom from the toils' he 'endured' at Troy; in fact, he is alluding to the first line of Aeschylus' *Agamemnon*, the very play that dramatises his death (1292n.). As in *Medea*, the protagonist controls the *skēnē*, but is powerless on the *eisodoi*; unlike Medea, however, Hecuba will leave through the *eisodos*, and will turn into a non-human being only outside the theatrical space (1252–95n., 1270n., 1273n.).

4 MYTH

Several archaic and classical texts narrated the apparition of Achilles to the Greek army and the sacrifice of Polyxena. The apparition of Achilles featured in the *Nostoi* (37–9n.),[36] and in the *Sack of Ilium* (*Iliupersis*) the Greeks sacrifice Polyxena on the tomb of Achilles.[37] Ibycus (307 *PMG*) is the first known author who names Neoptolemus as the sacrificer (cf. 523). According to other archaic sources, Achilles fell in love with Polyxena when he saw her in the course of his ambush against her brother Troilus.[38] In many versions of the story, love is the reason behind Achilles' request for Polyxena as a sacrificial victim.[39] *Hecuba* probably echoes this tradition when bridal imagery is employed to describe the sacrifice (523n.). On the other hand, the play innovates on the traditional story when it places the tomb of Achilles not near Troy but in the Thracian Chersonese (8n., 37–9n.).

Polydorus is a traditional character, but Euripides profoundly modifies the Homeric version of his story. In Homer, Polydorus is Priam's youngest son (*Il.* 20.407–10), and he is killed in battle by Achilles in front of Hector (*Il.* 20.412–22); Priam had tried in vain to prevent him from fighting. In *Hecuba*, Polydorus is actually too young to fight (13–15), and Priam, in an attempt to protect him, sends him off to Thrace, where he is killed by Polymestor. The play probably echoes a somewhat similar story narrated in the *Iliad* about Iphidamas, son of Theano, who was reared in Thrace by his maternal grandfather Kisses.[40] Euripides also innovates in relation to Homer by making Hecuba the daughter of the quasi-homonymous Kisseus (3n.). This may suggest that the Theano and Iphidamas story was among the models for Euripides' Polydorus plot.[41]

Polymestor is probably a non-traditional character. His name means 'someone who contrives many skilful plots' (connected with μήδομαι

---

[36] Achilles appeared to the Greeks also before the fall of Troy, in the *Little Iliad*: West 2003: 122–3 and 2013: 190.
[37] West 2003: 146–7 = West 2013: 241–3 = Bernabé 1996: 89 lines 22–3. For discussions of these traditions cf. also Jouan 1966: 368–71, Debiasi 2004: 177. In another version, Polyxena dies as a consequence of the wounds inflicted on her by Odysseus and Diomedes during the sack of Troy, and is buried by Neoptolemus: some scholars attribute this to the archaic poem *Cypria* (Bernabé 1996: 62 (fr. 34)), others, less convincingly, to a prose history of Cyprus (West 2013: 55 n. 1).
[38] The story is attested in written sources, and in one fifth-century BCE vase: Touchefeu-Meynier 1994: 431–2, Schwarz 2001: 43–5, Tuna-Nörling 2001, Sommerstein, Fitzpatrick and Talboy 2006: 42–7, 50. The Troilus episode was narrated in the *Cypria*: West 2003: 78–9 and 102–3 = West 2013: 121–2 = Bernabé 1996: 63 fr. 41.
[39] It is probable, but not certain, that this version was known in archaic Greece. Cf. Fantuzzi 2012: esp. 7 and 14–18, Philostr. *Her.* 51.2–6, Fantham 1982: 238 on Sen. *Tro.* 195, and below, section 7, 'Reception', on Seneca.
[40] Iphidamas eventually died at Troy, killed by Agamemnon: *Il.* 11.223–43.
[41] Gregory 1995: 394–5.

'I contrive') and sounds like an ironic parody of the names Polydorus ('someone who has many gifts') and Polyxena ('someone who has many *xenoi*'): the names of these children characterise their father Priam as having many *xenia* relationships.[42] Polymestor's name signals his untrustworthiness and his betrayal of the rules of *xenia*. The absence of pre-Euripidean sources for the story about Polymestor, the lack of a genealogy for him in the play, and his transparent name, a name that fits so well the requirements of this play, increase the likelihood that this character was invented specifically for this play.[43] This means that the audience cannot predict the exact outcome of Hecuba's revenge against him (1021–2n.). Polymestor's children do not have a name, and are introduced into the narrative only to be killed.

The final episode mentioned in the play is Hecuba's transformation into a dog. All datable sources for this story are later than Euripides (1252–95n.), but it is probable that Euripides did not invent it. First of all, the toponym Cynossema, where Hecuba's tomb is said to be located, was certainly in use before Euripides' play; some interpreters suggest that Hecuba's transformation was a local myth.[44] Secondly, the transformation may also be explained by an association with the goddess Hecate, who was at times imagined in dog-shape; Hecuba's name is etymologically connected with that of Hecate (1265n., 1270n.), and it is therefore plausible that Hecuba's transformation is traditional, and connected with Hecate's cult. Finally, Euripides alludes to the metamorphosis in a cryptic and compressed way: why does Hecuba climb up the mast of the Greek ship? How can the transformation into a dog make this climb or the fall into the sea easier (1263n.)? Euripides usually takes great care to provide rational explanations for the events he narrates. These puzzling elements, introduced in passing, may have been intended as allusions to other, now lost, oral and/or literary sources.

5 CHARACTERS AND RECIPROCITY: *CHARIS, XENIA, PHILIA*

All the characters in the play are linked by a web of obligations and favours.[45] Odysseus is in debt to Hecuba, who saved his life (239–50);

---

[42] Cf. 4 and 7, Schlesier 1988: 113 n. 8 and Zeitlin 1996: 172. Similar epithets (such as 'she who has many sorrows') are used for Hecuba: cf. 492, 722–3n. and 1162n. *Xenoi* often named their children after the host or the *xenia* relationship in general: Herman 1987: 19–21 and 1990: 349–52 and 358. Another son of Priam was called Mestor (*Il.* 24.257). Polymestor combines the names of several children of Priam, and kills one of them.

[43] Hall 1989: 107–10, Mossman 1995: 30–1, with references.

[44] Mossman 1995: 35.

[45] Cf. Adkins 1966: 194 and 207, MacLachlan 1993: 157–60, Stanton 1995: 21, 25 and 30. For an earlier version of the arguments presented in this section cf. Battezzato 2003b.

Polymestor, out of friendship with Priam, agreed to take care of Polydorus, and to safeguard his gold (4–12); Agamemnon receives Cassandra's sexual 'favours', which, according to Hecuba, puts him under the obligation of helping Cassandra's family (824–35). The text describes these links of obligation using terminology that is standard in Greek culture: *xenia* 'guest-friendship', *philia* 'friendship' (but also 'family relationship') and *charis* 'favour'. Utilitarian or commercial calculation of advantages and disadvantages is ideally banned from *xenia* or *philia* relationships.[46] *Philia* is the more general term: it includes the relationship with family members, friends and *xenoi*.[47] *Xenia* indicates a 'ritualised friendship', typically created when someone hosts a stranger. *Xenoi* are a sub-class of *philoi* bound by ethical rules, guaranteed by Zeus, to exchange gifts and to provide help, shelter and protection, not only to the person involved but also to their family and offspring.[48] *Charis* 'favour' is a term used to describe the feeling of gratitude and the specific acts performed by people who help their *philoi*, in material and non-material ways.[49] These practices were typical of (but not exclusive to) the aristocratic elite. In *Hecuba*, the expectations of reciprocity conspicuously and repeatedly fail: the war destroys the links of aristocratic obligation, and forces Hecuba to forge new and unexpected ways to enact her shocking revenge, in response to Polymestor's perverted reciprocity.[50] Hecuba is at the centre of this web of relations with Odysseus, Polyxena, Agamemnon and Polymestor.

Hecuba expects Odysseus to conform to the aristocratic values of reciprocity. When she meets him, she asks him to return a 'favour' (*charis*): she spared his life when he secretly entered Troy. She also adds that Greek laws forbid the killing of slaves (291n.). He does not feel the need to explain why this law does not apply in the circumstances of war: he focuses instead on his willingness to repay Hecuba with exactly the same favour. He will spare *her* life, if she wants (301–2), but will not spare Polyxena's. Even if he does not formally renounce his *charis* relationship with Hecuba, his insistence on precise equality recalls the exactitude of commercial exchanges, rather than *charis* (299–331n.). The chorus had already characterised Odysseus as someone who 'likes to give *charis* to the *dēmos*' (131–3n.), and Odysseus explicitly claims that the bond he feels to the

---

[46] Cf. 1187–1237n., Blundell 1989: 30–1.
[47] Blundell 1989: 39–59, Konstan 1997: 1–92.
[48] On *xenia* cf. Herman 1987, Kurke 1991: 135–59, Mitchell 1997, Vlassopoulos 2013: 131–2, and below, 79on., [794n.], 1133n., 1187–1237n. On the names Polydorus and Polyxena cf. above, section 4, 'Myth'.
[49] Cf. 137n., 216–95n., 254n., 276n., 299–331n.
[50] On reciprocity in Greece cf. Seaford 1994, von Reden 1995, Gill, Postlethwaite and Seaford 1998, Mueller 2001. Coo 2006 discusses offstage characters.

5 CHARACTERS AND RECIPROCITY: *CHARIS, XENIA, PHILIA*

Greek community is stronger than any private bond he can have with foreign aristocrats. He claims that Greeks should first and foremost give honour (316, 327) and *charis* (320) to their fallen soldiers, treating them as *philoi* (311). However, he chooses to characterise his speech in an aristocratic way, stressing the need to honour the *esthloi* (307 and 327), i.e. those who are 'noble'/'valiant'. This is precisely the term Hecuba chooses in her speech in praise of aristocracy (596–7). It is difficult to disagree with Odysseus' exhortation to honour the fallen warriors, but he carefully avoids explaining why human sacrifice in particular is the best way to honour them. Odysseus stresses both aristocratic and civic values, in contrast to Hecuba, who focuses only on obligations which link aristocrats belonging to different communities.

Polyxena defiantly proclaims her allegiance to aristocratic values, to the point of self-annihilation. Other noble characters in Euripides willingly surrender their lives in order to protect their family and/or civic community (see in particular the maidens in *Heraclidae, Erechtheus* and *Iphigenia at Aulis,* and Menoeceus in *Phoenician Women*).[51] Being of noble origin is often a necessary pre-requisite for the victim.[52] In *Hecuba,* it is nobility itself that becomes the reason for choosing death: Polyxena cannot accept life in slavery (342–78n.). In particular she rejects the possibility that she will be transformed into an object of commercial exchange: she, who was 'worthy of princes' (366), will not tolerate to be sold 'for a piece of silver' (360) and given as wife to a servant 'bought some place or other' (365). The chorus explicitly approve her choice, saying that she proved 'worthy' of her noble origin (380–1). Her free choice alleviates the responsibility of the Greeks, and discharges Hecuba from any obligation or impulse to avenge her death: the mother feels sorrow, but the aristocratic spirit displayed by Polyxena takes away some of the pain (589–92). Like all aristocratic gifts, Polyxena's self-sacrifice is not without recompense: the Greek army admire her because she gave her life without asking for any compensation. They not only give her dresses and 'ornaments' (578) but honour her in a way that is specifically appropriate for an aristocratic male, namely the ceremony of *phyllobolia,* the throwing of leaves, as when honouring a winning athlete (573–4n.). Polyxena preserves her noble status by offering her most precious possession, her life: the Greek leaders and army recognise her status. Even the baring of her breast during the sacrifice is part of this mechanism: by offering her body to the view of all, Polyxena is able to persuade the crowd not to disfigure or (as Hecuba fears, 605–6n.) rape her dead body. Polyxena rightly points out to her

---

[51] Cf. 258n., 342–78n.
[52] Allan and Wilkins on *Hcld.* 408–9, Henrichs 1981: 217, *Pho.* 942–6, and below, 142n.

mother that any attempt to resist the violence of the Greeks simply invites more violence (405–8). She thus manages to preserve part of her status precisely by persuading the Greeks that she has willingly chosen the fate that they were trying to impose on her.

Hecuba tries to make a similar claim to Agamemnon: she argues that Cassandra's relationship with the Greek king is a freely chosen one, in which Cassandra willingly gives her sexual *charis* to her master.[53] The ambiguity of the term *charis*, 'favour', helps Hecuba build her case: since Agamemnon received a *charis*, he must give back another favour (830n. and 831–2n.).[54] Hecuba uses the argument from *charis* (824–35) after using an argument from justice (787–805), just as she did with Odysseus. However, in the case of Odysseus and Hecuba, a clearly established (even if, as it turned out, unsatisfactory) *charis* relationship already existed. Hecuba has no *charis* relationship with Agamemnon: she is just 'a slave and an enemy' for him (741n.). Her best way to obtain Agamemnon's help is to establish a new relationship based on supplication, a humiliation that she initially resists (736–51n.). Agamemnon, just like Odysseus, refuses to reciprocate the favour, adducing motives taken from 'democratic' ideology: leaders must prove that their private interests do not clash with the interest of the community (216–95n.). Hecuba comments that Agamemnon is a 'slave to the crowd' (864–9n.), giving voice to her aristocratic point of view and suggesting that 'democratic' attitudes prevent aristocrats from acting honourably.[55]

Polymestor's breach of the norms of *charis* is far worse than those of Odysseus and Agamemnon, but, at first, he acts as the good *xenos* and offers his help to the Trojan *philoi* in misfortune (985). His position is, however, ambiguous from the start: he claims that the Greeks, as well as Hecuba, are his *philoi* (983–4), and in fact Agamemnon had already testified to that (858), but he had also insisted that one cannot be friends with the Greeks and the Trojans at the same time (859–60n.).

Hecuba explains to Polymestor that it is she, in spite of her present misfortune, who is going to provide material wealth to him; Polymestor will in turn pass it on to Polydorus (986–1018). The reversal in Polymestor's fortune is sudden, and his language changes, too. He abandons the language of friendship and *xenia*, and uses the language of hunting and animal fighting instead: he presents himself as a wild animal that attacks the dogs who killed its offspring (1056–9, 1077, 1173), but also as a hunter who attacks the wild animals (1174), that is, the Trojan women ('wild beasts': see 1072n., 1125–6n.). When Agamemnon arrives

---

[53] Scodel 1998, comparing Tecmessa in Sophocles' *Ajax*.
[54] Cf. Soph. *Ai.* 522, Eur. *Hel.* 1234, Blundell 1989: 75, Battezzato 2014a.
[55] On the political themes of the play see Morwood 2014.

5 CHARACTERS AND RECIPROCITY: *CHARIS, XENIA, PHILIA*

onstage, Polymestor switches linguistic tone again: he attempts to reaffirm his *philia* relationship with Agamemnon from the start, calling him 'dearest' (φίλτατε) (1114). He also explains that he wants a 'just' verdict (1131) and that his murder of Polydorus was done as a 'favour' (*charis*: 1175) to Agamemnon and the Greeks: Polydorus will not survive so as to cause another Trojan war. Hecuba has an easy rhetorical victory against Polymestor, debunking his argument about *charis*: had he really cared about the Greeks, he would have killed Polydorus at the beginning of the Trojan war, not at the end (1211–16), and he would have given Polydorus' money to the Greeks, who need it, being far away from home, rather than keeping it for himself (1217–23).

Hecuba thus demonstrates that 'the barbarian race would never be friends (φίλον) with the Greeks, nor could it be' (1199–1201). She summarises here another major theme of the play, the relationship between Greeks and non-Greeks. Hecuba, herself a barbarian, apparently sides with Agamemnon, who used 'barbarian' disparagingly in reference to Polymestor (1129n.).[56] As in many other plays by Euripides, a barbarian accuses the Greeks of failing to act on the moral standards they claim to uphold. Hecuba is however careful to phrase this in a way that might elicit Agamemnon's approval. She summarises what she has learned about the relationships between Greeks and non-Greeks in the course of the play.[57] She had repeatedly appealed to the *philia* and *charis* of the Greeks, unsuccessfully. The cultural reality of the fifth century BCE was of course much more nuanced: many elite Greeks had links of 'ritual friendship' with barbarians,[58] even if cultural barriers and political divergences could lead to misunderstandings, occasionally with disastrous consequences.[59] The reality of the play, too, is more nuanced than Hecuba implies: with Agamemnon playing the role of impartial judge (1109–13n., 1130n.), she cannot draw attention to the fact that the support of the Greek king (see 870–4 and 864–75n.) was crucial for the success of her revenge plot. Her words also suggest that the aristocratic obligations of *xenia* and *philia* do apply within the barbarian world, which makes Polymestor's crime an even worse one.

Agamemnon and Odysseus present themselves as supporters of the cultural superiority of the Greeks. Agamemnon, using the language of fifth-century ethnography, reproaches Polymestor, saying that 'perhaps killing guests is a light matter among you (Thracians)' (1247n.), whereas Odysseus accuses the barbarians of being 'incapable of treating your *philoi*

---

[56] Cf. also Barker 2009: 347–50. [57] Hall 1989: 161 and 195.
[58] Cf. above, at the beginning of this section, and 7n.
[59] Compare for instance the cases of Alcibiades (Xen. *Hell.* 1.1.9 and 1.3.12, Plut. *Alc.* 24–8 and 39.1, Mitchell 1997: 116–18 and 132–3) and Iphicrates (Dem. 23.129–32, Mitchell 1997: 139–42).

as *philoi*, of robbing the fallen soldiers of the honour due to them, with the result that 'Greece flourishes, and you get the results that correspond to your <bad> choices' (328–31n.). Both Agamemnon and Odysseus seem to know the Herodotean and Pindaric dictum that customs vary from land to land,[60] but they reject cultural relativism and insist that Greek values and customs are clearly superior. Odysseus and Agamemnon specifically stress that barbarian customs involve the breach of duties connected with *philia* and *xenia* relationships. This is particularly ironic since Odysseus and Agamemnon themselves breached their duties of reciprocity (*charis*) and *philia* to Hecuba when they rejected their obligations towards her.

6 HECUBA'S REVENGE

Polymestor's crime is horrible, but this does not necessarily justify Hecuba's own horrible revenge. In the Renaissance several critics expressed approval for her course of action.[61] In the seventeenth century, Vossius even considered Polymestor's punishment a 'symbolic image of divine vengeance'.[62] Divine approval for Hecuba's revenge is never explicit in the play, but the gods of Hades do allow Polydorus to appear to his mother, which sets in motion the revenge plot (47–50n.). Moreover, the lack of wind prevents the Greeks from departing from Thrace until the revenge is accomplished (900, 901, 1287–90n., 1289–90): the audience may suppose that this was ordained by the gods, who indirectly approved of the revenge (even if not necessarily of the specific method chosen by Hecuba).

Assessing the morality of Hecuba's revenge is bound to be influenced by one's views about justice and punishment, and by historic circumstances. Approval for Hecuba's revenge started to fade after the eighteenth-century Enlightenment, when many intellectuals advanced theories of punishment that disapproved of cruel punishments. Writing in 1831, Hermann admitted that Hecuba had a right to punish Polymestor, but stressed that killing innocent children and blinding the culprit were 'horrible crimes', appropriate for a 'wild beast'.[63] This trend continued in the twentieth century, when Gilbert Murray claimed that at the end of the play Hecuba was transformed into 'a kind of devil' and 'a kind of Hell-hound'.[64] Some scholars argued that Hecuba underwent a process of moral degradation during the play, from suffering woman to revengeful

---

[60] Cf. 798–805n., Hdt. 3.38, Pind. fr. 169a.1.   [61] Heath 1987a: 47.
[62] *Figura est vindictae divinae*. Vossius 1647: 51.   [63] Hermann 1831: xvii.
[64] Murray 1913: 89 and 90. Segal 1993: 179 speaks of 'Hecuba's almost demonic skill and resourcefulness in gaining revenge'. Heath 1987a: 62–4 lists many other similar judgements.

animal.[65] In the second part of the twentieth century others returned to interpretations more favourable to Hecuba, arguing that, from the point of view of the moral standards of fifth-century BCE Greece, her revenge was appropriate or justifiable.[66] In recent years, however, several scholars have stressed how Greek literary texts, from Homer to tragedy, problematise retaliatory violence.[67]

Modern scholars emphasise different aspects of ancient theories of punishment, which were in fact much debated in classical Athens.[68] Several ancient voices argued that milder punishments would create greater social benefits. In reconstructing the debate of 427 BCE about the fate of the defeated rebel city of Mytilene, Thucydides has one speaker, Diodotus, say that in earlier times punishments were much milder, and gradually became harsher and harsher. Diodotus argues that 'punishing in a moderate way' (μετρίως κολάζοντες: Thuc. 3.46.4) would be more politically expedient. Similarly, in Eur. *Or.* 512–17, Tyndareus praises the wisdom of the ancients, who punished the homicide with exile, not capital punishment.[69] Protagoras, in the Platonic dialogue that bears his name, argued that

> no one punishes a wrong-doer from the mere contemplation or on account of his wrong-doing, unless one takes unreasoning vengeance like a wild beast. But he who undertakes to punish with reason does not avenge himself for the past offence, since he cannot make what was done as though it had not come to pass; he looks rather to the future, and aims at preventing that particular person and others who see him punished from doing wrong again. (Pl. *Prt.* 324a6–b4, trans. Lamb 1967)

Hecuba's revenge clearly exceeds the limits suggested by Diodotus, Tyndareus and Protagoras. Some modern critics have however argued that killing the children of an enemy was not seen as morally problematic by fifth-century Athenians. It is true that, in tragedy, children are often killed from prudential motives, 'to avoid subsequent vengeance ... or to inflict greater sufferings by this means upon the primary object of

---

[65] Cf. the list in Heath 1987a: 63 and n. 122; see also Nussbaum 1986: 417, Gall 1997, Meltzer 2006: 144–5.
[66] See Adkins 1966: 205, Meridor 1978, Heath 1987a: 65, Kovacs 1987: 78–114, Mossman 1995: 177–201, Burnett 1998: 166–76, Gregory 1999: xxii–xxv, Matthiessen 2010: 24–5, 30–2.
[67] Cf. W. Allan 2013. See esp. Herman 2006: 184–215 and E. M. Harris 2013: 60–98 (arguing against the view, advanced by D. J. Cohen 1995 and others, that Athenians condoned revenge). On violence in Greek tragedy in general cf. Seidensticker and Vöhler 2006, Sommerstein 2010b: 30–46.
[68] See Allen 2000, D. J. Cohen 2005, and the previous note.
[69] Tyndareus alludes to the customs described in Homer: Willink *ad loc.*

vengeance'.⁷⁰ It is however worth noting that such motives are adduced by loathsome tyrants (Eurystheus in *Heraclidae*, Lycus in *Heracles*) or hateful characters whose cruelty and disrespect for the norms of reasonable human conduct are clearly stressed in the text (Menelaus in *Andromache*, Odysseus in *Trojan Women*).⁷¹ In *Hecuba* Polymestor argues that he killed Polydorus for prudential motives, for fear that the son of Priam, on reaching adulthood, would cause a new Trojan war (1136–44: see esp. 1136–7n.). The argument, as in the other examples from Euripides' plays, casts a negative light on the person who voices it, and is in any case rejected as invalid in the present instance by the judge of the 'trial', Agamemnon (1243–5; see also 1240–51n.).

If killing innocent children in order to avoid future harm for oneself is depicted as a morally wrong action in tragic texts, it is even more questionable to kill them when no danger to oneself is present, as in the case of Hecuba and Medea. In order to explain how the murder of the children can be considered acceptable, several interpreters refer to a couple of episodes of cruel revenge narrated in Herodotus. Hermotimos was castrated by Panionios, who sold him as a eunuch; Hermotimos was able to revenge himself on Panionios, forcing him to castrate his own children and, in turn, his children to castrate him (Hdt. 8.104–6). Hermotimos claims that his revenge was just (8.106.3) and Herodotus does not explicitly condemn him. However, this does not prove in any way that killing the children of one's enemy was a generally accepted practice: Herodotus himself notes that this was the 'greatest punishment' (μεγίστη τίσις) he knew of (8.105.1).⁷² The symbolic value of this narrative also makes it unlikely that this story can be taken at face value, or as a reliable standard for measuring 'the bounds prescribed by custom' in fifth-century Athenian morality.⁷³

The same applies to the other Herodotean episode often adduced as a parallel to Hecuba's revenge.⁷⁴ The Greeks, and in particular

---

⁷⁰ Mossman 1995: 189, arguing that this provides some justification for Hecuba's conduct. See also below, n. 75.

⁷¹ See *HF* 168–9, 545–7, *Hcld.* 467–70, 1000–4, *Tro.* 723, *Andr.* 519–22 (Mossman 1995: 189 n. 54). The principle is also mentioned in *Cypria* fr. 31 West 2003: 106–7 = West 2013: 128 and in Arist. *Rh.* 1395a.

⁷² He also has Hermotimos say that Panionios committed the 'most unholy acts' (ἔργων ἀνοσιωτάτων: 8.106.3).

⁷³ As Gregory 1999: xxxiii says. Mossman 1995: 189 and Gregory 1999: xxxiii n. 56 also claim that the story of Panionios and Hermotimos is evidence for generally accepted judgement on revenge in classical Greece. Hornblower 2003 demonstrates how the story symbolises the conflict between Ionian and Carian ethnic groups.

⁷⁴ Adduced by Mossman 1995: 176 and Matthiessen 2010: 25. For other horrible revenge stories in Herodotus, not adduced as parallels, cf. Hdt. 4.162–7, 200–1.

6 HECUBA'S REVENGE

Xanthippos (Pericles' father) and the Athenians, kill Artaÿktes, punishing him for his sacrilegious robbing of the tomb of the hero Protesilaos. They nail him to a plank, and stone his child to death in front of his own eyes (Hdt. 9.120). This story can be read as a symbol for the Persian defeat. Some have argued that it 'might imply Herodotus' approval of his [i.e. Artaÿktes'] punishment'.[75] However, this 'singular piece of Athenian brutality'[76] rather disturbingly suggests that the Athenian empire is going to be more and more like the Persian one.[77] The two Herodotean parallels do show that fifth-century audiences loved gruesome tales of revenge, but they fail to provide clear justification for Hecuba's course of action.

Polymestor's crime is described as exceptionally unholy (790, 792, 852). Polymestor himself, in his self-centred accusation speech, does not make the most of Hecuba's weak point, the killing of the children, and focuses on other, less effective, arguments (1132–82n.). Hecuba ignores the killing of Polymestor's children in her reply, and Agamemnon is only too happy to follow suit. The shocking nature of Hecuba's revenge, just like Hermotimos', is not lost on the audience, who have heard her announce a crime as horrifying as that of the women of Lemnos (886–7n.), but she successfully diverts the attention of Agamemnon (and the audience) away from it, and directs it towards Polymestor's crime.

Hecuba is different from most other ancient revenge plays in that the revenge plot is followed by a judicial procedure assessing the justice of the revenge. Among the other extant tragedies, this happens only in Aeschylus' *Oresteia*: in *Eumenides*, a jury presided over by Athena judges the appropriateness of Orestes' revenge and matricide. As in *Eumenides*, the verdict in *Hecuba* does not put a stop to the conflicts of the play. Hecuba starts to use the language of 'reciprocity of revenge' which she rejected at 262 (and which is so prominent in *Choephori*),[78] and stresses that suffering should be met by suffering (1256). Polymestor answers in kind, prophesying the deaths of both Hecuba and Agamemnon. He clearly presents Hecuba's metamorphosis as a kind of punishment.[79] Polymestor rejects any ethical interpretation of 'justice': he is indignant that he should 'give justice' to 'socially inferior people', in particular to a woman (1252–3). His reaction also shows how easily human interpretation transforms suffering into punishment and acts of revenge. Hecuba's transformation and Agamemnon's death at the hands of Clytemnestra are not

---

[75] Mossman 1995: 176.   [76] Derow 1995.   [77] Flower and Marincola 2002: 303.
[78] See Aesch. *Cho.* 144 τοὺς κτανόντας ἀντικατθανεῖν, 309–14. This language is explicitly disapproved by Tyndareus in Eur. *Or.* 508–9 ἀποκτείνειεν ... ἀνταποκτενεῖ. On the 'reciprocity of revenge' cf. Seaford 1994: 25–6, von Reden 1995: 15–18.
[79] See esp. 1252–95n., 1265n., 1270n., 1271n., 1272n., 1273n., 1274n., 1276n.

interpreted by the gods in this text. Hecuba's revenge is concluded by her death, after the end of the play, and her morally discredited enemy is able to interpret her death as an event that clouds her frightening success.

7 RECEPTION

The reception of *Hecuba* illuminates some of the major interpretive problems of the play.[80] Ancient adaptations focused on some of the spectacular and fantastic elements of the play (the ghosts; child-murder; Hecuba's transformation) and on the unorthodox mythical versions chosen (or invented) by Euripides; they also tried to refashion and simplify the ethical problems of the revenge play, while introducing other kinds of complexity.

Ennius (239–169 BCE), Pacuvius (c. 220–130 BCE) and Accius (170–c. 86 BCE) wrote Latin tragedies modelled on Euripides' play. Very little is known about Accius' version.[81] Ennius' version, known to us from only ten fragments, was apparently a rather free rendering of Euripides' text.[82] We have more information on Pacuvius' *Iliona*, if we can trust the version transmitted by a Latin mythographic source.[83] In Pacuvius' play, Polymestor has married Iliona, Polydorus' sister, but the identities of Iliona's brother and son were exchanged. When Troy falls, Agamemnon asks Polymestor to kill Polydorus, promising him 'great abundance of gold' and his daughter in marriage. Polymestor agrees, but unknowingly kills his own son. Polydorus learns the truth and blinds Polymestor before killing him. This version discards the troublesome spectacle of feminine violence, casting Polydorus, rather than Hecuba, as avenger. It also eliminates some of the moral complexities from the revenge plot: Polymestor himself kills his own son by mistake. The Polyxena plot is left out, simplifying some of the geographical problems involved in relocating Achilles' tomb to Thrace (37–9n.). The apparition of the ghost of Iliona's child (a scene that mirrors the appearance of Polydorus' ghost in *Hecuba*) was one of the most famous, and dramatically successful, passages of the play.

---

[80] On the reception of Euripides from antiquity to the present time cf. Mastronarde 2010: 1–15, Lauriola and Demetriou 2015. On fourth-century reception of Greek tragedy cf. Easterling 1993, Csapo, Goette, Green and Wilson 2014, Hanink 2014. On *Hecuba* cf. Heath 1987a: 41–3, Mossman 1995: 211–43 and 247–53, Dugale 2015, Foley 2015: 77–101.
[81] See Dangel 1995: 164 and 320, Jocelyn 1967: 304–5.
[82] See Jocelyn 1967: 104–6, 303–18, Manuwald 2012: 151–64.
[83] See Schierl 2006: 312–41, Manuwald 2000. The plot is reconstructed from Hyg. *fab.* 109. It is possible that Pacuvius adapted a Greek play and/or that Hyginus is offering a summary of a Greek play.

7 RECEPTION

The death of the child Polydorus is the focus of the most famous adaptation of the play, Virgil's narrative in Book 3 of the *Aeneid*.[84] In Virgil's version, Aeneas discovers the body of Polydorus by chance, when collecting branches for a sacrifice on the coast of Thrace. The branches of cornel and myrtle drip blood. They are the 'iron crop of spears' that killed the young boy; the spears 'grew up with sharp shafts' (*Aen.* 3.45–6).[85] Virgil seems to literalise one of Euripides' comparisons: Polydorus was growing 'like a shoot' (20n.). The spears seem to be 'grafted' into Polydorus' trunk.[86] Polydorus explains to Aeneas that he was murdered by Polymestor, who profaned the bond of hospitality in order to acquire Polydorus' gold. Aeneas gives proper burial to Polydorus and, following his advice,[87] leaves Thrace, apparently without completing the sacrifice that led him to meet Polydorus. Virgil's Aeneas even takes for granted that Polymestor's crime is motivated not only by profit, but also by his siding with the Greeks, a reason that is dismissed as false in *Hecuba* (1243–4).[88] The peculiarity of Virgil's version is that it preempts the plot of Euripides' *Hecuba*: if Polydorus was metamorphosed into a sort of plant, it was impossible for Hecuba to know his death; it was also impossible for her to avenge him. Not only that: Aeneas and the Trojan leader, as soon as they hear Polydorus' story, decide to 'leave the land of crime' (*Aen.* 3.60). They do not even consider the possibility, or the moral duty, of punishing Polymestor, nor does Polydorus ask them to do that. Virgil's version alludes to a previous literary text, but, paradoxically, is incompatible with the plot of the very text alluded to. Virgil also makes sure that the chronology of his narration is incompatible with that of Euripides: the action of Euripides' play takes place soon after the fall of Troy,[89] whereas Virgil's text implies that Aeneas stopped for a long time at Antandros before reaching Thrace (*Aen.* 3.5–12).[90] A story of cruel revenge was not best suited to Aeneas' rhetorical purpose in addressing Dido.

Ovid's version, as often, focuses on filling in the gaps in Virgil's adaptation, and correcting it.[91] In Book 13 of the *Metamorphoses*, Ovid conspicuously discards the Virgilian version of Polydorus' metamorphosis, and, in

---

[84] On Virgil and Greek tragedy in general see Hardie 1997, Panoussi 2009, with references. On Polydorus cf. Horsfall 2006: 50–87 on Verg. *Aen.* 3.13–68, with references.
[85] Here and below, the translations from *Aeneid* 3 are taken from Horsfall 2006.
[86] Coo 2007.
[87] Verg. *Aen.* 3.44: 'flee this land of cruelty, flee this shore of greed'.
[88] Verg. *Aen.* 3.54: Polymestor 'followed Agamemnon's cause and the winning side'.
[89] 32n.; 33–4n.; Battezzato 2014b.
[90] On the chronology cf. also Horsfall 2006: 45 on Verg. *Aen.* 3.8. Battezzato forthcoming-a discusses other allusions to *Hecuba* present in the text of the *Aeneid*.
[91] Casali 2007: 182–8.

his close adaptation of Euripides,[92] creates a much more compact and less ethically ambiguous version. Ovid eliminates Odysseus, Talthybius, Agamemnon and the Servant from his narrative. He also omits Polymestor's children: this allows him to discard, like Pacuvius, but less radically than Virgil, the ethically dubious narrative of child murder from the revenge plot. The epic genre allows him to change setting and scene, and so to gloss over some difficulties of Euripides' play, such as the location of Achilles' tomb.

Ovid, in accordance with the overall theme of his poem, makes the story of Hecuba's metamorphosis the starting and ending point of the narrative (*Met.* 13.404–7 and 567–75). His version is much less ambiguous than Euripides': thanks to the metamorphosis, Hecuba escapes the revenge of the Thracians who want to punish her for blinding Polymestor (*Met.* 13.565–71).[93] The transformation is unambiguously presented as a 'loss' of humanity and a fate that deserves pity (*Met.* 13.405, 13.575). Ovid thus moves in the same direction as Nicander (active *c.* 130 BCE) and Cicero, who suggested psychological reasons for Hecuba's transformation: Nicander wrote that she leapt into the sea and 'took the semblance of a Hyrcanian hound' after seeing the destruction of Troy and the death of Priam,[94] whereas Cicero asserts that she 'was transformed into a bitch as a consequence of the sorrow of her soul (*acerbitatem animi*) and her fury' (Cic. *Tusc.* 3.63). Ovid's version popularised Hecuba's story in the Middle Ages. Dante's famous mention of Hecuba in *Inferno* 30.16–21 clearly echoes Ovid's text.[95]

Seneca, like Ovid, simplifies the ethical dilemmas of *Hecuba* and rationalises some baffling elements of the plot while stressing the gory or fantastic elements of the story. His play *Trojan Women* combines the plots of Euripides' own *Trojan Women* with the narrative of Polyxena's death from *Hecuba*. Seneca replaces the death of Polydorus from *Hecuba* with that of Astyanax, killed by Ulysses (a crucial event in Euripides' *Trojan Women*).[96] The elimination of the Polymestor plot creates greater thematic coherence for the play, now focused on the sufferings of the Trojan

---

[92] For detailed analyses cf. Bömer 1982: 299–346, Galasso in Paduano and Galasso 1999: 1461–9, Hopkinson 2000: 22–7 and 165–86, Curley 2013: 101–14, 153–61, 185–91, Hardie 2015: 277–303. Ov. *Met.* 13.464 echoes the spurious line Eur. *Hec.* 214, which was clearly present in the text Ovid read.

[93] For this reason Ovid locates the metamorphosis on land, not at sea (*Met.* 13.571; contrast Eur. *Hec.* 1259–65).

[94] Translation and comments in Gow and Schofield 1953: 145 and 208 (fr. 62).

[95] 'Hecuba, sad, wretched and captive, after she had seen Polyxena slain and, forlorn, discerned her Polydorus on the sea-strand, she, driven mad, barked like a dog, so had the sorrow wrung her soul' (tr. Singleton 1977: 315–17).

[96] On Seneca's allusion to *Hecuba* and the poetic tradition in general cf. esp. Fantham 1982: 60–1, 71–5 and *passim*, Keulen 2001: 10–11 and *passim*.

prisoners. On the other hand, the disturbing revenge narrative is eliminated, as in Virgil: no revenge is possible for Hecuba against the Greeks. The absurdity of human sacrifice is restated by Seneca, in a complex web of allusions and 'corrections' to Euripides' version. In Euripides, Polyxena accepted the sacrifice without compensation for herself (342–78n.); the play never states clearly whether the sacrifice was necessary for the Greeks' voyage home.[97] Hecuba's indignant questioning of the necessity of human sacrifice in Euripides (260–1) is echoed and expanded by Agamemnon in Seneca: 'let the fleshy throats of Phrygian cattle be cut, and let blood flow that brings tears to no mother. What is that practice you speak of?' (Sen. *Tro.* 296–8).[98] The seer Calchas replies to Agamemnon, and Euripides' Hecuba: 'the fates (*fata*) grant a way to the Greeks at their customary price: the virgin must be sacrificed' (Sen. *Tro.* 360–1). Calchas also adds that Polyxena 'will be properly given in marriage' to Achilles (Sen. *Tro.* 364),[99] thus making explicit an element that is simply alluded to in Euripides' play.[100] Seneca makes Ulysses echo some of Polymestor's arguments for killing the heirs of the Trojan kings: Astyanax, if spared by the Greeks, would grow up to fight them again, as a future Hector (Sen. *Tro.* 524–55: compare Eur. *Hec.* 1138–41). Seneca's virtuoso display of allusion transfers a motif from the suppressed Polydorus plot, making it appear rhetorically less specious, even if probably equally odious. His version thus follows some of the main lines of the ancient reception of Euripides' play, simplifying and rationalising it, while at the same time inserting some new elements of literary and narrative complexity.

Hecuba was one of the most frequently read Greek plays in antiquity and during the Byzantine era;[101] it was the first play in most Byzantine manuscripts and Renaissance editions of Euripides, and one of the first to be translated into Latin, in the fourteenth century.[102] Erasmus' Latin translation, first published in 1506, was famous and influential,[103] and spurred a flurry of renderings of the play into modern languages, notably French, German, Italian and Spanish.[104] Many of these 'translations' are in fact free adaptations, with additions and changes to the play, often echoing Virgil, Ovid and other sources; some of the Renaissance versions

[97] Cf. 37–9n., 111–14, 538–41n., 900n., 902n., 1287–90n. In Ovid, honouring Achilles was the only reason for the sacrifice (*Met.* 13.445–8).
[98] Cf. also 258n. As in Euripides (*Hec.* 120–2), Agamemnon tries to avoid the sacrifice of Polyxena, and is accused of doing so out of love for Cassandra (Sen. *Tro.* 303–4). Here and below, the translation is from Fantham 1982.
[99] Cf. Sen. *Tro.* 888–902, 1120–64.   [100] Cf. 416n., 523n., 612n.
[101] Cf. below, section 8, 'Transmission of the Text'.
[102] Cf. Pertusi 1960: 120–52, Porro 1992.   [103] Mastronarde 2010: 9–10.
[104] See Heath 1987a: 53–4, Mossman 1995: 220–43, Garnier 1999, Matthiessen 2010: 61–5, Pollard 2012, Cuzzotti 2017. On Spanish translations see the next note.

emphasise the moral justification for Hecuba's revenge,[105] which was often praised by early modern scholars.[106]

Shakespeare cites Hecuba as an example of misfortune in *Titus Andronicus* (first performed *c.* 1593–4) and in *Hamlet* (first performed *c.* 1600–1).[107] Some scholars argue that Shakespeare never read Euripides' play,[108] and that he knew the story from Latin and/or more recent versions of the myth, in particular Ovid's *Metamorphoses*, a poem quoted at length by the characters of *Titus Andronicus*. It is however probable that he was familiar with (sections of) a Latin translation of *Hecuba*. Demetrius (*Titus Andronicus* 1.1.137–8) knows that Hecuba exacted her 'sharp revenge | upon the Thracian Tyrant in his Tent', as in Euripides. Ovid (*Met.* 13.547–71) never mentions a tent.[109] Hamlet was a student of the University of Wittenberg, which saw the first modern staging of Euripides' *Hecuba*, in the early sixteenth century.[110] This may be a coincidence, but it is a striking one.

A number of seventeenth-, eighteenth- and twentieth-century operas stage the story of Polydorus and Polyxena, often influenced by Virgil and Ovid as well as by Euripides. The Romantic operatic stage was less interested in this particular classical myth (and in classical myths in general).[111] Some recent publications provide good guidance to the history of modern performances and adaptations.[112]

8 TRANSMISSION OF THE TEXT

Hecuba was widely read in the Hellenistic and Imperial ages; it was part of the school syllabus in late antiquity (probably) and in the Byzantine era (certainly), along with *Orestes* and *Phoenician Women*.[113]

In antiquity, actors (possibly) and readers (certainly) added material that they considered appropriate for grammatical or aesthetic reasons, or in a misguided attempt to 'improve' the meaning of the texts, especially in

---

[105] Cf. Morenilla Talens 2014. [106] Cf. above, section 6, 'Hecuba's Revenge'.
[107] On *Hamlet* 2.2.414–28 cf. Pollard 2012, with references.
[108] Martindale and Martindale 1990: 43–4. [109] Pollard 2012: 1076 n. 76.
[110] Mossman 1995: 224, Pollard 2012: 1064.
[111] Cf. Reid and Rohmann 1993: 907–12.
[112] See Hall and Macintosh 2005: esp. 97–8, 252–3, 255, 510, Foley 2015: 77–101 and 127–30, and the 'Archive of performances of Greek and Roman drama' at the University of Oxford (http://www.apgrd.ox.ac.uk, accessed August 2017).
[113] Cf. W. S. Barrett 1964: 51–3, Cavallo 2002: 89–93. On the transmission of the texts from Athens to Alexandria cf. Griffith 1977: 226–34, Battezzato 2003a (in general), Battezzato 2008a (lyrical sections). On the transmission of Euripides in general see Finglass forthcoming.

plays that were often performed.[114] These inauthentic passages were probably inserted in copies that are at the origin of all our manuscript tradition, and/or quickly spread to all extant copies. In general, when scribes find additional lines (e.g. in the margins of their model, or in another copy of the same text), they prefer to err by including material of uncertain origin rather than omit a possibly genuine passage.[115]

The success of *Hecuba* with ancient readers and teachers created a demand for copies of the play. This explains the very high number of surviving ancient and medieval manuscripts of the text. A dozen ancient papyri[116] and about 200 (mostly Byzantine) manuscripts are extant. *Hecuba* was more often copied than *Orestes* (about 180 extant manuscripts) and *Phoenician Women* (about 130 manuscripts).[117] Manuscripts of the play were thus easily available: this meant that scribes, when copying a text, sometimes had a chance to check their copy not only against the manuscript they used as a model, but also against one or more other manuscripts. Readers and scholars did the same, adding variants in the margins or above the lines. When the copy was in its turn copied, the new scribe, in producing a new manuscript, incorporated the readings from annotations and corrections into his text, attempting to reproduce the 'best' text in front of him. This process, called 'contamination', means that any manuscript is not merely a copy of the one from which it was copied, plus possible additional mistakes, but rather a conflation of readings from several different ancestors. Contamination makes it difficult or impossible to establish a genealogical relationship between manuscripts, which can be grouped at most into loose 'families'. This type of textual transmission is generally called an 'open tradition' (as opposed to a 'closed tradition', in which every manuscript descends only from a single ancestor, in the absence of contamination).[118]

---

[114] The following lines are considered interpolated in this edition (see the notes *ad locc.*): 62–3, 73–8, 92–7, 145, 175–6, 211–15, 402–4, 412, 441–3, 490, 504, 531–3, 555–6, 599, 756–9, 793–7, 974, 1087, 1185–6. Other possible interpolations are: 90–1, 599–602, 831–2, 953, 973–5, 1173, 1174. On interpolations in tragedy see Mastronarde 1994: 39–49, with references.

[115] For this general principle and some striking examples cf. Aland and Aland 1981: 276, 285–9; see also Tarrant 2016: 85–104.

[116] Listed below, p. 29; Carrara 2005, Battezzato 2009b: 9–11.

[117] Cf. Matthiessen 2010: 75, Turyn 1957: 3–9, and the studies mentioned in the following note.

[118] On the concept of 'open tradition' see Pasquali 1952. W. S. Barrett 1964: 57–76, Di Benedetto 1965 and Zuntz 1965: 157 argued that the MS tradition of Euripides was an open one. Matthiessen 1974, Mastronarde and Bremer 1982 and Diggle 1991 are the principal studies on the manuscript tradition of *Hecuba*, *Phoenician Women* and *Orestes*, respectively. They conclusively demonstrate that many later, esp. thirteenth-century, manuscripts carry valuable ancient information; they suggest grouping the manuscripts into several families, renounce

The medieval manuscripts of *Hecuba* are thus not easily grouped; contamination is widespread, and manuscripts often report variant readings. Matthiessen 1974 offered the first systematic exploration of the extant manuscripts. Diggle 1984 consistently reports the readings of twenty-one manuscripts; he occasionally supplements them with readings taken from a group of thirty-two others, when he considers that those variant readings may go back to antiquity and thus represent what Euripides actually wrote. Matthiessen 2010 consistently reports the readings of twenty-seven manuscripts, plus occasional readings from thirteen others.[119]

The importance of this play in education created a demand for commentaries. Scholars of the Hellenistic, Imperial and Byzantine ages wrote notes or commentaries on *Hecuba*. The Hellenistic and Imperial commentaries were written on separate papyrus rolls from the texts of the plays, although scattered notes were occasionally added in the margins of a poetic text to help the reader. The invention of the codex created scope for more extensive annotations in the wider margins. These marginal notes, called scholia, were the result of the rephrasing, abridgement and rearrangement of earlier commentaries. Byzantine scholars wrote commentaries on a few selected plays, adopting the same format (marginal commentaries).[120] These sources help in the reconstruction of the original text of *Hecuba*: they paraphrase or quote the text of Euripides that was available at the time when the note was written, that is, in many cases, the text as it was current in the era of the Roman Empire.[121] The views of Didymus of Alexandria, a grammarian and commentator who lived in the first century BCE, are especially discussed in the scholia (see the *apparatus criticus* on 13 and 847n.). *Hecuba* was also widely quoted in antiquity and in the Byzantine era.[122] Quotations occasionally help us to recover the original text of the play, when transmitted in corrupt form in the manuscripts.[123]

---

a general stemma for the whole tradition, and argue that contamination was widespread.

[119] Cf. Matthiessen 1974 and 2010.

[120] Most of the old scholia on Euripides are published in Schwartz 1887: 9–91. The vast Byzantine material is available only in outdated or partial editions: Dindorf 1863: 200–516, Günther 1995, de Faveri 2002. A new, thorough edition of all extant scholia is being published online by D. J. Mastronarde (http://euripidesscholia.org/EurSchHome.html, accessed August 2017). On the formation of scholia on Euripides cf. W. S. Barrett 1964: 47–51 and 78–81, Dickey 2007: 31–4. On scholia in general see the recent surveys in Montana and Porro 2014, Montanari, Matthaios and Rengakos 2015.

[121] Cf. 13, 211, 457, 467, 580, 685, 700, 794, 853, 1023, 1041, 1100, 1112.

[122] The fullest list of ancient citations is offered by Matthiessen 2010.

[123] Cf. lines 293, 295, 569, 1112.

9 PRESENTATION OF TEXTUAL EVIDENCE IN THIS EDITION

The apparatus of the present edition, in accordance with the style of the series, does not report all the details of this very complex manuscript tradition. It aims to give the reader a sense of the complexities of the tradition by reporting readings from a selected group of pre-thirteenth century manuscripts (HMBO),[124] supplementing them, when necessary, from other more recent ones. The apparatus provides information on the manuscript evidence whenever the reading printed in the text is not found in the HMBO manuscripts, except for minor variants and orthographical divergences. These manuscripts provide the textual evidence necessary to reconstruct the original text of Euripides for most of the play, but supplementary evidence from other manuscripts needed to be used on more than thirty occasions. The sigla 'p'/'pp' designate readings found in one (p) or more (pp) manuscripts outside the group listed above: readers should consult Diggle 1984 and Matthiessen 2010 for more detailed information. These manuscripts often preserve ancient readings that are not transmitted in HMBO.

By analysing the textual information that has come down to us from antiquity (ancient manuscripts, quotations, etc.), scholars reconstruct the so-called *paradosis* ('what has been transmitted'). Word division, accents and the names of speakers are not part of the *paradosis*, and were introduced systematically by medieval scribes and scholars. Editors are free to change accents, word division and attribution of lines if doing so gives a better text (cf. 243n., 693n., 743n., 1000). The *paradosis* sometimes gives impossible meaning, language, metre or style. It is therefore necessary to recognise that the *paradosis* is corrupt and to 'conjecture' the original text (i.e. posit what the possible original reading was). Hermann, Porson, Bothe, Hartung, Nauck, Wecklein and Diggle are the modern scholars who have contributed most to restoring the original text of *Hecuba* by conjectural emendation.[125]

10 METRE AND LANGUAGE

The sections of Greek tragedy delivered by actors are very largely written in iambic trimeters: the iambic metron $\times - \cup -$ is repeated three times. This is the basic metrical structure:

$$\| \times - \cup - \times \vdots - \cup \vdots - \times - \cup \cap \|$$

---

[124] For details on these manuscripts cf. p. 29.
[125] Cf. the *apparatus criticus* of this edition. On the steps needed to prepare a critical edition see West 1973, Battezzato 2009d. On conjectures see Conte 2013.

The series of symbols indicates the abstract pattern of the iambic trimeter.[126] Each symbol of the abstract pattern designates an 'element'. The symbol × indicates an *anceps* element, that is, an element that can be implemented by either a long or short syllable. Tragic metre allows two short syllables to implement the first *anceps* element (i.e. for a verse to begin ⏑ ⏑ –); this happens frequently, but not exclusively, in the case of proper names (e.g. 3, 4, 7, 31, 442, 752, 766).[127] In the iambic trimeter, a long element (symbol –) may be implemented by a long syllable or two short ones. The implementation of a long element by two short syllables is called 'resolution'.[128] The final element of the line, indicated by the symbol ⌒, is *indifferens*: it does not matter whether it is implemented by a short or a long syllable, since it is followed by metrical pause. Every element preceding metrical pause is *indifferens*.

Long sections of *Hecuba* are written in anapaests. Anapaests can be recited (59–67, 98–153, 1293–5) or sung (68–72, [92–7], 79–89, 154–210, [211–15]).[129] The basic structure of the anapaestic metron is ⏑⏑ – ⏑⏑ –. The long elements may be implemented by two short syllables, and the two short elements may be combined into a single long syllable. In practice, therefore, the structure is ⏒ ⏕ ⏒ ⏕. In recited, as opposed to sung, anapaests (98–153n.), sequences of four short syllables are avoided ([62–3n.], [145n.]). Word-end occurs after each anapaestic metron, or, at the most, after a run-over of one short syllable. Anapaests are traditionally printed in dimeters (⏒ ⏕ ⏒ ⏕ | ⏒ ⏕ ⏒ ⏕) or monometers (⏒ ⏕ ⏒ ⏕). When a metrical pause occurs in recited anapaests, the dimeter is curtailed of one element at the end ('catalectic') and assumes the shape ⏒ – ⏒ – ⏑⏑ – ⌒ ‖ (e.g. 103 and 115; 98–153n.). This structure (catalectic anapaestic dimeter) is normally called 'paroemiac' (= the metre used 'in proverbs'). In recited anapaests, metrical pauses occur only after paroemiacs (146–7n.). A line break after a recited anapaestic dimeter or monometer does not correspond to a metrical pause. It would be impractical to group several anapaestic metra in a single line of printed text, inserting line breaks only where paroemiacs occur.

Sung anapaests are metrically freer to some extent (more resolutions, less strict rules about word-end, etc.: 59–97n. 'Metre'). They also avoid the characteristically Attic η corresponding to an original ᾱ. In these cases all

---

[126] Cf. the list of metrical symbols on pp. viii–ix.
[127] The second and third *ancipita* may be implemented by two short syllables only in the case of proper names, but this happens rarely, as in Eur. *Hipp.* 32.
[128] On the resolution rates and their evolution in Euripides see above, section 2, 'The Date of *Hecuba*'.
[129] In 154–210 the anapaests are interspersed with other types of cola: 154–215n. 'Metre'. Many lyric anapaests are present in 1059–84: see 1056–1108n. 'Metre'.

Greek dialects, except Ionic and Attic, present α. Sung sections of tragedy prefer the less 'parochial' α-vocalism: see e.g. 68 στεροπά, instead of Attic στεροπή.

Sung sections of this play use mostly Aeolic ('Metre' sections of 444–83n., 629–57n., 905–52n.) and dochmiac cola ('Metre' sections of 684–721n., 1023–34n., 1056–1108n.). These cola are often interspersed with different metrical structures, especially iambic, enoplian and anapaestic cola. The term 'colon' indicates a short metrical structure, combined with others (of similar or different rhythm) within a larger metrical structure, concluded by metrical pause. The symbol ‖ indicates metrical pause. If, within a lyric section, a metrical pause is detected by the presence of a short syllable where a long one is expected (*breuis in longo*), the symbol ‖^b is used. If a metrical pause is detected by the presence of a hiatus, the symbol ‖^h is used. If a metrical pause is detected on the basis of the fact that a pause is normally found in that position, the symbol ‖^c (= metrical pause detected thanks to the knowledge of ancient Greek metrical practice (*cognitio metrorum*)) is used. Pauses marked by ‖^b and ‖^h are to be taken as reasonably certain; pauses marked by ‖^c are considered probable by the present editor, but their presence cannot be considered certain. Metrical pauses at the end of a sung section (for instance at the end of a strophe or when the singing is interrupted by a spoken line) are marked by ‖‖. The sign ‖‖ indicates with certainty the presence of a metrical pause. Syllables preceding ‖ or ‖‖ are always scanned as *indifferentia*. Lyric sections consistently present the non-Attic α-vocalism.[130]

The commentary discusses in detail many problems of language and style. In addition to traditional grammatical concepts, it refers to a couple of concepts from pragmatics, 'topic' and 'focus'.[131] Linguistic pragmatics, broadly defined, discusses the relationship between linguistic context and meaning, with special attention to information structure and word order. 'Topic' is 'what the sentence is about',[132] that is a piece of given information, often already mentioned in the preceding context, and generally known to the speakers. In Greek it is normally placed at the beginning of the sentence. It may be implemented by a noun, pronoun, adjective or adverb (less frequently by a verb). For instance, at 589–90 'and now, speaking about what happened to you, I could not wipe it out of my mind so as not to mourn it', τὸ μὲν σὸν ... πάθος is the topic of the sentence. This informative function explains its position at the beginning of the

---

[130] This section is meant as a general introduction; for fuller information see West 1982: 77–137, Martinelli 1997, Mastronarde 2002: 97–108, Lourenço 2011, Battezzato 2014c.

[131] Cf. Dik 2007: 31–4 and *passim*, Battezzato 2008b: 88–95, Battezzato 2012: 311–16.

[132] Gundel and Fretheim 2004: 176.

sentence (see 589–90n.). 'Focus' is either a new piece of information, or a piece of information that is contrasted with other possible ones. At 1184 τὸ θῆλυ ... πᾶν ... γένος ('the entire race of women'), Greek, unlike English, places the emphasised adjective θῆλυ first, since the speaker contrasts the *female* race with that of men (contrastive focus, marked with italics in written English). Other linguistic and rhetorical concepts used in the commentary are either well known from traditional grammar,[133] or are explained in the notes.

---

[133] For general discussions of tragic language see Mastronarde 2002: 81–96, Battezzato 2012, Rutherford 2012, Battezzato forthcoming-b. On rhetorical terms see Lausberg 1998.

SYMBOLS, SIGLA AND ABBREVIATIONS USED IN THE EDITION OF THE GREEK TEXT

SYMBOLS AND ABBREVIATIONS USED IN THE MAIN GREEK TEXT

< >	words added by modern scholars
[ ]	words present in the manuscripts but considered not authentic by the editor
† †	words that cannot have been written by the author in that form; emendations have been suggested, but no single one stands out as convincing
ant.	antistrophe
astr.	astrophic song
ep.	epode
mes.	mesode
str.	strophe

SIGLA AND ABBREVIATIONS USED IN THE APPARATUS

ω	the reading of manuscripts HMBO (or those of them that are extant for any given line)
H	Hierosolymitanus τάφου 36 (lines 869–920 and 1125–73 only), 10th or 11th cent.
M	Marcianus gr. 471, 11th cent.
B	Parisinus gr. 2713 (lines 523–1295 only), 11th cent.
O	Laurentianus 31.10, copied c. 1175
Π	reading found in a fragmentary manuscript, normally written on papyrus, dating from the 2nd to the 6th cent. CE (Π^1: P. Oxy. 876; $\Pi^2 + \Pi^{10}$: P. Oxy. 877 + 4561; Π^5: P. Oxy. 3215 fr. 2; Π^7: P. Oxy. 4557; Π^8: P. Oxy. 4559; Π^9: P. Oxy. 4560; Π^{12}: P. Oxy. 4558)
p/pp	the reading of one (p) or more (pp) manuscripts later than ω, listed in Diggle 1984 and/or Matthiessen 2010, dating from the 13th to the 15th cent.
γρ	a reading which is not reported in the main text but only as a variant (in line, above the line, in the margin or in the scholium)
ac/pc	the reading of the MS before or after a correction by the scribe who wrote the text (e.g. M^{ac})

[1]	the reading of the MS after a correction by a scribe other than the one who wrote the text (e.g. M[1])
*	a letter that cannot be read with certainty
Σ	a reading attested in a scholium (either as a lemma, or in the body of the scholium, or inferred from the explanation in the scholium itself). For details see Diggle 1984, Schwartz 1887 and Matthiessen 2010.
test.	a reading attested in the indirect tradition (quotations from Euripides). For details see Diggle 1984 and Matthiessen 2010.

Square brackets around a MS siglum or sigla (e.g. [MB]) indicate that the original writing of that MS or MSS cannot be read with certainty. Square brackets around part of a reading reported in the apparatus indicate that the letter(s) are not extant or are not readable in a papyrus or MS, as a consequence of physical damage to the writing surface. The readings of MBO reported in this edition have all been checked on digital reproduction of the manuscripts.

om.	*omisit/omiserunt* (a manuscript, a papyrus or a quotation omits the word/words or line/lines)
del.	*delevit/deleverunt* (one or more modern scholars consider the word/words or line/lines not to be part of the original text by Euripides)

ΕΥΡΙΠΙΔΟΥ ΕΚΑΒΗ

ΤΑ ΤΟΥ ΔΡΑΜΑΤΟΣ ΠΡΟΣΩΠΑ

ΠΟΛΥΔΩΡΟΥ ΕΙΔΩΛΟΝ
ΕΚΑΒΗ
ΧΟΡΟΣ ΑΙΧΜΑΛΩΤΙΔΩΝ ΓΥΝΑΙΚΩΝ
ΠΟΛΥΞΕΝΗ
ΟΔΥΣΣΕΥΣ
ΤΑΛΘΥΒΙΟΣ
ΘΕΡΑΠΑΙΝΑ
ΑΓΑΜΕΜΝΩΝ
ΠΟΛΥΜΗΣΤΩΡ

Dramatis personas habent pp: om. ω

ΕΥΡΙΠΙΔΟΥ ΕΚΑΒΗ

ΠΟΛΥΔΩΡΟΥ ΕΙΔΩΛΟΝ
Ήκω νεκρῶν κευθμῶνα καὶ σκότου πύλας
λιπών, ἵν' Ἅιδης χωρὶς ᾤκισται θεῶν,
Πολύδωρος, Ἑκάβης παῖς γεγὼς τῆς Κισσέως
Πριάμου τε πατρός, ὅς μ', ἐπεὶ Φρυγῶν πόλιν
κίνδυνος ἔσχε δορὶ πεσεῖν Ἑλληνικῶι,   5
δείσας ὑπεξέπεμψε Τρωϊκῆς χθονὸς
Πολυμήστορος πρὸς δῶμα Θρηικίου ξένου,
ὃς τήνδ' ἀρίστην Χερσονησίαν πλάκα
σπείρει, φίλιππον λαὸν εὐθύνων δορί.
πολὺν δὲ σὺν ἐμοὶ χρυσὸν ἐκπέμπει λάθραι   10
πατήρ, ἵν', εἴ ποτ' Ἰλίου τείχη πέσοι,
τοῖς ζῶσιν εἴη παισὶ μὴ σπάνις βίου.
νεώτατος δ' ἦ Πριαμιδῶν, ὃ καί με γῆς
ὑπεξέπεμψεν· οὔτε γὰρ φέρειν ὅπλα
οὔτ' ἔγχος οἷός τ' ἦ νέωι βραχίονι.   15
ἕως μὲν οὖν γῆς ὄρθ' ἔκειθ' ὁρίσματα
πύργοι τ' ἄθραυστοι Τρωϊκῆς ἦσαν χθονὸς
Ἕκτωρ τ' ἀδελφὸς οὑμὸς ηὐτύχει δορί,
καλῶς παρ' ἀνδρὶ Θρηικὶ πατρώιωι ξένωι
τροφαῖσιν ὥς τις πτόρθος ηὐξόμην τάλας·   20
ἐπεὶ δὲ Τροία θ' Ἕκτορός τ' ἀπόλλυται
ψυχή πατρῶια θ' ἑστία κατεσκάφη
αὐτός τε βωμῶι πρὸς θεοδμήτωι πίτνει
σφαγεὶς Ἀχιλλέως παιδὸς ἐκ μιαιφόνου,
κτείνει με χρυσοῦ τὸν ταλαίπωρον χάριν   25
ξένος πατρῶιος καὶ κτανὼν ἐς οἶδμ' ἁλὸς
μεθῆχ', ἵν' αὐτὸς χρυσὸν ἐν δόμοις ἔχηι.
κεῖμαι δ' ἐπ' ἀκταῖς, ἄλλοτ' ἐν πόντου σάλωι,
πολλοῖς διαύλοις κυμάτων φορούμενος,
ἄκλαυτος ἄταφος· νῦν δ' ὑπὲρ μητρὸς φίλης   30

---

8 τήνδ' Hermann: τὴν ω   Χερσονησίαν test.: Χερρονησίαν ω   13 ἦ Didymus apud Σ: ἦν ω test.   16 ἔκειτ' ἐρείσματα Scaliger   18 ηὐτύχει pp: εὐτύχει ω   23 θεοδμήτωι M^γρO: λιθοδμήτωι M   30 ἄκλαυτος pp: ἄκλαυστος ω   ἀκλἄτ- M: ἄτ- ἀκλ- O

ΕΥΡΙΠΙΔΟΥ

Ἑκάβης ἀίσσω, σῶμ' ἐρημώσας ἐμόν,
τριταῖον ἤδη φέγγος αἰωρούμενος,
ὅσονπερ ἐν γῆι τῆιδε Χερσονησίαι
μήτηρ ἐμὴ δύστηνος ἐκ Τροίας πάρα.
πάντες δ' Ἀχαιοὶ ναῦς ἔχοντες ἥσυχοι 35
θάσσουσ' ἐπ' ἀκταῖς τῆσδε Θρηικίας χθονός.
ὁ Πηλέως γὰρ παῖς ὑπὲρ τύμβου φανεὶς
κατέσχ' Ἀχιλλεὺς πᾶν στράτευμ' Ἑλληνικόν,
πρὸς οἶκον εὐθύνοντας ἐναλίαν πλάτην·
αἰτεῖ δ' ἀδελφὴν τὴν ἐμὴν Πολυξένην 40
τύμβωι φίλον πρόσφαγμα καὶ γέρας λαβεῖν.
καὶ τεύξεται τοῦδ' οὐδ' ἀδώρητος φίλων
ἔσται πρὸς ἀνδρῶν· ἡ πεπρωμένη δ' ἄγει
θανεῖν ἀδελφὴν τῶιδ' ἐμὴν ἐν ἤματι.
δυοῖν δὲ παίδοιν δύο νεκρὼ κατόψεται 45
μήτηρ, ἐμοῦ τε τῆς τε δυστήνου κόρης.
φανήσομαι γάρ, ὡς τάφου τλήμων τύχω,
δούλης ποδῶν πάροιθεν ἐν κλυδωνίωι.
τοὺς γὰρ κάτω σθένοντας ἐξηιτησάμην
τύμβου κυρῆσαι κἀς χέρας μητρὸς πεσεῖν. 50
τοὐμὸν μὲν οὖν ὅσονπερ ἤθελον τυχεῖν
ἔσται· γεραιᾶι δ' ἐκποδὼν χωρήσομαι
Ἑκάβηι· περᾶι γὰρ ἥδ' ὑπὸ σκηνῆς πόδα
Ἀγαμέμνονος, φάντασμα δειμαίνουσ' ἐμόν.
φεῦ·
ὦ μῆτερ, ἥτις ἐκ τυραννικῶν δόμων 55
δούλειον ἦμαρ εἶδες, ὡς πράσσεις κακῶς
ὅσονπερ εὖ ποτ'· ἀντισηκώσας δέ σε
φθείρει θεῶν τις τῆς πάροιθ' εὐπραξίας.

ΕΚΑΒΗ
ἄγετ', ὦ παῖδες, τὴν γραῦν πρὸ δόμων,
ἄγετ' ὀρθοῦσαι τὴν ὁμόδουλον, 60
Τρωιάδες, ὑμῖν, πρόσθε δ' ἄνασσαν,
[λάβετε φέρετε πέμπετ' ἀείρετέ μου] 62–3

---

35 πάντες δ' O: πάντες τ' M   38 Ἑλληνικόν Ω: Ἀχαϊκόν M^γρ   44 τῶιδ' ἐμὴν ἐν ἤματι
Ο: τὴν ἐμὴν τῆιδ' ἡμέραι M   62–3 del. Bothe

ΕΚΑΒΗ 35

γεραιᾶς χειρὸς προσλαζύμεναι·
κἀγὼ σκολιῶι σκίπωνι χερὸς   65
διερειδομένη σπεύσω βραδύπουν
ἥλυσιν ἄρθρων προτιθεῖσα.

ὦ στεροπὰ Διός, ὦ σκοτία Νύξ,   astr.
τί ποτ' αἴρομαι ἔννυχος οὕτω
δείμασι φάσμασιν; ὦ πότνια Χθών,   70
μελανοπτερύγων μᾶτερ ὀνείρων,
ἀποπέμπομαι ἔννυχον ὄψιν
[ἣν περὶ παιδὸς ἐμοῦ τοῦ σωιζομένου κατὰ Θρήικην   73-4
ἀμφὶ Πολυξείνης τε φίλης θυγατρὸς δι' ὀνείρων   75-6
†εἶδον γὰρ φοβερὰν ὄψιν ἔμαθον ἐδάην†].   77-8
εἶδον γὰρ βαλιὰν ἔλαφον λύκου αἵμονι χαλᾶι   90
σφαζομέναν, ἀπ' ἐμῶν γονάτων σπασθεῖσαν ἀνοίκτως.   91
ὦ χθόνιοι θεοί, σώσατε παῖδ' ἐμόν,   79
ὃς μόνος οἴκων ἄγκυρ' ἔτ' ἐμῶν   80
τὰν χιονώδη Θρήικην κατέχει
ξείνου πατρίου φυλακαῖσιν.
ἔσται τι νέον·
ἥξει τι μέλος γοερὸν γοεραῖς.
οὔποτ' ἐμὰ φρὴν ὧδ' ἀλίαστον   85
φρίσσει ταρβεῖ.
ποῦ ποτε θείαν Ἑλένου ψυχὰν
καὶ Κασσάνδραν ἐσίδω, Τρωιάδες,
ὥς μοι κρίνωσιν ὀνείρους;   89

[καὶ τόδε δεῖμά μοι·   92
ἦλθ' ὑπὲρ ἄκρας τύμβου κορυφᾶς
φάντασμ' Ἀχιλέως· ᾔτει δὲ γέρας
τῶν πολυμόχθων τινὰ Τρωϊάδων.   95
ἀπ' ἐμᾶς οὖν ἀπ' ἐμᾶς τόδε παιδὸς
πέμψατε, δαίμονες, ἱκετεύω.]

---

66 διερειδομένη pp: -μένα ω   71 μᾶτερ O: μῆτερ M   73-8 del. Baier et
Wilamowitz   90-1 transposuit Wilamowitz: del. Baier et Wilamowitz
91 ἀνοίκτως Porson (cf. Σ): ἀνάγκαι οἰκτρῶς ω   80 ἄγκυρ' ἔτ' p: ἄγκυρά τ' ω
81 τὰν Battezzato: τὴν ω   85 ἀλίαστον Nauck: ἀλίαστος ω
88 Κασσάνδραν Hermann: Κασάνδραν pp: Κασσάνδρας O: Κασάνδρας M 92-7 del.
Baier et Wilamowitz   94 Ἀχιλέως pp: Ἀχιλλέως ω

ΧΟΡΟΣ

Ἑκάβη, σπουδῆι πρὸς σ' ἐλιάσθην
τὰς δεσποσύνους σκηνὰς προλιποῦσ',
ἵν' ἐκληρώθην καὶ προσετάχθην 100
δούλη, πόλεως ἀπελαυνομένη
τῆς Ἰλιάδος, λόγχης αἰχμῆι
δοριθήρατος πρὸς Ἀχαιῶν,
οὐδὲν παθέων ἀποκουφίζουσ'
ἀλλ' ἀγγελίας βάρος ἀραμένη 105
μέγα σοί τε, γύναι, κῆρυξ ἀχέων.
ἐν γὰρ Ἀχαιῶν πλήρει ξυνόδωι
λέγεται δόξαι σὴν παῖδ' Ἀχιλεῖ
σφάγιον θέσθαι. τύμβου δ' ἐπιβὰς
οἶσθ' ὅτε χρυσέοις ἐφάνη σὺν ὅπλοις, 110
τὰς ποντοπόρους δ' ἔσχε σχεδίας
λαίφη προτόνοις ἐπερειδομένας,
τάδε θωύσσων· Ποῖ δή, Δαναοί,
τὸν ἐμὸν τύμβον
στέλλεσθ' ἀγέραστον ἀφέντες; 115
πολλῆς δ' ἔριδος συνέπαισε κλύδων,
δόξα δ' ἐχώρει δίχ' ἂν' Ἑλλήνων
στρατὸν αἰχμητήν, τοῖς μὲν διδόναι
τύμβωι σφάγιον, τοῖς δ' οὐχὶ δοκοῦν.
ἦν δὲ τὸ μὲν σὸν σπεύδων ἀγαθὸν 120
τῆς μαντιπόλου Βάκχης ἀνέχων
λέκτρ' Ἀγαμέμνων· τὼ Θησείδα δ',
ὄζω Ἀθηνῶν, δισσῶν μύθων
ῥήτορες ἦσαν, γνώμηι δὲ μιᾶι
συνεχωρείτην τὸν Ἀχίλλειον 125
τύμβον στεφανοῦν αἵματι χλωρῶι,
τὰ δὲ Κασσάνδρας λέκτρ' οὐκ ἐφάτην
τῆς Ἀχιλείας
πρόσθεν θήσειν ποτὲ λόγχης.
σπουδαὶ δὲ λόγων κατατεινομένων 130
ἦσαν ἴσαι πως, πρὶν ὁ ποικιλόφρων
κόπις ἡδυλόγος δημοχαριστὴς
Λαερτιάδης πείθει στρατιὰν

---

105 ἀραμένη pp: ἀραμένα ω   116 συνέπαισε pp: συνέπεσε ω   127 Κασσάνδρας pp: Κασάνδρας ω   128 Ἀχιλείας pp: Ἀχιλλείας ω

μὴ τὸν ἄριστον Δαναῶν πάντων
δούλων σφαγίων οὕνεκ' ἀπωθεῖν, 135
μηδέ τιν' εἰπεῖν παρὰ Φερσεφόνηι
στάντα φθιμένων ὡς ἀχάριστοι
Δαναοὶ Δαναοῖς τοῖς οἰχομένοις
ὑπὲρ Ἑλλήνων
Τροίας πεδίων ἀπέβησαν. 140
ἥξει δ' Ὀδυσεὺς ὅσον οὐκ ἤδη
πῶλον ἀφέλξων σῶν ἀπὸ μαστῶν
ἔκ τε γεραιᾶς χερὸς ὁρμήσων.
ἀλλ' ἴθι ναούς, ἴθι πρὸς βωμούς,
[ἵζ' Ἀγαμέμνονος ἱκέτις γονάτων,] 145
κήρυσσε θεοὺς τούς τ' οὐρανίδας
τούς θ' ὑπὸ γαίας. ἢ γάρ σε λιταὶ
διακωλύσουσ' ὀρφανὸν εἶναι
παιδὸς μελέας ἢ δεῖ σ' ἐπιδεῖν
τύμβωι προπετῆ φοινισσομένην 150
αἵματι παρθένον ἐκ χρυσοφόρου 151–2
δειρῆς νασμῶι μελαναυγεῖ.

Εκ. οἲ ἐγὼ μελέα, τί ποτ' ἀπύσω; str.
ποίαν ἀχώ, ποῖον ὀδυρμόν, 155
δειλαία δειλαίου γήρως
<καὶ> δουλείας τᾶς οὐ τλατᾶς,
  τᾶς οὐ φερτᾶς; ὤιμοι μοι.
τίς ἀμύνει μοι; ποία γενεά,
ποία δὲ πόλις; φροῦδος πρέσβυς, 160
φροῦδοι παῖδες.
ποίαν – ἢ ταύταν ἢ κείναν; –
στείχω; ποῖ δὴ σωθῶ; ποῦ τις
θεῶν ἢ δαίμων ἐπαρωγός;
ὦ κάκ' ἐνεγκοῦσαι 165
Τρωιάδες, ὦ κάκ' ἐνεγκοῦσαι
πήματ', ἀπωλέσατ' ὠλέσατ'· οὐκέτι μοι 167–8
βίος ἀγαστὸς ἐν φάει.

136 Φερσεφόνηι M: Περσεφόνηι O   141 Ὀδυσεὺς pp: Ὀδυσσεὺς ω   145 del.
Heimsoeth   147 γαίας Porson: γαῖαν ω   150 τύμβωι pp: τύμβου ω   157 <καὶ>
Triclinius   158 φερτᾶς ω: φευκτᾶς Bothe   159 γενεά Porson: γέννα ω   163 δὴ
σωθῶ Diggle: δ' ἤσω ω   164 δαίμων Triclinius: δαιμόνων ω

ὦ τλάμων, ἄγησαί μοι πούς, mes.
ἄγησαι τᾶι γηραιᾶι 171
πρὸς τάνδ' αὐλάν. ὦ τέκνον, ὦ παῖ
δυστανοτάτας ματέρος, ἔξελθ'
ἔξελθ' οἴκων, ἄι' αὐδάν
[ὦ τέκνον, ὡς εἰδῆις οἵαν οἵαν 175
ἀίω φάμαν περὶ σᾶς ψυχᾶς].

ΠΟΛΥΞΕΝΗ
ἰώ
μᾶτερ μᾶτερ, τί βοᾶις; τί νέον
καρύξασ' οἴκων μ' ὥστ' ὄρνιν
θάμβει τῶιδ' ἐξέπταξας;
Εκ. οἴμοι τέκνον. 180
Πο. τί με δυσφημεῖς; φροίμιά μοι κακά.
Εκ. αἰαῖ σᾶς ψυχᾶς.
Πο. ἐξαύδα· μὴ κρύψηις δαρόν.
δειμαίνω δειμαίνω, μᾶτερ,
τί ποτ' ἀναστένεις. 185
Εκ. τέκνον τέκνον μελέας ματρός...
Πο. τί τόδ' ἀγγέλλεις;
Εκ. σφάξαι σ' Ἀργείων κοινά
συντείνει πρὸς τύμβον γνώμα
Πηλείαι γένναι. 190
Πο. οἴμοι, μᾶτερ, πῶς φθέγγηι;
ἀμέγαρτα κακῶν μάνυσόν μοι,
μάνυσον, μᾶτερ.
Εκ. αὐδῶ, παῖ, δυσφήμους φήμας,
ἀγγέλλουσ' Ἀργείων δόξαι 195
ψήφωι τᾶς σᾶς περὶ μοίρας.

Πο. ὦ δεινὰ παθοῦσ', ὦ παντλάμων, ant.
ὦ δυστάνου, μᾶτερ, βιοτᾶς,

---

171 γηραιᾶι Hermann: γραίαι ω   174 ἄι' αὐδάν Diggle: ἅιε ματέρος αὐδάν ω
175–6 post Hartung del. Schroeder   175 εἰδῆις M¹ pp: ἰδῆις ω   176 ἀίω ω:
κλαίω vel αὐδῶ Battezzato   177 ἰώ ω: del. Reisig: ἰώ ἰώ Hermann   186 τέκνον
τέκνον Hermann: ὦ τέκνον τέκνον ω   187 ἀγγέλλεις M¹ pp: ἀγγέλεις
ω   190 Πηλείαι Paley: Πηλεῖδα(ι) ω   195 ἀγγέλλουσ' M¹ pp: ἀγγέλους'
ω   196 ψήφωι ΟΣ: ψήφοις ΜΣ   περὶ μοίρας Page: περί μοι ψυχᾶς   198 ὦ
δυστάνου ω: τᾶς δυστάνου Hermann: ὦ δύστανος Wecklein

οἵαν οἵαν αὖ σοι λώβαν
⟨λύμαν τ'⟩ ἐχθίσταν ἀρρήταν τ' 200
ὦρσέν τις δαίμων, ⟨ὤιμοι⟩.
οὐκέτι σοι παῖς ἅδ' οὐκέτι δὴ
γήραι δειλαία δειλαίωι
συνδουλεύσω.
σκύμνον γάρ μ' ὥστ' οὐριθρέπταν 205
μόσχον δειλαία δειλαίαν 206
⟨— — — — ⏑ ⟩ ἐσόψηι 206b
χειρὸς ἀναρπαστὰν
σᾶς ἄπο λαιμότομόν θ' Ἅιδαι
γᾶς ὑποπεμπομέναν σκότον, ἔνθα νεκρῶν
μέτα τάλαινα κείσομαι. 210

[καὶ σοῦ μέν, μᾶτερ, δυστάνου
κλαίω πανοδύρτοις θρήνοις,
τὸν ἐμὸν δὲ βίον λώβαν λύμαν τ'
οὐ μετακλαίομαι, ἀλλὰ θανεῖν μοι
ξυντυχία κρείσσων ἐκύρησεν.] 215

Χο. καὶ μὴν Ὀδυσσεὺς ἔρχεται σπουδῆι ποδός,
Ἑκάβη, νέον τι πρὸς σὲ σημανῶν ἔπος.

ΟΔΥΣΣΕΥΣ
γύναι, δοκῶ μέν σ' εἰδέναι γνώμην στρατοῦ
ψῆφόν τε τὴν κρανθεῖσαν· ἀλλ' ὅμως φράσω.
ἔδοξ' Ἀχαιοῖς παῖδα σὴν Πολυξένην 220
σφάξαι πρὸς ὀρθὸν χῶμ' Ἀχιλλείου τάφου.
ἡμᾶς δὲ πομπούς καὶ κομιστῆρας κόρης
τάσσουσιν εἶναι· θύματος δ' ἐπιστάτης
ἱερεύς τ' ἐπέσται τοῦδε παῖς Ἀχιλλέως.

200 ⟨λύμαν τ'⟩ Battezzato: ⟨λώβαν⟩ Hermann   201 ὦρσεν τις O: ὦρσε τίς M   ⟨ὤιμοι⟩ Battezzato: ⟨ὤμοι⟩ Diggle   203 δειλαία δειλαίωι pp: δειλαίωι δειλαία ω   206b lacunam indicauit Murray: ⟨μάτηρ σκύμνον σὸν⟩ e.g. Battezzato   208 θ' Ἅιδαι Hermann: τ' ἀίδαν M: τ' ἀίδαι O: τ' αἰκῶς Battezzato   210 τάλαινα p: ἁ τάλαινα ω   211–15 del. Wilamowitz   211 σοῦ Heimsoeth (cf. Σ): σὲ ω   δυστάνου M: δύστανε O   212 πανοδύρτοις ω: πανδύρτοις Blomfield   213 τὸν ἐμὸν δὲ βίον ω: τοὐμοῦ δὲ βίου Reiske   215 ξυντυχία ω: πότμος Weil: δαίμων Nauck   224 ἐπέσται Nauck: ἐπέστη Π⁵ ω

ΕΥΡΙΠΙΔΟΥ

οἶσθ' οὖν ὃ δρᾶσον· μήτ' ἀποσπασθῆις βίαι 225
μήτ' ἐς χερῶν ἅμιλλαν ἐξέλθηις ἐμοί,
γίγνωσκε δ' ἀλκὴν καὶ παρουσίαν κακῶν
τῶν σῶν· σοφόν τοι κἂν κακοῖς ἃ δεῖ φρονεῖν.
Εκ. αἰαῖ· παρέστηχ', ὡς ἔοικ', ἀγὼν μέγας,
πλήρης στεναγμῶν οὐδὲ δακρύων κενός. 230
κἄγωγ' ἄρ' οὐκ ἔθνηισκον οὗ μ' ἐχρῆν θανεῖν,
οὐδ' ὤλεσέν με Ζεύς, τρέφει δ' ὅπως ὁρῶ
κακῶν κάκ' ἄλλα μείζον' ἡ τάλαιν' ἐγώ.
εἰ δ' ἔστι τοῖς δούλοισι τοὺς ἐλευθέρους
μὴ λυπρὰ μηδὲ καρδίας δηκτήρια 235
ἐξιστορῆσαι, †σοὶ μὲν εἰρῆσθαι† χρεών,
ἡμᾶς δ' ἀκοῦσαι τοὺς ἐρωτῶντας τάδε.
Οδ. ἔξεστ', ἐρώτα· τοῦ χρόνου γὰρ οὐ φθονῶ.
Εκ. οἶσθ' ἡνίκ' ἦλθες Ἰλίου κατάσκοπος
δυσχλαινίαι τ' ἄμορφος ὀμμάτων τ' ἄπο 240
φόνου σταλαγμοὶ σὴν κατέσταζον γένυν;
Οδ. οἶδ'· οὐ γὰρ ἄκρας καρδίας ἔψαυσέ μου.
Εκ. ἔγνω δέ σ' Ἑλένη καὶ μόνηι κατεῖπ' ἐμοί;
Οδ. μεμνήμεθ' ἐς κίνδυνον ἐλθόντες μέγαν.
Εκ. ἥψω δὲ γονάτων τῶν ἐμῶν ταπεινὸς ὤν; 245
Οδ. ὥστ' ἐνθανεῖν γε σοῖς πέπλοισι χεῖρ' ἐμήν. 246
Εκ. τί δῆτ' ἔλεξας δοῦλος ὢν ἐμὸς τότε; 249
Οδ. πολλῶν λόγων εὑρήμαθ' ὥστε μὴ θανεῖν. 250
Εκ. ἔσωσα δῆτά σ' ἐξέπεμψά τε χθονός; 247
Οδ. ὥστ' εἰσορᾶν γε φέγγος ἡλίου τόδε. 248
Εκ. οὔκουν κακύνηι τοῖσδε τοῖς βουλεύμασιν, 251
ὃς ἐξ ἐμοῦ μὲν ἔπαθες οἷα φὴις παθεῖν,
δρᾶις δ' οὐδὲν ἡμᾶς εὖ, κακῶς δ' ὅσον δύναι;
ἀχάριστον ὑμῶν σπέρμ', ὅσοι δημηγόρους
ζηλοῦτε τιμάς· μηδὲ γιγνώσκοισθέ μοι, 255
οἳ τοὺς φίλους βλάπτοντες οὐ φροντίζετε,
ἢν τοῖσι πολλοῖς πρὸς χάριν λέγητέ τι.
ἀτὰρ τί δὴ σόφισμα τοῦθ' ἡγούμενοι
ἐς τήνδε παῖδα ψῆφον ὥρισαν φόνου;

225 δρᾶσον Π⁵ Μ: δράσεις Π⁵ʸᵖ Μʸᵖ Ο   231 κἄγωγ' ἄρ' L. Dindorf: κἀγὼ γὰρ ω   236 σοὶ μὲν εἰρῆσθαι ω: σὲ μὲν ἀμείβεσθαι Herwerden   243 κατεῖπ' ἐμοί Brunck: κατεῖπέ μοι ω   249–50, 247–8 pp: 247–8, 249–50 ω   253 δύναι Porson: δύνηι ω   255 γιγνώσκοισθ' ἐμοί Wilamowitz

ΕΚΑΒΗ 41

πότερα τὸ χρή σφ' ἐπήγαγ' ἀνθρωποσφαγεῖν 260
πρὸς τύμβον, ἔνθα βουθυτεῖν μᾶλλον πρέπει;
ἢ τοὺς κτανόντας ἀνταποκτεῖναι θέλων
ἐς τήνδ' Ἀχιλλεὺς ἐνδίκως τείνει φόνον;
ἀλλ' οὐδὲν αὐτὸν ἥδε γ' εἴργασται κακόν.
Ἑλένην νιν αἰτεῖν χρῆν τάφωι προσφάγματα· 265
κείνη γὰρ ὤλεσέν νιν ἐς Τροίαν τ' ἄγει.
εἰ δ' αἰχμαλώτων χρή τιν' ἔκκριτον θανεῖν
κάλλει θ' ὑπερφέρουσαν, οὐχ ἡμῶν τόδε·
ἡ Τυνδαρὶς γὰρ εἶδος ἐκπρεπεστάτη,
ἀδικοῦσά θ' ἡμῶν οὐδὲν ἧσσον ηὑρέθη. 270
τῶι μὲν δικαίωι τόνδ' ἁμιλλῶμαι λόγον·
ἃ δ' ἀντιδοῦναι δεῖ σ' ἀπαιτούσης ἐμοῦ
ἄκουσον. ἥψω τῆς ἐμῆς, ὡς φήις, χερὸς
καὶ τῆσδε γραίας προσπίτνων παρηίδος·
ἀνθάπτομαί σου τῶνδε τῶν αὐτῶν ἐγὼ 275
χάριν τ' ἀπαιτῶ τὴν τόθ' ἱκετεύω τέ σε,
μή μου τὸ τέκνον ἐκ χερῶν ἀποσπάσηις
μηδὲ κτάνητε· τῶν τεθνηκότων ἅλις.
ταύτηι γέγηθα κἀπιλήθομαι κακῶν·
ἥδ' ἀντὶ πολλῶν ἐστί μοι παραψυχή, 280
πόλις, τιθήνη, βάκτρον, ἡγεμὼν ὁδοῦ.
οὐ τοὺς κρατοῦντας χρὴ κρατεῖν ἃ μὴ χρεὼν
οὐδ' εὐτυχοῦντας εὖ δοκεῖν πράξειν ἀεί·
κἀγὼ γὰρ ἦ ποτ' ἀλλὰ νῦν οὐκ εἴμ' ἔτι,
τὸν πάντα δ' ὄλβον ἧμαρ ἕν μ' ἀφείλετο. 285
ἀλλ', ὦ φίλον γένειον, αἰδέσθητί με,
οἴκτιρον· ἐλθὼν δ' εἰς Ἀχαιικὸν στρατὸν
παρηγόρησον ὡς ἀποκτείνειν φθόνος
γυναῖκας, ἃς τὸ πρῶτον οὐκ ἐκτείνατε
βωμῶν ἀποσπάσαντες ἀλλ' ὠικτίρατε. 290
νόμος δ' ἐν ὑμῖν τοῖς τ' ἐλευθέροις ἴσος
καὶ τοῖσι δούλοις αἵματος κεῖται πέρι.
τὸ δ' ἀξίωμα, κἂν κακῶς λέγηις, τὸ σὸν
πείσει· λόγος γὰρ ἔκ τ' ἀδοξούντων ἰὼν

260 χρή Nauck: χρῆν ω test.: χρεών Scaliger   ἀνθρωποσφαγεῖν ω: ἀνθρωποκτονεῖν Σ pp test.   269 ἐκπρεπεστάτη Μ: εὐπρεπεστάτη O   274 γραίας Valckenaer: γεραιᾶς ω   293 λέγηις Muretus (cf. test.): λέγηι ω test.

ΕΥΡΙΠΙΔΟΥ

κἀκ τῶν δοκούντων αὐτὸς οὐ ταὐτὸν σθένει. 295
Χο. οὐκ ἔστιν οὕτω στερρὸς ἀνθρώπου φύσις
ἥτις γόων σῶν καὶ μακρῶν ὀδυρμάτων
κλύουσα θρήνους οὐκ ἂν ἐκβάλοι δάκρυ.
Οδ. Ἑκάβη, διδάσκου, μηδὲ τῶι θυμουμένωι
τὸν εὖ λέγοντα δυσμενῆ ποιοῦ φρενός. 300
ἐγὼ τὸ μὲν σὸν σῶμ' ὑφ' οὗπερ ηὐτύχουν
σώιζειν ἕτοιμός εἰμι κοὐκ ἄλλως λέγω·
ἃ δ' εἶπον εἰς ἅπαντας οὐκ ἀρνήσομαι,
Τροίας ἁλούσης ἀνδρὶ τῶι πρώτωι στρατοῦ
σὴν παῖδα δοῦναι σφάγιον ἐξαιτουμένωι. 305
ἐν τῶιδε γὰρ κάμνουσιν αἱ πολλαὶ πόλεις,
ὅταν τις ἐσθλὸς καὶ πρόθυμος ὢν ἀνὴρ
μηδὲν φέρηται τῶν κακιόνων πλέον.
ἡμῖν δ' Ἀχιλλεὺς ἄξιος τιμῆς, γύναι,
θανὼν ὑπὲρ γῆς Ἑλλάδος κάλλιστ' ἀνήρ. 310
οὔκουν τόδ' αἰσχρόν, εἰ βλέποντι μὲν φίλωι
χρώμεσθ', ἐπεὶ δ' ὄλωλε μὴ χρώμεσθ' ἔτι;
εἶἑν· τί δῆτ' ἐρεῖ τις, ἤν τις αὖ φανῆι
στρατοῦ τ' ἄθροισις πολεμίων τ' ἀγωνία;
πότερα μαχούμεθ' ἢ φιλοψυχήσομεν, 315
τὸν κατθανόνθ' ὁρῶντες οὐ τιμώμενον;
καὶ μὴν ἔμοιγε ζῶντι μὲν καθ' ἡμέραν
κεἰ σμίκρ' ἔχοιμι πάντ' ἂν ἀρκούντως ἔχοι·
τύμβον δὲ βουλοίμην ἂν ἀξιούμενον
τὸν ἐμὸν ὁρᾶσθαι· διὰ μακροῦ γὰρ ἡ χάρις. 320
εἰ δ' οἰκτρὰ πάσχειν φήις, τάδ' ἀντάκουέ μου·
εἰσὶν παρ' ἡμῖν οὐδὲν ἧσσον ἄθλιαι
γραῖαι γυναῖκες ἠδὲ πρεσβῦται σέθεν,
νύμφαι τ' ἀρίστων νυμφίων τητώμεναι,
ὧν ἥδε κεύθει σώματ' Ἰδαία κόνις. 325
τόλμα τάδ'. ἡμεῖς δ', εἰ κακῶς νομίζομεν
τιμᾶν τὸν ἐσθλόν, ἀμαθίαν ὀφλήσομεν·
οἱ βάρβαροι δὲ μήτε τοὺς φίλους φίλους
ἡγεῖσθε μήτε τοὺς καλῶς τεθνηκότας
θαυμάζεθ', ὡς ἂν ἡ μὲν Ἑλλὰς εὐτυχῆι, 330

295 αὐτός test.: ὡὐτὸς p: αὐτὸς ω test.   300 φρενός Murray: φρενί ω

ΕΚΑΒΗ

ὑμεῖς δ' ἔχηθ' ὅμοια τοῖς βουλεύμασιν.
Χο. αἰαῖ· τὸ δοῦλον ὡς κακὸν πέφυκ' ἀεὶ
τολμᾶι θ' ἃ μὴ χρή, τῆι βίαι νικώμενον.
Εκ. ὦ θύγατερ, οὑμοὶ μὲν λόγοι πρὸς αἰθέρα
φροῦδοι μάτην ῥιφθέντες ἀμφὶ σοῦ φόνου· 335
σὺ δ', εἴ τι μείζω δύναμιν ἢ μήτηρ ἔχεις,
σπούδαζε πάσας ὥστ' ἀηδόνος στόμα
φθογγὰς ἱεῖσα, μὴ στερηθῆναι βίου.
πρόσπιπτε δ' οἰκτρῶς τοῦδ' Ὀδυσσέως γόνυ
καὶ πεῖθ' (ἔχεις δὲ πρόφασιν· ἔστι γὰρ τέκνα 340
καὶ τῶιδε) τὴν σὴν ὥστ' ἐποικτῖραι τύχην.
Πο. ὁρῶ σ', Ὀδυσσεῦ, δεξιὰν ὑφ' εἵματος
κρύπτοντα χεῖρα καὶ πρόσωπον ἔμπαλιν
στρέφοντα, μή σου προσθίγω γενειάδος.
θάρσει· πέφευγας τὸν ἐμὸν Ἱκέσιον Δία· 345
ὡς ἕψομαί γε τοῦ τ' ἀναγκαίου χάριν
θανεῖν τε χρήιζουσ'· εἰ δὲ μὴ βουλήσομαι,
κακὴ φανοῦμαι καὶ φιλόψυχος γυνή.
τί γάρ με δεῖ ζῆν; ἧι πατὴρ μὲν ἦν ἄναξ
Φρυγῶν ἁπάντων· τοῦτό μοι πρῶτον βίου. 350
ἔπειτ' ἐθρέφθην ἐλπίδων καλῶν ὕπο
βασιλεῦσι νύμφη, ζῆλον οὐ σμικρὸν γάμων
ἔχουσ', ὅτου δῶμ' ἑστίαν τ' ἀφίξομαι.
δέσποινα δ' ἡ δύστηνος Ἰδαίαισιν ἢ
γυναιξί, παρθένοις τ' ἀπόβλεπτος μέτα, 355
ἴση θεοῖσι πλὴν τὸ κατθανεῖν μόνον.
νῦν δ' εἰμὶ δούλη. πρῶτα μέν με τοὔνομα
θανεῖν ἐρᾶν τίθησιν οὐκ εἰωθὸς ὄν·
ἔπειτ' ἴσως ἂν δεσποτῶν ὠμῶν φρένας
τύχοιμ' ἄν, ὅστις ἀργύρου μ' ὠνήσεται, 360
τὴν Ἕκτορός τε χἀτέρων πολλῶν κάσιν,
προσθεὶς δ' ἀνάγκην σιτοποιὸν ἐν δόμοις
σαίρειν τε δῶμα κερκίσιν τ' ἐφεστάναι
λυπρὰν ἄγουσαν ἡμέραν μ' ἀναγκάσει·
λέχη δὲ τἀμὰ δοῦλος ὠνητός ποθεν 365
χρανεῖ, τυράννων πρόσθεν ἠξιωμένα.

332 πέφυκ' ἀεὶ pp test.: πεφυκέναι ω   333 τολμᾶν Reiske   335 ῥιφθέντες pp:
ῥιφέντες Μ: ῥηθέντες Ο   352 γάμων Σ pp: γάμου Ο: βίου Μ

οὐ δῆτ'· ἀφίημ' ὀμμάτων ἐλευθέρα
φέγγος τόδ', Ἅιδηι προστιθεῖσ' ἐμὸν δέμας.
ἄγ' οὖν μ', Ὀδυσσεῦ, καὶ διέργασαί μ' ἄγων·
οὔτ' ἐλπίδος γὰρ οὔτε του δόξης ὁρῶ 370
θάρσος παρ' ἡμῖν ὥς ποτ' εὖ πρᾶξαί με χρή.
μῆτερ, σὺ δ' ἡμῖν μηδὲν ἐμποδὼν γένηι
λέγουσα μηδὲ δρῶσα, συμβούλου δέ μοι
θανεῖν πρὶν αἰσχρῶν μὴ κατ' ἀξίαν τυχεῖν.
ὅστις γὰρ οὐκ εἴωθε γεύεσθαι κακῶν 375
φέρει μέν, ἀλγεῖ δ' αὐχέν' ἐντιθεὶς ζυγῶι·
θανὼν δ' ἂν εἴη μᾶλλον εὐτυχέστερος
ἢ ζῶν· τὸ γὰρ ζῆν μὴ καλῶς μέγας πόνος.
Χο. δεινὸς χαρακτὴρ κἀπίσημος ἐν βροτοῖς
ἐσθλῶν γενέσθαι, κἀπὶ μεῖζον ἔρχεται 380
τῆς εὐγενείας ὄνομα τοῖσιν ἀξίοις.
Εκ. καλῶς μὲν εἶπας, θύγατερ, ἀλλὰ τῶι καλῶι
λύπη πρόσεστιν. εἰ δὲ δεῖ τῶι Πηλέως
χάριν γενέσθαι παιδὶ καὶ ψόγον φυγεῖν
ὑμᾶς, Ὀδυσσεῦ, τήνδε μὲν μὴ κτείνετε, 385
ἡμᾶς δ' ἄγοντες πρὸς πυρὰν Ἀχιλλέως
κεντεῖτε, μὴ φείδεσθ'· ἐγὼ 'τεκον Πάριν,
ὃς παῖδα Θέτιδος ὤλεσεν τόξοις βαλών.
Οδ. οὐ σ', ὦ γεραιά, κατθανεῖν Ἀχιλλέως
φάντασμ' Ἀχαιοὺς ἀλλὰ τήνδ' ἠιτήσατο. 390
Εκ. ὑμεῖς δέ μ' ἀλλὰ θυγατρὶ συμφονεύσατε,
καὶ δὶς τόσον πῶμ' αἵματος γενήσεται
γαίαι νεκρῶι τε τῶι τάδ' ἐξαιτουμένωι.
Οδ. ἅλις κόρης σῆς θάνατος· οὐ προσοιστέος
ἄλλος πρὸς ἄλλωι· μηδὲ τόνδ' ὠφείλομεν. 395
Εκ. πολλή γ' ἀνάγκη θυγατρὶ συνθανεῖν ἐμέ.
Οδ. πῶς; οὐ γὰρ οἶδα δεσπότας κεκτημένος.
Εκ. ὅμοια· κισσὸς δρυὸς ὅπως τῆσδ' ἕξομαι.
Οδ. οὔκ, ἤν γε πείθηι τοῖσι σοῦ σοφωτέροις.
Εκ. ὡς τῆσδ' ἑκοῦσα παιδὸς οὐ μεθήσομαι. 400
Οδ. ἀλλ' οὐδ' ἐγὼ μὴν τήνδ' ἄπειμ' αὐτοῦ λιπών.

367 ἐλευθέρα Battezzato: ἐλεύθερον ω: ἐλευθέρων Blomfield: ἐλευθέρως Battezzato   369 ἄγ' οὖν μ' pp: ἄγου μ' M: ἀγοῦ μ' O   387 ἐγὼ 'τεκον Battezzato (cf. Dickey): ἐγὼ τεκον O: ἐγὼ τέκον M: ἐγὼ 'τεκον Dindorf   392 πῶμ' Porson: πόμ' ω   398 ὅμοια· Reiske (distinxit Jackson): ὁποῖα ω   ὅπως ω: ἐγὼ Sybel

Πο. μῆτερ, πιθοῦ μοι· [καὶ σύ, παῖ Λαερτίου,
χάλα τοκεῦσιν εἰκότως θυμουμένοις,
σύ τ', ὦ τάλαινα,] τοῖς κρατοῦσι μὴ μάχου.
βούληι πεσεῖν πρὸς οὖδας ἑλκῶσαί τε σὸν 405
γέροντα χρῶτα πρὸς βίαν ὠθουμένη
ἀσχημονῆσαί τ' ἐκ νέου βραχίονος
σπασθεῖσ', ἃ πείσηι; μὴ σύ γ'· οὐ γὰρ ἄξιον.
ἀλλ', ὦ φίλη μοι μῆτερ, ἡδίστην χέρα
δὸς καὶ παρειὰν προσβαλεῖν παρηίδι, 410
ὡς οὔποτ' αὖθις ἀλλὰ νῦν πανύστατον
[ἀκτῖνα κύκλον θ' ἡλίου προσόψομαι].
τέλος δέχηι δὴ τῶν ἐμῶν προσφθεγμάτων·
ὦ μῆτερ ὦ τεκοῦσ', ἄπειμι δὴ κάτω...
Εκ. ὦ θύγατερ, ἡμεῖς δ' ἐν φάει δουλεύσομεν. 415
Πο. ἄνυμφος ἀνυμέναιος ὧν μ' ἐχρῆν τυχεῖν.
Εκ. οἰκτρὰ σύ, τέκνον, ἀθλία δ' ἐγὼ γυνή.
Πο. ἐκεῖ δ' ἐν Ἅιδου κείσομαι χωρὶς σέθεν.
Εκ. οἴμοι· τί δράσω; ποῖ τελευτήσω βίον;
Πο. δούλη θανοῦμαι, πατρὸς οὖσ' ἐλευθέρου. 420
Εκ. ἡμεῖς δὲ πεντήκοντά γ' ἄμμοροι τέκνων.
Πο. τί σοι πρὸς Ἕκτορ' ἢ γέροντ' εἴπω πόσιν;
Εκ. ἄγγελλε πασῶν ἀθλιωτάτην ἐμέ.
Πο. ὦ στέρνα μαστοί θ', οἵ μ' ἐθρέψαθ' ἡδέως.
Εκ. ὦ τῆς ἀώρου θύγατερ ἀθλία τύχης. 425
Πο. χαῖρ', ὦ τεκοῦσα, χαῖρε Κασσάνδρα τέ μοι...
Εκ. χαίρουσιν ἄλλοι, μητρὶ δ' οὐκ ἔστιν τόδε.
Πο. ὅ τ' ἐν φιλίπποις Θρηιξὶ Πολύδωρος κάσις.
Εκ. εἰ ζῆι γ'· ἀπιστῶ δ'· ὧδε πάντα δυστυχῶ.
Πο. ζῆι καὶ θανούσης ὄμμα συγκλήισει τὸ σόν. 430
Εκ. τέθνηκ' ἔγωγε πρὶν θανεῖν κακῶν ὕπο.
Πο. κόμιζ', Ὀδυσσεῦ, μ' ἀμφιθεὶς κάραι πέπλον,
ὡς πρὶν σφαγῆναί γ' ἐκτέτηκα καρδίαν
θρήνοισι μητρὸς τήνδε τ' ἐκτήκω γόοις.
ὦ φῶς· προσειπεῖν γὰρ σὸν ὄνομ' ἔξεστί μοι, 435
μέτεστι δ' οὐδὲν πλὴν ὅσον χρόνον ξίφους
βαίνω μεταξὺ καὶ πυρᾶς Ἀχιλλέως.

402-4 καὶ σύ ... ὦ τάλαινα del. Battezzato 412 om. ω: del. Wecklein: habent
pp 415-16 post 420 traiecit Diggle 425 ἀθλία Markland: ἀθλίας O:
ἀθλίου Μ 427 τόδε O: χαρά Μ 428 Θρηιξὶ Hermann: Θραξὶ ω 432 κάραι
πέπλον Battezzato: κάρα πέπλον p: κάρα πέπλοις ω: κάραι πέπλους Kirchhoff

Εκ. οἴ 'γώ, προλείπω, λύεται δέ μου μέλη.
ὦ θύγατερ, ἄψαι μητρός, ἔκτεινον χέρα,
δός, μὴ λίπηις μ' ἄπαιδ'. ἀπωλόμην, φίλαι. 440
[ὡς τὴν Λάκαιναν σύγγονον Διοσκόροιν
Ἑλένην ἴδοιμι· διὰ καλῶν γὰρ ὀμμάτων
αἴσχιστα Τροίαν εἷλε τὴν εὐδαίμονα.]

Χο. αὔρα, ποντιὰς αὔρα, str. 1
ἅτε ποντοπόρους κομί- 445
ζεις θοὰς ἀκάτους ἐπ' οἶδμα λίμνας,
ποῖ με τὰν μελέαν πορεύ-
σεις; τῶι δουλόσυνος πρὸς οἶκον κτηθεῖσ' ἀφίξομαι; ἢ
Δωρίδος ὅρμον αἴας, 450
ἢ Φθιάδος ἔνθα τὸν
καλλίστων ὑδάτων πατέρα
φασὶν Ἀπιδανὸν πεδία λιπαίνειν, 453-4

ἢ νάσων, ἁλιήρει ant. 1
κῶπαι πεμπομένα, τάλαι- 456
ναν οἰκτρὰ βιοτὰν ἔχουσ' ἄοικος,
ἔνθα πρωτόγονός τε φοῖ-
νιξ δάφνα θ' ἱεροὺς ἀνέ-
σχε πτόρθους Λατοῖ φίλον ὠ- 460
δῖνος ἄγαλμα Δίας,
σὺν Δηλιάσιν τε κού-
ραισιν Ἀρτέμιδος θεᾶς
χρυσέαν τ' ἄμπυκα τόξα τ' εὐλογήσω; 464-5

ἢ Παλλάδος ἐν πόλει str. 2
τὰς καλλιδίφρους Ἀθα-
ναίας ἐν κροκέωι πέπλωι
ζεύξομαι ἆρα πώ-

438 μου M: μοι O   441-3 del. Hartung   456 πεμπομένα Willink: πεμπομέναν ω   457 οἰκτρὰ Battezzato: οἰκτρὰν ω   ἔχουσ' ἄοικος Willink: ἔχουσαν οἴκοις ω: ἔχουσ' ἐν οἴκοις Voss (ἐν ... οἴκοις ... ἔχουσα Σ)   460 φίλον Wecklein: φίλαι M: φίλα O   463 Ἀρτέμιδος O: Ἀρτέμιδος τε M   464-5 χρυσέαν τ' pp: χρυσέαν ω   467 τὰς Σ: τᾶς ω   καλλιδίφρους MΣ: καλλιδίφρου O   467-8 Ἀθαναίας ω: θεᾶς Lackner   469 ἆρα O: ἆρα M: ἅρματι pp: ἄρματα p: ἅρμα Fritzsche

λους ἐν δαιδαλέαισι ποι- 470
κίλλουσ' ἀνθοκρόκοισι πή-
ναις ἢ Τιτάνων γενεάν,
τὰν Ζεὺς ἀμφιπύρωι κοιμί-
ζει φλογμῶι Κρονίδας;

ὤιμοι τεκέων ἐμῶν, ant. 2
ὤιμοι πατέρων χθονός θ', 476
ἃ καπνῶι κατερείπεται
τυφομένα δορί-
κτητος Ἀργείων· ἐγὼ δ'
ἐν ξείναι χθονὶ δὴ κέκλη- 480
μαι δούλα, λιποῦσ' Ἀσίαν,
Εὐρώπας θεράπναν ἀλλά-
ξασ' Ἅιδα θαλάμους.

ΤΑΛΘΥΒΙΟΣ
ποῦ τὴν ἄνασσαν δή ποτ' οὖσαν Ἰλίου
Ἑκάβην ἂν ἐξεύροιμι, Τρωιάδες κόραι; 485
Χο. αὕτη πέλας σοῦ νῶτ' ἔχουσ' ἐπὶ χθονί,
Ταλθύβιε, κεῖται συγκεκλημένη πέπλοις.
Τα. ὦ Ζεῦ, τί λέξω; πότερά σ' ἀνθρώπους ὁρᾶν
ἢ δόξαν ἄλλως τήνδε κεκτῆσθαι μάτην
[ψευδῆ, δοκοῦντας δαιμόνων εἶναι γένος], 490
τύχην δὲ πάντα τἀν βροτοῖς ἐπισκοπεῖν;
οὐχ ἥδ' ἄνασσα τῶν πολυχρύσων Φρυγῶν;
οὐχ ἥδε Πριάμου τοῦ μέγ' ὀλβίου δάμαρ;
καὶ νῦν πόλις μὲν πᾶσ' ἀνέστηκεν δορί,
αὐτὴ δὲ δούλη γραῦς ἄπαις ἐπὶ χθονὶ 495
κεῖται, κόνει φύρουσα δύστηνον κάρα.
φεῦ φεῦ· γέρων μέν εἰμ', ὅμως δέ μοι θανεῖν
εἴη πρὶν αἰσχρᾶι περιπεσεῖν τύχηι τινί.
ἀνίστασ', ὦ δύστηνε, καὶ μετάρσιον
πλευρὰν ἔπαιρε καὶ τὸ πάλλευκον κάρα. 500
Εκ. ἔα· τίς οὗτος σῶμα τοὐμὸν οὐκ ἐᾶι

477 καπνῶι om. p: del. Lackner   479 Ἀργείων Hermann: Ἀργείων
ω   482 θεράπναν Purgold: θεράπναν Ω: θεράπαιναν Σ   483 Ἅιδα Canter: Ἀΐδα
ω   487 συγκεκλημένη Hermann: συγκεκλημένη Μ: συγκεκλιμένη
Ο   489 κεκτῆσθαι μάτην ω: κεκτῆσθαι βροτοὺς Apitz: κεκτῆσθαί ποτε
Battezzato   490 del. Nauck

ΕΥΡΙΠΙΔΟΥ

κεῖσθαι; τί κινεῖς μ', ὅστις εἶ, λυπουμένην;
Τα. Ταλθύβιος ἥκω, Δαναϊδῶν ὑπηρέτης
[Ἀγαμέμνονος πέμψαντος, ὦ γύναι, μέτα].
Εκ. ὦ φίλτατ', ἆρα κἄμ' ἐπισφάξαι τάφωι 505
δοκοῦν Ἀχαιοῖς ἦλθες; ὡς φίλ' ἂν λέγοις.
σπεύδωμεν, ἐγκονῶμεν· ἡγοῦ μοι, γέρον.
Τα. σὴν παῖδα κατθανοῦσαν ὡς θάψηις, γύναι,
ἥκω μεταστείχων σε· πέμπουσιν δέ με
δισσοί τ' Ἀτρεῖδαι καὶ λεὼς Ἀχαιικός. 510
Εκ. οἴμοι, τί λέξεις; οὐκ ἄρ' ὡς θανουμένους
μετῆλθες ἡμᾶς ἀλλὰ σημανῶν κακά;
ὄλωλας, ὦ παῖ, μητρὸς ἁρπασθεῖσ' ἄπο,
ἡμεῖς δ' ἄτεκνοι τοὐπὶ σ', ὦ τάλαιν' ἐγώ.
πῶς καί νιν ἐξεπράξατ'; ἆρ' αἰδούμενοι; 515
ἢ πρὸς τὸ δεινὸν ἦλθεθ' ὡς ἐχθράν, γέρον,
κτείνοντες; εἰπέ, καίπερ οὐ λέξων φίλα.
Τα. διπλᾶ με χρήιζεις δάκρυα κερδᾶναι, γύναι,
σῆς παιδὸς οἴκτωι· νῦν τε γὰρ λέγων κακὰ
τέγξω τόδ' ὄμμα πρὸς τάφωι θ' ὅτ' ὤλλυτο. 520
παρῆν μὲν ὄχλος πᾶς Ἀχαιικοῦ στρατοῦ
πλήρης πρὸ τύμβου σῆς κόρης ἐπὶ σφαγάς,
λαβὼν δ' Ἀχιλλέως παῖς Πολυξένην χερὸς
ἔστησ' ἐπ' ἄκρου χώματος, πέλας δ' ἐγώ·
λεκτοί τ' Ἀχαιῶν ἔκκριτοι νεανίαι, 525
σκίρτημα μόσχου σῆς καθέξοντες χεροῖν,
ἕσποντο. πλῆρες δ' ἐν χεροῖν λαβὼν δέπας
πάγχρυσον αἴρει χειρὶ παῖς Ἀχιλλέως
χοὰς θανόντι πατρί· σημαίνει δέ μοι
σιγὴν Ἀχαιῶν παντὶ κηρῦξαι στρατῶι. 530
[κἀγὼ καταστὰς εἶπον ἐν μέσοις τάδε·
Σιγᾶτ', Ἀχαιοί, σῖγα πᾶς ἔστω λεώς,
σίγα σιώπα. νήνεμον δ' ἔστησ' ὄχλον.]
ὁ δ' εἶπεν· Ὦ παῖ Πηλέως, πατὴρ δ' ἐμός,
δέξαι χοάς μοι τάσδε κηλητηρίους, 535
νεκρῶν ἀγωγούς· ἐλθὲ δ', ὡς πίηις μέλαν
κόρης ἀκραιφνὲς αἷμ' ὅ σοι δωρούμεθα.

504 del. Jenni   512 σημανῶν pp: σημαίνων ω   531-3 del. Battezzato
531 καταστὰς MB: παραστὰς O   535 μοι pp: μου ω

ΕΚΑΒΗ 49

στρατός τε κἀγώ· πρευμενὴς δ' ἡμῖν γενοῦ
λῦσαί τε πρύμνας καὶ χαλινωτήρια
νεῶν δὸς ἡμῖν πρευμενοῦς τ' ἀπ' Ἰλίου 540
νόστου τυχόντας πάντας ἐς πάτραν μολεῖν.
τοσαῦτ' ἔλεξε, πᾶς δ' ἐπηύξατο στρατός.
εἶτ' ἀμφίχρυσον φάσγανον κώπης λαβὼν
ἐξεῖλκε κολεοῦ, λογάσι δ' Ἀργείων στρατοῦ
νεανίαις ἔνευσε παρθένον λαβεῖν. 545
ἡ δ', ὡς ἐφράσθη, τόνδ' ἐσήμηνεν λόγον·
Ὦ τὴν ἐμὴν πέρσαντες Ἀργεῖοι πόλιν,
ἑκοῦσα θνῄσκω· μή τις ἅψηται χροὸς
τοὐμοῦ· παρέξω γὰρ δέρην εὐκαρδίως.
ἐλευθέραν δέ μ', ὡς ἐλευθέρα θάνω, 550
πρὸς θεῶν, μεθέντες κτείνατ'· ἐν νεκροῖσι γὰρ
δούλη κεκλῆσθαι βασιλὶς οὖσ' αἰσχύνομαι.
λαοὶ δ' ἐπερρόθησαν Ἀγαμέμνων τ' ἄναξ
εἶπεν μεθεῖναι παρθένον νεανίαις.
[οἱ δ', ὡς τάχιστ' ἤκουσαν ὑστάτην ὄπα, 555
μεθῆκαν, οὗπερ καὶ μέγιστον ἦν κράτος.]
κἀπεὶ τόδ' εἰσήκουσε δεσποτῶν ἔπος,
λαβοῦσα πέπλους ἐξ ἄκρας ἐπωμίδος
ἔρρηξε λαγόνας ἐς μέσας παρ' ὀμφαλὸν
μαστούς τ' ἔδειξε στέρνα θ' ὡς ἀγάλματος 560
κάλλιστα, καὶ καθεῖσα πρὸς γαῖαν γόνυ
ἔλεξε πάντων τλημονέστατον λόγον·
Ἰδού, τόδ' εἰ μὲν στέρνον, ὦ νεανία,
παίειν προθυμῇ, παῖσον, εἰ δ' ὑπ' αὐχένα
χρῄζεις πάρεστι λαιμὸς εὐτρεπὴς ὅδε. 565
ὁ δ' οὐ θέλων τε καὶ θέλων οἴκτωι κόρης
τέμνει σιδήρωι πνεύματος διαρροάς·
κρουνοὶ δ' ἐχώρουν. ἡ δὲ καὶ θνῄσκουσ' ὅμως
πολλὴν πρόνοιαν εἶχεν εὐσχήμων πεσεῖν,
κρύπτουσ' ἃ κρύπτειν ὄμματ' ἀρσένων χρεών. 570
ἐπεὶ δ' ἀφῆκε πνεῦμα θανασίμωι σφαγῇ,
οὐδεὶς τὸν αὐτὸν εἶχεν Ἀργείων πόνον,

540 πρευμενοῦς ω: ἡσύχου Kovacs 555–6 del. Jacobs 559 μέσας Brunck: μέσον
ω 569 εὐσχήμων test.: εὐσχήμως Β: εὐσχημόνως Ο: εὐστήμως Μ 570 del. quidam
apud scholium κρύπτουσ' pp test.: κρύπτειν θ' ω

50 ΕΥΡΙΠΙΔΟΥ

ἀλλ' οἱ μὲν αὐτῶν τὴν θανοῦσαν ἐκ χερῶν
φύλλοις ἔβαλλον, οἱ δὲ πληροῦσιν πυρὰν
κορμοὺς φέροντες πευκίνους, ὁ δ' οὐ φέρων 575
πρὸς τοῦ φέροντος τοιάδ' ἤκουεν κακά·
Ἕστηκας, ὦ κάκιστε, τῆι νεάνιδι
οὐ πέπλον οὐδὲ κόσμον ἐν χεροῖν ἔχων;
οὐκ εἶ τι δώσων τῆι περίσσ' εὐκαρδίωι
ψυχήν τ' ἀρίστηι; τοιάδ' ἀμφὶ σῆς λέγων 580
παιδὸς θανούσης εὐτεκνωτάτην τέ σε
πασῶν γυναικῶν δυστυχεστάτην θ' ὁρῶ.
Χο. δεινόν τι πῆμα Πριαμίδαις ἐπέζεσεν
πόλει τε τῆμῆι θεῶν ἀνάγκαισιν τόδε.
Εκ. ὦ θύγατερ, οὐκ οἶδ' εἰς ὅ τι βλέψω κακῶν, 585
πολλῶν παρόντων· ἢν γὰρ ἅψωμαί τινος,
τόδ' οὐκ ἐᾶι με, παρακαλεῖ δ' ἐκεῖθεν αὖ
λύπη τις ἄλλη διάδοχος κακῶν κακοῖς.
καὶ νῦν τὸ μὲν σὸν ὥστε μὴ στένειν πάθος
οὐκ ἂν δυναίμην ἐξαλείψασθαι φρενός· 590
τὸ δ' αὖ λίαν παρεῖλες ἀγγελθεῖσά μοι
γενναῖος. οὔκουν δεινόν, εἰ γῆ μὲν κακὴ
τυχοῦσα καιροῦ θεόθεν εὖ στάχυν φέρει,
χρηστὴ δ' ἁμαρτοῦσ' ὧν χρεὼν αὐτὴν τυχεῖν
κακὸν δίδωσι καρπόν, ἄνθρωποι δ' ἀεὶ 595
ὁ μὲν πονηρὸς οὐδὲν ἄλλο πλὴν κακός,
ὁ δ' ἐσθλὸς ἐσθλὸς οὐδὲ συμφορᾶς ὕπο
φύσιν διέφθειρ' ἀλλὰ χρηστός ἐστ' ἀεί;
[ἆρ' οἱ τεκόντες διαφέρουσιν ἢ τροφαί;]
ἔχει γε μέντοι καὶ τὸ θρεφθῆναι καλῶς 600
δίδαξιν ἐσθλοῦ· τοῦτο δ' ἤν τις εὖ μάθηι,
οἶδεν τό γ' αἰσχρὸν κανόνι τοῦ καλοῦ μαθών.
καὶ ταῦτα μὲν δὴ νοῦς ἐτόξευσεν μάτην·
σὺ δ' ἐλθὲ καὶ σήμηνον Ἀργείοις τάδε,
μὴ θιγγάνειν μοι μηδέν' ἀλλ' εἴργειν ὄχλον 605
τῆς παιδός. ἔν τοι μυρίωι στρατεύματι

580 λέγων ΜΒΣ: λέγον Ο: κλύων Wecklein: κλυὼν Battezzato   581 τέ σε Reiske: δέ
σε ω: λέγω Wecklein   582 θ' ὁρῶ ω: δέ σε Wecklein: τ' ἐρῶ Battezzato
584 ἀνάγκαισιν Herwerden: ἀναγκαῖον ωΣ   595 ἄνθρωποι Hermann: ἀνθρώποις ω
599 del. Battezzato: 599–602 del. Sakorraphos   600 γε μέντοι Ο: γε τοί τι
ΜΒ   605 μοι p: μου ω

ΕΚΑΒΗ 51

ἀκόλαστος ὄχλος ναυτική τ' ἀναρχία
κρείσσων πυρός, κακὸς δ' ὁ μή τι δρῶν κακόν.
σὺ δ' αὖ λαβοῦσα τεῦχος, ἀρχαία λάτρι,
βάψασ' ἔνεγκε δεῦρο ποντίας ἁλός, 610
ὡς παῖδα λουτροῖς τοῖς πανυστάτοις ἐμήν,
νύμφην τ' ἄνυμφον παρθένον τ' ἀπάρθενον,
λούσω προθῶμαί θ' ὡς μὲν ἀξία – πόθεν;
οὐκ ἂν δυναίμην – ὡς δ' ἔχω (τί γὰρ πάθω;),
κόσμον γ' ἀγείρασ' αἰχμαλωτίδων πάρα, 615
αἵ μοι πάρεδροι τῶνδ' ἔσω σκηνωμάτων
ναίουσιν, εἴ τις τοὺς νεωστὶ δεσπότας
λαθοῦσ' ἔχει τι κλέμμα τῶν αὑτῆς δόμων.
ὦ σχήματ' οἴκων, ὦ ποτ' εὐτυχεῖς δόμοι,
ὦ πλεῖστ' ἔχων μάλιστά τ' εὐτεκνώτατε 620
Πρίαμε, γεραιά θ' ἥδ' ἐγὼ μήτηρ τέκνων,
ὡς ἐς τὸ μηδὲν ἥκομεν, φρονήματος
τοῦ πρὶν στερέντες. εἶτα δῆτ' ὀγκούμεθα,
ὁ μέν τις ἡμῶν πλουσίοισι δώμασιν,
ὁ δ' ἐν πολίταις τίμιος κεκλημένος; 625
τὰ δ' οὐδέν, ἄλλως φροντίδων βουλεύματα
γλώσσης τε κόμποι. κεῖνος ὀλβιώτατος
ὅτωι κατ' ἦμαρ τυγχάνει μηδὲν κακόν.

Χο. ἐμοὶ χρῆν συμφοράν, str.
ἐμοὶ χρῆν πημονὰν γενέσθαι, 630
Ἰδαίαν ὅτε πρῶτον ὕλαν
Ἀλέξανδρος εἰλατίναν
ἐτάμεθ', ἅλιον ἐπ' οἶδμα ναυστολήσων 633-4
Ἑλένας ἐπὶ λέκτρα, τὰν 635
      καλλίσταν ὁ χρυσοφαὴς
Ἅλιος αὐγάζει.

πόνοι γὰρ καὶ πόνων ant.
ἀνάγκαι κρείσσονες κυκλοῦνται·
κοινὸν δ' ἐξ ἰδίας ἀνοίας 640

---

615 κόσμον γ' Wakefield: κόσμον τ' ω   620 μάλιστά τ' Harry: κάλλιστά τ' pp: κάλλιστά κ' ΜΒΟ^pc: κάλλιστ' O^ac   624 πλουσίοισι δώμασιν Bothe: πλουσίοις ἐν δώμασιν ω   639 κρείσσονες MB: μείζονες O

κακὸν τᾶι Σιμουντίδι γᾶι
ὀλέθριον ἔμολε συμφορᾶι τ' ἔπ' ἄλλων. 642-3
ἐκρίθη δ' ἔρις, ἅν ἐν Ἴ-
δαι κρίνει τρισσὰς μακάρων 645
παῖδας ἀνὴρ βούτας,

ἐπὶ δορὶ καὶ φόνωι καὶ ἐμῶν μελάθρων λώβαι· ep. 647-8
στένει δὲ καί τις ἀμφὶ τὸν εὔροον Εὐρώταν 649-50
Λάκαινα πολυδάκρυτος ἐν δόμοις κόρα, 651-2
πολιόν τ' ἐπὶ κρᾶτα μάτηρ τέκνων θανόντων 653-4
τίθεται χέρα δρύπτεταί τε <δίπτυχον> παρειάν, 655
δίαιμον ὄνυχα τιθεμένα σπαραγμοῖς. 656-7

ΘΕΡΑΠΑΙΝΑ
γυναῖκες, Ἑκάβη ποῦ ποθ' ἡ παναθλία,
ἡ πάντα νικῶσ' ἄνδρα καὶ θῆλυν σπορὰν
κακοῖσιν; οὐδεὶς στέφανον ἀνθαιρήσεται. 660
Χο. τί δ', ὦ τάλαινα σῆς κακογλώσσου βοῆς;
ὡς οὔποθ' εὕδει λυπρά μοι κηρύγματα.
Θε. Ἑκάβηι φέρω τόδ' ἄλγος· ἐν κακοῖσι δὲ
οὐ ῥάιδιον βροτοῖσιν εὐφημεῖν στόμα.
Χο. καὶ μὴν περῶσα τυγχάνει δόμων ὕπο 665
ἥδ', ἐς δὲ καιρὸν σοῖσι φαίνεται λόγοις.
Θε. ὦ παντάλαινα κἄτι μᾶλλον ἢ λέγω,
δέσποιν', ὄλωλας κοὐκέτ' εἶ, βλέπουσα φῶς,
ἄπαις ἄνανδρος ἄπολις ἐξεφθαρμένη.
Εκ. οὐ καινὸν εἶπας, εἰδόσιν δ' ὠνείδισας. 670
ἀτὰρ τί νεκρὸν τόνδε μοι Πολυξένης
ἥκεις κομίζουσ', ἧς ἀπηγγέλθη τάφος
πάντων Ἀχαιῶν διὰ χερὸς σπουδὴν ἔχειν;
Θε. ἥδ' οὐδὲν οἶδεν, ἀλλά μοι Πολυξένην
θρηνεῖ, νέων δὲ πημάτων οὐχ ἅπτεται. 675
Εκ. οἲ 'γὼ τάλαινα· μῶν τὸ βακχεῖον κάρα
τῆς θεσπιωιδοῦ δεῦρο Κασσάνδρας φέρεις;
Θε. ζῶσαν λέλακας, τὸν θανόντα δ' οὐ στένεις

643 συμφορᾶι τ' ἔπ' ἄλλων Stinton: συμφορά τ' ἀπ' ἄλλων ΩΣ   649-50 εὔροον Hermann: εὔρροον p: εὔρουν ω   655 τε <δίπτυχον> Diggle: τε pp: om. ω   656 δίαιμον ω: δίδυμον Β^(γρ)Ο^(γρ)   662 μοι Herwerden: σου ω   665 ὕπο Β¹ pp: ὕπερ Π⁷ ΜΟ[Β]

ΕΚΑΒΗ 53

τόνδ᾽· ἀλλ᾽ ἄθρησον σῶμα γυμνωθὲν νεκροῦ,
εἴ σοι φανεῖται θαῦμα καὶ παρ᾽ ἐλπίδας. 680
Εκ. οἴμοι, βλέπω δὴ παῖδ᾽ ἐμὸν τεθνηκότα,
Πολύδωρον, ὅν μοι Θρῇξ ἔσωιζ᾽ οἴκοις ἀνήρ.
ἀπωλόμην δύστηνος, οὐκέτ᾽ εἰμὶ δή.

ὦ τέκνον τέκνον, astr.
αἰαῖ, κατάρχομαι νόμον 685
βακχεῖον, ἐξ ἀλάστορος
ἀρτιμαθὴς κακῶν.
Θε. ἔγνως γὰρ ἄτην παιδός, ὦ δύστηνε σύ.
Εκ. ἄπιστ᾽ ἄπιστα, καινὰ καινὰ δέρκομαι.
ἕτερα δ᾽ ἀφ᾽ ἑτέρων κακὰ κακῶν κυρεῖ, 690
οὐδέ ποτ᾽ ἀστένακτος ἀδάκρυτος ἁ-
μέρα ᾽πισχήσει.
Χο. δείν᾽, ὦ τάλαινα, δεινὰ πάσχομεν κακά.
Εκ. ὦ τέκνον τέκνον ταλαίνας ματρός,
τίνι μόρωι θνῄσκεις, τίνι πότμωι κεῖσαι, 695-6
πρὸς τίνος ἀνθρώπων;
Θε. οὐκ οἶδ᾽· ἐπ᾽ ἀκταῖς νιν κυρῶ θαλασσίαις.
Εκ. ἔκβλητον ἢ πέσημα φοινίου δορὸς
ἐν ψαμάθωι λευρᾶι; 700
Θε. πόντου νιν ἐξήνεγκε πελάγιος κλύδων.
Εκ. ὤιμοι αἰαῖ,
ἔμαθον ἐνύπνιον ὀμμάτων
ἐμῶν ὄψιν (οὔ με παρέβα φάντασμα μελανόπτερον), 705
ἃν ἐσεῖδον ἀμφὶ σέ,
ὦ τέκνον, οὐκέτ᾽ ὄντα Διὸς ἐν φάει.
Χο. τίς γάρ νιν ἔκτειν᾽· οἶσθ᾽ ὀνειρόφρων φράσαι;
Εκ. ἐμὸς ἐμὸς ξένος, Θρῄκιος ἱππότας, 709-10

685 νόμον ΒΣ: νόμων Μ: γόον Ο   686 βακχεῖον ωΣ: βακχείων p   690 ἀφ᾽ Μ: ἐφ᾽ ΒΟ   691 ἀστένακτος ἀδάκρυτος Hermann: ἀδάκρυτος ἀστένακτος ωΣ: ἀδάκρυτον ἀστένακτον pp   692 ᾽πισχήσει Bothe et Hermann: μ᾽ ἐπισχήσει ω: με σχήσει Blaydes   693 choro tribuunt MO: famulae et choro (θε. χο.) tribuit B: famulae tribuunt pp   698 θαλασσίοις Hartung   699 φοινίου pp: φονίου ω   700 Hecubae continuant p et 'quidam' apud Σ: famulae tribuunt ω   704-5 φάντασμα Matthiae: φάσμα ω: φάμα Willink   706-7 ἀμφὶ σέ, ὦ ... ὄντα Murray: ἀμφί σ᾽, ὦ ... ὄντα ΜΒ: ἀμφί σ᾽, ὦ ... ἐόντα Ο: ἀμφὶ σοῦ ... ὄντος Wecklein: ἀμφὶ σοῦ, ὦ ... ὄντος Diggle   708 choro tribuunt pp: famulae tribuunt ω

ΕΥΡΙΠΙΔΟΥ

ἵν' ὁ γέρων πατὴρ ἔθετό νιν κρύψας. 711-12
Χο. οἴμοι, τί λέξεις; χρυσὸν ὡς ἔχοι κτανών;
Εκ. ἄρρητ' ἀνωνόμαστα, θαυμάτων πέρα,
οὐχ ὅσι' οὐδ' ἀνεκτά. ποῦ δίκα ξένων; 715
ὦ κατάρατ' ἀνδρῶν, ὡς διεμοιράσω 716-17
χρόα, σιδαρέωι τεμὼν φασγάνωι 718-19
μέλεα τοῦδε παιδὸς οὐδ' ὤικτισας. 720-1

Χο. ὦ τλῆμον, ὥς σε πολυπονωτάτην βροτῶν
δαίμων ἔθηκεν ὅστις ἐστί σοι βαρύς.
ἀλλ' εἰσορῶ γὰρ τοῦδε δεσπότου δέμας
Ἀγαμέμνονος, τοὐνθένδε σιγῶμεν, φίλαι. 725

ΑΓΑΜΕΜΝΩΝ
Ἑκάβη, τί μέλλεις παῖδα σὴν κρύπτειν τάφωι
ἐλθοῦσ' ἐφ' οἷσπερ Ταλθύβιος ἤγγειλέ μοι
μὴ θιγγάνειν σῆς μηδέν' Ἀργείων κόρης;
ἡμεῖς μὲν οὖν εἰῶμεν οὐδ' ἐψαύομεν·
σὺ δὲ σχολάζεις, ὥστε θαυμάζειν ἐμέ. 730
ἥκω δ' ἀποστελῶν σε· τἀκεῖθεν γὰρ εὖ
πεπραγμέν' ἐστίν, εἴ τι τῶνδ' ἐστὶν καλῶς.
ἔα· τίν' ἄνδρα τόνδ' ἐπὶ σκηναῖς ὁρῶ
θανόντα Τρώων; οὐ γὰρ Ἀργεῖον πέπλοι
δέμας περιπτύσσοντες ἀγγέλλουσί μοι. 735
Εκ. δύστην', ἐμαυτὴν γὰρ λέγω λέγουσα σέ,
Ἑκάβη, τί δράσω; πότερα προσπέσω γόνυ
Ἀγαμέμνονος τοῦδ' ἢ φέρω σιγῆι κακά;
Αγ. τί μοι προσώπωι νῶτον ἐγκλίνασα σὸν
δύρηι, τὸ πραχθὲν δ' οὐ λέγεις; τίς ἔσθ' ὅδε; 740
Εκ. ἀλλ' εἴ με δούλην πολεμίαν θ' ἡγούμενος
γονάτων ἀπώσαιτ', ἄλγος ἂν προσθείμεθ' ἄν.
Αγ. οὔτοι πέφυκα μάντις, ὥστε μὴ κλυὼν
ἐξιστορῆσαι σῶν ὁδὸν βουλευμάτων.
Εκ. ἆρ' ἐκλογίζομαί γε πρὸς τὸ δυσμενὲς 745
μᾶλλον φρένας τοῦδ', ὄντος οὐχὶ δυσμενοῦς;
Αγ. εἴ τοί με βούληι τῶνδε μηδὲν εἰδέναι,

718-19 σιδαρέωι Π⁷ ΒΟ: σιδηρέωι Μ 720-1 ὤικτισας ΒΟ: οἰκτίσω Μ 729 εἰῶμεν Nauck: ἐῶμεν ω οὐδ' ἐψαύομεν Bothe: οὐδὲ ψαύομεν ω 740 πραχθὲν ΜΟ: κραθὲν Π¹ Β: κρανθὲν pp 742 προσθείμεθ' ἄν Μ: προσθείμεθα ΒΟ 743 κλυὼν West: κλύων ω

ἐς ταὐτὸν ἥκεις· καὶ γὰρ οὐδ' ἐγὼ κλυεῖν.
Εκ. οὐκ ἂν δυναίμην τοῦδε τιμωρεῖν ἄτερ
τέκνοισι τοῖς ἐμοῖσι. τί στρέφω τάδε; 750
τολμᾶν ἀνάγκη, κἂν τύχω κἂν μὴ τύχω.
Ἀγάμεμνον, ἱκετεύω σε τῶνδε γουνάτων
καὶ σοῦ γενείου δεξιᾶς τ' εὐδαίμονος.
Αγ. τί χρῆμα μαστεύουσα; μῶν ἐλεύθερον
αἰῶνα θέσθαι; ῥάιδιον γάρ ἐστί σοι. 755
[Εκ. οὐ δῆτα· τοὺς κακοὺς δὲ τιμωρουμένη
αἰῶνα τὸν σύμπαντα δουλεύειν θέλω.
Αγ. καὶ δὴ τίν' ἡμᾶς εἰς ἐπάρκεσιν καλεῖς;
Εκ. οὐδέν τι τούτων ὧν σὺ δοξάζεις, ἄναξ.]
Εκ. ὁρᾶις νεκρὸν τόνδ' οὗ καταστάζω δάκρυ; 760
Αγ. ὁρῶ· τὸ μέντοι μέλλον οὐκ ἔχω μαθεῖν.
Εκ. τοῦτόν ποτ' ἔτεκον κἄφερον ζώνης ὕπο.
Αγ. ἔστιν δὲ τίς σῶν οὗτος, ὦ τλῆμον, τέκνων;
Εκ. οὐ τῶν θανόντων Πριαμιδῶν ὑπ' Ἰλίωι.
Αγ. ἦ γάρ τιν' ἄλλον ἔτεκες ἢ κείνους, γύναι; 765
Εκ. ἀνόνητά γ', ὡς ἔοικε, τόνδ' ὃν εἰσορᾶις.
Αγ. ποῦ δ' ὢν ἐτύγχαν', ἡνίκ' ὤλλυτο πτόλις;
Εκ. πατήρ νιν ἐξέπεμψεν ὀρρωδῶν θανεῖν.
Αγ. ποῖ τῶν τότ' ὄντων χωρίσας τέκνων μόνον;
Εκ. ἐς τήνδε χώραν, οὗπερ ηὑρέθη θανών. 770
Αγ. πρὸς ἄνδρ' ὃς ἄρχει τῆσδε Πολυμήστωρ χθονός;
Εκ. ἐνταῦθ' ἐπέμφθη πικροτάτου χρυσοῦ φύλαξ.
Αγ. θνήισκει δὲ πρὸς τοῦ καὶ τίνος πότμου τυχών;
Εκ. τίνος γ' ὑπ' ἄλλου; Θρῆιξ νιν ὤλεσε ξένος.
Αγ. ὦ τλῆμον· ἦ που χρυσὸν ἠράσθη λαβεῖν; 775
Εκ. τοιαῦτ', ἐπειδὴ συμφορὰν ἔγνω Φρυγῶν.
Αγ. ηὗρες δὲ ποῦ νιν; ἢ τίς ἤνεγκεν νεκρόν;
Εκ. ἥδ', ἐντυχοῦσα ποντίας ἀκτῆς ἔπι.
Αγ. τοῦτον ματεύουσ' ἢ πονοῦσ' ἄλλον πόνον;
Εκ. λούτρ' ὤιχετ' οἴσουσ' ἐξ ἁλὸς Πολυξένηι. 780
Αγ. κτανών νιν, ὡς ἔοικεν, ἐκβάλλει ξένος.
Εκ. θαλασσόπλαγκτόν γ', ὧδε διατεμὼν χρόα.
Αγ. ὦ σχετλία σὺ τῶν ἀμετρήτων πόνων.
Εκ. ὄλωλα κοὐδὲν λοιπόν, Ἀγάμεμνον, κακῶν.
Αγ. φεῦ φεῦ· τίς οὕτω δυστυχὴς ἔφυ γυνή; 785

748 κλυεῖν West: κλύειν ω   756–9 om. Π⁷ et Π¹², fortasse etiam Π⁸: del. Hughes et Nodar: 756–9 habent pp: solum 759 habent ω: 756–8 del. Nauck: 759 del. Hartung   761 μαθεῖν Π⁷Π¹² M: φράσαι BO

Εκ. οὐκ ἔστιν, εἰ μὴ τὴν Τύχην αὐτὴν λέγοις.
ἀλλ' ὧνπερ οὕνεκ' ἀμφὶ σὸν πίπτω γόνυ
ἄκουσον. εἰ μὲν ὅσιά σοι παθεῖν δοκῶ,
στέργοιμ' ἄν· εἰ δὲ τοὔμπαλιν, σύ μοι γενοῦ
τιμωρὸς ἀνδρὸς ἀνοσιωτάτου ξένου, 790
ὃς οὔτε τοὺς γῆς νέρθεν οὔτε τοὺς ἄνω
δείσας δέδρακεν ἔργον ἀνοσιώτατον
[κοινῆς τραπέζης πολλάκις τυχὼν ἐμοὶ
ξενίας τ' ἀριθμῶι πρῶτα τῶν ἐμῶν ξένων·
τυχὼν δ' ὅσων δεῖ καὶ λαβὼν προμηθίαν 795
ἔκτεινε· τύμβου δ', εἰ κτανεῖν ἐβούλετο,
οὐκ ἠξίωσεν ἀλλ' ἀφῆκε πόντιον].
ἡμεῖς μὲν οὖν δοῦλοί τε κἀσθενεῖς ἴσως·
ἀλλ' οἱ θεοὶ σθένουσι χὠ κείνων κρατῶν
νόμος· νόμωι γὰρ τοὺς θεοὺς ἡγούμεθα 800
καὶ ζῶμεν ἄδικα καὶ δίκαι' ὡρισμένοι·
ὃς ἐς σ' ἀνελθὼν εἰ διαφθαρήσεται
καὶ μὴ δίκην δώσουσιν οἵτινες ξένους
κτείνουσιν ἢ θεῶν ἱερὰ τολμῶσιν φέρειν,
οὐκ ἔστιν οὐδὲν τῶν ἐν ἀνθρώποις ἴσον. 805
ταῦτ' οὖν ἐν αἰσχρῶι θέμενος αἰδέσθητί με,
οἴκτιρον ἡμᾶς, ὡς γραφεύς τ' ἀποσταθεὶς
ἰδοῦ με κἀνάθρησον οἷ' ἔχω κακά.
τύραννος ἦ ποτ' ἀλλὰ νῦν δούλη σέθεν,
εὔπαις ποτ' οὖσα, νῦν δὲ γραῦς ἄπαις θ' ἅμα, 810
ἄπολις ἔρημος ἀθλιωτάτη βροτῶν.
οἴμοι τάλαινα, ποῖ μ' ὑπεξάγεις πόδα;
ἔοικα πράξειν οὐδέν· ὦ τάλαιν' ἐγώ.
τί δῆτα θνητοὶ τἄλλα μὲν μαθήματα
μοχθοῦμεν ὡς χρὴ πάντα καὶ ματεύομεν, 815
Πειθὼ δὲ τὴν τύραννον ἀνθρώποις μόνην
οὐδέν τι μᾶλλον ἐς τέλος σπουδάζομεν
μισθοὺς διδόντες μανθάνειν, ἵν' ἦν ποτε
πείθειν ἅ τις βούλοιτο τυγχάνειν θ' ἅμα;
τί οὖν ἔτ' ἄν τις ἐλπίσαι πράξειν καλῶς; 820
οἱ μὲν γὰρ ὄντες παῖδες οὐκέτ' εἰσί μοι,

793-7 del. Nauck: 794-5 del. Matthiae: 794-7 del. Dindorf   794 ξένων BO:
φίλων ΜΣ   805 ἀνθρώποισι σῶν Kayser   818 ἦν Elmsley: ἢ O: *(*) MB

ΕΚΑΒΗ 57

αὐτὴ δ' ἐπ' αἰσχροῖς αἰχμάλωτος οἴχομαι,
καπνὸν δὲ πόλεως τόνδ' ὑπερθρώισκονθ' ὁρῶ.
καὶ μὴν ἴσως μὲν τοῦ λόγου κενὸν τόδε,
Κύπριν προβάλλειν, ἀλλ' ὅμως εἰρήσεται· 825
πρὸς σοῖσι πλευροῖς παῖς ἐμὴ κοιμίζεται
ἡ φοιβάς, ἣν καλοῦσι Κασσάνδραν Φρύγες.
ποῦ τὰς φίλας δῆτ' εὐφρόνας λέξεις, ἄναξ;
ἦ τῶν ἐν εὐνῆι φιλτάτων ἀσπασμάτων
χάριν τίν' ἕξει παῖς ἐμή, κείνης δ' ἐγώ; 830
ἐκ τοῦ σκότου τε τῶν τε νυκτερησίων
φίλτρων μεγίστη γίγνεται βροτοῖς χάρις.
ἄκουε δή νυν. τὸν θανόντα τόνδ' ὁρᾶις;
τοῦτον καλῶς δρῶν ὄντα κηδεστὴν σέθεν
δράσεις. ἑνός μοι μῦθος ἐνδεὴς ἔτι. 835
εἴ μοι γένοιτο φθόγγος ἐν βραχίοσιν
καὶ χερσὶ καὶ κόμαισι καὶ ποδῶν βάσει
ἢ Δαιδάλου τέχναισιν ἢ θεῶν τινος,
ὡς πάνθ' ἁμαρτῆι σῶν ἔχοιτο γουνάτων
κλαίοντ' ἐπισκήπτοντα παντοίους λόγους. 840
ὦ δέσποτ', ὦ μέγιστον Ἕλλησιν φάος,
πιθοῦ, παράσχες χεῖρα τῆι πρεσβύτιδι
τιμωρόν, εἰ καὶ μηδέν ἐστιν ἀλλ' ὅμως.
ἐσθλοῦ γὰρ ἀνδρὸς τῆι δίκηι θ' ὑπηρετεῖν
καὶ τοὺς κακοὺς δρᾶν πανταχοῦ κακῶς ἀεί. 845
Χο. δεινόν γε, θνητοῖς ὡς ἅπαντα συμπίτνει·
καινὰς ἀνάγκας οἱ νόμοι διώρισαν,
φίλους τιθέντες τούς γε πολεμιωτάτους
ἐχθρούς τε τοὺς πρὶν εὐμενεῖς ποιούμενοι.
Αγ. ἐγώ σε καὶ σὸν παῖδα καὶ τύχας σέθεν, 850
Ἑκάβη, δι' οἴκτου χεῖρά θ' ἱκεσίαν ἔχω,
καὶ βούλομαι θεῶν θ' οὕνεκ' ἀνόσιον ξένον
καὶ τοῦ δικαίου τήνδε σοι δοῦναι δίκην,
εἴ πως φανείη γ' ὥστε σοί τ' ἔχειν καλῶς

824 κενὸν ω: ξένον Nauck   828 λέξεις Diggle: δείξεις ω test.   829 ἦ ω: ἢ Diggle   830 τιν' Porson   831–2 del. Matthiae   831 νυκτερησίων Nauck: νυκτέρων p test.: νυκτέρων βροτοῖς ω test.: νυκτέρων πάνυ pp: νυκτέρων ἀσπασμάτων (om. τῶν τε) pp: νυκτέρων τ' ἀσπασμάτων (om. τῶν τε) pp   833 δή νυν Matthiae: δὴ νῦν ω   837 ποδῶν βάσει MB: βαδίσμασιν O   839 ἁμαρτῆι Barrett: ὁμαρτῆι ω   842 παράσχες MO: πάρασχε B   847 καινὰς Battezzato: καὶ τὰς ω   853 δίκην ΟΣ: χάριν MB

στρατῶι τε μὴ δόξαιμι Κασσάνδρας χάριν 855
Θρήικης ἄνακτι τόνδε βουλεῦσαι φόνον.
ἔστιν γὰρ ἧι ταραγμὸς ἐμπέπτωκέ μοι·
τὸν ἄνδρα τοῦτον φίλιον ἡγεῖται στρατός,
τὸν κατθανόντα δ' ἐχθρόν· εἰ δὲ σοὶ φίλος
ὅδ' ἐστί, χωρὶς τοῦτο κοὐ κοινὸν στρατῶι. 860
πρὸς ταῦτα φρόντιζ'· ὡς θέλοντα μέν μ' ἔχεις
σοὶ ξυμπονῆσαι καὶ ταχὺν προσαρκέσαι,
βραδὺν δ', Ἀχαιοῖς εἰ διαβληθήσομαι.
Εκ. φεῦ.
οὐκ ἔστι θνητῶν ὅστις ἔστ' ἐλεύθερος·
ἢ χρημάτων γὰρ δοῦλός ἐστιν ἢ τύχης 865
ἢ πλῆθος αὐτὸν πόλεος ἢ νόμων γραφαὶ
εἴργουσι χρῆσθαι μὴ κατὰ γνώμην τρόποις.
ἐπεὶ δὲ ταρβεῖς τῶι τ' ὄχλωι πλέον νέμεις,
ἐγώ σε θήσω τοῦδ' ἐλεύθερον φόβου.
σύνισθι μὲν γάρ, ἤν τι βουλεύσω κακὸν 870
τῶι τόνδ' ἀποκτείναντι, συνδράσηις δὲ μή.
ἢν δ' ἐξ Ἀχαιῶν θόρυβος ἢ 'πικουρία
πάσχοντος ἀνδρὸς Θρηικὸς οἷα πείσεται
φανῆι τις, εἶργε μὴ δοκῶν ἐμὴν χάριν.
τὰ δ' ἄλλα – θάρσει – πάντ' ἐγὼ θήσω καλῶς. 875
Αγ. πῶς οὖν; τί δράσεις; πότερα φάσγανον χερὶ
λαβοῦσα γραῖαι φῶτα βάρβαρον κτενεῖς
ἢ φαρμάκοισιν ἢ 'πικουρίαι τίνι;
τίς σοι ξυνέσται χείρ; πόθεν κτήσηι φίλους;
Εκ. στέγαι κεκεύθασ' αἵδε Τρωιάδων ὄχλον. 880
Αγ. τὰς αἰχμαλώτους εἶπας, Ἑλλήνων ἄγραν;
Εκ. σὺν ταῖσδε τὸν ἐμῶν φονέα τιμωρήσομαι.
Αγ. καὶ πῶς γυναιξὶν ἀρσένων ἔσται κράτος;
Εκ. δεινὸν τὸ πλῆθος σὺν δόλωι τε δύσμαχον.
Αγ. δεινόν· τὸ μέντοι θῆλυ μέμφομαι γένος. 885
Εκ. τί δ'; οὐ γυναῖκες εἷλον Αἰγύπτου τέκνα
καὶ Λῆμνον ἄρδην ἀρσένων ἐξώικισαν;
ἀλλ' ὣς γενέσθω· τόνδε μὲν μέθες λόγον,
πέμψον δέ μοι τήνδ' ἀσφαλῶς διὰ στρατοῦ

859 δὲ σοὶ ω: δ' ἐμοὶ Elmsley 864 ἔστι θνητῶν ω: ἔστιν ἀνδρῶν test. 866 πόλεος pp: πόλεως ω 875 distinxit Reiske 878 τίνι Barnes: τινί ω 882 ἐμῶν Scaliger: ἐμὸν ω 885 γένος ω: σθένος Jenni

ΕΚΑΒΗ

γυναῖκα. καὶ σὺ Θρηικὶ πλαθεῖσα ξένωι 890
λέξον· Καλεῖ σ᾽ ἄνασσα δή ποτ᾽ Ἰλίου
Ἑκάβη, σὸν οὐκ ἔλασσον ἢ κείνης χρέος,
καὶ παῖδας, ὡς δεῖ καὶ τέκν᾽ εἰδέναι λόγους
τοὺς ἐξ ἐκείνης. τὸν δὲ τῆς νεοσφαγοῦς
Πολυξένης ἐπίσχες, Ἀγάμεμνον, τάφον, 895
ὡς τώδ᾽ ἀδελφὼ πλησίον μιᾶι φλογί,
δισσὴ μέριμνα μητρί, κρυφθῆτον χθονί.
Αγ. ἔσται τάδ᾽ οὕτω· καὶ γὰρ εἰ μὲν ἦν στρατῶι
πλοῦς, οὐκ ἂν εἶχον τήνδε σοι δοῦναι χάριν·
νῦν δ᾽, οὐ γὰρ ἵησ᾽ οὐρίους πνοὰς θεός, 900
μένειν ἀνάγκη <ς> πλοῦν ὁρῶντας ἡσύχους.
γένοιτο δ᾽ εὖ πως· πᾶσι γὰρ κοινὸν τόδε,
ἰδίαι θ᾽ ἑκάστωι καὶ πόλει, τὸν μὲν κακὸν
κακόν τι πάσχειν, τὸν δὲ χρηστὸν εὐτυχεῖν.

Χο. σὺ μέν, ὦ πατρὶς Ἰλιάς, str. 1
τῶν ἀπορθήτων πόλις οὐκέτι λέξηι· 906
τοῖον Ἑλλάνων νέφος ἀμφί σε κρύπτει 907–8
δορὶ δὴ δορὶ πέρσαν.
ἀπὸ δὲ στεφάναν κέκαρ- 910
σαι πύργων, κατὰ δ᾽ αἰθάλου
κηλῖδ᾽ οἰκτροτάταν κέχρωσαι.
τάλαιν᾽, οὐκέτι σ᾽ ἐμβατεύσω.

μεσονύκτιος ὠλλύμαν, ant. 1
ἦμος ἐκ δείπνων ὕπνος ἡδὺς ἐπ᾽ ὄσσοις 915
σκίδναται, μολπᾶν δ᾽ ἄπο καὶ χοροποιὸν 916–17
θυσίαν καταπαύσας
πόσις ἐν θαλάμοις ἔκει-
το, ξυστὸν δ᾽ ἐπὶ πασσάλωι, 920
ναύταν οὐκέθ᾽ ὁρῶν ὅμιλον
Τροίαν Ἰλιάδ᾽ ἐμβεβῶτα.

901 <ς> Battezzato ὁρῶντας ἡσύχους Markland: ὁρῶντας ἥσυχον ω: ὁρῶντ᾽ ἐς ἥσυχον Murray   907–8 τοῖον H: τοῖον δ᾽ MBO   911 αἰθάλου Canter: αἰθάλωι Triclinius: αἰθάλου καπνοῦ ω   916–17 μολπᾶν [B] pp: μολπᾶν HMO   χοροποιὸν H^pc O: χοροποιῶν MB: χαροποιῶν H^ac   918 θυσίαν HMO: θυσιᾶν B   921 ναυτᾶν Σ   922 Τροίαν Ἰλιάδ᾽ ω: Ἰλιάδ᾽ pp: χώραν Ἰλιάδ᾽ Battezzato   ἐμβεβῶτα pp: ἐμβεβαῶτα ω, fortasse recte

ΕΥΡΙΠΙΔΟΥ

ἐγὼ δὲ πλόκαμον ἀναδέτοις   str. 2
μίτραισιν ἐρρυθμιζόμαν
χρυσέων ἐνόπτρων λεύσσουσ' ἀτέρμονας εἰς αὐγάς,   925–6
ἐπιδέμνιος ὡς πέσοιμ' ἐς εὐνάν.
ἀνὰ δὲ κέλαδος ἔμολε πόλιν·
κέλευσμα δ' ἦν κατ' ἄστυ Τροίας τόδ'· Ὦ
   παῖδες Ἑλλάνων, πότε δὴ πότε τὰν   930
   Ἰλιάδα σκοπιὰν
πέρσαντες ἥξετ' οἴκους;

λέχη δὲ φίλια μονόπεπλος   ant. 2
λιποῦσα, Δωρὶς ὡς κόρα,
σεμνὰν προσίζουσ' οὐκ ἤνυσ' Ἄρτεμιν ἁ τλάμων·   935–6
ἄγομαι δὲ θανόντ' ἰδοῦσ' ἀκοίταν
τὸν ἐμὸν ἅλιον ἐπὶ πέλαγος·
πόλιν δ' ἀποσκοποῦσ', ἐπεὶ νόστιμον
   ναῦς ἐκίνησεν πόδα καί μ' ἀπὸ γᾶς   940
   ὥρισεν Ἰλιάδος,
τάλαιν' ἀπεῖπον ἄλγει,

τὰν τοῖν Διοσκούροιν Ἑλέναν κάσιν Ἰ-   ep. 943–4
   δαῖόν τε βούταν Αἰνόπαριν κατάραι διδοῦσα,   945
ἐπεί με γᾶς ἐκ πατρίας ἀπώλεσεν   946–7
ἐξώικισέν τ' οἴκων γάμος οὐ γάμος ἀλλ'
   ἀλάστορός τις οἰζύς·
ἃν μήτε πέλαγος ἅλιον ἀπαγάγοι πάλιν   950–1
μήτε πατρῶιον ἵκοιτ' ἐς οἶκον.

ΠΟΛΥΜΗΣΤΩΡ
ὦ φίλτατ' ἀνδρῶν Πρίαμε, φιλτάτη δὲ σύ,
Ἑκάβη, δακρύω σ' εἰσορῶν πόλιν τε σὴν
τήν τ' ἀρτίως θανοῦσαν ἔκγονον σέθεν.   955
φεῦ·
οὐκ ἔστιν οὐδὲν πιστόν, οὔτ' εὐδοξία
οὔτ' αὖ καλῶς πράσσοντα μὴ πράξειν κακῶς.

932 οἴκους Triclinius: ἐς οἴκους ω   939 δ' Willink: τ' ω   946–7 γᾶς ω: γαίας Diggle   πατρίας Dindorf: πατρώιας ω   ἀπώλεσεν ω: ἀπούρισεν M^γρ
948 ἐξώικισέν Porson: ἐξώικισέ ω   953 del. Nauck

ΕΚΑΒΗ

φύρουσι δ' αυτά θεοί πάλιν τε και πρόσω
ταραγμὸν ἐντιθέντες, ὡς ἀγνωσίαι
σέβωμεν αὐτούς. ἀλλὰ ταῦτα μὲν τί δεῖ 960
θρηνεῖν, προκόπτοντ᾽ οὐδὲν ἐς πρόσθεν κακῶν;
σὺ δ᾽, εἴ τι μέμφηι τῆς ἐμῆς ἀπουσίας,
σχές· τυγχάνω γὰρ ἐν μέσοις Θρήικης ὅροις
ἀπών, ὅτ᾽ ἦλθες δεῦρ᾽· ἐπεὶ δ᾽ ἀφικόμην,
ἤδη πόδ᾽ ἔξω δωμάτων αἴροντί μοι 965
ἐς ταὐτὸν ἥδε συμπίτνει δμωὶς σέθεν,
λέγουσα μύθους ὧν κλυὼν ἀφικόμην.

Εκ. αἰσχύνομαί σε προσβλέπειν ἐναντίον,
Πολυμῆστορ, ἐν τοιοῖσδε κειμένη κακοῖς.
ὅτωι γὰρ ὤφθην εὐτυχοῦσ᾽, αἰδώς μ᾽ ἔχει 970
ἐν τῶιδε πότμωι τυγχάνουσ᾽ ἵν᾽ εἰμὶ νῦν,
κοὐκ ἂν δυναίμην προσβλέπειν ὀρθαῖς κόραις.
ἀλλ᾽ αὐτὸ μὴ δύσνοιαν ἡγήσηι σέθεν,
[Πολυμῆστορ· ἄλλως δ᾽ αἴτιόν τι καὶ νόμος,]
γυναῖκας ἀνδρῶν μὴ βλέπειν ἐναντίον. 975

Πο. καὶ θαῦμά γ᾽ οὐδέν. ἀλλὰ τίς χρεία σ᾽ ἐμοῦ;
τί χρῆμ᾽ ἐπέμψω τὸν ἐμὸν ἐκ δόμων πόδα;

Εκ. ἴδιον ἐμαυτῆς δή τι πρὸς σὲ βούλομαι
καὶ παῖδας εἰπεῖν σούς· ὀπάονας δέ μοι
χωρὶς κέλευσον τῶνδ᾽ ἀποστῆναι δόμων. 980

Πο. χωρεῖτ᾽· ἐν ἀσφαλεῖ γὰρ ἥδ᾽ ἐρημία.
φίλη μὲν εἶ σύ, προσφιλὲς δέ μοι τόδε
στράτευμ᾽ Ἀχαιῶν. ἀλλὰ σημαίνειν σε χρή·
τί χρὴ τὸν εὖ πράσσοντα μὴ πράσσουσιν εὖ
φίλοις ἐπαρκεῖν; ὡς ἕτοιμός εἰμ᾽ ἐγώ. 985

Εκ. πρῶτον μὲν εἰπὲ παῖδ᾽ ὃν ἐξ ἐμῆς χερὸς
Πολύδωρον ἔκ τε πατρὸς ἐν δόμοις ἔχεις
εἰ ζῆι· τὰ δ᾽ ἄλλα δεύτερόν σ᾽ ἐρήσομαι.

Πο. μάλιστα· τοὐκείνου μὲν εὐτυχεῖς μέρος.

Εκ. ὦ φίλταθ᾽, ὡς εὖ κἀξίως λέγεις σέθεν. 990

Πο. τί δῆτα βούληι δεύτερον μαθεῖν ἐμοῦ;

Εκ. εἰ τῆς τεκούσης τῆσδε μέμνηταί τί που.

Πο. καὶ δεῦρό γ᾽ ὡς σὲ κρύφιος ἐζήτει μολεῖν.

958 αὐτὰ p^{γρ}: αὗτα pp: αὖθ᾽ οἱ MO: αὖ τοι B   967 κλυὼν West: κλύων ω   974 del. Battezzato: 973–5 del. Hartung: 974–5 del. Diggle   982 μὲν pp: μὲν ἡμῖν ω   992 που Herwerden: μου ω

Εκ. χρυσός δὲ σῶς ὃν ἦλθεν ἐκ Τροίας ἔχων;
Πο. σῶς, ἐν δόμοις γε τοῖς ἐμοῖς φρουρούμενος. 995
Εκ. σῶσόν νυν αὐτὸν μηδ' ἔρα τῶν πλησίον.
Πο. ἥκιστ'· ὀναίμην τοῦ παρόντος, ὦ γύναι.
Εκ. οἶσθ' οὖν ἃ λέξαι σοί τε καὶ παισὶν θέλω;
Πο. οὐκ οἶδα· τῶι σῶι τοῦτο σημανεῖς λόγωι.
Εκ. ἔστ', ὦ φιληθεὶς ὡς σὺ νῦν ἐμοὶ φιλῆι ... 1000
Πο. τί χρῆμ' ὃ κἀμὲ καὶ τέκν' εἰδέναι χρεών;
Εκ. χρυσοῦ παλαιαὶ Πριαμιδῶν κατώρυχες.
Πο. ταῦτ' ἔσθ' ἃ βούληι παιδὶ σημῆναι σέθεν;
Εκ. μάλιστα, διὰ σοῦ γ'· εἶ γὰρ εὐσεβὴς ἀνήρ.
Πο. τί δῆτα τέκνων τῶνδε δεῖ παρουσίας; 1005
Εκ. ἄμεινον, ἢν σὺ κατθάνηις, τούσδ' εἰδέναι.
Πο. καλῶς ἔλεξας· τῆιδε καὶ σοφώτερον.
Εκ. οἶσθ' οὖν Ἀθάνας Ἰλιάδος ἵνα στέγαι;
Πο. ἐνταῦθ' ὁ χρυσός ἐστι; σημεῖον δὲ τί;
Εκ. μέλαινα πέτρα γῆς ὑπερτέλλουσ' ἄνω. 1010
Πο. ἔτ' οὖν τι βούληι τῶν ἐκεῖ φράζειν ἐμοί;
Εκ. σῶσαί σε χρήμαθ' οἷς συνεξῆλθον θέλω.
Πο. ποῦ δῆτα; πέπλων ἐντὸς ἢ κρύψασ' ἔχεις;
Εκ. σκύλων ἐν ὄχλωι ταῖσδε σώιζεται στέγαις.
Πο. ποῦ δ'; αἵδ' Ἀχαιῶν ναύλοχοι περιπτυχαί. 1015
Εκ. ἴδιαι γυναικῶν αἰχμαλωτίδων στέγαι.
Πο. τἄνδον δὲ πιστὰ κἀρσένων ἐρημία;
Εκ. οὐδεὶς Ἀχαιῶν ἔνδον ἀλλ' ἡμεῖς μόναι.
ἀλλ' ἕρπ' ἐς οἴκους· καὶ γὰρ Ἀργεῖοι νεῶν
λῦσαι ποθοῦσιν οἴκαδ' ἐκ Τροίας πόδα· 1020
ὡς πάντα πράξας ὧν σε δεῖ στείχηις πάλιν
ξὺν παισὶν οὗπερ τὸν ἐμὸν ὤικισας γόνον.

Χο. οὔπω δέδωκας ἀλλ' ἴσως δώσεις δίκην· astr.
ἀλίμενόν τις ὡς ἐς ἄντλον πεσὼν 1024–5
λέχριος ἐκπεσῆι φίλας καρδίας, 1026–7
ἀμέρσας βίοτον. ὃ γὰρ ὑπέγγυον 1028–9
Δίκαι καὶ θεοῖσιν οὐ ξυμπίτνει, 1030
ὀλέθριον ὀλέθριον κακόν.

996 νυν pp: νῦν ω   998 ἃ ω: ὃ p   999 τοῦτο ω: ταῦτα Brunck   1000 ἔστ', ὦ Hermann: ἔστω ω   1007 distinxit Boissonade   1008 Ἰλιάδος Scaliger: Ἰλίας ω   1013 ἦ Μ^{pc}: ἢ Μ^{ac}BO   1023 choro tribuunt BO: Hecubae continuant M et 'quidam' apud Σ   1024–5 πεσὼν pp: ἐμπεσὼν ω   1028–9 βίοτον. ὃ Matthiae: βίοτον. τὸ ω: βίον. τὸ Hermann   1030 οὐ ΩΣ: οὔ Hemsterhuys

ΕΚΑΒΗ 63

ψεύσει σ' οδού τήσδ' ελπίς ή σ' επήγαγεν
θανάσιμον προς Άΐδαν, ώ τάλας,
άπολέμωι δε χειρί λείψεις βίον.

Πο. ώιμοι, τυφλοΰμαι φέγγος ομμάτων τάλας. 1035
Χο. ήκούσατ' ανδρός Θρηικός οίμωγήν, φίλαι;
Πο. ώιμοι μάλ' αύθις, τέκνα, δυστήνου σφαγής.
Χο. φίλαι, πέπρακται καίν' έσω δόμων κακά.
Πο. άλλ' ούτι μή φύγητε λαιψηρώι ποδί·
βάλλων γάρ οίκων τώνδ' άναρρήξω μυχούς. 1040
ιδού, βαρείας χειρός όρμαται βέλος.
Χο. βούλεσθ' έπεσπέσωμεν; ώς ακμή καλεί
Έκάβηι παρεΐναι Τρωιάσιν τε συμμάχους.
Εκ. άρασσε, φείδου μηδέν, έκβάλλων πύλας·
ου γάρ ποτ' όμμα λαμπρόν ένθήσεις κόραις, 1045
ου παίδας όψηι ζώντας ους έκτειν' εγώ.
Χο. ή γάρ καθεΐλες Θρήικα και κρατείς ξένον,
δέσποινα, και δέδρακας οίάπερ λέγεις;
Εκ. όψηι νιν αύτίκ' όντα δωμάτων πάρος
τυφλόν τυφλώι στείχοντα παραφόρωι ποδί, 1050
παίδων τε δισσών σώμαθ', ους έκτειν' εγώ
σύν ταΐσδ' άρίσταις Τρωιάσιν· δίκην δέ μοι
δέδωκε. χωρεί δ', ώς οράις, όδ' έκ δόμων.
άλλ' έκποδών άπειμι κάποστήσομαι
θυμώι ζέοντι Θρηικί δυσμαχωτάτωι. 1055

Πο. ώιμοι εγώ, πάι βώ, πάι στώ, πάι κέλσω, astr. 1056–7
τετράποδος βάσιν θηρός όρεστέρου
τιθέμενος έπί χείρα κατ' ίχνος; ποίαν
– ή ταύταν ή τάνδ'; – έξαλλάξω, τάς 1060
άνδροφόνους μάρψαι χρήιζων Ίλιάδας,
αϊ με διώλεσαν;
τάλαιναι κόραι τάλαιναι Φρυγών,
ώ κατάρατοι,

1033 ώ Triclinius: ίώ ω   1041 Polymestori continuat pars Σ: choro tribuunt MO:
semichoro B   1047 ξένον Hermann: ξένου ω   1052 ταΐσδ' Hermann: ταΐς
ω   1055 θυμώι ω: θυμόν Ruhnken   ζέοντι pp: ρέοντι ω   1059 κατ' ίχνος ω:
καί ίχνος Porson   1063 τάλαιναι κόραι τάλαιναι Φρυγών Seidler et Hermann:
τάλαιναι τάλαιναι κόραι Φρυγών ω

ΕΥΡΙΠΙΔΟΥ

ποῖ καί με φυγᾶι πτώσσουσι μυχῶν; 1065
εἴθε μοι ὀμμάτων αἱματόεν βλέφαρον
ἀκέσαι' ἀκέσαιο, τυφλόν, Ἅλιε,
φέγγος ἀπαλλάξας.
ἆ ἆ,
σῖγα· κρυπτὰν βάσιν αἰσθάνομαι
τάνδε γυναικῶν. πᾶι πόδ' ἐπάιξας 1070
σαρκῶν ὀστέων τ' ἐμπλησθῶ,
θοίναν ἀγρίων θηρῶν τιθέμενος,
ἀρνύμενος λώβας λύμας <τ'> ἀντίποιν'
ἐμᾶς, ὦ τάλας;
ποῖ πᾶι φέρομαι τέκν' ἔρημα λιπὼν 1075
Βάκχαις Ἅιδα διαμοιρᾶσαι
σφακτά, κυσίν τε φοινίαν δαῖτ' ἀνημέροις, οὐρείαν τ' ἐκβολάν;
πᾶι στῶ, πᾶι βῶ, πᾶι κάμψω,
ναῦς ὅπως ποντίοις πείσμασιν λινόκροκον 1080
φᾶρος στέλλων, ἐπὶ τάνδε συθεὶς 1081-2
τέκνων ἐμῶν φύλαξ ὀλέθριον κοίταν; 1083-4

Χο. ὦ τλῆμον, ὥς σοι δύσφορ' εἴργασται κακά· 1085
δράσαντι δ' αἰσχρὰ δεινὰ τἀπιτίμια
[δαίμων ἔδωκεν ὅστις ἐστί σοι βαρύς].

Πο. αἰαῖ ἰὼ Θρήικης λογχοφόρον ἔνο- astr. 1088-9
πλον εὔιππον Ἄρει κάτοχον γένος. 1090
ἰὼ Ἀχαιοί, 1091
ἰὼ Ἀτρεῖδαι· 1091b
βοὰν βοάν, αὐτῶ βοάν·
ὦ ἴτε μόλετε πρὸς θεῶν.
κλύει τις ἢ οὐδεὶς ἀρκέσει; τί μέλλετε;
γυναῖκες ὤλεσάν με, 1095

1069 σίγα σίγα O   1072 τιθέμενος θηρῶν Seidler   1073 ἀρνύμενος λώβας λύμας <τ'> Hadley (λώβας iam Bothe): ἀρνύμενος λώβαν λύμας ω: ἀρνυμένων λώβαν, λύμας Battezzato   1074 ὦ Seidler et Hermann: ἰὼ ω   1076 Ἅιδα Diggle: Ἅιδου ω   1077 σφακτά Hermann: σφακτάν ω   1077-8 ἀνημέροις Battezzato: ἀνήμερον ω   1078 οὐρείαν τ' MB: οὐρίαν τ' O: ὀρείαν τ' pp: τ' οὐρείαν Hermann: τ' ὄρειον Diggle   1079 πᾶι στῶ, πᾶι βῶ, πᾶι κάμψω p: πᾶι στῶ, πᾶι κάμψω, πᾶι βῶ ω: πᾶι βῶ, πᾶι στῶ, πᾶι κάμψω Porson: πᾶι στῶ, πᾶι κάμψω Nauck   1087 del. Hermann

ΕΚΑΒΗ 65

γυναῖκες αἰχμαλωτίδες·
δεινὰ δεινὰ πεπόνθαμεν.
ὤιμοι ἐμᾶς λώβας.
ποῖ τράπωμαι, ποῖ πορευθῶ;
ἀμπτάμενος οὐράνιον ὑψιπετὲς ἐς μέλαθρον, 1100-1
Ὠαρίων ἢ Σείριος ἔνθα πυρὸς φλογέας ἀφίησιν 1102-3
ὄσσων αὐγάς, ἢ τὸν ἐς Ἅιδα 1104-5
μελάγχρωτα πορθμὸν ἄιξω τάλας;
Χο. συγγνωσθ᾽, ὅταν τις κρείσσον᾽ ἢ φέρειν κακὰ
πάθηι, ταλαίνης ἐξαπαλλάξαι ζόης.
Αγ. κραυγῆς ἀκούσας ἦλθον· οὐ γὰρ ἥσυχος
πέτρας ὀρείας παῖς λέλακ᾽ ἀνὰ στρατὸν 1110
Ἠχὼ διδοῦσα θόρυβον· εἰ δὲ μὴ Φρυγῶν
πύργους πεσόντας ἦισμεν Ἑλλήνων δορί,
φόβον παρέσχ᾽ ἂν οὐ μέσως ὅδε κτύπος.
Πο. ὦ φίλτατ᾽, ἠισθόμην γάρ, Ἀγάμεμνον, σέθεν
φωνῆς ἀκούσας, εἰσορᾶις ἃ πάσχομεν; 1115
Αγ. ἔα·
Πολυμῆστορ ὦ δύστηνε, τίς σ᾽ ἀπώλεσεν;
τίς ὄμμ᾽ ἔθηκε τυφλὸν αἱμάξας κόρας
παῖδάς τε τούσδ᾽ ἔκτεινεν; ἦ μέγαν χόλον
σοὶ καὶ τέκνοισιν εἶχεν ὅστις ἦν ἄρα.
Πο. Ἑκάβη με σὺν γυναιξὶν αἰχμαλωτίσιν 1120
ἀπώλεσ᾽ – οὐκ ἀπώλεσ᾽ ἀλλὰ μειζόνως.
Αγ. τί φήις; σὺ τοὔργον εἴργασαι τόδ᾽, ὡς λέγει;
σὺ τόλμαν, Ἑκάβη, τήνδ᾽ ἔτλης ἀμήχανον;
Πο. ὤιμοι, τί λέξεις; ἦ γὰρ ἐγγύς ἐστί που;
σήμηνον, εἰπὲ ποῦ 'σθ᾽, ἵν᾽ ἁρπάσας χεροῖν 1125
διασπάσωμαι καὶ καθαιμάξω χρόα.
Αγ. οὗτος, τί πάσχεις; Πο. πρὸς θεῶν σε λίσσομαι,
μέθες μ᾽ ἐφεῖναι τῆιδε μαργῶσαν χέρα.
Αγ. ἴσχ᾽· ἐκβαλὼν δὲ καρδίας τὸ βάρβαρον
λέγ᾽, ὡς ἀκούσας σοῦ τε τῆσδέ τ᾽ ἐν μέρει 1130
κρίνω δικαίως ἀνθ᾽ ὅτου πάσχεις τάδε.
Πο. λέγοιμ᾽ ἄν. ἦν τις Πριαμιδῶν νεώτατος,

1097 δεινὰ δεινὰ ω: δεινὰ Hermann et Bothe   1100–1 ἀμπτάμενος Σ: αἰθέρ᾽ ἀμπτάμενος ω   1102–3 Ὠαρίων [MB]Σ p^γρ : ὦ Ὠρίων O   ἢ ω: καὶ Battezzato   1104–5 Ἅιδα Pflugk: Ἅίδαν pp: Ἀίδαν ω   1108 ζόης p^γρ: ζοῆς pp: ζώης ω   1112 ἦισμεν Σ test.: ἴσμεν ω   1113 παρέσχ᾽ ἂν Heath et Markland: παρέσχεν ἂν MO: παρέσχεν B   1115 φωνὴν Blaydes

ΕΥΡΙΠΙΔΟΥ

Πολύδωρος, Ἑκάβης παῖς, ὃν ἐκ Τροίας ἐμοὶ
πατὴρ δίδωσι Πρίαμος ἐν δόμοις τρέφειν,
ὕποπτος ὢν δὴ Τρωϊκῆς ἁλώσεως. 1135
τοῦτον κατέκτειν'· ἀνθ' ὅτου δ' ἔκτεινά νιν
ἄκουσον, ὡς εὖ καὶ σοφῆι προμηθίαι.
ἔδεισα μή σοι πολέμιος λειφθεὶς ὁ παῖς
Τροίαν ἀθροίσηι καὶ ξυνοικίσηι πάλιν,
γνόντες δ' Ἀχαιοὶ ζῶντα Πριαμιδῶν τινα 1140
Φρυγῶν ἐς αἶαν αὖθις ἄρειαν στόλον,
κἄπειτα Θρήικης πεδία τρίβοιεν τάδε
λεηλατοῦντες, γείτοσιν δ' εἴη κακὸν
Τρώων, ἐν ὧιπερ νῦν, ἄναξ, ἐκάμνομεν.
Ἑκάβη δὲ παιδὸς γνοῦσα θανάσιμον μόρον 1145
λόγωι με τοιῶιδ' ἤγαγ', ὡς κεκρυμμένας
θήκας φράσουσα Πριαμιδῶν ἐν Ἰλίωι
χρυσοῦ· μόνον δὲ σὺν τέκνοισί μ' εἰσάγει
δόμους, ἵν' ἄλλος μή τις εἰδείη τάδε.
ἵζω δὲ κλίνης ἐν μέσωι κάμψας γόνυ· 1150
πολλαὶ δέ, χειρὸς αἱ μὲν ἐξ ἀριστερᾶς,
αἱ δ' ἔνθεν, ὡς δὴ παρὰ φίλωι Τρώων κόραι
θάκους ἔχουσαι κερκίδ' Ἠδωνῆς χερὸς
ἤινουν, ὑπ' αὐγὰς τούσδε λεύσσουσαι πέπλους·
ἄλλαι δὲ κάμακε Θρηικίω θεώμεναι 1155
γυμνόν μ' ἔθηκαν διπτύχου στολίσματος.
ὅσαι δὲ τοκάδες ἦσαν, ἐκπαγλούμεναι
τέκν' ἐν χεροῖν ἔπαλλον, ὡς πρόσω πατρὸς
γένοιντο, διαδοχαῖσ' ἀμείβουσαι χερῶν.
κᾆτ' ἐκ γαληνῶν πῶς δοκεῖς προσφθεγμάτων 1160
εὐθὺς λαβοῦσαι φάσγαν' ἐκ πέπλων ποθὲν
κεντοῦσι παῖδας, αἱ δὲ πολυπόδων δίκην
ξυναρπάσασαι τὰς ἐμὰς εἶχον χέρας
καὶ κῶλα· παισὶ δ' ἀρκέσαι χρῄζων ἐμοῖς,
εἰ μὲν πρόσωπον ἐξανισταίην ἐμὸν 1165

1141 ἄρειαν Σ pp: αἴρειαν O: αἴροιαν HMB   στόλον H^{γρ}MB: δόρυ HM^{γρ}O
1151 χειρὸς Milton: χεῖρες ωΣ   1153 θάκους Hermann: θάκουν ωΣ
1154 ἤινουν Hermann: ἤινουν θ' ωΣ   1155 del. quidam apud Σ κάμακε Θρηικίω
Hartung: κάμακα Θρηικίαν fere ωΣ   1156 στολίσματος ωΣ: στοχίσματος Σ^{γρ}:
στοχάσματος Hartung   1159 διαδοχαῖσ' Elmsley: διαδοχαῖς MBO: διαδοχαῖσιν
H   χερῶν O: χερ** H^{ac}: χεροῖν H^{pc} vel H^1: διὰ χερός MB   1162 πολυπόδων
Verrall: πολεμίων ω

κόμης κατεΐχον, εἰ δὲ κινοίην χέρας
πλήθει γυναικῶν οὐδὲν ἤνυτον τάλας.
τὸ λοίσθιον δέ, πῆμα πήματος πλέον,
ἐξειργάσαντο δείν'· ἐμῶν γὰρ ὀμμάτων
πόρπας λαβοῦσαι τὰς ταλαιπώρους κόρας   1170
κεντοῦσιν αἱμάσσουσιν· εἶτ' ἀνὰ στέγας
φυγάδες ἔβησαν. ἐκ δὲ πηδήσας ἐγὼ
θὴρ ὣς διώκω τὰς μιαιφόνους κύνας,
ἅπαντ' ἐρευνῶν τοῖχον, ὡς κυνηγέτης
βάλλων ἀράσσων. τοιάδε σπεύδων χάριν   1175
πέπονθα τὴν σήν, πολέμιόν γε σὸν κτανών,
Ἀγάμεμνον. ὡς δὲ μὴ μακροὺς τείνω λόγους,
εἴ τις γυναῖκας τῶν πρὶν εἴρηκεν κακῶς
ἢ νῦν λέγων ἔστιν τις ἢ μέλλει λέγειν,
ἅπαντα ταῦτα συντεμὼν ἐγὼ φράσω·   1180
γένος γὰρ οὔτε πόντος οὔτε γῆ τρέφει
τοιόνδ'· ὁ δ' αἰεὶ ξυντυχὼν ἐπίσταται.
Χο. μηδὲν θρασύνου μηδὲ τοῖς σαυτοῦ κακοῖς
τὸ θῆλυ συνθεὶς ὧδε πᾶν μέμψηι γένος.
[πολλαὶ γὰρ ἡμῶν· αἱ μέν εἰσ' ἐπίφθονοι,   1185
αἱ δ' εἰς ἀριθμὸν τῶν κακῶν πεφύκαμεν.]
Εκ. Ἀγάμεμνον, ἀνθρώποισιν οὐκ ἐχρῆν ποτε
τῶν πραγμάτων τὴν γλῶσσαν ἰσχύειν πλέον·
ἀλλ' εἴτε χρήστ' ἔδρασε χρήστ' ἔδει λέγειν,
εἴτ' αὖ πονηρὰ τοὺς λόγους εἶναι σαθρούς,   1190
καὶ μὴ δύνασθαι τἄδικ' εὖ λέγειν ποτέ.
σοφοὶ μὲν οὖν εἰσ' οἱ τάδ' ἠκριβωκότες,
ἀλλ' οὐ δύνανται διὰ τέλους εἶναι σοφοί,
κακῶς δ' ἀπώλοντ'· οὔτις ἐξήλυξέ πω.
καί μοι τὸ μὲν σὸν ὧδε φροιμίοις ἔχει·   1195
πρὸς τόνδε δ' εἶμι καὶ λόγοις ἀμείψομαι·
ὃς φὴις Ἀχαιῶν πόνον ἀπαλλάσσων διπλοῦν
Ἀγαμέμνονός θ' ἕκατι παῖδ' ἐμὸν κτανεῖν.
ἀλλ', ὦ κάκιστε, πρῶτον οὔποτ' ἂν φίλον

1167 ἤνυτον Porson: ἤν*τον H: ἤνυον MBO   1173 del. Barrett   1174 del.
Prinz   ἐρευνῶ Barrett   1176 γε Diggle: τε Ω: τὸν p   1185–6 del.
Dindorf   1185 πολλαὶ γὰρ ἡμῶν· αἱ μέν εἰσ' ἐπίφθονοι BO: πολλαὶ γὰρ ἡμῶν· εἰσ'
ἐπίφθονοι Μ: πολλαὶ γὰρ ἡμῶν οὐδέν εἰσ' ἐπίφθονοι Musgrave: πολλαὶ γάρ· αἱ μὲν
<οὐδέν> εἰσ' ἐπίφθονοι Porson   1194 ἀπώλοντ'· οὔτις Ο: ἀπώλοντο κοὔτις
MB   1195 ὧδε pp: ὥδ' ἐν ΩΣ

ΕΥΡΙΠΙΔΟΥ

τὸ βάρβαρον γένοιτ' ἂν Ἕλλησιν γένος 1200
οὐδ' ἂν δύναιτο. τίνα δὲ καὶ σπεύδων χάριν
πρόθυμος ἦσθα; πότερα κηδεύσων τινὰ
ἢ συγγενὴς ὢν ἢ τίν' αἰτίαν ἔχων;
ἢ σῆς ἔμελλον γῆς τεμεῖν βλαστήματα
πλεύσαντες αὖθις; τίνα δοκεῖς πείσειν τάδε; 1205
ὁ χρυσός, εἰ βούλοιο τἀληθῆ λέγειν,
ἔκτεινε τὸν ἐμὸν παῖδα καὶ κέρδη τὰ σά.
ἐπεὶ δίδαξον τοῦτο· πῶς, ὅτ' ηὐτύχει
Τροία, πέριξ δὲ πύργος εἶχ' ἔτι πτόλιν,
ἔζη τε Πρίαμος Ἕκτορός τ' ἤνθει δόρυ, 1210
τί οὐ τότ', εἴπερ τῶιδ' ἐβουλήθης χάριν
θέσθαι, τρέφων τὸν παῖδα κἀν δόμοις ἔχων
ἔκτεινας ἢ ζῶντ' ἦλθες Ἀργείοις ἄγων;
ἀλλ' ἡνίχ' ἡμεῖς οὐκέτ' ἦμεν ἐν φάει,
καπνὸς δ' ἐσήμην' ἄστυ πολεμίοις ὕπο, 1215
ξένον κατέκτας σὴν μολόντ' ἐφ' ἑστίαν.
πρὸς τοῖσδε νῦν ἄκουσον ὡς φαίνηι κακός·
χρῆν σ', εἴπερ ἦσθα τοῖς Ἀχαιοῖσιν φίλος,
τὸν χρυσὸν ὃν φὴις οὐ σὸν ἀλλὰ τοῦδ' ἔχειν
δοῦναι φέροντα πενομένοις τε καὶ χρόνον 1220
πολὺν πατρώιας γῆς ἀπεξενωμένοις·
σὺ δ' οὐδὲ νῦν πω σῆς ἀπαλλάξαι χερὸς
τολμᾶις, ἔχων δὲ καρτερεῖς ἔτ' ἐν δόμοις.
καὶ μὴν τρέφων μὲν ὥς σε παῖδ' ἐχρῆν τρέφειν
σώσας τε τὸν ἐμόν, εἶχες ἂν καλὸν κλέος· 1225
ἐν τοῖς κακοῖς γὰρ ἀγαθοὶ σαφέστατοι
φίλοι· τὰ χρηστὰ δ' αὔθ' ἕκαστ' ἔχει φίλους.
εἰ δ' ἐσπάνιζες χρημάτων, ὁ δ' ηὐτύχει,
θησαυρὸς ἄν σοι παῖς ὑπῆρχ' οὑμὸς μέγας·
νῦν δ' οὔτ' ἐκεῖνον ἄνδρ' ἔχεις σαυτῶι φίλον 1230
χρυσοῦ τ' ὄνησις οἴχεται παῖδές τε σοὶ
αὐτός τε πράσσεις ὧδε. σοὶ δ' ἐγὼ λέγω,
Ἀγάμεμνον· εἰ τῶιδ' ἀρκέσεις, κακὸς φανῆι·
οὔτ' εὐσεβῆ γὰρ οὔτε πιστὸν οἷς ἐχρῆν,

1201 οὐδ' Dindorf: οὔτ' ω   1202 τινὶ Kovacs   1209 πτόλιν Ο: πόλιν MB   1211 τί Wecklein: τί δ' ω   1215 καπνὸς p^{γρ}: καπνῶι ω   ἐσήμην' MB: ἐσήμαιν' Ο: ἐπήμην' p^{γρ} πολεμίοις Schenkl: πολεμίων ωΣ   1217 φαίνηι Gloël: φανῆι pp: φανῆις ω

ΕΚΑΒΗ

	οὐχ ὅσιον, οὐ δίκαιον εὖ δράσεις ξένον·	1235
	αὐτὸν δὲ χαίρειν τοῖς κακοῖς σε φήσομεν	
	τοιοῦτον ὄντα· δεσπότας δ' οὐ λοιδορῶ.	
Χο.	φεῦ φεῦ· βροτοῖσιν ὡς τὰ χρηστὰ πράγματα	
	χρηστῶν ἀφορμὰς ἐνδίδωσ' ἀεὶ λόγων.	
Αγ.	ἀχθεινὰ μέν μοι τἀλλότρια κρίνειν κακά,	1240
	ὅμως δ' ἀνάγκη· καὶ γὰρ αἰσχύνην φέρει	
	πρᾶγμ' ἐς χέρας λαβόντ' ἀπώσασθαι τόδε.	
	ἐμοὶ δ', ἵν' εἰδῇς, οὔτ' ἐμὴν δοκεῖς χάριν	
	οὔτ' οὖν Ἀχαιῶν ἄνδρ' ἀποκτεῖναι ξένον,	
	ἀλλ' ὡς ἔχηις τὸν χρυσὸν ἐν δόμοισι σοῖς.	1245
	λέγεις δὲ σαυτῶι πρόσφορ' ἐν κακοῖσιν ὤν.	
	τάχ' οὖν παρ' ὑμῖν ῥάιδιον ξενοκτονεῖν·	
	ἡμῖν δέ γ' αἰσχρὸν τοῖσιν Ἕλλησιν τόδε.	
	πῶς οὖν σε κρίνας μὴ ἀδικεῖν φύγω ψόγον;	
	οὐκ ἂν δυναίμην. ἀλλ' ἐπεὶ τὰ μὴ καλὰ	1250
	πράσσειν ἐτόλμας, τλῆθι καὶ τὰ μὴ φίλα.	
Πο.	οἴμοι, γυναικός, ὡς ἔοιχ', ἡσσώμενος	
	δούλης ὑφέξω τοῖς κακίοσιν δίκην.	
Εκ.	οὔκουν δικαίως, εἴπερ εἰργάσω κακά;	
Πο.	οἴμοι τέκνων τῶνδ' ὀμμάτων τ' ἐμῶν τάλας.	1255
Εκ.	ἀλγεῖς; τί δ'; ἦ 'μὲ παιδὸς οὐκ ἀλγεῖν δοκεῖς;	
Πο.	χαίρεις ὑβρίζουσ' εἰς ἔμ', ὦ πανοῦργε σύ;	
Εκ.	οὐ γάρ με χαίρειν χρή σε τιμωρουμένην;	
Πο.	ἀλλ' οὐ τάχ', ἡνίκ' ἄν σε ποντία νοτίς ...	
Εκ.	μῶν ναυστολήσηι γῆς ὅρους Ἑλληνίδος;	1260
Πο.	κρύψηι μὲν οὖν πεσοῦσαν ἐκ καρχησίων.	
Εκ.	πρὸς τοῦ βιαίων τυγχάνουσαν ἁλμάτων;	
Πο.	αὐτὴ πρὸς ἱστὸν ναὸς ἀμβήσηι ποδί.	
Εκ.	ὑποπτέροις νώτοισιν ἢ ποίωι τρόπωι;	
Πο.	κύων γενήσηι πύρσ' ἔχουσα δέργματα.	1265
Εκ.	πῶς δ' οἶσθα μορφῆς τῆς ἐμῆς μετάστασιν;	
Πο.	ὁ Θρηιξὶ μάντις εἶπε Διόνυσος τάδε.	
Εκ.	σοὶ δ' οὐκ ἔχρησεν οὐδὲν ὧν ἔχεις κακῶν;	
Πο.	οὐ γάρ ποτ' ἂν σύ μ' εἷλες ὧδε σὺν δόλωι.	
Εκ.	θανοῦσα δ' ἢ ζῶσ' ἐνθάδ' ἐκπλήσω φάτιν;	1270
Πο.	θανοῦσα· τύμβωι δ' ὄνομα σῶι κεκλήσεται ...	

1254 Hecubae tribuit p: Agamemnoni tribuerunt ω   1256 τί δ'; ἦ 'μὲ Bothe: τί δαί με Β: τί δέ με ΜΟ: τί δὴ με p   1257 interrogationis nota distinxit Weil   1258 χρή pp: χρῆν ω   1263 ναὸς Π¹⁰ ω: νηὸς pp   ἀμβήσηι B: ἐμβήσηι ΜΟΣ   1270 φάτιν Weil: βίον ω

Εκ. μορφῆς ἐπωιδὸν μή τι τῆς ἐμῆς ἐρεῖς;
Πο. κυνὸς ταλαίνης σῆμα, ναυτίλοις τέκμαρ.
Εκ. οὐδὲν μέλει μοι, σοῦ γέ μοι δόντος δίκην.
Πο. καὶ σήν γ' ἀνάγκη παῖδα Κασσάνδραν θανεῖν. 1275
Εκ. ἀπέπτυσ'· αὐτῶι ταῦτα σοὶ δίδωμ' ἔχειν.
Πο. κτενεῖ νιν ἡ τοῦδ' ἄλοχος, οἰκουρὸς πικρά.
Εκ. μήπω μανείη Τυνδαρὶς τοσόνδε παῖς.
Πο. καὐτόν γε τοῦτον, πέλεκυν ἐξάρασ' ἄνω.
Αγ. οὗτος σύ, μαίνηι καὶ κακῶν ἐρᾶις τυχεῖν; 1280
Πο. κτεῖν', ὡς ἐν Ἄργει φόνια λουτρά σ' ἀμμένει.
Αγ. οὐχ ἕλξετ' αὐτόν, δμῶες, ἐκποδὼν βίαι;
Πο. ἀλγεῖς ἀκούων;   Αγ. οὐκ ἐφέξετε στόμα;
Πο. ἐγκλῄετ'· εἴρηται γάρ.   Αγ. οὐχ ὅσον τάχος
νήσων ἐρήμων αὐτὸν ἐκβαλεῖτέ ποι, 1285
ἐπείπερ οὕτω καὶ λίαν θρασυστομεῖ;
Ἑκάβη, σὺ δ', ὦ τάλαινα, διπτύχους νεκροὺς
στείχουσα θάπτε· δεσποτῶν δ' ὑμᾶς χρεὼν
σκηναῖς πελάζειν, Τρωιάδες· καὶ γὰρ πνοὰς
πρὸς οἶκον ἤδη τάσδε πομπίμους ὁρῶ. 1290
εὖ δ' ἐς πάτραν πλεύσαιμεν, εὖ δὲ τἀν δόμοις
ἔχοντ' ἴδοιμεν τῶνδ' ἀφειμένοι πόνων.
Χο. ἴτε πρὸς λιμένας σκηνάς τε, φίλαι,
τῶν δεσποσύνων πειρασόμεναι
μόχθων· στερρὰ γὰρ ἀνάγκη. 1295

1272 μ[ή] Π²: ἢ ωΣ   1278 Agamemnoni tribuit Weil   1279 γε pp et fortasse
Π²: σε ωΣ: τε pp: om. Σ: δὲ pp   1281 ἀμμένει p: ἀναμένει BO:
ἀναμενεῖ M   1284 ἐγκλῄετ' Dindorf: ἐγκλείετ' ω   1285 ποι O: που MB

COMMENTARY

1–97 PROLOGUE

1–58 Monologue of Polydorus

The play begins with a narrative monologue in iambic trimeters, delivered on an empty stage, as in most plays by Euripides: Mastronarde on *Med.* 1–48, Allan on *Hel.* 1–67. Polydorus, like divine prologue-speakers, does not reappear as a speaking character in the rest of the play: cf. *Hippolytus, Ion*, and (in dialogic prologues) *Alcestis, Trojan Women*. Polydorus, appearing as the ghost of a deceased person, has special contact with and assistance from the gods (49–52). His account of the past, and his predictions, are authoritative ('Staging', below; 40–1, 47–50), even if he leaves considerable space for surprises in the narrative (43n.).

The crucial literary models for this speech are *Iliad* 23, which narrates the funeral of Patroclus (cf. 518–82n.) and the apparition of his ghost to Achilles, and Sophocles' *Polyxena* (1–2n.). Patroclus asks to be buried; he is barred from reaching Hades by the spirits of the dead (*Il.* 23.71–3). Euripides corrects this belief about the afterlife: Polydorus has reached the underworld before burial, like the suitors in *Od.* 24.1–204 (cf. Aristonicus in sch. *Il.* 23.73).

Staging

The play is set on the Gallipoli peninsula (8n., 33–4, 37–9n.). The *skēnē* represents Agamemnon's tent, where Hecuba is also lodged (53–4; cf. 1016n.). The chorus too say that the slaves are sharing the tents with their respective masters (99–101, 1288–9), as in the *Trojan Women* (176–8). In *Hecuba*, the Greek masters are in any case absent from the tents (1018), since they *all* assembled to discuss Achilles' request (107) and, later, to attend the sacrifice of Polyxena (522). On the position of the tent cf. also 616n. and 880.

Polydorus describes himself as 'flying over my mother' (30n., 31n.). He probably appears on the *skēnē* roof, also known as *theologeion*: Mastronarde 1990: 276. Alternatively, Polydorus may also appear on the *mēchanē* (Jouanna 1982: 51–2, Mastronarde 1990: 277 n. 91), even if this would be unique at the very beginning of a play. Some scholars argue that Polydorus, as he comes from the underworld, must arrive onstage walking on ground level (Heath 1987b: 165), through one of the *eisodoi* (Di Benedetto and Medda 1997: 129) or through a 'subterranean entrance' (Lane 2007: 293–4). However, 30–1 ὑπὲρ μητρὸς φίλης ... ἀίσσω and especially 32 αἰωρούμενος 'suspended' clearly indicate that he is in a higher position when speaking those lines. Euripides modifies Homeric representations of ghosts and dreams appearing over the head of a sleeper: *Il.* 2.20, 23.68 (Patroclus' ghost), *Od.* 4.803. See also 52–3n. and Introduction, section 3.2, 'Stage Movements'.

1–2 Ἥκω ... | λιπών 'I have come here, leaving ...' Polydorus stresses that he was able to leave Hades (an exceptional event), and mentions the setting only at 8. The passage seems to allude to Sophocles' *Polyxena*, where the ψυχή of Achilles probably appeared onstage in the prologue saying 'I have come here leaving (λιποῦσα ... ἦλθον) the black lake-shores deep below, unvisited by Apollo' (fr. 523.1–2: trans. Sommerstein, Fitzpatrick and Talboy 2006: 52–7, 69–70, 76–7; see above, Introduction, section 2). Many characters in Euripides begin their speeches by giving similar indications, esp. in prologues: cf. 503, *Tro.* 1 ἥκω λιπών, *Ion* 5 ἥκω, *Ba.* 1 ἥκω.

σκότου πύλας 'the gates of darkness', cf. 209. 'Darkness' designates 'death' or 'Hades' by metonymy, 'the substitution of one word for another to which it stands in some close relation' (Smyth §3033): see 460–1n., 567n., 1153n., Nagy 2015, Matzner 2016. Euripides adapts the epic and tragic phrase 'Gates of Hades' (*Il.* 5.646, 23.71, Aesch. *Ag.* 1291).

2 ἵν' Ἅιδης χωρὶς ᾤκισται θεῶν 'where Hades has fixed his dwelling, separate from the <other> gods'. Hades was allotted the nether world: *Il.* 15.191.

3 'I, Polydorus, the son born from Hecuba, the <daughter> of Kisseus'. The name Kisseus recalls, with minimal variation, that of Kisses, a Thracian king, father to Theano (*Il.* 6.298–9, 11.221–4). In the *Iliad* (16.718), Hecuba's father is Dymas. Giving a Thracian father to Hecuba fits the setting of the play, making the choice of Polymestor as a warden of Hecuba's child more plausible, and aggravating Polymestor's breach of hospitality. Hecuba and Theano are closely connected, and exchange roles in *Il.* 6.269–310: Gregory 1995. The name Kisseus is related to κισσός 'ivy' and may suggest a connection with Dionysus, recipient of special cult in Thrace: cf. 1267n., Schlesier 1988: 112 n. 3, Zeitlin 1996: 177 and n. 12.

4–5 ἐπεὶ Φρυγῶν πόλιν | κίνδυνος ἔσχε δορὶ πεσεῖν Ἑλληνικῶι 'when the danger of falling under the spear of the Greeks came upon the Phrygians' city'.

6 ὑπεξέπεμψε 'sent away (-εξ-) secretly (ὑπ-)'. Cf. 10n., 13.

7 'to the house of Polymestor, our Thracian *xenos* [host, friend]'. *Xenia* indicates a 'ritualised friendship' between people belonging to different cities; the link is religiously sanctioned (in particular by Zeus). On *xenia* see Introduction, section 5.

8 τήνδ' ἀρίστην Χερσονησίαν πλάκα 'this splendid plain of Chersonese'. 'Chersonese' means 'peninsula'. Here it refers to the

Thracian headland (nowadays part of European Turkey) that runs along the Hellespont, north of Troy. The phrase, with the deictic τήνδ' (conjectured by Hermann), identifies the setting of the play for the audience (cf. 33–6 and 37–9n.), as is regularly the case in Euripides' prologues (Barrett on *Hipp.* 12). The MS text τὴν ἀρίστην inappropriately implies that the Chersonese is elsewhere. The Thracian Chersonese is 'splendid' because of its fertility, like that of Thrace as a whole (*Il.* 20.485). Athenian colonies in the peninsula were strategically and politically important when this play was staged: Mitchell 1997: 134–47, Archibald 1998: 112–20. Some Athenians viewed Thrace as a barbaric country, while others (esp. from the elite) saw it as a land of political, economic and military opportunities: Archibald 1998: 96–102, Sears 2013, Vlassopoulos 2013: 119–28. The anti-Thracian undertones of the plot of *Hecuba* are presented from a (Trojan) aristocratic point of view: the combination within the same play of popular prejudice against Thracians and of an elitist viewpoint questions both these ideologies (299–331n., 1187–1237n., 1199–1204n.).

9 φίλιππον 'horse-loving'. Thracians were famous for rearing horses: cf. 710, 1090 and *Il.* 13.4, 14.227 ἐφ' ἱπποπόλων Θρηικῶν.

10 ἐκπέμπει λάθραι 'sent away secretly' (cf. 6n.). The historic present highlights the crucial narrative point (527–9n., 937n.): sending the gold causes the death of Polydorus.

11–12 ἵν', εἴ ποτ' Ἰλίου τείχη πέσοι, | τοῖς ζῶσιν εἴη παισὶ μὴ σπάνις βίου 'so that, should the walls of Troy fall, <his> surviving children would not lack resources to support them'.

παισί is here a poetic plural (265n.), referring to Polydorus himself.

βίου 'means of living'.

13 νεώτατος ... Πριαμιδῶν Polydorus is the youngest of Priam's children: *Il.* 20.409 and Introduction, section 4.

ἦ, not ἦν, is the old Attic form of the 1st p. sg. of the imperfect of εἰμί, regularly used by Euripides, and should be printed throughout the play (15, 284, 354, 809): Barrett on *Hipp.* 700.

ὃ καί 'and this in fact is the reason why'. For ὅ 'wherefore' cf. Mastronarde on *Pho.* 155. καί does not emphasise the following με, but indicates that the relative clause 'contains an addition to the information contained in the main clause' (Denniston 294–5). Cf. 515–17n.

με: enclitic pronouns tend towards second position in the clause (Wackernagel's law: Goldstein 2016). They do not intrude between the relative (or interrogative) pronoun and the adverbial καί which modifies the entire relative (or interrogative) clause: 515, 1065, Barrett on *Hipp.* 92, K–G II.255.

14–15 οὔτε ... νέωι βραχίονι: the 'youthful arm' here indicates helplessness, not youthful strength, as in *Suppl.* 738; see also 407n.

16–17 'As long as the boundaries of <our> country stayed firm, and the towers of the Trojan land stood unbroken'. 'Trojan land' in fact means Troy by synecdoche, as in *Tro.* 4–5: Diggle 1981: 67.

μὲν οὖν is used to mark a transition to a new subject: cf. 798, 1192 and Denniston 472–3.

ὁρίσματα is an abstract term for ὅρος 'boundary stone': Long 1968: 18–21 and 35–46. Boundaries here coincide with the city walls.

18 'and my brother Hector was successful with his spear'. Hector's recorded success in the *Iliad* lasted in fact only the few days when Achilles abstained from fighting (*Il.* 7–19), but Polydorus, like Priam in *Il.* 22.56–65 and Andromache in *Il.* 24.728–30, implies that the siege against Troy lasted so many years thanks to Hector's prowess.

ηὐτύχει: verbs in ευ- normally take the temporal augment in ηυ- in the Classical period, and should be so printed throughout the play (301, 1208, 1228): Mastronarde 1989, Threatte 1996: 482–3. The diphthong ηυ- was later shortened to ευ-, a form often found in medieval MSS.

19 παρ' ἀνδρὶ Θρηικὶ πατρώιωι ξένωι 'in the house of the Thracian guest of my father'. ἀνδρί is in apposition to ξένωι: cf. 644–6n., 790n., 1252–3n.

20 'I was growing like a plant that is nourished, unhappy me'.

τροφαῖσιν indicates the series of acts entailed in the nurturing of a young child: Aesch. *Ag.* 1159 ἠνυτόμαν τροφαῖς, Eur. *Tro.* 1187.

ὥς τις πτόρθος: young people are often compared to growing plants: 123n., 592–8n., Eur. fr. 481.8 πτόρθον, 360.22–3, *Il.* 18.56–7, *Od.* 6.157.

21–2 Ἕκτορός τ' ἀπόλλυται | ψυχή 'and the life of Hector was destroyed'. The ψυχή is the vital impulse that animates the body: 87–9n., *Andr.* 611 ψυχὰς ... ἀπώλεσας, *Hel.* 52–3 ψυχαὶ δὲ πολλαὶ ... ἔθανον, *Tro.* 1214–15.

ἀπόλλυται, in the singular, refers to two subjects, Τροία and ψυχή: 459–60 ἀνέσχε, *HF* 774–6 ὁ χρυσὸς ἅ τ' εὐτυχία ... ἐξάγεται ... ἐφέλκων, K–G 1.79–80, Smyth §966. For the historic present cf. 527–9n.

22 πατρῶια θ' ἑστία κατεσκάφη 'and the hearth of my father was razed to the ground'.

23–4 'and my father himself falls at the altar of the gods, slaughtered by the murderous son of Achilles [i.e. Neoptolemus]'. The episode was narrated in the *Iliupersis*: 'Neoptolemus kills Priam, who has fled to the altar of Zeus of the Courtyard' (Proclus' summary: trans. West 2003: 145; see West 2013: 234). On Neoptolemus' notorious bloodlust cf. 566n. Bloodshed at the altar is the worst possible offence against a god: even the murderous tyrant Lycus (*HF* 238–51) and the treacherous Menelaus (*Andr.* 366–83) refrain from killing their enemies at an altar.

αὐτός τε: the notion of 'father' is supplied from the adjective πατρῴια at 22: Cooper and Krüger 1998: 978.

θεοδμήτωι 'built for the gods, sacred'. This alludes to the Homeric phrase about the Trojan 'walls built by the gods' (*Il.* 8.519 θεοδμήτων ἐπὶ πύργων), with a variation in meaning: θεόδμητος almost comes to mean 'sacred' (as in Pind. *Ol.* 3.7). As in many compound adjectives, the second element is redundant: 470–2n. The adjective stresses Neoptolemus' sacrilege.

πίτνει: this alternative present-tense formation (scanned ⌣ –) is often used in poetry for πίπτει (scanned – –): Mastronarde on *Pho.* 293, metre; Schwyzer 1939: 695.

Ἀχιλλέως: the vowels -έω- form a single syllable by synizesis: [94n.], 551n.

ἐκ with genitive indicates the agent: Moorhouse 1982: 109.

25–7 'The house-guest of my father kills me, unhappy me, for the gold, and, after killing me, throws <me> to the swelling of the sea, so that he can keep the gold in his palace.'

25 For the word order cf. 44n.

25–6 κτείνει με ... καὶ κτανών: the repetition mimics a simple, oral narrative style: Mastronarde on *Pho.* 22.

26 οἶδμ' ἁλός is a slightly redundant poetic phrase (cf. 634, 446, 701n., 938, *Hel.* 400) since οἶδμα alone can mean 'sea' (*Pho.* 202).

28–9 'I lie <sometimes> on the shore, sometimes in the rolling swell of the sea, transported by the incessant ebb and flow of the waves'.

ἄλλοτ' 'sometimes' refers both to ἐπ' ἀκταῖς and to ἐν πόντου σάλωι, and must be translated twice in English (the so-called ἀπὸ κοινοῦ construction): cf. 370–1n.

διαύλοις 'to-and-fro': a double course, as in a race in a Greek stadium, from one point to another and back. Polydorus in fact returns to the Thracian shore, more or less where Polymestor cast him out to sea.

30 ἄκλαυτος ἄταφος: Polydorus adapts for himself Achilles' words for Patroclus in *Il.* 22.386 κεῖται πὰρ νήεσσι νέκυς ἄκλαυτος ἄθαπτος. Two or three adjectives beginning with privative alpha are often placed in rhetorically prominent positions in Greek poetry, to pathetic effect: 669n., *Il.* 9.63, Fraenkel on Aesch. *Ag.* 412–13, Soph. *Ant.* 29 ἄκλαυτον ἄταφον. Like Patroclus (1–58n.), Polydorus desires lamentation and burial in order to complete his transition to the underworld.

ὑπὲρ μητρὸς φίλης: ὑπέρ + gen. indicates the position occupied by ghosts hovering above the head of the living person they want to communicate with: cf. 1–58n., Richardson on *Il.* 23.68 = 24.682 στῆ δ' ἄρ' ὑπὲρ κεφαλῆς (the ghost of the dead Patroclus, appearing to Achilles in a dream).

31 ἀίσσω 'I dart', 'I glide', 'I fly' describes the quick movements of the souls of the dead: *Od.* 10.495 σκιαὶ ἀΐσσουσιν 'they flit as shadows'.

σῶμ' ἐρημώσας ἐμόν 'having left my corpse': the soul of Polydorus, appearing onstage, is his real self, i.e. the entity that can say 'I'.

32 τριταῖον ἤδη φέγγος 'for three days already', accusative of duration. φέγγος 'light', 'daylight' is often used to mean 'a day': see Barrett on *Hipp*. 275 τριταίαν ... ἡμέραν. The 'third day' is particularly apt for supernatural or magical events: Alcestis can speak only on the third day after returning from Hades (*Alc.* 1146 τρίτον ... φάος); a ghost appears to the mother of Demaratus on the third day from her wedding (Hdt. 6.69.1). For 'three times' in cult cf. Soph. *Ant.* 431.

αἰωρούμενος 'suspended': cf. 1–58n. 'Staging'.

33–4 'for as much time as my unhappy mother has been here in this land of Chersonese, <having arrived> from Troy'. Cf. 37–9n.

ὅσονπερ is an accusative of duration, parallel to 32 τριταῖον ... φέγγος.

πάρα 'is present', equivalent to πάρεστι.

35–6 ἥσυχοι | θάσσουσ': the phrase here indicates inertia: cf. 90 1 n., *Hcld.* 477 ἥσυχον μένειν. In other contexts, it may indicate imperturbability and detachment: *Ba.* 622 ἥσυχος θάσσων, *Tro.* 985.

37–9 'For the son of Peleus, Achilles, having made his apparition over his tomb, held back the whole Greek army, as they were guiding their ships towards home.' In the archaic epic poem *Nostoi* the ghost of Achilles appears to Agamemnon and his soldiers 'and tries to prevent them <from sailing> by foretelling what will happen' (trans. West 2003: 155; see West 2013: 258–9); a similar apparition was narrated in Sophocles' *Polyxena* (1–2n.). Here, Achilles stops the Greek fleet with his apparition and his request for honours. The Greeks later pray for his protection while returning to Greece (538–41n.), but Achilles is not said to stop the winds on this occasion (cf. 111–12n.); later in the course of the play Agamemnon mentions lack of winds as a reason for not leaving (900, 1289–90).

Homer locates Achilles' tomb in the Troad: *Il.* 23.125–6 and 245–8, *Od.* 24.82, Cook 1973: 159–64, Burgess 2009: 111–26. Euripides locates it in the Thracian Chersonese (8n., 33–6), across the Hellespont from Troy, stressing this innovation from the start. The audience is reminded of the Thracian setting at 962–3, 1088–90.

Ἀχιλλεύς is in apposition to 37 ὁ Πηλέως ... παῖς.

εὐθύνοντας 'guiding', a plural participle, referring to the plural 'the Greeks' implicit in the collective noun στράτευμ' (38): Smyth §1044.

ἐναλίαν πλάτην: lit. 'the oar used in the sea', 'the maritime plank'. 'Oar' is used by synecdoche for 'ship': see *Hel.* 191, Schein on Soph. *Phil.* 220. As often, the adjective 'maritime' is ornamental and does not contrast this type of oar with a different one: 26n.

40–1 'He asks to get my sister Polyxena as a pleasing sacrifice and gift of honour to his tomb.' Polydorus testifies that Achilles requests Polyxena in particular, not just any prisoner: this statement, from a person coming from the underworld, and speaking in the prologue, is authoritative for the audience: 113–15n.

γέρας is an allusion to, or rather 'grim parody' (King 1985: 51) of, *Il.* 1. 118–87: in the *Iliad* Achilles protects a young prisoner, Chryseis, whereas here he demands the sacrifice of another (Polyxena). Cf. [94–5], 113–15n., 306–8n. This dead Euripidean Achilles alludes to both the beginning and the end of the *Iliad*: he asks for special honours (306–8n.; *Il.* 1.163–8) but also wants a human sacrifice (260n., 342–78n., *Il.* 18.336–7, 23.22–3 and 175–6). He does not seem to feel the bitter disillusionment about rank and honours that he expresses, after his death, at *Od.* 11.489–91 (551–2n.).

43 ἡ πεπρωμένη 'the allotted <portion>', 'fate'. The term μοῖρα is understood here. Fate, in archaic and classical Greek literature, is not imagined as preventing individuals from acting freely; moreover, it indicates the general direction of events only, not all minute details of each action. Polyxena's free choice of death (342–78n., 367–8n., 548–9n.) and the exact denouement of the action are not predicted by Polydorus, leaving considerable scope for suspense. Cf. *Ion* 1388, where the protagonist chooses a course of action because he claims 'I would not go against what is fated [τὰ ... πεπρωμέν(α)]'. On fate in tragedy cf. Williams 1993: 138–41, Sewell-Rutter 2007: 136–50, Cairns 2012: 141–8.

44 For the interlaced word order cf. *HF* 1139 μιᾶς ἅπαντα χειρὸς ἔργα σῆς τάδε, Diggle 1994: 97, 152, 419–20.

45 Wordplay with numbers is a favourite stylistic feature of classical poetry: 124–5, *Andr.* 516, *Ion* 466.

47–50 Polydorus announces that his body will be found thanks to divine intervention, and he gives specific details of the future action; contrast the lack of details about Polyxena's fate (43n.). In this way, the highly unlikely circumstances of the finding of his body will not appear implausible, but divinely ordained. Many passages in Euripides are devised so that unlikely events may appear plausible: Scodel 1999: esp. 118–19, 122.

48 'in front of the feet of a slave woman, by the seashore', anticipating the appearance of this minor character at 658–701.

49 τοὺς γὰρ κάτω σθένοντας 'those who have power down below', i.e. the gods of the underworld. σθένος ('strength, power') is a defining quality of the gods: 799–800n., *Ba.* 884, *IA* 1090–5, Riedweg 1990: 46.

50 κἄς = καὶ ἐς.

51–2 τοὐμόν ... ἔσται 'and so my lot will be to get what I wanted'.

τοὐμόν 'my situation, my lot': Diggle 1981: 106–7.

μὲν οὖν: 16–17n.

52–3 γεραιᾶι δ' ἐκποδὼν χωρήσομαι | Ἑκάβηι 'I will get out of the way of the aged Hecuba'. Polydorus stands aside while Hecuba enters: for this convention of stage action, often signalled by ἐκποδών, cf. 1054, Garvie on Aesch. *Cho.* 20, Taplin 1977: 334–5.

53–4 Hecuba probably appears in the *skēnē* door; she cannot see her son. Alternatively, she might appear slightly later, at 59, but the effect of Polydorus' words is much more forceful if the audience can see her already at this point.

περᾷ ... πόδα 'moves <her> foot', 'walks'. περᾶν, usually intransitive ('to go across'), is here used causatively, 'to make the foot go across': cf. 1070n., Finglass on Soph. *Ai.* 40, K–G 1.299.

ὑπὸ σκηνῆς 'from under the tent', as if the tent covered Hecuba: cf. *Andr.* 441 ὑπὸ πτερῶν σπάσας, *HF* 296.

φάντασμα δειμαίνουσ' ἐμόν 'frightened at seeing me in her dream'. φάντασμα means 'vision seen in a dream' (704–5n., Kyriakou on *IT* 42–3, Aesch. *Sept.* 710 ἐνύπνια φαντάσματα).

55 φεῦ 'alas', expressing grief. For other usages cf. 864n.

ἐκ τυραννικῶν δόμων: in English one needs to add a verb indicating movement or change. The phrase means 'leaving your royal palaces', i.e. 'losing your former status of queen'. For this usage of ἐκ cf. 915, 1160n., Moorhouse 1982: 109.

56 δούλειον ἦμαρ 'the day of slavery', a Homeric expression (cf. Graziosi and Haubold on *Il.* 6.463 δούλιον ἦμαρ) imitated in *Andr.* 99, *Tro.* 1330.

57–8 ἀντισηκώσας δέ σε | φθείρει θεῶν τις τῆς πάροιθ' εὐπραξίας 'one of the gods brings ruin <to you>, compensating you for your former good fortune'. ἀντισηκόω 'I counterbalance, compensate' is construed with the genitive τῆς πάροιθ' εὐπραξίας. Hecuba and Priam are the standard mythical example for a change of fortune: 61n.

59–97 Hecuba's Monody

Hecuba arrives onstage, accompanied by young female attendants (59). A vision (70 φάσμασιν, 72 ἔννυχον ὄψιν), which she saw in a dream (71 ὀνείρων), has frightened her. She fears for her son Polydorus (79–86) and asks for help from Helenos and Cassandra, who will interpret her dream (87–9). The dream is a consequence of Polydorus' apparition (30n., 53–4n., 704–5n.). Hecuba is clearly not aware of what Polydorus said in the prologue, as is the rule for offstage characters: at most they hear a summons or noises (*Hcld.* 642–53, Mastronarde 1979: 28–30).

An interpolator added some verses in order to create pathos ([62–3]) or to make explicit certain details of the plot ([73–8n.], 90–1n., [92–7n.]) ; some interpreters oppose the deletions (Brillante 1988, Matthiessen), but the case is very strong (Bremer 1971). The spurious lines 73–8, 92–7 and 211–15 would allow two actors to perform 59–215 as a bravura piece, eliminating the parodos (98–153), and providing the audience with a general understanding of the plot.

The dream narrative follows a traditional pattern: a mysterious dream makes the dreamer fear about the future; interpretations are offered, but the wrong one is chosen; the events fulfil the dream; the dreamer at last realises the correct interpretation. Hecuba initially imagines that the dream is about Polydorus (79–86), but after the parodos her attention shifts to the imminent death of Polyxena. At 142 and 205–210 Euripides has the chorus and Polyxena describe the death of Polyxena with images and metaphors that recall Hecuba's dream (even if they have no knowledge of it). The prophetic dream is finally understood by Hecuba at 702–8 (cf. esp. 703–4 ἔμαθον ... ὄψιν, 708 οἶσθ' ὀνειρόφρων φράσαι;).

The same pattern is found in other dream narratives: Aesch. *Cho.* 32–6 (dream and fear), 38–46 (wrong interpretation), 540–52 (Orestes interprets the dream correctly), 928–9 (Clytemnestra understands the correct interpretation); Eur. *IT* 44–55 (dream), 42–3 (fear and pain), 55–8 (wrong interpretation), 467–71 (fulfilment) (the correct interpretation is never made explicit in the play); Soph. *El.* 417–25 (dream), 427 (fear), 459–60 (correct interpretation), 644–7 (Clytemnestra is uncertain as to the interpretation of the dream). The pattern is frequently found in Herodotus: dreams cause fear (1.39.2, 1.107.1–2, 3.30.3), are interpreted incorrectly (1.209.5, 6.107.2) and, finally, correctly (1.210.1, 3.125.4, 6.108.1 συνεβάλετο).

Greek tragedy and Herodotus asked their audiences to be active interpreters of dreams: at times the wrong interpretation is not spelled out (Soph. *El.*), at times the correct one is not (Eur. *IT*), even if both interpretations are important for understanding the actions and the intentions of the characters. The audience is normally told the actual content of the dream. The only tragic instance where this does not happen is Aesch. *Sept.* 710, but the dream was probably narrated in a previous play in the trilogy (Sommerstein 2010a: 88; for the opposite view, cf. Hutchinson *ad loc.*). This constant tragic practice supports the authenticity of 90–1.

Dodds 1951: 102–34, Brillante 1991, Walde 2001, Näf 2004 and W. V. Harris 2009 offer guidance on the interpretative issues and the vast bibliography on dreams in Greek antiquity. On this particular dream see also Jouanna 1982.

Metre

From a metrical point of view, the whole section 59–215 is a large, mainly anapaestic, block, formed by a monody (59–97), the parodos (98–153) and a lyric dialogue (154–215). The parodos is, uniquely, recited

COMMENTARY: 59-97

(cf. 98–153n. and Introduction, section 10), and is contrasted with the preceding and following sections, sung by the actors. Long sections (mostly) in anapaests, leading to the parodos after a prologue section in trimeters, are found also at *Med.* 96–130 and *Tro.* 98–152 (also delivered by Hecuba).

In the monody, after an initial section in recited anapaests (59–67), Hecuba switches to lyric (sung) anapaests (68–72, 79–89, [92–7]) and (sung) hexameters ([73–78], 90–1). The dactylic rhythm of many anapaests in 68–72 prepares for the hexameters.

As a rule anapaests present word-end after each anapaestic metron (diaeresis); a word may run over to the next metron by a short syllable in recited anapaests. This constraint is much weakened in lyric anapaests. In this passage, lack of word-end at the end of anapaestic metra is found only in paroemiacs (69, 72, 89) and in the interpolated line [96]. The paroemiac at [97], an interpolated line, has a shape unparalleled in Euripides; the closest parallel is *IT* 215 ⏑ ⏑ – – – ⏑ ⏑ ⏑ ⏑ – ⌢ |||. Conjectures have been advanced to improve metre and style ([96–7n.]). The metrical rules for anapaests in Attic tragedy are discussed in detail in Dale 1968: 47–68, West 1982: 121–4, Diggle 1981: 95–7, Martinelli 1997: 184–9, Lourenço 2011: 45–51.

The final syllables of 69 αἴρομαι and 72 ἀποπέμπομαι are shortened in front of a word-initial vowel (shortening in hiatus: see West 1982: 11–12). At 79 θεοί is to be measured as one syllable (synizesis: 55.1n.).

Hexameters are used in many passages of tragic lyric (Lourenço 2011: 66), esp. for narrating prophecies and forebodings (Pretagostini 1995: 175–6).

	– ⏑ ⏑ – ⏑ ⏑ – ⏑ ⏑ – –	2 an
68	ὦ στεροπὰ Διός, ὦ σκοτία Νύξ,	
	⏑ ⏑ – ⏑ ⏑ – ⏑ ⏑ – ⌢ ‖ᶜ	paroemiac ‖ᶜ
69	τί ποτ' αἴρομαι ἔννυχος οὕτω	
	– ⏑ ⏑ – ⏑ ⏑ – ⏑ ⏑ – –	2 an
70	δείμασι φάσμασιν; ὦ πότνια Χθών,	
	⏑ ⏑ – ⏑ ⏑ – – ⏑ ⏑ – –	2 an
71	μελανοπτερύγων μᾶτερ ὀνείρων,	
	⏑ ⏑ – ⏑ ⏑ – ⏑ ⏑ – ⌢ ‖ᵇ	paroemiac ‖ᵇ
72	ἀποπέμπομαι ἔννυχον ὄψιν	
	– ⏑⏑ – ⏑ ⏑ – – – ⏑ ⏑ – ⏑ ⏑ – ⌢ ‖ᶜ	dactylic hexameter ‖
73–4	[ἣν περὶ παιδὸς ἐμοῦ τοῦ σωιζομένου κατὰ Θρήικην	

COMMENTARY: 59-97   81

75-6 — ◡ ◡ — — — ◡ ◡ — ◡ ◡ — ◡ ◡ — ⌒ ||ᶜ   dactylic hexameter ||ᶜ
      ἀμφὶ Πολυξείνης τε φίλης θυγατρὸς δι' ὀνείρων

77-8 — — — ◡ ◡ — — ◡ ◡ ◡ ◡ ◡ ◡ —   [corrupt]
      †εἶδον γὰρ φοβερὰν ὄψιν ἔμαθον ἐδάην†].

      — — — ◡ ◡ — ◡ ◡ — ◡ ◡ — ◡ ◡ — ⌒ ||ᶜ   dactylic hexameter ||ᶜ
90   εἶδον γὰρ βαλιὰν ἔλαφον λύκου αἵμονι χαλᾶι

      — ◡ ◡ — ◡ — ◡ ◡ — — — ◡ ◡ — ⌒ ||ᶜ   dactylic hexameter ||ᶜ
91   σφαζομέναν, ἀπ' ἐμῶν γονάτων σπασθεῖσαν ἀνοίκτως.

      — ◡ ◡ — — ◡ ◡ — ◡ ◡   2 an
79   ὦ χθόνιοι θεοί, σώσατε παῖδ' ἐμόν,

      — ◡ ◡ — — — — ◡ ◡ —   2 an
80   ὃς μόνος οἴκων ἄγκυρ' ἔτ' ἐμῶν

      — ◡ ◡ — — — — ◡ ◡ —   2 an
81   τὰν χιονώδη Θρήικην κατέχει

      — — ◡ ◡ — ◡ ◡ — ⌒ ||ᵇ   paroemiac ||ᵇ
82   ξείνου πατρίου φυλακαῖσιν.

      — — ◡ ◡ ⌒ ||ᵇ   an ||ᵇ
83   ἔσται τι νέον·

      — — ◡ ◡ — ◡ ◡ — ◡ ◡ —   2 an
84   ἥξει τι μέλος γοερὸν γοεραῖς.

      — ◡ ◡ — — — ◡ ◡ — —   2 an
85   οὔποτ' ἐμὰ φρὴν ὧδ' ἀλίαστον

      — — — —   an
86   φρίσσει ταρβεῖ.

      — ◡ ◡ — — ◡ ◡ — — —   2 an
87   ποῦ ποτε θείαν Ἑλένου ψυχὰν

      — — — — ◡ ◡ — — ◡ ◡   2 an
88   καὶ Κασσάνδραν ἐσίδω, Τρωιάδες,

      — — — — ◡ ◡ — ⌒ ||| paroemiac |||
89   ὥς μοι κρίνωσιν ὀνείρους;

      — ◡ ◡ — ◡ ◡   an
92   [καὶ τόδε δεῖμά μοι·

      — ◡ ◡ — — — — ◡ ◡ —   2 an
93   ἦλθ' ὑπὲρ ἄκρας τύμβου κορυφᾶς

82   COMMENTARY: 59–67

94	‒ ‒ ⏑ ⏑ ‒ ‒ ‒ ‒ ⏑ ⏑ ‒ φάντασμ' Ἀχιλέως· ἤιτει δὲ γέρας	2 an
95	‒ ⏑ ⏑ ‒ ‒ ⏑ ⏑ ‒ ⏑ ⏑ ‒ τῶν πολυμόχθων τινὰ Τρωϊάδων.	2 an
96	⏑ ⏑ ‒ ‒ ⏑ ⏑ ‒ ⏑ ⏑ ‒ ‒ ἀπ' ἐμᾶς οὖν ἀπ' ἐμᾶς τόδε παιδός	2 an
97	‒ ⏑ ⏑ ‒ ⏑ ⏑ ⏑ ⏑ ‒ ⌢ ||| πέμψατε, δαίμονες, ἱκετεύω.]	paroemiac |||

59–60 ἄγετ'... ἄγετ': repetition of a word at the beginning of two consecutive cola is characteristic of Euripides' style, esp. in lyric and anapaests: 165–8n., 170–1, 202–3, 1095–6n., Diggle 1994: 370.

60–1 τὴν ὁμόδουλον, | Τρωιάδες, ὑμῖν 'the woman who shares her slavery with you, Trojan women'. The dative ὑμῖν is construed with the prefix ὁμο-: cf. 331 ὅμοια τοῖς βουλεύμασιν.

61 πρόσθε δ' ἄνασσαν: many tragic characters comment on losing their regal status (354–5n., *Andr.* 65 τῆι πρόσθ' ἀνάσσηι τῆιδε, νῦν δὲ δυστυχεῖ), but the cases of Hecuba (492, 891) and Priam (620–1) attracted general reflections already in antiquity: Arist. *Eth. Nic.* 1100a5–9, 1101a6–8, Nussbaum 1986: 327–40.

[62–3] An interpolator, imitating *Suppl.* 275–6, *Hipp.* 198 and 1361, wrote a metrically faulty line. In recited anapaests, series of four short syllables (λάβετε φέ-), not to mention six (λάβετε φέρετε), are severely limited (cf. [145n.]). Moreover, a word break between the two short syllables of an anapaest (-τε φέ-) is avoided: Barrett on *Hipp.* 1364–7, Diggle 1994: 315.

64 'taking her by her old arm'.

γεραιᾶς is scanned as ⏑ ⏑ ‒, with correption (='shortening') of the diphthong αι in front of a vowel: West 1982: 11, Barrett on *Hipp.* 170–1.

64–5 χειρὸς ... χερός: for the unstressed repetition cf. 526–8n.

65–7 lit. 'and I, leaning on the bent rod of your arm, will hasten the slow-moving step of <my> limbs, putting <it> forward'.

σκολιῶι σκίπωνι χερός: the arm is compared to a bent rod, because of its function and shape. Matthiessen and others interpret the line as 'leaning on the crooked rod which I have in my hand', but this would make Hecuba's call for help at 59–61 superfluous. The 'representative' singular χερός may indicate the (plural) hands of the servant women: cf. *Med.* 1069–70 δότ', ὦ τέκνα, ... δεξιὰν χέρα, Barrett on *Hipp.* 1131–4, Moorhouse 1982: 1. The gen. explains the meaning of a noun used metaphorically, as in *Med.* 107 νέφος οἰμωγῆς 'cloud of lament, lament that is like a cloud'.

σπεύσω gives a paradoxical contrast with βραδυ- 'slow-': cf. Augustus' motto σπεῦδε βραδέως (Suet. *Aug.* 25.4, Polyaenus, *Strat.* 8.24.4).

ἄρθρων: the genitive is redundant after the adjective βραδύπουν 'slow-footed': 26n., *Tro.* 232 ταχύπουν ἴχνος, *Pho.* 1549 πόδα... τυφλόπουν.

68 ὦ στεροπὰ Διός 'O dazzling light of Zeus' indicates the daylight, as στεροπᾶι in Soph. *Trach.* 99. The text alludes to and modifies the meaning of a Homeric expression designating lightning: *Il.* 10.154, 11.66 στεροπή... Διός, 16.298 στεροπηγερέτα Ζεύς.

70 δείμασι φάσμασιν: the two terms in asyndeton (cf. 86n.) express a single concept (436–7n.), 'fearful apparitions', 'fearful dreams'. On φάσμασιν cf. 54n.

Χθών 'Earth' sends dreams also in *IT* 1261–2. Here Earth probably refers to the underworld (71 μελανοπτερύγων). The 'land of dreams' (δῆμον ὀνείρων) is associated with the underworld already in *Od.* 24.12.

71 μελανοπτερύγων: dreams have wings (*IT* 571), and inauspicious dreams have dark ones (705, Jouanna 1982: 47); black is the colour of the earth and of the night, and it has obvious sinister connotations (Aesch. *Ag.* 770, Eur. *HF* 780).

72 ἀποπέμπομαι 'I avert', a magic and religious term indicating the attempt, by means of a prayer or curse, to divert towards someone else an ill omen or a possible future evil, esp. if sent by supernatural forces: Fraenkel on Aesch. *Ag.* 1573, Finglass on Soph. *El.* 647 ἔμπαλιν μέθες. By uttering the word ἀποπέμπομαι Hecuba enacts the ritual (which fails): 1276n.

[73–8] The lines are inconsistent with 79–82, where Hecuba reveals that the dream made her fear for Polydorus. Line 77, as transmitted in the MSS, is metrically unacceptable, and syntactically incorrect: γάρ is impossible in a relative clause, and in any case cannot be placed so late in the sentence. The original form of 77 was probably φοβερὰν ἐδάην (an anapaest). It was corrupted by the insertion of a fragment from 90 (εἶδον γάρ) and by the addition of glosses (ἔμαθον is a gloss on ἐδάην: cf. the scholia on Pind. *Ol.* 7.98a and 168a Drachmann, Hsch. δ 21, 26, 37 Latte; ὄψιν is also an addition explaining φοβεράν).

ἐδάην usually means 'I learned', 'I understood'. In the context, it would be better if ἐδάην meant 'I perceived', 'I saw' (the vision), as in Bacchyl. 5.64 ψυχὰς ἐδάη (Heracles 'perceived the spirits', i.e. he saw them), but the interpolator might have intended to indicate that Hecuba deciphered the dream.

90–1 'for I saw a dappled hind being slaughtered [lit. 'sacrificed'] by the eager (?) claws of a wolf, after having been pitilessly torn away from my knees'. The lines imitate *Od.* 19.228, ἐν προτέροισι πόδεσσι κύων ἔχε ποικίλον ἐλλόν 'a hound held a dappled deer in its forepaws', a description of the image on the golden brooch of Odysseus. The allusion can be read as a foreshadowing of the role of Odysseus in sacrificing Polyxena (cf. 141–3). A memory of her dream makes Hecuba guess the identity of the killer of Polydorus (709): the dream must have included some (indirect) description of the killer. In fact this dream is a complex allusion to the deaths of both children.

The audience might interpret the lines as referring primarily to Polyxena: (a) girls are often compared to young animals (cf. 142n. 'filly', 177–9n. 'bird', 205n. 'whelp', 206n. 'heifer'); for a hind cf. the Iphigenia myth (*IT* 28); (b) σπασθεῖσαν looks forward to 142, 207, 408, 513; (c) the sacrificial language (σφαζομέναν) alludes to the death of Polyxena, announced in 41 πρόσφαγμα; (d) violent young men are compared to wolves: cf. *Il.* 16.352 and in the dream narrated in [Eur.] *Rhes.* 783.

The lines in fact suit Polydorus as well: (a) boys too are compared to young animals (142n.); Iliadic warriors, when killed or chased by a more powerful enemy, are compared to male (*Il.* 22.189) and female deer (*Il.* 11.113); (b) Polydorus too was taken away from his mother (13–14, 768–9), even if no violence was involved; (c) the death of Polydorus is not presented in sacrificial language, but his corpse was subjected to 'unholy' abuse (714–21); (d) Polymestor is explicitly compared to a wild animal who walks on all fours and wants to feed on human flesh (1056–8, 1070–4, 1125–6). The dream can be read also as a reference to the death of the children of Polymestor: (a) they are compared to prey eaten by dogs and birds (1077–8); (b) they are taken away from his lap (1157–9); (c) they are 'sacrificed' (1037, 1077); (d) they are killed by murderous dogs (1173).

As Wilamowitz-Moellendorff 1909: 446–51 = Wilamowitz-Moellendorff 1962: 225–9 saw, 90–1 were displaced by 73–7; the presence of εἶδον γάρ in 77 is a relic of a variant reading indicating the original position of the lines. The interpolator who wrote 92–7 moved 90–1 to the position they have in medieval MSS. Wilamowitz considered 90–1 spurious as well, but that requires the intervention of two different interpolators. Moreover, a mention of the content of the dream is to be expected (59–97n.), and the narrative is compatible with the imagery of the play.

αἵμονι means either 'eager' or 'bloody'. The adjective occurs elsewhere only in *Il.* 5.49 αἵμονα θήρης (of a warrior), 'eager for the hunt'. Cf. the root of ἵμερος 'desire', Weiss 1998: 55–6, Beekes 2010 s.v. αἵμων. The Homeric scholia interpret αἵμονα θήρης as 'expert in hunting', which makes sense in the Homeric context (cf. *Il.* 5.51 ἐσθλὸν θηρητῆρα 'good hunter', and 10.360 εἰδότε θήρης) but is etymologically unexplained and may be a simple guess. Alternatively, Euripides may have used αἵμων to mean 'bloody': cf. ὁμαίμων, συνομαίμων, συναίμων and πολυαίμων, Chantraine 1968–80 s.v. αἵμα.

χαλᾶι (= Attic χηλῆι) 'claw' (Mastronarde on *Pho.* 1024–5). 'Although real wolves tear at their prey with their teeth, this is a dream wolf that uses its paws like hands' (Gregory), like the wolf of *Od.* 19.228 (90–1n.).

ἀνοίκτως: Porson's conjecture restores good metre and meaning, and is supported by ἀνηλεῶς in a scholium (in Σ *Tro.* 786 ἀνηλεεῖς explains ἄνοικτος).

79 'O gods below the Earth, save my son', i.e. 'spare him'. The gods of the underworld were considered to be unmoved by human acts of worship (cf. Aesch. fr. 161). Only in extreme situations, as here, would someone address them with a prayer; the name Hades is in any case normally avoided, as here, in favour of euphemistic terms: cf. Allan and Kannicht on *Hel.* 969, fr. 448a56–7, Finglass on Soph. *El.* 110. On the gods of the underworld cf. Burkert 1985: 200–2.

80 οἴκων ἄγκυρ' ... ἐμῶν 'anchor of my household', a common maritime metaphor: fr. 866.2 ἄγκυρα στέγης (cf. 281n.), Pearson on Soph. fr. 685 ἀλλ' εἰσὶ μητρὶ παῖδες ἄγκυραι βίου.

81 τὰν χιονώδη Θρήικην 'snowy Thrace', a traditional qualification: *Il.* 14.227 Θρηικῶν ὄρεα νιφόεντα, Eur. *Andr.* 215. These lines are probably sung, and it is necessary to introduce the form τάν (= Attic τήν). The stem of Θρήικην has eta in the first syllable in all dialects, and in lyric passages of tragedy: fr. 752g2, g10, Björck 1950: 354–5. The final syllable maintains the epic eta even in lyric passages: Aesch. *Pers.* 566 Θρήικης, West 1990: xxvi.

κατέχει 'dwells in, occupies'.

82 'under the protection of a guest-friend of his father'.

83 τι νέον 'something untoward', a negative meaning attested especially when νέον is accompanied by τί or τι (177, 217, LSJ s.v. II.2).

84 γοερὸν γοεραῖς: 154–215n.

85–6 'my mind has never shuddered, has never felt fear so continuously'. οὔποτ' with the present tense indicates an action that began in the past and continues in the present: Smyth §1885.

φρήν is often designated as the part of the human mind which feels fear: *Il.* 1.555 δέδοικα κατὰ φρένα, Aesch. *Pers.* 115, Sullivan 1997: 33–6.

ἀλίαστον 'without stopping', adverbial accusative, as in *Il.* 24.549 ἄνσχεο, μηδ' ἀλίαστον ὀδύρεο. The meaning of this epic word is disputed: 'that does not move aside, that does not go back' (λιάζομαι, cf. 98), i.e. 'inescapable, never ending'. Cf. Silk 1983: 315–16, Chantraine 1968–1980 and Beekes 2010 s.v. λιάζομαι, Kannicht 2004 on Eur. fr. 1095b. The MS text ἀλίαστος is problematic. φρήν and other mental 'organs' are often said to be 'unbending' (Eur. *Hipp.* 1268 ἄκαμπτον φρένα, Aesch. *PV* 163) but it is difficult to find adjectives such as ἀλίαστος or ἄκαμπτος used predicatively with verbs other than 'to be, become'. Homeric usage also favours Nauck's conjecture ἀλίαστον.

86 φρίσσει ταρβεῖ '<my mind> shudders, fears'. Tragic language often favours asyndeton between near-synonyms, esp. in connection with real or threatened violence: 387, 507, 840n., 1171, 1175n., Bond on *HF* 602, Mastronarde on *Pho.* 1193.

87–9 'Where can I ever see the divine spirit of Helenus, or Cassandra, Trojan women, so that they can interpret <my> dreams for me?' Hecuba's children Helenus and Cassandra were both skilled prophets, as stated for Helenus in the *Iliad* (6.76) and for both siblings in the *Cypria* (West 2013: 83–5). Cassandra was Agamemnon's slave and concubine (824–32, Aesch. *Ag.* 950–5). According to a probable reconstruction of the *Nostoi*, Helenus survived the fall of the city and was a slave to Neoptolemus (Apollod. *Epit.* 6.12, West 2013: 179–81 and 262–3).

καί is apparently used in the meaning of Latin *uel* ('and/or'): see 1102–4n. and Diggle 1994: 198.

Hecuba's monody ends in a question which amounts to a request to Helenus and Cassandra to appear onstage. In their stead the chorus enter (98), as is normal at this point of the play. The entrance of the 'wrong' person, who gives surprising news, is a frequent device in tragedy: Taplin 1977: 11–12. Hecuba's request loses relevance after the parodos, which seems to offer the right interpretation of the dream (90–1n.).

θείαν Ἑλένου ψυχάν: Helenus has a 'divine spirit' because he has access to what the gods have to say, like Tiresias, θεῖον ... μάντιν (Soph. *OT* 298), and Theonoe (*Hel.* 13–14): Dodds 1951: 139. Philosophical reflection attributed divine minds also to other human beings: Eur. fr. 1018 ὁ νοῦς γὰρ ἡμῶν ἐστιν ἐν ἑκάστωι θεός, Emp. 31 A 32. Cf. also 21–2n.

Κασσάνδραν: the accusative is preferable to the genitive, as it introduces a characteristic *uariatio* (642–3n., 659n., 916–18n., 1200, Breitenbach 1934: 210) after Ἑλένου ψυχάν. 'Cassandra' must be spelled with two sigmas: Fraenkel on Aesch. *Ag.* 1035.

[92–7] 'This too is a cause of fear for me: the ghost of Achilles appeared above the very top of his tomb. He asked for one of the much-suffering Trojan women as a gift in his honour. O gods, avert this from my child, from my child: I supplicate you.' These lines are unlikely to be authentic: they take away the surprise element from the parodos announcement, are metrically dubious ([96–7n.]: cf. 59–97n. 'Metre') and often re-elaborate phrases from other sections of the play ([93n.], [94–5n.], [96–7n.]). It is absurd to have Hecuba add this devastating piece of news as an afterthought. Moreover, 59–87 presuppose that Hecuba has just been awoken by the ominous dream.

[93] ἦλθ' ὑπὲρ ἄκρας τύμβου κορυφᾶς rephrases 109 τύμβου δ' ἐπιβάς. The tomb is implicitly (and exaggeratedly) compared to a mountain, by way of an allusion to a Homeric phrase typically used for Mount Olympus (*Il.* 1.499 ἀκροτάτηι κορυφῆι πολυδειράδος Οὐλύμποιο).

[94] Ἀχιλέως is to be scanned as ⌣ ⌣ –. Cf. 23–4n. for the synizesis of εω, 108 and 128 for the single lambda.

[94–5] ἤιτει δὲ γέρας | τῶν πολυμόχθων τινὰ Τρωϊάδων rephrases 40–1 αἰτεῖ ... | ... γέρας λαβεῖν (cf. 115 ἀγέραστον). Hecuba (cf. the chorus in 113–15) here implies that Achilles did not specify the identity of the victim; Polydorus (40–1) and Odysseus (305, 390) state that Achilles asked specifically for Polyxena.

[96–7] ἀπ' ἐμᾶς οὖν ἀπ' ἐμᾶς τόδε παιδός | πέμψατε echoes ἀποπέμπομαι 72n. Bothe's conjecture ἀπ' ἐμᾶς ἀπ' ἐμᾶς οὖν restores good metre (59–97n. 'Metre') and style, but there is not much point in improving the text of interpolated lines.

[97] δαίμονες: 163–4n.

98–153 PARODOS

The chorus arrive onstage in order to bring an important piece of news, as in *El.* 169, fr. 752f15–35. Many other tragic choruses arrive onstage in order to help or show sympathy to the main characters: Pattoni 1989, Mastronarde 2010: 127–9.

The chorus present the meeting of the Greek army as a quasi-democratic assembly. Agamemnon, as often in the *Iliad*, fails to persuade the army leaders. Only the leaders speak, and they do so with freedom and frankness, as in Homer (*Il.* 2.50–397, 18.249–313, Schofield 1986) and in democratic Athens (234–7n.). In the end, the demagogue Odysseus persuades the 'army' (133). The decision is not sanctioned by a vote, as for instance in the Athenian *ekklēsia*, or by other means of approval, such as shouting (553n., *Il.* 2.394, 18.310, Plut. *Lyc.* 26.3–5). The lack of a final vote or acclamation recalls some Homeric army meetings, and differs from the formal procedures of a polis assembly: *Il.* 1.304–5, 9.173, Raaflaub 1997: 642.

The chorus act and speak like other tragic messengers (98n., 104–6n., 108–9n.), and, like them, quote direct speeches (113–15: cf. 518–82n.). Moreover, their narrative, like those of many tragic messengers, is mostly factual, but occasionally includes moral judgement on some of the events or characters (131–3: cf. *Or.* 889–94, 903, de Jong 1991: 77–9). In one case, they either manipulate the facts or are economical with the truth (113–15n.).

The metre is non-lyric anapaests (59–97n. 'Metre'). The colometry printed here divides the anapaests into dimeters, except for the monometers at 114, 128, 139, and for the paroemiacs, marking end of period, at

103, 115, 129, 140, 153. Many other parodoi begin with recited anapaests (*Alc.* 77–85), but this is the only extant one that does not include a lyric section. This was probably not unique: Arist. *Poet.* 1452b22–3 defined the parodos as 'the first utterance (λέξις) of the chorus', presumably implying that it did not need to be sung (Dale 1969: 35–6, Rode 1971: 89, Battezzato 2005: 151).

98 σπουδῆι πρός σ' ἐλιάσθην 'I came back to you in a hurry'. The verb λιάζομαι implies that the person is not where he or she is supposed to be: 85–6n. The chorus women slipped away (from the meeting) unnoticed by their masters (Mossman 1995: 70–1), but this is 'only a slight and glancing detail' (Easterling 1987: 24): neither Odysseus nor Agamemnon comments on the fact that the women are not where they should be. They are in fact in front of the tent of their master (1–58n.). Haste is a sign of care and urgency (216–17, *Hipp.* 902–3, *Andr.* 880, Taplin 1977: 147), especially common in the case of messengers (Aesch. *Pers.* 247–8, Eur. *Hipp.* 1151–2, Griffith on Soph. *Ant.* 223–6).

99–102 'having left the tent of my master, where I was assigned by lot and ordered to go as a slave, after I was driven away from the city of Ilium'. The lines identify the chorus for the audience, as usual in the parodos (*Pho.* 202–7).

Ἰλιάδος 'Iliadic', gen. sg. of the feminine adjective: cf. 1008n.

102–3 λόγχης αἰχμῆι | δοριθήρατος πρὸς Ἀχαιῶν 'captured by the point of the spear, by the action of the Achaeans'. Poetic language favours redundant expressions: the genitive in the phrase λόγχης αἰχμῆι 'by the point of the spear' repeats the idea expressed by the first element of the compound adjective δοριθήρατος 'captured by the spear'.

104–6 οὐδὲν παθέων ἀποκουφίζουσ' | ἀλλ' ἀγγελίας βάρος ἀραμένη | μέγα σοί τε, γύναι, κῆρυξ ἀχέων 'not lightening your suffering, but taking up the great burden of an announcement and as a herald of sorrows for you, my lady'. The participles ἀποκουφίζουσ' and ἀραμένη qualify the main verb at 98 ἐλιάσθην 'I came back'. Messengers are often reluctant to announce bad news: 518n. 'Weight' is a frequent metaphor for suffering: Eur. *Alc.* 353, *Hipp.* 259, Soph. *Ant.* 1273.

κῆρυξ: this traditional accentuation of the word (Herodian vol. II 9. 18–29) is preferable to the accentuation κήρυξ propounded by West 1990: xlviii and others: see Probert 2003: 84, Battezzato 2009a: 191–7.

107 'in the full assembly of the Greeks'. The chorus use the language of fifth-century politics: 522, Xen. [*Ath. Pol.*] 2.17 ἐν πλήρει τῶι δήμωι 'in a full assembly meeting', LSJ. s.v. πλήρης III.1.

108–9 λέγεται δόξαι σὴν παῖδ' Ἀχιλεῖ | σφάγιον θέσθαι 'it is said that it has been decided to offer your daughter as a sacrificial offering to Achilles'. The chorus concisely deliver the main piece of news before embarking on the detailed narrative. So do tragic messengers, normally in a short dialogue before the narrative *rhēsis*: 484–628n., 508–10.

δόξαι 'it seemed right', 'it has been decided', the technical term for political decision: the chorus leave out a dative which would normally indicate who took the decision. On breaking the news, they prefer to let Hecuba judge for herself the responsibility of individual Greek leaders, on the basis of the detailed narration that follows; contrast 678–80n. On impersonal constructions in messenger narratives cf. J. Barrett 2002: 34–6, 120–1, 202.

109–10 τύμβου δ' ἐπιβάς | οἶσθ' ὅτε χρυσέοις ἐφάνη σὺν ὅπλοις 'do you know when he appeared with his golden armour, over his tomb?' The main sentence is a question and ends at 115; it includes a direct speech (cf. 929–30n.) at 114–15, which is itself a question. On Achilles' apparition cf. 1–58n., 37–9n. Hephaestus used gold in the fabrication of the shield and/or armour of Achilles, both for the original set (*El.* 443–4, *IA* 1071–2 χρυσέων ὅπλων Ἡφαιστοπόνων) and the replacement he created at the request of Thetis (*Il.* 18.475, 20.272, Edwards 1991: 202). Gold is the default material of divine objects: 463–5n.

τύμβου δ' ἐπιβάς: lit. 'having mounted upon his tomb'. From a syntactic point of view, the participial phrase refers to the subject of ἐφάνη, and does not go with οἶσθ'. The phenomenon is called 'left dislocation' in modern linguistics. For similar dislocations, placing syntactic material of the subordinate clause before the subordinating conjunction (here ὅτε), cf. *Med.* 669 παίδων ἐρευνῶν σπέρμ' ὅπως γένοιτό μοι, *Hipp.* 604 οὐκ ἔστ' ἀκούσας δεῖν' ὅπως σιγήσομαι.

οἶσθ': 239, 1008n. By using this turn of phrase, the chorus assume that Hecuba knows part of the news that they are in fact delivering to her.

110 χρυσέοις is probably to be scanned as – –. The υ of χρύσεος is always long in Homer, and much more frequently long than short in tragedy. If that was the case here, εοι coalesced into one syllable (synizesis: cf. [94n.], 464–5 χρυσέαν, 551n., 922n.). Alternatively, one may scan χρυσέοις as ⏑ ⏑ –: the υ of χρύσεος is occasionally short in Pindar and tragedy (Page on *Med.* 633–4).

111–12 'and when he stopped the seafaring ships that had their sails pressed against the forestays'. On Achilles' orders cf. 37–9n.

σχεδίας: lit. 'rafts'. The forestays are the ropes that reach from masthead to prow. The sails 'billow forth to the forestays', i.e. the ships are departing with a favourable wind: Diggle 1994: 435.

113–15 Ποῖ δή, Δαναοί, | τὸν ἐμὸν τύμβον | στέλλεσθ' ἀγέραστον ἀφέντες; 'Where do you hasten to, you Greeks, leaving my tomb without a γέρας [= unhonoured]?' Achilles is ironically made to repeat the point made by Agamemnon against Achilles himself in *Il.* 1.118–19, where he asked the Greeks: 'Prepare for me a γέρας, so that I will not be the only one of the Argives to be ἀγέραστος, since that is not appropriate (οὐδὲ ἔοικε).'

Achilles has now taken on Agamemnon's ruthless persona (40–1n.). The chorus (unlike Polydorus: 40–1n.) do not report Achilles as specifying that the victim had to be Polyxena. The chorus try to spare Hecuba the details of the bad news and speak in vague terms, whenever possible (104–6n., 108–9n.). In the debate that follows (116–40) 'Agamemnon's opposition takes for granted that a close relative of Cassandra is in question' (Scodel 1999: 118). Hecuba, apparently ignoring Achilles' specific request, later suggests that Odysseus should find a different sacrificial victim (Helen: 265–70; cf. [94–5n.]). Only at 305 and 389–90 does Odysseus reveal to her that Achilles requested Polyxena in particular. On the location of Achilles' tomb cf. 37–9n., 386.

116 'the wave of a great quarrel clashed together'. The army is compared to a stormy sea: cf. [531–3n.], 1160n. συμπαίω is used intransitively.

117–18 δόξα ... αἰχμητήν 'Opinion was moving in two different directions among the the spear-wielding army of the Greeks.'

ἐχώρει δίχ' 'was moving at variance', a reformulation of Homeric phrases: *Il.* 18.510 δίχα δέ σφισιν ἥνδανε βουλή, 21.386, LSJ s.v. δίχα I.2.

στρατὸν αἰχμητήν: the noun αἰχμητής is used as an adjective, as in Pind. *Pyth.* 1.5: 274–5n.

118–19 τοῖς μὲν διδόναι | τύμβωι σφάγιον, τοῖς δ' οὐχὶ δοκοῦν 'because to some it seemed right to give a sacrificial victim to the tomb, to others it did not'.

δοκοῦν is an accusative absolute (neuter participle of the impersonal δοκέω): 505–6, Smyth §2076A.

120–2 ἦν δὲ ... Ἀγαμέμνων 'Agamemnon was the one who was active promoting what is good for you, remaining constant to the bed of the prophetic bacchant', i.e. Cassandra. 'Bed' is a metonymy (1–2n.) for 'sexual relationship'.

ἦν ... σπεύδων is a periphrastic form, used in particular when the action expressed by the verb in the participle (here σπεύδων) is the 'topic' of the sentence (cf. Introduction, section 10). The sentence answers the question: 'Who was active in promoting what is good for Hecuba?' Cf. Soph. *Ai.* 1324, Gonda 1959, Diggle 1981: 103, K–G I.38–9.

ἀνέχων 'remaining constant to, protecting': cf. Finglass 2009b: 85–9 discussing Soph. *Ai.* 211–12 ἐπεὶ σε λέχος δουριάλωτον | στέρξας ἀνέχει (or, according to the interpretation favoured by Finglass, στέρξασαν ἔχει) θούριος Αἴας.

122 τὼ Θησεῖδα 'the two sons of Theseus': Acamas and Demophon. Two Attic vases of 490–480 BCE depict them as involved in the sacrifice of Polyxena (Kron 1981: 438, 443). They are not mentioned in the *Iliad*. The poems of the archaic epic cycle *Sack of Ilium* and *Little Iliad* included accounts of their participation in the Trojan war: West 2003: 134–7, 146–7, 150–3, Cingano 2007.

123 ὄζω Ἀθηνῶν 'the two scions of Athens', lit. 'the two branches of Athens'. This metaphor (cf. 20n.) imitates the epic formula ὄζος Ἄρηος (*Il.* 2.540), where however ὄζος in origin was probably an etymologically different word meaning 'servant' (of a god): cf. Aesch. *Ag.* 231 ἀόζοις, Chantraine 1968–80, Beekes 2010 s.vv. ἄοζος and ὄζος. Ancient interpreters of the epic phrase took ὄζος to mean 'branch', 'offspring' (Hsch. ο 132), and Euripides gives us the first attestation of this interpretation: in the present context, the meaning 'servant of a god' is impossible. The final vowel of ὄζω is shortened in front of the initial vowel of Ἀθηνῶν: cf. 59–97n. 'Metre'.

123–4 δισσῶν ... μιᾶι: 45n.

125–6 'they concurred in the opinion that <one> should crown the tomb of Achilles with fresh blood'. The subject of the infinitive στεφανοῦν, not expressed, is clearly understood from the context: Smyth §931. στέφανος, στεφανόω and cognates are often used as metaphorical designation for cult actions at a tomb or altar: Griffith on Soph. *Ant.* 429–31, Finglass on Soph. *El.* 53.

χλωρῶι: the original meaning is 'yellow, green'. The adjective is often used metaphorically to mean 'fresh', 'alive', 'moist': Soph. *Trach.* 1055 χλωρὸν αἷμα, Mastronarde on *Med.* 906, Clarke 2004: 133–7.

127–9 'and they said that <one> should never put the bed of Cassandra before the spear of Achilles', that is, one should not value the sexual relationship with Cassandra more than Achilles' prowess. The sons of Theseus leave the subject of θήσειν undetermined (125–6n.); the resulting turn of phrase however clearly alludes to Agamemnon. 'This argument is clearly meant to "correct" (and thereby strongly evoke) the disastrous position adopted' in *Iliad* 1 (King 1985: 54), when Agamemnon's desire for the 'bed' (*Il.* 1.31) of Briseis was considered more important than Achilles. On Achilles' famous 'spear' see Janko on *Il.* 16.130–54.

οὐκ ἐφάτην ... θήσειν ποτέ: in Greek the negative οὐκ accompanies the verb of saying (ἐφάτην) rather than the infinitive, as in English: Smyth §§ 2691–3.

130–1 σπουδαὶ δὲ λόγων κατατεινομένων | ἦσαν ἴσαι πως 'support for the contested arguments was more or less equal'. σπουδαί 'support, zeal' is a distributive plural (Smyth §1004), referring to the support each Greek army member gave to each of the arguments.

131–3 ὁ ποικιλόφρων | κόπις ἡδυλόγος δημοχαριστής | Λαερτιάδης 'the astute, liar, sweet-tongued, crowd-pleaser son of Laertes'. The first and third epithets echo, with variations, Homeric epithets of Odysseus; the second and fourth are less traditional. Odysseus is often negatively characterised in Greek tragedy: Worman 2002: 108–48, Schein on Soph. *Phil.* 96–9 and his introduction, 20–1.

ποικιλόφρων 'having an intricate mind, astute' echoes, with variation, the epic epithet of Odysseus ποικιλομήτης. For an accumulation of (teasing) insulting epithets see Athena's address to Odysseus in *Od.* 13.293 σχέτλιε, ποικιλομῆτα, δόλων ἆατ'.

κόπις 'liar' is a word not attested in epic, used here for designating a typical characteristic of Odysseus in epic (*Od.* 13.293–5, 19.203). Grammatically, it is a noun used in apposition: 790n.

ἡδυλόγος is a variation on the epic epithet ἡδυεπής (*Il.* 1.248), used in reference to Nestor, whose eloquence is also praised as 'sweeter than honey' (*Il.* 1.249). Odysseus too is traditionally portrayed as a good orator: *Il.* 3.216–24. His sweet tongue, however, is here presented as deceptive and dangerous, like the 'honey-sweet voice' (μελίγηρυν ... ὄπ(α)) of the Sirens (*Od.* 12.187) and the 'mild words' of Medea (*Med.* 776 μαλθακοὺς ... λόγους, 316).

δημοχαριστής: Odysseus is presented as a person whose *charis* is directed towards the demos, not his peers (254n.). In fact, in opposition to Agamemnon, he argues that *charis* is due to the best fighters (137–40) and, in opposition to Hecuba, that this attitude is profitable for the collectivity as a whole (299–331n.).

134–5 μὴ τὸν ἄριστον Δαναῶν πάντων | δούλων σφαγίων οὕνεκ' ἀπωθεῖν 'that <one> should not spurn the best of all the Greeks to avoid sacrificing a slave'. The text alludes again to the *Iliad*: Achilles is 'the best of the Achaeans' (303–5, *Il.* 1.244), but other heroes also aspired to that position (*Il.* 1.91, Nagy 1979: 26–41).

δούλων σφαγίων is a poetic plural, referring to a single slave: 265n.

136–7 μηδέ τιν' εἰπεῖν παρὰ Φερσεφόνηι | στάντα φθιμένων 'so that none of the dead people would say, standing in front of Persephone'. The genitive φθιμένων depends on τιν'. The enclitic τις is placed as second element in the clause, often in hyperbaton from other related elements of the sentence: *Alc.* 513, *Med.* 283, *Suppl.* 90–1, Diggle 1994: 170 and 260. People stand up when speaking before (παρά: LSJ B II.3) a person of authority or to a large audience, except under special circumstances: cf. [531–3n.], Edwards 1991 and Coray 2009 on *Il.* 19.77.

137–40 'that the Greeks left the flatlands of Troy without showing gratitude to the Greeks who died fighting for the Hellenes'. The polyptoton Δαναοὶ Δαναοῖς (cf. Mastronarde on *Pho.* 536–8, 881) and the use of the synonym Ἑλλήνων make the threefold repetition of the same concept stylistically elegant.

137 ἀχάριστοι: a crucial theme in the play: 216–95n., 299–331n., 830n. and Introduction, section 5. The adjective is to be connected with 140 ἀπέβησαν, 'they left without showing gratitude'. In *Il.* 9.316–20 Achilles himself complains that there is no *charis* in fighting against the enemies, since valiant and cowardly soldiers get identical rewards (cf. 306–8n.). Agamemnon, here and in the *Iliad*, is the person who deprives Achilles of the *charis* that is due to him.

COMMENTARY: 141-153

141 ὅσον οὐκ ἤδη 'almost immediately', 'in no time', 'almost', a prose usage: Thuc. 6.57.2, 8.96.3, Xen. *Hell.* 6.2.24, Dodds on *Ba.* 1076.

142 πῶλον 'the filly', i.e. Polyxena. Virgins are often metaphorically represented as fillies (Anacreon 417.1 *PMG*, Eur. *Hipp.* 546, *Andr.* 621) or untamed animals (Aesch. *Ag.* 245, Ar. *Lys.* 217): see Wohl 1998: 221 n. 71, Hunter on Ap. Rhod. *Arg.* 3.4–5 ἀδμῆτας ... παρθενικάς. πῶλος is used also for young boys: Orestes in Aesch. *Cho.* 794 and the virgin Menoeceus (Mastronarde on *Pho.* 947). Cf. 90–1n.

143 ἔκ τε γεραιᾶς χερὸς ὁρμήσων 'and in order to take her from your hand', lit. 'and in order to set her in rapid motion away from your hand' (Smyth §2044). The text uses a more generic word (ὁρμάω) instead of a more specific one ('dragging', 'tearing away', as 142 ἀφέλξων), as often in tragedy: 154, 155n., 716–21n., Bruhn 1899: 136–8.

144 Polyxena can be saved only by divine intervention, but at 163–4 Hecuba claims not to know which god can help her. In fact altars and temples do not seem to be present in the inhabited area where the play is set. Divine absence (488–91n., 1287–90n., contrast 900.) is opposed to the efficacious presence of the hero Achilles (538–41n.): Segal 1993: 215–26, Mastronarde 2010: 202–4.

[145] 'sit as a suppliant at Agamemnon's knees'. Agamemnon has already failed to save Polyxena (120–2): it does not make sense for the chorus to advise Hecuba to supplicate him. An interpolator wrote a metrically dubious line ([62–3n.]) in order to insert an allusion to Hecuba's supplication of Agamemnon at 752–845 (which occurs for completely different reasons). Mercier 1994 claims that the line is authentic, but fails to note that Agamemnon does not need to be convinced to help Polyxena. Hecuba will later supplicate Odysseus, who had the power to stop the sacrifice: 293–4n.

146–7 κήρυσσε θεοὺς τούς τ' οὐρανίδας | τούς θ' ὑπὸ γαίας 'call upon the gods, both those in the sky and those under the earth', a typical polar expression: cf. 791n., fr. 912.6–8.

ὑπὸ γαίας: the MS text ὑπὸ γαῖαν scans only if one assumes that a metrical pause followed γαῖαν. In recitative anapaests, however, a metrical pause occurs only after paroemiacs as a rule: Diggle 1981: 97, Mastronarde on *Med.* 184–204. Porson's conjecture ὑπὸ γαίας restores good metre and syntax: cf. ὑπὸ χθονός at Eur. fr. 450.1, Soph. *Ant.* 65. The error may have several causes: ὑπό + gen. often means 'from under' (53–4n.), and is less commonly used locally of place 'under which'; the phrase ὑπὸ γαῖαν 'under the earth' (not 'towards the underworld'), attested already in *Il.* 19.259, became standard in prose: LSJ s.v. ὑπό A I. 1–2, C I.2, Moorhouse 1982: 128–9.

147–53 'Either your prayers will be able to avoid your being deprived of your unhappy daughter, or you must see the young girl reddened with blood <flowing> in a dark-shining stream from her neck adorned with gold, while she is bent over the tomb' of Achilles. For the accumulation of circumstantial phrases in 150–2 cf. 205–10, Aesch. *Ag.* 231–4.

It is a recurring rhetorical device to end a speech with a pair of alternatives, which conveys a sense of urgency (as here) or menace, or strengthens a statement: *Il.* 12.328, 13. 327 εἴδομεν ἠέ τωι εὖχος ὀρέξομεν ἠέ τις ἡμῖν, Eur. *Alc.* 627–8 φημὶ τοιούτους γάμους | λύειν βροτοῖσιν, ἢ γαμεῖν οὐκ ἄξιον, *El.* 583–4.

150 τύμβωι προπετῆ: like a victim inclined towards the altar: cf. 524n. and Aesch. *Ag.* 232–5 ὕπερθε βωμοῦ | πέπλοισι περιπετῆ ... | προνωπῆ λαβεῖν ἀέρδην. The details of the actual sacrifice in fact will differ: Polyxena is placed above the tomb (524) but, when Neoptolemus' helpers seize her (presumably in order to hold her over the tomb), she asks to be left free (544–70). For the dative of direction τύμβωι compare perhaps the dative after περιπετής in Aesch. *Ag.* 233, as interpreted by Lloyd-Jones 1952: 132–4 'with her arms flung about his robes' (an interpretation challenged by Medda 2012: 91–9). The adjective προπετής normally takes a prepositional phrase: Parker on *Alc.* 909–10 πολιάς ἐπὶ χαίτας ... προπετής 'drooping towards grey hair', Xen. *Hell.* 6.5.24 προπετεῖς ἦσαν εἰς τὸ ἰέναι 'inclined to go', Pl. *Leg.* 792d5–6.

151–3 ἐκ χρυσοφόρου | δειρῆς νασμῶι μελαναυγεῖ: the preposition ἐκ implies a verb of 'flowing' 'coming from', as in *Tro.* 574–6 σκύλοις ... ἀπὸ Τροίας, Diggle 1981: 28–9, 69. Polyxena is imagined as still wearing gold, as appropriate for a princess. In fact the Trojan slaves do not seem to have much of value with them: 613–18n., 617–18n., 1013n.

μελαναυγεῖ 'dark-shining' is a vivid description of the gleaming of a dark liquid, imitating the epic phrases μέλαν αἷμα (536–7n.), αἷμα κελαινόν (*Il.* 1.303), αἷμα κελαινεφές (*Il.* 4.140). Euripides uses several other similar, but less paradoxical, compounds: *Alc.* 261 κυαναυγέσι, *Hel.* 179 κυανοειδές and 1502 κυανόχροα. The fifth-century BCE hexameters from Selinus published in Jordan and Kotansky 2011: 57, col. i.8 use the phrase μελαναυγέι χώρωι (followed by νασμοῦ in line 11). Bremmer 2013: 25 argues that the hexameters imitate this passage of Euripides, but it is probable that the ritual hexameters had a much earlier origin, and that Euripides echoes traditional language.

154–443 FIRST EPISODE

After the parodos, the unannounced entrance of a new character usually marks the beginning of the first episode. In fact Polyxena will enter only at 176, after being summoned. Odysseus will arrive later, announced by the chorus (216n.).

154–215 Lyric Duet between Hecuba and Polyxena

Hecuba reacts to the news with a long lyric section, lamenting her hopelessness and the fate of Polyxena, whom she invites to come onstage. After an initial dialogue with her mother (177–96), Polyxena laments her own fate and expresses pity for Hecuba (197–210). The section displays some typical characteristics of Euripidean lyric language: pathetic repetitions (160–1, 167–8n., 170–2, 199, 202–3), use of connected metaphors (esp. animal metaphors: 177–9n., 205n., 206n.), poetic compound adjectives (205n., 208n.), lexical innovations (177–9n.), Homeric allusions (183n.) and poetic paraphrases of fifth-century language (188–90n., 195–6n.; cf. 98–153 *passim*). The passage is very simple in content and syntax, relying for its pathetic effect on the rhythmic and lexical repetitions and the virtuoso performance of the singers.

Metre

The lament is mostly in sung anapaests. Two dactylic sections (165–69~207–10) are clearly in responsion. It is likely that the whole section 154–69~197–215 was written as a strophic pair, even if the details are uncertain in some points (200–1, 206). The long mesode 170–96 is in any case very unusual.

In this passage, lack of word-end at end of anapaestic metra (diaeresis: cf. 59–97n. 'Metre') is found only in dimeters (e.g. 156, 170, 194–5, 203, 206) and paroemiacs (e.g. 171, 179, 188) consisting of long syllables.

The interpolated line 215 (- ⏑ ⏑ - - - - ⏑ ⏑ - ⌒ |||) is metrically suspect, lacking diaeresis while being not predominantly spondaic (Parker 1958: 83, Lourenço 2011: 46 and n. 77). It is true that a non-catalectic anapaest may be followed by metrical pause (146–7n., *Hipp.* 1377), but 215, if authentic, would be the only non-catalectic dimeter to end a whole lyrical section.

For 4da^^ and 5da^^ cf. respectively *Pho.* 192 and *El.* 452~464, Lourenço 2011: 67 and 69. Lourenço 2011: 65, following Diggle and others, interprets 167–9~209–10 as 5da kδ. At 164 θεῶν is to be scanned as one syllable (551n.).

Strophe and Antistrophe: 154–69~197–215

    ⏕ _ ⏑⏑_ ⏕ _ _ _   2 an
154   οἲ ἐγὼ μελέα, τί ποτ' ἀπύσω;
197   ὦ δεινὰ παθοῦσ', ὦ παντλάμων,

    _ _ _ _ _ ⏕ ⏔ _   2 an
155   ποίαν ἀχώ, ποῖον ὀδυρμόν,
198   ὦ δυστάνου, μᾶτερ, βιοτᾶς,

COMMENTARY: 154-215

	$- - - \; - \; - - \quad - \; -$	2 an
156	δειλαία δειλαίου γήρως	
199	οἴαν οἴαν αὖ σοι λώβαν	
	$- \; - - - \; - \; - \; - -$	2 an
157	<καὶ> δουλείας τᾶς οὐ τλατᾶς,	
200	<λύμαν τ'> ἐχθίσταν ἀρρήταν τ'	
	$- - - \; - - - \; \frown \; \|^{c}$	paroemiac $\|^{c}$
158	τᾶς οὐ φερτᾶς· ὤιμοι μοι.	
201	ὦρσέν τις δαίμων, <ὤιμοι>	
	$\underline{\smile\smile} \; \overline{\smile\smile} - - \; - - \; \smile\smile -$	2 an
159	τίς ἀμύνει μοι; ποία γενεά,	
202	οὐκέτι σοι παῖς ἅδ᾽ οὐκέτι δή	
	$- - \; \underline{\smile\smile} \; - \; - - \; - -$	2 an
160	ποία δὲ πόλις; φροῦδος πρέσβυς,	
203	γήραι δειλαία δειλαίωι	
	$- - \; - -$	an
161	φροῦδοι παῖδες.	
204	συνδουλεύσω.	
	$- - \; - \; - - - -$	2 an
162	ποίαν – ἢ ταύταν ἢ κείναν; –	
205	σκύμνον γάρ μ' ὥστ' οὐριθρέπταν	
	$- - \; - \; - - \; - \; - -$	2 an
163	στείχω; ποῖ δὴ σωθῶ; ποῦ τις	
206	μόσχον δειλαία δειλαίαν	
	$- - - - \; \smile\smile - \; \frown \; \|^{b1}$	paroemiac $\|^{b1}$
164	θεῶν ἢ δαίμων ἐπαρωγός;	
206b	< – – – – ⏑ > ἐσόψηι	
	$- \smile \; \smile - \; - -$	D (= δ)
165	ὦ κάκ᾽ ἐνεγκοῦσαι	
207	χειρὸς ἀναρπαστάν	
	$- \smile\smile \; - \; \smile \; \smile - \; - -$	4 da^^
166	Τρωιάδες, ὦ κάκ᾽ ἐνεγκοῦσαι	
208	σᾶς ἄπο λαιμότομόν θ᾽ Ἄιδαι	
	$- \smile \; \smile \; - \smile\smile \; - \; \smile\smile \; - \smile\smile -$	5 da^^
167–8	πήματ᾽, ἀπωλέσατ᾽ ὠλέσατ᾽· οὐκέτι μοι	
209	γᾶς ὑποπεμπομέναν σκότον, ἔνθα νεκρῶν	

COMMENTARY: 154–215   97

169 ⏑⏑⏑ − ⏑ − ⏑⌢ ||| lecythion |||
     βίος ἀγαστὸς ἐν φάει.
210 μέτα τάλαινα κείσομαι.

Mesode: 170–96

− − − − − − −   2 an
170 ὦ τλάμων ἄγησαί μοι πούς,

− − − − − − − ||ᶜ   paroemiac ||ᶜ
171 ἄγησαι τᾶι γηραιᾶι

− − − − − ⏑ ⏑ − −   2 an
172 πρὸς τάνδ' αὐλάν. ὦ τέκνον, ὦ παῖ

− − ⏑ ⏑ − − ⏑ ⏑ − −   2 an
173 δυστανοτάτας ματέρος, ἔξελθ'

− − − − ⏑ ⏑ −⌢ ||| paroemiac |||
174   ἔξελθ' οἴκων, ἆι' αὐδάν.

− ⏑ − − − − − −   − 2 an
175 [ὦ τέκνον, ὡς εἰδῆις οἴαν οἴαν

⏑ ⏑ − − − ⏑ ⏑ − − −   2 an
176 ἀίω φάμαν περὶ σᾶς ψυχᾶς].

ἰώ   extra metrum

− − − − ⏑ ⏑ − ⏑ ⏑−   2 an
177 μᾶτερ μᾶτερ, τί βοᾶις; τί νέον

− − − − − − − −   2 an
178 καρύξασ' οἴκων μ' ὥστ' ὄρνιν

− − − − − −⌢ ||ᵇ   paroemiac ||ᵇ
179 θάμβει τῶιδ' ἐξέπταξας;

− − − −   an
180 οἴμοι τέκνον.

⏑ ⏑ − − − − ⏑ ⏑ − ⏑⌢ ||ᵇʰ   an δ ||ᵇʰ
181 τί με δυσφημεῖς; φροίμιά μοι κακά.

− − − − −   δ
182 αἰαῖ σᾶς ψυχᾶς.

− − − − − − −   2 an
183 ἐξαύδα· μὴ κρύψηις δαρόν.

98   COMMENTARY: 154–215

184	– – – – – – – – δειμαίνω δειμαίνω, μᾶτερ,	2 an
185	∪ ∪ ∪ – ∪ – τί ποτ' ἀναστένεις.	δ
186	– – – – ∪ ∪– – – τέκνον τέκνον μελέας ματρός ...	2 an
187	∪ ∪ – – – τί τόδ' ἀγγέλλεις;	an
188	– – – – – – – σφάξαι σ' Ἀργείων κοινά	paroemiac
189	– – – – – – – – συντείνει πρὸς τύμβον γνώμα	2 an
190	– – – – ⌒ ‖ʰ Πηλείαι γένναι.	δ ‖ʰ
191	– – – – – – – ⌒ ‖ʰ οἴμοι, μᾶτερ, πῶς φθέγγηι;	paroemiac ‖ʰ
192	∪ ∪ – ∪ ∪ – – – – – ἀμέγαρτα κακῶν μάνυσόν μοι,	2 an
193	– – – – – μάνυσον, μᾶτερ.‖ᵇ	δ ‖ᵇ
194	– – – – – – – – αὐδῶ, παῖ, δυσφήμους φήμας,	2 an
195	– – – – – – – – ἀγγέλλουσ' Ἀργείων δόξαι	2 an
196	– – – – ∪ ∪ – ⌒ ‖‖ ψήφωι τᾶς σᾶς περὶ μοίρας.	paroemiac ‖‖

Spurious ending: [211–15]

211	– – – – – – – – [καὶ σοῦ μέν, μᾶτερ, δυστάνου	2 an
212	– – ∪ ∪ – – – ⌒ ‖ᶜ κλαίω πανοδύρτοις θρήνοις,	paroemiac ‖ᶜ
213	∪ ∪ – ∪ ∪ – – – – τὸν ἐμὸν δὲ βίον λώβαν λύμαν τ'	2 an

COMMENTARY: 154-163

214   οὐ μετακλαίομαι, ἀλλὰ θανεῖν μοι   – ⏑ ⏑ – ⏑ ⏑   – ⏑   ⏑ – –   2 an

215   ξυντυχία κρείσσων ἐκύρησεν.]   – ⏑ ⏑ –   – –   ⏑ ⏑ – ⏒ ||| 2 an |||

154 οἲ ἐγὼ μελέα 'alas, unhappy me', a typical beginning for an actor's song in tragedy: *Med.* 96 ἰώ, δύστανος ἐγὼ μελέα τε πόνων, *Hipp.* 1347-8 αἰαῖ αἰαῖ· | δύστανος ἐγώ.

τί ποτ' ἀπύσω; 'what shall I say?', aor. subj. from ἠπύω 'I call', in tragedy often 'I say', with 'Doric' alpha. Many lyric sections include similar rhetorical questions with the subjunctive, especially at the beginning: 162-3n., 1056-7n.

155 ποίαν ἀχώ, ποῖον ὀδυρμόν 'what sound, what lament' (i.e. 'shall I utter': supply ἀπύσω from 154). ἀχώ is the 'Doric' accusative of Attic ἠχώ 'echo'. Tragic language often uses the word ἠχώ 'echo' in the more general sense (143n.) of 'sound': Soph. *El.* 109. The symmetry of syntax and metre, often with words scanning – – or ⏑ ⏑ –, is frequent in adjacent anapaestic metra: 157-8, 159-61, 177, 186, 199, 206, *Med.* 99, 111, 131.

156-8 'unhappy because of an unhappy old age, and of a condition of slavery that cannot be endured, that cannot be suffered'. γήρως and δουλείας are genitives of cause: 182, 475-6, Smyth §1435, Moorhouse 1982: 71-2.

δουλείας τᾶς οὐ τλατᾶς, | τᾶς οὐ φερτᾶς: the repeated article is usual in a series of epithets: fr. 781.15-17 τὰν Διὸς οὐρανίαν ἀείδομεν | τὰν ἐρώτων πότνιαν, τὰν παρθένοις | γαμήλιον Ἀφροδίταν, *Hipp.* 151-2, 538-40.

οὐ τλατᾶς ... οὐ φερτᾶς: Bothe's conjecture οὐ φευκτᾶς 'that cannot be avoided' has a good parallel at Soph. *Ai.* 222 ἄτλατον οὐδὲ φευκτάν 'unbearable and unavoidable' (cf. Finglass *ad loc.*), but φευκτᾶς is less apt here, where Hecuba is still (vainly) trying to escape from her fate (159-63). She often uses synonyms and repeated phrases (160-1, 163-4, 165-7, etc.).

159-61 'Who defends me? Which family, which city? The old man <is> gone, gone <are> the children.' Neither Priam (πρέσβυς) nor Hector is there to help Hecuba.

ἀμύνει is present (ῡ) not future (ῠ). The future is more idiomatic in English for an imminent danger: Smyth §1879.

γενεά restores the necessary long final syllable (Diggle 1981: 97).

160-1 φροῦδος ... φροῦδοι 'gone away'. This adjective is often used in poignant verbless sentences: 334-5, *Med.* 139, *Andr.* 1078 φρούδη μὲν αὐδή, φροῦδα δ' ἄρθρα. On comic parody see Introduction, section 2.

162-3 ποίαν – ἢ ταύταν ἢ κείναν; – | στείχω; 'Which way shall I go? This way or that?' A single sentence includes two questions: 1059-60n. στείχω is deliberative subjunctive (1056–7n.). The accusative of direction ποίαν implies ὁδόν (Smyth §1027b, K–G II.558–9); it is functionally comparable to adverbs (Schwyzer 1939: 621). In some cases feminine adjectives or pronouns in the accusative function as indefinite abstracts: Fraenkel on Aesch. *Ag.* 916, Cooper and Krüger 2002: 1915–16.

ποῖ δὴ σωθῶ; 'To which safe place can I go?' σωθῶ is aor. subj. from σώιζω, a verb which often implies 'a sense of motion to a place' (LSJ s.v. II.2), as in *Pho.* 725 δεῦρο σωθήσηι. The transmitted text ποῖ δ' ἤσω is impossible because the *active* future of ἵημι cannot have the meaning 'To which place shall I hasten myself?' (which is expressed by the intransitive middle: LSJ s.v. ἵημι II.1): Diggle 1994: 16–17.

163–4 ποῦ τις | θεῶν ἢ δαίμων ἐπαρωγός; 'Where is one of the gods or a *daimōn* who can help me?' *daimōn* is mostly used as a synonym of 'god', especially when it is not possible to determine the identity of the divine being: see Flower and Marincola 2002 on Hdt. 9.76.2 τοὺς οὔτε δαιμόνων οὔτε θεῶν ὄπιν ἔχοντας. In these passages and at *Med.* 1391 τίς ... θεὸς ἢ δαίμων, *El.* 1234–5, the speakers do not imply a sharp difference between *daimones* and gods; rather, they try to cover all possible names of divine beings: Fraenkel on Aesch. *Ag.* 160. Pl. *Symp.* 202d–e was especially influential in spreading the idea that *daimones* are intermediate beings, facilitating the communication between men and gods: Burkert 1985: 179–81, 331–2, Mikalson 1991: 22–9.

165–8 People who bring ill tidings are often censured for doing so: 661. For the pattern of iteration see *Hipp.* 836 τὸ κατὰ γᾶς θέλω, τὸ κατὰ γᾶς κνέφας.

167–8 ἀπωλέσατ' ὠλέσατ': in anadiplosis, the preverb is felt to modify the meaning of both verbs, even if not repeated, as in *Ba.* 1065 κατῆγεν ἦγεν ἦγεν: Watkins 1967, Diggle 1994: 389–90.

167–9 οὐκέτι μοι | βίος ἀγαστὸς ἐν φάει 'life under the sun does not give me delight any more', another redundant expression typical of lyric language: the Greeks considered 'life' as identical with the condition of being 'under the sun' (248n., 367–8n., 415).

170–2 'unhappy foot, lead me, lead me, an old woman, to this dwelling' (i.e. the tent where Polyxena sleeps). Hecuba addresses her foot again at *Tro.* 1275 ἀλλ', ὦ γεραιὲ πούς, ἐπίσπευσον μόλις. See also *Ion* 1041 ἄγ', ὦ γεραιὲ πούς. The address to a part of the body is a tragic adaptation of a feature of Homeric style, the address to one's heart: *Od.* 20.18, Parker on *Alc.* 837. For a comic parody, see Ar. *Ach.* 480–8.

ἄγησαι corresponds to Attic ἥγησαι, aor. imp. 2nd p. sg. from ἡγέομαι. On the repetition cf. 59–6on.

172–3 ὦ τέκνον, ὦ παῖ | δυστανοτάτας ματέρος is a tragic phrase (186, 694, *Tro.* 790) with a Homeric pedigree (*Il.* 6.127 δυστήνων ... παῖδες).

173–4 The passage uses conventional tragic language (*Tro.* 1303 ὦ τέκνα, κλύετε, μάθετε ματρὸς αὐδάν). The parody in Ar. *Nub.* 1165–6 ὦ τέκνον, ὦ παῖ, ἔξελθ' οἴκων, | ἄιε σοῦ πατρός (Introduction, section 2) assures us of the genuineness of (at least part) of these lines.

174–6 The MS text is metrically and stylistically suspicious: it contains some semantically vacuous repetitions (ματέρος in 173 and 174; ὦ τέκνον in 172 and 175, ἄιε in 174 and ἀίω in 176) and material which reappears again later (182, 196, 199; cf. *HF* 136 οἴους οἴους ὀλέσασα). Moreover, if ἄιε ματέρος αὐδάν is genuine, the alpha in ἀίω must be scanned as long, as at Aesch. *Suppl.* 59 and 759, Soph. *OC* 304, not as short, as always in Euripides. Several attempts at rewriting have been advanced, and the text cannot be considered certain.

177 ἰώ | μᾶτερ μᾶτερ: as at *Pho.* 304 ἰὼ τέκνον, the interjection ἰώ is pronounced by the character arriving onstage, in response to a summons. ἰώ is *extra metrum* in anapaests: cf. the instances in Diggle 1994: 118–19.

τί βοᾶις; 'what are you shouting?' Polyxena enters onstage as if reacting to a βοή, that is a cry for help to the community: 1088–98n., Aesch. *Cho.* 885, Eur. *Hcld.* 73, *Hipp.* 790, Taplin 1977: 218–21. Her formulation shows concern for her mother but can also be interpreted, more generically, as an information-seeking question ('what are you saying?').

177–9 τί ... ἐξέπταξας; 'What piece of bad news are you announcing? You scared me out of the house like a bird with these alarming shouts.' The interrogative pronoun is governed by the participle καρύξασ' (= Attic κηρύξασα, from κηρύσσω), and does not go with the main verb ἐξέπταξας (2nd p. sg. ind. aor. from ἐκπτήσσω, a compound verb probably created by Euripides for this passage), a construction impossible in English: 448–9n., Smyth §§2643–4, K–G II.519–21.

τί νέον: cf. 83n.

ὥστ' ὄρνιν ... ἐξέπταξας: the animal imagery (cf. 205–6) suggests helplessness, esp. in connection with ἐξέπταξας. πτήσσω is the verb regularly used for cowering birds: Bond on *HF* 974 ὄρνις ὣς ἔπτηξ', Finglass on Soph. *Ai.* 169–71. On ὥστ' cf. 205n.

θάμβει τῶιδ': lit. 'with this amazement', in reference to Hecuba's shouts.

181 τί με δυσφημεῖς; φροίμιά μοι κακά 'Why do you use words of ill omen in speaking of me? The prelude <is> an unhappy one for me.' For φροίμια cf. 1195n.

182 αἰαῖ σᾶς ψυχᾶς 'alas for your life'. For genitive of cause after exclamations cf. 156–8n., 475.

183 ἐξαύδα· μὴ κρύψηις δαρόν 'speak; do not conceal this for a long time' (i.e. 'any longer'). Polyxena alludes to a Homeric phrase that Thetis uses twice in addressing the weeping Achilles: *Il.* 1.363 ἐξαύδα, μὴ κεῦθε νόωι, 18.74 (echoed by Achilles in 16.19 addressing Patroclus who cries 'like a small girl' (16.7–8)). Polyxena's motherly attitude foreshadows the future role reversal in 402–34, where she guides (and consoles: 430) her mother.

δαρόν: a non-Attic poetic form (cf. epic δηρός), which tragedy uses also in non-lyric sections: *Or.* 55, Björck 1950: 126.

184–5 'I feel fear, fear, mother, for whatever it is that you are lamenting.' The verb of fearing, δειμαίνω, introduces an indirect question: Smyth §2669.

ἀναστένεις: the present tense is used in reference to an impending action (159–61n.).

186: 172–3n.

188–90 'the common decision of the Greeks leads <them> to sacrifice you, <taking you> to the tomb, <in honour of> the progeny of Peleus'. On this usage of πρός + acc., which implies a verb of movement, see Finglass on Soph. *El.* 931 πρὸς τάφον κτερίσματα, Diggle 1981: 28–9.

Ἀργείων designates the whole Greek army, as usual in epic (*Il.* 9.518 and 522) and in this play (195, 479, 544), not the Argive contingents in particular.

κοινά ... γνώμα: this phrase from contemporary political language refers to decisions taken 'in common' by a group of allies (Hdt. 5.63.3 κοινῆι γνώμηι, Thuc. 5.38.1 ἄνευ κοινῆς γνώμης), as is the case here, in reference to the Greek army (a federation of different kingdoms).

Πηλείαι γένναι: Achilles. Πηλείαι is the dative from the adjective Πήλειος (shortened from epic Πηλήϊος). The adjective, as at *Il.* 18.60 δόμον Πηλήϊον 'the house of Peleus', Eur. *IT* 170–1 Ἀγαμεμνόνιον | θάλος 'the scion of Agamemnon', is used where (in non-poetic Greek) one would expect the genitive of the proper name. The MS text Πηλεῖδα (= Attic Πηλείδου) γένναι 'to the progeny of the son of Peleus' designates in fact Neoptolemus, a meaning impossible in the context.

192–3 'reveal to me <my> unenviable sufferings, reveal <them>, mother'.

ἀμέγαρτα κακῶν: lit. 'things that, among sufferings, do not cause envy'. κακῶν is partitive genitive, as in 716. The unusual phrase suggests some sort of superlative, as *Suppl.* 807 τὰ κύντατ' ἄλγη κακῶν.

194 δυσφήμους φήμας 'ill-omened messages'. Oxymoron is frequent in lyric passages: *Hel.* 213 αἰὼν δυσαίων, Mastronarde on *Pho.* 1047 γάμους δυσγάμους.

195–6 'announcing that the vote of the Greeks has taken a decision about your destiny'.

δόξαι 'that it seemed best' is an impersonal inf. aor. from δοκέω, a political idiom already used in poetry in Aesch. *Suppl.* 605 ἔδοξεν Ἀργείοισιν. Cf. 119.

Ἀργείων ... ψήφωι 'to the vote of the Argives', a poetic paraphrase for 'the Greeks', stressing the quasi-democratic nature of the Greek decision-making procedures.

197–210 Polyxena focuses on her mother's suffering rather than on her own, with graphic descriptions of the fate that awaits them. Like many other tragic characters, she prefers to face the grim reality rather than soothe her family with wishful thinking.

198 ὦ δυστάνου μᾶτερ βιοτᾶς 'oh mother, you that have an unhappy life'. δυστάνου ... βιοτᾶς is a genitive of quality, cf. Finglass on Soph. *Ai.* 1004 ὦ δυσθέατον ὄμμα καὶ τόλμης πικρᾶς, Smyth §1320, Moorhouse 1982: 56.

199–200 λώβαν | <λύμαν τ'>: the phrase is found also at 1073; the interpolator reused it at [213]. Interpolators often lift stylish phrases from authentic passages: 174–6n.

201 ὤιμοι 'alas': this was the ancient form, overwhelmingly supported in the most ancient and accurate MSS of archaic and classical poetry, and it is adopted throughout the text. οἴμοι is also attested as a genuine classical form, whereas the spelling ὤμοι is less securely attested for classical authors: Finglass 2009a: 206–12.

202–4 'I, the daughter you see here, will not be a slave with you, wretched one, in your wretched old age, not any more, not any more.' On the pattern of repetition cf. 154–215n.

παῖς ἄδ': lit. 'this daughter', in agreement with the (unexpressed) subject 'I': 992n.

205–10 'You, the wretched <mother>, will see me, wretched me, <your> whelp, < ... > snatched up from your hand like a heifer reared on the mountains, and sent to the darkness of the earth, with the throat cut, to Hades, where I will lie among the dead in my misery.' σκύμνον is in apposition to μ', followed by the comparison ὥστ' οὐριθρέπταν | μόσχον. The sentence continues with adjectives (207 ἀναρπαστάν, 208 λαιμότομον) and participles (209 ὑποπεμπομέναν) in agreement with μ(ε) ... δειλαίαν. The MS text gives dubious syntax at 205–6: σκύμνον and μόσχον both refer to Polyxena. The text remains uncertain.

205 σκύμνον 'whelp, cub' is used elsewhere in reference to human beings: *Andr.* 1169–70 τὸν Ἀχίλλειον | σκύμνον (Neoptolemus, with pitying connotations), *Or.* 1386–7 Λήδας | σκύμνον (Helen), Willink on *Or.* 1211–13.

ὥστ' means 'like', in imitation of epic usage (ὥς + generalising epic τε = 'as it is generally the case'): 178, LSJ s.v. A 1.

οὐριθρέπταν: cows were reared in the mountains (*IA* 575).

206 μόσχον 'heifer', a metaphor or comparison frequently used in describing the victim of human sacrifices: 526n., *IT* 359–60, *IA* 1081–3 (Iphigenia).

207–8 χειρὸς ἀναρπαστάν | σᾶς ἄπο: for the anastrophe χειρὸς ... σᾶς ἄπο cf. 292n. Polyxena's prophecy echoes Hecuba's dream: cf. 91

σπασθεῖσαν, and 408 σπασθεῖσ', when in fact Polyxena's self-sacrifice prevents the fulfilment of the prediction.

208 λαιμότομον 'with the throat cut' (cf. *IA* 776 λαιμοτόμους κεφαλάς). When the adjective has an active meaning, 'throat-cutting' (*IT* 444–5 λαιμοτόμωι | ... χειρί), the accent is paroxytone (λαιμοτόμος): Probert 2003: 92 and 107–8.

Ἅιδαι: dative of the person to whom one is sent, as in *Il.* 1.3 Ἄϊδι προΐαψεν (other victims of Achilles): Smyth §§1475 and 1485, *IT* 159 Ἀίδαι πέμψας. The form Ἅιδαι (to be scanned – –) gives perfect metrical responsion here, whereas Ἀίδαι ⏑ ⏑ – does not.

209 γᾶς ... σκότον: accusative of direction (Smyth §1588). Cf. the phrase γῆς ὑπὸ ζόφον at Aesch. *Pers.* 839 and Eur. *Hipp.* 1416. For the accumulation of dative and accusative of direction cf. *HF* 1156 ἐς ὄμμαθ' ἥξει φιλτάτωι ξένων ἐμῶν, Aesch. *Pers.* 222.

210 μέτα refers to νεκρῶν (anastrophe: 207–8, 292n.).

κείσομαι seems to allude to the theme of the 'bride of Hades' (E. Cingano, personal communication): a young woman dies before marriage, and Hades is her bridegroom. κεῖμαι may allude to sexual congress. Polyxena's sacrifice corresponds to a marriage to Achilles (cf. 337–8n., 416n., 523n., 612n.).

[211–15] Stylistic and metrical infelicities mar this spurious passage, which also includes a spoiler, inappropriately communicating to Hecuba (and to the audience) Polyxena's surprising decision to accept death: 342–5n., Wilamowitz-Moellendorff 1909: 449–50 = Wilamowitz-Moellendorff 1962: 228.

[211–12] σοῦ ... μᾶτερ, δυστάνου | κλαίω: Matthiessen and others construe σοῦ with κλαίω, ('I weep for you, mother'), on the analogy of other verbs of weeping which take the genitive (*IA* 370 Ἑλλάδος ... στένω 'I weep for Greece', K–G 1.388). This blurs the crucial contrast between the survival of Hecuba and the death of Polyxena. Supplying βίον from the following clause ('I weep for your unhappy life, mother') gives better meaning but is syntactically harsh. Either way, the text is infelicitous (contrast *Hipp.* 1409 στένω σε μᾶλλον ἢ 'μὲ τῆς ἁμαρτίας).

[212] πανοδύρτοις 'all-plaintive'. The form πανόδυρτος is well attested in later Greek (Meleager, *AP* 7.476.9), but not in tragedy; it is quite possible that an interpolator used it here. Blomfield conjectured πανδύρτοις, creating a rhythmically effective series of long syllables, imitative of lament; for a similar corruption cf. Soph. *El.* 1077 ἁ πάνδυρτος [Porson: πανόδυρτος MSS] ἀηδών, Aesch. *Pers.* 941.

[213–14] τὸν ἐμὸν δὲ βίον λώβαν λύμαν τ' | οὐ μετακλαίομαι 'I do not weep afterwards for my life, <which consists in> dishonour and indignity'. μετα- is extremely strange in the context, since Polyxena is not dead. Kovacs prints Willink's conjecture μέγα κλαίομαι 'I do not weep greatly for my life', which suggests that (contrary to the general thrust of the argument) Polyxena does indeed weep for her life, but only a little. Reiske's conjecture τοὐμοῦ δὲ βίου gives smoother syntax ('I weep for the dishonour and indignity of my life'). One would have expected Polyxena to say that she does not weep for her death: cf. Polyxena's statement in Ov. *Met.* 13.464, *non mea mors illi, uerum sua uita gemenda est* 'she [= Hecuba] ought to cry for her life, not for my death'.

[214–15] θανεῖν μοι | ξυντυχία κρείσσων ἐκύρησεν 'to die is a better event for me'. The word ξυντυχία 'event, circumstance' is semantically inept. Cf. 154–215 'Metre'.

216–443 *Dialogue between Odysseus, Hecuba and Polyxena*

This is one of the earliest scenes in Greek tragedy where three actors actually engage in a three-way dialogue (cf. *Hcld.* 646–701, Seidensticker 1971: 203–4, 210–11). This allows the poet to change the character of the scene. The first part (216–331) is indeed similar to a formal debate (*agōn*) (Mossman 1995: 55), a set-piece in Greek tragedy (1130-1251n.). Hecuba's mention of an ἀγὼν μέγας, 'a great trial' (229), is an instance of Euripidean misdirection; it (falsely) suggests that an *agōn* scene is about to occur (as at Aesch. *Eum.* 677; cf. Soph. *Ai.* 1163). However, from a formal point of view, the scene lacks 'the angry dialogue after the speeches which is normal in the *agōn*' (Lloyd 1992: 8). The content of Hecuba's speech also differs from those in *agōn* scenes: she abandons arguments on 'justice' (271) and unexpectedly turns her accusation of Odysseus into a passionate supplication speech (275n.). Odysseus' rejection (299–331) does not lead to an altercation, but to the introduction into the dialogue of the third speaking actor, playing Polyxena. Hecuba vainly asks her daughter to supplicate Odysseus; Polyxena's refusal of supplication (342–5n.) and acceptance of her fate lead to the farewell scene (409–43).

216–95 The debate between Hecuba and Odysseus introduces some of the play's crucial themes: human sacrifice, *charis* and reciprocity, aristocratic and democratic codes of conduct.

Hecuba saved Odysseus's life in the past (239n.). This was a favour (χάριν 276) and must be reciprocated (Soph. *Ai.* 522 '*charis* always generates *charis*'; cf. Blundell 1989: 75, 231; 299–331n.). Odysseus has failed to do so (254 ἀχάριστον), and has ignored the fact that Hecuba's act of *charis* established a *philia* relationship between them (Connor 1971: 98 n. 16, Stanton 1995: 21–2). For Hecuba, *philia* between aristocrats of different, even opposed, communities is a stronger bond than those linking the members of the community itself (cf. 864–9n., 1187–1237n.).

Odysseus, however, seeks to obtain *charis* from the *dēmos* (257 τοῖσι πολλοῖς πρὸς χάριν 'to please the masses', a phrase that takes up 132 δημοχαριστής 'who pleases the demos'). The passage alludes to fifth-century BCE political debate. Odysseus renounces his aristocratic network of *philoi*, which includes Hecuba, just as democratic leaders such as Pericles and the demagogue Cleon, in their desire to appear impartial, are said to have renounced ties of friendship (Plut. *Per.* 7.5, *prae. ger. reip.* 800b–c, 806f–807e). This may not be historically completely accurate for Cleon (Hornblower 1983: 123), but it reflects fifth-century perceptions (Connor 1971: 121–8). The atrocity of sacrificing the guiltless Polyxena, recommended by the 'demagogue' Odysseus (254n., 258n.), can be compared to the 'cruel and extraordinary decision' supported by Cleon 'to destroy an entire city [Mytilene] rather than those who were guilty' (Thuc. 3.36.4). Hecuba ends her speech appealing to Odysseus' aristocratic pride and prestige, claiming that it could be a decisive factor in changing the decision of the Greeks (293–5). Hecuba can be compared to the Plataeans and Melians in Thucydides (3.53.4 and 5.86), who speak 'to an audience whom they have no chance of persuading and who have them entirely in their power' (Macleod 1983: 155). Odysseus will respond only in part to her accusations, and will appeal to both aristocratic and democratic political values to justify his position (299–331n.).

216 καὶ μήν: this combination of particles is often used in entrance announcements (665; Denniston 331, 356 and 586). As a rule, entrances are always announced except at the beginning of an episode, after a parodos or a stasimon, when an entrance is expected: 484 and Hamilton 1978: 69–70. This shows that Euripides saw 154, not 216, as the beginning of the first episode.

σπουδῆι ποδός 'with speediness of foot', i.e. 'walking speedily': 98n.

217 νέον τι ... ἔπος: 83n.

218–28 Odysseus' curt speech is devoid of any sympathy for Hecuba's suffering. When he assumes Hecuba's point of view (225–8), he simply invites her to consider what is rational (228 σοφόν) and proper (228 ἃ δεῖ). Moreover, he masks a threat of physical violence as a piece of friendly advice (226–7). The later revelation of Odysseus' indebtedness to Hecuba (239–53) exposes his coolness as self-serving ingratitude.

219 ψῆφόν τε τὴν κρανθεῖσαν 'and the vote passed' by the army. Odysseus uses standard political terminology (see also 218 γνώμην, 220 ἔδοξ'): Aesch. *Suppl.* 943 ψῆφος κέκρανται, Eur. *Andr.* 1272, *Tro.* 785. On κραίνω cf. 740n.

221 ὀρθὸν χῶμ' 'the upright tumulus': 524n.

223–4 θύματος δ' ἐπιστάτης | ἱερεύς τ' ἐπέσται 'he will be in charge as overseer and priest at the sacrifice'. For ἔπειμι with a predicative nominative see Aesch. *Pers.* 827–8 κολαστής ... ἔπεστι. The MS reading ἐπέστη 'was in charge' is stylistically objectionable: the verb ἐφίστημι is always followed by the dative or genitive of the supervised action or duty in all other passages in tragedy where it has this meaning. The only exceptions occur when the participle is used instead of a noun (*Alc.* 547 τοῖς... ἐφεστῶσιν 'those in charge', Soph. *Ai.* 1072). The aorist tense of ἐπέστη is another difficulty: this usually implies that the overseen action was already taking place (363, *Suppl.* 763). Here, the aorist ἐπέστη could be allowed to stand only if translated, uniquely, as a passive 'was put in charge', not 'was in charge'. It is true that the wordplay ἐπιστάτης... ἐπέστη would be etymologically sounder, but this kind of exactitude is not required in poetry (Aesch. *Ag.* 687–90) or in ancient etymological explanations in general (Plato, *Cratylus*; Ademollo 2011: 12–14).

225 οἶσθ' οὖν ὃ δρᾶσον 'you know what you must do'. Greek admits imperative forms (δρᾶσον) in relative clauses (K–G 1.239). This idiom is common in Euripides and comedy: Stevens 1976: 36, Diggle 1994: 500, Mastronarde on *Med.* 600. The idiom can be interpreted as a question (Eur. *Suppl.* 932–3, Ar. *Eq.* 1158, *Pax* 1061: an answer follows), or as a statement (*Hcld.* 451: the following sentence begins with γάρ). Here a statement conveys the confidence of Odysseus that Hecuba will not reject his suggestion.

μήτ' ἀποσπασθῇς βίαι 'do not be forcibly separated' from Polyxena, 'do not make us drag you away from her by force' (2nd p. sg. aor. subj. pass. from ἀποσπάω); cf. 513n., *Tro.* 617.

227 ἀλκὴν καὶ παρουσίαν κακῶν 'the strength and the presence of your misfortunes', i.e. 'the strength of your present misfortunes'. The genitive κακῶν depends on ἀλκήν, '(aggressive) strength', as in Eur. fr. 1059.1 δεινὴ μὲν ἀλκὴ κυμάτων θαλασσίων: Battezzato 2000c: 225. Others interpret 'recognize [her] strength', 'meaning that she should recognize her weakness' (Gregory *ad loc.*), intending ἀλκήν as a *vox media* (a word that can have a positive or negative meaning depending on the context), 'strength or weakness': cf. Eur. *Pho.* 1654, *Il.* 9.34 ἀλκὴν μέν μοι... ὀνείδισας, Smyth §3018.0, K–G II.569–70.

228 σοφόν τοι κἂν κακοῖς ἃ δεῖ φρονεῖν 'it is wise to think appropriate thoughts even in misfortune'. Odysseus reminds Hecuba that she has a duty to think and behave properly (ἃ δεῖ φρονεῖν 'to think what one must'), probably implying that this is what a former queen is expected to do. Odysseus interprets 'wisdom' as expediency; Hecuba rejects his interpretation (258n.) and assimilates Odysseus' self-serving 'wisdom' to Polymestor's (1007n., 1136–7n., 1192–3). On the fifth-century debate on σοφία compare *Med.* 190, 292–305, *Ba.* 395, 655–6, 877, Guthrie 1969: 27–30. The particle τοι conveys the nuance 'do not forget, please' (Denniston 542).

229–33 These words of desperation are not addressed to Odysseus, but may have been heard by him. They are not meant as an aside, in a strict sense, but they sound like a monologue: 736–51n.

229 παρίστηχ' 'has arrived', intrans. pf. from παρίστημι.

ἀγὼν μέγας: 216–443n.

230 'full of groans nor void of tears'. Cf. 860n.

231–3 'And now, as for myself, I understand that I did not die when I should have, and that Zeus did not kill me, but keeps me alive so that I see other evils, greater than <my past> evils, wretched me.'

κἄγωγ': the stressed form (κἄγωγ' = καὶ ἔγωγε) here indicates a change of topic (see Introduction, section 10, Dik 2007: 48 n. 9).

ἄρ' indicates that 'the reality of a past event is presented as apprehended ... at the moment of speaking' (Denniston 36); cf. 511. On the word order cf. Dik 2007: 2–83.

οὗ 'when'. Hecuba imagines that her death would have been less painful had she died earlier; this is a variation on the heroic motif whereby an earlier death in battle is declared preferable, for a warrior, to a later and less noble death (Garvie on Aesch. *Cho.* 345–53; cf. *Od.* 24.30–4, Eur. *Andr.* 1182–3).

οὐδ' ὤλεσέν με Ζεύς, τρέφει δ': Hecuba subversively rephrases the Homeric epithet διοτρεφής 'nourished by Zeus', commonly used in reference to kings: *Il.* 1.176 διοτρεφέων βασιλήων, 5.464 ὦ υἱεῖς Πριάμοιο διοτρεφέος βασιλῆος, West 1997: 133–4. Zeus nourishes her, as the wife of a king, but Zeus's nourishment gives her suffering instead of protection. On Hecuba's unending series of sufferings cf. 585–8n.

234–7 Hecuba asks Odysseus for permission to question him gently. Slaves do not ask questions of their masters, but the Greeks granted their slaves some rights denied to them in other communities, e.g. protection against homicide (cf. 291n.). In principle, freedom of speech (παρρησία) was an exclusive right of free citizens: *Hipp.* 422 (the first extant occurrence of παρρησία), *Ion* 670–5, Mastronarde on *Pho.* 391–5, Foucault 2001, Sluiter and Rosen 2004. Some sources claim, with polemical exaggeration, that the Athenian democracy was so extreme that it granted παρρησία (Dem. 9.3) and ἰσηγορία, 'equality of free speech' (Gray 2007 and Marr and Rhodes 2008 on Xen. [*Ath. Pol.*] 1.12) even to slaves and foreigners.

236 †σοὶ μὲν εἰρῆσθαι† χρεών: the MS reading is ungrammatical and does not make sense in the context. The perfect infinitive εἰρῆσθαι lacks a subject (237 τάδε is the object of the participle ἐρωτῶντας). Moreover, it normally refers to something that has already been said (Eur. *El.* 667, Soph. *OT* 553), which is the opposite of what is required here. We expect Hecuba to say 'you must answer', as in Herwerden's conjecture (σὲ μὲν ἀμείβεσθαι), which is however very far from the transmitted reading.

237 'and we, who ask these questions, must listen'. ἡμᾶς is the subject, not the object of ἀκοῦσαι, which takes the 'gen. of person from whom it is heard' (LSJ s.v. ἀκούω 1.1). Hecuba uses the plural masculine form in reference to herself, as is normal in generalisations: 798, Barrett on *Hipp.* 287, Smyth §1009.

238 Odysseus puts himself up for cross-questioning. Sophists such as Gorgias and Protagoras prided themselves on their ability to answer whatever question the audience asked; Socrates, taking advantage of this, cross-questions them: Pl. *Grg.* 447c, *Prt.* 328e–329b, Gorgias 82 A 1a D–K, McCabe 2008: 98–100. As in Platonic dialogues, Hecuba's relentless questions lead up to a point she wanted her opponent to concede, and conclude with a general reflection. On Hecuba and the sophists, cf. 787–845n., 798–805n., 816n., 817–18n.

239 οἶσθ' ἡνίκ': on οἶσθα-questions see 109–10, 760n., 1008n.

Ἰλίου κατάσκοπος 'as a spy to reconnoitre Troy'. Odysseus entered the city in disguise, dressed in rags (240n.); Helen recognised him and denounced him to Hecuba. The queen accepted Odysseus' supplication and agreed to conceal his identity. Euripides manipulates the episode narrated by Helen at *Od.* 4.242–58: in that version, Hecuba is absent, and Helen does not betray Odysseus because she hoped for the victory of the Greeks (S. West in Heubeck, West and Hainsworth 1988 and de Jong 2001 *ad loc.*). The episode is mentioned also in the *Little Iliad* (fr. 8: West 2003: 122–3, 130–1) and in [Eur.] *Rhes.* 498–507 and 710–19. In all these versions, Odysseus wounds himself as part of his disguise (cf. 241; Fantuzzi 1996). The scholia on *Hecuba* 241 criticise Euripides for his implausible alteration of the Homeric narrative: unlike Helen, Hecuba had no reason not to denounce Odysseus.

240 δυσχλαινίαι τ' ἄμορφος 'and <you were> unsightly because of <your> miserable dress', an adaptation of *Od.* 4.245, where Odysseus, in disguise at Troy (239n.), wears σπεῖρα κάκ' 'ugly rags'. The clause lacks a verb. One can supply a past tense of a verb such as 'you appeared', 'you were': Smyth §§948, 3018i, Cooper and Krüger 2002: 2681. Alternatively, one can supply 'you came' from 239 ('and <you came> with an unsightly appearance in your miserable dress').

241 φόνου 'blood': *IT* 72. Odysseus wounded the area around his eyes; he drips blood to his chin.

242 οὐ γὰρ ἄκρας καρδίας ἔψαυσέ μου 'that circumstance touched not the surface of my heart', i.e. it touched the heart deep inside. Compare 230n. and Aesch. *Ag.* 805 οὐκ ἀπ' ἄκρας φρενός.

243 μόνηι κατεῖπ' ἐμοί 'she revealed <this> to *me* alone'. A personal pronoun reinforced by μόνος is normally non-enclitic. The non-enclitic form is metrically guaranteed in several instances where the adjective μόνος comes second: Soph. *OC* 83 ἐμοῦ μόνης, Eur. *Hcld.* 807, K–G 1.557–9,

Probert 2003: 144. This explains why it is better to interpret the *paradosis* (Introduction, section 9) as κατεῖπ' ἐμοί, with Brunck, rather than as κατεῖπέ μοι, with the medieval MSS.

244 Odysseus switches to the first person plural, implying that Hecuba shares his view: cf. 370–1n., 806–8n.

245 Suppliants usually make contact with knees, chin and the right hand of the person they are supplicating: *Suppl.* 277–9, *HF* 1206–10, *IA* 909–11, Gould 1973: 76 = Gould 2001: 26, Naiden 2006: 44–55. In some cases the supplication was 'figurative' (Gould 2001: 27), i.e. the suppliant simply described his or her action in words, when he or she was prevented by the circumstances from making physical contact with the person supplicated (*Od.* 6.141–7). The next line shows that the supplication was not figurative in this case. Cf. 275, 752–3n.

246 'to the point that, in fact, my hand died in your *peplos*'. The bold metaphor (ἐνθανεῖν 'to die in', i.e. 'to grow torpid') lacks precise parallels. Euripides seems to invert the Homeric phrase ἔν τ' ἄρα οἱ φῦ χειρί '(s)he took his hand', a phrase in which, like some modern scholars (Coray 2009 on *Il.* 19.7), he took ἐν with φῦ: *Ion* 891 λευκοῖς δ' ἐμφὺς καρποῖσιν. Instead of ἐμφύω 'I cling to' (φύω 'I give birth, I grow'), Euripides uses ἐνθνῄσκω (θνῄσκω 'I die'). Other modern scholars take ἐν with χειρί in Homer: Graziosi and Haubold on *Il.* 6.253.

249–50, 247–8 This order of lines, preserved in a few later MSS, gives a much better sequence of thought. Lines 247–8 mark the completion of Hecuba's supplication, and should come at the end. It is rhetorically weak for Hecuba to conclude her questions by going back in time to the moment when Odysseus pleaded with her. She needs him to admit that she saved his life, in order to reproach him with ingratitude (252). The error probably arose from the identical line beginnings at 246 and 248, ὥστ'.

249 The positions of slave and master are inverted now. Hecuba will later claim that Agamemnon is a slave even when he is king: cf. 864–75n.

250 πολλῶν λόγων εὑρήμαθ' 'contrivances consisting in many words', i.e. rhetorical expedients. Odysseus implies that the words of a suppliant (such as Hecuba now) should not be trusted.

247 Ancient sources considered harsh series of *s*-sounds to be a peculiarity of the style of Euripides: Mastronarde on *Med.* 476.

248 'to the effect that I now see the light of the sun', i.e. 'that I am alive'. With φέγγος ... τόδε compare φάος ... τόδε 'this light' = 'the light that shines now' (367–8n.).

251 'Well, are you not ashamed of these decisions?', i.e. the resolution to kill Polyxena that he supported. For κακύνομαι 'feel ashamed of', cf. Barrett on *Hipp.* 685–6. οὔκουν in questions can be translated as 'well, why': *Hcld.* 111, Denniston 431.

252 ἐξ ἐμοῦ μὲν ἔπαθες οἷα φῂς παθεῖν 'you received from me the treatment that you admit you in fact received'. This is a modification of an otherwise euphemistic or ominous turn of phrase ('you suffered what you suffered': 873n.); the modification highlights Odysseus' admission that Hecuba dealt with him with exceptional generosity.

253 δύναι 'you can', contracted 2nd p. sg. from δύναμαι. The normal Homeric and Attic form is the uncontracted δύνασαι (*Il.* 1.393, Soph. *Ai.* 1164, Ar. *Ach.* 291). For similar contracted forms cf. Aesch. *Eum.* 86, 581 ἐπίσται 'you know'.

254: 131–3n.

ἀχάριστον ὑμῶν σπέρμ᾽, ὅσοι 'your race is ungrateful, you who ...' For similar invectives cf. *Tro.* 424–6 (on heralds), fr. 282.2 (against 'the race of athletes'). Demagogues are ungrateful towards friends (256n.), but speak to please the crowd (257 πρὸς χάριν). On *charis* cf. 137n., 216–95n., 299–331n.

255 μηδὲ γιγνώσκοισθέ μοι 'my wish is that you should not be known, as far as I am concerned', i.e. 'I wish I might have nothing further to do with you'. Here, the dative of interest μοι (Cooper and Krüger 1998: 280, 282–3) comes close in meaning to a dative of agent proper (George 2005: 78–102). A dative of agent is rare with verbs in the present tense (see Thuc. 4.62.1 εὖ βουλευομένοις εὑρίσκεται, Smyth §1490) but common with verbal adjectives (Smyth §1488). The present optative expresses a wish referring to the future; this wish is probably felt to be unattainable (Smyth §1818).

256 'you who do not care about hurting your friends'. Cf. 216–95n., 299–331n.

258 τί δὴ σόφισμα τοῦθ᾽ ἡγούμενοι 'what clever idea did they think this was?' (for the syntax of the participle cf. 177–9n.). The word σόφισμα and its cognates can be used in a positive (Aesch. *PV* 470) or, as here, derogatory (Eur. *Ba.* 30, Ar. *Av.* 430) sense: see Dover on Ar. *Nub.* 205, 331, Mastronarde on *Pho.* 65. Hecuba exploits the ambiguity: the Greeks considered human sacrifice a cunning contrivance, but in fact it is an atrocity that allows the real culprit (Helen) to walk away scot-free.

260 τὸ χρή 'what must be', 'fate'. Monosyllabic χρεών (Scaliger) is also possible, but more distant from the MS text χρῆν: cf. Diggle 1981: 93.

σφ᾽ 'them', the Greeks. This form is normally used as a singular pronoun (masc./fem. 3rd p. accusative), but occasionally also as a plural form for both animate genders: *Med.* 1401, K–B 1.593.

ἀνθρωποσφαγεῖν 'to sacrifice a human being', a word coined by Euripides. The verbal novelty stresses the peculiarity of the situation. Human sacrifice is a frequent theme in Euripides: Mastronarde on *Pho.* 834–1018, O'Connor-Visser 1987, Sonnino 2010: 120–4. The Iphigenia myth is a crucial instance of human sacrifice for the tragic genre, and Polyxena's sacrifice is meant to allude to it (518–82n., 560n.). The animal substitution in the Iphigenia myth is often read as a sign of historical progress from human to animal sacrifice; this myth was designed to produce the 'cultic illusion of death without actual loss of human life', creating the impression of immortality (Henrichs 1981: 202). But Hecuba points out that in this case it is human sacrifice that replaces animal sacrifice: human civilisation proceeds towards practices that are less and less morally acceptable, abandoning the 'appropriate' (261 πρέπει) ancient customs. For a similarly pessimistic view of human progress cf. Thuc. 3.45, where Diodotus argues that the punishment inflicted on offenders has become harsher and harsher with time.

262–70 Hecuba's argument has a pedantic ring: if criterion A (guilt) is applied, Helen has to be the victim (262–6); if criterion B (beauty) is applied, Helen has to be the victim (267–9), and besides she was more guilty even on criterion A (270). A famous instance of similar rhetorical and philosophical overkill is Gorgias 82 B 3 D-K: Battezzato 2000c: 225–6.

262 τοὺς κτανόντας ἀνταποκτεῖναι θέλων 'in his desire to kill in return those who caused his death'. See Introduction, section 6 and n. 78.

263 ἐς τήνδ' Ἀχιλλεὺς ἐνδίκως τείνει φόνον; 'is Achilles justified in aiming the death sentence at *this* <woman>?', as if shooting an arrow (LSJ s.v. τείνω A I.4). Achilles was conspicuously not an archer when alive; archery was disparaged as a less heroic way of fighting (*Il.* 11.385–90, Bond on *HF* 159ff.). In death, Achilles fights from a distance, in a way that Hecuba implies to be less than heroic.

265 The asyndeton with the preceding sentence is contrastive (Smyth §2167d; Mastronarde on *Pho.* 456): 'on the contrary, he should have asked for Helen as a sacrificial victim for his tomb'.

νιν: Achilles. Tragedy uses νιν (Doric for Homeric μιν) as a masculine and feminine accusative (and, occasionally, neuter) pronoun, both for singular and plural: K–B 1.592, Stockert on *IA* 327 and 552.

προσφάγματα 'as a sacrificial victim'. For the poetic plural cf. 134–5, [402], 557, 750, 1195n., *Hipp.* 11 Πιτθέως παιδεύματα 'persons reared by Pittheus' (in reference to Hippolytus alone), Smyth §1007, Cooper and Krüger 2002: 1933–4, Wackernagel 2009: 126–32.

266 ἐς Τροίαν τ' ἄγει 'and brought him to Troy'. Preposition and noun are taken as a single unit, and τ' is placed after it: 520, *Alc.* 446, Denniston 516–17. The alternation aorist (ὤλεσεν)/present (ἄγει) is common: 571–4, 935–7, 1162–9, K–G 1.132–4, Fraenkel on Aesch. *Ag.* 1383. The effect of ἄγει is still present: Achilles is not buried at home, but in Asia (*IT* 988 διὰ πόνων τ' ἄγει, *Ba.* 465, K–G 1.136). Hecuba inverts the chronological order (Helen made Achilles come to Troy first and then caused his death). This figure of speech is called *hysteron proteron*; it emphasises the important fact first (the death of Achilles): 17–8, 21, Battezzato 2008b: 13–51.

268 οὐχ ἡμῶν τόδε 'this quality does not belong to us'. τόδε refers to a concept present in the previous clause (extraordinary beauty), even if not expressed by a neuter word: Smyth §1253. For τόδε instead of τοῦτο cf. Smyth §1247.

269 ἡ Τυνδαρίς 'the daughter of Tyndareus', i.e. Helen (here) or Clytemnestra (1278).

εἶδος ἐκπρεπεστάτη '<is> outstanding for physical beauty', a phrase used also to describe Alcestis (*Alc.* 333). On Helen's famed beauty cf. 635–7, *Il.* 3.156–8, Eur. *Andr.* 629–30, *Hel.* 27, Blondell 2013.

270 οὐδὲν ἧσσον 'not less', as in 322, Aesch. *Ag.* 1391.

271 τῶι μὲν δικαίωι τόνδ' ἁμιλλῶμαι λόγον 'In making this speech, I contend on the ground of what is just.' τόνδ' ... λόγον is an internal accusative; ἁμιλλάομαι means 'to compete', 'to strive' (Kannicht and Allan on *Hel.* 165), and τῶι ... δικαίωι is an instrumental dative as at *HF* 1255 ὡς ἁμιλληθῶ λόγοις 'so that I will compete with my speech'. ἅμιλλα ... λόγων is almost a technical and metatheatrical term for 'an *agōn*' (216–443n.): Mastronarde on *Med.* 546.

272 ἀντιδοῦναι 'to give in return', a basic duty for people who have a relation based on reciprocity (216–95n., 262n., 299–331n.).

273 ἄκουσον 'listen'. Formulaic at the beginning of a section in a *rhēsis*: cf. 788, 1137, 1217.

274–5 On supplication cf. 245n. The gestures are not gender-specific: both Hecuba and Odysseus touch the hand(s) and cheek(s) of the person supplicated. At 245 Hecuba added that Odysseus also touched her knees; she will touch Agamemnon's knees, chin and hand at 752–3.

τῆσδε γραίας ... παρηίδος 'this old cheek', genitive of contact with 273 ἥψω. For τῆσδε = 'my' cf. 519–20n. The noun γραῖα 'old woman' is used as an adjective: *Ion* 1213 γραῖαν ὠλένην.

275 ἀνθάπτομαί σου τῶνδε τῶν αὐτῶν ἐγώ 'I touch in return the same parts of your body'. The genitive τῶνδε τῶν αὐτῶν (part) is in apposition to σου (whole): K–G 1.289–90, *Ba.* 619.

276 χάριν τ' ἀπαιτῶ τὴν τόθ' 'and I demand back the favour I did to you then'. Hecuba's insistence on her right to a corresponding favour will be taken literally by Odysseus, as a strategy to avoid returning the favour at all: 299–331n.

278 τῶν τεθνηκότων ἅλις 'there are enough dead people'. The series of sentences in asyndeton at 278–82 is rhetorically striking. Cf. 394n.

279 The line is almost identical to *Or.* 66 ταύτηι γέγηθε κἀπιλήθεται κακῶν. Repetition or near-repetition of lines, esp. from different plays, is a genuine feature of Euripidean writing practice (805n.), but some instances of repetition are interpolated: [504n.], Mastronarde on *Pho.* 143.

281 This asyndetic list is emotionally charged and conveys the sense of the paramount importance of Polyxena for her mother. The ancient rhetorical tradition called this figure of style ἐπιμονή 'persistence': cf. Eur. fr. 866: 'this woman is my nurse, | mother, sister, servant, anchor of my household', Graziosi and Haubold on *Il.* 6.429–30, Eur. *Hcld.* 224, 229–30, Soph. *OT* 1284, Bond on *HF* 224.

282 οὐ τοὺς κρατοῦντας χρὴ κρατεῖν ἃ μὴ χρεών 'those who have power should not exercise a power that it is not right <to exercise>'.

ἃ is cognate accusative after κρατεῖν: cf. Aesch. *Ag.* 1470–1 κράτος ... κρατύνεις.

χρεών 'what is right'. It indicates what social conventions and morality require (cf. 236, 570) and comes close in meaning to πρέπει (261).

283 οὐδ' εὐτυχοῦντας εὖ δοκεῖν πράξειν ἀεί 'nor should people in prosperity expect to be prosperous for ever'. This traditional piece of advice on the mutability of fortune is often coupled with advice against wrongdoing (282) and the remark that a single day (285n.) may change the life of a person: Steiner 2010 on *Od.* 18.130–7, Noussia-Fantuzzi 2010 on Solon fr. 13.25–36 West. The phrases εὐτυχοῦντας and εὖ ... πράξειν have the same meaning, as in *Tro.* 509–10 τῶν δ' εὐδαιμόνων | μηδένα νομίζετ' εὐτυχεῖν, πρὶν ἂν θάνηι, where Hecuba rephrases a related general reflection also attributed to Solon (Hdt. 1.32.7; cf. 623–5n.).

284 ἦ ποτ' ἀλλὰ νῦν οὐκ εἴμ' ἔτι 'I existed once, but now I do not exist anymore'. Hecuba equates her present misfortune with symbolic death, as in 668n., *Hipp.* 357 οὐκέτ' εἴμ'. Others understand ἦ as 'I was prosperous/ powerful', supplying εὐτυχοῦσα or κρατοῦσα *vel sim.* from the previous lines, which somewhat lessens Hecuba's misfortune.

285 Human beings are by nature 'ephemeral', that is 'precarious', dependent on what happens day by day (623–5n.); Fränkel 1946 explores the importance of this theme in Greek literature from Homer onwards. A single day may make a person prosper, or ruin him or her for ever; tragic plots focus on events lasting 'one day only': Mastronarde on *Pho.* 1689.

286 ὦ φίλον γένειον: lit. 'O dear chin'; Hecuba touches Odysseus' chin (245n., 274–5n.).

286–7 αἰδέσθητί με, | οἴκτιρον: the suppliant deserves respect (αἰδέομαι: Cairns 1993: 280 n. 53); the person suffering unjustly deserves pity (οἰκτίρω). On the ancient concept of pity cf. Konstan 2001 and Sternberg 2005.

288 παρηγόρησον ὡς 'advise them that', 'address them saying that'. Gregory, after Paley, translates 'talk them over [to the idea] that', comparing παρειπεῖν 'to win over' for the force of παρά. Odysseus should make the assembly take a vote on a matter already decided. This may recall the

Athenian procedure of ἀναψηφίζειν 'put to the vote again' (Hornblower on Thuc. 3.36.6 and 6.14), a process which involved a considerable risk of (at least) losing face for the proponent.

φθόνος '<is> cause for indignation'. Hecuba does not state but implies that it is the gods who feel *phthonos*. φθόνος θεῶν is a frequently attested phrase and concept: *Alc.* 1135, *Or.* 974, Fisher 1992: 360–2 and 433–4. The powerless often hope for divine *phthonos*, which 'focuses on recognised moral offences on the part of human beings' (Cairns 1996: 18).

290 βωμῶν ἀποσπάσαντες: an act of impiety that ruthless people threaten to enact against suppliants (Eur. *Hcld.* 249, Hdt. 6.81), and the Greeks actually performed at Troy (935–6n., *Little Iliad* fr. 25 in West 2003: 136–9), where they even killed suppliants at the altar (23–4n., *Tro.* 562–3).

291 νόμος ... ἴσος: an allusion to *isonomia*, a byword for democracy in Greek political theory (805n., 234–7n.). Hecuba anachronistically alludes to contemporary Athenian legal practices (Morrow 1937). Antiph. 5.48 claims that 'the vote (of the jury) has the same power' (ἡ ψῆφος ἴσον δύναται) 'over the killer of a slave as over the killer of a free man', an exaggeration, since the courts judging these cases were different (Gagarin 1997 *ad loc.*; E. M. Harris 2015: 20–1). Dem. 21.46–50 mentions a law restraining acts of *hybris* against slaves, and slave-owners punished people who murdered their slaves (Pl. *Euthphr.* 3e–4d). It is however doubtful whether the homicide law was 'the same' (ἴσος) for slaves and free citizens. Legal action against the killer had to be taken by the owner of the slave; only few such cases were likely to be discussed in court, e.g. when someone killed someone else's slave (MacDowell 1963: 21–2; Antiph. 6.4).

292 αἵματος ... πέρι 'on blood crimes', 'on homicide'. When disyllabic prepositions are placed after the word they govern (anastrophe), they receive a paroxytone accent (Smyth §175b). Anastrophe is common in poetry, but restricted in prose. Prepositions in anastrophe can be separated by one or more words (hyperbaton). For other examples and discussions cf. 749n., Devine and Stephens 2000: 11–12, 211–22, Baechle 2007: 139–207, esp. 194.

293–4 τὸ δ' ἀξίωμα, κἂν κακῶς λέγηις, τὸ σόν | πείσει 'your prestige, even if you do not speak well, will carry conviction'. Hecuba uses fifth-century political language to express the aristocratic point of view that social prestige (ἀξίωμα) per se can influence decisions. This is denied by democratic leaders. At Thuc. 2.37.1, Pericles claims that, in a democracy, the obscurity of a citizen's ἀξίωμα does not bar him from benefiting the polis; Theseus in *Suppl.* 433–41 states that social position does not influence political or judicial assemblies, whereas the Argive herald complains that in democratic constitutions 'a man from the lower classes enjoys prestige (ἀξίωμα)' (424–5): see Macleod 1983: 150, Hornblower on Thuc. 2.37.1, Morwood 2009: 357. In fact, Hecuba's point of view is in part vindicated by the actual workings of democracy: Thucydides notes that the ἀξίωμα of Pericles (2.65.8) and Alcibiades (5.43.2 'the ἀξίωμα of his ancestors', 6.15.3) helped them to acquire prominent positions in the polis, and that this could lead to the 'rule by the first man' (2.65.9: cf. Hdt. 3.83.4) or even 'tyranny' (6.15.4). Many Athenian democratic leaders came from elite families: Rhodes 1986, Ober 1989.

294–5 λόγος ... αὐτός [= ὁ αὐτός] 'the same speech', 'the same argument'.

ἔκ τ' ἀδοξούντων ἰών | κἀκ τῶν δοκούντων 'if it comes from people of no consequence or from important people'. κἀκ = καὶ ἐκ. For καί introducing an alternative ('or') cf. Soph. *Phil.* 1082 θερμὸν καὶ παγετῶδες 'hot or icy, as the case may be' (Denniston 292).

296–8 The chorus leader delivers a 'tag', as usual after long speeches, esp. in *agōn* scenes (332–3, 1183–6, *Med.* 520–1). This chorus side with Hecuba, and indicate the emotional reaction expected of Odysseus and of the theatrical audience (Riedweg 2000: 30–1). Odysseus is not impressed.

στερρός 'harsh, unfeeling'. Cf. 1293–5n.

ἥτις ... οὐκ ἂν ἐκβάλοι δάκρυ 'who ... would not weep'. For the potential optative with ἄν in similar relative clauses see *El.* 903 οὐκ ἔστιν οὐδεὶς ὅστις ἂν μέμψαιτό σε, Cooper and Krüger 2002: 2470–1, Smyth §2556a.

γόων ... ὀδυρμάτων: genitives of explanation, defining θρήνους at 298 ('your mourning cries consisting in laments and long wailings'): *Tro.* 609 θρήνων τ' ὀδυρμοί, *Hipp.* 161–4; cf. Moorhouse 1982: 53. In fact Odysseus has not heard Hecuba 'lament' at 154–96 (cf. 433–4). By 'lament' the chorus leader refers generically to a speech that arouses pity, or has mournful content: at *Tro.* 684–5 the chorus describe Andromache, who has just finished her *rhēsis*, as θρηνοῦσα ... | τὸ σόν 'lamenting your destiny'.

299–331 In his response to Hecuba's accusation of acting as a demagogue, Odysseus uses fifth-century democratic rhetoric, arguing that he acted for the common good (306, 330), in contrast to leaders from an aristocratic background, who bestow favours on specific individuals or families: 216–95n., von Reden 1995: 110. Odysseus also claims that he prefers honour for his tomb over excessive wealth (317–20): similarly, Pericles urged Athenians to pursue honour (τιμᾶσθαι) over riches (κερδαίνειν: Thuc. 2.44.4, cf. Eur. *Suppl.* 875–7, Aesch. *Ag.* 773–81). Nonetheless, Odysseus in fact uses aristocratic language throughout. The city must honour 'the noble ones' over 'those who are worse' (307–8 ἐσθλός ... τῶν κακιόνων, 327 τὸν ἐσθλόν): ἐσθλός and κακός are often used to distinguish 'aristocratic' and 'non-aristocratic' people (596–7, *Hipp.* 409–12, *Andr.* 772). For Odysseus, though, being 'noble' is not enough: one must also fight valorously (307 πρόθυμος, 329 καλῶς). This is true friendship (311 φίλωι), not the simple aristocratic *philia* extolled by Hecuba. Odysseus stresses that the barbarians, unlike the

Greeks, are prisoners of their aristocratic, anti-communitarian way of thinking, and do not know how to distinguish and honour those who are truly φίλοι (328–30). Greeks and non-Greeks are separated by a gulf: Hecuba will turn this argument against Polymestor (1199–1204n.).

As for Hecuba's argument based on *charis*, Odysseus answers by claiming that he is ready to render *charis* for *charis* in precisely the same amount: Hecuba saved his life, and Odysseus will save hers, not Polyxena's. This precise reckoning of favours is typical of commercial exchanges and is a complete denial of the logic of reciprocity and *charis*. Friends are supposed to return favours that are similar, not exactly identical, in kind and quantity: *Or.* 640–68, Introduction, section 5, Blundell 1989: 32–4, von Reden 1995: 3, 26 and 88.

299–300 τῶι θυμουμένωι ... φρενός 'because of the anger of <your> mind'. Hecuba's two main emotions are sorrow and anger. After her revenge, anger will be the defining emotion of Polymestor, not of Hecuba (1054–5n., Konstan 2006: 62–6). τῶι θυμουμένωι is a neuter form of the participle used as an abstract noun ('anger'), a stylistic feature characteristic of Euripides and of intellectually ambitious prose: Thuc. 5.9.6, Barrett on *Hipp.* 248 τὸ ... μαινόμενον, *Alc.* 797, *Or.* 210, Denniston 1952: 36–7, K–G 1.267–8. φρενός qualifies the neuter participle τῶι θυμουμένωι, a structure 'effectively reversing the normal relation between substantive and attribute' (Rusten 1989: 22): cf. Thuc. 7.68.1 τῆς γνώμης τὸ θυμούμενον, 2.59.3, Gagarin 1997 on Antipho 2.3.3 τὸ θυμούμενον τῆς γνώμης. In τῶι θυμουμένωι ... φρενός, five words separate the participle and the genitive; for similar hyperbata, encircling a whole sentence or line, cf. 1252–3n., *Alc.* 1072–4 ὥστε σὴν | ἐς φῶς πορεῦσαι νερτέρων ἐκ δωμάτων | γυναῖκα, Finglass on Soph. *El.* 78, 1349–50 οὗ τὸ Φωκέων πέδον | ὑπεξεπέμφθην σῆι προμηθίαι χεροῖν (οὗ ... χεροῖν 'at whose hands'). On hyperbaton in general cf. 44n., 690n. φρενός is Murray's conjecture for the awkward double dative of the MS text τῶι θυμουμένωι ... φρενί. The corruption was caused by failure to link the genitive φρενός with the distant participle.

τὸν εὖ λέγοντα δυσμενῆ ποιοῦ 'do not consider hostile a person that gives good advice'. Odysseus will not give bad (293–4n.) but good advice, as he has always done.

301 ὑφ᾽ οὗπερ ηὐτύχουν: the intransitive verb (εὐτυχέω 'to prosper') is treated as having a passive meaning ('to be the recipient of an action that brings good fortune'). On the augment in ηὐ- cf. 18n.

302 κοὐκ ἄλλως λέγω 'and I do not deny it' (as in *El.* 1035, *Hel.* 1106, *Pho.* 359). Odysseus presents himself as faithful to his own words with both Hecuba and the Greeks (303 εἰς ἅπαντας). The present tense refers to an action that will continue in the future (cf. οὐκ ἀρνήσομαι: 'I do not say otherwise now (and I will not say otherwise in the future)': Smyth §1879.

303–5 ἅ... εἶπον... δοῦναι 'the advice I offered, <namely> to give...' The infinitive δοῦναι is in apposition to ἅ (Smyth §1987).

ἀνδρὶ τῶι πρώτωι στρατοῦ: Achilles (134n.)

305 σὴν παῖδα δοῦναι σφάγιον ἐξαιτουμένωι 'to give him your daughter as a sacrificial victim, since he demands her'. Odysseus here and at 390, like Polydorus (40–1), claims that Achilles asked for Polyxena specifically; the chorus reported a generic request for 'a gift' (113–15n.)

306–8 'For this is where many cities get into difficulties, when someone who is a brave and zealous man does not get a greater reward than his inferiors.' Odysseus, in claiming special honours for Achilles, voices the argument put forward by Achilles himself at *Il.* 1.163–8 and 9.316–20: Achilles, the best Greek warrior, should receive a greater share of honour (and loot); under bad leaders, such as Agamemnon, 'the *kakos* and the *esthlos* are equally honoured' (*Il.* 9.319). Cf. 137n.

ἐν τῶιδε... κάμνουσιν: ἐν τῶιδε looks forward to ὅταν: 'under this circumstance..., namely when...'. For κάμνω + ἐν with dative 'to get into difficulties', 'to be in trouble', as in 1143–4n.: cf. *IA* 966 ἐν τῶιδ' ἔκαμνε, *Med.* 768 ἧι... ἐκάμνομεν.

310 κάλλιστ': a death in battle is considered 'beautiful': 329, *Il.* 22.73, Tyrt. 10.1, Eur. *Or.* 1152 καλῶς θανόντες.

311–12 εἰ βλέποντι μὲν φίλωι | χρώμεσθ', ἐπεὶ δ' ὄλωλε μὴ χρώμεσθ' ἔτι 'if we treat him as a friend when he is alive, but do not do so any more when he dies'. φίλωι is to be taken with both instances of χρώμεσθ'. A person must honour one's *philoi* (friends and family) after death (Soph. *Ant.* 73), esp. if the dead are regarded as having reached heroic status (313–16n., *HF* 1331–7).

313–16 Odysseus argues that the expectation of posthumous honours is one of the prime incentives that motivate soldiers. The tombs of fallen soldiers receive special honours (Soph. *Ant.* 194–7, Macleod 1983: 155). At Athens, the fallen were remembered in a funeral oration at the Kerameikos cemetery and received heroic cult: Hornblower on Thuc. 2. 34–46.

313 εἶέν 'well then'. The particle here indicates that the speaker grants, for the sake of the argument, the point made by his opponent: cf. Stockert on *IA* 1185.

313–14 ἤν τις αὖ φανῆι | στρατοῦ τ' ἄθροισις πολεμίων τ' ἀγωνία 'if some occasion arises again for mustering the army or for fighting the enemies'.

315 φιλοψυχήσομεν 'shall we cling to our life?' This implies that the soldiers will try to preserve their lives by cowardly action, as in Tyrt. 10.18 μηδὲ φιλοψυχεῖτ' ἀνδράσι μαρνάμενοι. Cf. 346–8n.

317–18 καθ' ἡμέραν | κεἰ σμίκρ' ἔχοιμι πάντ' ἂν ἀρκούντως ἔχοι 'even if I had a little day by day, that would be completely sufficient'. καθ' ἡμέραν is emphasised by being placed before the subordinating conjunction κεἰ (= καὶ εἰ): cf. 802, *HF* 499, *Ion* 521, K–G II.598–9. Enjoying one's fate καθ' ἡμέραν 'day by day' is what wise human beings should do: 285n., Aesch. *Pers.* 841, Eur. *Alc.* 788. Frugality is presented positively here (299–331n., fr. 714), but the epic Odysseus aims at restoring his prosperity by plundering his neighbours: *Od.* 23.355–8. The audience could suspect that Odysseus was being hypocritical here. Compare Clytemnestra at Aesch. *Ag.* 1574–6: 'even if I have a small part of my patrimony, it completely suffices me, provided that I can put an end to the madness of mutual slaughter that is affecting our palace'.

319–20 Odysseus, after his death, wants to 'see' (ὁρᾶσθαι, cf. 316 ὁρῶντες) his tomb honoured. Oedipus imagines he will 'see' his parents in Hades: Soph. *OT* 1371–3, Dover 1974: 243–6, 261–8.

χάρις: cf. 299–331n.

321–5 At Thuc. 3.67.3 the Thebans use the sufferings of their side as an argument to support their demand for cruel punishment of the helpless Plataean war prisoners.

322–3 οὐδὲν ἧσσον ἄθλιαι ... σέθεν 'not less unhappy than you'. σέθεν (= Attic σοῦ) is the Homeric form of the genitive.

γραῖαι γυναῖκες ἠδὲ πρεσβῦται 'old women and old men'. ἠδέ 'and' is an epicism, rarely used in tragedy; it is used to link a pair of strictly connected terms: *HF* 30, *IA* 812, Denniston 287–8. Euripides here echoes the Homeric phrases ἀνέρες ἠδὲ γυναῖκες (*Il.* 15.683) and νέοι ἠδὲ γέροντες (*Il.* 2.789).

325 ὧν ... σώματ' 'whose bodies'.

ἥδε ... Ἰδαία κόνις 'this dust of Mount Ida'. For the interlaced hyperbata cf. 44n. ἥδε implies that the speaker can see Mount Ida, in the Troad, not that the audience can see it, nor that the play is set on Trojan land (cf. 823n.).

326 τόλμα τάδ' 'endure this fate of yours'. For τολμάω 'to endure' cf. 333, *Alc.* 276, and contrast 1123. The imperative in contrastive asyndeton marks the end of this section, and leads to the final general reflection as in *Alc.* 703 σίγα.

327 ἀμαθίαν ὀφλήσομεν 'we will incur the charge of senseless behaviour'. ἀμαθία does not simply indicate lack of knowledge, but 'moral insensitivity', and morally insensible people: *El.* 294, Bond on *HF* 347, Mastronarde 2010: 164, 190.

328–31 'You barbarians! Carry on not regarding your friends as friends and not admiring those who died a glorious death [cf. 310n.], so that Greece flourishes, and you get the results that correspond to your <bad> choices.' ἡγεῖσθε and θαυμάζεθ' are imperatives, accompanied by a subject (οἱ βάρβαροι), which expresses an insult. At 426–8 the nominative construed with the imperative is a term indicating a family relation, expressing affection.

Odysseus means that the barbarians do not treat their friends as they should, and that they fail to fulfil the basic duty 'to be a friend to one's friends': 299–331n., Bond on *HF* 585 τοῖς φίλοις <τ'> εἶναι φίλον, *Suppl.* 867, *IT* 610. Odysseus resorts to generalisations because he cannot point to any specific failure of the Trojans to honour their fallen soldiers. Hecuba is in fact opposed to honouring a *Greek* warrior, Achilles. On Greeks and barbarians cf. 1129n., 1199–1204n. and Introduction, section 5.

330–1 ὡς ἂν ... εὐτυχῇ | ... ἔχηθ': final clauses (Smyth §2201a).

332–3 The choral 'tag' (296–8n.) discusses slavery, a crucial theme in the play (864–9n., 1293–5n.).

τὸ δοῦλον ὡς κακὸν πέφυκ' ἀεί 'What an evil thing the condition of slavery is under all circumstances!' τὸ δοῦλον is a neuter adjective used to express an abstract concept (299–300n., fr. 217, *Tro.* 614–15); in 332, it is almost personified ('the slaves'). ὡς κακόν 'how bad!' introduces the interjection; the 'topic' (589–90n.) τὸ δοῦλον is placed at sentence-beginning. The exclamative infinitive πεφυκέναι, transmitted by part of the MS tradition, gives inappropriate meaning (surprise or indignation: Smyth §2015) and dubious syntax (one would need to conjecture τολμᾶν at 333 for syntactic regularity).

334–5 Hecuba abandons her supplication of Odysseus and loses physical contact with him. She now addresses Polyxena, whom she urges to resume supplication (339). Odysseus' hand is free at 342.

οὑμοὶ μὲν λόγοι πρὸς αἰθέρα | φροῦδοι μάτην ῥιφθέντες ἀμφὶ σοῦ φόνου 'my words about your murder, uttered in vain, went away to the sky'. The form ῥιφθέντες is probably to be preferred over ῥιφέντες: Kannicht 2004 on fr. 489. φροῦδοι (160–1n.), μάτην (*Med.* 1404 μάτην ἔπος ἔρριπται) and πρὸς αἰθέρα (Bond on *HF* 510) all stress the vanity of Hecuba's efforts; for similar redundancy cf. 489n., Aesch. *Cho.* 845–6, Eur. *Andr.* 1218–20.

337–8 σπούδαζε πάσας ὥστ' ἀηδόνος στόμα | φθογγὰς ἱεῖσα 'make effort to utter all <sorts of> voices, <singing> like the mouth of a nightingale'. Polyxena is compared to a bird: the more varied her singing is, the better chance she has of finding the right note to convince Odysseus. σπούδαζε is to be taken with the participle ἱεῖσα (contrast 817–18 σπουδάζομεν and the infinitive μανθάνειν). The nightingale sings a proverbially melodious (Ar. *Av.* 659–60), often mournful song (*Od.* 19. 518–24, Finglass on Soph. *El.* 107 and 145–52). πάσας ... φθογγάς rephrases the epithet for Procne's voice at *Od.* 19.521 πολυηχέα 'many-toned' (or, in a variant reading, πολυδευκέα, 'which imitates many (voices)': see Ael. *NA* 5.38): Polyxena will need to surpass Procne, and use 'all kinds of voices', not just 'many'. Procne turns into a nightingale after killing her son; this myth is not explicitly alluded to here. Polyxena's death will in fact be in lieu of marriage (416n., 523n., 612n.). For ὥστ' cf. 205n.

339–41 Polyxena is asked to point out that Odysseus' child, Telemachus, can suffer the same fate as that planned by Penelope's suitors, i.e. being murdered (*Od.* 4.663–74, 16.342–86). Suppliants often stress similarities in the family situation of the supplicated person in order to elicit pity: *Il.* 24.486–7, Eur. *Suppl.* 55. Hecuba may know that Odysseus has only one son: τέκνα can be interpreted as a poetic plural (265n.).

340 ἔχεις δὲ πρόφασιν 'you have an opportunity' to support your argument. πρόφασις is used here in a rhetorical sense, 'a starting point for your speech', as in Ion of Chios fr. 26.2 West πρόφασις παντοδαπῶν λογίων 'an opportunity for all kinds of learned speeches [or 'learned speakers']'. This sense is attested for ἀφορμαί (cf. 1238–9n.) and the two words are used as near synonyms in Dem. 18.156 τὰς ἀφορμὰς ταύτας καὶ τὰς προφάσεις αὐτῶι παρασχών.

340–1 πεῖθ'... τὴν σὴν ὥστ' ἐποικτῖραι τύχην 'persuade him to take pity on your fate'. πείθω can take ὥστε and infinitive (*Hel.* 1039–40) as well as the simple infinitive (*Hel.* 1396), with no difference in meaning.

342–78 Polyxena surprisingly consents to die. In Euripides, the victim of human sacrifices accepts her death voluntarily (cf. 260n., *Hcld.* 500–34, a speech very similar to Polyxena's in content and form: cf. Allan *ad loc.*). Similarly, according to some ancient sources, victims expressed assent to their sacrifice: cf. Aesch. *Ag.* 1297–8 'you [Cassandra] walk without fear in the direction of the altar, like a cow driven by a god', Burkert 1966, Naiden 2006: esp. 65. Polyxena's speech displays shocking rationality in discussing disturbing choices (cf. 349n., *Med.* 364–409). Like many female (*Hcld.* 513, *HF* 308, *IA* 1376) and male (Finglass on Soph. *Ai.* 479–80) aristocratic characters in tragedy, she prefers death over loss of status or reputation (349–68 and 374–8; cf. 359n.). Megara and Iphigenia, in similar situations, accept death as a 'necessity' (*HF* 282, cf. *Hec.* 346), as something 'impossible' to avoid (*IA* 1370).

342–5 Polyxena describes Odysseus' gestures, marking them as significant stage actions (for the general principle cf. Taplin 1977: 38–9). She surprisingly disobeys Hecuba's invitation and refuses to supplicate Odysseus: Iphigenia similarly surprises her mother at *IA* 1368–70. Odysseus wants to avoid supplication and acts so that Polyxena will not be able to touch his hand or chin; he even avoides eye contact. Avoidance of eye contact may originate out of modesty (968–75n., Soph. *Ant.* 441, Mueller 2011), shame (Allan on *Hcld.* 887, 942–4) or hostility (*Pho.* 454–8), and is more common when a character arrives onstage, rather than in mid-scene.

345 θάρσει 'do not worry'. Cf. 875n.

πέφευγας τὸν ἐμὸν Ἱκέσιον Δία: lit. 'you have escaped my Zeus of Supplication', i.e. 'you are free from my supplication, which Zeus of Supplication would have supported'. At *Andr.* 603, Peleus tells Menelaus that Helen left τὸν σὸν ... Φίλιον 'your [*sc.* Zeus] of Friendship', i.e. 'your marriage, protected by Zeus of Friendship' (cf. Stevens *ad loc.*). Zeus is traditionally thought to protect suppliants: *Od.* 13.213, Aesch. *Suppl.* 616, Eur. fr. 661.15.

346–8 A passage imitated by the Stoic philosopher Cleanthes: cf. 369n., Cleanthes fr. 2 in Powell 1925: 229.

τοῦ τ' ἀναγκαίου χάριν | θανεῖν τε χρῄζουσ' 'because it is necessary and because I want to die'. The prepositional phrase (τοῦ ... ἀναγκαίου χάριν) and the participle (χρῄζουσ') are treated as syntactically parallel (τ' ... τε), since they both express cause: 916–18, 1197–8n., Diggle 1994: 53.

φιλόψυχος: Polyxena, like other self-sacrificing virgins, does not want to appear too attached to life: *Hcld.* 533 μὴ φιλοψυχοῦσ', *IA* 1385 οὐδέ τοί <τι> λίαν ἐμὲ φιλοψυχεῖν χρεών. These young girls implicitly compare themselves to fighting warriors (cf. 315n.). In *Hcld.* and *IA*, they actually help their fellow citizens or their allies to overcome enemies in battle; by contrast, Polyxena dies to honour the most powerful soldier who fought against her city.

349 τί γάρ με δεῖ ζῆν; 'Why should I go on living?' Polyxena adopts the rhetoric of the 'desperation speech' (Fowler 1987: 30–2; *Alc.* 960, *Andr.* 404, *HF* 1301), but will keep her tone perfectly calm and rational (cf. 350 πρῶτον, 351 ἔπειτ').

350 τοῦτό μοι πρῶτον βίου 'this was the first thing in my life', both chronologically (cf. 351 ἔπειτ') and for its importance (Mastronarde on *Pho.* 886).

351–3 'After that, I was raised with the fair hope of becoming the wife of a king, causing no small rivalry for my wedding <since I made people wonder> whose hearth and home I would go to.' Suitors competed in myth (Hes. frr. 196–204 Merkelbach–West) and real life (Hdt. 6.126–30) for noble and/or rich marriageable girls. In fact, Greek heroes often became kings by marrying a princess, by matrilinear transmission of the throne, rather than inheriting a kingdom from their fathers (Finkelberg 1991). ζῆλον 'rivalry' implies that people were uncertain as to the outcome of the competition for marrying Polyxena. The indirect question ὅτου δῶμ' ἑστίαν τ' ἀφίξομαι depends 'on an idea involved in the principal verb' (Smyth §2669). Polyxena stresses the feasibility of this potential outcome by using the indicative ἀφίξομαι instead of the optative (K–G II.537–8, Smyth §2678), which would have been more common after a main verb in the secondary tense.

354–5 δέσποινα δ' ἡ δύστηνος Ἰδαίαισιν ἦ | γυναιξί, παρθένοις τ' ἀπόβλεπτος μέτα 'I was a princess among the women of Ida, wretched me, and admired among the young girls'. παρθένοις is governed by μέτα (anastrophe for μετά: cf. 292n.): fr. 360.26 μετ' ἀνδράσιν πρέποι. ἀπόβλεπτος 'gazed upon', 'an object of admiration' is better referred to παρθένοις alone than to Ἰδαίαισιν... γυναιξὶ as well: Polyxena is admired in her age-class, as a marriageable girl: cf. *Od.* 6.27–35 and 283–4, Theocr. 18.22–37. It would be improper for her to suggest that she competed with married women for male attention.

356 ἴση θεοῖσι: Euripides, like Sappho before him, uses the Homeric epithet ἰσόθεος for women as well as for men: Sapph. 68.a3 ἴσαν θέοισιν, Eur. *Hel.* 819 θεοῖς ἴση. Polyxena has royal status, a condition 'equal to that of the gods' (*Tro.* 1169 ἰσοθέου τυραννίδος). Polyxena's specification, 'with the only exception of death', poignantly and ominously recalls Hecuba's words to Hector in *Il.* 22.434–6: the Trojans 'welcomed you like a god;... now death and fate have reached you'. On ἰσόθεος and related expressions in Homer and tragedy cf. Furley 2000: 10–11, Garvie on Aesch. *Pers.* 633–9.

πλήν + inf. means 'except so much as to': Mastronarde on *Pho.* 501–2.

357 τοὔνομα 'the name', i.e. 'the simple fact that I am called a slave', even before she experiences the 'reality' of the slavery: cf. Mastronarde on *Med.* 125–6 πρῶτα μὲν... τοὔνομα 'first of all, the mere name'. For the opposition ὄνομα/ἔργον 'word/deed' cf. 798–805n.

358 οὐκ εἰωθὸς ὄν 'since it is not habitual' for me, i.e. 'since I am not used to it'. The participle εἰωθός is used as an adjective: Dover on Ar. *Ran.* 721, K–G 1.39.

359–64 'Moreover, there is a good chance that I will get a harsh master, someone who will buy me for silver, me, the sister of Hector and of many others, and, imposing on me the task of preparing bread in his mansion, will force me to to sweep the floor of the house, and to work at the loom, living a life of misery.'

359 δεσποτῶν ὠμῶν φρένας: lit. 'masters harsh in their attitude'. Clytemnestra, urging Cassandra, Polyxena's sister, to accept slavery, notes that the newly rich are the harshest masters of all (Aesch. *Ag.* 1035–46). Polyxena echoes Clytemnestra's language (*Ag.* 1045 ὠμοί τε δούλοις) while rejecting her argument.

φρένας is accusative of respect after ὠμῶν (Smyth §1601).

360 ὅστις: the relative pronoun in the singular refers to a member of the class of the plural antecedent, δεσποτῶν (359): cf. K–G 1.56–7, Smyth §2502c, Mastronarde on *Med.* 220.

361 Polyxena alludes to the fifty children of Priam (cf. Graziosi and Haubold on *Il.* 6.244), but tactfully leaves out the fact that thirty-one of them (Richardson on *Il.* 24.496–7) were not Hecuba's children. Cf. 421n., 620, 821.

362 δ' 'and' connects the verbs ὠνήσεται and ἀναγκάσει.

προσθείς ... ἀνάγκην σιτοποιόν 'adding the obligation to prepare bread'. ἀνάγκη 'necessity, coercion' is used almost as a synonym of slavery (1293–5n.). σιτοποιός, a prose word (Hdt. 7.187.1), conveys the sense of degradation felt by Polyxena here, and by Hecuba at *Tro.* 494 σιτοποιεῖν, in reference to the slavery of Andromache. Euripides here, in line with a fifth-century stylistic trend (16–17n., 299–300n., 332–3n., 607–8n., 945n.), uses an abstract term. Its reference is explained by the defining adjective: *Suppl.* 39 ἀνάγκας ἱκεσίους 'the obligation to help the suppliants' (Collard *ad loc.*), Denniston 1952: 35–6. For the periphrasis προσθείς ... ἀνάγκην cf. *HF* 710 ἀνάγκην προστίθης, Barrett on *Hipp.* 282. Euripides could have written the simpler καὶ σιτοποιεῖν ἐν δόμοις μ' ἀναγκάσας (cf. *Hel.* 427 φυλάσσειν τἄμ' ἀναγκάσας λέχη).

363 Bread making and floor sweeping (*Andr.* 166 σαίρειν τε δῶμα, echoed here) are servile tasks. Princesses and queens did work at the loom at Troy (*Il.* 3.125, 22.440), but 'weaving under the order of another woman' (*Il.* 6.456: the imagined fate of Andromache) is a sign of servile status. Electra considers wearing only home-made clothes a crucial sign of her poverty and loss of status (*El.* 307–8).

364 λυπρὰν ἄγουσαν ἡμέραν 'living a miserable life'; ἡμέρα is a metonym for 'life': Mastronarde on *Med.* 651.

365 λέχη δὲ τἀμά 'as for my marriage bed' resumes the topic of marriage (352).

ὠνητός ποθεν 'bought some place or other'. A master is likely to value less a slave bought on the market (*Alc.* 676) than one born in his own house (Soph. *OT* 1123).

366 χρανεῖ 'will defile it', fut. from χραίνω.

τυράννων πρόσθεν ἠξιωμένα 'which (i.e. λέχη) had been previously deemed worthy of kings'. Cf. *Tro.* 484–6.

367–8 ἀφίημ' ὀμμάτων ἐλευθέρα | φέγγος τόδ' 'I freely discard this light of day from my eyes'. 'To leave the light of day' means 'to die': *Or.* 954. For ἐλευθέρα (predicative: 'as a free person', i.e. 'freely') cf. 550 ἐλευθέρα θάνω, fr. 472e40–1 ἐλεύθεροι ... θανούμεθα. The MSS read ἐλεύθερον | φέγγος τόδε 'I discard this free light of the day', but the light of day, and, by extension, the life of human beings is not free in general, nor is it free for Polyxena. ἐλευθέρα was corrupted because of assimilation to the following φέγγος. Alternatively, one could also read ἐλευθέρως: *Hcld.* 559 ἐλευθέρως θάνω, *Or.* 1170–1 ἐλευθέρως | ψυχὴν ἀφήσω. Blomfield conjectured ἐλευθέρων, 'I discard this light of day from my free eyes'. However, the adjective 'free', so placed, lacks contrastive emphasis; moreover, one would have expected the reverse corruption, from ἐλεύθερον to ἐλευθέρων.

369 ἄγ' οὖν μ', Ὀδυσσεῦ, καὶ διέργασαί μ' ἄγων 'then lead me, Odysseus, and, leading me, bring me to my death'. Cleanthes fr. 2 in Powell 1925: 229 ἄγου δέ μ', ὦ Ζεῦ (346–8n.) appears to imitate the variant ἄγου μ' ('take me with you', cf. *Alc.* 382), but ἄγ' is the correct reading here, in view of the following ἄγων (for the rhetoric cf. 25–6n.). For οὖν with imperatives cf. [96], 806, *Andr.* 316.

370–1 'I do not see that we have any confident hope or expectation of a future happy lot for me'. Polyxena switches from ἡμῖν to με: she implies that the other prisoners lack hope, but stresses that it is she in particular who has no prospects for the future. For similar changes from singular to plural see 244n., 806–8n., Bond on *HF* 858 μαρτυρόμεσθα δρῶσ'.

ἐλπίδος ... θάρσος 'the confidence to hope', i.e. 'a confident hope'.

του is the gen. indefinite adj., more commonly found in the form τινος. It is to be taken with both ἐλπίδος and δόξης (the so-called ἀπὸ κοινοῦ construction): cf. *Med.* 1330, Bond on *HF* 238.

χρή means 'it must happen', 'it is fated that': Barrett on *Hipp.* 41.

372–3 μῆτερ 'you, mother'. The structure vocative + personal pronoun (referring to the same person as the vocative) + δέ usually indicates a change of addressee, as in fact here: cf. 1287, *Hel.* 1392, Denniston 189. This applies also when the vocative is placed after the pronoun and δέ: *El.* 598, *Hel.* 1436.

ἡμῖν μηδὲν ἐμποδὼν γένηι | λέγουσα μηδὲ δρῶσα 'do not try to stop me with words or deeds'. Euripides avoids the straightforward parallelism μήτε λέγουσα μήτε δρῶσα. μηδέν colours both γένηι and λέγουσα (Denniston 194). Euripides occasionally employs even bolder constructions: 370–1n., *Tro.* 477 Τρωιὰς οὐδ' Ἑλληνὶς οὐδὲ βάρβαρος.

373–4 συμβούλου ... τυχεῖν 'and agree with me in my wish of dying before suffering shameful experiences, in a way that is unworthy <of me>'. Cf. 381, 408, 613.

375–8 Polyxena ends her speech with a general reflection, as tragic characters often do: 293–4, 627–8, 844–5, Mastronarde on *Pho.* 438–42. She strengthens the heroic concept that 'an ignoble life is a great pain' (378: cf. 342–78n.) with a more subtle, and very aristocratic, paradox: the suffering of the commoners is less painful to them because they are used to misery (*Tro.* 637–40, Cropp on *IT* 1117–21).

376 αὐχέν' ἐντιθεὶς ζυγῶι 'submitting <his> neck to the yoke', a frequent metaphor: *Tro.* 678, Fraenkel on Aesch. *Ag.* 218.

377 μᾶλλον εὐτυχέστερος 'happier'. For this form of reinforced comparative cf. Aesch. *Sept.* 673 μᾶλλον ἐνδικώτερος, K–G 1.26, and 620–1n.

379–81 The chorus leader, as often, generalises (296–8n.). She concurs with Polyxena's aristocratic view, but introduces the themes of worth and, by allusion, money, which will be central to the second half of the play (772, 1187–1237n.,1229n.).

379–80 δεινὸς χαρακτὴρ κἀπίσημος ἐν βροτοῖς | ἐσθλῶν γενέσθαι 'to be born of noble parents is an extraordinary and notable mark of distinction among human beings'. δεινός often introduces general reflections: 846n.

χαρακτήρ, from χαράσσω 'to engrave, to carve', is also the sign incised on coins (*Med.* 519, *El.* 559 and Seaford 1998: 137–8); cf. also κἀπίσημος (= καὶ ἐπίσημος) 'bearing a sign'.

380–1 κἀπὶ μεῖζον ἔρχεται | τῆς εὐγενείας ὄνομα τοῖσιν ἀξίοις 'and the renown given by noble birth becomes greater for those who deserve it', i.e. people who prove by their deeds that they are worthy of their noble birth acquire even greater fame.

382–3 τῶι καλῶι | λύπη πρόσεστιν: Iolaus feels pride and sorrow for the self-sacrifice of Heracles' daughter in the parallel scene at *Hcld.* 541–2 οὐδ' αἰσχύνομαι | τοῖς σοῖς λόγοισι, τῆι τύχηι δ' ἀλγύνομαι 'I am proud of what you said, but I suffer for your fate'. For mixed emotions of admiration and sorrow cf. 581–2, 589–92, *IA* 1404–32.

384 χάριν ... ψόγον: Hecuba is forced to accept Odysseus' point about the nature of *charis* (299–331n., 320), but reminds him of her earlier observation that human sacrifice may bring disapproval (260n.). She now tones down her statement, suggesting human (ψόγον) rather than divine disapproval (cf. 288n. φθόνος). Odysseus concedes that he is reluctant to sacrifice the girl (394–5n.).

386 πρὸς πυράν 'to the pyre'. Here and at 437, πυρά refers by synecdoche (cf. 16–17n., 1066–8n.) to the tumulus built over the pyre, as at Soph. *El.* 901. On the location of Achilles' tomb, cf. 37–9n.

387 κεντεῖτε, μὴ φείδεσθ' 'stab me, do not spare me'. At *Pho.* 968–9, Creon, like Hecuba, states his willingness to die for the polis in place of his offspring. For two verbs in asyndeton at line beginning cf. 86n.

ἐγὼ 'τεκον Πάριν 'I gave birth to Paris'. Hecuba had argued that Helen, not the Trojan prisoners, was to blame for the war (262–70n., 266n.). She now takes upon herself the blame, an argument that Helen will in fact use against her at *Tro.* 919–22. A prophecy, never mentioned in this play, warned Hecuba of the ills that Paris' birth would cause: *Andr.* 293–300, Kannicht 2004 on fr. 62e–h.

ἐγὼ 'τεκον: word-initial ε or short α can be elided after a word ending in a long vowel or diphthong ('prodelision'): Platnauer 1960, K–B I.241–2, Eur. fr. 266.3 ἐγὼ 'τεκον. If the elided vowel is accented, as here (ἔτεκον), a preceding oxytone accent (ἐγώ) does not become grave (ἐγὼ): cf. Probert 2003: 40–1.

388 παῖδα Θέτιδος: the story that Paris killed Achilles with arrows is alluded to at *Il.* 22.358–60 (de Jong 2012 *ad loc.*) and attested in the archaic epic poem *Aithiopis*: West 2003: 112–13, Burgess 2009.

389–90 'the apparition of Achilles did not ask the Greeks that you should die, old woman, but that this girl (τήνδ') should': 113–15n., 305n. The enjambment Ἀχιλλέως | φάντασμ' separates strictly connected words: 731–2n., *El.* 1020–1 Ἀχιλλέως | λέκτροισι, Battezzato 2008b: 111–16. On φάντασμα cf. 53–4n.

391 'then at least kill me together with my daughter'. The collocation δέ ... ἀλλά 'then at least' is normally found with imperatives, introducing an alternative request: Mastronarde on *Med.* 942, Denniston 10.

392 δὶς τόσον πῶμ' αἵματος 'twice as much blood to drink': the blood of two people.

393 τάδ' 'these offerings'. Hecuba uses a vague neuter plural, as if to suggest that her death was part of Achilles' request, which was not the case.

394 ἅλις κόρης σῆς θανάτος: Odysseus uses one of Hecuba's arguments (278n.) against her.

394–5 οὐ προσοιστέος | ἄλλος πρὸς ἄλλωι 'we must not add death on death'. A contrastive (278–9) or, as here, explanatory (*Alc.* 334, *Hel.* 143) asyndeton is frequent after a verbless sentence with ἅλις.

μηδὲ τόνδ' ὠφείλομεν 'I wish that we did not have <to add> this one either'. The imperfect of ὀφείλω (here ὠφείλομεν) expresses a contrary-to-fact wish, in Homeric style (*Il.* 6.350, Goodwin 1912: §734–5), with προσφέρειν understood from 394. The aorist ὤφελον, also Homeric, is more usual in classical Greek in this meaning (Mastronarde on *Med.* 1). Odysseus' reluctance is consistent with his earlier statement that he acts under the orders of the army (218–22); the chorus, on the contrary, stressed his crucial role in deciding the death of Polyxena (131–43). For μηδέ 'not either' cf. 255, Denniston 190, Fraenkel on Aesch. *Ag.* 1498.

397 'How come? I am not aware that I acquired masters.' Odysseus reacts to ἀνάγκη (396), a word which implies 'slavery' (362n., 1293–5n.). δεσπότας κεκτημένος is a pun, reversing the usual relationship between master and slave: cf. 448–9 δουλόσυνος ... κτηθεῖσ(α), Ar. *Plut.* 4 τῶι κεκτημένωι 'to the master' (of a slave).

398 ὅμοια 'it does not matter', a complete sentence, as ὅμοιον in *Suppl.* 1069. The MS text ὁποῖα 'like' is intolerable with ὅπως 'like' in the same sentence. In *Tro.* 146–8 (ὡσεὶ ... ὅπως) the text is suspect.

κισσὸς δρυὸς ὅπως τῆσδ' ἕξομαι 'I will cling to her like ivy to oak'. The adverb ὅπως comes often after the word it refers to: cf. 1079–81n. and ὥστε at 205n. The roles of mother and daughter are reversed: the young Polyxena is compared to an oak (a proverbially old tree). At *Med.* 1213 Creon clings to his dying daughter like ivy to laurel tree.

399 σοφωτέροις 'to people wiser than you'. On *sophia* cf. 228n., 1007n., 1187–1237n.

400 ὡς at sentence-beginning marks a 'strong asseveration' (Mastronarde on *Med.* 609) and can be translated as 'bear well in mind that', as if εὖ ἴσθι preceded: K–G II.372, Diggle 1981: 88.

401 ἀλλ' οὐδ' ἐγὼ μὴν τήνδ' ἄπειμ' αὐτοῦ λιπών 'but *I* will not go away and leave this woman here either'. For the interlaced word order (the participle λιπών governs τήνδ'), cf. 44n., *Andr.* 918 καί μ' ἔρημον οἴχεται λιπών, Stinton 1990: 102.

402–4 [καὶ σύ, παῖ Λαερτίου, | χάλα τοκεῦσιν εἰκότως θυμουμένοις, | σύ τ', ὦ τάλαινα,] 'and you, son of Laertes, yield to a parent who is reasonably angry, and you, unhappy one'. These words are unlikely to be part of the original text. The adverb εἰκότως 'reasonably' is too weak for the context, and θυμουμένοις 'angry' does not correspond to Hecuba's feelings in the scene: she is suicidal and desperate, rather than angry. Moreover, the imperative πιθοῦ is normally placed immediately before the order or advice given by the speaker (*Cycl.* 309–10, *Hcld.* 174–75, *Or.* 1101); if it is not, the advice occurs before the imperative πιθοῦ (*Alc.* 1097–1101, *Hipp.* 891–92). Finally, the reference of χάλα is unexpressed and unclear (contrast fr. 716.2–3 φρονήματος | χάλα). Polyxena does not ask Odysseus to 'give way' or 'relent' towards Hecuba and accept Hecuba's request to spare her daughter. The lines may have been introduced in order to explain Odysseus' inaction until 432, when Polyxena addresses him after taking leave from her mother. For interpolations starting at mid-line cf. *Alc.* 795–6, Diggle 1994: 162.

τοκεῦσιν: poetic plural (265n.)

405–6 ἑλκῶσαί τε σὸν | γέροντα χρῶτα 'and wound your own old body'. Polyxena uses active verbs (here ἑλκῶσαι, 407 ἀσχημονῆσαι), presenting Hecuba's ill treatment at the hands of the Greeks as self-wounding. The harsh enjambment after σόν (389–90n.) reinforces the point.

407 ἀσχημονῆσαι 'disgrace yourself'.

ἐκ νέου βραχίονος 'as a consequence of the action of a youthful arm', i.e. 'by the arms of young (soldiers)' (14–15n.) indicates the complement of agent (23–4n.), in reference to 408 σπασθεῖσ'.

408 σπασθεῖσ': 207–8n.

ἃ πείσηι '<abuses> that you will suffer' if you do not let me go. The antecedent of the relative pronoun ἅ is omitted, as often: it is in apposition to the sentences of 405–7.

μὴ σύ γ' 'don't *you*, please!', a colloquial expression: Mastronarde on *Pho.* 532, Collard 2005: 367.

409–11 ἡδίστην ... πανύστατον 'give me your beloved hand, and allow me to press my cheek to yours, for <I will> never <do it> again, but this is the very last time'. The imperative δός takes two different constructions (zeugma: 954–5n.): the simple accusative ('give me your hand') and the infinitive ('allow me to ...'). For the gesture cf. *Ion* 1438, *Pho.* 306–9.

[412] An interpolator provided a finite verb for the elliptical sentence in 411, changing its meaning (W. S. Barrett 2007: 68–72): 'For I will never see again the ray and the orb of the sun, but this is the very last time.' For similar interpolations cf. *Or.* 139, *Ba.* 1028, Willink on *Or.* 1024. The absence of 412 from the earliest manuscripts is a strong argument against its authenticity: Mastronarde on *Pho.* 1346. It is rhetorically stronger to have Polyxena focus on her request of a last embrace rather than let her expand on the farewell to the sun: Ferrari 1985: 45–6, Kovacs 1996: 60–1. Lines 411–12 occur in almost identical form at *Alc.* 207–8 (cf. Parker *ad loc.*). Tragic characters facing death often bid farewell to the light of day (435, *Alc.* 244, *IA* 1506, Aesch. *Ag.* 1323–4); interpolators occasionally expanded these passages (Finglass on Soph. *Ai.* 856–8).

414 ὦ μῆτερ ὦ τεκοῦσ' 'O mother that gave me life'. The repeated ὦ may link syntactically connected words, e.g. adjective and noun/proper name: *Cycl.* 266 ὦ κάλλιστον ὦ Κυκλώπιον, *Tro.* 601 ὦ πατρίς ὦ μελέα, *Ion* 112–14, Liapis on [Eur.] *Rhes.* 357–9. The redundant participle τεκοῦσ' (*Pho.* 1270, Battezzato 2008b: 6–7) stresses the bond of affection (421n.).

415–22 Diggle transposes 415–16 after 420, making ἐκεῖ (418) refer to κάτω (414). However, the series of vocatives in 414–15 is typical of tragic dialogue (424–5, *Med.* 1363–4, *Pho.* 1270–2 ὦ τεκοῦσα μῆτερ ... ὦ θύγατερ, 1701–2), and the reference of ἐκεῖ (418) is made clear by ἐν Ἅιδου in the same line: Mastronarde 1988: 157.

415 ἡμεῖς δ' ἐν φάει δουλεύσομεν 'we, on the contrary, will be slaves under the light' of the sun, i.e. 'I will keep on living, but as a slave' (cf. 167–9n.). Hecuba contrasts ἐν φάει with 414 κάτω.

416 ἄνυμφος ἀνυμέναιος ὦν μ' ἐχρῆν τυχεῖν 'deprived of the husband and of the nuptial song that I should have had as my lot'. The syntax continues 414. ὦν is a gen. of separation after adjectives with alpha privative (Smyth §1428, Cooper and Krüger 2002: 2087–8) and refers to the nouns νυμφίος and ὑμέναιος implied by ἄνυμφος ἀνυμέναιος (709–12n.). Young women facing death often voice similar regrets, whether they die willingly (*Hcld.* 579, 591, *IA* 1398) or are subject to violence (Soph. *Ant.* 813–16). Polyxena's death deprives her of marriage, but can be seen as a sort of wedding to Achilles (523n., 612n.).

417 For the ellipsis of εἶ 'you are' cf. 240n.

419 τί δράσω; cf. 736–7n.

ποῖ τελευτήσω βίον; 'Where will I go to end my life?' The verb implies that Hecuba will move somewhere else to die; this explains ποῖ 'to what place'. Hecuba, like the chorus (447 ποῖ), does not know her final destination as a slave; Polymestor's revelation will come as a complete surprise (1259–73).

420 Polyxena stresses that she is now a slave (as in 357–8), rather than drawing attention to the freedom of her choice (367–8n., 550).

421 Hecuba in fact bore only nineteen of Priam's fifty children (361n.). She presents herself as mother of all of them in her feelings, thus displaying extreme devotion to her husband (*Andr.* 222–7).

422–3 Tragic characters imagine that, after death, it will be possible to speak to the dead in the underworld: Soph. *Ai.* 865.

423 Cf. 786n., 811.

424 Breastfeeding creates a bond of affection that mothers often recall in the proximity of death: *Il.* 22.80, Garvie on Aesch. *Cho.* 896–8, Mastronarde on *Pho.* 1568. Here Polyxena inverts the *topos*, thanking Hecuba for her motherly cares.

425 ὦ τῆς ἀώρου θύγατερ ἀθλία τύχης 'O my daughter, unhappy because of your untimely lot!' For the genitive cf. 156–8n. The MSS assimilate the ending of the adjective ἀθλία to that of τύχης, with a clumsy accumulation of adjectives in asyndeton. 'Untimely death' is a frequent theme in farewell scenes (*Or.* 1029–30, *IA* 1218) and funerary epigrams (Noussia-Fantuzzi 2010: 389 on Solon 27.18 West).

426–8 Κασσάνδρα ... κάσις: in the nominative, cf. 328–31n.

χαῖρε ... μοι 'farewell'. μοι is an ethical dative (Smyth §1486), implying 'please do this for me'.

χαίρουσιν ἄλλοι 'other people feel joy', a pun on 426 χαῖρ᾽ 'farewell' (formally an imperative from χαίρω 'I rejoice'). Similar wordplay occurs often: *Pho.* 618, *Or.* 1083, Fraenkel on Aesch. *Ag.* 251ff.

Θρηιξί: on the form with eta (Hermann: MSS Θραξί) cf. 81n.

429–30 For the audience, Polyxena's attempt to comfort Hecuba must be tragically ironic: Hecuba will in fact bury her son, an experience perceived as a reversal of the natural order of things (*Tro.* 1181–6).

431 Hecuba's sorrows make her see herself as a dead person before her actual death (cf. 668n., 784), like Antigone (Soph. *Ant.* 559–60) and Helen (*Hel.* 286).

432 ἀμφιθεὶς κάραι πέπλον 'putting my cloak around my head', in shame (972n.). For the singular πέπλον cf. *IT* 1218 πέπλον ὀμμάτων προθέσθαι. For the construction cf. *Med.* 787 λαβοῦσα κόσμον ἀμφιθῆι χροΐ, *Ion* 1433. The majority MS reading ἀμφιθεὶς κάρα πέπλοις construes the verb with the accusative of object encircled and the instrumental dative, as with περιβάλλω: *Cycl.* 330 δοραῖσι θηρῶν σῶμα περιβαλὼν ἐμόν, Garvie on Aesch. *Cho.* 576. However, περιβάλλω is distant from ἀμφιτίθημι in etymology and meaning. The majority MS text presumably arose from an accidental omission of the iota in κάραι, and from a subsequent attempt to make sense of the text.

Polyxena asks Odysseus to veil her 'because' (433 ὡς ... γ᾽) she feels she is already dead, even before being sacrificed (cf. 431n.). People on the verge of death (Eur. *Hipp.* 1458, Pl. *Phd.* 118a6–12) as well as dead bodies (*Tro.* 627) are often veiled. Veiling occurs frequently in tragedy, with different symbolic implications, such as shame or grief: Telò 2002: 38–75, Cairns 2011.

433–4 ἐκτέτηκα καρδίαν | θρήνοισι μητρὸς τήνδε τ᾽ ἐκτήκω γόοις 'I am melted in my heart by my mother's wails, and I melt her with my laments'. ἐκτέτηκα is a perfect intransitive from the verb ἐκτήκω 'to melt', an intensified form of τήκω (cf. Bond on *HF* 18). These verbs may indicate emotional distress or the wasting away of the body through grief or tears (*Or.* 134–5 ὄμμα δ' ἐκτήξουσ' ἐμὸν | δακρύοις). A comparable repeated emphasis on τήκω occurs in *Od.* 19.204–9, in reference to Penelope 'melting' beside the disguised Odysseus (R. Hunter, personal communication).

435: [412n.].

436–7 μέτεστι δ' οὐδὲν πλὴν ὅσον χρόνον ξίφους | βαίνω μεταξὺ καὶ πυρᾶς Ἀχιλλέως 'I have a share in the light <of the sun> [i.e. of life] only for the time that it takes me to walk from here to the sword and the pyre of Achilles'. The two elements ξίφους … καὶ πυρᾶς Ἀχιλλέως express a single concept (hendiadys), 'Achilles' pyre, where I will be killed by the sword': cf. 70n., 227n., *Pho.* 365, Sansone 1984. Both genitives indicate the point of arrival. The point of departure is to be understood from the context, as in the other occurrence of μεταξύ 'between' as a preposition in tragedy, Soph. *OC* 290–1 τὰ δὲ | μεταξὺ τούτου 'for the time between <the present and> that moment'. Usually, when two words in the genitive depend upon the preposition μεταξύ, they indicate the limits of the action in space or time (Thuc. 1.97.1 μεταξὺ τοῦδε τοῦ πολέμου καὶ τοῦ Μηδικοῦ).

438 λύεται δέ μου μέλη 'my limbs are loosened'. Hecuba falls to the ground (cf. 486–7n., 495–6, 499–502), as Iolaus does at *Hcld.* 602–3 λύεται μέλη | λύπηι: Telò 2002: 18–37. Hecuba's language echoes Homeric phrases such as λύντο δὲ γυῖα (*Il.* 7.16) and λῦσε δὲ γυῖα (*Il.* 4.469), mostly used to describe the collapsing to the ground of dying warriors, and λύτο γούνατα καὶ φίλον ἦτορ, which usually suggests the overwhelming psychological effect of strong emotions (*Il.* 21.114, *Od.* 4.703, 5.297). Hecuba is lying on the ground when the *Trojan Women* begins (*Tro.* 37).

[441–3] 'I wish that I could see Helen of Sparta, the sister of the two Dioscuri, in this condition: for with her fair eyes she seized the rich city of Troy in the most dishonourable way.' The etymology Ἑλένην … εἷλε is repeated in *Tro.* 892, and echoes that of Aesch. *Ag.* 687–90 Ἑλέναν … ἑλέπτολις. Helen's eyes cause ruin, as at Aesch. *Ag.* 742 and *Tro.*772–3 ὄλοιο· καλλίστων γὰρ ὀμμάτων ἄπο | αἰσχρῶς τὰ κλεινὰ πεδί᾽ ἀπώλεσας Φρυγῶν, a possible model for the interpolator. The lines are unlikely to be by Euripides: it is implausible that Hecuba, after falling to the ground and saying 'I am done for', would resume speaking with such fierceness (Finglass 2006: 258–60). In the next episode, her characterisation as extremely dejected is consistent with 438–40, not [441–3]: she is wrapped tightly in her robes (486–7: cf. Polyxena at 432) and resists Talthybius' attempt to engage her in conversation and make her sit up (499–507). It is possible that an actor interpolated the lines in order to expand his role, adapting 943–4 τὰν τοῖν Διοσκούροιν Ἑλέναν κάσιν.

ὥς 'so', i.e. taken to her death like Polyxena. The form ὥς for οὕτως rarely occurs in Attic, except in some set phrases (888n., LSJ s.v. ὡς Aa 1–2, Fraenkel on Aesch. *Ag.* 930).

444–83 FIRST STASIMON

The chorus imagine their future life in Greece. The stasimon is a variation on the so-called 'escape odes' (cf. Barrett on *Hipp.* 732–75, Swift 2009), in which choruses express their wish to reach fantastic destinations (sky, etc.). Here the chorus select real-world destinations such as the Peloponnese, Thessaly, Delos and Athens, but imagine that, even as slaves, they will perform ritual acts that are normally reserved for free women (see esp. 455–74). Only at 457 and 475–83 do they realistically mourn their fate.

The imagination of the chorus is not inconsistent with possible (if unlikely) scenarios in Greek epic or tragedy (462–3n.). They imagine they will sing for Artemis in Delos (455–65). Similarly, in *IT* 123–31, a chorus of slave women (*IT* 131 δούλα, 1111–16) sing a cult song for Artemis/Dictynna. The chorus of the *Phoenician Women* describe themselves as 'slave<s> to Phoebus' (221 Φοίβωι λάτρις), and hope that they will 'become a chorus' in Delphi (234–8). Here, the Trojan women imagine they will weave a *peplos* for Athena in Athens (466–74). In *Iliad* 6.288–95, Hecuba offers Athena a *peplos* woven by Phoenician women that Paris had abducted (or bought?) as slaves (cf. Graziosi and Haubold *ad loc.*): the chorus imagine that they will perform the ritual acts that slave women perform in Troy. Cf. also the story about the Locrian Maidens, who acted as slaves in the Temple of Athena at Troy (1008n., Timaeus 566 F 146).

In a very similar passage of the *Trojan Women* (176–229), the chorus wonder where in Greece they will be taken as slaves, and 'rank some possible destinations in terms of their desirability (202–29)' (Gibert 2011: 389), listing Corinth, Athens (top choice), Sparta (envisaged as the worst possibility), Thessaly, Sicily and Thurii. Ranking is not explicit in this stasimon of *Hecuba*, but the chorus' hostility to Sparta (649–57), the order of places and the distribution of descriptive adjectives suggests a similar judgement: Dorian Greece (worst), (Aeolic) Thessaly (third best? 452 καλλίστων ὑδάτων), (Ionian) Delos (second best, 460–1 φίλον ... ἄγαλμα, 465 εὐλογήσω), (Attic) Athens (best destination, 467–8 καλλιδίφρους ... κροκέωι). Mastronarde 2010: 143 suggests that 'the first three stanzas ... display an assimilation to the native Greek point of view ... This hybrid viewpoint can in part be ascribed to the Hellenic (and in the second strophe Attic) chauvinism of Attic tragedy.' On ethnicity and Panhellenic appeal see also Visvardi 2011.

COMMENTARY: 444-83   133

The chorus do not sing in praise of Polyxena, as other choruses do
under similar circumstances (*Hcld.* 621-8, *Pho.* 1054-66; Rosivach 1975,
Mossman 1995: 77-81). The only choral praise for Polyxena, warm but
brief, occurs at 379-81. Polyxena's self-sacrifice does not provide any
benefit for the community: 260n., 346-8n.

Metre

The stasimon is in Aeolic metre (cf. in general Itsumi 1984, Lourenço
2011 91-116). The cola are often linked by word-overlap of one
syllable ('dovetailing': West 1982: 6 and 117): 447-9, 458-60,
471-2, 480-1.

The last long element of a glyconic is resolved at 452 and 453, a feature
frequent in later plays of Euripides (*IT* 1106, Itsumi 1984: 78).
The dodrans (469~478) is followed by glyconic, with dovetailing, as
here, in *Hel.* 517. The Aeolic hexasyllable (474~483) is identical to the
glyconic minus the last two elements, which may suggest a clausular
rhythm: cf. Lourenço 2011: 111, and *Alc.* 270.

The clausular rhythm suggests that period-end occurred at 446~457
(glyconic ba = phalaecian), 450~461 (aristophanean). At 464-5 χρυσέαν
measures – – (synizesis of εα). At 449 ἀφίξομαι measures ⏑ – ⏑ ⏑ (shortening
in hiatus: 59-97n. 'Metre'). Soph. *Phil.* 1125-6~1148-9 provides two solid
parallels for the responsion between – ⏑ and ⏑ – at 446~457. Willink 2005:
502-3 suggested τάλαιναν πόνοις βιοτὰν ἔχουσ' ἄοικος in order to achieve
exact responsion in the first two elements at 446~457.

First Strophe and First Antistrophe: 444-54~455-66

	– – – ⏑ ⏑ – ⌒ ‖ʰ¹	pherecratean ‖ʰ¹
444	αὔρα, ποντιὰς αὔρα,	
455	ἢ νάσων, ἁλιήρει	

	– ⏓ – ⏑ ⏑ – ⏑ –	glyconic
445	ἅτε ποντοπόρους κομί-	
456	κώπαι πεμπομένα, τάλαι-	

	⏓ ⏓ – ⏑ ⏑ – ⏑ – ⏑ – ⌒ ‖ᵇ²	glyconic ba ‖ᵇ²
446	ζεις θοὰς ἀκάτους ἐπ' οἶδμα λίμνας,	
457	ναν οἰκτρὰ βιοτὰν ἔχουσ' ἄοικος,	

	– ⏑ – ⏑⏑ – ⏑ –	glyconic
447	ποῖ με τὰν μελέαν πορεύ-	
458	ἔνθα πρωτόγονός τε φοῖ-	

COMMENTARY: 444–83

	− − − ⏑ ⏑ − ⏑ −	glyconic
448	σεις; τῶι δουλόσυνος πρὸς οἷ-	
459	νιξ δάφνα θ' ἱεροὺς ἀνέ-	
	− − − ⏓ − ⏑ ⏑ −	wilamowitzian
449	κον κτηθεῖσ' ἀφίξομαι; ἢ	
460	σχε πτόρθους Λατοῖ φίλον ὠ-	
	− ⏑ ⏑ − ⏑ − ⌒ ||ᶜ	aristophanean ||ᶜ
450	Δωρίδος ὅρμον αἴας,	
461	δῖνος ἄγαλμα Δίας·	
	− − ⏑⏑ − ⏑ −	telesillean
451	ἢ Φθιάδος ἔνθα τὸν	
462	σὺν Δηλιάσιν τε κού-	
	− ⏒ − ⏑ ⏑ − ⏑ ⏓	glyconic
452	καλλίστων ὑδάτων πατέρα	
463	ραισιν Ἀρτέμιδος θεᾶς	
	− ⏓ − ⏑ ⏑ − ⏑ ⏓ ⏑ − ⌒ |||	glyconic ba |||
453–4	φασὶν Ἀπιδανὸν πεδία λιπαίνειν,	
464–5	χρυσέαν τ' ἄμπυκα τόξα τ' εὐλογήσω·	

Second Strophe and Second Antistrophe: 466–74~475–83

	− − ⏑ ⏑ − ⏑ ⌒ ||ᶜ?	telesillean ||ᶜ?
466	ἢ Παλλάδος ἐν πόλει	
475	ὤιμοι τεκέων ἐμῶν,	
	− − ⏑ ⏑ − ⏑ −	telesillean
467	τὰς καλλιδίφρους Ἀθα-	
476	ὤιμοι πατέρων χθονός θ',	
	− − − ⏑ ⏑ − ⏑ ⌒ ||ᶜ?	glyconic ||ᶜ?
468	ναίας ἐν κροκέωι πέπλωι	
477	ἃ καπνῶι κατερείπεται	
	− ⏑ ⏑ − ⏑ −	dodrans
469	ζεύξομαι ἆρα πώ-	
478	τυφομένα δορί-	
	− ⏑ − ⏑ ⏑ − ⏑ −	glyconic
470	λους ἐν δαιδαλέαισι ποι-	
479	κτητος Ἀργείων· ἐγὼ δ'	

	− − − ⏑ ⏑ − ⏑ −	glyconic
471	κίλλουσ᾽ ἀνθοκρόκοισι πή-	
480	ἐν ξείναι χθονὶ δὴ κέκλη-	
	− − − ⏑ − ⏑ ⏑ ⌢ ||^{c?}	wilamowitzian ||^{c?}
472	ναις ἢ Τιτάνων γενεάν,	
481	μαι δούλα, λιποῦσ᾽ Ἀσίαν,	
	− − − ⏑ ⏑ − − −	glyconic
473	τὰν Ζεὺς ἀμφιπύρωι κοιμί-	
482	Εὐρώπας θεραπνᾶν ἀλλά-	
	− − − ⏑ ⏑ ⌢ |||	Aeolic hexasyllable |||
474	ζει φλογμῶι Κρονίδας;	
483	ξασ᾽ Ἄιδα θαλάμους.	

444–6 'wind, wind of the sea, you who carry the swift sea-crossing ships over the swelling of the deep'. The stasimon begins in hymnic style, with reduplication of the vocative, and a relative sentence, introduced by the epic form ἅτε (fem. from ὅστε), listing the usual actions or powers of supernatural beings: Willink on *Or.* 321–3 Εὐμενίδες, αἵτε ..., *Ion* 907–8, Diggle 1994: 325.

ποντιάς is a recherché form, used also by Pindar (*Nem.* 4.36), and equivalent to ποντία (fem. from πόντιος: 610, Pind. *Nem.* 5.36): Chantraine 1933: 37–58.

οἴδμα 26n.

448–9 τῶι δουλόσυνος πρὸς οἶ|κον κτηθεῖσ᾽ ἀφίξομαι; 'Bought by whom as a slave shall I arrive to <his> house?' The interrogative pronoun τῶι (dat. of τίς) 'by whom?' is connected with the participle κτηθεῖσ᾽ 'bought', rather than with the main verb: 177–9n. For the dative of agent (255n.) with the participle cf. Aesch. *Sept.* 691 Φοίβωι στυγηθέν, George 2005: 51–9, 78–102.

δουλόσυνος 'as a slave', a poetic adjective coined by Euripides, equivalent to δοῦλος/δούλιος: cf. μαντόσυνον 'oracular' (*Andr.* 1032), κηδοσύνωι 'anxious' (*Or.* 1017), Chantraine 1933: 210–11.

κτηθεῖσ᾽ 'acquired, bought', an aor. passive form of the middle κτάομαι 'I acquire': cf. Thuc. 1.123.1 ἐκτήθη, Smyth §813.

449–54 ἢ | Δωρίδος ὅρμον αἴας ... πεδία λιπαίνειν 'either to a harbour of the Dorian land or to <one> of <the land of> Phthia, where they say that Apidanus, the father of the most beautiful waters, fertilises the plains'. As in *Tro.* 234, the chorus of Trojan slaves designate as 'Dorian' the area where Agamemnon and Menelaus had their kingdoms, the Peloponnese: cf. Soph. *OC* 1301 'Dorian Argos', Rosivach 1975: 354–5.

451 ἢ Φθιάδος: supply ὅρμον αἴας from the previous line. Phthia, in Thessaly, is the kingdom of Peleus and Achilles (*Il.* 1.155–71).

453–4 Ἀπιδανόν: the Apidanus is a tributary of the main river of Thessaly, the Peneius. Its name is not attested in Greek poetry before Euripides.

λιπαίνειν: in *Ba.* 572–5 Euripides transfers the same praise to the Lydias, a Macedonian river.

455–65 The chorus describe possible future choral song and dances: their present performance is an allusion to and a partial enactment of their future one. Henrichs 1994 and 1996 studies this technique, which he calls 'choral projection'. On Delos cf. also *IT* 1096–1105. Other choral festivals mentioned in Euripides' stasima include *Hel.* 1465–74, *Hcld.* 777–83, *El.* 167–80.

455–7 ἢ νάσων, ἁλιήρει | κώπαι πεμπομένα, τάλαι|ναν οἰκτρὰ βιοτὰν ἔχουσ᾽ ἄοικος 'or <shall I arrive> at <the harbour> of the island, carried by the oar that rows in the sea, having a miserable life, pitiable, deprived of a house ... ?'

νάσων (= Attic νήσων) is a poetic plural (265n.) referring to Delos.

πεμπομένα ... ἔχουσ᾽ are in agreement with the subject of 449 ἀφίξομαι. For two adjectives referring to the same noun or pronoun cf. *Suppl.* 1131 ἐγὼ δ᾽ ἔρημος ἀθλίου πατρὸς τάλας, Diggle 1994: 95, 418. For the interlaced order, often corrupted in MSS, cf. 44n., 401n. The MSS corrupt the endings of the participles πεμπομένα ... ἔχουσα to the accusative, under the influence of τάλαιναν ... βιοτάν: Willink 2005: 501–2. In the MS text, πεμπομένα and ἔχουσα continue the syntax of 447–8 ποῖ με ... πορεύσεις;, ignoring the syntax of 448–54.

458–61 'where the first palm tree and the first bay tree that was born raised their sacred branches for Leto, as a fond homage to Zeus's offspring'.

πρωτόγονός τε φοῖ|νιξ δάφνα θ᾽: Leto gave birth to Apollo and Artemis in a kneeling position, leaning on the palm and the bay tree, which the chorus imagine were first brought into existence on this occasion. The palm is a traditional element of the story (Richardson 2010 on *Hymn.Hom.Ap.* 16–19, 117), but the bay tree (*Ion* 919–22), sacred to Apollo, and sometimes the olive tree, are mentioned: *IT* 1099–1102 φοίνικά θ᾽ ... δάφναν τ᾽ ... καὶ ... θαλλὸν ... ἐλαίας, Λατοῦς ὠδῖνι φίλον, which rephrases the present passage.

φοῖνιξ: on the accent see on κῆρυξ, 104–6n.

ἀνέσχε: the singular verb is to be understood with both subjects: 21–2n.

460–1 φίλον ὠ|δῖνος ἄγαλμα Δίας: the phrase is an internal apposition, referring to the effect of the action described in the main verb ἀνέσχε: Barrett on *Hipp.* 752–7, Aesch. *Cho.* 199–200 συμπενθεῖν ἐμοί, | ἄγαλμα τύμβου τοῦδε. Gregory and others take the phrase as an apposition to φοῖνιξ δάφνα θ', which is grammatically possible, but merely focuses on the trees; if the phrase is an apposition to the sentence it emphasises their miraculous action.

φίλον: for the word order cf. 44n. The MSS text φίλαι arose by assimilation to the dative ending of Λατοῖ.

ὠδῖνος: lit. 'birth-pangs' by metonymy designates the product of birth-pangs, i.e. the newborn gods.

ἄγαλμα 'what pleases', 'delight': Griffith on *Ant.* 704, Wilamowitz and Bond on *HF* 49.

Δίας: genitive of the adjective Δῖος. In tragedy it can mean 'pertaining to Zeus' (*Alc.* 5, *Ba.* 245), as here, and for this reason should be capitalised. In epic the adjective is used in the less specific meaning 'godlike', and is not capitalised. Both meanings are etymological: Chantraine 1968–80 and Beekes 2010 s.v.

462–3 σὺν Δηλιάσιν τε κού|ραισιν 'and <where> with the Delian maidens', who sing in honour of the gods in the island, generation after generation, making sure that songs for the gods will never cease: *Hymn. Hom.Ap.* 156–76, Bond on *HF* 687–90. The slave women imagine that they, as *hierodouloi*, will be able to take part in rituals that are in fact reserved to free women. For slave women taking part in cult, see the chorus of *Choephori*; for *hierodouloi*, compare the chorus of *Phoenician Women*: Battezzato 2016: 142–4.

463–5 Ἀρτέμιδος ... εὐλογήσω; 'shall I praise the golden diadem and the bow and arrows of the goddess Artemis?' Divine objects are typically made of gold: Eur. *Med.* 633–4 (Aphrodite's arrows), *Il.* 24.341 (Hermes' uncomfortable golden sandals). In epic, Artemis is called χρυσηλάκατος 'of the golden distaff' (*Il.* 16.183). τόξα 'bow', esp. in the plural, often refers to the arrows as well.

467–70 τὰς καλλιδίφρους Ἀθα|ναίας ἐν κροκέωι πέπλωι | ζεύξομαι ἆρα πώ|λους 'shall I yoke the horses of Athena, the goddess that has a beautiful chariot, in her saffron-coloured *peplos*?' The saffron-coloured *peplos* was traditionally offered to the goddess at the Athenian Panathenaea: cf. Strattis fr. 31, Vian 1952: 251–3, Barber 1992. The weaver is imagined as performing the action she creates on the woven *peplos*.

τὰς καλλιδίφρους Ἀθαναίας ... πώλους: six words separate the adjective from the noun: cf. 1081–4, *Pho.* 808–10 Καδμογενῆ ... γένναν (nine words), *IA* 1036–39 τίν' ... ἰαχάν (fourteen words), Breitenbach 1934: 242–7. The intervening words are combined into two strictly connected phrases (ἐν κροκέωι πέπλωι and ζεύξομαι ἆρα), which makes interpretation of the syntax easier.

467 καλλιδίφρους 'that have a beautiful chariot'. Cf. *Il.* 7.139 καλλίζωνοί τε γυναῖκες 'and women who have beautiful girdles', Eur. *Ion* 189 καλλιβλέφαρον φῶς 'the light [= face] that has beautiful eyelashes', Kannicht on *Hel.* 1. The chariot belongs to Athena, who is often portrayed riding on it (Demargne 1984: 974 and 990). The audience could (but need not) transfer the adjective to Ἀθαναίας, the genitive defining πώλους. For the figure of speech ('enallage' or 'hypallage') see Mastronarde on *Pho.* 1351 λευκοπήχεις κτύπους χεροῖν, Bers 1974, Smyth §3027.

467–8 Ἀθα|ναίας refers 'in common' (370–1n.) to τὰς καλλιδίφρους ... πώλους and to ἐν κροκέωι πέπλωι.

469 ἄρα is never elsewhere placed so late in the sentence (eleventh word): cf. *Or.* 1512 (fourth word) and Denniston 49. The position of ἄρα, etymologically related and similar, in tragic usage, to ἆρα, is much freer: *Ion* 790, Denniston 41. The text is doubtful, but no satisfactory conjecture has been advanced.

470–2 ἐν δαιδαλέαισι ποι|κίλλουσ᾽ ἀνθοκρόκοισι πή|ναις 'creating an image of different colours with artistically interwoven flowery threads'.

δαιδαλέαισι 'well wrought', in connection with the mythical artist Daedalus.

ἀνθοκρόκοισι 'of the colours of flowers', lit. 'with a weft of flowers', cf. κρόκη 'weft, thread', κρέκω 'to weave' (not related to κρόκος 'saffron'). The second element of the compound is redundant, esp. in this context (πήναις): 473–4n., Pind. *Ol.* 6.39 φοινικόκροκον ζώναν 'a crimson girdle', Aesch. *Sept.* 857 μελάγκροκον 'black'.

472 Τιτάνων γενεάν 'the race of Titans'. The battle against the Giants (not Titans) was traditionally represented on the *peplos* for Athena: Strattis fr. 73 K–A, Stamatopoulou 2012: 72–3. According to traditional accounts, Athena was not yet born when Zeus fought with the Titans: Hes. *Th.* 886–900 and 617–720, Vian 1952: 169–83. The conflation of Titans and Giants becomes common in Hellenistic and especially Roman literature, but Athena's involvement in the Titanomachy is already securely attested in Epicharmus 135 K–A and Eur. *IT* 222–4: Battezzato 2016: 144–6.

473–4 'which Zeus, son of Cronus, puts to sleep with his blaze that has fire at both ends'. Zeus's thunderbolt is imagined as a shaft burning at both ends; he used it in the battle against the Giants (*Ion* 212 κεραυνὸν ἀμφίπυρον, West 2007: 251–3). Here, the second part of the compound adjective (-πύρωι) repeats an idea already expressed in the noun φλογμῶι: cf. 470–2n., 701n., Soph. *OT* 518 βίου ... τοῦ μακραίωνος.

τάν 'which' (= Attic τήν). In imitation of Homeric language, tragedians use tau-forms of the article as relatives, especially when metrically convenient (cf. 635, where ἄν cannot be substituted for τάν). In trimeters, Euripides uses them only when metrically necessary: K–G 1.587–8, Diggle 1994: 32–3, 466–7. The regular relative pronoun ἄν would be metrically acceptable in this passage.

κοιμίζει 'puts to sleep', in fact 'defeats', as in *Pho.* 184 (of the thunderbolt). The verb can be a euphemism for 'to kill' (*Tro.* 594). However, Titans and supernatural beings such as Ate (Aesch. *Cho.* 1076 μετακοιμισθέν) cannot be killed, but only imprisoned or made inactive.

475–8 'Alas for my children, alas for my fathers and my country, which is in ruins, consumed in smoke'. For the genitive of cause cf. 182n.

478–9 δορί|κτητος Ἀργείων 'conquered by the spear of the Argives'. The genitive Ἀργείων refers to the first part of the compound adjective, as in Soph. *Ai.* 508 πολλῶν ἐτῶν κληροῦχον 'whose allotted portion is many years' (= old). The genitive does not indicate the agent; it indicates the agent only with adjectives formed with a negative prefix: *OC* 1722–3 κακῶν δυσάλωτος 'not touched by sorrows', Moorhouse 1982: 68–9, K–G 1.401–2.

480–1 κέκλη|μαι δούλα: the chorus will not escape the name that Polyxena avoids with her death (551–2n.).

482–3 Εὐρώπας θεραπνᾶν ἀλλά|ξασ' Ἅιδα θαλάμους 'reaching a dwelling in Europe in exchange for the realms of Hades'. The chorus refer to their defeated city, and the possibility of being killed (at the fall of Troy, or here in Thrace), as the 'realm of Hades'. 'This acknowledges the chorus' unheroic fate as survivors in exile and slavery' (D. J. Mastronarde, personal communication).

θεραπνᾶν is the 'Doric' genitive plural of θεράπνη 'dwelling'. The MSS MO read Εὐρώπας θεράπναν ἀλλάξασ', Ἅιδα θαλάμους 'reaching Europe, the realm of Hades', which gives acceptable grammar but a less apt meaning: death is naturally associated with Troy, rather than with Europe. Euripides wrote no accents, and we are free to accent the words as it seems best.

ἀλλάξασ' 'exchanging', i.e. 'leaving': *IT* 135 ἐξαλλάξασ' 'having left', Soph. *Ant.* 945 ἀλλάξαι. The genitive θεραπνᾶν indicates what is taken in exchange: Aesch. *PV* 966–7 τῆς σῆς λατρείας τὴν ἐμὴν δυσπραξίαν | ... οὐκ ἂν ἀλλάξαιμ' ἐγώ 'I would not give my misfortune in exchange for your slavery'. Verbs of exchanging are also often used with the accusative of what is taken/reached and the genitive of what is left: 1059–60n., *IT* 396–7 Ἀσιήτιδα γαῖαν Εὐρώπας διαμείψας. Euripides avoided the possible, but less recherché, construction Εὐρώπας θεράπναν ἀλλάξασ' Ἅιδα θαλάμων.

484–628 SECOND EPISODE

The messenger narrative, followed by Hecuba's comments, is the focus of the episode. The messenger arrives after the choral song, as usual (de Jong 1991: 119 n. 6, Taplin 1977: 80–5 and 167–9). He has a specific message to give: Agamemnon orders Hecuba to bury her daughter (508–10). The addressees of messenger speeches are usually either onstage (*Med.* 1121) or arrive onstage from the *skēnē* (658–83n., *Hipp.* 1153–62, *Pho.*

1067–76). Here, Hecuba is onstage, but not immediately visible to the messenger (484–7): this prompts him to comment on Hecuba's state and the human condition in general (488–98). The messenger, as usual, first delivers a condensed version of his message (508–10, cf. *Med.* 1125–6, *Hipp.* 1162–3). In response to Hecuba's request, and out of admiration for Polyxena's bravery, he then gives a detailed narration of the offstage events (558–71). Hecuba responds with a long *rhēsis* and gives orders for Polyxena's burial to the messenger and a Servant (603–18). The scene concludes the section of the play about Polyxena, whose body will not be seen again (954–5n.), as usual in the case of human sacrifices (Taplin 1977: 171).

484 Talthybius was familiar as Agamemnon's herald (*Il.* 1.320, Hdt. 7.134.1, Eur. *Or.* 888), and is a character in *Trojan Women*. Here and at *Tro.* 426 he is presented as a 'servant' or 'helper' ὑπηρέτης (503), a term which also applies to free men (Pylades at Eur. *El.* 821 and Philoctetes at Soph. *Phil.* 53). Talthybius and Λίχας ὁ κῆρυξ (Soph. *Trach.* 189, cf. 229) are the only tragic messengers to have a name; as heralds, they are in a socially subordinate condition, but above servile status.

ποτ' οὖσαν 'who once was': 821n.

486–7 'She lies near you, Talthybius, with her back on the ground, wrapped up in her clothes.' The text makes explicit Hecuba's stage movement alluded to at 438. Soph. *El.* 1474 αὕτη πέλας σοῦ uses similar language for similar staging (678–80n.): Clytemnestra's corpse is close to, but not seen by, Aegisthus. In other cases, a form of οὗτος combines with πέλας to describe the arrival of a character onstage (*Andr.* 545, *Suppl.* 1031).

συγκεκλῃμένη: the correct classical Attic spelling is κλῄω (root *κλᾱϝι-). The shift to κλείω occurred in the fourth century BCE: 430, 1284, Barrett on *Hipp.* 498–9, Threatte 1980: 369–70.

488–91 'O Zeus, what shall I say? <Shall I say> that you look over human beings, or that you got this futile reputation falsely, and that chance takes care of all human things?' Some characters in Euripides claim that, if the gods fail to help them, 'chance' will prove to be a goddess, stronger than the gods themselves (Odysseus in *Cycl.* 606–7); others forcefully state that, since the gods exist, chance cannot exist (fr. 820b); others still are uncertain (fr. 901). In itself, *tychē* does not mean 'absence of causal connections', but 'is what just happens', 'the element of human existence that humans do not control' (Nussbaum 1986: 89 n. *, 318–43). Euripides even uses phrases such as 'the *tychē* of a god' (*Med.* 671), or 'necessary *tychai*', i.e. 'necessity' (*IA* 511). The specialised meaning 'chance', 'events not caused by deliberate divine or human action' is first attested in the fifth century: Eur. *Pho.* 1202, Thuc. 1.140.1. On *tychē* in Greek thought cf. also Gomme and Sandbach 1973 on Men. *Aspis* 147–8, Versnel 2011: 277–8.

Here Talthybius implies that it is not clear to him why Zeus would humiliate Hecuba thus. The chorus of *Hecuba* (629–48, 943–52), like that of Aeschylus' *Agamemnon* (362–4, 399–402), have a clear explanation for the sufferings of the Trojans: it was Paris' fault (at Aesch. *Ag.* 367–8 and 699–716 the elders also blamed the Trojans collectively). Talthybius, out of sympathy with Hecuba, avoids suggesting this explanation, and prefers calling into doubt divine control over human events, and divine support for the Greeks. The interpolated line 490 makes him doubt the very existence of the gods, a separate and very different claim.

τί λέξω: aorist deliberative subjunctive (1056–7n.).

ὁρᾶν 'to watch over'. In this meaning, the simplex is securely attested (*Ba.* 394, fr. 255.3), but less frequently used than the compound verb (cf. 491 ἐπισκοπεῖν). This is a feature of high style: Finglass on Soph. *Ai.* 1376–7. Supervising men's actions is a traditional responsibility of Zeus: *Od.* 13.213–14 Ζεύς ... ὅς τε καὶ ἄλλους | ἀνθρώπους ἐφορᾶι καὶ τείνυται, ὅς τις ἁμάρτηι, Finglass on Soph. *El.* 175 Ζεύς, ὃς ἐφορᾶι πάντα.

δόξαν ἄλλως τήνδε 'this mistaken reputation', 'this thought that is merely an opinion'. For ἄλλως 'mistakenly' cf. *Cycl.* 355. Here it modifies δόξαν and is best translated as an adjective: cf. 626, *Tro.* 476 ἀριθμὸν ἄλλως 'mere number', Diggle 1981: 102.

μάτην 'falsely', 'with no real substance', cf. *Ion* 275. This is very close in meaning to ἄλλως. For analogous examples of redundancy cf. 335 φροῦδοι μάτην, Ar. *Vesp.* 929 διὰ κενῆς ἄλλως. μάτην is however often used as a gloss on ἄλλως and may have replaced an adverb such as e.g. ποτε.

[490] The interpolated line makes Talthybius doubt the very existence of the gods, as Bellerophon does, to his peril, in fr. 286. The line is syntactically irregular: ἀνθρώπους, the object of ὁρᾶν in 488, becomes the subject of κεκτῆσθαι (489), a very harsh change. Moreover, δόξαν τήνδε κτάομαι means 'I acquire this reputation' (*Hcld.* 165–6, fr. 1007d, 1043); it cannot mean 'to form an opinion', as required by the context.

ψευδῆ 'false'. This adjective is inelegantly redundant after ἄλλως and μάτην.

492 οὐχ ἥδ' ἄνασσα: the context (Hecuba is not a queen any more) clearly indicates that one must supply the imperfect of εἰμί (240n.).

τῶν πολυχρύσων Φρυγῶν 'of the Phrygians who are rich in gold', a *topos* of tragedy (Allan on *Hel.* 928, *Andr.* 2) and epic, even if in the *Iliad* many comment on the fact that the war has greatly reduced the wealth of Troy (9.401–3, 18.288–92).

494 'and now the whole city has been depopulated because of the war'. ἀνέστηκεν is pf. from ἀνίστημι (LSJ s.v. III.2); the intransitive pf. corresponds to a passive in English. Cf. the adjective ἀνάστατος, 'laid waste': Soph. *Trach.* 240 ἀνάστατον δορί.

495 Cf. 281n.

496 κόνει φύρουσα δύστηνον κάρα 'sullying her miserable head with dust', as Priam did when Hector died (*Il.* 22.414). At *Od.* 24.316–17, Laertes does the same, fearing that his son is dead.

497–8 Being old, Talthybius will die soon in any case; he wishes 'all the same' (ὅμως) to die before suffering such evils as those that affect Hecuba (so Weil). Other interpreters think that by 'all the same' Talthybius means that he, *qua* old, should in fact be more attached to life than a young person (Arist. *Rh.* 1389b32–5). This would however characterise the herald negatively (as 'too attached to life': 315n., 346–8n.).

Talthybius is careful to soften this ill-omened death wish and mention of future evils (1006n.) with the pious indefinite τινί (902n.). Only the gods know what the future has in store.

499–500 μετάρσιον | πλευρὰν ἔπαιρε καὶ τὸ πάλλευκον κάρα 'lift your chest and your all-white head <so as to make it> raised from the ground'. The adjective μετάρσιον 'raised from the ground' is proleptic, that is, it expresses the result of the action of the governing verb (1032–3n., K–G 1.276, Smyth §1579).

501–2 'Ah! Who is this person who does not let my body rest on the ground? Why do you disturb me, whoever you are, in my distress?' Hecuba at first hears Talthybius but does not see or recognise him; ἔα signals the first, partial contact (cf. 733–4n.). Her third-person address, later changing to a second-person address, is in any case meant as disparaging; cf. Easterling on Soph. *Trach.* 1238–40.

503 ὑπηρέτης: 484n.

[504] Ἀγαμέμνονος πέμψαντος, ὦ γύναι, μέτα 'since Agamemnon sent me <for you>, woman'. The line is linguistically very dubious: μέτα is meant as the preverb of μεταπέμψαντος, separated (tmesis: 907–8n., 1172n.) and postponed (anastrophe), a structure which occurs in epic, but is rare in other genres, and never securely attested in tragedy (Diggle *apud* Mastronarde on *Pho.* 1317). The line also disrupts the sequence 503 Δαναϊδῶν ... 506 Ἀχαιοῖς, and makes 509–10 redundant. It may have been fabricated from *Alc.* 66–7 Εὐρυσθέως πέμψαντος ἵππειον μετὰ | ὄχημα, where however μετά is a preposition. On repeated lines cf. 279n.

505 ὦ φίλτατ' 'O dearest <man>' is the formula normally used in tragedy to greet a messenger who brings good news, or someone whose arrival was hoped for: cf. 1114, Gregor 1957. Hecuba interrupts Talthybius, assuming he has come to kill her; Talthybius will answer her second question of 502 at 508.

505–6 κἄμ᾽ [= καὶ ἐμέ] **ἐπισφάξαι τάφωι | δοκοῦν Ἀχαιοῖς** 'because it has been decided by the Greeks to sacrifice me as well on the tomb'.

δοκοῦν: 118–19n.

COMMENTARY: 506–582   143

506 ὡς φίλ' ἂν λέγοις 'how your words would please me!' (contrast 517). ὡς introduces an exclamation with ἂν and the optative, as in Eur. *Hel.* 540, Soph. *Trach.* 734.

507 σπεύδωμεν, ἐγκονῶμεν: for the asyndeton cf. 387n.

508 σὴν παῖδα κατθανοῦσαν is the object of the verb θάψῃς, and is placed before the subordinating conjunction ὡς, in 'focus' position (Introduction, section 10), answering Hecuba's question at 502.

509 ἥκω μεταστείχων σε 'I have come searching for you'.

510 δισσοί ... Ἀτρεῖδαι 'the two sons of Atreus', Agamemnon and Menelaus. This phrase is a tragic (not epic) phrase (Soph. *Ai.* 57, 947–8, Eur. *Or.* 818) created in imitation of Aesch. *Ag.* 122–3 (cf. Fraenkel *ad loc.*).

511 τί λέξεις; 'a horrified "what do you mean to say?"' (Mastronarde on *Pho.* 1274; cf. 713, Barrett on *Hipp.* 353).

ἆρ': 231–3n.

θανουμένους: 237n.

513 μητρός ... ἄπο: 292n.

ἁρπασθεῖσ' 'snatched away'. Hecuba considers that her daughter has been taken from her by *force majeure*. Ployxena in fact followed Odysseus willingly; he only threatened to use violence (225n.). Cf. 142, 207–8n.

514 ἄτεκνοι τοὐπὶ σ' 'without children, as far as you are concerned'. Hecuba corrects Talthybius' ἄπαις (495). Helenus (87), Cassandra and, as far as Hecuba knows, Polydorus are still alive.

515–17 'How did you actually kill her? Did you show respect? Or did you approach the horrific act by killing her as someone you hated, old man? Speak, even if you are not going to say words that will please me.'

καί following an interrogative is often used when 'the questioner asks for supplementary information'; the position after the interrogative 'gives stress to the addition' (Denniston 312; cf. 13n., 1065, 1201).

νιν: 265n.

τὸ δεινόν: the sacrifice, here a euphemistic phrase, as at *Med.* 403. The phrase is used in a similar context at *Hcld.* 562: cf. Wilkins *ad loc.*, Soph. fr. 351.1.

518–82 Talthybius delivers one of the most vivid and powerful messenger speeches in tragedy. Its power derives from an impressive combination of violence and eroticism (523n., 558–61), the stimulation of mixed emotions (581–2, 589–92), stylistic bravura (567n., 568n.), and the complex reworking of three crucial texts in Greek literature: Patroclus' funeral in *Iliad* 23, which includes the only narration of human sacrifice in Homeric epic (40–1n., 527–9n.), the summoning of the dead in *Odyssey* 11 (527–9n., 536n., 536–7n., 551–2n.) and, above all, the narration of Iphigenia's sacrifice in Aeschylus' *Agamemnon* (526n., 544–5n., 558–61n., 560n., Thalmann 1993: 142–8, Mossman 1995: 142–63).

Talthybius is emotionally involved in what he reports to a greater extent than is usual with messengers. Paradoxically, Hecuba, unlike Talthybius (518), feels that the report has lessened, not increased, her suffering (591–2).

Talthybius gives his report a dramatic, rather than simply narrative, character by repeatedly reporting direct speeches: 534–41, 547–52, 563–5, 577–80, de Jong 1991: 131–9. His skilled rhetoric succeeds in presenting Agamemnon as attentive to Polyxena's wishes (553–4), Neoptolemus as an unwilling killer (566) and the Greek army as admiring and compassionate (572–80). The stress on pity, and the subtly slanted narrative, inconspicuously deflect the guilt of killing Polyxena to unnamed parties, as is to be expected from the spokesman of the Greeks. On human sacrifice in Greece cf. 260n., Bonnechère 1994.

The Latin narratives of Polyxena's death subtly rework and interpret this passage, stressing the erotic and wedding imagery, the paradoxical pity of the Greeks, and the courage of the victim: see Ov. *Met.* 13.449–82 and Sen. *Tro.* 1118–64; cf. Introduction, section 7, 523n., 566n., 568–70, Catull. 64. 362–70.

518 'You want me to earn a double amount of tears, woman.' As Arist. *Rh.* 1370b25–6 notes, 'there is a certain pleasure in lamentations and suffering' (*Il.* 23.10, Cropp on *El.* 126 πολύδακρυν ἁδονάν, Finglass on Soph. *El.* 286). Talthybius sympathises with Hecuba's point of view. He is reluctant to tell his story, like the messengers at Aesch. *Ag.* 636–49, Eur. *Pho.* 1209–18. He expects tears will bring pain to him, not relief, and highlights his feelings of compassion for Polyxena. Retelling a painful tale, esp. about personal misfortunes, brings new pain, as Odysseus stressed in a much-imitated passage, *Od.* 9.12–13: cf. Kannicht and Allan on *Hel.* 143 οὐ διπλᾶ χρῄζω στένειν, 770, Verg. *Aen.* 2.3. Here, κερδᾶναι is ironic: cf. Ar. *Nub.* 1064.

519 λέγων κακά 'telling the terrible facts', as in Eur. *Andr.* 973 ἐμὰς λέγων τύχας, 'narrating my misfortunes', *Od.*14.197 λέγων ἐμὰ κήδεα.

519–20 'I will moisten my eye <with tears> now, just as <I moistened it> at the tomb when she died'. For τε ... τε 'just as' cf. Denniston 515.

τόδ᾽ 'this' refers to a part of the body of the speaker, as at 274, *Med.* 1378 τῇδε ... χερί.

522 πλήρης: cf. 107n.

523 λαβών ... Πολυξένην χερός 'taking Polyxena by the hand'. A soldier is shown leading Polyxena by the hand to the tomb of Achilles on a sarcophagus (early fifth century BCE) and two Attic vases (around 500–480 BCE): Touchefeu-Meynier 1994: 432 nos. 21, 22 and 24, Durand and Lissarrague 1999: 96–7, 100–1, Rose 2014: 72–103. The gesture may be seen also as an allusion to a wedding ceremony: 337–8n., 416n., 612n., Mossman 1995: 148–50, 154–5, Sommerstein,

Fitzpatrick and Talboy 2006: 42–3. Sen. *Tro.* 1132–6 makes the reference to a wedding explicit. On the love story between Polyxena and Achilles see Introduction, section 4, nn. 38–9.

Ἀχιλλέως παῖς: Neoptolemus: see Introduction, section 4.

524 ἔστησ᾽ ἐπ᾽ ἄκρου χώματος 'he placed her on top of the mound', so that the blood would fall on the altar, as in the sacrifice of Iphigenia (Aesch. *Ag.* 232 ὕπερθε βωμοῦ, Eur. *El.* 1022 ὑπερτείνας πυρᾶς, *IT* 26 ὑπὲρ πυρᾶς). Polyxena is shown in this position in archaic paintings: cf. Maas 1951, Touchefeu-Meynier 1994: 433 no. 26, Durand and Lissarrague 1999: 90 and 94, Medda 2012. Cf. 150n.

πέλας stresses the trustworthiness of Talthybius' eyewitness report, as in *Hipp.* 1196: de Jong 1991: 9–12.

525 'selected young boys, chosen from among the Achaeans'. The redundancy is characteristic of tragic style: 26n., 37–9n., Soph. *Ai.* 710 θοᾶν ὠκυάλων νεῶν.

526 'who would restrain with <their> hands a leap of your heifer'. Polyxena is compared to a heifer (206n.) who might leap in fear as death approaches. This passage reworks Aesch. *Ag.* 231–43 (cf. 544–5n.), where Agamemnon orders his *ministers* (231 ἀόζοις) to lift Iphigenia over the altar and gag her mouth; she can only move her eyes. Cf. 558–61n.

526–8 χεροῖν ... ἐν χεροῖν ... χειρί: for the repetition cf. 64–5, 1025–7n., *Ba.* 647, Diggle on *Phaeth.* 56, Pickering 2003: 490–1.

527–9 The messenger does not specify whether Neoptolemus pours wine, as was normally the case over a sacrificial pyre (λοιβαί or σπονδαί: *Il.* 1.462–3, 11.774–5, *Od.* 3.459–60), or a mixture of other liquids, as in libations for the dead, which were poured on to the ground (χοαί including honey, milk, wine and water: cf. *Od.* 11.26–8 and Garvie on Aesch. *Pers.* 611–18). In *Il.* 23.218–21, Achilles pours wine on to the ground from a golden goblet, in honour of Patroclus, whose body is burning on the pyre; Achilles had already put amphorae full of oil and honey on the pyre (23.170). The ceremony, both in *Hecuba* and in the *Iliad*, is a (human) sacrifice as well as a libation for a dead hero, and includes elements of both types of ritual. On libations cf. Burkert 1985: 70–3, Simon 2004.

αἴρει 'he lifted up'. In messenger speeches the historical present highlights salient moments in the narration: cf. 567 τέμνει, 937n., de Jong 1991: 38–45, Rijksbaron 2006 and 2015, Boter 2012.

χοὰς θανόντι πατρί 'as libations to <his> late father'.

χοάς is in apposition to 527 δέπας, as in *Pho.* 933 αἷμα γῆι δοῦναι χοάς (a description of another human sacrifice).

[531–3] These lines are unlikely to be authentic. Talthybius four times orders the crowd to be silent (532–3 Σιγᾶτ᾽ ... σῖγα ... | σῖγα σιώπα), and describes the silence again at 533 (νήνεμον δ᾽ ἔστησ᾽ ὄχλον). Such orders are normally given only once; they are occasionally repeated twice in a messenger speech (*Suppl.* 669–70 Σιγᾶτε, λαοί, σῖγα, Καδμείων στίχες, | ἀκούσαθ᾽) and in dialogue (*HF* 1067, *Or.* 140, 1311), to convey a sense of urgency, esp. when the interlocutor seems unwilling to be quiet immediately. Four repetitions of the order of silence are not attested and do not here seem to serve any particular point. In *Pho.* 1224 (κελεύσας σῖγα κηρῦξαι στρατῷ, cf. here 530) the messenger simply refers to the order issued to the heralds to impose silence, without specifying that the order was carried out and obeyed; the actual words of the heralds are not reported (as in *Il.* 2.280, 23.567–9). Lines 531–3 may have been added by an actor wanting to expand his part (cf. [490n.], [504n.], [555–6n.]).

καταστάς 'taking my stand', as often in similar descriptions of speakers: 136–7n., Garvie on Aesch. *Pers.* 295 λέξον καταστάς, LSJ s.v. καθίστημι B 1b. The variant reading παραστάς 'standing by', adapts the the epic formula εἶπε παραστάς (*Il.* 6.75, etc.), never used of messengers. A similar false variant παρασταθείς is attested for *Or.* 365 κατασταθείς.

σῖγα 'in silence', adverb.

σίγα 'be quiet', imperative from σιγάω.

νήνεμον δ᾽ ἔστησ᾽ ὄχλον 'I stilled the crowd and made it calm'. νήνεμον lit. 'windless' is used metaphorically (cf. 1160n.); syntactically, it is a proleptic adjective (499–500n.).

534–41 Neoptolemus' prayer to Achilles is divided into invocation (534), offering (535–7) and request for help (538–41). Neoptolemus imagines that Achilles will actually come (536n.). Requests to dead heroes are similarly structured in other tragic prayers, with similar appeals for their presence and help: Garvie on Aesch. *Pers.* 623–80, Bond on *HF* 490–6, Cropp on *El.* 677–84. On direct speeches in messenger narratives cf. 518–82n. and 929–30n.

534 **Ὦ παῖ Πηλέως, πατὴρ δ᾽ ἐμός** 'O son of Peleus, O father of mine'. 'Δέ is regularly used to link different relations of the same person standing in apposition to each other' (Garvie on Aesch. *Cho.* 190; cf. Fraenkel on Aesch. *Ag.* 1585).

535 **δέξαι ... μοι** 'please accept from me'. The dative indicates 'the person from whom something is accepted but also additionally suggests that that person is proffering the thing accepted and urging its acceptance' (Cooper and Krüger 2002: 2122): Collard, Cropp and Gibert 2004: 248 on Eur. fr. 757.920 ταῦτά μοι [Valckenaer: μου MSS] δέξαι, γύναι, *Il.* 2.186 δέξατό οἱ σκῆπτρον, Astydamas *TrGF* 60 F 2.1 δέξαι κυνῆν μοι. MSS ω read μου, which can be taken as genitive of origin ('from me': Soph. *OT* 1163), or as a specification of χοάς 'these libations of mine'. However, the alternative reading μοι can be explained only as a survival of the original text: there was no reason for ancient scribes or scholars to alter a transmitted genitive μου.

κλητηρίους 'that appease' your wrath. Atossa calls the libations offered to the dead Darius παιδὸς πατρὶ πρευμενεῖς χοάς (*Pers.* 609) 'libations that induce softness of temper for the father of my son'.

536 νεκρῶν ἀγωγούς 'that lead the dead' to the world of the living: prayers, like laments (Aesch. *Pers.* 687 ψυχαγωγοῖς ... γόοις) and sacrifices (*Od.* 11.34–7), are imagined to be capable of conjuring up the dead.

ἐλθέ 'come'. Dead heroes are invited to come and help in Aesch. *Pers.* 658–9 ἴθι ἱκοῦ | ἐλθ', Eur. *HF* 494, *El.* 680. According to *Od.* 11.492–3, Achilles in Hades has no knowledge of his son's fate; this prayer from Neoptolemus, addressed to his father, challenges the *Odyssey* narration.

536–7 ὡς πίῃς μέλαν | κόρης ἀκραιφνὲς αἷμ' 'to drink the pure black blood of the girl', as the souls of the dead do in *Od.* 11.98 πίεν αἷμα κελαινόν, 11.153 πίεν αἷμα κελαινεφές. In other human sacrifices (*Pho.* 933: 527–9n.), it is the earth that drinks the blood. The blood is ἀκραιφνές 'pure', i.e. 'undefiled', as the wine libation for Darios at Aesch. *Pers.* 614–15 ἀκήρατόν τε ... | ποτόν: Garvie *ad loc.* and Beekes 2010 s.v. ἀκήρατος. The adjective also alludes to Polyxena's virginity (*Alc.* 1052 ἀκραιφνής), a frequent precondition for human sacrifice (Aesch. *Ag.* 245, Eur. *Pho.* 943).

538–41 πρευμενὴς δ' ἡμῖν γενοῦ | ... πρευμενοῦς ... νόστου 'be favourable to us ... a favourable homeward voyage'. The repetition is pointed: πρευμενοῦς is placed in emphatic position at clause beginning (540–1 πρευμενοῦς τ' ... μολεῖν), as in Aesch. *Ag.* 973–4 Ζεῦ Ζεῦ τέλειε, τὰς ἐμὰς εὐχὰς τέλει | ... τελεῖν, and it is meant to stress the similarity between the hero and the favour he is asked to grant. πρευμενοῦς means 'favourable' here as in Aesch. *Suppl.* 138–40 τελευτὰς ... πρευμενεῖς, *Ag.* 1647 πρευμενεῖ τύχῃ. Kovacs 1996: 65 suggests substituting πρευμενοῦς with ἡσύχου ('i.e. without railery'), claiming that Achilles, 'a hero with only local influence', cannot protect the Greeks in their journey home. This limitation is not perceived by Neoptolemus. Achilles was worshipped as Ποντάρχης 'lord of the sea/of Pontus' in the Black Sea, and had some sort of divine cult: Burgess 2009: 128–9.

539 χαλινωτήρια 'mooring cables'.

541 πάντας 'all of us' (supply ἡμᾶς from 540 ἡμῖν). In fact very many Greeks will *not* be able to arrive home at all (*Od.* 1.6–9, Aesch. *Ag.* 648–80). It may not have been in Achilles' power to overcome divine hostility against some individual Greeks (*Tro.* 74–97). The unanswered prayer highlights the futility, or worse, of the sacrifice: for many of the Greeks it would have been better not to leave Troy at all (1287–90n. 1292n.).

543–4 ἀμφίχρυσον φάσγανον κώπης λαβὼν | ἐξεῖλκε κολεοῦ 'he grabbed the golden sword by the hilt, and took it out of its scabbard'. ἀμφίχρυσον 'gilded all over' must refer to the sword's hilt (so the scholium) or to gold decorations on the blade: gold is not a suitable material for the blade itself.

φάσγανον is accusative of the whole, κώπης genitive of the part seized; they both depend from λαβών.

544–5 λογάσι ... ἔνευσε ... λαβεῖν: a close imitation of Aeschylus' description of the sacrifice of Iphigenia: *Ag.* 231–4 φράσεν δ' ἀόζοις ... | λαβεῖν, cf. 518–82n., 526n.

λογάσι ... νεανίαις 'chosen young men'.

546 ὡς ἐφράσθη 'as soon as she perceived <this>'. This aorist passive is used in a middle sense: *Od.* 19.485, Hdt. 1.84.4, Smyth §814.

548–9 ἑκοῦσα θνῄσκω· μή τις ἅψηται χροός | τοὐμοῦ 'I die of my own will; let no one touch my body': Euripides has Polyxena rephrase in compact form *Hcld.* 530–1 ἥδε γὰρ ψυχὴ πάρα | ἑκοῦσα κοὐκ ἄκουσα, 550–1 τὴν ἐμὴν ψυχὴν ἐγώ | δίδωμ' ἑκοῦσα. Polyxena's sacrifice is more disturbing, as she accepts it not in order to save her family, as Heracles' daughter does in *Heraclidae*, but to preserve her own 'freedom' and nobility: cf. 342–78n. 346–8n., 367–8n. Ov. *Met.* 13.466–9 makes Polyxena explicitly mention that physical contact with the Greeks may involve sexual contamination, an act to be avoided in order not to offend Achilles. Euripides will reuse a similar cluster of motives in fr. 175 (from *Antigone* or *Antiope*: these plays were probably [*Antigone*] or certainly [*Antiope*] staged later than *Hecuba*), where a woman demands not to be touched by slaves, accepts her fate willingly (11 ἑκοῦσα), and recognises that it is 'folly' (13 ἀμαθίαν: 228n.) for a person of high birth to fight against fate: Collard and Cropp 2008a: 203–5.

550: 367–8n., 420n.

551 θεῶν: measured as one syllable (synizesis: cf. Battezzato 2000d).

551–2 ἐν νεκροῖσι γὰρ | δούλη κεκλῆσθαι βασιλὶς οὖσ' αἰσχύνομαι 'I, being a queen, am ashamed of being called a slave woman among the dead'. In *Od.* 11.489–91, the *psychē* of the dead Achilles said he preferred to be a poor man's slave on earth rather than the king of the dead, but Polyxena prefers the opposite.

553 ἐπερρόθησαν 'clamoured in approval', an imitation of Homeric scenes: cf. *Il.* 1.22 πάντες ἐπηυφήμησαν Ἀχαιοί, Mastronarde on *Pho.* 1238 and above, 98–153n.

[555–6] As at 531–3, an interpolator wrote a short passage to explain exactly how an order from an army leader was carried out. The language and style of 555–6 do not match Euripides' standards. The phrase ὑστάτην ὄπα 'his latest words' inappropriately suggest that Agamemnon is about to die: cf. 411, Eur. *Hipp.* 1097, Soph. *Ai.* 864 τοῦθ' ὑμῖν Αἴας τοὔπος ὕστατον θροεῖ. The relative clause of 556 is an uninformative afterthought, and inappropriately paraphrases a Homeric formula normally used in reference to Zeus (*Il.* 2.118 τοῦ γὰρ κράτος ἐστὶ μέγιστον). For καί cf. 13n.

558–61 λαβοῦσα ... κάλλιστα 'Taking her robes, she tore them from the top of the shoulder to mid-waist, near the navel, and showed her breasts and chest, which were very beautiful, like those of a statue.' Polyxena's gesture is a provocation and, at the same time, a way of appealing to the crowd. The sacrifice would have probably entailed the loosening or ripping off of her clothes by violence; the bared breasts often symbolise physical violence in Greek visual arts (B. Cohen 1997: 77). Polyxena here freely performs the act, avoiding physical contact and violence, in a surprising and puzzling gesture. The Greek army react by a gesture of gratitude: far from performing acts of necrophilia, as Hecuba seems to fear (605–6n.), they are shocked and placated by Polyxena's courage (568–70n.), and make her the object of special, almost heroic honours (573–4n.). Polyxena's gesture certainly arouses 'pathos' (Mossman 1995: 159) and pity (O'Sullivan 2008: 195), but that does not cancel the obvious erotic associations of that gesture (*Andr.* 627–31, Scodel 1996: 123), which some find even 'voyeuristic' (Hall 2006: 130). Euripides may have been inspired by a painting by Polygnotus: Stieber 2011: 215–18.

The scene repeatedly alludes to Aeschylus' narration of the sacrifice of Iphigenia (524n., 526n., 544–5n., 560n.). It is possible that Euripides interpreted Aesch. *Ag.* 239 κρόκου βαφὰς δ' ἐς πέδον χέουσα as 'letting her saffron-dyed robes fall to the ground' (as Fraenkel *ad loc.* did). If he interpreted it as 'letting the robes hang to the ground' (Lloyd-Jones 1952, Denniston and Page *ad loc.*), he intentionally misread the passage and 'improved' on it in his intertextual allusion, which he makes stronger by rephrasing the simile of Aesch. *Ag.* 242 (560n.).

559 λαγόνας 'waist, flanks' is 'more often neutral ... than erotic ... in tone' (Sider 1997 on Phld. *ep.* 12.2), but can have sexual overtones (Chaerem. *TrGF* 71 F 14.3, [Luc.] *Am.* 14).

560 ὡς ἀγάλματος is reminiscent of Aesch. *Ag.* 242 πρέπουσα τώς [Maas: θ' ὥς MSS] ἐν γραφαῖς, where Iphigenia is compared to a painting (O'Sullivan 2008). Here the comparison objectifies the person who is the focus of erotic gaze, as in Eur. fr. 125, Pl. *Chrm.* 154c8.

561 καθεῖσα πρὸς γαῖαν γόνυ 'lowering the knee to the ground', from καθίημι, as at *IT* 332–3 ἐς δὲ γῆν γόνυ | καμάτωι καθεῖσαν.

562 τλημονέστατον here probably means 'the most steadfast' as at *Hcld.* 570–1 τλημονεστάτην ... | πασῶν γυναικῶν (also in reference to a self-sacrificing maiden), cf. Aesch. *Ag.* 1302; 'the most unhappy' (cf. *Med.* 1067–8), also a possible translation, gives less credit to Polyxena's courage.

563–5 Polyxena's language is similar to that of Andromache (*Andr.* 411–12) and Amphitryon (*HF* 319–20 ἰδού, πάρεστιν ἥδε φασγάνωι δέρη | κεντεῖν φονεύειν ἱέναι πέτρας ἄπο) when they, under threats of violence, leave the altar and offer themselves to their enemies: she speaks as if it is only her free decision that allows the Greeks to attack her.

566 οὐ θέλων τε καὶ θέλων 'not willing and willing', a phrase echoing a Homeric oxymoron (*Il.* 4.43 ἑκὼν ἀέκοντί γε θυμῶι), often taken up in tragedy: Cropp on *IT* 512 οὐχ ἑκὼν ἑκών. Talthybius uses it to soften Neoptolemus' guilt. Ov. *Met.* 13.475–6 and Sen. *Tro.* 1154 similarly present Neoptolemus as reluctant to strike Polyxena, which, as the messenger in Seneca notes, is paradoxical, considering Neoptolemus' notorious bloodlust: 23–4n.

567 'He cuts her wind-pipe with his iron.' For the historical present cf. 527–9n. The phrasing combines traditional poetic language (the metonymy σιδήρωι 'iron' = 'sword': *Il.* 18.34, Eur. *Suppl.* 678) with a neologism suggesting a precise medical description of human physiology: cf. Hippoc. *Vic.* 1.9.3 τοῦ πνεύματος διεξόδους, 1.23.2 Joly, Craik 2001: 91.

568 κρουνοὶ δ' ἐχώρουν 'the springs <of blood> were flowing'. The metaphor 'rivers of blood' is rare and striking in Greek: cf. Soph. *Ant.* 1238 ὀξεῖαν ... ῥοήν, Liapis on [Eur.] *Rhes.* 790 θερμός ... κρουνός, two passages that rephrase Aesch. *Ag.* 1389 ὀξεῖαν αἵματος σφαγήν. Talthybius euphemistically omits the word 'blood'.

568–70 ἡ δὲ ... χρεών: Polyxena covers her genitals (570), a gesture praised by ancient commentators (Heath 1987a: 42), although some unnamed ancient scholars deleted 570, considering it in bad taste. The passage was often imitated in ancient literature (Bömer 1982 on Ov. *Met.* 13.479–80), notably in the description of Caesar's death (Suet. *Iul.* 82.2): Polyxena's courage (Mastronarde 2010: 267–9) makes her into a suitable role model for men.

569 εὐσχήμων, an adj. in reference to Polyxena, is better translated as an adverb, 'decently'.

570 'hiding from the eyes of men what it was proper to hide'. κρύπτω takes the double accusative.

571: ἀφῆκε: 367–8n.

θανασίμωι σφαγῆι 'because of the deadly wound': cf. 1037n., *Ion* 1250.

573–4 *Phyllobolia*, the act of pelting with leaves, flowers or garlands, was performed in honour of winners in athletic competitions: Pind. *Pyth.* 9.123–4, Eratosth. *FGrHist* 241 F 14. It was also a way of honouring heroic or military successes: Pind. *Pyth.* 4.240. *Phyllobolia* is an act of consecration parallel to the throwing of barley grains over the sacrificial victim (Burkert 1983: 5 n. 16). Philicus *SH* 680.53 is the only other instance of *phyllobolia* referring to a female person or goddess without male companions.

575 κορμούς ... πευκίνους 'pine-logs'.

ὁ δ' οὐ φέρων 'anyone who did not bring', a generalising singular: *Med.* 86 τοῦ πέλας, Smyth §996, K–G 1.13–14, Cooper and Krüger 1998: 80.

576 τοιάδ' ἤκουεν κακά 'received accusations such as these'. τοιάδ' refers to the reported speech that follows (*Med.* 1207, *El.* 804, *IT* 364). Cf. 580n.

578 'Garments' (πέπλον) and 'ornaments' (κόσμον) are offered in funerals: 615–18, *Tro.* 1143–4.

580 τοιάδ'... λέγων 'as I report such events'. τοιάδ' refers to what has been said before: *Alc.* 950, *Hipp.* 655. Wecklein noted that one would expect the messenger to say 'having heard [κλύων or, better, κλυών: 743n.] these words' of praise from the army. If one prints κλυών in 580, τοιάδε refers to the preceding direct speech as in Aesch. *Ag.* 156. This however entails further, less plausible, changes; Wecklein eliminated σε from 581, which is crucial to make clear the reference of εὐτεκνωτάτην. Alternatively, one could consider writing τ' ἐρῶ at 582 (future for present: Smyth §1915).

581 εὐτεκνωτάτην 'the person who has the best children', cf. καλλίπαις 'having good children' in Aesch. *Ag.* 762, Eur. *HF* 839. The messenger ends his narrative with a comment, as messengers normally do (de Jong 1991: 106–10), restating his sympathy for Hecuba.

583–4 'This has seethed up as a terrible, mysterious (τι) suffering against the family of Priam and my city, under divine compulsion.' The metaphor of 'boiling' (ἐπιζέω) is less unusual in Greek than in English: cf. 1054–5n., *IT* 987–8 δεινή τις [cf. τι in 583 and 902n.] ὀργὴ δαιμόνων ἐπέζεσεν | πρὸς Ταντάλειον σπέρμα, Aesch. fr. 451i.2–3. On divine ἀνάγκη cf. 847n.; for the syntax cf. *Andr.* 132 δεσποτᾶν ἀνάγκαις.

585–8 Sorrows are metaphorically described as surrounding Hecuba and competing for her attention (587 οὐκ ἐᾶι... παρακαλεῖ): 639n., 784n.

586–8 'Whenever I touch [or "perceive"] one, this one does not let me go, but another grief calls me from the other side, succeeding sorrows with sorrows.'

ἄψωμαι: after 585 βλέψω, the audience expect the metaphorical meaning of ἅπτομαι 'to perceive, grasp' (cf. 675n.), but Hecuba continues as if she had used it in the literal meaning of 'touching' (273): the personified sorrow clutches at her (οὐκ ἐᾶι, cf. Soph. *Phil.* 817).

διάδοχος κακῶν: for the genitive cf. Soph. *Phil.* 867 φέγγος ὕπνου διάδοχον 'light that comes after sleep'.

κακοῖς 'with sorrows' is a dative indicating the instrument used for performing the action (Smyth §1507). For similar combinations cf. *Suppl.* 71–2 γόων γόοις [Valckenaer: γόων γόων MS L] | διάδοχος 'succeeding groans with groans', *Andr.* 802–3. The phrase imitates that of another slave woman, Briseis lamenting over the death of Patroclus: *Il.* 19.290 ὥς μοι δέχεται κακὸν ἐκ κακοῦ αἰεί.

589–90 'and now I could not wipe out of my mind what happened to you, so as not to mourn it'.

τὸ μὲν σὸν... πάθος is the topic of the sentence; this explains its position at sentence-beginning (cf. Introduction, section 10).

ἐξαλείψασθαι: as in Pl. *Tht.* 187b1, the mind is imagined as a board or wall from which signs (= thoughts) can be wiped away.

591–2 τὸ δ' αὖ λίαν παρεῖλες ἀγγελθεῖσά μοι | γενναῖος 'on the other hand, you have taken away the excess <of grief>, because you have been reported to me <to have been> noble'. For παρεῖλες 'to remove (grief)' cf. *Hipp.* 1105 λύπας παραιρεῖ.

592–8 For Hecuba, aristocrats inevitably possess an unfaltering inborn virtue. She recalls the traditional comparison between human beings and live plants (20n., *Il.* 6.146–9, Pind. *Nem.* 6.8–11, Eur. fr. 415) only to reject it: plants depend on external circumstances, unlike noble human beings. Other Euripidean characters, by contrast, argue that aristocratic origins do not guarantee moral excellence: *El.* 367–72.

592 δεινόν: 846n.

592–4 κακή ... χρηστή: 'bad' and 'good' have moral as well as social ('commoner'/'aristocrat') connotations: 299–331n.

τυχοῦσα καιροῦ θεόθεν 'if it [= the earth] receives from the gods what is appropriate' (e.g. the right amount of rain and sunshine). καιρός is 'what is appropriate': Barrett on *Hipp.* 386–7.

595 ἄνθρωποι 'as for human beings'. A nominative at sentence-beginning can be picked up by nouns or pronouns in different cases later in the sentence (Cooper and Krüger 1998: 101–2). ἄνθρωποι is the topic of the sentence (589–90n.), placed at its left periphery in the least-marked case (nominative), followed by a list of items (596 ὁ μὲν πονηρός, 597 ὁ δ' ἐσθλός) in 'partitive apposition' (Smyth §981).

596 'the evil one is nothing else but bad'. πλήν here is not used as a preposition, which would require a genitive, but as a conjunction, 'except', linking the two nominatives πονηρός and κακός (Smyth §2966).

597–8 'the noble one is noble, nor does he spoil his nature under adverse circumstances, but is always worthy'. The aorist διέφθειρ' expresses a general truth ('gnomic aorist': Smyth §1931).

[599] 'Do parents make a difference or the way people are raised?' The line does not belong to this context: Hecuba clearly states in 592–8 that birth does make a difference. The line was added by someone who misunderstood 600–2.

600–2 'Yet a good upbringing too can teach one nobility: if someone learns this well, he knows what is shameful, learning it by the yardstick of what is honourable.' Hecuba concedes that someone who is not noble by birth might be able to show bravery or virtue. The teachability of virtue or wisdom is a much-debated theme in fifth-century thought: *Hipp.* 79–80, *Suppl.* 911–17, Pl. *Prt.* 319a3–329d2, Guthrie 1969: 250–60. Many scholars consider 599–602 spurious, claiming that they are inconsistent with Hecuba's view and/or discuss a different issue, 'the source of our knowledge of good and ill' (W. S. Barrett 2007: 473). The inconsistency is removed if 599 is deleted. There is no change of subject matter if we understand that 600–2 are about good action: 602 αἰσχρόν is what brings bad reputation, not 'ill' in general.

603 'in any case, my mind shot these thoughts wide of the mark'. Thoughts or words are often metaphorically described as arrows (Aesch. *Suppl.* 446, Eur. *Andr.* 365) or spears (Eur. *Suppl.* 456). Hecuba acknowledges that her digression is not strictly relevant to her argument. καὶ ... μὲν δή is progressive ('in any case'), and looks forward to δέ in 604 (σὺ δ' ἔλθὲ), as in *Alc.* 156–7: Denniston 258, 392–3, 396–7.

605–6 μὴ θιγγάνειν ... τῆς παιδός 'that no one touches her, and that <they> [= the Argive leaders] keep the crowd away from my child'. The subject of the second infinitive (εἴργειν) has to be supplied from the context (604 Ἀργείοις), and is different from the subject (μηδέν') of the first one (θιγγάνειν). For similar changes of grammatical subjects cf. Finglass on Soph. *Ai.* 457–9. For Hecuba, the contact of male soldiers with the naked corpse of the young woman is sexually inappropriate, possibly suggestive of necrophilia (558–61n.).

τῆς παιδός is governed both by θιγγάνειν (partitive gen.) and εἴργειν (gen. of separation).

μοι is a dative of interest (translated as a possessive adjective above: '*my* child').

606–8 ἔν τοι μυρίωι στρατεύματι | ἀκόλαστος ὄχλος ναυτική τ' ἀναρχία | κρείσσων πυρός 'In a large army, you know, the crowd is undisciplined and the mariners who do not obey their leaders are worse than fire.' ἀκόλαστος is predicative to ὄχλος ('the crowd is undisciplined'). It would also be possible to interpret ἀκόλαστος and ναυτική as attributive, and κρείσσων as predicative to both nouns: 'In a large army, you know, the undisciplined crowd and the mariners who do not obey their leaders are worse than fire.' In this case, each singular subject has a singular predicate (κρείσσων). Cf. also Smyth §1053, K–G 1.79–80, Cooper and Krüger 1998: 935. The combination τ' (607) ... δ' (608) indicates contrast, not simply addition (Denniston 513–14).

ναυτική ... ἀναρχία: the adjective defines the identity of the people referred to, whereas the abstract noun ἀναρχία designates their characteristics: 362n., Mastronarde on *Pho.* 655 Βάκχιον χόρευμα 'Bacchus who is worshipped in dancing'. Hecuba, like other characters in tragedy (*IA* 914, *Suppl.* 509), shares the anti-democratic feeling of the Athenian oligarchic elite against the socially underprivileged sailors: Gray 2007 and Marr and Rhodes 2008 on [Xen.] *Ath. Pol.* 1.2.

608 κρείσσων πυρός 'stronger than fire', i.e. 'worse than fire', as in 638–9 πόνων ἀνάγκαι κρείσσονες, Soph. *OT* 176 κρείσσων ... πυρός, 1374 κρεῖσσον' ἀγχόνης.

κακὸς δ' ὁ μή τι δρῶν κακόν 'and whoever does not do something bad is bad'. Hecuba attributes to the mob a complete subversion of linguistic and moral standards, such as that described in Thuc. 3.82.4–6 and Pl. *Resp.* 488d1–489a2. Fifth-century philosophers noted that in some circumstances (theatre, sport) acting unjustly is 'just' (Gorgias 82 B 23).

609 Hecuba addresses a previously unmentioned Servant: 'no particular attention is paid to the servants until there is some purpose in doing so' (Taplin 1977: 79, cf. Aesch. *Ag.* 908–9). The servant will reappear, as a speaking actor, at 658 (Introduction, section 3.2). Talthybius probably exits at this point (617–18n.), rather than at the end of the scene (628).

609–10 'and you, old servant of mine, take a vessel, dip it <into seawater> and bring some seawater here'. The participles λαβοῦσα ... βάψασ' describe two actions that take place in succession (Smyth §2056, §2147f–g, K–G II.103–4): the aorist imperative ἔνεγκε (cf. φέρω) marks the end of the sequence. ποντίας ἁλός is partitive genitive.

611 The washing of a corpse before the funeral is traditionally done by female relatives (Griffith on Soph. *Ant.* 900–3). In this context (416n., 612n.), this action recalls also the prenuptial bath, another task performed by mothers (Mastronarde on *Med.* 1025–7, *Pho.* 347–8).

παῖδα ... ἐμήν is governed by λούσω in 613.

612 Polyxena, a virgin, is a 'bride' to Achilles, and hence 'not a virgin' (ἀπάρθενον, cf. Theocr. 2.41). In fact she is killed, and does not become a 'bride'. The alpha privative retains its original meaning. In other similar paradoxical expressions, it almost amounts to a pejorative prefix: Fehling 1968, Finglass on Soph. *El.* 1154 μήτηρ ἀμήτωρ.

613–18 Hecuba needs to borrow items for the funeral from her fellow prisoners. This is a moving contrast with her previous affluence. Lysias uses a similar real-life situation for analogous pathetic effects in 12.18: Polemarchos' family was rich, but they were not allowed to use their luxury goods for the *ekphora*, and had to borrow funeral robes from friends. Hecuba fears that her offering is not enough for the ritual: she apologises to the dead and explains that she cannot do more: cf. Soph. *El.* 450–2.

613 προθῶμαι: subj. aor. from προτίθημι. The πρόθεσις ('laying out') of the body is an essential part of funerary rituals: cf. *Alc.* 664, *Pho.* 1319. This raises the expectation of a funerary lament later in the play, which will in fact be for Polydorus (672–3n.).

613–14 ὡς μὲν ἀξία ... πάθω; 'as she deserves – how could I do this? I could not – but as I can (what else am I to do?)'. The sentence is interrupted by πόθεν; and continues with ὡς δ' ἔχω ('as I can', 'according to my means') taking up the main verb προθῶμαι.

πόθεν; 'where from?' acquires the meaning of 'there is no way I can do this'.

τί ... πάθω; 'what is to happen to me?', i.e. 'what else am I to do?' Both πόθεν; and this phrase are colloquial: Stevens 1976: 57–8, Mastronarde on *Pho.* 894–5.

615 κόσμον γ᾽ ἀγείρασ᾽ 'by collecting adornments'; γε accompanies an 'epexegetic' participial clause, which explains ὡς ... ἔχω: Denniston 139. The MSS have τ᾽ instead of γ᾽, which gives weaker meaning ('as I can and by collecting adornments'): Diggle 1994: 203. κόσμον is 'funeral attire' (clothes and other adornments): Parker on *Alc.* 149.

616 πάρεδροι 'who dwell nearby': 1–58n.

617–18 εἴ τις τοὺς νεωστὶ δεσπότας | λαθοῦσ᾽ ἔχει τι κλέμμα τῶν αὐτῆς δόμων 'if one [i.e. of the Trojans prisoners] keeps some object stolen from her own house, having escaped the notice of the new masters'. Hecuba can say this with less concern if Talthybius left at 609. κλέμμα 'thing stolen' is paradoxical and pathetic in the context. Cf. 1014n.

619 ὦ σχήματ᾽ οἴκων 'O beauty of my palace'. The periphrasis σχῆμα ('form', 'appearance', i.e. 'beauty') + gen. is employed in a similar way at *Med.* 1072 σχῆμα ... τέκνων. It can assume a variety of other connotations: Mastronarde on *Pho.* 250–2. For the poetic plural see 265n.

620–1 ὦ πλεῖστ᾽ ἔχων μάλιστά τ᾽ εὐτεκνώτατε | Πρίαμε 'O Priam, you who had so many possessions, and were very blessed with children'. Having many fine children (581n.) is considered a blessing, and Priam had very many (361n., 421n.). This seems to correct Priam's scathing comments at *Il.* 24.253–62, where he accused most of them of being cowardly, and vastly inferior to Hector. The participle ἔχων refers to the past (821n.). μάλιστα reinforces the superlative εὐτεκνώτατε, as in *Hipp.* 1421 μάλιστα φίλτατος: 377n., Smyth §1090. For the enjambment cf. *Andr.* 1073–4 γέρον | Πηλεῦ. In the MS text ὦ πλεῖστ᾽ ἔχων κάλλιστά τ᾽, εὐτεκνώτατε 'you who had very many and very fine possessions, most blessed with children' two attributes (ἔχων and εὐτεκνώτατε) of the vocative Πρίαμε are linked in asyndeton. The frequent combination πλεῖστ(α) ... κάλλιστα (Ar. *Ran.* 1254–5, Lys. 2.42, Pl. *Phd.* 85a1, *Grg.* 490d8) may have contributed to the corruption. Diggle 1994: 232–3 lists other objections to the MS text.

622–3 'how we have come to nothing, robbed of our previous pride'.

φρονήματος 'pride', almost 'conceit' (cf. 623 ὀγκούμεθα).

623–5 Hecuba denounces the vanity of the aristocratic condition, apparently dismissing the trait that was crucial to her identity (216–95n., 293–4n., 592–8n.), and also to Polyxena's (342–78n., 375–8n.). The theme of man's ephemeral nature (285n.) is here used to make an egalitarian point: like Croesus, who 'thought he was the happiest (ὀλβιώτατον) of all human beings' (Hdt. 1.34.1: cf. Hdt. 1. 30–2), Hecuba learns that high social status and wealth do not entail happiness (283n., 956–61n., 627–8n.). She thus appropriates the

Herodotean Solon's statement about the mutability of fortune. Hecuba will in fact express aristocratic sentiments again at 866–7 and 1187–1237n.

ὀγκούμεθα...; 'are we proud...?' ὄγκος 'bulk', and (ἐξ)ὀγκόω 'to make bigger, swollen', are often used metaphorically (Soph. *OC* 1162, Eur. *Andr.* 703).

ὁ μέν τις ἡμῶν... | ὁ δ': this is a list of items in partitive apposition to an understood 'we' (to be inferred from 623 ὀγκούμεθα, and made explicit in 624 ἡμῶν): cf. 595n. The combination of τις and definite article designates 'a particular, but anonymous individual' (Allan on *Hel.* 1597–9): Smyth §1108 (specifically on ὁ μέν τις... ὁ δέ).

πλουσίοισι δώμασιν | ... κεκλημένος: the dative ('because of his rich household') and the participle explain the reasons why people are proud (623 ὀγκούμεθα): for similar asymmetric syntax cf. 346–8n., 1197–8n. The MS text πλουσίοις ἐν δώμασιν ('in his rich household') gives inappropriate sense.

626–7 τὰ δ'... κόμποι 'these things are nothing: they are vain thoughts of our conceited minds and verbal boasts'.

ἄλλως: 488–9n.

βουλεύματα usually means 'decisions, deliberations' (*Med.* 1044), but it comes close here to 'thoughts, mental activity' (744n.).

γλώσσης... κόμποι: the same phrase occurs in Soph. *Ant.* 127.

627–8 Many tragic characters claim that happiness depends on what happens 'day by day' (κατ' ἦμαρ: cf. Dodds on *Ba.* 910–11, 424–6, Bond on *HF* 503–5). Hecuba pessimistically states that the happiest person (ὀλβιώτατος) cannot do better than avoid suffering each day (cf. Eur. fr. 714, Soph. *OC* 1211–38). Hecuba enters the tent.

629–57 SECOND STASIMON

The chorus recall the origin of the sorrows of Troy: echoing Homeric passages (631–5n.; cf. also Hdt. 1.1.1–1.5.1), they state that it all started when Paris, the 'cowherd', 'judged the three daughters of the blessed gods on Mount Ida' (644–6). The condemnation of Paris (and Helen: 262–70n., 943–52n.) is a Homeric *topos* (640n., *Il.* 3.39–57, 3.100). The chorus stress that, as a consequence of what he did, they have a fate that is even worse than the normal 'cycle of human affairs' (639n.).

In the epode, the chorus imagine the grief and pain of Spartan women, who have lost their loved ones (649–52). This may be read as a 'humanistic', anti-war statement: war hurts the winners too. On the other hand, by specifically mentioning that Spartan women cry by the Eurotas (649–50), the Trojan chorus fully appropriate the Athenian point of view: the enemies of the Trojans are the enemies of the

Athenians. In the Peloponnesian War, the Spartans repeatedly invaded Attica and forced the Athenians to take refuge within the walls. This ambiguous sympathy for the suffering of the enemies might seem to be an instance of *Schadenfreude* – Sparta, the city that attacked Athens, is suffering the bitter consequences of its aggression – but this suggestion entails the risky allusion to a possible Spartan victory. Euripides corrects this impression by creating a parallel between Troy and Sparta, designating each city by its respective river (641 τᾶι Σιμουντίδι γᾶι and 649–50 ἀμφὶ τὸν εὔροον Εὐρώταν) and stressing how both cities are affected by the suffering caused by war. In the third stasimon the Trojan women compare themselves to Dorian girls (934). But the implications of these political allusions, as often, remain unspoken: it is left to the audience to imagine whether it will be Sparta or Athens that will suffer the fate of Troy.

Metre

Iambic (ba, cr, ia) and Aeolic (dodrans, telesillean, hipponactean, wilamowitzian) cola are combined in the strophic pair. At 637–646 (end of strophe), the dodrans (normally – ᴗ ᴗ – ᴗ –, cf. 469–478) is 'dragged' (i.e. it has a long penultimate syllable instead of a short one), taking the form – ᴗ ᴗ – – –, as in Ar. *Av.* 676 (first line of a lyric section, cf. also below, 1098): West 1982: 116. The epode continues the mixture of double-short (Aeolic cola: ibycean, telesillean) and single-short (iambic cola: ia, ba, ithyphallic) rhythms. The basic form of the ibycean is – ᴗ ᴗ – ᴗ ᴗ – ᴗ –. Its 'dragged' version (– ᴗ ᴗ – ᴗ ᴗ – – –) is very common in Euripides: *HF* 1185–7 (preceded by an iambic penthemimer, × – ᴗ – ×, as here), Itsumi 1984: 71–2, Lourenço 2011: 77 and 102–4.

The telesillean (when beginning with two short syllables, as always in this stasimon) and the ibycean have a clear rythmic affinity with the enoplian genus of cola. For enoplian analyses of some cola in the epode cf. Itsumi 1991–3: 246 and 251–2, Diggle 1994: 236, Lourenço 2011: 85 and 187 (who interprets 647–8 and 649–50 as iambelegus + sp). It is possible that each colon of the epode ended in a metrical pause.

Strophe and Antistrophe: 629–37~638–46

   ᴗ – – – ᴗ –   ba cr
629 ἐμοὶ χρῆν συμφοράν,
638 πόνοι γὰρ καὶ πόνων

   ᴗ – – – ᴗ – ᴗ – ⌒ ||ʰ¹   ba cr ba ||ʰ¹
630 ἐμοὶ χρῆν πημονὰν γενέσθαι,
639 ἀνάγκαι κρείσσονες κυκλοῦνται·

— — — ⏑ ⏑ — ⏑ — ⌒ ‖c?	hipponactean ‖c?
631 Ἰδαίαν ὅτε πρῶτον ὕλαν	
640 κοινὸν δ' ἐξ ἰδίας ἀνοίας	
⏑ — — ⏑ — ⏑ ⏑ ⌒ ‖h2	wilamowitzian ‖h2
632 Ἀλέξανδρος εἰλατίναν	
641 κακὸν τᾶι Σιμουντίδι γᾶι	
⏑ ⏑ ⏑ ⏑ ⏑ ⏑ ⏑ — ⏑ — ⏑ — ⌒ ‖c?	2 ia ba ‖c?
633–4 ἐτάμεθ', ἅλιον ἐπ' οἶδμα ναυστολήσων	
642–3 ὀλέθριον ἔμολε συμφορᾶι τ' ἔπ' ἄλλων,	
⏑ ⏑ — ⏑ ⏑ — ⏑ —	telesillean
635 Ἑλένας ἐπὶ λέκτρα, τὰν	
644 ἐκρίθη δ' ἔρις, ἂν ἐν Ἴ-	
— — — × — ⏑ ⏑—	wilamowitzian
636 καλλίσταν ὁ χρυσοφαὴς	
645 δαι κρίνει τρισσὰς μακάρων	
— ⏑ ⏑ — — ⌒ ‖‖	dragged dodrans ‖‖
637 Ἅλιος αὐγάζει.	
646 παῖδας ἀνὴρ βούτας,	

Epode: 647–57

⏑ ⏑ ⏑ ⏑ — ⏑ — ⏑ ⏑ — ⏑ ⏑ — — ⌒ ‖c?	penth ibycean ‖c?
647–8 ἐπὶ δορὶ καὶ φόνωι καὶ ἐμῶν μελάθρων λώβαι·	
⏑ — ⏑ — ⏑ ⏑ — ⏑ — — ⏑ ⏑ — — ⌒ ‖c?	penth ibycean ‖c?
649–50 στένει δὲ καί τις ἀμφὶ τὸν εὔροον Εὐρώταν	
⏑ — ⏑ ⏑ ⏑ — ⏑ — ⏑ — ⏑ ⌒ ‖c?	3 ia ‖c?
651–2 Λάκαινα πολυδάκρυτος ἐν δόμοις κόρα,	
⏑ ⏑ — ⏑ ⏑ — ⏑ — — ⏑ — ⏑ — ⌒ ‖c?	telesillean cr ba ‖c?
653–4 πολιόν τ' ἐπὶ κρᾶτα μάτηρ τέκνων θανόντων	
⏑ ⏑ — ⏑ ⏑ — ⏑ — ⏑ <— ⏑ —> ⏑ — ⌒ ‖c?	telesillean ia ba ‖c?
655 τίθεται χέρα δρύπτεταί τε <δίπτυχον> παρειάν,	
⏑ — ⏑ ⏑ ⏑ ⏑ ⏑ ⏑ — ⏑ — ⌒ ‖‖	2 ia ba ‖‖
656–7 δίαιμον ὄνυχα τιθεμένα σπαραγμοῖς.	

629–30 ἐμοὶ χρῆν … ἐμοὶ χρῆν: the repetition, in anaphora (475–6, 1095–6, Diggle 1994: 370), stresses the ineluctability of Trojan misery (*Hcld.* 449 χρῆν χρῆν).

631–5 ὅτε πρῶτον ... λέκτρα 'from the very first moment when Alexander cut the forest of firs of Mount Ida to sail over the waves of the sea to the bed of Helen'. The chorus echo *Il.* 5.62–3 νῆας ... | ἀρχεκάκους (cf. also *Il.* 22.115–16), stating that all troubles began when Paris built his ships for travelling to Greece. They then go back in time to the Judgement of Paris (644–6). The chronological inversion has a famous parallel in *Med.* 1–13, where the nurse starts her narration from the construction of Jason's ship. In *Andr.* 274–308, at the beginning of the stasimon, the chorus declare the Judgement of Paris to be the origin of all Trojan suffering; cf. also *Tro.* 919.

631 Ἰδαίαν ... ὕλαν: the text adapts the Homeric phrase Ἰδαίων ὀρέων (*Il.* 8.170, etc.) 'wooded mountains'/'Mount Ida'. The juncture of ὕλαν 'wood' and Ἰδαίαν calls attention to the etymology: ἴδη means 'timber tree'.

632 εἰλατίναν 'of fir'; fir was commonly used in ship-building (*Od.* 5.239).

633–4 ἐτάμεθ' (= ἐτάμετο) 'he cut', 3rd p. middle aor. from τέμνω.
ἅλιον ἐπ' οἶδμα: 26n.

635 τάν 'whom': 473–4n.

636 καλλίσταν: 269n.
χρυσοφαής: the sun (χρυσωπόν: *El.* 740) and the stars are 'golden' (*El.* 54).

639 κρείσσονες 'worse': 608n.
κυκλοῦνται: the 'circle of human affairs' (κύκλος τῶν ἀνθρωπηίων ... πρηγμάτων) 'does not allow the same people to be in good fortune all the time' (Hdt. 1.207.2): cf. Pearson on Soph. fr. 871.

640–3 'but, from the folly of a single individual, a shared misery came, bringing ruin to the land of Simois, and resulting in disaster for others'.

640 κοινόν ... ἰδίας: the opposition between public and private is a crucial fifth-century concept: 902–3n., Thuc. 8.1.2 καὶ ἰδίαι ἕκαστος καὶ ἡ πόλις, 6.41.2, Eur. *Pho.* 1206, *Suppl.* 129; cf. already *Od.* 3.82.
ἀνοίας: Helen (Graziosi and Haubold on *Il.* 6.356) and the Homeric narrator (*Il.* 24.28) describe Paris' actions, respectively his abduction of Helen (cf. 633–7) and his choice of Aphrodite in the Judgement (cf. 644–6), as ἄτη 'ruinous folly'.

641 τᾶι Σιμουντίδι γᾶι 'the land of Simois', one of the rivers of Troy. Σιμουντίς is the contracted form of the adjective derived from the name of the river.

642–3 συμφορᾶι τ' ἐπ' ἄλλων: ἐπί is construed with the dative συμφορᾶι, indicating an end or purpose: LSJ s.v. ἐπί B III.2, Soph. *Phil.* 151 ἐπί σῶι ... καιρῶι. The genitive ἄλλων depends on συμφορᾶι: for the word order cf. Eur. *Or.* 94 τάφον ... πρὸς κασιγνήτης, Jebb on Soph. *OT* 178. The prepositional phrase συμφορᾶι ... ἐπ' ἄλλων is paired with the adjectival phrase 641–2 τᾶι Σιμουντίδι γᾶι | ὀλέθριον (Stinton 1990: 72). For similar syntactic variations cf. 916–18n. The MS text συμφορά τ' ἀπ' ἄλλων 'and disaster came from others' (the Greeks? the Trojans? the gods?) relieves Paris from part of the guilt, destroying the rhetoric of the whole stasimon.

644–6 ἃν ἐν Ἴ|δαι κρίνει ... βούτας '(the contest) which the herdsman judged on Ida between the three daughters of the blessed ones'. The verb takes the accusative of both the dispute judged ('the quarrel that he judges', cf. *Od.* 12.440, Ar. *Ran.* 873 ἀγῶνα κρῖναι, Eur. *Hcld.* 179), and the people who are judged (*IA* 71–2 ὁ τὰς θεὰς | κρίνας). This bold combination is in part eased by the fact that the first object is expressed by a relative pronoun. Compare other double accusative constructions: *Alc.* 733 εἰ μή σ' ἀδελφῆς αἷμα τιμωρήσεται, *Od.* 15.236–7 ἐτείσατο ἔργον ἀεικὲς | ἀντίθεον Νηλῆα, Jacquinod 1989: 248, 252–3, K–G I.320–8. On the Judgement of Paris cf. Richardson on *Il.* 24.27–30, Eur. *Tro.* 924–90, Stinton 1990: 17–75.

ἀνὴρ βούτας: lit. 'a man, a herdsman'; for this type of apposition cf. 790n. Paris had been abandoned at birth and was working as a cowherd when he judged the three goddesses (*Andr.* 280–3). Paris the cowherd appeared onstage in Euripides' *Alexandros* (Collard and Cropp 2008a: 33–75). He is disparagingly so called in other contexts also (945, *IA* 180).

647–8 'which resulted in war, death, and the ruin of my household'. For ἐπί + dat. cf. 642–3n. The syntax runs over from the antistrophe to the epode. This is rare in tragedy, but not in archaic lyric (Barrett on *Hipp.* 129–30). The break is never harsh in tragedy: for a prepositional phrase, as here, cf. Aesch. *Ag.* 238. A participial clause is added in 943–9, *Hipp.* 131, *Suppl.* 47, *El.* 157.

649–50 ἀμφὶ τὸν εὔροον Εὐρώταν: the Homeric epithet ἐΰρροος (*Il.* 7.329) is applied to the Eurotas, the river of Sparta (*Andr.* 437, *Tro.* 210–11), suggesting a punning etymology, echoing another Homeric adjective for rivers, εὑρείτης (*Il.* 6.34 Σατνιόεντος ἐϋρρεῖταο, Eur. *Tro.* 810). The non-contracted form εὔροον, conjectured by Hermann, gives the correct metrical shape and restores the form current in classical Greek: Soph. *Phil.* 491–2 εὔροον | Σπερχειόν, K–B I.270.

651–2 πολυδάκρυτος 'full of tears' (cf. *Od.* 19.213 πολυδακρύτοιο γόοιο, Aesch. *Cho.* 333, Emp. 31 B 62.1 D–K πολυκλαύτων ... γυναικῶν), not 'much wept' (as in *Il.* 24.620). As normal for adjectives in -τος, the basic meaning is 'such that there is much weeping'; the adjective acquires an 'active' or 'passive' meaning according to the context: Fraenkel on Aesch. *Ag.* 12, Barrett on *Hipp.* 677–9.

653–7 'the mother of dead children lays her hand on her grey head, and scratches her two cheeks, making her nail bloody by tearing' (tr. Diggle 1994: 234 adapted). Diggle 1994: 234–6 shows that τε at 655 is necessary for the syntax, and that the addition of δίπτυχον (cf. *Tro.* 280 δίπτυχον παρειάν) restores good metre. Female mourners usually beat their head with their hands and tear their cheeks: *El.* 146–9, *Tro.* 279–80, *Hel.* 372–4 (with similar language).

655–7 τίθεται ... τιθεμένα: 1024–7n.

658–904 THIRD EPISODE

The episode is divided into two sections: an announcement scene, which, after an introduction (658–83), takes the form of a lyric exchange (684–721), and a supplication scene (722–904).

658–83 Dialogue between Chorus Leader, Servant and Hecuba

The Servant returns onstage to announce the death of Polydorus. This section recalls the preparation for a messenger scene (684–721n.), and would suggest that the Servant is about to deliver a report. Messengers are normally characters who have not been onstage previously, but for exceptions see e.g. *El.* 766. Instead of a speech, what follows is a lyric dialogue. The Servant asks for Hecuba, who appears onstage (cf. *Hipp.* 1153–5). She then warns Hecuba that she is bringing bad news, without giving details (667–9). This is a tactful regular practice in Euripides: *Med.* 1122–3, *Hipp.* 1157–9, cf. Soph. *OT* 1223–31 (good news is announced right away: cf. e.g. *Hcld.* 784–6). Hecuba tries to guess what happened (μῶν: 676, cf. *Hipp.* 1160), but fails to imagine the extent of the disaster, as often: *Hipp.* 1160–1, 1164–5 (ironic and insulting, a parody of the usual development), *Tro.* 712. The messenger at that point usually corrects the addressee and starts his or her narrative. Here the Servant chooses to reveal the body, an insensitive course of action (678–80n.).

659 πάντα ... ἄνδρα καὶ θῆλυν σποράν 'every man and female offspring', that is, 'every man and woman'. Tragic language is fond of such polar expressions where two (or more) opposed terms subsume every possibility: Wilamowitz on *HF* 1106, Barrett on *Hipp.* 441–2, 1277–80. For variations in the second element see 1200, Bond on *HF* 536 τὸ θῆλυ ... ἀρσένων.

659–60 νικῶσ' ... | κακοῖσιν 'defeating ... with <her> misfortunes'. The crucial qualification is delayed by four intervening words and enjambment: this stresses Hecuba's paradoxical victory.

στέφανον 'crown', indicating victory (Pind. *Ol.* 8.76). Cassandra will echo and reverse this claim at *Tro.* 401.

661 τί δ', ὦ τάλαινα σῆς κακογλώσσου βοῆς; 'What do you mean, you wretched with your ill-omened cry?' For the genitive cf. 156–8n. Her tongue is not εὔφημος (664).

662 '<I say this> because painful announcements never cease for me.' For ὡς in this meaning after a question cf. 985, 1042. ὡς could also be taken as exclamatory (cf. 506), stressing 'never'; with exclamatory ὡς the emphasis is normally on a term expressing quality ('good', 'bad', 'suffer') rather than on adverbs. εὕδειν 'to sleep' metaphorically means 'to cease': Collard on *Suppl.* 1147.

μοι 'for me'. The MSS read σου 'your painful announcements never sleep' but: (a) this implies that the Servant brought bad news in the past, which is not the case: οὔποτε + pres. ind. usually refers to a past action continuing (or repeated) in the present (85–6, *Ion* 1435), which may also go on in the future (Aesch. *Eum.* 175 οὔποτ' ἐλευθεροῦται, Eur. fr. 518.5); (b) 663 'I bring this suffering to Hecuba' implies a correction of a claim by the coryphaeus in 662 that the bad news affected her (μοι), not Hecuba.

665 καὶ μήν: 216n.

δόμων ὕπο 'from under the house', 53–4n. The reading ὕπερ gives impossible meaning ('above the house': *El.* 1233, *HF* 817). ὕπο may be a (good) Byzantine conjecture.

666 ἐς δὲ καιρὸν σοῖσι φαίνεται λόγοις 'and she makes her appearance at the right moment for <hearing> your message'. Several other comparable entries take place 'at the right moment' in tragedy: 966, *Hipp.* 899, *HF* 701, Soph. *Ai.* 1168.

667 παντάλαινα κἄτι μᾶλλον ἢ λέγω 'completely wretched and even more <completely wretched> than I can say', an extreme form of superlative: *Alc.* 1082, *Hipp.* 914 φίλους γε, κἄτι μᾶλλον ἢ φίλους. Language at its most hyperbolic cannot match the extreme situation of Hecuba: for this concept see *Suppl.* 844, *HF* 916, *IT* 1321, *Pho.* 389.

668 ὀλωλας κοὐκέτ' εἶ, βλέπουσα φῶς 'you are dead and do not exist anymore, even if you see the light of the day'. For the paradox cf. 431n. Hecuba wishes to die (386–96, 505–11) and is often said to be symbolically dead (168, 231–2, 431, 784, 1214). βλέπουσα φῶς is a concessive participle: for the absence of ὅμως see *El.* 551, Smyth §2066. It may also be taken as expressing time, 'while you see the light of the day', as the participle in *Tro.* 442.

669 Four words in apposition form a single line ('tetracolon'), an impressive stylistic feature: see 811, Soph. *Ant.* 1071 ἄμοιρον, ἀκτέριστον, ἀνόσιον νέκυν. For three-word trimeters cf. *Hipp.* 1406, Marcovich 1984.

ἄπαις ἄνανδρος ἄπολις: 3on.

670 εἰδόσιν δ' ὠνείδισας 'and you taunt people who know' how things are: a highly ironic occurrence of a turn of phrase often used to apologise (*Il.* 23.787) or rebuke (*Il.* 10. 250) someone for repeating what is well known: Friis-Johansen and Whittle on Aesch. *Suppl.* 742. Hecuba agrees with what the Servant says about her current situation at 667–9, but does not in fact 'know' what happened. On the masculine generalising plural εἰδόσιν see Barrett on *Hipp.* 287, Smyth §1009.

672-3 ἧς ἀπηγγέλθη τάφος | πάντων Ἀχαιῶν διὰ χερὸς σπουδὴν ἔχειν 'whose funeral rites were reported to be the object of care at the hand of all the Greeks'. σπουδήν ἔχειν usually means 'to have concern for': *Alc.* 778, *Med.* 557. However, several phrases with ἔχω and the accusative may be used in both active and passive sense, according to the context: 351–3n., *Or.* 1069 μομφὴν ἔχω 'I have cause to reproach', *Hcld.* 974 ἕξεις μέμψιν 'you will be reproached', Mastronarde on *Pho.* 773. The Greeks built the funeral pyre; they were not to touch Polyxena's body (548–9, 605–6, 726–9).

674 ἥδ' 'this woman'. Demonstratives are often used disparagingly of a character present onstage, but not directly addressed, even if he or she is supposed to hear the remark: 1196, Eur. *Hipp.* 1038, Soph. *OT* 1160, Bain 1977: 71–3, Battezzato 1995: 111. The servant is not able to deliver the news with tact (678–8on., 688n., 693n., contrast 658–83n.).

675 ἅπτεται 'grasps'.

676–7 Hecuba cannot imagine that Polydorus, who is supposed to be far away, could be the corpse in front of her; Cassandra is the only other close relative left to her.

μῶν: 1260n.

βακχεῖον 'Bacchic', that is 'inspired by god', 'prophetic'. See the cognate words used similarly at 121, *Tro.* 341, 366–7.

κάρα 'head', a periphrasis referring to the whole person: Griffith on Soph. *Ant.* 1, Eur. *Ion* 1476.

δεῦρο 'here'. For its unusual position in the middle of a syntactically unrelated phrase see *Hcld.* 136 πέμπει Μυκηνῶν δεῦρό μ' Εὐρυσθεὺς ἄναξ, *Andr.* 150 ἀπαρχὰς δεῦρ' ἔχουσ' ἀφικόμην.

678–80 The Servant uncovers the corpse of Polydorus. This brutal gesture characterises her as unperceptive (674n., 688n., 693n.), and lacking in verbal skills, in contrast to the professional messenger Talthybius, who is brief and direct (508–10), but compassionate (518–20, 580–2). Corpses, especially disfigured ones, were normally kept veiled onstage, for decency's sake (Soph. *Ai.* 915–19, 1003–5); special care was taken to avoid shocking mothers with the view of their dead children (*Suppl.* 944–5). When parents had to see the bodies of their children, cautious and lengthy verbal preparation preceded visual revelation (see the special cases of *HF* 1089–1145 and *Ba.* 1264–85). The closest parallel for this scene is Soph. *El.* 1458–78, where Orestes shocks Aegisthus with the unexpected view of Clytemnestra's body, a deliberately planned act of hostility. Compare also 703 with Soph. *El.* 1479–81.

681 οἴμοι, βλέπω δή 'alas, I do see'. The particle δή takes up ἄθρησον: *Suppl.* 1009 ὁρᾷς ... 1012 ὁρῶ δή ..., Denniston 214–15.

683: 668n.

684–721 Lyric Dialogue (amoibaion)

Euripides often chooses a short lyric dialogue (*amoibaion*) as an alternative to a messenger scene (*Tro.* 239–91, Popp 1971: 261–4). In an *amoibaion*, sung and recited sections create an alternation between the delivery of information and highly emotional reactions. This scene is unusual in that visual contact with the body of Polydorus becomes a substitute for a verbal announcement of his death. Hecuba addresses her dead son in a lament, asking *him* questions about his death; the Servant fills in the details, answering the questions directed to Polydorus. Hecuba's dialogue with her son's body mixes formulas of lament (685n.) and questions which it would be normal to ask of a messenger. Compare 695 τίνι μόρωι θνήισκεις ...; with Eur. *Ba.* 1041 τίνι μόρωι θνήισκει;, *HF* 919, Aesch. *Pers.* 446, Soph. *Ant.* 1314. For 697 cf. *Hipp.* 1164.

The Servant and the chorus recite in iambic trimeters. Hecuba's trimeters were probably sung, but could have been also recited or chanted: Dale 1968: 86 and 208; Parker on *Alc.* 213–37 (metre), Moore 2008. Hecuba certainly sings the rest of the lyric sections.

Metre

684	− − − − ⌒ ‖ᵇ ὦ τέκνον τέκνον,	δ ‖ᵇ
685	⌣ − ⌣ − ⌣ − ⌣ − αἰαῖ, κατάρχομαι νόμον	2 ia
686	− − ⌣ − ⌣ − ⌣ ⌒ ‖ᵇ βακχεῖον, ἐξ ἀλάστορος	2 ia ‖ᵇ
687	− ⌣ ⌣ − ⌣ ⌒ ‖‖ ἀρτιμαθὴς κακῶν.	δ ‖‖
688	− − ⌣ − − − ⌣ − − − ⌣ ⌒ ‖ᵇʰ ἔγνως γὰρ ἄτην παιδός, ὦ δύστηνε σύ.	ia trim (recited) ‖ᵇʰ
689	⌣ − ⌣ − ⌣ − ⌣ − ⌣ − ⌣ ⌒ ‖ʰ ἄπιστ' ἄπιστα, καινὰ καινὰ δέρκομαι.	ia trim (sung?) ‖ʰ
690	⌣ ⌣ ⌣ − ⌣ ⌣ − ⌣ ⌣ − ⌣ − ⌣ ⌒ ‖ʰ ἕτερα δ' ἀφ' ἑτέρων κακὰ κακῶν κυρεῖ,	2 δ ‖ʰ
691	− ⌣ − ⌣ − ⌣ ⌣ ⌣ − ⌣ − οὐδέ ποτ' ἀστένακτος ἀδάκρυτος ἀ-	2 δ
692	⌣ − − − ⌒ ‖‖ μέρα 'πισχήσει.	δ ‖‖

COMMENTARY: 684–721

	− − ◡ − ◡ − ◡ − ◡ − ◡ ⁀ ‖^bh	ia trim (recited) ‖^bh
693	δείν', ὦ τάλαινα, δεινὰ πάσχομεν κακά.	
	− − − − − ◡ − − − −	2 δ
694	ὦ τέκνον τέκνον ταλαίνας ματρός,	
	◡ ◡ ◡ − − − ◡ ◡ ◡ − − −	2 δ
695–6	τίνι μόρωι θνήισκεις, τίνι πότμωι κεῖσαι,	
	− ◡ ◡ − − ⁀ ‖‖‖	δ ‖‖‖
697	πρὸς τίνος ἀνθρώπων;	
	− − ◡ − − − − ◡ − ◡ − ◡ ⁀ ‖^c	ia trim (recited) ‖^c
698	οὐκ οἶδ'· ἐπ' ἀκταῖς νιν κυρῶ θαλασσίαις.	
	− − ◡ − ◡ − ◡ − ◡ − ◡ ⁀ ‖^b	ia trim (sung?) ‖^b
699	ἔκβλητον ἢ πέσημα φοινίου δορὸς	
	− ◡ ◡ − − ⁀ ‖‖‖	δ ‖‖‖
700	ἐν ψαμάθωι λευρᾶι;	
	− − ◡ − − − ◡ ◡ ◡ − ◡ ⁀ ‖^c	ia trim (recited) ‖^c
701	πόντου νιν ἐξήνεγκε πελάγιος κλύδων.	
	× × × × ‖^h	exclamations *extra metrum* ‖^h
702	ὤιμοι αἰαῖ,	
	◡ ◡◡ ◡◡ ◡◡ − ◡ −	2 ia
703	ἔμαθον ἐνύπνιον ὀμμάτων	
	◡ − − ◡ − ◡ ◡ ◡ − − −	2 δ
704	ἐμῶν ὄψιν (οὔ με παρέβα φάντα-	
	◡ ◡ ◡ − ◡ ⁀ ‖^b	δ ‖^b
705	σμα μελανόπτερον)	
	− ◡ − ◡ − ◡ ⁀ ‖^bh	lecythion ‖^bh
706	ἃν ἐσεῖδον ἀμφὶ σέ,	
	− ◡ ◡ − ◡ − ◡ ◡ − ◡ ⁀ ‖‖‖	2 δ ‖‖‖
707	ὦ τέκνον, οὐκέτ' ὄντα Διὸς ἐν φάει.	
	− − ◡ − − − ◡ − ◡ − ◡ ⁀ ‖^h	ia trim (recited) ‖^h
708	τίς γάρ νιν ἔκτειν'; οἶσθ' ὀνειρόφρων φράσαι;	
	◡ ◡ ◡ − ◡ − − ◡ ◡ − ◡ −	2 δ
709–10	ἐμὸς ἐμὸς ξένος, Θρήικιος ἱππότας,	
	◡ ◡ ◡ − ◡ − ◡ ◡ ◡ − − ⁀ ‖‖‖	2 δ ‖‖‖
711–12	ἵν' ὁ γέρων πατὴρ ἔθετό νιν κρύψας.	

_ _ ⏑ _ _ _ ⏑ _ ⏑ _ ⏑ ⌒ ‖ᶜ	ia trim (recited) ‖ᶜ
713 οἴμοι, τί λέξεις; χρυσὸν ὡς ἔχοι κτανών;	
_ _ ⏑ _ ⏑ _ ⏑ _ ⏑ _ ⏑ ⌒ ‖ᵇʰ	ia trim (sung?) ‖ᵇʰ
714 ἄρρητ' ἀνωνόμαστα, θαυμάτων πέρα,	
_ ⏑⏑ _ ⏑ _ ⏑ _ ⏑ _ ⏑ _	δ kδ
715 οὐχ ὅσι' οὐδ' ἀνεκτά. ποῦ δίκα ξένων;	
_ ⏑⏑ _ _ _ ⏑⏑ _ _	2 δ
716–17 ὦ κατάρατ' ἀνδρῶν, ὡς διεμοιράσω	
⏑⏑ ⏑ _ ⏑ _ ⏑ _ _ ⏑ _	2 δ
718–19 χρόα, σιδαρέωι τεμὼν φασγάνωι	
⏑⏑⏑ _ ⏑ _ ⏑ _ _ ⏑ ⌒ ‖‖	2 δ ‖‖
720–21 μέλεα τοῦδε παιδὸς οὐδ' ὤικτισας.	

685 κατάρχομαι 'I begin', a meta-performative statement marking the start of the lament, as in *Andr.* 1199, *Or.* 960. See also *Tro.* 147–8 ἐξάρξω ... μολπάν, delivered by Hecuba.

685–6 νόμον | βακχεῖον 'a Bacchic song': cf. 3n. Dionysiac music was considered very emotional: Soph. *Trach.* 216–21, Bierl 1991: 86. The variant γόον βακχεῖον is not implausible: *Or.* 960 κατάρχομαι στεναγμόν, *Pho.* 1489–90 βάκχα νεκύ|ων.

686–7 ἐξ ἀλάστορος | ἀρτιμαθὴς κακῶν 'having learned only now the evils caused by an avenging spirit'. At *Hipp.* 820 Theseus imagines that his misfortune is an 'inexpressible stain from some avenging spirit (ἐξ ἀλαστόρων τινός)'. An ἀλάστωρ is often imagined to be the cause of unexplainable misfortune: 949, *Or.* 337, *IA* 878, Gagné 2013: 398–9. For ἐκ see Diggle 1981: 28–9. Tragic characters learn too late: *Alc.* 940 and *Ba.* 1296 ἄρτι μανθάνω, *Med.* 85. For the compound adjective, compare ἀρτιτρεφής (*Sept.* 350), ἀρτιθανής (*Alc.* 600).

688 ἔγνως γὰρ ἄτην παιδός, ὦ δύστηνε σύ '<You say this> because you understood your child's fate, unhappy you.' ἔγνως takes up ἀρτιμαθής. On this meaning of γάρ see Denniston 75, Soph. *OT* 1115–17. Editors print the line as a question, but this is less appropriate here: a rhetorical question, giving 'the grounds for an implied assent' (Denniston 76), would be otiose; a rhetorical question expressing surprise (*Alc.* 1089), disbelief (*HF* 610) or irony (*Alc.* 711, Denniston 77–8) would be illogical; nor is the servant woman asking an information-seeking question (*Hcld.* 672, Denniston 81–6).

689 ἄπιστ' ἄπιστα 'incredible, incredible things', a frequent reaction to unexpected news: Aesch. *Ag.* 268, Eur. *IT* 1293, *Hel.* 1520, Stinton 1990: 236–64.

690 The double hyperbaton emphasises the adjectives: Eur. *Andr.* 1144 κραυγὴ δ' ἐν εὐφήμοισι δύσφημος δόμοις, Devine and Stephens 2000: 127.

691–2 οὐδέ ποτ' ἀστένακτος ἀδάκρυτος ἁ|μέρα 'πισχήσει 'nor will a day without groans and tears stop them' (= the misfortunes, 690 κακά). The MS text οὐδέ ποτ' ἀδάκρυτος ἀστένακτος ἁμέρα μ'ἐπισχήσει is metrically dubious and syntactically very difficult ('nor will a day without groans and tears stop me' (from crying?)). Many interpret 'πισχήσει as an intransitive form, 'will continue, pass' (Gregory, referring to LSJ s.v. ἐπέχω vi.2b), but secure classical parallels are lacking. For the interpolation of a personal pronoun see Diggle 1994: 363. Blaydes conjectured ἁμέρα με σχήσει ('never a day without tears will have me'), which also gives possible meaning and good metre, even if a precise parallel for 'a day will have me' is lacking: see 970, LSJ s.v. ἔχω A 1.8. For the interpolation of a preverb see *Or.* 1658, *Hipp.* 965.

693 δείν', ὦ τάλαινα, δεινὰ πάσχομεν κακά 'terrible, poor woman, terrible are the woes we suffer'. Polymestor's δεινὰ δεινὰ πεπόνθαμεν (1097) highlights the reversal of situation. The sharing tone of the 'we' in 693 fits better with the attribution of the line to the chorus (ὡ) than to the insensitive slave girl (678–80n., 688n.) (D. Mastronarde, personal communication). The names of speakers are often the guesswork of ancient or medieval scholars and scribes, replacing earlier sigla that indicated a change of speaker: West 1973: 55, Marshall 2004, Gammacurta 2006: 240–6.

695–6 θνήισκεις ... ; 'are you dead?' The present tense indicates the enduring effect of an action that has taken place in the past: 1134n., Smyth §1887a, Moorhouse 1982: 183–4, K–G I 136.

κεῖσαι ... ; 'do you lie dead?'

698 νιν κυρῶ 'I found him': 695–6n.

699–700 'Was he thrown away or was he killed by a murderous spear on the smooth sand?' For ἔκβλητον compare 1077–8n. ἐκβολάν. πέσημα 'what has fallen' (cf. πίπτω) means 'corpse' (*HF* 1131, *Pho.* 1701), just like πτῶμα: Friis-Johansen and Whittle on Aesch. *Suppl.* 661–2. The genitive indicates the agent responsible for the action of the verbal root 'to fall': K–G I.333, Bruhn 1899: 139.

701 πόντου ... πελάγιος κλύδων 'the marine wave of the sea', a redundant expression: 26n., *Hipp.* 753–4 πόντιον | κῦμ' ἁλίκτυπον ἅλμας, *Med.* 211–12, Breitenbach 1934: 193–4.

703–4 ἐνύπνιον ὀμμάτων | ἐμῶν ὄψιν 'the dream image seen by my eyes'. ὄψις often designates a vision in a dream: 72, *IT* 151, Aesch. *Sept.* 710 ἐνυπνίων φαντασμάτων ὄψεις, *Ag.* 425, *PV* 645. For the etymological play ὀμμάτων [root *oπ-] ... ὄψιν see Seaford on *Cycl.* 459 and 628, *Or.* 513.

704–5 οὔ με παρέβα φάντα|σμα μελανόπτερον 'the dream vision with dark wings has not escaped me'. For the meaning of παρέβα see Soph.

Trach. 226 παρῆλθε, *Il.* 1.132 οὐ παρελεύσεαι. The sentence means almost the same thing as ἔμαθον ... ὄψιν: for the redundancy see Eur. *Hcld.* 778, Soph. *Phil.* 205–9. For φάντασμα 'vision in a dream' see 53–4n. The MS reading φάσμα has the same meaning (70, *IT* 42, 1262) but is metrically awkward here. For the corruption see Eur. *Or.* 407, Aesch. *Sept.* 710. By reusing the imagery of 71, Hecuba stresses that she is now able to understand the dream she could not interpret at the beginning of the play.

706 ἀμφὶ σέ 'about you'. The accusative with ἀμφί is an epic usage imitated in tragedy: *Il.* 18.339–40 ἀμφὶ δὲ σὲ Τρωιαὶ καὶ Δαρδανίδες ... | κλαύσονται, Eur. *Tro.* 511–14 ἀμφί μοι Ἴλιον ... ἄισον ... ὠιδάν, Mastronarde on *Pho.* 1028, Soph. *Trach.* 937. Wecklein conjectured the more common genitive case.

707 οὐκέτ' ὄντα Διὸς ἐν φάει 'you who are not in the light of Zeus any more'. For Zeus and the light of the day see *IA* 1507–8 ἰὼ λαμπαδοῦχος ἀμέρα Διός τε φέγγος. The usual phrase refers to the light of the day or of the sun: 169, 415, *Hel.* 530, *Hipp.* 4. The transferral is due to the equivalence between Zeus and *aithēr* (Aesch. fr. 70, Eur. frr. 839, 877, 941) and between *aithēr* and light (Aesch. *PV* 1091–2, Eur. *Pho.* 3, Janko on *Il.* 13.837 ἵκετ' αἰθέρα καὶ Διὸς αὐγάς). In classical Greece Zeus is never securely identified with the Sun: Pherecydes 7 A 9 D–K, Schibli 1990: 44 n. 92, 61 n. 25.

708 οἶσθ' ... φράσαι; 'Can you tell me?', a typical question to a messenger: Aesch. *Pers.* 479 οἶσθα σημῆναι τορῶς; (after a question), *IT* 248, *Ion* 800–1.

ὀνειρόφρων 'inspired by the dream', a unique formation: compare Pind. *Ol.* 6.41 θεόφρονα κοῦρον 'a child inspired by the god', Smyth §897 (2).

709–12 Θρήικιος ἱππότας, | ἵν' 'the horseman of Thrace, where ...' The relative adverb refers to the noun 'Thrace' implied by the adjective Θρήικιος 'Thracian': Diggle 1994: 443 n. 5, Bers 1974: 21–7.

713 τί λέξεις; 511n.

ἔχοι the main verb is in a secondary tense (708 ἔκτειν(ε)), which explains the optative.

714 ἄρρητ' ἀνωνόμαστα 'impossible to say and to name'. For the paired adjectives cf. 669n., *Suppl.* 966 ἄπαις ἄτεκνος, *Ion* 782.

θαυμάτων πέρα 'beyond marvels', worse than what would cause astonishment. The crime exceeds what human mind and language can imagine and express: *IT* 839–40 θαυμάτων πέρα, *Ba.* 667 θαυμάτων τε κρείσσονα, 667n., 689.

715 ποῦ δίκα ξένων; 'Where is the justice that protects guests?': an indignant question, similar to Croesus' cry from the pyre: 'Where is the *charis* of the gods?' (Bacchyl. 3.38).

716 ὦ κατάρατ' ἀνδρῶν 'you, cursed among men' (1064n.). κατάρατος was probably an insult in everyday language; it occurs in Euripides (*Med.*

162, *Hec.* 1064, *Hel.* 54) and, frequently, in comedy and the orators, but only once in Sophocles (*OT* 1342), never in Aeschylus. Euripides also uses it to express commiseration: *Hipp.* 1362.

716–21 ὡς διεμοιράσω ... παιδός 'how you rent the child's flesh and cut his limbs with the iron sword' (Kovacs). Cf. 782. At 1076–7, Polymestor fears that Hecuba and the Trojan women will do the same to his children; Polymestor in his turn will attempt to tear the women apart too (1125–6; cf. also 1070–4). In fact Polydorus' body does not appear to have been dismembered: it is recovered in one piece (contrast *Ba.* 1125–43, 1216–20) and Hecuba does not make further references to the supposed dismembering. Hecuba resorts to the language of epic to describe the horror of violence: *Il.* 13.501, 16.761 ταμέειν χρόα νηλέϊ χαλκῶι. She uses a range of specific terms (hyponyms) to indicate 'killing' in general: compare 143n., 155n., Eur. *Hipp.* 1376 διαμοιρᾶσαι, and διαρραίω in *Il.* 24.355, *Od.* 1.251, 16.128. Schlesier 1988: 127–32 and Zeitlin 1996: 178–83 suggest that this detail echoes Aeschylus' *Edonians* (frr. 57–67), where the Thracian king Lycurgus rejected Dionysus, was blinded by Zeus (*Il.* 6.130–40) and, in a state of madness induced by Dionysus, killed and dismembered his son Dryas (Apollod. 3.5.1; cf. Soph. *Ant.* 955–65).

720–1 οὐδ' ὤικτισας 'and did not take pity on him'. The variant ὠικτίσω (2nd p. ind. aor. middle) has the same meaning: Aesch. *Suppl.* 1031, Thuc. 2.51.6. On synonymous middle and active verbs see R. J. Allan 2003: 203–10. The ending in -ω probably arose because of assimilation to the ending of διεμοιράσω.

722–904 Dialogue between Hecuba and Agamemnon

722–3 Hecuba is not simply the most unhappy woman (659–60, 667, 785–6): she is called πολυπονωτάτην, an adjective which ironically reverses the names of her children Polyxena and Polydorus (Introduction, section 4 and note 42).

For divine hostility as an explanation for suffering see 686–7n. For the text see [1087n.]

724–5 After an *amoibaion* or *kommos*, the entrance onstage of actors is always announced: Hamilton 1978: 68–9.

τοῦδε δεσπότου δέμας | Ἀγαμέμνονος 'the figure of my master Agamemnon, who is here (τοῦδε)'. The periphrasis (on which see Bond on *HF* 1036) here suggests solemnity.

726 κρύπτειν τάφωι 'to cover with a tumulus', as in *El.* 1277 καλύψουσιν τάφωι. The more usual phrase is κρύπτειν χθονί 'to cover with earth': 896–7n. Tumulus and pyre are not mutually exclusive: *Alc.* 608 πρὸς τάφον τε καὶ πυράν.

727–8 ἐφ' οἷσπερ ... κόρης 'according to what Talthybius announced, that no one of the Argives should touch your daughter'. ἐφ' οἷς 'according to the agreement which' is a phrase much used in prose (LSJ s.v. ἐπί III.3) and in Euripides (*HF* 706).

729 εἰῶμεν οὐδ' ἐψαύομεν 'we let her be and did not touch her'. οὐδ' ἐψαύομεν is to be preferred to οὐδὲ ψαύομεν because, in tragic trimeters, 'when the anceps of the third metron is occupied by a long syllable, this syllable and the one following belong to the same word [here: ἐψαύ-], unless one of them is a monosyllable' (West 1987: 25). This rule is called Porson's law: see Devine and Stephens 1984: 6, Battezzato 2009c. The slight correction εἰῶμεν (Nauck: ἐῶμεν MSS) harmonises the tenses. For the easy confusion between ει and ε see Threatte 1980: 172–7 and 299–30.

731–2 τἀκεῖθεν γάρ εὖ | πεπραγμέν' ἐστίν, εἴ τι τῶνδ' ἐστὶν καλῶς 'things over there have been brought to completion well, if there is anything that is fine among those things'. Agamemnon uses euphemistic language, stressing his misgivings about the sacrifice and its efficacy: cf. 120–2 and, for the language, *Hel.* 27, 952, *Or.* 17. For the monosyllable in enjambment see 405, *Med.* 1053 (δὲ μή), *Hcld.* 1016 (μὲν οὐ), Battezzato 2008b: 103–38.

733–4 ἔα· τίν' ἄνδρα τόνδ' ἐπὶ σκηναῖς ὁρῶ | θανόντα Τρώων; 'Ah! Who is this man that I see here in front of the tent, dead? He is one of the Trojans.' Agamemnon, on entering onstage, did not see Polydorus. The exclamation ἔα is often used as a sign that the 'partial vision' of a character entering onstage has ended: Mastronarde 1979: 22–6.

734–5 οὐ γάρ ... ἀγγέλλουσί μοι 'The clothes that wrap his body announce to me that he is not an Argive.' The metaphorical use of ἀγγέλλουσι continues the archaic usage of ἄγγελος in riddles or enigmatic expressions: Thgn. 549, Aesch. *Suppl.* 180 with Friis Johansen and Whittle *ad loc.*, Eur. *Hcld.* 656 βοήν ... ἄγγελον φόβου. The silent clothes, distinguishably barbarian (Hall 1989: 136), 'speak'.

736–51 Hecuba speaks to herself; Agamemnon does not hear what she says, while the audience does ('aside'). Asides are exceptional in Greek tragedy (Bain 1977: 13–66). This passage is even more remarkable in that two trains of thought, Agamemnon's and Hecuba's, develop in parallel, up to the point where the possibility of contact is almost broken; the complexity of this passage is enhanced by the fact that Hecuba, debating with herself about Agamemnon's sympathy, delays verbal contact with Agamemnon, but the delay in fact risks alienating him. Usually, monologue and comment on it are differently intertwined: for instance, characters onstage often comment on an offstage monologue (Soph. *Ai.* 333–45, Eur. *Med.* 96–172), or a character hears and comments on a monologue but is not taken into account by the soliloquising person (e.g. Aesch. *Ag.* 1072–1139, Eur. *Hipp.* 208–43, 337–43, 916–31, *Pho.* 604–7, *Or.* 257–61). The innovative aside technique here offers a framework for a very traditional type of Homeric-style monologue, where a character considers two alternative options: de Jong 2012 on *Il.* 22.91–137. In Homer, the turning point is marked by the phrase ἀλλὰ τίη μοι ταῦτα φίλος διελέξατο θυμός; (*Il.* 11.407, 17.97, 21.562, 22.122), alluded to here at 750 τί στρέφω τάδε; (cf. 960–1, *Med.* 1049). Supplication is humiliating, and characters of high social standing resort to it only in extreme circumstances: *Suppl.* 164–7 'I consider it shameful (ἐν μὲν αἰσχύναις ἔχω) to fall on the ground and to embrace your knee with my hand: I am an old man, and was once a prosperous king; however, it is now necessary (ἀνάγκη, cf. 751 ἀνάγκη) to yield to my misfortunes', *Hel.* 512 (ἀναγκαίως ἔχει), 947–9, *Pho.* 1622–4, *Or.* 671–3.

736–7 δύστην', ἐμαυτὴν γὰρ λέγω λέγουσα σέ, | Ἑκάβη, τί δράσω; 'You, wretched Hecuba – for, when I say you, I mean myself – what shall I do?' Hecuba addresses herself in the vocative, 'as if another person' (Paley), an elaborate procedure signalling the split in her own mind. For similar monologic addresses to oneself see *Med.* 402, Men. *Sam.* 326. For the distance between δύστηνε and Ἑκάβη see *Med.* 1306–7, Diggle 1994: 167.

γάρ explains the reason for the vocative chosen: cf. *Med.* 465–6, *Andr.* 64, *Hel.* 1193, Diggle 1994: 1–2.

τί δράσω; is an aporetic question (= 'I do not know what to do'): 419, *Alc.* 380, *Med.* 1042. In monologues, it may introduce one or more deliberative questions, listing possible courses of action: Mastronarde on *Pho.* 1310–11, 1615–20, Soph. *OC* 1254–6.

740 πραχθέν 'what happened', as in *Hipp.* 842. The variant reading κρανθέν 'what was brought to completion' (cf. *Ion* 77) is less apt. κραίνω is normally used of bringing to completion what the gods or fate or the rulers have ordained, which is not the case here: Eur. *Hipp.* 1255–6, 1345–6, Fraenkel on Aesch. *Ag.* 369, Bain 1977: 14 n. 1.

741 πολεμίαν θ' ἡγούμενος: Euripides reuses the same phrase in *Tro.* 915, reversing the roles: Helen fears that Menelaus will not listen to her, and will favour Hecuba in the debate.

742 On the repetition of ἄν see Barrett on *Hipp.* 270.

743 οὔτοι πέφυκα μάντις 'I am not a seer'. Monologues sound illogical or hard to understand to people who do not hear them distinctly: see Aesch. *Ag.* 1112–13, 1130–1, Eur. *Ion* 255 (ἀνερμήνευτα), *Hipp.* 212–36, 346 οὐ μάντις εἰμὶ τἀφανῆ γνῶναι σαφῶς. Agamemnon indirectly complains that Hecuba is not addressing him clearly, remarking sarcastically that he (unlike his bedfellow Cassandra) lacks mantic skills. He does not apparently understand Hecuba's precise words, but simply perceives a lament (740 δύρηι).

μὴ κλυών 'if I do not hear' (what you say). κλυών is the aorist participle of κλύω, whereas κλύων is the present: West 1984: 175. Euripides simply wrote

ΚΛΥωΝ without accents. Context usually indicates whether we should interpret the word as aorist or present.

744 ἐξιστορῆσαι: lit. 'to know after asking', as in Aesch. *Sept.* 506 ἐξιστορῆσαι μοῖραν 'to know one's destiny', Hdt. 7.195.

σῶν ὁδὸν βουλευμάτων 'the path of your ideas'. Intellectual activities are often compared to travelling: Parmenides 28 B 2 D–K, Eur. *Hipp.* 290 γνώμης ὁδόν, Soph. *OT* 67. Song or speech are often imagined as a 'road': Pind. *Ol.* 1.110 ὁδὸν λόγων, Eur. *Pho.* 911, Fraenkel on Aesch. *Ag.* 1154.

745–6 ἆρ' ἐκλογίζομαί ... δυσμενοῦς; 'Am I estimating that his attitude is inclined towards hostility more than it is in reality, while he is in fact not hostile?' For πρὸς τὸ δυσμενές compare Hdt. 4.137.3 τετραμμένοι πρὸς ταύτην τὴν γνώμην, Eur. *Or.* 606, Cooper and Krüger 2002: 2808.

μᾶλλον 'more' (than it is in reality), 'too much'. See Smyth §1082, K–G II.305–7, Cooper and Krüger 2002: 2190.

748 ἐς ταὐτὸν ἥκεις 'you have come to the same point', that is, 'our purposes coincide': Barrett on *Hipp.* 273.

καὶ γὰρ οὐδ' ἐγὼ κλυεῖν 'for I do not <want> to listen either'.

κλυεῖν is aor. inf., as opposed to κλύειν, pres. inf.: 743n. and West 1984: 179.

749 τοῦδε τιμωρεῖν ἄτερ 'to obtain revenge without his help'. There is only one other instance in surviving tragedy where ἄτερ in anastrophe is separated from its genitive by an interposed word: Soph. *Phil.* 812 σοῦ μολεῖν ἄτερ. Cf. 292n.

750 τέκνοισι τοῖς ἐμοῖσι: in fact punishing Polymestor is a revenge for the death of Polydorus only. This may be taken as a poetic plural (265n.), referring in fact to one person only (*IA* 1015), but it also suggests that Hecuba sees revenge on Polymestor as a compensation for both deaths (882).

τί στρέφω τάδε; 'Why do I turn this over in my mind?' For the rhetoric see 736–51n. For στρέφω cf. LSJ s.v. VI, Soph. *Ant.* 231 τοιαῦθ' ἑλίσσων, 158, *OT* 300.

751 κἄν τύχω κἄν μὴ τύχω 'whether I have success or not'. For similar phrases cf. *IA* 1271 κἄν θέλω κἄν μὴ θέλω, *Cycl.* 332, *Tro.* 647, 914.

752–3 Hecuba's words here imply that the supplication involves physical contact: 274–5n., 812, Mercier 1993: 152 n. 8.

754 μαστεύουσα 'seeking'. The verbs ματεύω (779) and μαστεύω are etymologically distinct (Beekes 2010 s.vv.) but are used interchangeably in poetry: Mastronarde on *Pho.* 36, Finglass on Soph. *El.* 1107.

μῶν 'here expresses incredulity at the thought of a positive answer' (Mastronarde on *Med.* 567; cf. Barrett on *Hipp.* 794).

755 αἰῶνα, in general 'lifetime' ([757]), here means 'life, destiny, lot', as in fr. 30.2 (exile is οἰκτρός τις αἰών), *Andr.* 1215 τίν' αἰῶν' ... ἕξεις;

ῥᾴδιον γάρ ἐστί σοι 'it is easy for you' (to obtain freedom). For the syntax, see Eur. *Tro.* 1057, Ar. *Vesp.* 706. Agamemnon suggests that freedom is attainable for Hecuba, who is his slave (53), but refrains from an explicit promise, purposely omitting the crucial pronoun ἐμοί.

[756–9] These inauthentic lines were probably written by someone who considered the transition between 755 and 760 too abrupt. They add nothing essential to the argument, and 759 is especially uninformative. Their omission in Π⁷ (Π⁸) Π¹² cannot be explained on palaeographic grounds, and strongly supports the case for deletion. By contrast, the similarity between οὐ δῆτα and οὐδέν at 756–8 explains the omission of 756–8 in MBO.

Several other arrangements of the lines have been suggested: see Diggle's apparatus and Mastronarde 1988: 157 (who considers 756–9 authentic). If we do not delete 756–9, the stichomythia does not start until 761; for similar irregularities see *Alc.* 1130–40, Mastronarde on *Pho.* 710–11. For καὶ δή in a surprised question cf. *Hel.* 101, Denniston 250.

[756–7] Here Hecuba claims she does not care to be set free, provided the killer of her son is punished (cf. Garvie on Aesch. *Cho.* 438, Soph. *El.* 399, Eur. *Or.* 1116–17). In the rest of the play Hecuba associates punishment with Agamemnon's intervention (749, 790, 843). It would be rhetorically less apt if she attributed to herself the enactment of the revenge here, instead of asking for Agamemnon's help.

αἰῶνα τὸν σύμπαντα 'my whole life', a stylistically choicer phrase than the one frequently used in comedy and prose, ἄπαντα/πάντα τὸν βίον (Ar. *Eq.* 391, *Av.* 41, Pl. *Symp.* 216e4, etc.).

[759] οὐδέν τι τούτων ὧν σὺ δοξάζεις 'not a single one of the requests you imagine'. For οὐδέν τι see *Hel.* 1197 οὐδέν τι χαίρω σοῖς λόγοις (see Allan *ad loc.*), Hdt. 5.65.1, 6.3. The plural τούτων awkwardly refers to the possibility of freedom mentioned in 754–5 and to Hecuba's requests implicit in Agamemnon's question at 758 ('what help do you ask of us?').

760 ὁρᾷς νεκρὸν τόνδ' ... ; In stichomythia, characters may answer a question (see 754–5) by asking another question, forcing 'the dialogue-partner to participate in the unfolding of the answer' (Mastronarde 1979: 43); a detailed narrative unfolds, starting from the origin of the present situation, unknown to the dialogue-partner (in this case, Agamemnon). For similar questions answering questions see *Suppl.* 116 οἶσθα, *Hel.* 797 ὁρᾷς. In some cases the 'answering' question is delayed: see *IA* 319–322. See 239n.

νεκρὸν τόνδ' οὗ καταστάζω δάκρυ 'this corpse, over which I shed tears'. The genitive οὗ is construed with the preverb κατα-, and indicates the direction of the movement, as in *IT* 72 βωμὸς Ἕλλην οὗ καταστάζει φόνος, *Hel.* 985, *HF* 934, and καταχέω 'to pour over' (LSJ s.v. 1). In other passages, the accusative, not the genitive, is used to express the direction of the movement: 241, *IT* 308.

761 τὸ μέντοι μέλλον οὐκ ἔχω μαθεῖν 'Nevertheless I am not able to understand what comes after that'. The reading μαθεῖν is to be preferred to φράσαι: Agamemnon wants to 'know' (ἐξιστορῆσαι 744, εἰδέναι 747). For οὐκ ἔχω μαθεῖν in a similar context see *Pho.* 410. The phrase οὐκ ἔχω φράσαι is more appropriate after a question: *Ion* 540, 803, *Hcld.* 669. For comparable corruptions see Eur. *Pho.* 36, 387.

762 For the *hysteron proteron* see 266n.

κἄφερον ζώνης ὕπο 'I carried him under my girdle' (= in my womb): LSJ s.v. ζώνη I.2, Aesch. *Cho.* 992, *Eum.* 607–8.

763 'which one of your children is this one <you mentioned>, poor woman?' On the hyperbaton σῶν ... τέκνων cf. 299–300n.

765 ἦ γάρ indicates that Agamemnon is surprised by what he heard, and by the possible affirmative answer to his question: Denniston 284–5, Barrett on *Hipp.* 702–3.

766 ἀνόνητά γ' 'yes, to no purpose'. The pains taken to give birth and to nurture the son have been spent in vain, as he died prematurely: for the *topos* see Eur. *Hipp.* 1144–5 ὦ τάλαινα μᾶτερ, | ἔτεκες ἀνόνατα, *El.* 507–8, Aesch. *Cho.* 752, Soph. *El.* 1143–5. Children are supposed to help their parents in old age, and can be defined as 'advantageous' to them: Austin and Olson on Ar. *Th.* 469, Philemo fr. 143 K–A.

768 ὀρρωδῶν θανεῖν 'fearing that he [= Polydorus] would die' at the fall of the city.

771 'to the man who rules this land, Polymestor'. The name Πολυμήστωρ, in apposition to the accusative ἄνδρα, is inserted in the relative clause in the nominative case: for the syntax cf. *Hipp.* 101, K–G II. 419–20, Smyth §2539.

772 πικροτάτου χρυσοῦ φύλαξ 'to guard the gold that gave him so much pain' (lit. 'that was so bitter').

775 ὦ τλῆμον 'The brute!' (Collard), in reference to Polymestor. For the meaning see e.g. *Hel.* 109 and *IA* 1253.

776 τοιαῦτ' 'exactly', as in *El.* 645 (τοιαῦτα· μισεῖται γὰρ ἀνόσιος γυνή) and *Andr.* 910 (τοιαῦτα ταῦτα), both times in stichomythia.

συμφοράν ... Φρυγῶν 'the misfortune of the Phrygians', i.e. the fall of Troy.

778 ἥδ' is a deictic referring to the Servant, present onstage from 658.

779 ματεύουσ': 753–4n.

781 'Our guest-friend killed him and threw out his corpse, as seems clear to me.' Agamemnon stresses the link of *xenia*, which makes the crime even more heinous. Polydorus' body is thrown out, in the hope of erasing all traces of the murder. Lack of burial is a sign of dishonour: *Andr.*

1156–7, *Tro.* 448–50, *Pho.* 1630. Polymestor fears that his children too will be left unburied, and will be prey to wild beasts (1077–8).

782 θαλασσόπλαγκτόν γ' 'yes, <so that> he was tossed on the sea'. Hecuba continues Agamemnon's syntax, adding a confirmatory γ': Denniston 130–1. The adjective θαλασσόπλαγκτον here is proleptic (499–500n.), in reference to νιν 781. The adjective is used in reference to ships at Aesch. *PV* 467.

782 διατεμών χρόα: 716–21n.

783 'Unhappy you for your countless woes!' Cf. 425n.

784 κοὐδὲν λοιπόν ... κακῶν 'and not a single one of <all possible> evils remains <to happen>'. Hecuba is in the same position as Oedipus (Soph. *OT* 1284–5 and 1496 τί γὰρ κακῶν ἄπεστι;), Antigone (Soph. *Ant.* 4–6) and Heracles (*HF* 1245 γέμω κακῶν δὴ κοὐκέτ᾽ ἔσθ᾽ ὅπηι τεθῆι). Earlier Hecuba said that if Agamemnon refused to help her that would 'add another sorrow' (742), which would imply that further sorrows are still possible. On the number of her sorrows see also 585–8n. Hecuba presents her situation differently, according to the rhetorical demands of the context.

785 φεῦ φεῦ· τίς οὕτω δυστυχὴς ἔφυ γυνή; The question implies (and receives) a negative answer, just like *HF* 1195 φεῦ φεῦ· τίς ἀνδρῶν ὧδε δυσδαίμων ἔφυ; The paradox of these tragic characters (and of the tragic genre) is that each of them claims that his/her fate is unique, whereas in fact several such stories have tragic potential: see Arist. *Poet.* 1453a17–22.

786 'There is no one, unless you mean Misfortune in person'. Τύχη is a *vox media*, meaning both 'good luck' and 'bad luck' (*Held.* 714): there was a goddess Τύχη but not one called Δυστυχία (Herzog-Hauser 1948: 1647). Paradoxes of this type occur in *TrGF* vol. II fr. 534 'no man would speak ill of him, not even if he was more spiteful than Envy', Pl. *Resp.* 487a6 οὐδ᾽ ἂν ὁ Μῶμος ... μέμψαιτο, Call. fr. 393, and (frequently) in Latin comedy (Plaut. *Asin.* 267 *ego illos lubentiores faciam quam Lubentia est,* Fraenkel 2007: 10).

787–845 Hecuba answers Agamemnon at 786, and then starts a long speech, in the style of courtroom prosecution. Hecuba omits the narration of events (a stock element in judicial oratory) because this was covered in the stichomythia. She can launch straight into her plea (787–811), asking Agamemnon to punish Polymestor. She quotes the relevant law (*nomos*), which is of divine origin. No human law is enforceable against Polymestor, who would be his own judge in Thrace. Hecuba's theories on law and the gods allude to contemporary sophistic and philosophic reflections (798–805n.). She ends her (first) plea with an emotional recollection of her misfortunes (806–11). Her speech would have ended here, but Agamemnon moves away, silently rejecting her supplication (812n.). Hecuba then soliloquises on her desperate situation, and on the need to learn 'Persuasion', which reigns over human beings (814–23). She addresses Agamemnon again at 826, where she starts a new *peroratio*, using personal arguments: Hecuba refers to the sexual relationship between Agamemnon and Cassandra (824–32), claiming that this creates a sort of family bond between the Greek king and her (833–5). She ends her speech imagining a new, quasi-magical supplication of Agamemnon with every part of her body (836–40), and appeals again to justice and the law (841–5).

Divine law is vulnerable to human ethical choices, and Agamemnon's refusal to enact justice creates a crucial ethical and theological dilemma (Nussbaum 1986: 400–4, 415–17). Hecuba's speech is at the same time a display of rhetorical technique and a questioning of its effectiveness. The highly rhetorical first section is denounced as artless by Hecuba herself, who argues that she needs rhetoric (814–19): she pretends to speak as if the appeal to a divinely sanctioned and universal law would suffice – but in fact it does not. Hecuba's second attempt, making use of more mundane arguments, is even more rhetorically crafted, but equally ineffective. On this speech see Kirkwood 1947: 65–8, Lanza 1963, Reckford 1985: 119–21, Battezzato 2008b: 53–7 and 72–6, Mastronarde 2010: 231–3.

787 ἀμφὶ σὸν πίπτω γόνυ: on supplication see 245n., 752–3n. The same words occur in *Hel.* 894.

790 τιμωρὸς ἀνδρὸς ἀνοσιωτάτου ξένου 'punisher of my most impious guest-friend'. ἀνδρὸς ... ξένου is a single phrase: see 1244, *Hcld.* 244, Soph. *Trach.* 40, Hdt. 1.199.1. ξένος is a substantive, and ἀνήρ a substantive 'used as an attributive to another substantive' (Smyth §986, K–G 1.271–2, LSJ s.v. ἀνήρ VI.1; Dodds on *Ba.* 1024–6). See also ἀνὴρ βούτας (646), Θρῆιξ ... ἀνήρ (682), ἀνδρὸς Θρηικός (873, 1036), and 19n. Other scholars print a comma after ἀνδρός and translate 'my avenger on that man, that most unholy ally' (Collard).

791 οὔτε τοὺς γῆς νέρθεν οὔτε τοὺς ἄνω 'neither those below the earth nor those above'. The context makes clear that the gods are meant: Aesch. *Cho.* 165 κῆρυξ μέγιστε τῶν ἄνω τε καὶ κάτω, *Pers.* 619 (see 622), Eur. *Alc.* 14. More frequently, οἱ κάτω and οἱ ἄνω mean 'the dead and the living' (Soph. *Ant.* 75, 1068). Here, the emphasis on ἀνοσιώτατον (790, 792) and the mention of 'fear' (792 δείσας) favour a reference to the gods (see 852, Soph. *Ant.* 1071 ἀνόσιον, *Od.* 14.389 Δία ξένιον δείσας, Aesch. *Suppl.* 755–6).

[793–7] Poor syntax and content show that these lines are not by Euripides. There are four main problems: (a) τυχὼν δ' ὅσων δεῖ (795) is a useless repetition of 793–4, expressing the same concept with the same word (τυχών 793 and 795); (b) in 794 ξενίας and τῶν ἐμῶν ξένων are impossibly redundant ([794n.]); (c) in 794 the word πρῶτα is syntactically very awkward ([794n.]); (d) in 796, εἰ κτανεῖν ἐβούλετο is absurd in context

(Hecuba could not say that 'if he wanted to kill him' he had at least to bury him) and syntactically irregular ([796–7n.]). The superlative ἀνοσιώτατον at 792 is a rhetorically fitting conclusion for the sentence: see *Med.* 408–9, 796 (ἔργον ἀνοσιώτατον), 1328, *Or.* 592. The phrase ἔργον ἀνοσιώτατον does not make explicit the nature of the crime, and this could have led the interpolator to add 793–7 (D. Mastronarde, personal communication). As often, the interpolator reused phrases from other plays of Euripides (κοινῆς τραπέζης at 793 occurs at *Ion* 652 and *Or.* 9). These lines may have been interpolated by actors, but the low quality of the syntax suggests that the interpolation is more likely to have been inserted by readers or teachers.

[794] ξενίας τ' ἀριθμῶι πρῶτα τῶν ἐμῶν ξένων 'and <was> first of my guest-friends in the rank of guest-friendship'. It is absurd to stress that Polymestor was *the first* among Hecuba's *xenoi*, as if another, less prominent, *xenos* would be justified in killing Hecuba's child. Moreover, the syntax is unsatisfactory: the interpolator meant the line to be equivalent to ξενίας τ' ἀριθμῶι πρῶτος ὢν ἐμῶν ξένων (Porson), but πρῶτα as an adverb sits ill with the verb 'to be'. It is not equivalent to τὰ πρῶτα 'of the first rank' (as in *Med.* 917, LSJ s.v. πρότερος II.3) because of the lack of article. Some interpreters (scholium in MSS MB on 794, Handley, Matthiessen) think that ξενίας is syntactically dependent on τυχών in 793, and coordinated with τραπέζης but, if so, πρῶτα would mean, absurdly, 'having met my friendship for the first time'.

ξένων: the variant φίλων is a gloss (cf. Hsch. ξ 29, 30) or an attempt to correct the clumsiness of the repetition.

[795] λαβὼν προμηθίαν 'having made a shrewd plan'. προμηθία means 'shrewd cautiousness': 1136–7, Aesch. *Suppl.* 178 τἀπὶ χέρσου νῦν προμηθίαν λαβών ('taking into consideration the situation on land'). For similar periphrases with λαμβάνω and a noun indicating intellectual activity see Eur. *Hipp.* 1027 ἔννοιαν λαβεῖν, Soph. *Trach.* 669–70, *Phil.* 1078. Here the phrase corresponds to προμηθέομαι, and is used without a direct object: cf. Hp. *Vict.* 3.72 ἀλλὰ χρὴ προμηθεῖσθαι corresponding to 3.77 ἢν μή που προμηθείηι χρέηται.

[796–7] τύμβου δ', εἰ κτανεῖν ἐβούλετο, | οὐκ ἠξίωσεν, ἀλλ' ἀφῆκε πόντιον: the interpolator mixed two sentences: 'if he wanted to kill him, he had the duty to bury him' and 'after killing him, he did not even bury him'. Sentences such as Lys. 32.23 εἰ ἐβούλετο δίκαιος εἶναι … ἐξῆν αὐτῶι … μισθῶσαι τὸν οἶκον are not a good parallel, because in those cases the protasis is counterfactual (Wakker 1994: 144–6).

798–805 In a complex section, dense with literary and philosophic allusions, Hecuba claims that power is essential to enforce justice, but also that the gods and *nomos* ('law', but also 'convention') have power. Hecuba sees no contradiction between the power of the gods and that of

nomos (799–800n.). She implies that Agamemnon should enforce *nomos*; otherwise, 'equality' (= 'justice') will be lost. Does *nomos* mean 'law' or 'convention' in this passage? Does Agamemnon's failure to enforce *nomos* imply that the gods do not exist?

Hecuba starts with a rhetorical artifice and a literary allusion. At 798–801 she delivers a *Priamel*, that is a 'series of detached statements illustrating either by analogy or by contrast a rule of wisdom in which the passage culminates' (Dodds on *Ba.* 902–11; cf. Race 1982: 1–17 and 95–8). Here the *Priamel* is compressed to just two statements, and alludes to a famous passage by Pindar (fr. 169a.1–4) which said that 'Law (νόμος), the king of all, | of mortals and immortals, | guides them as it justifies the utmost violence | with a sovereign hand' (tr. Race). Herodotus and Callicles in Plato quote this fragment, claiming that it refers, respectively, to 'convention, usage' and to the 'right of the stronger', bending the meaning to their rhetorical purposes: Asheri, Lloyd and Corcella 2007 on Hdt. 3.38.4, Dodds on Pl. *Grg.* 484b1–c3; cf. Guthrie 1969: 131–4. Modern scholars are divided as to whether Pindar meant 'convention' or 'law', but the second meaning is more likely (Lloyd-Jones 1972: 55 = Lloyd-Jones 1990: 163–4). On *nomos* see esp. Heinimann 1945: 59–89, Ostwald 1986: 84–136, Allen 2005.

Hecuba's complex allusion to a widely discussed text is capped by an even more ambiguous statement: we believe in the gods νόμωι (800). She is not alone in claiming that *nomos* defines what is just: Lys. 2.19 ἀνθρώποις προσήκει νόμωι ὁρίσαι τὸ δίκαιον. However, her distinction recalls the sophistic one between what is φύσει, 'by nature', and νόμωι, 'by (human) convention (only, and not in fact)' (Heinimann 1945, Guthrie 1969: 55–134, Long 2005). If we translate νόμωι as 'by convention' in 800, the lines imply that (a) belief in the gods and (b) definition of what is right and what is wrong are purely human conventions. Both opinions occur in Pl. *Leg.* 889e2–7: 'these people say that the gods exist by artifice (τέχνηι), not by nature, but by some laws/conventions (τισιν νόμοις), ... and that what is right (τὰ ... δίκαια) does not exist at all by nature (φύσει)', on which see Sedley 2013. The two opinions are widely attested in earlier texts, already in the fifth century BCE: (a) Critias *TrGF* 43 F 19.25–6; (b) Archelaus 60 A 1 τὸ δίκαιον εἶναι καὶ τὸ αἰσχρὸν οὐ φύσει, ἀλλὰ νόμωι, Hippias 86 C 1, Antipho 87 B 44 D–K, cols. 1.23–2.1, Pl. *Grg.* 482c4–483c6, *Tht.* 172a1–c1, *Resp.* Books 1–2. Some scholars have argued that the idea of atheism arose from the debate on *nomos* and *physis* (Winiarczyk 1990). On atheism in antiquity see Whitmarsh 2015. On atheism in Euripides see Riedweg 1990, Mastronarde 2010: 2, 154, 177.

An 'atheistic' reading of Hecuba's speech is linguistically possible but unlikely in the context: the logic of Hecuba's speech implies that she means to defend the existence of gods and their support of law. Some interpreters have suggested that Euripides here means the audience to understand that Hecuba's language tricks her into saying the opposite of what she means (Heinimann 1945: 121) and that by *nomos* the text (but not necessarily Hecuba) means 'convention' (Ostwald 1969: 38, Nussbaum 1986: 400 and 403). If gods exist only in human beliefs, they will be not there to help her. *Ba.* 274–85 uses Prodicus' atheistic arguments (Dodds *ad loc.*, Guthrie 1969: 241–2, Henrichs 1975: 109–15) in order to *affirm* the divinity of Dionysus. Here too, Euripides is provocatively using a sophistic slogan (νόμωι) to affirm the existence of the gods in the strongest possible terms. An avant-garde philosophical soundbite is cleverly inserted in a theodicy delivered by a barbarian aristocrat.

798–801 'It may very well be true that we are in slavery, and without power, but the gods do have power, and so does the law (*nomos*) that rules over them: for it is thanks to the law (*nomos*) that we believe in the gods and conduct our lives distinguishing what is right and what is wrong.'

798 μὲν οὖν: οὖν is retrospective, resuming the topic of Hecuba's powerlessness, discussed in 752–86; μέν is prospective, and prepares for the objection stated at 799 ἀλλ': Denniston 472.

κἀσθενεῖς: the law is of special help to those who are 'weak' (ἀσθενεῖς): see *Suppl.* 433–4 'if the laws are written down, the weak and the rich (ὅ τ' ἀσθενής | ὁ πλούσιός τε) have the same chances in court' and esp. Pl. *Grg.* 483b4–6 'it is the weak (οἱ ἀσθενεῖς ἄνθρωποι) who have established the laws, and the multitude (οἱ πολλοί)'. Slaves are by definition 'weak' (*Ion* 983 τὸ δοῦλον ἀσθενές). Hecuba's extreme situation is in fact representative of the human condition generally: human beings are the gods' slaves (Heraclitus 22 B 53 D–K, Eur. *Hipp.* 88, 460, *Or.* 418), and are weak in comparison with them (799–800n., Ar. *Av.* 685–9). On the masculine δοῦλοι see 237n.

ἴσως: lit. 'perhaps'. The adverb is introduced to reject an argument ('it may be true that ...'), as in Aesch. *PV* 317, Eur. *IA* 849.

799 σθένουσι: on divine σθένος cf. 49n.

799–800 χὠ κείνων κρατῶν | νόμος: κράτος, like σθένος, is a divine quality: *Alc.* 251 τοὺς κρατοῦντας ... θεούς, LSJ s.v. κρείσσων I 2, and Aesch. *PV* 903, Eur. *Ion* 973, fr. 972. *Nomos* and other personifications are occasionally said to have power over the gods: Pind. fr. 169a1–2, *IT* 1486 τὸ γὰρ χρεὼν σοῦ τε καὶ θεῶν κρατεῖ, *Alc.* 965. This usage seems to rule out the interpretation 'the powerful law of the gods' (so e.g. Hartung). Human beings who seek to be more powerful than the gods are however impious: *Hipp.* 474–5 οὐκ ἄλλο πλὴν ὕβρις | τάδ' ἐστί, κρείσσω δαιμόνων εἶναι θέλειν, *Suppl.* 216–17, *Tro.* 948–9, 964. The passage does not imply that the power of *nomos* questions divine power. This is a sort of 'rhetorical superlative' (Battezzato 2008b: 53–80) meant 'to dignify some particular abstraction by conferring on it Zeus' title of "ruler of gods and men"' (Lloyd-Jones 1972: 48 = Lloyd-Jones 1990: 157): Heraclitus 22 B 53, Eur. fr. 136.1. It does not imply that a conflict for supremacy between *nomos* and the gods exists.

νόμωι γὰρ τοὺς θεοὺς ἡγούμεθα: this is one of the earliest securely dated instances of the phrase ἡγεῖσθαι θεούς 'to believe in the gods': cf. Ar. *Eq.* 32 (424 BCE), Yunis 1988: 63–6. The dative νόμωι means 'because of the law' rather than 'by convention': 798–805n. See also Thuc. 5.105.2 ἡγούμεθα γὰρ τὸ ... θεῖον δόξηι ... ἄρχειν.

801 ἄδικα καὶ δίκαι' ὡρισμένοι: Hecuba uses the language of philosophers and lawgivers: 798-805n., Arist. *Eth. Nic.* 1132b22–3 ὡρίζοντο ... τὸ δίκαιον, Dem. 24.79 ἃ δίκαι' ὡρίσατ' αὐτὸς ἐν τῶι νόμωι. Unjust people do not respect these boundaries (fr. 419.2–3); those without power must suffer what is just as well as what is unjust (Aesch. *Cho.* 78).

ὡρισμένοι: transitive middle. This form of the verb, in a different meaning, occurs in Dem. 31.5 ὡρισμένος τὴν οἰκίαν 'having marked the house with *horoi*'. This is a 'mental process' middle: cf. Hdt. 1.170.1 γνώμην ... ἀποδέξασθαι 'to give one's opinion', Thuc.1.87.2, Smyth §1721, R. J. Allan 2003: 64–76.

802–5 'And if this law, when referred to you, is made void, and those who kill their guest-friends and dare to rob what is sacred to the gods are not punished, there is no justice in human affairs.'

802 ὅς 'and this (law)': Smyth §2490.

ἀνελθών: lit. 'when it comes up to you'. The verb is used as synonymous with ἀνενεχθείς 'having been referred': cf. *Suppl.* 562 and Diggle 1994: 287.

διαφθαρήσεται: according to Hecuba, divine law depends on human action. Theseus concurs: *Suppl.* 561–3 'it will not be reported to the Greeks that the ancient law of the gods, which was referred to me (εἰς ἔμ' ἐλθών) and the city of Pandion, was destroyed (διεφθάρη)'. Belief in the gods depends on tangible signs of their action: Eur. *El.* 583–4, *Ba.* 1326, Ar. *Eq.* 32, Thgn. 747–52, Riedweg 1990. Human action is a sign of divine presence, not a substitute for it; even if Agamemnon fails to offer his help, Hecuba will be able to punish Polymestor. On 'divine enforcement of law' see Dover 1974: 257–61.

804 Agamemnon must punish actions that go against what is ὅσιον 'sanctioned by divine law' (788, 790, 852; cf. 1232n.) and what is ἱερόν 'under divine protection', that is he must punish every kind of unjust action: cf. Thuc. 2.52.3 ἐς ὀλιγωρίαν ἐτράποντο καὶ ἱερῶν καὶ ὁσίων ὁμοίως. On ὅσιος and ἱερός see Peels 2016: 207–30. In the fourth century ἱερόσυλος 'temple robber' became a colloquial insult: Ar. *Plut.* 30, Lys. 30.21. See already Hipponax fr. 118.1 West θεόσυλιν.

805 τῶν ἐν ἀνθρώποις 'in human life', 'in what human beings experience/control', as in fr. 1030 ἀρετὴ μέγιστον τῶν ἐν ἀνθρώποις καλόν, *Med.* 948, *Pho.* 440.

ἴσον 'right'. τὸ ἴσον means 'what is equitable', 'justice': 291–2. Archaic and classical political thought stresses the link between justice and equality: Mastronarde on *Pho.* 538 τὸ γὰρ ἴσον νόμιμον ἀνθρώποις ἔφυ, Collard on *Suppl.* 429–32 and 438–41, Vlastos 1953, Ostwald 1969: 96–160. Diggle prints Kayser's ἀνθρώποισι σῶν 'nothing is safe for mortals' but the parallels above show that ἴσον is in keeping with classical political and philosophical thought. Fr. 1048.1 repeats this line (279n.), confirming the reading ἀνθρώποις ἴσον.

806 ἐν αἰσχρῶι θέμενος 'considering shameful' what Polymestor did. For τίθημι ἐν followed by an abstract noun see *Alc.* 1037 οὐδ' ἐν αἰσχροῖσιν τιθείς, *Suppl.* 164 ἐν αἰσχύναις ἔχω, and Mastronarde on *Pho.* 1276. For the middle τίθεμαι see Soph. *Phil.* 473, 875–6.

806–7 αἰδέσθητι ... | οἴκτιρον: cf. 286–7n.

806–8 με ... ἡμᾶς ... με 'me ... us ... me'. All three pronouns refer to Hecuba; here the variation does not seem to convey any special point: see K-G I.83–4, Bond on *HF* 858; contrast 244n., 370–1n.

ὡς γραφεύς τ' ἀποσταθείς 'moving away <from me>, like a painter'. Distance gives a better view and comprehension: Eur. *Ion* 585, Pl. *Tht.* 208e7–10, Hor. *Ars* 361–2. The viewer should be moved to compassion, but in effect Hecuba unwittingly suggests and anticipates Agamemnon's rejection of her supplication, which will take place precisely when he moves away (812).

ἰδοῦ με κἀνάθρησον οἷ' ἔχω κακά 'look at me and contemplate how much I suffer'. The imperative of a verb of looking is used to arouse pity in Soph. *Ant.* 940–2 λεύσσετε ... οἷα ... πάσχω, Eur. *Med.* 161 λεύσσεθ' ἃ πάσχω, *Pho.* 611. Hippolytus, knowing that his father would not respond to such an imperative, conjures up the image of another self that, standing at a distance, will look at his own sufferings (*Hipp.* 1078–9).

811: for the rhetoric cf. 669n.

812 ποῖ μ' ὑπεξάγεις πόδα; 'Where do you direct your foot, taking it away from me?', that is, 'Where do you go? You extricate yourself from my supplication.' Tragedians use ἄγω with an accusative meaning 'foot', 'leg', as a periphrasis for 'going' (*Ba.* 169 κῶλον ἄγει ταχύπουν). Here ὑπεξάγω πόδα is used as equivalent to ὑπεκτρέχω 'to escape from', taking the accusative: Soph. *Ant.* 1086, Eur. *Med.* 524, *Pho.* 873 θεοὺς ὑπεκδραμούμενοι, Jacquinod 1989: 106–7.

813 ἔοικα 'it seems clear that I': 781n.

814 τἄλλα μὲν μαθήματα 'the other types of knowledge'. Like Theseus in *Hipp.* 916–20, Hecuba complains that human beings disregard the most important lesson to be learned (according to Theseus, teaching good sense to injudicious people).

815 ὡς χρή 'as one should', as in *Or.* 652.

816 'Persuasion, the only queen of mankind'. *Peithō* was a goddess: Buxton 1982: 31–45. Asking the help of Persuasion is itself a rhetorical ploy: Aesch. *Eum.* 885, Hdt. 8.111, Thuc. 3.53.4, Macleod 1983: 156. For Hecuba's speech as rhetorically highly elaborate see 787–845n. and 798–805n. Hecuba will later allude (implicitly) to erotic *Peithō* at 824–32.

817–18 οὐδέν τι μᾶλλον ἐς τέλος σπουδάζομεν | ... μανθάνειν '(Why) do we not make any extra effort <in order> to learn <it> [= persuasion] to the full?' For οὐδέν τι μᾶλλον compare *Alc.* 522, *Hipp.* 344, fr. 795.5.

μισθοὺς διδόντες 'paying money'. Another allusion to the sophists (cf. 798–805n.), who charged a fee for teaching the ability to persuade: Dodds on Pl. *Grg.* 519b3–521a1, Guthrie 1969: 38, 42, 45, 275. As if to prove her point, Hecuba will soon claim that one of her arguments is not apt to convince her audience (824); she will also deprecate rhetorical ability, another rhetorical move (1187–94n.).

ἵν' ἦν 'so that it would be possible'. The imperfect means that the goal has not been and cannot be achieved: Eur. *Hipp.* 647, fr. 439, K–G II. 388–9.

820 τις 'someone', that is Hecuba herself. For this usage see K–G I.662, Finglass on Soph. *Ai.* 403 ποῖ τις οὖν φύγηι;, Ar. *Thesm.* 603 ποῖ τις τρέψεται;

ἐλπίσαι 'could expect' (3rd p. sg. aor. opt.: K–B II.73–4, Smyth §668).

821 'the children that I had, I do not have any more'. The participle ὄντες refers to the past: 484, 620, K–G I.200, Diggle 1994: 233 n. 13.

822 ἐπ' αἰσχροῖς 'in circumstances that bring disgrace upon me': see *Hipp.* 511, *Andr.* 1111.

823 'I see smoke here rising from the city'. Smoke on the tragic scene is usually caused by fire visible to the audience: see e.g. the torches in *Tro.* 1256–9 and 1298–9, *Or.* 1541–3. However, it is doubtful whether the audience saw smoke at this point: it would be absurd if it appeared only now, and puzzling if it was seen from the beginning of the play. Smoke is mentioned also at 477, 911–12, 1215, but not as something visible to the characters or chorus. On the difficulty of reconstructing how fire and earthquakes were staged see Bond on *HF* 904–5, Goldhill 1986: 276–86.

824 καὶ μὴν ἴσως μέν 'and yet it is possible that'. For καὶ μὴν ... μέν see 1224, fr. 201.1. μέν is answered by ἀλλ' ὅμως, as at *Hipp.* 47: Denniston 6. Diggle writes and punctuates καὶ μὴν (ἴσως μὲν τοῦ λόγου ξένον τόδε, | Κύπριν προβάλλειν, ἀλλ' ὅμως εἰρήσεται) | πρὸς σοῖσι πλευροῖς, but a semantically relevant section of the sentence must occur before the parenthesis starts: the sentence should start at least with a pronoun, an adverb, or a conjunction, as in *Andr.* 732 καὶ νῦν μέν, *El.* 102 νῦν οὖν, *Tro.* 647 ἔνθα, *Ion* 444 εἰ δ', and the beginning of the parenthetic passage should be clearly marked (e.g. by γάρ). It is better to accept καὶ μὴν ... μέν here, an attested combination which gives good sense.

τοῦ λόγου κενὸν τόδε 'this part of the speech <is> ineffective'. τόδε is construed with τοῦ λόγου (see *Ion* 363 οἶσθ' οὖν ὃ κάμνει τοῦ λόγου μάλιστά σοι;), and κενόν is predicative. For κενός in reference to λόγος *vel sim.* see *Suppl.* 849 ('false'), fr. 494.2 ('ineffective'), fr. 757.852 ('wasted'). τόδε introduces what will be mentioned later in the speech: Smyth §1245. Nauck suggested correcting κενόν to ξένον 'extraneous', but in fact Hecuba's argument, if convincing, would be highly relevant.

825 Κύπριν προβάλλειν 'to put forward Cypris', i.e. to advance the argument of sex. For the verb in this meaning cf. Soph. *Trach.* 810.

ἀλλ' ὅμως εἰρήσεται 'but it will be mentioned nonetheless'.

826 The asyndeton emphasises the new point, as if introducing a direct speech: 220, *Hcld.* 928–9, *Ba.* 776–7.

πρὸς σοῖσι πλευροῖς ... κοιμίζεται 'sleeps by your side', a euphemism for 'having sex'. See the similarly phrased passage Soph. *Trach.* 1225–6 τοῖς ἐμοῖς πλευροῖς ὁμοῦ | κλιθεῖσαν, and Eur. *Alc.* 366–7, *Andr.* 390, *Pho.* 54.

827 ἡ φοιβάς, ἣν καλοῦσι Κασσάνδραν Φρύγες 'the woman inspired by Phoebus whom Phrygians call Cassandra'. For similarly redundant introductions of a name see *Il.* 5.305–6, 11.756–8, Soph. *OT* 1451–2. φοιβάς 'the woman of/inspired by Phoebus' is especially appropriate for Cassandra, whom Apollo loved unrequitedly: Aesch. *Ag.* 1080–3, 1202–12.

828 ποῦ τὰς φίλας δῆτ' εὐφρόνας λέξεις ... ; 'What value will you put on those nights of love?' (Diggle 1994: 237). λέξεις here means 'reckon, estimate' (cf. 906), and, combined with an adverb of place, indicates the value given to a person or a thing: Diggle compares Soph. *Ant.* 183 τοῦτον οὐδαμοῦ λέγω 'I count him for nothing', *Phil.* 451 ποῦ χρὴ τίθεσθαι ταῦτα...;, Eur. *Alc.* 322, *Andr.* 210.

829–30 ἢ τῶν ἐν εὐνῆι φιλτάτων ἀσπασμάτων | χάριν τίν' ἕξει παῖς ἐμή, κείνης δ' ἐγώ; 'or what gratitude will my daughter acquire in exchange for her pleasurable embraces in bed? And <what gratitude will> I <acquire> in exchange for her?' The questions imply a negative answer: 'we will not have anything in exchange, if you do not punish Polymestor'. See *Suppl.* 127 τὸ δ' Ἄργος ἡμῖν ποῦ 'στιν; ἢ κόμποι μάτην;. Diggle 1994: 237–8 argues for ἦ ... τιν', objecting to the late position of interrogative τίν'. See however *Ion* 433–4, *Suppl.* 450–1, Dik 2007: 136–66, Battezzato 2008b: 85–96. Diggle's ἦ ... τιν' implies a positive answer ('we will have something in exchange'), which is too optimistic in the context.

830 χάριν 'gratitude' but also 'pleasure'. In Hecuba's view, Cassandra obviously does not get pleasure from her union with Agamemnon (Eur. *Tro.* 665–6, Soph. fr. 583.11–2). The only *charis* a woman can get under these circumstances is help for herself or her family: Soph. *Ai.* 522. Hecuba pretends not to know that Agamemnon got Cassandra by force: Scodel 1998: 137–44. On the treatment of female war prisoners see Pritchett 1991: 38–42. On *charis* see 299–331n., Introduction, section 5.

831–2 The association between darkness, night and sex is obvious and frequent: *Hipp.* 106, fr. 524 'Cypris by nature loves darkness'. Scholars have advanced objections against the authenticity of 831–2: (a) the variants in the MS tradition are suspicious; (b) φίλτρων and χάρις both mean 'love'; (c) the lines are not coherent with the context; (d) Hecuba's words are those of a procuress (a charge reported but refuted in scholium MB 825: see Scodel 1998: 137–8). However: (a) similar variants also occur in authentic lines (*Pho.* 572, 748, 915, 1597, 1599); when the rare word νυκτερησίων was corrupted (see below), scribes attempted to patch the metre with inappropriate supplements; (b) χάρις means 'debt of gratitude' at 832; (c) the lines expand the concept of 830; for a similar expansion see *IA* 977–80; (d) allusive references to sex are well possible in Euripides: see fr. 323, *Hipp.* 966–70.

ἐκ τοῦ σκότου τε: the enclitic τε is placed after the whole prepositional phrase: cf. Aesch. *Eum.* 291, Thuc. 3.64.5, Denniston 517 section iii, K–G II.245.

νυκτερησίων 'nocturnal'. Nauck's conjecture restores meaning and metre to a passage which was evidently corrupt in antiquity. Cf. Austin and Olson on Ar. *Thesm.* 204 νυκτερήσια (Bothe). The suffix -ησιος is found in words such as φιλοτήσιος (*Od.* 11.246), ἡμερήσιος (Aesch. *Ag.* 22) and βροτήσιος (Hes. *Op.* 773): Schwyzer 1939: 466.

φίλτρων 'charms'. For the metaphor see Eur. fr. 323, Stevens on *Andr.* 540.

χάρις 'favour', 'gratitude', not 'erotic pleasure': for this meaning, in an erotic context, see Eur. *Andr.* 1253 τῆς ἐμῆς εὐνῆς χάριν, Soph. *Ai.* 522.

833 τὸν θανόντα τόνδ' ὁρᾶις; 'Do you see the body which is here?' (taking up 760).

834 κηδεστήν designates 'any male affine' (Thompson 1971: 110), here 'wife's brother'. Hecuba speaks as if Cassandra were lawfully wedded to Agamemnon. This is what Cassandra pretends (and Hecuba denies) at *Tro.* 311–13 and 345–7. Hecuba assumes that Agamemnon had a quasi-marital obligation towards Cassandra. Her argument is rhetorically skilful, but legally specious. Concubinage was formalised in Athens, but only in some circumstances: Todd 2007 on Lys. 1.31. Moreover, Athenian concubines (παλλακαί) were free women or 'slave women on whom their master had conferred this status' (A. R. W. Harrison 1968: 15).

835 ἑνός μοι μῦθος ἐνδεής ἔτι 'my speech lacks only one further point'. This introduces the whole final section: compare *Hipp.* 1021.

836–40 Hecuba imagines a fantastic transformation of her body: her every limb would supplicate Agamemnon, thanks to a prodigy such as that operated by Daedalus on his statues, which moved (Eur. fr. 372, Pl. *Euthphr.* 11c7–d2, *Meno* 97d5–e4) and spoke (Pl. Com. fr. 204.2–3): Faraone 1992: 18–35 and 94–112, Morris 1992: 215–37. Some interpreters have seen her desire as a grotesque degradation (Michelini 1982:

152, Nussbaum 1986: 415), but Hecuba needs extraordinary rhetoric (814–19) and body language to convince the Greek king. Homer offered the model for an imagined *bodily* transformation required to perform an impossible task: the poet would need ten tongues, ten mouths and a heart of bronze, if he were to list all the soldiers fighting at Troy (*Il.* 2.484–93). The impossible multiplication of supplicating powers is taken up at *El.* 332–5, where Electra's whole body, hands, tongue, mind and shaved head, supplicates (332 ἱκετεύω) the stranger (in fact, Orestes). Similarly, Admetus and Iphigenia wish that they had the powers of persuasion and incantation that Orpheus had: *Alc.* 357; *IA* 1211–14. Hecuba's rhetoric cannot achieve Daedalus' magic, but the miracle she evokes gives an impressive close to her speech. By mentioning Daedalus, Hecuba also implicitly compares herself to a statue, and alludes to the similar comparison used for Polyxena at 560. Hecuba had presented herself as a painter's subject at 807 (Gödde 2000: 86–94).

836 γένοιτο: the optative expresses an unattainable wish referring to the future (255n.).

837 κόμαισι 'in my hair'. Only the hands have a formal role in supplication, as a rule; arms, feet and hair determine identity (*Od.* 4.149–50, Garvie on Aesch. *Cho.* 164–245) and symbolise the whole body.

ποδῶν βάσει: lit. 'in the step of my feet', i.e. 'in my feet which walk'. βάσις means 'step', 'foot': note *Tro.* 333–4 ποδῶν | φέρουσα φιλτάταν βάσιν, Mastronarde on *Pho.* 303 ποδὸς βάσιν.

839 ἁμαρτῆι 'at the same time'. On the correct spelling see Barrett on *Hipp.* 1194–7.

ἔχοιτο γουνάτων 'so that they [= the body parts] would cling to your knees'.

840 κλαίοντ' ἐπισκήπτοντα 'uttering among weeps and implorations'. Cf. 387n., Aeschin. 3.157 κλαίοντας, ἱκετεύοντας … ἐπισκήπτοντας.

842–3 παράσχες χεῖρα τῆι πρεσβύτιδι | τιμωρόν 'offer your hand to <this> old woman so that it will punish' Polymestor, i.e. 'offer me your help in punishing him'. The form πάρασχε is impossible in classical Greek: Battezzato 2009a: 181–91.

843 εἰ καὶ μηδέν ἐστιν 'although it is nothing' (Collard). Hecuba flatters Agamemnon's pride: punishing Polymestor will not take him much effort. The usual translation (Gregory: 'even if she is nothing', in reference to Hecuba) is incompatible with Hecuba's suggestion that Agamemnon consider Polydorus his relation by marriage (834).

ἀλλ' ὅμως 'however, <do it> all the same' (i.e. παράσχες χεῖρα). For this elliptical phrase see Mastronarde on *Pho.* 1069, Willink on *Or.* 1023.

844–5 The final general reflection (375–8n.) is an indirect and polite way of implying that Agamemnon has the moral obligation to help Hecuba.

846 δεινόν γε ... ὡς 'it is extraordinary how'. δεινόν often introduces a general reflection: 592, Diggle on *Phaeth.* 164.

θνητοῖς ... ἅπαντα συμπίτνει 'all sorts of things happen to mortals'. For the thought see Soph. *Ai.* 646–7 and 679–83. For συμπίπτω 'to happen' see Aesch. *Eum.* 337, Lys. 19.24. For πάντα 'all sorts of things' see *Hcld.* 841, *Hipp.* 918. Collard and Kovacs interpret 'all things come together' (cf. 966, 1029, Aesch. *Cho.* 299), but the point here is that *incredible* things happen, not that everything comes together at the same point.

847 καινὰς ἀνάγκας οἱ νόμοι διώρισαν 'the laws determine new [or "unexpected"] obligations'. The chorus allude to 751 τολμᾶν ἀνάγκη, where Hecuba states that she is forced to supplicate Agamemnon. For the resulting asyndeton compare fr. 196.1–2. For ἀνάγκας 'obligations', 'something unpleasant imposed on us', see 362, 584, Eur. *Suppl.* 39 ἀνάγκας ἱκεσίους, Thuc. 3.82.2 ἀκουσίους ἀνάγκας. For καινάς 'new and strange', with a negative connotation, see Soph. *Trach.* 613, Eur. *HF* 1118, 1177.

The MS text is problematic in its vagueness: 'and the laws determine the obligations'. In the first century BCE, Didymus (scholium M on 847) found the text illogical, arguing that subject and object should have been reversed. Kovacs and others interpret ἀνάγκας as 'our closest ties' (cf. also Cropp forthcoming), but that would have been ἀναγκαιότητας (as in Lys. 32.5: note the variant ἀνάγκας) or τοὺς ἀναγκαίους. See LSJ s.v. ἀναγκαῖος II.5 'related by blood', *Alc.* 533, *Andr.* 671. Several other conjectures have been advanced.

οἱ νόμοι: the chorus are alluding to the law to which Hecuba appealed in 800. This forces Hecuba to pursue the punishment of Polymestor.

διώρισαν 'determine' (gnomic aorist: Smyth §1931). Gods or abstract concepts are often the subject when (δι)ορίζω is used in this meaning: Eur. *IT* 979 Apollo ὥρισεν σωτηρίαν, Chaerem. 71 F 42 συμφορὰς δαίμον[ες δι]ώρισαν, Xen. *Hell.* 7.1.2, Pl. *Leg.* 864e6 ὁ νόμος ὥρισεν.

848–9 Friendship depends on circumstances. Bias, one of the Seven sages, famously said that men should 'love their friends as if they would some day hate them' (Diog. Laert. 1.87, trans. Hicks), a maxim echoed in Soph. *Ai.* 679–80 'my enemy should be hated as one who will later behave as a friend' (trans. Finglass: see his note and Jebb *ad loc.*; *OC* 609–15).

τιθέντες ... ποιούμενοι 'making ... making'.

850–63 Agamemnon's answer is divided into two sections: (a) a long sentence (850–6), in which, thanks to irregular syntax (852–5n.), he shifts from an apparent benevolence towards Hecuba to a prudent, not to say self-serving, refusal to act; a similar shift occurred in Odysseus' speech: compare 301 and 850; (b) a series of short sentences, rhetorically balanced in a quasi-Gorgianic style: cf. the rhyme ταχύν ... βραδύν (862–3), the parallelism ξυμπονῆσαι and προσαρκέσαι (cf. Fehling 1969:

258–60, and 1250–1n.), the polyptoton φίλιον ... στρατός, | ... φίλος | ... στρατῶι (cf. e.g. Gorgias 82 B 11b § 7 καὶ δὴ τοίνυν σύνειμι καὶ σύνεστι κἀκεῖνος ἐμοὶ κἀκείνωι ἐγώ). Agamemnon's language characterises him as one of those who are (deplorably) 'good at speaking', such as the sons of Theseus (123–4) and Odysseus (132, 254). Hecuba is of course far from rhetorically inept (870–1n.).

851 δι' οἴκτου ... ἔχω 'I take pity': Barrett on *Hipp.* 542–4.

852–5 βούλομαι ... δόξαιμι 'in consideration both of the gods and of justice, I want the impious guest-friend to pay this punishment to you, if it might possibly appear both that things go well for you, and I did not give the army the impression that...' The indicative βούλομαι in the apodosis is followed by a more tentative optative in the protasis: Smyth §2359–60, K–G II.478. The elaborate and irregular syntax and the cautious wording are signs of Agamemnon's difficulty and insincerity. The optative δόξαιμι, assimilated to φανείη, is syntactically coordinated with the infinitive ἔχειν, signalling a stronger degree of uncertainty. For the optative in consecutive clauses cf. Cooper and Krüger 1998: 1047–8, K–G II.513.

852–3 θεῶν ... τοῦ δικαίου are construed with οὕνεκ(α).
ἀνόσιον ξένον is the subject of δοῦναι.

854 φανείη 'it would appear'. Agamemnon prefers the impersonal form, avoiding responsibility.

855 Κασσάνδρας χάριν 'for Cassandra's sake'. The formulaic phrase takes up the theme of *charis*: 830n., Introduction, section 5.

857 ἔστιν γὰρ ἧι ταραγμὸς ἐμπέπτωκέ μοι 'there is a point where inquietude hits me', i.e. 'which makes me uneasy'. Agamemnon uses standard epic and tragic style, stressing that his emotions originate outside of himself: *Il.* 17.625 δέος ἔμπεσε θυμῶι, Aesch. *Ag.* 341 ἔρως δὲ μή τις ... ἐμπίπτηι στρατῶι.

859–60 εἰ δὲ σοὶ φίλος | ὅδ' ἐστί 'if he [i.e. Polydorus] is dear to you'. Agamemnon tacitly rejects Hecuba's argument, and stresses the distance between barbarians and Greeks, with pedantic insistence on the obvious *philia* between Polydorus and his mother. εἰ means 'if, as in fact is the case' (LSJ s.v. VI). Elmsley's conjecture δ' ἐμοί implies that Agamemnon, just when he refuses to give help, accepts Hecuba's argument (834n.) that Polydorus is an affine of his.

860 χωρὶς τοῦτο κοὐ κοινὸν στρατῶι 'this <is> separate, and not common to the army'. Agamemnon is overstating the obvious in order to shift attention away from his responsibility. His formal style has many parallels in Euripides (23on., Denniston on *El.* 985–7, fr. 371.1 ζῶντα κοὐ τεθνηκότα, fr. 635.3 δυστυχὲς κοὐκ εὐτυχές) and echoes the philosophical usage of χωρίς 'differently' introducing subtle (or obvious) distinctions: Austin and Olson on Ar. *Thesm.* 11, Parker on *Alc.* 528.

863 βραδύν 'slow'. Agamemnon prefers a euphemism to a negative statement. 'Slow' means 'inactive': Ar. *Ran.* 1427–8 ὠφελεῖν πάτραν | βραδὺς φανεῖται, μεγάλα δὲ βλάπτειν ταχύς, Soph. *OC* 306–7.
εἰ διαβληθήσομαι 'if I am unjustly accused'. What most worries Agamemnon is public opinion and criticism: 1240–51n.

864–75 Hecuba's answer focuses on one of the main themes of the play: the interaction between social constraints and individual freedom. Polyxena's voluntary sacrifice gave a paradoxical answer to the problem. Hecuba chose revenge over freedom (755) and now shows to Agamemnon that she is psychologically and ethically superior to him: it is she, the slave, who makes her master 'free'. Her master, a king, is not free (see K–A on Philem. fr. 31). In plotting her revenge, she must resort to female deception (884), which evokes disturbing parallels (886–7n.). Hecuba instantly comes up with a plan which she does not reveal (compare *Andr.* 262–5), heightening the suspense; she surpasses Agamemnon in caution, and Medea in quickness of execution (*Med.* 368–409, 764–810). Agamemnon's astonishment at 1122–3 is not feigned: he is genuinely disconcerted and surprised by the violence, speed and effectiveness of Hecuba's actions.

864–9 Hecuba mentions four types of slavery: being a slave to (a) money (fr. 1029.2); (b) *tychē* 'chance' (*HF* 1357, *El.* 892, *Or.* 716); (c) 'the populace' (868: cf. Eur. *IA* 450, fr. 1029.3, Ar. *Eq.* 44, [Xen.] *Ath. Pol.* 1.18); (d) written laws (Hdt. 7.104.4–5, Pl. *Cri.* 50e4). The concepts (a) and (b) are commonplace; points (c) and (d) express potentially antidemocratic sentiments. Hecuba is after all a queen. In Athenian democratic ideology, freedom defined the power of the *dēmos* ([Xen.] *Ath. Pol.* 1.8). This definition was contested precisely in elitist circles: Ober 1998, Raaflaub 2004: 225–47. Hecuba is stating that the rule of the mass in fact restricts freedom. Unlike Callicles in Plato's *Gorgias* and Thrasymachus in the *Republic*, she suggests that the power of the *dēmos* obstructs conventional piety and justice (on law and democracy see 1253n., Ar. *Eccl.* 944–5). Fearing his subjects, the king is a 'slave to his own slaves', an elitist concept Hecuba alludes to, but opportunely does not elaborate: Eur. *Hel.* 1428, *Ba.* 803, [Xen.] *Ath. Pol.* 1.11 τοῖς ἀνδραπόδοις δουλεύειν.

864 φεῦ 'Ah!' Exclamations are often used to introduce emphatically a general reflection: 956, *Od.* 1.32 ὦ πόποι, Eur. *El.* 367, Battezzato 1995: 105–7.

866–7 νόμων γραφαὶ | εἴργουσι χρῆσθαι μὴ κατὰ γνώμην τρόποις 'written laws prevent him from following the ways of life that are in accordance with his mind'. Hecuba complains that the democratic laws coerce aristocrats, and assumes that Agamemnon would follow his character, as other immoralists (often aristocratic ones) did in fifth-century Athens: Thuc. 6.15.3 ταῖς ἐπιθυμίαις ... ἐχρῆτο Alcibiades 'indulged his tastes', Ar. *Nub.* 1078 χρῶ τῆι φύσει, ... νόμιζε μηδὲν αἰσχρόν 'follow your nature, ...

consider nothing shameful', Thuc. 2.53.4 θεῶν δὲ φόβος ἢ ἀνθρώπων νόμος οὐδεὶς ἀπεῖργε (speaking of Athenians during the plague).

μὴ κατὰ γνώμην: a common phrase (*Andr.* 737 κατὰ γνώμην ἐμήν), which here qualifies τρόποις. The negative μή is normally present in Greek in infinitive clauses introduced by verbs of prevention, but should be omitted in English: Smyth §2739, Cooper and Krüger 1998: 789–90 and 1123–5. The negative is normally attached to the verb, but here it is placed next to the element that is especially negated (implying a contrast with 'ways of life imposed on him'): Soph. *Phil.* 66–7 εἰ δ' ἐργάσηι | μὴ ταῦτα, Smyth §2690a.

868 ὄχλωι 'the populace', a word with negative connotations: Eur. *Hipp.* 986–9, *Suppl.* 411 (the Theban envoy, a negative character), Thuc. 4.28.3. Hecuba disparagingly uses ὄχλος to designate the Greek army (605, 607), whereas Agamemnon and the Greeks normally use the neutral στρατός and its cognates. Talthybius uses ὄχλος non-disparagingly at 521 (cf. [533]); so does Hecuba in reference to the Trojan women (880; see also 1014).

870–4 '<I say this> [i.e. 869 'I will free you from this fear'] because I ask you to share in the knowledge, if I plan some harm for the man who killed this <person> [i.e. Polydorus], but not in the action. If some uproar or help should materialise from the Greeks, when the Thracian man suffers what he will suffer, prevent <them>, without letting <them> notice <that you are doing it> as a favour for me.' γάρ means 'I say this because' (Denniston 60). In Greek, a command can be introduced by γάρ (*Hcld.* 153 φέρ' ἀντίθες γάρ, cf. *Cycl.* 313–14), whereas in English it is necessary to rephrase the imperative ('I ask you to') or to omit γάρ from the translation.

870–1 σύνισθι ... συνδράσηις: Hecuba ably contrasts two verbs formed with the same preverb: see Hdt. 1.142.4 ὁμολογέουσι κατὰ γλῶσσαν οὐδέν, σφίσι δὲ ὁμοφωνέουσι, and Democr. 68 B 65 πολυνοΐην, οὐ πολυμαθίην, Fehling 1969: 246.

873 πάσχοντος ἀνδρὸς Θρηικὸς οἷα πείσεται is an ominous turn of phrase, which euphemistically avoids specifying his punishment: see Mastronarde on *Med.* 889, *El.* 1141, Johnstone 1980: 53–4.

874 ἐμὴν χάριν: 855n.

875 τὰ δ' ἄλλα ... πάντ' ἐγὼ θήσω καλῶς 'I'll take good care of all the rest'. Such sweeping statements are often euphemistic (*Hipp.* 709 (Phaedra, alluding to her suicide)) or will be refuted by the events (Aesch. *Ag.* 1673, Eur. *Med.* 926). Cf. Fraenkel on Aesch. *Ag.* 913, Diggle 1994: 263–5.

θάρσει 'fear not!', parenthetic: Soph. *OC* 1185, Eur. *El.* 1319–20. Hecuba, the slave, reassures the master, taking up what her daughter had said to Odysseus at 345 (Kovacs 1987: 104).

876–8 Women resort to poison or deceit, not violence: fr. 464, *Med.* 376–85, *IT* 1032.

πῶς οὖν; τί δράσεις; 'How then? What will you do?' The same phrase occurs in *Hipp.* 598; note also Eur. *Med.* 1376, Soph. *OC* 652. The elliptical πῶς οὖν; is a question expressing surprise and disbelief; in Euripides and Plato, it always introduces a second question.

ἢ 'πικουρίαι τίνι; 'or with what help <will you kill him>?' For the position of the interrogative adjective see 829–30n.

879 τίς σοι ξυνέσται χείρ; 'What hand will be with you?' Agamemnon uses 'hand' implying 'men who can help with their physical force', as the following φίλους makes clear: *Hcld.* 337 πολλῆι … χειρί 'with a large number of soldiers'. The element of gender reversal implied by female violence is emphasised here and at 880–7; cf. also 1034n.

880–2 Hecuba now reveals that the slave women will be part of her revenge plan. Like Medea (364–409, 764–810), she has worked out the details of her plot in her mind, before revealing it at the right moment.

τὸν ἐμῶν φονέα τιμωρήσομαι 'I will punish the killer of my <children>.' On the plural see 750n. The adjective ἐμῶν is used substantively, which would normally require an article (Smyth §1021, 1130, K–G 1.594), but tragic language is at times surprisingly sparing with articles: Diggle 1994: 25, K–G 1.608–9. Tragedy occasionally admits the prosody φονέα, as here, instead of the usual Attic prosody φονέα (from φονῆα): *El.* 599, 763, Smyth §277a, K–B 1.448.

884 'the crowd <is> frightening, and difficult to fight against, if assisted by deceit'. Hecuba assumes that she will have many helpers, whereas Polymestor will be alone: 979–81n.

885 δεινόν a speaker in a stichomythia often takes up a word used by the other, as at *El.* 769–70, *IT* 920–1.

θῆλυ … γένος 'the female sex' (lit. 'race'). Misogynistic attitudes considered women as a separate 'race', stressing their difference from and inferiority to men: see 1183–4, Eur. *Med.* 574, 909, Hes. *Th.* 590, *LfgrE* s.v. γένος B 4, Loraux 1993: 72–110. Diggle prints Jenni's σθένος, for which compare fr. 199.1–2 τὸ δ' ἀσθενές μου καὶ τὸ θῆλυ σώματος | κακῶς ἐμέμφθης 'you were wrong to blame my body's weakness and femininity' (tr. Collard and Cropp 2008a). σθένος however does not answer Hecuba's new point about the number of women.

μέμφομαι 'I have little consideration for', cf. Pl. *Euthd.* 305b6 μεμφόμενος τὴν φιλοσοφίαν (in reference to 304e6–305a1), *Grg.* 470a1–2 μέμφηι τὴν τοιαύτην δύναμιν. See already Hdt. 1.77.1 and 7.49.1 'to complain about the army', i.e. 'to consider the army insufficient'.

886–7 The Danaids, daughters of Danaus, were forced to marry their cousins, sons of Aegyptus, and killed them on their wedding night: Aesch. *Suppl. passim, PV* 853–69, Garvie 1969: 163–83. The women of Lemnos, rejected by their husbands in favour of concubines, killed them all and 'Lemnian evils' became a byword for horrific crimes: Garvie on

Aesch. *Cho.* 631–8, Hdt. 6.138 (who also narrates a similar crime committed by men in Lemnos). On the intertextual relationship with *Choephori* cf. 1177–82n., 953–1295n., Thalmann 1993: 150–2. These examples of extreme female violence threaten the whole male 'race': Hecuba is aiming to punish a single man, but chooses mythical examples that stress her threat.

Λῆμνον ἄρδην ἀρσένων ἐξώικισαν; 'did they not completely depopulate Lemnos of men'? ἐξοικίζω 'to settle away from, to banish from' is construed here as κενόω 'to empty' (Aesch. *Suppl.* 659–60 μήποτε λοιμὸς ἀνδρῶν | τάνδε πόλιν κενῶσαι) with the genitive of the people that have been taken away, and the accusative of the land that has been emptied, whereas the people normally go in the accusative (946–8 με ... ἐξώικισεν ... οἴκων, Thuc. 6.76.2 ἡμᾶς ... ἐξοικίσαι).

888 ὡς γενέσθω 'let it be so', a phrase occurring also at *IT* 603, *Tro.* 726. Hecuba starts giving orders to Agamemnon, revealing her queenly attitude and dominant character.

891–4 The precise wording is important for the plot to succeed (see Garvie on Aesch. *Cho.* 773, Eur. *El.* 651–4), and for this reason Hecuba tells the slave woman the exact words she needs to repeat, as a direct speech. Euripides resorts to a quasi-Homeric technique: *Od.* 16.284–94 and 19.4–13. Direct speech is rarely quoted in tragedy outside messengers' speeches: de Jong 1991: 131–9 and 199–201.

892 σὸν οὐκ ἔλασσον ἢ κείνης χρέος 'because of a matter that concerns you not less than her'. On the accusative see Smyth §991b, 1607.

893–4 Hecuba, by requesting the presence of the children of Polymestor, indirectly suggests that she will reveal to him some important and confidential piece of news (1005–7).

896–7 The two siblings must be cremated and buried together, like Orestes and Electra (Eur. *Or.* 1041–55, Soph. *El.* 1165–9). This motif is attested also for Achilles and Patroclus (*Il.* 23.91–2, 243–4, *Od.* 24.76–7) and, very frequently, for spouses (*Alc.* 363–8, *Suppl.* 990–1030, 1064–71, *Hel.* 985–90). On the play on numbers (two children, a single pyre) see 45n., Barrett on *Hipp.* 1403, Diggle 1994: 351.

κρυφθῆτον χθονί (so that) 'they could be covered by the earth' (= could be buried), a traditional poetic phrase: Aesch. *Ag.* 455, Pind. *Nem.* 8.38.

899 οὐκ ἂν εἶχον 'I would not have been able to'.

900 θεός 'god', 'a god', in reference to an unspecified divine intervention: Eur. *Alc.* 514, *Hipp.* 867, Hdt. 1.32.9 ὁ θεός, T. Harrison 2000: 171–5.

901 μένειν ἀνάγκη <ʼς> πλοῦν ὁρῶντας ἡσύχους 'it is necessary <for us> to wait, staying idle, and look for <an opportunity to> sail'. Agamemnon characteristically attempts to shift responsibility away from himself to the army (855–60, 1249). As at 899, πλοῦς without qualifications means '(opportunity) to sail'. For ὁρῶντας ἐς 'looking for', 'waiting for', 'being ready to' cf. LSJ s.v. 1.1 and 3, Eur. fr. 162.1 ἀνδρὸς δ' ὁρῶντος εἰς Κύπριν, Friis-Johansen and Whittle on Aesch. *Suppl.* 725. For prodelision of ἐς (often corrupted or omitted in MSS) see *Ion* 1562, *Cycl.* 240, 387n. For ἡσύχους with μένειν see 35–6n. The MS text μένειν ἀνάγκη πλοῦν ὁρῶντας ἥσυχον 'it is necessary to wait for a quiet sailing, seeing it' gives poor meaning, and implies that the Greeks were blocked by storms, not by lack of winds.

902 γένοιτο δ' εὖ πως 'let us hope that <things> will turn out for the good, somehow'. The indefinite adverb πως alludes to divine intervention: Fraenkel on Aesch. *Ag.* 182–3, Garvie on Aesch. *Cho.* 957–9, Eur. *Hel.* 712. Agamemnon assumes that a god has stopped the winds (900), evidently to help Hecuba in her revenge. The prayer is formulaic: Aesch. *Ag.* 217, 1249 ἀλλὰ μὴ γένοιτό πως, *Suppl.* 454 γένοιτο δ' εὖ, Eur. *Suppl.* 603.

902–3 πᾶσι γὰρ κοινὸν τόδε, | ἰδίαι θ' ἑκάστωι καὶ πόλει 'this is common to all, both privately to everyone and to the city' (cf. 640n.). Agamemnon's language is full of antitheses and repetitions (850–63n., 860n.). For κοινόν 'what is in the public interest' see Hdt. 3.82.3, Eur. *Suppl.* 538.

903–4 That it is just to punish the wicked is said in similar language at 1085–6 and 1250–1 (1086n.). That noble human beings should prosper is not borne out by the plot of the play: it certainly does not apply well to Polyxena (377, 581–2, 595–8). Agamemnon implies that he is χρηστός, but that might be doubted (850–63). On the concluding general reflections cf. 375–8n.

904 Agamemnon leaves from the parodos by which he entered. He is accompanied by his attendants, and by the servants who carry Polydorus' body, taking it where Polyxena's is, in order to prepare a common burial (896–7, 1287–8). Hecuba possibly goes back inside the tent.

Mossman 1995: 60 claims that Polydorus' body remains onstage, arguing that Polymestor mistakes it for that of Polyxena. However, it would be hard to explain why Hecuba does not refer to the body in her speech against the murderer (compare 1212–13, 1224–5, 1228–30 with 760–3, 833). Hecuba could have made very effective use of a revelation of the body, as in Soph. *El.* 1466–77. No deictics point to its presence onstage after 904 (953n., 954–5n.). As Mossmann notes, only two corpses are misidentified in Greek tragedy, that of Polydorus at 671–82 and that of Clytemnestra in Soph. *El.* 1466–77. In both cases, however, a correct identification follows. Polydorus' body is carried away at this stage; no misidentification is likely to have occurred.

905-52 THIRD STASIMON

The third stasimon narrates the sack of Ilium, a topic treated previously in epic (see esp. the *Sack of Ilium*) and lyric poetry (Stesich. frr. 98–164 Finglass) and very popular in art: Finglass and Davies 2014: 395–402. Euripides takes up the theme again at *Tro.* 511–67, *IA* 751–800 and, in more allusive terms, *Andr.* 1009–18.

Here, the first strophe introduces the topic, and laments the fate of Troy. The first antistrophe and the second strophe describe the moment immediately before the sack of Ilium from the point of view of a (young?) Trojan housewife, who is getting ready to go to bed with her husband. The second antistrophe describes the fate of the Trojans. The stasimon ends with a curse on Helen and Paris, in the epode. The depiction of collective grief is contrasted with a scene of everyday sensuality, elaborately described. The sack is thus narrated through the eyes of the victims. This gives an unprecedented twist to the *topos* of the wealthy Trojans punished because of their sexual misdemeanours, embodied in Paris. Here the chorus members dissociate themselves from Paris (943–52), but cherish the memory of the past moments of intimacy with their husbands, in the luxurious setting of their home (923–6n.).

The chorus also claim that Troy 'will not be counted any more among unsacked cities', thus suggesting a parallel with Athens and Sparta, which claimed they were never sacked by their enemies (at least in mythical times). The claim is not true for Troy, as Heracles had already sacked it (906n.). The selective memory of the chorus stresses the parallelism between the suffering of Troy and that of Athens and Sparta, already alluded to in the epode of the second stasimon (649–57). The women of the chorus compare themselves to 'Spartan girls' (934n.), thus suggesting a possible similar fate for Sparta, which prided itself on having never been subject to invasion, even if it lacked city walls. The text only hints at this, by associating Spartans and Trojan women. The chorus invite the Greek audience to participate in the fate of the vanquished Trojans. The text of Euripides impersonates the defeated, even if the author and the audience belong to the country of the conquerors. Athens had a colony, Sigeum, in the Trojan land (Aesch. *Eum.* 397–402). The text suggests new possible narratives, hinting that the Peloponnesian war might be seen as some sort of re-enactment of the earlier one.

The stasimon is exceptional also for its narrative technique. The toilette of the Trojan lady is presented as a long 'still frame', whereas details of the fall of Troy are either suppressed (the Trojan horse) or merely hinted at (the celebrations for the supposed end of the war: 916–17). This technique is not common in Euripides, who often presents extensive and continuous narratives, esp. on Trojan topics: *Andr.* 274–92, *Tro.* 511–67, *IA* 751–800 (cast in the future), *Hel.* 1301–68, Panagl 1971.

In contrast to the later, so-called 'dithyrambic', style, the syntax is relatively simple, with short sentences clearly balanced. The vocabulary has only a few of the newly coined compound adjectives that will make late Euripidean lyrics linguistically demanding. On the other hand the influence of lyric and epic poetry is still strong (907–8n., 910–11n., 915n., 945n.), in part because of the 'epic' content.

Verbal echoes in responding metrical positions are not frequent: 913 ἐμβατεύσω ~ 922 ἐμβεβῶτα and the anagrammatic 925–6 ἀτέρμονας ~ 935–6 Ἄρτεμιν (ἆ τλάμων).

Metre

The first strophic pair includes Aeolic, enoplian and dactylo-epitrite cola, which reappear in the second pair and in the epode. For other metrical discussions and analyses see Lourenço 2011: 188–9, Parker 1997: 443, Stinton 1990: 131.

First Strophe and First Antistrophe: 905–13~914–22

	⏑ ⏑ – ⏑ ⏑ – ⏑ –	telesillean
905	σὺ μέν, ὦ πατρὶς Ἰλιάς,	
914	μεσονύκτιος ὠλλύμαν,	
	– ⏑ – – ⏑ ⏑ – ⏑ ⏑ – –	tro D –
906	τῶν ἀπορθήτων πόλις οὐκέτι λέξηι·	
915	ἦμος ἐκ δείπνων ὕπνος ἡδὺς ἐπ' ὄσσοις	
	– ⏑ – – ⏑ ⏑ – ⏑ ⏑ – –	tro D –
907–8	τοῖον Ἑλλάνων νέφος ἀμφί σε κρύπτει	
916–17	σκίδναται, μολπᾶν δ' ἄπο καὶ χοροποιὸν	
	⏑ ⏑ – ⏑ ⏑ – ⁀ ‖ᵇ¹	telesillean^ ‖ᵇ¹
909	δορὶ δὴ δορὶ πέρσαν.	
918	θυσίαν καταπαύσας	
	⏑ ⏑ – ⏑ ⏑ – ⏑ –	telesillean
910	ἀπὸ δὲ στεφάναν κέκαρ-	
919	πόσις ἐν θαλάμοις ἔκει-	
	– – – ⏑ ⏑ – ⏑ –	glyconic
911	σαι πύργων, κατὰ δ' αἰθάλου	
920	το, ξυστὸν δ' ἐπὶ πασσάλωι,	

COMMENTARY: 905-52   195

	— — _ ᴗ ᴗ — ᴗ — —	hipponactean
912	κηλῖδ' οἰκτροτάταν κέχρωσαι.	
921	ναύταν οὐκέθ' ὁρῶν ὅμιλον	
	ᴗ̆ — _ — ᴗ ᴗ _ — ᴗ — ⌢ ‖‖	hipponactean ‖‖
913	τάλαιν', οὐκέτι σ' ἐμβατεύσω.	
922	Τροίαν Ἰλιάδ' ἐμβεβῶτα.	

Second Strophe and Second Antistrophe: 923-32~933-42

	ᴗ — ᴗ ᴗ ᴗ ᴗ ᴗ ᴗ ᴗ —	2 ia
923	ἐγὼ δὲ πλόκαμον ἀναδέτοις	
933	λέχη δὲ φίλια μονόπεπλος	
	ᴗ — ᴗ — ᴗ — — ᴗ —	2 ia
924	μίτραισιν ἐρρυθμιζόμαν	
934	λιποῦσα, Δωρὶς ὡς κόρα,	
	— — ᴗ — _ — — ᴗ — ᴗ ᴗ — — —	ia wilamowitzian sp
925-6	χρυσέων ἐνόπτρων λεύσσουσ' ἀτέρμονας εἰς αὐγάς,	
935-6	σεμνὰν προσίζουσ' οὐκ ἤνυσ' Ἄρτεμιν ἁ τλάμων·	
	ᴗ ᴗ — ᴗ ᴗ — ᴗ — ᴗ — —	telesillean ba
927	ἐπιδέμνιος ὡς πέσοιμ' ἐς εὐνάν.	
937	ἄγομαι δὲ θανόντ' ἰδοῦσ' ἀκοίταν	
	ᴗ ᴗ ᴗ ᴗ ᴗ ᴗ ᴗ ᴗ ᴗ ᴗ ⌢ ‖ᶜ?	2 ia ‖ᶜ?
928	ἀνὰ δὲ κέλαδος ἔμολε πόλιν·	
938	τὸν ἐμὸν ἅλιον ἐπὶ πέλαγος·	
	ᴗ — ᴗ _ ᴗ — ᴗ — — ᴗ —	2 ia cr
929	κέλευσμα δ' ἦν κατ' ἄστυ Τροίας τόδ'· Ὦ	
939	πόλιν δ' ἀποσκοποῦσ', ἐπεὶ νόστιμον	
	— ᴗ — — ᴗ ᴗ — ᴗ ᴗ —	tro D
930	παῖδες Ἑλλάνων, πότε δὴ πότε τὰν	
940	ναῦς ἐκίνησεν πόδα καί μ' ἀπὸ γᾶς	
	— ᴗ ᴗ — ᴗ ᴗ —	D
931	Ἰλιάδα σκοπιὰν	
941	ὥρισεν Ἰλιάδος,	
	ᴗ̆ — ᴗ — ᴗ — ⌢ ‖‖	ia ba ‖‖
932	πέρσαντες ἥξετ' οἴκους;	
942	τάλαιν' ἀπεῖπον ἄλγει,	

Epode: 943-52

943-4	– – ⏑ – – – ⏑ ⏑ – ⏑⏑ – τὰν τοῖν Διοσκούροιν Ἑλέναν κάσιν ἴ-	iambelegus
945	– – ⏑ – – – ⏑ ⏑ – ⏑ ⏑ – ⏑ – ⌢ ‖ʰ δαῖόν τε βούταν Αἰνόπαριν κατάραι διδοῦσα,	iambelegus ba ‖ʰ
946-7	⏑ – ⏑ – – ⏑ ⏑ – ⏑ – ⏑ ⌢ ‖ᵇ ἐπεί με γᾶς ἐκ πατρίας ἀπώλεσεν	ia cho ia ‖ᵇ
948	– – ⏑ – – – ⏑ ⏑ – ⏑ ⏑ – ἐξώικισέν τ' οἴκων γάμος οὐ γάμος ἀλλ'	iambelegus
949	⏑ – ⏑ – ⏑ – ⌢ ‖ᶜ ἀλάστορός τις οἰζύς·	ia ba ‖ᶜ
950-1	– – ⏑ ⏑⏑ ⏑ ⏑⏑⏑⏑ ⏑ ⏑ – ⏑ – ἂν μήτε πέλαγος ἅλιον ἀπαγάγοι πάλιν	3 ia
952	– ⏑ ⏑ – ⏑ ⏑ – ⏑ – ⌢ ‖‖ μήτε πατρῶιον ἵκοιτ' ἐς οἶκον.	alcaic decasyllable ‖‖

905 σὺ μέν: many lyric songs begin with an apostrophe (444, *Med.* 1251 *Hipp.* 525, Kranz 1933: 238–9). Invocations to places and cities occur often in Euripidean lyrics: *Med.* 645 ὦ πατρίς, *Hipp.* 555–6 ὦ Θήβας ἱερὸν τεῖχος. Troy is here personified and compared to a woman: 910–11n., 911–12n.

906 'you will not be counted any more among unsacked cities'. In fact, according to other mythical narratives, Troy had already been sacked by Heracles: *Il.* 5.638–42, Pind. *Ol.* 8.31–46, Eur. *Andr.* 797–801. Athenian ideology found ways to claim, in spite of the Persian invasion, that Athens had never been sacked: Aesch. *Pers.* 348, Eur. *Med.* 825–6, Strabo 8.33. Similar claims were made by the Spartans: Dinarchus 1.73, Lys. 33.7.

907–8 νέφος: the metaphor has its origins in epic and lyric poetry: *Il.* 17.243 πολέμοιο νέφος, Pind. *Isthm.* 7.27, Mastronarde on *Pho.* 250–1 νέφος ἀσπίδων.

ἀμφί σε κρύπτει: preverb (ἀμφί) and verb (κρύπτει) are separated ('tmesis') by one or more words (in tragedy often a single enclitic word, as here): see 1172n. All the verbs in this sentence are in tmesis, while the object is sandwiched between preverb and verb (910–11 ἀπὸ ... κεκάρσαι, 911–12 κατὰ ... κέχρωσαι, see later in the stasimon 928 ἀνὰ ... ἔμολε, an intransitive verb which surrounds its subject). This adds to the Homeric flavour of the stasimon.

909 δορὶ δὴ δορί: for this kind of anadiplosis see 930n., Alc. 222 πόριζε δὴ πόριζε.

πέρσαν 'which destroyed you': neut. aor. ptcp. from πέρθω in reference to νέφος (907–8). This verb recalls the name of the epic poem *Sack of Ilium* (Ἰλίου πέρσις) (905–52n.).

910–11 ἀπὸ δὲ στεφάναν κέκαρ|σαι πύργων 'you were shorn of your crown of towers'. στεφάναν is an accusative depending on the passive verb; in the active, the verb takes two objects, one of a person and one of an object (Smyth §1632, K–G I.325–9). The image of the 'crown of towers' is first found in compressed form at *Il.* 19.99 ἐυστεφάνωι ἐνὶ Θήβηι. Cf. Pind. *Ol.* 8.32, Soph. *Ant.* 122, Eur. *Tro.* 784, Mastronarde on *Pho.* 832–3. A similar metaphor is found with κρήδεμνον, which means both 'head-binding/veil' (*Il.* 14.184, Eur. *Pho.* 1490) and 'towers' of a city (Janko on *Il.* 16.100; Eur. *Tro.* 508). The semantic field of κείρω ('shear', 'ravage', also 'slaughter': Soph. *Ai.* 55) is appropriate both to the 'normal' and to the metaphorical meaning of στεφάναν. The city is implicitly compared to a woman in mourning, whose 'head-ornaments' are shorn. Similarly complex metaphors with κείρω and δρέπω are found at Eur. *HF* 875–6 (ἀποκείρεται σὸν ἄνθος πόλεος, 'the flower of your city' = 'its most valiant man') and Aesch. *Suppl.* 663.

911–12 κατὰ δ'αἰθάλου | κηλῖδ'... κέχρωσαι 'you have been smeared with the stain of smoke'. κατὰ ... κέχρωσαι is perfect passive from καταχρώιζω 'touch' and κηλῖδ' is an internal accusative: Smyth §§1620, 1631–2. The chorus carry on consistently the comparison between Troy and a woman: κηλίς is often associated with blood (Eur. *IT* 1200, Antipho 3.3.11) and sexual contamination (Soph. *OT* 1384).

914 μεσονύκτιος ὠλλύμαν: Troy fell at midnight, according to the *Little Iliad*: cf. fr. 14 West 2003 νὺξ μὲν ἔην μεσάτη, λαμπρὰ δ' ἐπέτελλε σελήνη (reported by the scholium on Σ on the present passage). On the date of the fall of Troy see also 1102–4n.

915 ὕπνος ἡδύς: the phrase is derived from epic: *Il.* 4.131, *LfgrE* s.vv. ἡδύς B 4, γλυκύς B 2b. The epic colour is varied by Euripides, who uses a non-epic scansion (ὕπνος = ⏑ ⏑).

916–17 σκίδναται occurs in this meaning, 'to spread, to emanate', in reference to light (Aesch. *Pers.* 502, *Il.* 8.1), sound (Hes. *Th.* 41–2) and smell (*h.hom.Cer.* 278). 'Sleep' is elsewhere conceived as a substance that is poured over the eyes: cf. *Il.* 24.445 ὕπνον ἔχευε, Pind. *Pyth.* 1.8. Sophocles used the same verb of dispelling sleep: *Trach.* 989–90 σκεδάσαι τῶιδ' ἀπὸ κρατὸς βλεφάρων θ' ὕπνον 'to dispel sleep from his head and eyes'.

916–18 μολπᾶν δ' ἄπο καὶ χοροποιὸν | θυσίαν καταπαύσας 'after the songs and after finishing the sacrifice that is accompanied by dancing'. For the participle linked to a prepositional phrase see 346–8n. On χοροποιόν see Mastronarde on *Pho.* 788.

920 ξυστὸν δ' ἐπὶ πασσάλωι 'the spear <was> on the peg' not only because the Greeks had departed (fr. 369.1) but also because it was night: Gow on Theocr. 24.43.

921 ναύταν... ὅμιλον 'the crowd of sailors'. The noun ναύτης 'sailor' is here used attributively (cf. 644–6n., 790n.), as often happens with 'substantives denoting *occupation, condition,* or *age*' in combination with nouns such as 'man' (Smyth §986) or 'people' (*Suppl.* 509 and Diggle 1994: 219).

922 Τροίαν Ἰλιάδ' 'the part of the Troad in front of Ilium'. For the redundancy cf. *Andr.* 151 ἐκ Λακαίνης Σπαρτιάτιδος χθονός, *Tro.* 9–10 ὁ ... Παρνάσιος | Φωκεύς. Τροία can be both the city and the region, just as Ἄργος is: Finglass on Soph. *El.* 4, Eur. *IT* 508–10. The boundaries of the Troad were subject to debate in early historiography: Jacoby on *FGrH* 1 F 221–7 and 5 F 9, Strabo 13.1.4. Herodotus apparently differentiates between the 'Trojan territory' (5.26) and the 'territory of Ilium' (7.42). Ilium and Troy, and the connected adjectives, however, were often used interchangeably (*El.* 3–5), which makes the redundancy of this passage suspect. Euripides may have written something like χώραν Ἰλιάδ' (cf. *Hcld.* 31 and *Pho.* 246).

ἐμβεβῶτα echoes 913 ἐμβατεύσω, in the same metrical position. The echo stresses the contrast between the inevitability of exile (913) and the illusion of the Trojans at the fake departure of the Greeks. The variant ἐμβεβαῶτα is the epic form of the perfect participle, and would scan here only with epic synizesis, a type not normally found in tragedy: see Garvie on Aesch. *Cho.* 410 κέαρ, Björck 1950: 168.

923–6 The toilette suggests luxury and refinement, and, ultimately, seduction. Helen eagerly adopted this Oriental habit (*Or.* 1110–4, *Tro.* 991–7, 1107).

πλόκαμον... ἐρρυθμιζόμαν 'I was arranging my hair' in front of a mirror: cf. Jason's bride (*Med.* 1161) and Clytemnestra (*El.* 1071).

ἀναδέτοις | μίτραισιν 'with head-bands tied up', keeping the hair off the face. *Mitrai* came from Asia (Hdt. 1.195.1, Sappho fr. 98a.10–11) and their use in Greece is generally restricted to women or cross-dressing men (Ar. *Thesm.* 257, 941, Eur. *Ba.* 833, 929). The same word may designate girdles (*Il.* 4.137), or other kinds of fillets (Pind. *Ol.* 9.84, Eur. *El.* 162). See Gow on Theocr. 17.19. Mirrors and head-bands are associated in a list of implements used by women in Ar. fr. 332.1–2 K–A.

χρυσέων ἐνόπτρων λεύσσουσ' ἀτέρμονας εἰς αὐγάς 'looking at the boundless gleam of my golden mirror'. ἀτέρμων is probably an ornamental adjective, describing with exaggeration the endlessness (in time? or in space?) of the rays: Empedocles 31 B 84.6 D–K says that the light of a lantern, compared to an eye, 'shines with endless beams' (λάμπεσκεν ... ἀτείρεσιν ἀκτίνεσσι). Fire or *aithēr* is boundless: Empedocles 31 B 135.2 D–K διά τ' εὐρυμέδοντος | αἰθέρος ἠνεκέως τέταται διά τ' ἀπλέτου αὐγῆς, 17.18 ἠέρος ἄπλετον ὕψος. For golden mirrors compare *Tro.* 1106 χρύσεα δ' ἔνοπτρα.

927 ἐπιδέμνιος ὡς πέσοιμ' ἐς εὐνάν: for the redundancy cf. *Andr.* 104 ἀγάγετ' εὐναίαν [~ ἐπιδέμνιος] ἐς θαλάμους [~ ἐς εὐνάν] Ἑλέναν, a passage closely echoed at 950. ἐπιδέμνιος 'on the bed' is a *hapax*.

928 κέλαδος: the shouting of the Greeks is also the turning point in the narrative of the fall of Troy in *Tro.* 555.

929–30 Ὦ | παῖδες Ἑλλάνων 'you children of the Greeks'. The periphrasis has its origin in epic, but makes its appearance in tragic diction as well: *Il.* 2.551, Aesch. *Pers.* 402 (ὦ παῖδες Ἑλλήνων), Eur. *Andr.* 1124, *Ba.* 37. On direct speeches in tragedy, with special attention to lyric passages, cf. Bers 1997: 23–115.

930 πότε δὴ πότε 'when, when?' For the repetition see 909n., *El.* 727 τότε δὴ τότε, *Or.* 1483, *Hcld.* 873 νῦν δὴ νῦν, Diggle 1994: 296.

932 ἥξετ' οἴκους; 'will you get home?' The accusative indicates the goal: Smyth §1588. The *nostos* is a recurring theme in the play (109–15, 444–83, 898–901, 1289–92) as it is in epic (*Il.* 2.288, 354–6). Fate determined the time of the sack of Troy: *Il.* 16.707–9, 21.517.

933 The woman did get to the bed and began (the preliminaries of) her love-making. This is implied by the phrase 'I left the marriage-bed I loved'. The love-making, interrupted by the shout of the attacking Greeks, is left tactfully understood.

μονόπεπλος 'wearing only the *peplos*', not the upper garment: she is in a hurry. Pindar uses ἄπεπλος ('without the upper garment') of Alcmena rushing out of bed out of fear: Pind. *Nem.* 1.50, fr. 52u.14. Similar adjectives are often used to the same effect: Ap. Rhod. *Arg.* 3.646 οἰέανος, Plut. *Ant.* 83.1 μονοχίτων, [Arist.] *Ath. Pol.* 25.4 μονοχίτων (Ephialtes as a suppliant). For related *topoi* ('without footwear'= 'in a hurry') see Aesch. *PV* 135, West on Hes. *Op.* 345, Theocr. 24.36.

934 Δωρὶς ὡς κόρα: the Dorian dress-code for women had disturbing connotations for non-Dorian Greeks: (a) immodesty: Dorian unmarried girls and women usually wore only the *peplos*, and this was considered provocative (Anacr. fr. 399 *PMG*, Soph. fr. 872 (of Hermione), Pythainetos *FGrHist* 299 F 3); (b) impropriety (Ibyc. 339 *PMG*, Eur. *Andr.* 595–600, Plut. *Com. Lyc. Num.* 3.5–9); (c) aggressiveness. According to Hdt. 5.87–89 and Duris *FGrHist* 76 F 24 (a fragment reported in the scholium on the present passage) the Athenian women, when their men died in a battle with the Aeginetans in the early sixth century BCE, used the brooch-pins of their Dorian dress to kill the only survivor. Consequently, the Athenians made their women adopt the Ionian fashion, while Argives and Aeginetans increased the size of the brooch-pins. Nudity and physical exercise were associated (*Andr.* 595–600), thus creating the image of an aggressive and threatening virgin/woman.

The women of the chorus would not have dared to appear in public wearing only a *peplos*, if not for the extraordinary circumstances (the sack of the city). They thus present themselves as modest, in contrast with the characterisation of Dorian women. The aggressiveness implied in the Dorian robe is acted out at 1169–71, when the Trojan women use their brooch-pins to blind Polymestor. See Battezzato 1999–2000. The interplay of Troy and Sparta was already explored in the second stasimon: 629–57n.

935–6 σεμνὰν προσίζουσ' οὐκ ἤνυσ' Ἄρτεμιν 'I did not gain anything from taking refuge at the altar of Artemis', the goddess that protected their city. In the parallel stasimon of the *Trojan Women*, the women were celebrating Artemis (551–5) at the moment of the final attack of the Greeks; cf. also Finglass and Davies 2014: 446–7 on Stesich. fr. 114.9–12. The Trojan women were dragged away from the altars, when not killed or raped: 29on., *Tro.* 70, 501, 562. *Il.* 4.56 οὐκ ἀνύω φθονέουσ(α) ('I do not gain anything by refusing') is a precise parallel for the construction of ἀνύω with the participle and for the presence of οὐ where οὐδέν is usual: see also 1167 and Hdt. 9.66.1 πολλὰ ἀπαγορεύων οὐδέν ἤνυε. The accusative Ἄρτεμιν depends on προσίζω as at Aesch. *Suppl.* 189, Eur. fr. 554a.2. The god stands for the altar: *Hcld.* 238–9 Ζεὺς ἐφ' οὗ σὺ βώμιος | θακεῖς.

937 ἄγομαι 'I was dragged away'. The historical present (527–9n.) is not uncommon in lyric narrations: *Hel.* 1323–40. For its use in messenger speeches see 1148n.

938 ἅλιον ἐπὶ πέλαγος 'maritime sea': 701n.

939 πόλιν δ' ἀποσκοποῦσ' 'and, gazing back at the city'. δ' (Willink) makes the syntax smoother, making clear that this is a new sentence, with a new main verb. τ' (MSS) suggests a coordination between ἀποσκοποῦσα and ἰδοῦσα (937); in fact the coordination must link ἄγομαι (937) with ἀπεῖπον (942).

939–40 νόστιμον | ναῦς ἐκίνησεν πόδα 'the ship set its course for home' (Collard). Periphrases with πούς are very frequent to indicate movement (965n. and 1058), and are at times used in reference to objects, concepts (*Ba.* 889) or animals (*Ion* 162). The usage is made easier here since πούς is also a technical term for the two lower corners of a ship's sail or sheet: 1020. For predicative νόστιμον see *Alc.* 1153.

942 ἀπεῖπον ἄλγει: lit. 'I was unable to answer to the pain', i.e. 'I could not cope with the pain', 'I fainted because of the pain'. Eur. *Or.* 91 ἀπείρηκεν κακοῖς is similar; cf. also Soph. *Trach.* 789.

943–52 The epode is in the form of a *propemptikon*, a prayer normally meant to wish someone a safe voyage overseas (Sappho fr. 5). Here however the chorus wish for the shipwreck or death of the travellers (950–2): Hipponax fr. 115 West, Eur. *Tro.* 1100–17 (the chorus wish shipwreck for Menelaus and Helen sailing away from Troy), Hor. *Epod.* 10. The chorus paradoxically mention Helen's brothers the Dioscuri (943–4), who protect sailors (*El.* 990–3, Allan and Kannicht on *Hel.* 1500), before expressing the wish that Helen's voyage will end in ruin. A similar paradoxical *propemptikon* occurs at *IT* 439–46: the chorus wish Helen to arrive safely at the land of the Taurians, where she will be sacrificed. Contrast *Hel.* 1451–1511, where the chorus wish Helen a safe trip to Greece from Egypt, with the help of the Dioscuri. For the syntactic connection between antistrophe and epode cf. 647–8n.

945 βούταν: 644–6n.

Αἰνόπαριν 'terrible Paris', 'Paris cause of evil'. Euripides imitates Alcm. 77 *PMG* Δύσπαρις, Αἰνόπαρις, κακὸν Ἑλλάδι βωτιανείραι, who in turns echoes the tradition originating in *Il.* 3.39 Δύσπαρι, 13.769; see also Aesch. *Ag.* 713 Πάριν τὸν αἰνόλεκτρον and Eur. *Hel.* 1120 Πάρις αἰνόγαμος. Similar deformations are Δυσελένη (*Or.* 1387, *IA* 1316), Κακοΐλιον οὐκ ὀνομαστήν (*Od.* 19.260), Ἄϊρος (*Od.* 18.73).

κατάραι διδοῦσα 'cursing' Paris and Helen for the suffering they caused. The periphrasis δίδωμι + abstract noun/*nomen actionis* in the dative case suggests deliberate action ('to abandon X to the curse'): for the stylistic effects of periphrases cf. 362n. For other examples see LSJ s.v. δίδωμι II.1, Mastronarde on *Pho.* 994 δειλίαι δίδωσι.

946–7 με γᾶς ἐκ πατρίας ἀπώλεσεν 'destroyed me <and took me> away from my homeland'. (ἐξ)ἀπολλύναι can be construed with a phrase indicating motion from a place: cf. *Il.* 18.290 ἐξαπόλωλε δόμων κειμήλια καλά, *Od.* 20.357, Xen. *Smp.* 1.15. The sense 'to disappear' is paralleled by the fifth-century colloquial use of φθείρεσθαι ('to go to hell from ...', i.e. 'to go out of ...', 'to leave'): *Andr.* 708 εἰ μὴ φθερῆι τῆσδ' ... ἀπὸ στέγης, *HF* 1290, Stevens 1976: 17–18.

The variant reading ἀπούρισεν 'wafted (me) away (from my homeland)' is attractive, but οὐρίζω and its compounds are generally used of bringing to a *safe* destination: Aesch. *Cho.* 317, 814, Eur. *Andr.* 610, Soph. *Trach.* 827.

948 γάμος οὐ γάμος 'a marriage that turned out to be something different from a marriage', i.e. 'something completely different and terrible', a turn of phrase often used in Euripides: *Hel.* 1134 γέρας οὐ γέρας ἀλλ' ἔριν, Mastronarde on *Pho.* 1495 ἔρις οὐκ ἔρις ἀλλὰ ... φόνος. See also 566n., 612n., 1121n.

948–9 ἀλλ' | ἀλάστορος τίς οἰζύς 'but woe inflicted by an avenging spirit'. Helen is referred to as οἰζύς at Aesch. *Ag.* 1461 (Fraenkel *ad loc.*, Thalmann 1993: 134). As at *Andr.* 103–4 Πάρις οὐ γάμον ἀλλά τιν' ἄταν | ἀγάγετ' ... Ἑλέναν, divine intervention is considered responsible for these events. ἀλάστορος is probably the genitive of ἀλάστωρ: cf. 686–7, *Hipp.* 820 κηλὶς ... ἐξ ἀλαστόρων τινός, and phrases such as θεῶν ἀνάγκαισιν (583–4n.). Alternatively, it could be the nominative of the securely attested adjective ἀλάστορος, -ον 'under the influence of an avenging spirit': Soph. *Ant.* 974, Aesch. fr. 92a.

950–2 ἂν μήτε ... ἀπαγάγοι ... | μήτε ... ἵκοιτ': ἂν probably picks up Ἑλέναν of 943–4, syntactically prominent at the beginning of the epode (Panagl 1971: 28). The clause μήτε ... ἵκοιτ' implies a relative pronoun as a subject, omitted in the Greek: Smyth §2517. For a personal wish at the end of a choral passage see *Alc.* 604, Kranz 1933: 122 and 179.

πέλαγος ἅλιον: 701n., 938.

953–1295 EXODOS

The long final section of the play is formally complex and varied. Euripides offers us a deception scene (953–1022); a brief astrophic song, which some interpreters consider equivalent to a fifth stasimon (1023–34n.); a short dialogue in trimeters (1035–55); the monody of Polymestor (1056–1108); an *agōn* scene, where Agamemnon acquits Hecuba of having wrongfully punished Polymestor (1109–1251); a final dialogue which hints at what will happen after the end of the play (1252–95). No god appears to tell future events, as in *Heracles, Trojan women, Phoenician Women*, in the satyr drama *Cyclops*, and in the pro-satyric *Alcestis* (where however Heracles, in his capacity of supernatural hero, gives orders to Admetus). The only trace of divine presence in the exodos of *Hecuba* occurs when Polymestor recalls a prophecy he has received from Dionysus (Segal 1993: 214–26 and 1267n.).

The formal complexity of the exodos has a structural function: the introduction onstage of an important new character (Polymestor). This is rare at such a late stage in a play. The best parallels are Theseus, appearing at *HF* 1163, and Teucer, appearing at Soph. *Ai.* 974. One can compare also Orestes in *Andr.* 881 and Eurystheus at *Hcld.* 983, two plays composed shortly before *Hecuba*. However, Orestes soon leaves the stage, and Eurystheus arrives when the play is almost over. By contrast, the entire final section of *Hecuba* hinges on Polymestor, who has been an (absent) focus of attention from 682 on. In this long final scene, Euripides condenses several different tragic forms: Polymestor, in his *agōn* speech, takes up the role of the messenger (1132–82n.).

Now that we finally meet him, Polymestor is at pains to present himself in a completely different way from what we know about him: he poses as a true friend of Hecuba and (later) Agamemnon. Tragic writers created many scenes using the type of the 'untrustworthy friend', or 'false friend' (Pattoni 2007): a character who pretends to be friends with the protagonist, but is in fact treacherous. Oceanus in *Prometheus*, Menelaus in *Orestes*, Neoptolemus in (the first part of) *Philoctetes*, Creon in *Oedipus at Colonus* and, in some ways, Odysseus in *Hecuba* all stress their loyalty to

Prometheus, Orestes, Philoctetes, Oedipus and Hecuba, respectively; they claim to participate in the suffering of the protagonist and are willing to help, even if in fact they are prepared to do very little, except what is to their personal advantage. Polymestor is a *doubly* false friend, to both Hecuba and Agamemnon. The false friend usurps the signs of true friendship, such as empathy (954–5: cf. Eur. *Or.* 682, Soph. *OC* 744–5 'I suffer greatly because of your misfortune, old man, seeing that you are an unhappy exile ...'), offers of help or claims to have helped in the past (960–97, 1137–9, 1175–6: cf. *Or.* 684–6), claims of friendship (953–4, 982, 1114: cf. Eur. *Or.* 482, Soph. *Phil.* 671–3) and formal addresses (953–4, 1114: cf. Soph. *OC* 740–2). We encounter all these signs in Polymestor's scene. There is ample scope for subtle variation in these scenes. Neoptolemus in Sophocles' *Philoctetes* and (to a lesser degree) Oceanus in *Prometheus* are morally complex characters. Polymestor is not. The falsity of his factual statements makes us immediately doubt the sincerity of his proffer of help. As soon as Agamemnon appears, Polymestor claims that he has acted as a true friend to the Greek king. This volte-face exposes his treachery.

Polymestor can be easily turned into a caricature of the tragic victim. *Cycl.* 663–701 (the blinding of Polyphemus), a play probably written after *Hecuba* (1035n., 1039n., cf. Introduction, section 1, n. 6, section 2, nn. 18–21), imitates the present scene, building on the very similarity of the names Polyphemus and Polymestor. The blinding scene in *Hecuba* is also a re-enactment of Agamemnon's death, and an allusion to Aeschylus' representation of it (*Hec.* 1035–7 and Aesch. *Ag.* 1343–5). The audience does not know that, unlike Agamemnon, Polymestor will not be killed, and Euripides plays on the ambiguous language of Hecuba and the chorus (1021–34) to leave open that possibility, which suggests a strict similarity with *Agamemnon*. The links between Agamemnon and Polymestor are close: the Thracian king will predict Agamemnon's fate with language that is reminiscent of Aeschylus (1281: cf. Aesch. *Cho.* 491, *Eum.* 461). Agamemnon himself will echo the language of punishment and retribution that Clytemnestra has used against him in the *Agamemnon* (1250–1: cf. Aesch. *Ag.* 1525–30, and also *Cho.* 930). In his last line in the play he hopes to 'find everything in order at home, free from the suffering we experience now' (1292n.), ominously echoing the first line of Aeschylus' *Agamemnon*. This is a clear instance of tragic irony: the audience knows well the fate that is in store for the character.

953–1022 Dialogue between Hecuba and Polymestor

953–60 Polymestor combines two common ways of beginning a speech: a greeting (953–5) and a general reflection introduced by an exclamation

(864, *Andr.* 183). The words φεῦ· οὐκ ἔστ(ιν) ('there is no one/nothing that...') are a common way of emphasising a *gnōmē*: 864, *El.* 367, *Or.* 1155 (see also *Or.* 1, *Andr.* 986). The gnomic passage would have been unusual after a stasimon, and coming from someone who had just arrived onstage: see however *Med.* 446.

953 It may seem strange that Polymestor addresses Priam, who is absent and dead, putting him on the same level as Hecuba, who is in front of him; Nauck deleted the line. Polymestor is in fact adopting a mannered pose, pretending empathy, and adopting the language of passages such as 621–2, *Hipp.* 1092–7, *Tro.* 740–1. Another objection to Nauck's deletion is that Polyxena is not present onstage (954–5n.), and her name cannot be eliminated from Polymestor's speech, unless one deletes 953–5. Polymestor arrives onstage accompanied by his two sons, a number of attendants and Hecuba's servant (966n.).

954–5 σ' εἰσορῶν ... ἔκγονον σέθεν 'seeing you, your city, and that your daughter has just died'. εἰσορῶν means 'seeing' in reference to Hecuba and the city (823n.), and 'realising' in reference to Polyxena, with a shift in syntax (cf. Eur. *Pho.* 949–51, Soph. *OC* 1357, Bruhn 1899: 114) and meaning (cf. Mastronarde on *Pho.* 1350–1). For the usage of εἰσοράω 'I see, I realise' followed (or not) by a participle see LSJ s.v. 1b and 3, and *Ion* 967–8: Creusa: 'Why do you cover your head and cry, old man?'; Old Man: 'Because I see your misfortune and that of your father' (σὲ καὶ πατέρα σὸν δυστυχοῦντας εἰσορῶν) (who is in fact dead, and absent from the stage). It is unlikely that Polymestor has seen Polyxena on his way to the camp (Collard) or that she is onstage now (see 904n.).

956–61 Polymestor remarks on divine cruelty in order to reassure Hecuba of his sympathy, feigning the same sentiment that Talthybius genuinely expressed at 488–96 (compare the literal φύρειν of 496 with 958). Polymestor's religious sentiment in itself is not sceptical or anti-religious: Greek gods are entitled to use means fair and foul to ensure that men respect them, and divine ταραγμός explains mutability of fortune and social instability: Solon in Hdt. 1.32.1 (cf. 623–5n.), Kannicht on *Hel.* 711–21, *Suppl.* 552 τρυφᾶι δ' ὁ δαίμων, *IT* 572–3. On the reliability of the gods, by contrast, cf. the pious statements at Eur. *Ba.* 883, Pind. *Nem.* 10.54.

956 οὐκ ἔστιν οὐδὲν πιστόν 'nothing is to be relied upon', ironically referring to Polymestor's own action, and ironically forgotten by him at 1017. Victims are often convinced of their safety in deception scenes: see 981, 1017, fr. 223.58 and 71–4.

957 οὔτ' αὖ καλῶς πράσσοντα μὴ πράξειν κακῶς 'nor again <should one rely on the fact that> if someone is doing well he will not suffer in the future'. The infinitive is the subject of ἔστιν ... πιστόν, to be understood from 956. The subject of the infinitive goes in the accusative: Ar. *Plut.* 552

πτωχοῦ μὲν γὰρ βίος ... ζῆν ἐστιν μηδὲν ἔχοντα, K–G II.4. πράσσοντα is a generalising (impersonal) masculine singular as in Ar. *Plut.* 552 ἔχοντα: Smyth §2052a.

958 πάλιν τε καὶ πρόσω 'back and forth', i.e. 'confusingly'. A phrase that refers to space is used metaphorically: cf. Eur. *Ba.* 349 ἄνω κάτω τὰ πάντα συγχέας 'turning everything upside down', Pind. *Ol.* 12.5–6 'human expectations roll often up and at other times down (πόλλ' ἄνω, τὰ δ' αὖ κάτω)'.

959 ἀγνωσίαι 'because of our ignorance'. Religious cult is the only way for humankind to exert influence on the gods and prevent the very reversals of fortune that the gods themselves bring about precisely to foster religious cult. This remark too backfires on Polymestor: see 1268–9.

961 προκόπτοντ' οὐδέν 'making no progress'. προκόπτοντ' ('cutting one's way through', 'advancing') refers to the unexpressed indefinite subject of θρηνεῖν: Smyth §§937a, 1980. Similar expressions occur in *Hipp.* 824 ἐκπερᾶσαι κῦμα τῆσδε συμφορᾶς, fr. 757.927.

ἐς πρόσθεν κακῶν 'beyond one's sorrows', which are conceived of as a road that one has to travel through until the end (for road metaphors cf. 744n.). πρόσω, similar in meaning to ἐς πρόσθεν, is used with a genitive expressing the field one is progressing through (*Alc.* 911 βιότου τε πρόσω 'and advanced in age', Hdt. 3.56.1 ἐς τὸ πρόσω τε οὐδὲν προεκόπτετο τῶν πρηγμάτων 'and nothing made progress in their affairs') or, as here, what one has left behind: *Andr.* 1220 κόμπων μεταρσίων πρόσω 'far from lofty and fine-sounding words' (Lloyd), *IT* 839–40 θαυμάτων πέρα καὶ λόγου πρόσω. ἐς (τὸ) πρόσθεν is followed only by genitives expressing the field one is progressing through (not the situation one is trying to escape from, as here): Pl. *Prt.* 339d3–4 ὀλίγον δὲ τοῦ ποιήματος εἰς τὸ πρόσθεν προελθών, Hdt. 3.154.1 αἱ ἀγαθοεργίαι ἐς τὸ πρόσω μεγάθεος τιμῶνται.

962–7 Polymestor implies that, had he been at home when Hecuba arrived in Thrace, he would have been informed of her arrival even without Hecuba sending a messenger (963–4). He had returned, and was about to leave again (964–5), presumably to visit Hecuba, when the messenger arrived. The irony in this story is that he would not otherwise have brought his children with him. Polymestor makes up this story to present himself as a 'decent man who looks after his friends as soon as he hears they are in trouble' (Kovacs 1996: 68).

963 ἐν μέσοις Θρῄκης ὅροις 'in the middle of Thrace's boundaries', in effect simply 'in Thrace': cf. 16, *Tro.* 1069 τέρμονα τε πρωτόβολον ἔωι, *Ba.* 961 διὰ μέσης ... Θηβαίας χθονός. Phrases like ὅροι χώρας are often used as equivalents of χώρα, in reference to leaving or entering: Barrett on *Hipp.* 1158–9. The king of Thrace did not have a single capital city but had to visit several settlements, following a specific ritual: Mitchell 1997: 135–6, Theopompus *FGrHist* 115 F 31.

965 ἤδη πόδ' ἔξω δωμάτων αἴροντί μοι 'when I was already leaving [lit. "moving my foot out of"] the house'. αἴρειν πόδα and similar expressions are normally used of departure (*Tro.* 342, *Hel.* 1627, Kovacs 1996: 68), but see Soph. *Ant.* 224 δύσπνους ἱκάνω κοῦφον ἐξάρας πόδα.

966 ἐς ταὐτόν... συμπίτνει 'arrives at the same time'; for the idiom see 748, 666, 1030. For the historical present cf. 527–9n.

ἥδε... δμωὶς σέθεν 'this servant of yours'. The demonstrative ἥδε implies the presence onstage of the Servant, who was sent to fetch Polymestor at 890–4.

967 κλυών is an aor. ptcp.: 743n. Compare 1109 ἀκούσας ἦλθον.

968–75 Hecuba cannot look Polymestor straight in the eyes; her refusal foreshadows *his* future blindness (on the symbolism of averting the gaze see 972n.). Shame is one of the motives behind Polyxena's decision to sacrifice herself (374, 551–2) and is now turned into a tool of the deception. Hecuba makes Polymestor feel secure in order to surprise him off his guard, as is common in tragic intrigues (1007n.).

970 αἰδώς μ' ἔχει 'I feel shame of', 'I am ashamed to'; at the same place in the line at Aesch. fr. 132c.12, Eur. *Or.* 460, *Ba.* 828. ὀφθῆναι is to be understood from ὤφθην ('I am ashamed to be seen in my present condition by someone who...'), as at Eur. *Med.* 758, Soph. *Ant.* 404: K–G II.565–6, Smyth §3018a–b. The verb is more commonly explicit in the main clause, and implicit in the subordinate; here we have the opposite because the subordinate clause precedes. This explanation is easier than to assume the need to supply a genitive from ὅτωι: 'I feel shame of someone who saw me prosperous' (Fix). Omission of a genitive is very rare: Mastronarde on *Med.* 753 and 758.

971 τυγχάνουσ': the nominative comes naturally after αἰδώς μ' ἔχει, which is felt as equivalent to αἰσχύνομαι: Barrett on *Hipp.* 23, *Cycl.* 330–1, K–G II.105–7, Moorhouse 1982: 21–2. The nominative was the default case for a 'prominent' element of the sentence (the so-called 'logical subject'). These are not irregular or colloquial constructions, and occur in all stylistic registers of classical Greek (epic, tragedy, historiography, comedy, etc.). The term 'anacoluthon' is often misleading: see Slings 1992: 96–101 and 1997: 192–213.

972 ὀρθαῖς κόραις 'with my eyes straight at you'. Lowering the eyes is a sign of shame: *IA* 851 ὀρθοῖς ὄμμασιν, *Or.* 468–9, *Med.* 470, *Hipp.* 946–7, Cairns 2005: 129–30, Mueller 2011. Sometimes characters onstage veil themselves out of shame: 432n., Bond on *HF* 1160–2. Bond and Kovacs 1987: 106 assume that Hecuba is veiled here, but no textual elements support this suggestion. αἰδώς is associated with veiling already at Hes. *Op.* 197–200.

Averting the gaze had also other connotations in Greek culture, and Hecuba's explicit motivation is not necessarily the most important factor.

In Homer characters avert the gaze or cover the face 'to prevent leakage [= unintended self-disclosure] though eye contact' (Lateiner 1995: 84, cf. *Od.* 16.477). Preventing Polymestor from suspecting Hecuba's true feelings is probably a motive in the present passage. Hecuba also avoids Polymestor's gaze because he is polluted, having murdered her son: this is explicitly given as the reason for avoiding someone's gaze at *HF* 1161–2, *Or.* 459–61. Similarly, Lysias feels the need to apologise when he cross-examines his brother's murderer: Lys. 12.24.

973–5 'do not think that this is <a sign of> hostile attitude against you, that women do not look at men straight into their eyes' (the translation omits 974, a spurious line). The sentence includes a generalising feminine plural ('women' at 975: cf. 67on., Aesch. *Eum.* 100, Eur. *El.* 265). Failure to understand this invited the interpolation of 974. The addition of 974 makes Hecuba contradict 968–72, where she implied that she would have looked at Polymestor had she not fallen from her royal status. ἄλλως 'besides' in 974 vacuously introduces a more general point, not a more specific one, as it normally does (Eur. *Suppl.* 417, *Ion* 618, *IA* 491, Soph. *OT* 1114, *El.* 1324, fr. 64.3). In addition, τι at 974 greatly weakens the point and the rhetoric of the sentence. Line 974 also contains a highly unusual repetition of the vocative of a proper name within a short speech. Such repetitions only occur for special reasons: for example, at *Or.* 477–81 the repetition is explained by the interruption of the dialogue at 478–80. Hartung's deletion of 973–5 gives a plausible text at a higher cost. Diggle deletes 974–5, but 973 does not join well with 'no wonder' (976).

976 θαῦμά γ' οὐδέν 'no wonder!' was probably an expression frequent in spoken Attic: Aesch. fr. 47a.827 (in a satyr play), Ar. *Vesp.* 1139, *Plut.* 99, Eur. *El.* 284 and Stevens 1976: 14. However, its tone is not informal or frivolous, as it also occurs in serious contexts (Soph. *OT* 1132 and 1319).

τίς χρεία σ' ἐμοῦ 'why do you need me?' We must supply ἔχει: Soph. *Phil.* 646 ὅτου σε χρεία ... ἔχει, Ar. *Ach.* 454 τί ... σε τοῦδ' ἔχει πλέκους χρέος; The phrase recalls Homeric usages: *Il.* 11.606 τί δέ σε χρεὼ ἐμεῖο;

977 'Why did you make me come here from my dwellings?' For ἐπέμψω 'you made someone arrive here' see Soph. *OC* 602. Polymestor mixes colloquial expressions (τί χρῆμα; 'what thing?', i.e. 'why?': Stevens 1976: 22) with a stylish periphrasis (τὸν ἐμὸν ... πόδα 'my step', i.e. 'me').

979–81 The guards are dismissed, as in other deception scenes: Aesch. *Cho.* 766–73, Eur. fr. 223.69–72. See Taplin 1977: 79–80.

ἐρημία 'isolation', helpful in deception scenes; see 1017 and *IT* 1197.

982 φίλη ... προσφιλές: Polymestor considers the Greeks especially friendly: cf. Soph. *Ant.* 898–9 φίλη μὲν ἥξειν πατρί, προσφιλὴς δὲ σοί, | μῆτερ, φίλη δὲ σοί, κασίγνητον κάρα, *OT* 133 ἐπαξίως ... ἀξίως.

984 τί χρή followed by the infinitive is an information-seeking question. Since Euripides did not write punctuation marks, we need to decide whether τί χρή here starts a direct (Eur. *Alc.* 153) or indirect question (Aesch. *PV* 659). A direct question is better: in indirect questions the pronoun ὅ τι (Aesch. *PV* 295 σήμαιν(ε), Eur. *IT* 767–8 σήμαινε, *IA* 1014) is much more common than τί. An indirect question would also make Polymestor's offer less 'vivid', contrary to his intentions.

τὸν εὖ πράσσοντα μὴ πράσσουσιν εὖ: Polymestor's elaborate rhetoric is similar to Agamemnon's (858–9).

985 ὡς ἕτοιμός εἰμ' ἐγώ recalls the empty promises of Agamemnon at 861–2. The reciprocity of ξένοι or φίλοι is often stressed by pointed repetition: Hdt. 7.237.3 ξεῖνος δὲ ξείνωι εὖ πρήσσοντί ἐστι εὐμενέστατον πάντων.

986 παῖδ' is placed before the relative pronoun ὅν, in emphatic position, as the 'topic' of the sentence ('as far as my son is concerned'): Introduction, section 10. Receiving a child from the hands of the parents was a semi-formal commitment to raise him or her: Aesch. *Cho.* 750 and 762.

989 μάλιστα 'yes indeed'; colloquial, as at 1004: Stevens 1976: 16. Cf. 997n.

τοὐκείνου [= τὸ ἐκείνου] **εὐτυχεῖς μέρος** 'you are happy as far as his lot <is concerned>', accusative of respect, as in Soph. *Trach.* 1215 τοὐμὸν μέρος, *Ant.* 1062.

990 ὡς εὖ κἀξίως λέγεις σέθεν 'how well you speak, and in manner that is worthy of you', an ironic statement: 956n., 997n.

992 εἰ τῆς τεκούσης τῆσδε μέμνηταί τί που 'if he by any chance (που) gives any (τι) thoughts to his mother, i.e. me'. For πού τι see Thuc. 2.87.2, for εἴ που Soph. *El.* 1473. που ironically emphasises the feigned uncertainty of Hecuba. The transmitted μου is redundant and linguistically dubious, since τῆς τεκούσης τῆσδε by itself means μου: K–G 1.630, Moorhouse 1982: 155.

993 Polydorus (as a ghost) has in fact managed to 'see' Hecuba, and in secret (= without Polymestor's knowing).

994 ὃν ... ἔχων: lit. 'having which', i.e. 'with which'. The relative pronoun is governed by the participle, not by the main verb of the relative clause: Smyth §2543, K–G 11.100–1, 177–9n.

996 μηδ' ἔρα τῶν πλησίον 'and do not covet your neighbours' property'. The Greek is compressed for τῶν τῶν πλησίον (χρημάτων): see *Hel.* 915–16 τὰ τῶν πέλας | ... ἀποδοῦναι πάλιν, *HF* 590–1 διώλεσαν πόλιν | ἐφ' ἁρπαγαῖσι τῶν πέλας 'to rob their neighbours', or, rather, 'their neighbours' property'. On the ideology of moderation see 997n.

997 ἥκιστ' 'surely not'. Colloquial again (989n.): Stevens 1976: 14; Collard 2005: 361.

ὀναίμην τοῦ παρόντος 'may I profit from what I have!', i.e. 'may I be content with what I have!' Greedy Polymestor (1204–23) thinks that he can manipulate irony and language, defeating Hecuba, but he will soon be trapped by her, both physically and verbally. He pretends to praise moderation, a value often celebrated by Greek writers (Solon 4.9–10 West, Aesch. *Ag.* 750–80, Mastronarde on *Pho.* 539–40), who criticise πλεονεξία (Thuc. 3.45.4, Hornblower on Thuc. 3.84.1) and the love for absent riches (Pind. *Pyth.* 3.20 ἤρατο τῶν ἀπεόντων). Thracians are stereotypically greedy: Ar. *Ach.* 159–71, Hall 1989: 103–10. For the language of the wish see LSJ s.v. ὀνίνημι II.2 and Fraenkel on Aesch. *Ag.* 350, Kannicht on *Hel.* 645. The asyndeton is paralleled at *Alc.* 334.

998–1000 This passage combines two ways of introducing a narrative account in stichomythia, the οἶσθα-question (*Hipp.* 91–2, Mastronarde 1979: 43–4, 49–50) and the 'statement of existence' technique (1132n.). The revelation of the subject is skilfully postponed by Hecuba until 1002, slightly forcing the syntax of the sentence.

οἶσθ᾽ οὖν ...; 'Do you know ... ?' For similar 'empty' questions ('Do you know what?') see Collard on *Suppl.* 932, Soph. *OT* 1517. The question has the function of enticing the listener, or of introducing a sensitive topic with caution (*Ion* 363).

ἅ ... τοῦτο: the lack of grammatical agreement is regular even in connected syntax (595n., Eur. *HF* 195–7, Griffith on Soph. *Ant.* 707–9 ὅστις ... οὗτοι) and it is easier here with intervening sentence boundary (*Med.* 754–5 Medea: τί ... πάθοις; | Aegeus: ἃ τοῖσι δυσσεβοῦσι γίγνεται βροτῶν). The plural pronoun is placed first here because Hecuba prefers to be vague; in other cases the singular comes first, as the less marked number.

ἔστ᾽, ὦ φιληθεὶς ὡς σὺ νῦν ἐμοὶ φιλῆι ...: on the ominous tautologous phrase see 873n., 1021–2n., *IA* 649. Hecuba does not consider Polymestor a friend, and speaks in a way that will deceive him (but not the audience). The verb ἔστι 'there are' is followed by a subject in the plural (κατώρυχες in 1002): this is the so-called 'Pindaric construction' (Smyth §961, Mastronarde on *Pho.* 349). The interruption of the syntax makes the change of number easier.

1002 κατώρυχες 'caves' (be they natural or artificial), where the treasure is hidden: 1008n.

1004 εὐσεβής: 1232n. Hecuba ironically insists that Polymestor is 'pious', whereas in fact he broke a god-sanctioned law (790, 792 and *passim*).

1005 τί ... δεῖ ...: 984n.

1006 ἢν σὺ κατθάνηις 'if you were to die'. Mentioning death is ominous, and Hecuba plays with that fear here, just like the chorus at Aesch. *Ag.* 1652–3. Words that evoke death or misfortune are taboo: 1275–6, Eur. *Hipp.* 723–4, Soph. *Ai.* 362–3, 589–91.

τούσδ᾽: a word-final long syllable is not normally allowed in this metrical position (Porson's law: 729n.), but an elided trochee-shaped 'non-lexical' word (pronoun, particle, etc.) is acceptable: Eur. *Hipp.* 1151 τόνδ᾽ εἰσορῶ,

Pho. 897, Soph. *OT* 831, Devine and Stephens 1984: 6 and 136–7 and 1994: 343.

1007 τῇδε καὶ σοφώτερον 'this way is also wiser'. Hecuba is able to turn *sophia* to her advantage (contrast 258 σόφισμα). In deception scenes the victim often agrees that the arrangements that will lead to his or her defeat are 'wise' or 'correct': *Ba.* 824, *IT* 1180. These statements can also be read as a metaliterary allusion to the 'cleverness' of the plot designed by the playwright.

1008 στέγαι 'roofed building'. This probably refers to the temple of Athena at Troy, which was very prominent in the Trojan saga (Redfield 2003: 85–150, Rose 2014: 59–60). Polymestor asks for a sign that tells him where in the temple the treasure is. στέγη 'roof, roofed place' in the plural normally means 'house' (LSJ s.v. II.3). Other words normally meaning 'house' are often used for 'temple': see οἶκος at *Ion* 458, *Pho.* 1373, δῶμα at *IT* 1307, *Pho.* 606, δόμος or δόμοι at *IT* 1040, *Ion* 129. οἶσθα-questions refer to something well known, and are a rhetorical means to attract the attention and the collaboration of the addressee in the conversation: 110, 239, *Suppl.* 116, *Ion* 936, 987, Mastronarde 1979: 43 nn. 23–4 (contrast 998–1000n.). The adverb ἐνταῦθα shows that Polymestor knows what Hecuba is talking about (see ἐνταῦθα in *Suppl.* 118, *Ion* 939, 989).

Ἰλιάδος is the normal form of the feminine adjective (masc. Ἰλιεύς): 99–102n. The MSS offer Ἰλίας here, but the adjective Ἴλιος is apparently not attested elsewhere.

1010 μέλαινα πέτρα: the 'black stone' that signals the presence of the treasure bears an uncomfortable resemblance to the μελανοκάρδιος πέτρα of Styx mentioned at Ar. *Ran.* 470. Unlike the proverbial 'white stones' (= gold and silver) mentioned in Eur. fr. 1007, it will not make Polymestor wealthy.

1011 The pretext to make Polymestor go inside is added almost casually, and only because Polymestor asks the leave-taking question 'Is there anything else you want to tell me?' (as in *Suppl.* 1180). Polymestor is the maker of his own undoing, and his greed leads him to ask the wrong question.

1012 χρήμαθ' 'property', 'objects'. Polymestor takes the word in its financial meaning, 'property/money' (*El.* 941, *Pho.* 439). It may refer to the swords and the brooches hidden in Hecuba's *peploi* (1013, 1161 and 1170).

1013 ποῦ δῆτα; πέπλων ἐντὸς ἢ κρύψασ' ἔχεις; 'Where then? Do you keep it hidden in your *peploi*?' ἢ introduces a surmise after a first general question, as at *Cycl.* 129, *Andr.* 1062, *IT* 503, 1168. For the postponement of ἢ see Eur. *El.* 967 τί δῆτα δρῶμεν; μῆτερ' ἢ φονεύσομεν; and Pl. *Leg.* 935d4, *Resp.* 469c8, Denniston 283–4. πέπλων ἐντός here is to be taken as a strictly connected phrase. Hiding a small object in one's *peplos* is natural enough:

Or. 1457–8, [Eur.] *Rhes.* 713–14 ξιφήρης | κρύφιος ἐν πέπλοις. ἤ would be less appropriate, since there is no real alternative: πέπλων ἐντός 'inside your *peploi*' is in fact a form of hiding (κρύψασ').

The interplay of hiding and appearing is prominent in *Hecuba*. Polydorus is 'hidden' in Thrace (711). The failure of Polymestor to keep 'hidden' the treasure (Polydorus) that was given to him is punished because Polydorus comes 'in secret' (κρύφιος 993) to Hecuba (and is 'uncovered' in front of her: 679) and reveals the crime. Polymestor is lured with the prospect of more 'hidden' gold (1013, 1146), and punishment consists in blinding him (another form of 'concealing'). On the Trojan side too, 'hiding' and 'covering' are associated with decorum (Polyxena hides 'what has to be kept hidden': 570) but also with death (570 again, 726, 897; Hecuba is 'covered' by the sea when she dies: 1261; Troy is 'hidden' by the cloud of enemies: 907–8). Odysseus hides his hand in the *peplos* (343) to avoid supplication (Agamemnon will help Hecuba 'without seeming' to do so: 874 μὴ δοκῶν).

1014 σκύλων ἐν ὄχλωι: lit. 'in the crowd of spoils'. ὄχλος 'crowd' is rare in reference to material objects: cf. Eur. *Suppl.* 681 (chariots), Soph. fr. 828d (food), Thuc. 1.49.3 (ships).

σώιζεται: Hecuba plays with Polymestor, using for this 'treasure' the verb 'to keep safe' (also σῶς: 994–5), alluding to Polymestor's failure to 'keep safe' (682, 1225) Polydorus, his 'treasure' (1229).

1015 αἵδ' Ἀχαιῶν ναύλοχοι περιπτυχαί 'These <are> the enclosures of the Greeks that give <them> safe anchorage.' The reference of the abstract noun περιπτυχαί 'the things that enfold' is explained by the defining adjective ναύλοχοι: 362n. περιπτυχή is attested only in Euripides or in parodies of and quotations from him (Ar. *Av.* 1241, Mastronarde on *Pho.* 1357).

1016 ἴδιαι 'by themselves', 'private' (adj. fem. pl.). There is little difference in meaning if we read ἰδίαι (adverb), but the adjective is more natural after the verb 'to be'. In the prologue Polydorus stated that Hecuba shares the tent with Agamemnon (53–4). Here, Hecuba is probably lying to lure her victim into the *skēnē*, as often in similar deception scenes (*El.* 1128–31). It is highly unlikely that the audience would question the credibility of Polydorus, a prologue speaker, protected by the gods (49–50; cf. also 99–102n.). In any case, minor inconsistencies do occur in Euripides: Mastronarde on *Pho.* 26.

1017 πιστά: 956n.

κἀρσένων ἐρημία 'and a place where there are no men'. Pind. *Isthm.* 2.33 οὐ γὰρ πάγος οὐδὲ προσάντης ἁ κέλευθος γίνεται offers a syntactic parallel for the coupling of adjective and noun as predicative elements.

1019–22 Deception scenes often end with lines directed to a character who is leaving the stage to be punished. Their purpose may be twofold, as here: (a) injunction to leave (*El.* 1139 χώρει πένητας ἐς δόμους, *HF* 726, *Or.* 1337); in the present passage the speaker gives the motive for leaving; (b) allusion to the killing/punishment/kidnapping in 'riddling' words (1021–2n. and *Or.* 1343). The wording is kept inexplicit (Polymestor has not said that Polydorus is dead: 1022), but is ominous enough. Polymestor is probably imagined as losing dialogic contact at some point, probably around 1021; he may enter the tent just a moment before Hecuba, who utters the last few parting words. See Bain 1977: 34, 70–1; Taplin 1977: 221–2; Mastronarde 1979: 26–30.

1021–2 ὡς ... γόνον 'so that you, ..., accompanied by your children, will go back to the place where you settled my offspring'. Hecuba and the chorus seem to imply (here and in the lyric passage that follows) that Polymestor is to be killed (see 1028–9n., 1032–3). The audience was probably unaware of the outcome, because the story of Polymestor was either little known or had been invented by Euripides (see Introduction, section 4). A comparable ambiguity is exploited at a similar point of the plot in Soph. *OT* 1183 ὦ φῶς, τελευταῖόν σε προσβλέψαιμι νῦν (similar language at *Ai.* 856:[412n.]). Misdirection is a common technique in tragedy and epic: *Or.* 1491, 1589–90, Dodds on *Ba.* 52, Scodel 1999: 77–83 and 120–33.

πάντα πράξας ὧν σε δεῖ 'after getting all the rewards [or "sufferings"] that you must get [or "suffer"]'. The genitive ὧν is governed by πάντα, as in [Eur.] *Rhes.* 300 πάντ' ἀκούσας ὧν ἐφιέμην μαθεῖν, *Andr.* 1001 δείξω γαμεῖν σφε μηδέν' ὧν ἐχρῆν ἐμέ. For the 'attraction' of the relative see Soph. *OT* 862 οὐδὲν γὰρ ἂν πράξαιμ' ἂν ὧν οὐ σοὶ φίλον, K–G II.408. 'The ominous use of χρή or δεῖ is virtually a formula in ambiguous speech to a victim' (Bond on *HF* 726): *El.* 1141, *Ba.* 964, *IA* 673, 721. See 873n., 998–1000n. Hecuba is deliberately using ambiguous language, which fools Polymestor, but is transparent to the audience and the chorus.

1023–34 Astrophic Lyric Section Sung by the Chorus

'When the pace is quickening' (Taplin 1977: 347), Aeschylus and especially Euripides employ short astrophic choral passages to 'cover' the time when the stage is empty: Aesch. *Ag.* 1331–42, *Cho.* 855–68, Eur. *HF* 1016–38, *Ion* 1229–49, *Ba.* 1153–64. At times the scene includes a dialogue with a character inside the *skēnē* (*HF* 875–909). Sophocles uses this device at *Ai.* 866–78 and *Trach.* 205–24. See Kranz 1933: 177, 202, Rode 1971: 86, 92–4. Some scholars consider this astrophic passage as equivalent to a stasimon; this is mostly a problem in nomenclature.

The chorus take Hecuba's words at face value and seem to imply that Polymestor is about to die (1033–4). However, the language of this astrophic piece, rather than referential, is allusive (which, at times, makes the interpretation uncertain). The chorus, just like the audience, were not cognizant of Hecuba's plans, and Euripides takes advantage of this information gap: he gives the chorus words that fit both Polymestor's death, which is what audience and chorus would expect, and Polymestor's punishment as it is enacted in the play. The metaphor of a 'harbourless flood' (1024–7n.) aptly describes the situation of Polymestor, trapped in a confined space, and unable to find escape, but does not give away the outcome of the assault on him. The phrase ἐκπεσῆι φίλας καρδίας (1024–7n.) indicates that Polymestor is not going to achieve the goal he wished for, but also recalls by allusion an Iliadic phrase that refers to death. Justice and the gods bring a 'disastrous [or "deadly"] ruin' (1031). The reference to a 'pledge' (1029) refers primarily to Polymestor's debt to Justice and the gods, but also recalls the gold of Polydorus, a pledge of the friendship between Polymestor and the Trojans (1228–32). Wildberg 2002: 183–94 offers an extensive discussion of this brief choral passage.

Metre

Dochmii with resolved first longum (⏑ ⏑ ⏑ – ⏑ –) alternate with others with no resolution (⏑ – – ⏑ –) and iambics. On 1028–31 see *ad loc*. Note the 'dovetailing' (word-end occurs after the first or second syllable of the second metrical unit) of dochmiac metra at 1030, 1033 (two syllables) and 1034.

1023	– – ⏑ – ⏑ – ⏑ – – – ⏑ ⌒ ‖^c οὔπω δέδωκας ἀλλ᾽ ἴσως δώσεις δίκην·	ia trim (recited) ‖^c
1024–5	⏑ ⏑ ⏑ – ⏑ – ⏑ – – ⏑ – ἀλίμενόν τις ὡς ἐς ἄντλον πεσών	2 δ
1026–7	⏑ ⏑ ⏑ – ⏑ – ⏑ – – ⏑ – λέχριος ἐκπεσῆι φίλας καρδίας,	2 δ
1028–9	⏑ – – ⏑ ⏑ ⏑ ⏑ ⏑ ⏑ – ⏑ – ἀμέρσας βίοτον. ὃ γὰρ ὑπέγγυον	2 δ
1030	⏑ – – ⏑ – ⏑ – – ⏑ ⌒ ‖^h Δίκαι καὶ θεοῖσιν οὐ ξυμπίτνει,	2 δ ‖^h
1031	⏑ ⏑ ⏑ ⏑ ⏑ ⏑ ⏑ – ⏑ ⌒ ‖^c ὀλέθριον ὀλέθριον κακόν.	2 ia ‖^c
1032	– – ⏑ – – – ⏑ – ⏑ – ⏑ ⌒ ‖^c ψεύσει σ᾽ ὁδοῦ τῆσδ᾽ ἐλπὶς ἥ σ᾽ ἐπήγαγεν	ia trim (recited) ‖^c

```
           ∪ ∪ ∪ −   ∪ − ∪ − − ∪ −              2 δ
1033    θανάσιμον πρὸς Ἀΐδαν, ὦ τάλας,

           ∪ ∪ ∪ −   ∪ − ∪ − − ∪ ⌒ |||           2 δ |||
1034    ἀπολέμωι δὲ χειρὶ λείψεις βίον.
```

1023 Actors and choruses on occasion recite a single iambic trimeter to introduce a dochmiac section: 1032–3n., *El.* 1168, *Pho.* 145.

ἴσως δώσεις δίκην 'you will be punished, I think'. ἴσως (lit. 'perhaps') is used as an ironical understatement, as in *HF* 726–7, *El.* 242. See also τάχα at 1259 (ironical and threatening) and *Hel.* 452, οἶμαι 'I believe' in *Ba.* 321 (Stevens 1976: 23–4).

1024–7 In due course, Hecuba will suffer an analogous fate: she too will fall into the sea (1259, 1262n.), and find no safe harbour.

ἀλίμενόν τις ὡς ἐς ἄντλον πεσών 'just like someone that falls into harbourless water'. The word ἄντλος 'bilge, bilge water' is a common metaphor for a difficult situation (Aesch. *Sept.* 796, Eur. *Hcld.* 168), but occurs in poetry also for 'large mass of water, flood' (Pind. *Ol.* 9.53, 'the floodwater', in the narrative about Deucalion). The text reshapes an epic phrase: *Od.* 15.479 ἄντλωι ... πεσοῦσ(α).

λέχριος 'sideways' (an adjective in the Greek). According to the metaphor, Polymestor fails to proceed straight on his path (*Med.* 1168–9 λεχρία ... | χωρεῖ) and falls into open water. The word is used metaphorically at Soph. *Ant.* 1344–5 πάντα γὰρ | λέχρια τἂν χεροῖν.

ἐκπεσῆι φίλας καρδίας 'you will fall short of <what your> heart <desires>'. ἐκπίπτω 'to fall out of' + gen. means in fact 'to fail to attain': Thuc. 8.81.2 ἵνα ... τῶν ὑπαρχουσῶν ἐλπίδων ἐκπίπτοιεν. For 'heart' = 'what one's heart wants' see Soph. *Ant.* 1105–6 καρδίας τ' ἐξίσταμαι | τὸ δρᾶν 'but I do retract from my heart's <resolve> to keep on doing <as I have been>' (Griffith *ad loc.*). The repetition πεσών ... ἐκπεσῆι is unobjectionable in Greek: 655–7, Aesch. *Ag.* 1608–9, ἡψάμην ... ξυνάψας, Eur. *IT* 338–9 ἀποτείσει ... τίνουσα, Diggle 1981: 66–7 and 120. 'One's heart' (φίλα καρδία) echoes the Homeric phrases φίλον κῆρ (see also Aesch. *Cho.* 410) and φίλον ἦτορ.

1028–9 ἀμέρσας βίοτον 'because you have taken away a life' (Wildberg 2002: 189) rather than 'having deprived <yourself> of <your own> life' (LSJ I.3; cf. *Hipp.* 1367 ὀλέσας βίοτον 'having lost my own life', *Alc.* 534 ὤλεσεν βίον). The first interpretation is grammatically easier, even if Euripides leaves the audience puzzled and does not specify whose life is taken away. The echo of the Homeric phrase *Il.* 22.58 φίλης αἰῶνος ἀμερθῆις (aor. pass.) does not imply that we should interpret the active aorist ἀμέρσας as having a reflexive sense here. The sentence suggests the punishment of Polymestor the audience expects, that is death (1021–2n.). For ἀμέρδω 'to deprive' with the accusative of the thing taken away see *h. Hom. Cer.* 312.

1028–31 ὃ γὰρ ὑπέγγυον | Δίκαι καὶ θεοῖσιν οὐ ξυμπίτνει, | ὀλέθριον ὀλέθριον κακόν 'accountable behaviour that is not in accordance with justice and the gods <is> a deadly, deadly misfortune'. Polymestor's behaviour is 'accountable', 'under a pledge' (ὑπέγγυον), but his actions do not agree with justice and the god. The neuter pronoun is generalising. This is the least unsatisfactory interpretation of a difficult passage. Cf. Wildberg 2002: 193. For this meaning of συμπίπτω cf. 966, Hdt. 6.18 ὥστε συμπεσεῖν τὸ πάθος τῶι χρηστηρίωι. For the repetition ὀλέθριον ὀλέθριον see 909n., 930n., *Or.* 1364.

Human justice and divine law protected the *xenia* bond between Polymestor and the family of Priam. Polymestor will be punished for breaking his pledge. This may allude to the Delphic saying 'where a pledge is, ruin is near' (ἐγγύα, πάρα δ' ἄτα): cf. Eur. fr. 923, Cratinus iunior 12 K–A, Epicharm. 257 K–A, Pl. *Chrm.* 165a3–4. The Delphic saying probably alluded to financial debt, but was reinterpreted in different ways in antiquity.

Δίκαι καὶ θεοῖσιν 'justice and the gods' are often thought of as working together (Aesch. *Cho.* 148, Eur. *Andr.* 439, fr. 584), esp. after the accomplishment of revenge (*El.* 771, *HF* 739). The MS text is metrically impossible (βίοτον. τό = ⏑ ⏑ – ⏑, where ⏑ ⏑ ⏑ ⏑ or ⏑ – ⏑ is needed) and syntactically dubious: it would leave ὀλέθριον ὀλέθριον κακόν as a bald apposition to the sentence. Matthiae's conjecture (βίοτον. ὃ), printed in the text, assumes an easy corruption (assimilation of ὃ, mistaken for the article ὁ, to τό).

1032–3 ψεύσει σ' ὁδοῦ τῆσδ' ἐλπὶς ἥ σ' ἐπήγαγεν | θανάσιμον πρὸς Ἅιδαν 'your hope <to find the Trojan gold>, which has conducted you to your death in Hades, will cheat you of this course of action'. Deceitful hope (a familiar concept in Greek thought: Collard on *Suppl.* 479) has led Polymestor to death. At *Med.* 766 and *Or.* 550 ὁδός indicates a course of action. Others take ὁδοῦ τῆσδ' with ἐλπίς: 'the hope of this course of action will cheat you'.

ψεύσει is fut. act., 3rd p. sg., with a genitive of what one is cheated of: Ar. *Th.* 870 μὴ ψεῦσον ὦ Ζεῦ τῆς ἐπιούσης ἐλπίδος 'Zeus, do not deceive me and deprive me of what I hope to obtain', LSJ s.v. I.3.

The Attic forms τῆσδ', ἥ, ἐπήγαγεν (instead of 'Doric' τᾶσδ', ἅ, ἐπάγαγεν) show that this line is a recited trimeter; however, the line is syntactically linked to the following dochmiacs, which (we assume) were always sung in tragedy. A change in delivery within the same sentence is remarkable, but can be paralleled: *Pho.* 145. In other passages a speaker completes a recited line by another speaker, and then moves on to lyric delivery: *HF* 910–14, *Ion* 1452–3. The present passage is harsher as it occurs not at the beginning, but in the middle of a lyric passage. See also [Eur.] *Rhes.* 697.

θανάσιμον 'so that you will die' (θανάσιμος = 'dead': Schein on Soph. *Phil.* 819). The adjective (with σε) is used predicatively, and describes the effect of the verb: 499–500n., Parker on *Alc.* 34–7, Mastronarde on *Med.* 436–7. The word 'Hades' here counts as a cretic (Ἅϊδαν = – ⏑ –). Other scansions (Ἅιδαν = – –, cf. 208 Ἅιδαι = – – –) and analyses are possible, but would disrupt the regularity of the dochmiac pattern observed in the rest of this short song: Conomis 1964: 33, Diggle 1981: 21.

1034 ἀπολέμωι δὲ χειρί 'and by a non-military hand', as in *Ion* 216–18 Βρόμιος ... ἀπολέμοισι κισσίνοισι βάκτροις [= thyrsi] ἐναίρει, *Ba.* 736 χειρὸς ἀσιδήρου μέτα. Contrast 879n. Martial prowess in women is threatening, and the Trojan captives cross the boundary of proper behaviour (see the threatening mythological examples of 886–7). In the eyes of the audience, their violence is perhaps mitigated by the fact that they are barbarians who direct their violence towards an even more threatening barbarian. On the deceptive femininity of the Trojan women see also 1157n.

1035–55 Dialogue between Hecuba and Polymestor

1035–41 Polymestor cries from within. Death or severe physical injures are not acted out onstage. Instead of (or in addition to) presenting a messenger scene, playwrights can make the audience participate in the development of the action by allowing them to hear the dialogue that takes place inside the *skēnē*, or at least the shouts of the person punished (1037n.). Euripides plays with the convention here, just as he will in the Helen scene in *Or.* 1296–1316. Polymestor, contrary to expectations and to the conventional conclusion of these scenes, is not killed. He has the opportunity to threaten Hecuba and the other slave women, just like the protagonist of Euripides' *Cyclops*. Here, as in Aeschylus' *Choephori*, Sophocles' *Electra* and Euripides' *Antiope* (fr. 223), the chorus are hoping that the act of violence will be successful; in other passages playwrights have to find ways to explain the failure of the chorus to intervene (see esp. Aesch. *Ag.* 1346–71). Here the chorus wonder whether it would be useful to go inside to help Hecuba (1042–3), but this is clearly not necessary: she comes back onstage right away (1044). Polymestor himself will take up the role of a messenger at 1150–82, relating in detail what happened inside the *skēnē*. On these scenes see Taplin 1977: 323, Di Benedetto and Medda 1997: 58–65 and 69, Mastronarde on *Med.* 1270a and 1275.

1035 ὤιμοι, τυφλοῦμαι φέγγος ὀμμάτων τάλας: lit. 'ah, I am blinded in the light of my eyes, wretched me'. φέγγος is accusative of respect: Soph. *OT* 371 τυφλὸς τά τ' ὦτα τόν τε νοῦν τά τ' ὄμματ' εἶ, Smyth §1601a. The sentence recalls Aesch. *Ag.* 1343 ὤιμοι, πέπληγμαι καιρίαν πληγὴν ἔσω (Meridor 1975: 5–6, Thalmann 1993: 149) and is parodied in *Cycl.* 663 ὤιμοι κατηνθρακώμεθ' ὀφθαλμοῦ σέλας 'ah, they burn out the brightness of my eye', where Euripides employs a suitably coarser and more specific verb.

φέγγος ὀμμάτων 'the shine of my eyes': the eyes were conceived as a source of light. Only what emits light can perceive it: see 367-8, 1066-8, 1105, Janko on *Il.* 13.837, Plat. *Tim.* 45b-46a.

1037 ὤιμοι μάλ' αὖθις 'ah, I cry again'. Two cries at least is the norm, as here, and the speakers often comment on the repetition: Aesch. *Ag.* 1343-5, Soph. *El.* 1415-16, Eur. *Med.* 1270a-78, *Cycl.* 663, 665-8. In his later speech to Agamemnon, Polymestor reverses the sequence of the crimes, and makes the point that blinding is the last and most horrific crime (1162, 1168-71; cf. 1255). σφαγή and cognates are also used for the death of Priam (24), Polyxena (41, 135, 260, etc.), and by Polymestor of the death of his own children, here and at 1077. Polymestor thus highlights the correspondence between his punishment and the misfortunes of Hecuba. The vagueness of the bare σφαγή might be meant to include Polymestor's blinding as well as the children's death (so Weil). For σφαγή = 'wound' see 571n., Soph. *Trach.* 573, Eur. *El.* 1228.

1038 καίν'...κακά 'surprising...tribulations' hints at the unexpectedness of the outcome, both for the chorus and the audience: 83n., 1021-2n.

1039 ἀλλ' οὔτι μὴ φύγητε 'but you will not be able to escape, be sure of that'. There is an element of wish-fulfilment in this statement of Polymestor. The blinded Cyclops addresses the same phrase to Odysseus and his companions at *Cycl.* 666 (cf. already Aesch. *Sept.* 199 οὔ τι μὴ φύγηι μόρον). The construction οὐ μή + aor. (or, less frequently, pres.) subj. expresses 'an unequivocal negative future statement' (Collard on *Suppl.* 1069, Smyth §§1804, 1919, 2755a). The idiom is attested first in the fifth century, and is often used by Euripides. On the similar idiom οὐ μή + fut. expressing prohibition see 1282n., Barrett on *Hipp.* 212-14.

λαιψηρῶι ποδί 'with swift foot'. This image is part of the traditional Greek poetic language: *Il.* 15.269 Ἕκτωρ λαιψηρὰ πόδας καὶ γούνατ' ἐνώμα, Pind. *Nem.* 10.63, Eur. *El.* 549, *Hel.* 555.

1040 'I will strike and break open all the corners of this tent'. βάλλων means 'hitting' rather than 'throwing': see the etymological explanation implied in βέλος 1041n., and βάλλων ἀράσσων 'throwing and pounding' in 1175 (referring to this scene, and in the context of hunting imagery). The same phrase refers to throwing arrows and stones at *Andr.* 1154 and *IT* 310 (cf. 318-19) respectively.

1041 ἰδού 'look, here it is'. Here and in some other passages ἰδού signals that the speaker is going to accomplish an action that has been announced or promised: *IT* 791 ἰδού, φέρω σοι δέλτον ἀποδίδωμί τε, taking up ἀποδώσω from 745, *Andr.* 411. Here βέλος takes up βάλλων (1040). In other cases ἰδού follows immediately the event it draws attention to: *El.* 749, *HF* 904-5.

The MSS wrongly give the line to the chorus: the chorus may comment on offstage noises (see ἰδού in *El.* 749) but cannot describe Polymestor's actions while they are taking place (ὁρμᾶται), since he is inside the tent.

βαρείας χειρὸς ὁρμᾶται βέλος 'the missile <consisting> of my heavy [i.e. strong] fist', see 65–7n. Polymestor, with self-aggrandising language, adapts the epic expression χειρὶ παχείηι (*Il.* 5.309, *Od.* 19.448); cf. 1128 μαργῶσαν χέρα. The scholium takes βέλος to refer to sticks and stones that Polymestor throws at the Trojan women: 'the missile is being thrown from my hand'. In principle that is possible (1040n., Soph. *OT* 151–3, K–G I. 394–5), but the text does not mention arrows or stones.

1042 βούλεσθ' ἐπεσπέσωμεν; 'Do you want us to break in?', 'Do you think we should break in?': a self-addressed question from the chorus leader to the chorus in its entirety. ἐπεσπέσωμεν is a deliberative subjunctive in a question ('shall we break in?': 1056–7n.), introduced by 'do you want?'; the two verbs form a single sentence: Smyth §1806, Stevens 1976: 60–1.

1042–3 ἀκμὴ καλεῖ | Ἑκάβηι παρεῖναι Τρωιάσιν τε συμμάχους 'The occasion (ἀκμή) requires us to assist Hecuba and the Trojan women, as allies in their battle'. The chorus echo the language of the irresolute chorus at Aesch. *Ag.* 1353 τὸ μὴ μέλλειν δ' ἀκμή 'this is the time not to be hesitant'. The chorus of *Agamemnon* fail to stop the murder, that of *Hecuba* to help the queen to bring about Polymestor's punishment.

1044–6 Polymestor is the addressee of Hecuba's words, but he is out of dialogic and, because of his blindness, visual contact (1059–61, 1069–70, 1124). Hecuba mockingly incites her victim to useless violence, inverting the pattern of similar revenge scenes, where the chorus and/or other women present onstage pray for the killing (Aesch. *Cho.* 855–68) or incite to violence those who carry out the attack behind the *skēnē* (Eur. *Or.* 1302 φονεύετε, *Cycl.* 654–62, Soph. *El.* 1415–6).

ἄρασσε, φείδου μηδέν, ἐκβάλλων πύλας 'Go on, hit the door, smash it!' Polymestor cannot find his way out. Hecuba enters onstage and closes the *skēnē* door behind her. This passage shows that the door of the supposed tent was in fact imagined as more substantial than just a piece of fabric.

The meaning of the verb ἀράσσειν 'to smash' fades into 'to batter (on the door)/to knock vigorously (at the door)': Eur. *IT* 1308, Ar. *Eccl.* 977, Gow on Theocr. 2.6. Here ἄρασσε ... ἐκβάλλων means 'hit the door so violently as to break it open'; see 1040n. and, for (ἐκ)βάλλειν 'to break down a door', Eur. *HF* 999, *Or.* 1474–5, Lys. 3.23. For the coupling of (ἐκ)βάλλειν and ἀράσσειν see 1175n. The phrase φείδου μηδέν 'do not spare anything, be relentless' reinforces an imperative: Eur. *Med.* 401, *HF* 1400, Soph. *Ai.* 115.

οὐ γάρ ποτ' ὄμμα λαμπρὸν ... ἐγώ 'you will never put back the bright power of sight into the pupils of <your> eyes, nor will you see your children alive: I have killed them'. Hecuba scornfully plays on the double meaning of 'you will not see your children alive': he will not see them because he is blind, and because they are dead. She manipulates the language of passages such as *Med.* 803–4 οὔτ' ἐξ ἐμοῦ γὰρ παῖδας ὄψεταί ποτε | ζῶντας.

1047 ἦ γὰρ καθεῖλες Θρῆικα καὶ κρατεῖς ξένον ... ; 'Did you really get the better of your Thracian ally? Do you have mastery over him?' For the word order ξένον ... Θρῆικα cf. 1224–5, *Hipp.* 1260 οὔθ' ἥδομαι τοῖσδ' οὔτ' ἐπάχθομαι κακοῖς, Bruhn 1899: 93–4. The verb κρατεῖς here takes the accusative, as in *Alc.* 490 κρατήσας δεσπότην. The MSS read ξένου, an easy assimilation to the common genitive construction after κρατεῖς, suggesting that two different people are meant. For ἦ γάρ 'really?' see 765n. and 1124.

1050 τυφλῶι ... παραφόρωι ποδί 'with blind, staggering foot'. It is a Euripidean mannerism to use 'blind' of bodily parts other than the eye: for τυφλῶι ποδί Eur. *Pho.* 834, 1540, 1549 πόδα ... τυφλόπουν, 1699 τυφλὴν χεῖρ(α), Soph. *OC* 182–3 ἀμαυρῶι κώλωι.

1051–3 As Hecuba's words make clear, Polymestor enters onstage. The audience could see the inside of the tent, as Hecuba announced that the chorus would see the dead children. Mossman 1995: 65–6 and Gregory argue that the *ekkyklēma* was used, and Polymestor was rolled out onstage along with his children. That device, however, as used in *Hipp.* 808–1101 (see Barrett on *Hipp.* 811) and *HF* 1029–38, allows the audience to see what is inside the *skēnē* while the characters are imagined to be still *inside* the building (palace, house, etc.) which the *skēnē* represents: cf. Ar. *Ach.* 409, Austin and Olson on *Thesm.* 96 and 265, Taplin 1977: 442–3. In the present scene, it is quite clear that Polymestor leaves the tent and moves freely on centre stage; Hecuba steps aside to avoid meeting him (1054–5n.). Moreover, no reference to the presence of Polymestor's children onstage is made in the rest of the play, not even at the end, when Agamemnon orders every person present onstage to move (1284–92). Forgetting the dead children in plain view at the end of the play, or sending them to a desert island with Polymestor (1284–6), would be very awkward.

1054–5 Hecuba moves to the side, leaving space for Polymestor, as made clear by ἐκποδών: cf. 52–3n., *El.* 107–11, Bain 1977: 91–2, Mastronarde 1979: 23, Battezzato 1995: 45.

θυμῶι ζέοντι Θρηικὶ δυσμαχωτάτωι 'the Thracian, seething with anger; it is very difficult to fight against him'. θυμῶι is dative of cause (Smyth §1517). For the combination of datives cf. Soph. *Trach.* 445–6 τὠμῶι γ' ἀνδρὶ τῆιδε τῆι νόσωι | ληφθέντι. Hecuba and the women were able to overcome Polymestor by guile, but are not a match for his strength, especially now that his anger is unleashed. The implication is that he is like a wild beast, whose force is aroused by the wounds that make him angry, like the wounded lion of *Il.* 20.164–73. The metaphor of 'seething' with rage has precise parallels: 583–4n., Aesch. *PV* 370 ἐξαναζέσει χόλον, Soph. *OC* 434 ἕζει θυμός, Aesch. *Sept.* 708–9, W. V. Harris 2001: 68. Anger is implicitly compared to fire already at *Il.* 9.678 σβέσσαι χόλον 'quenching one's anger'. Ruhnken conjectured θυμὸν ζέοντι (see Aesch. *PV* 370 and his emendation on Ap. Rhod. *Arg.* 4.391), making the syntax easier. The reading of ὦ, ῥέοντι 'drenched in rage', is weaker and strained (contrast *Hel.* 1602 'drenched in blood' and LSJ s.v. ῥέω 1.1a).

1056–1108 Monody of Polymestor

This monody parallels the lyric sections sung by Hecuba and Polyxena at the beginning of the play: Polymestor's suffering is presented as a compensation for Hecuba's. The astrophic form gives room for expression of extreme emotions, not reined in by a symmetrical form. This is one of the earliest surviving astrophic monodies of Euripides: compare the song of the fatally wounded Hippolytus in *Hipp.* 1347–88, another entrance monody delivered by a physically suffering male character. The emotionalism of monodies usually suits female characters or 'marginal' males, esp. barbarians, as here; note however, besides Hippolytus, Theseus in *Hipp.* 817–51 (Hall 1989: 112) and several male characters in Sophocles (Battezzato 2005: 156–7, Nooter 2012). Style (short staccato sentences), metre (dochmiacs; polymetry), content (threats; descriptions of violence), and probably music, reinforced the shocking staging: the audience saw a blind actor, with a bloodied mask, moving frantically on all fours, against the background of his slaughtered children. On monodies in tragedy see Barner 1971, Hall 1999 and 2002.

Metre

This section is in dochmiacs, with the addition of anapaests, a frequent combination: see 182–93, West 1982: 112, 121 and 123, Parker 1997: 57–8. The metrical interpretation is often uncertain, and alternative analyses are possible (cf. Lourenço 2011: 190–1). The presence of an Aeolic colon (1097) among dochmiacs and iambics is rare (*Tro.* 314~331, *Ba.* 1156, West 1982: 113). Lines 1102–3 are a series of seven dactyls: cf. Aesch. *Pers.* 864~872, 905. Shortening in hiatus, a phenomenon rare in dochmiacs (Conomis 1964: 40–2), occurs at 1056 and 1098 ὤιμοι, 1066 μοι, 1088 αἰαῖ ἰώ. At 1094, ἦ οὐδείς counts as two syllables (synecphonesis: 1249n.). The long alpha in Ἄρει (1090) is unique in Euripides, but frequent in Aeschylus (*Sept.* 469) and Sophocles (*El.* 96).

COMMENTARY: 1056–1108   221

	– ᴗ ᴗ – – – – – – – –	2 δ
1056–7	ὤιμοι ἐγώ, πᾶι βῶ, πᾶι στῶ, πᾶι κέλσω,	
	– ᴗ ᴗ – ᴗ – – ᴗ ᴗ – ᴗ –	2 δ
1058	τετράποδος βάσιν θηρὸς ὀρεστέρου	
	ᴗ ᴗ ᴗ ᴗ ᴗ ᴗ – ᴗ ᴗ ᴗ – – –	2 δ
1059	τιθέμενος ἐπὶ χεῖρα κατ᾽ ἴχνος· ποίαν	
	– – – – – – – – – –	2 δ
1060	– ἢ ταύταν ἢ τάνδ᾽· – ἐξαλλάξω, τὰς	
	– ᴗ ᴗ – – – – – – ᴗ ᴗ ᴗ	2 δ
1061	ἀνδροφόνους μάρψαι χρήιζων Ἰλιάδας,	
	– ᴗ ᴗ – ᴗ –	δ
1062	αἵ με διώλεσαν;	
	ᴗ – – ᴗ – ᴗ – – ᴗ –	2 δ
1063	τάλαιναι κόραι τάλαιναι Φρυγῶν,	
	– ᴗ ᴗ – –	an
1064	ὦ κατάρατοι,	
	– – ᴗ ᴗ – – – ᴗ ᴗ –	2 an
1065	ποῖ καί με φυγᾶι πτώσσουσι μυχῶν;	
	– ᴗ ᴗ – ᴗ – – ᴗ ᴗ – ᴗ ᴗ ᴗ	2 δ
1066	εἴθε μοι ὀμμάτων αἱματόεν βλέφαρον	
	ᴗ ᴗ – ᴗ ᴗ – ᴗ ᴗ ᴗ – ᴗ ⌒ ||ᵇ	an δ ||ᵇ
1067	ἀκέσαι᾽ ἀκέσαιο, τυφλόν, Ἅλιε,	
	– ᴗ ᴗ – – ⌒ ||ᶜ	δ ||ᶜ
1068	φέγγος ἀπαλλάξας.	
	× × ||ᶜ	extra metrum ||ᶜ
1069	ἆ ἆ,	
	– – – – ᴗ ᴗ – ᴗ ᴗ –	2 an
1069b	σίγα· κρυπτὰν βάσιν αἰσθάνομαι	
	– – ᴗ ᴗ – – – ᴗ ᴗ – –	2 an
1070	τάνδε γυναικῶν. πᾶι πόδ᾽ ἐπάιξας	
	– – – – – – ⌒ ||ᶜ	paroemiac ||ᶜ
1071	σαρκῶν ὀστέων τ᾽ ἐμπλησθῶ,	
	– – – ᴗ – – – ᴗ ᴗ ᴗ ⌒ ||ᵇ	2 δ ||ᵇ
1072	θοίναν ἀγρίων θηρῶν τιθέμενος,	

	− ⏑⏑ − − − − − − ⏑ −	2 δ
1073	ἀρνύμενος λώβας λύμας <τ᾽> ἀντίποιν᾽	
	⏑ − − ⏑ −	δ
1074	ἐμᾶς, ὦ τάλας;	
	− − ⏑ ⏑ − ⏑ ⏑ − ⏑ ⏑ −	2 an
1075	ποῖ πᾶι φέρομαι τέκν᾽ ἔρημα λιπών	
	− − − − ⏑ ⏑ − − −	2 an
1076	Βάκχαις Ἅιδα διαμοιρᾶσαι	
	− ⏑ ⏑ − ⏑ − ⏑ − − ⏑ −	2 δ
1077	σφακτά, κυσίν τε φοινίαν δαῖτ᾽ ἀνη-	
	⏑ − − − − − ⏑ ⌒ ǁ^c	δ cr ǁ^c
1078	μέροις οὐρείαν τ᾽ ἐκβολάν;	
	− − − − − − ⌒ ǁ^c	paroemiac ǁ^c
1079	πᾶι στῶ, πᾶι βῶ, πᾶι κάμψω,	
	− ⏑ − − ⏑ − − ⏑ ⏑ ⏑ −	4 cr
1080	ναῦς ὅπως ποντίοις πείσμασιν λινόκροκον	
	− − − − ⏑ ⏑ − ⏑ ⏑ −	2 an
1081–2	φᾶρος στέλλων, ἐπὶ τάνδε συθεὶς	
	⏑ − ⏑ − ⏑ − ⏑ ⏑ ⏑ − − ⌒ ǁǁǁ	kδ δ ǁ
1083–4	τέκνων ἐμῶν φύλαξ ὀλέθριον κοίταν;	
	Recited iambic trimeters: 1085–7	
	⏑ ⏑ ⏑ − − − − ⏑ ⏑ ⏑ ⏑ −	δ hδ
1088–9	αἰαῖ ἰὼ Θρήικης λογχοφόρον ἔνο-	
	⏑ − − ⏑ − − ⏑ ⏑ − ⏑ ⌒ ǁ^b	2 δ ǁ^b
1090	πλον εὔιππον Ἄρει κάτοχον γένος.	
	⏑ − ⏑ − ⌒ ǁ^h	penth ǁ^h
1091	ἰὼ Ἀχαιοί,	
	⏑ − ⏑ − ⌒ ǁ^c	penth ǁ^c
1091b	ἰὼ Ἀτρεῖδαι·	
	⏑ − ⏑ − ⏑ − − ⏑ ⌒ ǁ^c	ia δ ǁ^c
1092	βοὰν βοάν, αὐτῶ βοάν·	
	− ⏑ ⏑ ⏑ ⏑ ⏑ − ⏑ −	ia cr
1093	ὦ ἴτε μόλετε πρὸς θεῶν.	
	⏑ − ⏑ − − − ⏑ − ⏑ − ⏑ ⌒ ǁ^b	trim ia ǁ^b
1094	κλύει τις ἢ οὐδεὶς ἀρκέσει; τί μέλλετε;	

COMMENTARY: 1056-1059

	⏑ – ⏑ – ⏑ – ⌒ ‖ᵇ	ia ba ‖ᵇ
1095	γυναῖκες ὤλεσάν με,	
	⏑ – ⏑ – ⏑ – ⏑ ⌒ ‖ᶜ	2 ia ‖ᶜ
1096	γυναῖκες αἰχμαλωτίδες·	
	– ⏑ – ⏑ ⏑ – ⏑ ⌒ ‖ᵇ	glyconic ‖ᵇ
1097	δεινὰ δεινὰ πεπόνθαμεν.	
	– ⏑ ⏑ – – –	δ
1098	ὤιμοι ἐμᾶς λώβας.	
	– ⏑ – – – ⏑ – ⌒ ‖ʰ	2 tro ‖ʰ
1099	ποῖ τράπωμαι, ποῖ πορευθῶ;	
	– ⏑ ⏑ ⏑ – ⏑ ⏑ ⏑ – ⏑ ⏑ ⏑ – ⏑ ⏑ ⏑	4 cr
1100–1	ἀμπτάμενος οὐράνιον ὑψιπετὲς ἐς μέλαθρον,	
	– ⏑ ⏑ – – – ⏑ ⏑ – ⏑ ⏑ – ⏑ ⏑ – ⏑ ⏑ – ⌒ ‖ᵇ	7 da‖ᵇ
1102–3	Ὠαρίων ἢ Σείριος ἔνθα πυρὸς φλογέας ἀφίησιν	
	– – – – – ⏑ ⏑ – –	2 an
1104–5	ὅσσων αὐγάς, ἢ τὸν ἐς Ἅιδα	
	⏑ – – ⏑ – ⏑ – – ⏑ ⌒ ‖‖	2 δ ‖‖
1106	μελάγχρωτα πορθμὸν ἄιξω τάλας;	

1056–7 πᾶι βῶ, πᾶι στῶ, πᾶι κέλσω 'Where shall I go? Where shall I find a place to stand? Where shall I land?' Similar series of questions in asyndeton, with deliberative subjunctives (Smyth §1805) occur at the beginning of several monodies: *Alc.* 862–3 ἰὼ μοί μοι, αἰαῖ <αἰαῖ>. | ποῖ βῶ; ποῖ στῶ; τί λέγω; τί δὲ μή;, *Tro.* 110–11, Soph. *OT* 1309–10.

πᾶι κέλσω 'where shall I land?' The verb κέλλω implies a comparison with a ship (1024–7n. and 1079–81n.)

1058–9 τετράποδος βάσιν θηρὸς ὀρεστέρου | τιθέμενος ἐπὶ χεῖρα κατ' ἴχνος 'walking like a four-footed wild animal, leaning on my hands, on their track'. Like the Pythia at Aesch. *Eum.* 34–7, Polymestor walks on all fours. The Pythia was reduced to walking like an animal by psychological and religious shock; Polymestor by blindness and shock. The scene is imitated in [Eur.] *Rhes.* 208–15, with verbal echoes (*Rhes.* 211–12 τετράπουν μιμήσομαι | λύκου κέλευθον).

βάσιν ... τιθέμενος: lit. 'placing the step'. The active of τίθημι is more common in such locutions (*Andr.* 546), but cf. *HF* 108–9 ἀμφὶ βάκτροις ἔρεισμα θέμενος and *Anth. Pal.* 7.464.2 θεμέναν ἴχνος. For similar variations in voice see Diggle 1994: 263–5 and 720–1n.

ἐπὶ χεῖρα: lit. 'leaning on my hand', as at Eur. *El.* 840 ὄνυχας ἐπ' ἄκρους στάς, Aesch. *Pers.* 930 ἐπὶ γόνυ κέκλιται, Mastronarde on *Pho.* 1400–1 ἐπὶ σκέλος | πάλιν χωρεῖ, LSJ s.v. πούς 1.6b. The singular χεῖρα in reference to both hands is common: *IT* 269.

κατ' ἴχνος 'on <their> track'. Polymestor stresses from the start that he is pursuing the Trojan women (1060–3), and κατ' ἴχνος is the phrase for 'on the track', continuing the assimilation of Polymestor to a wild beast: Aesch. *Ag.* 695 κατ' ἴχνος πλατᾶν ἄφαντον, Soph. *Ai.* 32 κατ' ἴχνος ἄισσω, Eur. *Tro.* 1003 (alluding to Aesch. *Ag.* 695), [Eur.] *Rhes.* 690 ἕρπε πᾶς κατ' ἴχνος αὐτῶν. Most editors print Porson's conjecture καὶ ἴχνος '(leaning on my hand) and foot' (a very common metaphorical meaning of ἴχνος). However, mention of the use of hands for walking is enough to convey the meaning, as at Aesch. *Eum.* 37 τρέχω δὲ χερσίν, οὐ ποδωκείαι σκελῶν.

1059–60 ποίαν | – ἢ ταύταν ἢ τάνδ'; – ἐξαλλάξω 'Which way shall I go? This way or that?' As at 162–3, a single sentence encompasses two questions (ποίαν ἐξαλλάξω; and ἢ ταύταν ἢ τάνδ' ἐξαλλάξω;). The verbal echo stresses the reversal of roles: it is now Polymestor who suffers, not Hecuba. For the syntax cf. *Andr.* 848–50 ποῦ δ' ἐκ πέτρας ἀερθῶ, | <ἢ> κατὰ πόντον ἢ καθ' ὕλαν ὀρέων, | ἵνα νερτέροισι μέλω; and Kannicht on *Hel.* 873, Diggle 1994: 428–9.

ἐξαλλάξω 'shall I go' (aor. subj.). The verb means 'exchanging/changing', and it often takes the accusative of what is left behind (482–3n., *IT* 135, *Ion* 918). For the meaning here cf. παραλλάσσειν 'to escape' (Aesch. *Ag.* 424) and Eur. *Or.* 272 εἰ μὴ 'ξαμείψει 'if she does not exchange place', i.e. 'if she does not go away'. The accusatives of direction ποίαν – ἢ ταύταν ἢ τάνδ'; – are feminine because they imply ὁδόν (Smyth §1027b, K–G II.558–9); they are functionally comparable to adverbs (Schwyzer 1939: 621).

1061 ἀνδροφόνους 'man-killing'. In the *Iliad*, this adjective usually qualifies male characters, esp. Hector and Ares (*LfgrE* s.v. B 1a α–β). Pind. *Pyth.* 4.252 uses it in reference to the women of Lemnos, with the meaning 'killers of their husbands'. Hecuba compared her revenge to the crime of the women of Lemnos (887); the element of gender reversal is clear from the Iliadic allusion. ἀνδροφόνος was the legal word for 'murderer' in Athens (Dem. 23.28), and was considered one of the ἀπόρρητα, the insults actionable under Attic law (Lys. 10.7). It is not used elsewhere in Attic drama, and is generally rare in non-epic poetry (see Tyrt. 19.9 West).

1063 'cruel girls, cruel girls of the Phrygians': 775n. For the anadiplosis see 695–6, *Med.* 1273 ἀκούεις βοάν ἀκούεις τέκνων, *Or.* 1541, Diggle 1994: 297 and 376–7. The MS text gives inferior style and acceptable, but less regular, metre (δ hδ, cf. 1088–9).

1064 ὦ κατάρατοι 'you cursed ones'. Polymestor uses of Hecuba the word she used of him (716n.).

1065 ποῖ καί με φυγᾶι πτώσσουσι μυχῶν; 'To which nook <of the tent> did they flee and now hide in avoidance of me?' For πτώσσω 'crouch (in hiding)' and the accusative of the person (or the thing) one runs away from see *Il.* 20.427, *Od.* 22.304. ποῖ... μυχῶν (cf. *HF* 74 ποῖ... γῆς; 'where on earth?') indicates the place where the women went hiding (πτώσσουσι). On the position of με cf. 13n.

1066–8 The passage foreshadows the allusion to the myth of Orion (1100–6n., 1102–4n., Zeitlin 1996: 181 and 185–6, Schlesier 1988: 132). Oenopion blinded Orion as a punishment for raping Oenopion's daughter Merope. Orion was healed when he met the Sun at the place where it rises (Hes. fr. 148a Merkelbach–West) and was eventually transformed into a star. The Sun is compared to an 'eye' (Soph. *Ant.* 104, Aesch. *PV* 91); it was an especially important divinity for Thracians (Soph. fr. 582, Ar. *Pax* 406–11).

ὀμμάτων αἱματόεν βλέφαρον: lit. 'the bloodied eyelid of the eyes'. The word βλέφαρον 'eyelid' is used as a synecdoche for 'eye' (*Cycl.* 673 τυφλοῖ βλέφαρον). The genitive ὀμμάτων repeats the concept expressed by βλέφαρον: *Alc.* 925 λέκτρων κοίτας, *IA* 233 ὄψιν ὀμμάτων, Mastronarde on *Pho.* 308–9.

τυφλόν... φέγγος 'the blind... light' (= 'blindness'). φέγγος may mean 'eyes', 'eyesight' (1035), just as φάεα (plural from φάος/φῶς) means 'eyes' at *Od.* 16.15. The paradoxical phrase τυφλόν φέγγος thus means 'the blinded eye', 'blindness', as in Eur. *Pho.* 377 σκότον δεδορκώς, Soph. *OT* 419 βλέποντα... σκότον.

1070 πόδ' ἐπάιξας 'rushing', 'moving my foot in haste'. ἐπαΐσσω is usually intransitive: cf. 53–4n.

1071 σαρκῶν ὀστέων τ' ἐμπλησθῶ 'can I get my fill of their flesh and bones?' (subj. aor. pass. from ἐμπίμπλημι). Euripides makes Polymestor echo the language and the practice of the Homeric Cyclops, who ate ἔγκατά τε σάρκας τε καὶ ὀστέα μυελόεντα (*Od.* 9.293), and thus 'filled up his great belly' (9.296 μεγάλην ἐμπλήσατο νηδύν). Cannibalistic wishes are a sign of extreme hate (Hecuba at *Il.* 24.212–13), as well as of lack of humanity and piety; the bones are in fact reserved to the gods (Hes. *Th.* 557). On the earth, only animals and uncivilised beings, such as the Cyclops, eat them.

1072 θοίναν ἀγρίων θηρῶν τιθέμενος 'preparing a banquet of wild beasts'. The objective genitive (Smyth §§1331–3) designates what is going to be eaten, i.e. the Trojan women, imagined as wild animals: see Eur. *Or.* 814–15 οἰκτρότατα θοινάματα καὶ | σφάγια γενναίων τεκέων and fr. 145.1 παρθένου θοινάματα, Soph. *Ai.* 1294. The phrase τίθεμαι δαῖτα means 'preparing a banquet' (probably) at *Il.* 7.475 (cf. *IA* 722 θοίνην ποῦ γυναιξὶ θήσομεν;) and 'taking part in a banquet' at *Od.* 17.269.

1073–4 ἀρνύμενος λώβας λύμας <τ'> ἀντίποιν' | ἐμᾶς 'trying to exact the punishment for my ruin and my defilement'. ἄρνυσθαι, 'to obtain', is construed with the accusative of the punishment (Soph. *El.* 34 δίκας ἀροίμην) or of what one gains (μισθόν at *Il.* 12.435 and Pl. *Prt.* 349a, τιμήν at *Il.* 1.159). Cf. Soph. *El.* 592 ἀντίποινα λαμβάνεις and Diggle 1994: 517. λώβας and λύμας (gen. sg.) designate the crime, and depend on ἀντίποιν(α), as at Aesch. *Eum.* 268 ἀντίποιν(α) [Schütz: ἀντιποίνους MSS] ... δύας, *Pers.* 476. Cf. [213-14]. The MS text ἀρνύμενος λώβαν λύμας ἀντίποιν' ἐμᾶς gives impossible meaning: 'obtaining dishonour for myself, <that is> punishment for my defilement'. Alternatively one could read ἀρνυμένων λώβαν [as in *Eum.* 168 ἀρόμενον ἄγος 'having acquired pollution'], λύμας ἀντίποιν' ἐμᾶς, '(the beasts) who suffer ruin, in punishment for my defilement'.

1075 ποῖ πᾶι φέρομαι 'where, which way am I going?' The two adverbs have very similar meaning, as in *Tro.* 190–1 τῶι δ' ἁ τλάμων | ποῦ πᾶι γαίας δουλεύσω γραῦς...; (πᾶι 'where'). For double questions see also *Alc.* 213 τίς ἂν πᾶι πόρος κακῶν γένοιτο ...; The double question suggests an agitated state of mind in all these passages. 'φέρομαι as a verb of motion with personal subject implies lack of rational or prudent control' (Mastronarde on *Pho.* 1489–90).

1076 Βάκχαις Ἅιδα 'bacchants of Hades'. The phrase is deliberately ambiguous. The genitive may designate the divinity causing possession: Eur. *Ion* 552 Μαινάσιν γε Βακχίου, Friis-Johansen and Whittle on Aesch. *Suppl.* 564 θυιὰς Ἥρας. However, in some passages Ἅιδα/Ἅιδου comes close to having a metaphorical meaning, 'hellish' (483, Fraenkel on Aesch. *Ag.* 1235). The force of the metaphor and the original meaning is however not completely lost: Seaford on *Cycl.* 396–7 τῶι θεοστυγεῖ | Ἅιδου μαγείρωι, *HF* 562, *IT* 286. Euripides repeats the phrase at *HF* 1119 εἰ μηκέθ' Ἅιδου βάκχος εἶ, and, with a different meaning, at *Pho.* 1489 βάκχα νεκύων ('frantic mourner of the dead': Mastronarde *ad loc.*)

διαμοιρᾶσαι: 716-21n.

1077–8 κυσίν τε φοινίαν δαῖτ' ἀνη|μέροις, οὐρείαν τ' ἐκβολάν 'a murderous meal for wild dogs, something cast out on the mountains'. The passage imitates *Il.* 1.4–5 in a version which was later adopted by Zenodotus, αὐτοὺς δὲ ἑλώρια τεῦχε κύνεσσι | οἰωνοῖσί τε δαῖτα (πᾶσι MSS and Aristarchus). Other tragic passages also allude to the reading δαῖτα, esp. Aesch. *Suppl.* 800–1 κυσίν δ' ἔπειθ' ἕλωρα κἀπιχωρίοις | ὄρνισι δεῖπνον, Soph. *Ai.* 830 ῥιφθῶ κυσίν πρόβλητος οἰωνοῖς θ' ἕλωρ, *Phil.* 954–8, Eur. *Ion* 504–5 πτανοῖς ἐξόρισεν | θοίναν θηρσί τε φοινίαν δαῖτα. See Pfeiffer 1968: 111–13, West 2001: 173. The crucial point is that δαῖτα rarely designates what animals eat (*Il.* 24.43, Aesch. *Ag.* 731), which may explain why someone created the variant πᾶσι at *Il.* 1.5.

ἀνημέροις 'wild', in a strong negative sense, cf. Aesch. *Eum.* 803 βρωτῆρας αἰχμὰς σπερμάτων ἀνημέρους, Clearchus fr. 32 Wehrli τῶν θηρῶν τοὺς ἀνημερωτάτους. Cf. also 1173 τὰς μιαιφόνους κύνας, *Il.* 22.66–7 κύνες ... | ὠμησταὶ ἐρύουσιν, Soph. *Ant.* 697. For the chiastic word order see *Ion*

1092–3 γάμους Κύπριδος ἀθέμιτος ἀνοσίους. The MS text ἀνή||μερόν οὐρείαν τ' ἐκβολάν is metrically dubious (an cr after a series of dochmii). The dative ἀνημέροις was erroneously assimilated to the preceding and following accusatives. Several editors print Hermann's suggestion ἀνή||μερόν τ' οὐρείαν ἐκβολάν (... | δ cr), which gives tautologous meaning: the mountains are obviously wild.

οὐρείαν 'on the mountains'. Abandoning a corpse to the wild beasts (who live on the mountains) is the ultimate savagery (or punishment): *Tro.* 448–50, *Suppl.* 47. The bodies of traitors and executed criminals were thrown into the *barathron* under Athenian law: Allen 2000: 216–23.

ἐκβολάν 'what is thrown away'. ἐκβάλλειν and cognates are used to designate the expulsion of the corpse from the polis: 699, 781, *Pho.* 1630.

1079–81 πᾶι στῶ ... στέλλων 'Where shall I find a place to stand? Where shall I go? Where shall I stop like a ship, using the maritime mooring cables, furling the sail made of woven flax?' Polymestor adopts a chiastic order (staying/going/staying), repeating the questions of 1056–7 (going/staying/going) in reverse order.

πᾶι κάμψω 'where shall I stop?' It presupposes the phrase κάμψαι γόνυ, 'to bend one's knee' reaching a resting position: 1150, *Il.* 7.118, *LfgrE s.v.* κάμπτω B 2, Aesch. *PV* 396, Soph. *OC* 19, 85. The choice of verb may also suggest nautical imagery ('where shall I turn?'), echoing 1056–7 πᾶι κέλσω.

ναῦς ὅπως 'like a ship', cf. 398n.

πείσμασιν 'using the mooring cables'. Most interpreters translate πεῖσμα as if it had the same meaning as κάλως, 'reefing cable, cable used to manoeuvre the sails'. However, πεῖσμα regularly means 'mooring cable', from Homer to Callimachus: Aesch. *Pers.* 113, *Ag.* 195, Eur. *Hipp.* 761–3, Casson 1971: 48 n. 43 and 259–60 n. 3.

λινόκροκον 'made of woven flax', as was often the case for sails: Aesch. *PV* 468 λινόπτερ' ηὗρε ναυτίλων ὀχήματα, Eur. *IT* 410 λινοπόροις <σὺν> αὔραις.

φᾶρος στέλλων 'furling the sail' (on the phrase see Friis Johansen and Whittle on Aesch. *Suppl.* 723). φᾶρος refers to any large piece of cloth (*Od.* 5.258), which could be made into sails (Bacchyl. 17.5 τηλαυγεῖ γὰρ [ἐν] φάρεϊ).

1081–4 ἐπὶ τάνδε συθεὶς | τέκνων ἐμῶν φύλαξ ὀλέθριον κοίταν 'rushing to this deadly resting place of my children in order to protect them'. On the wide separation between τάνδε and κοίταν see *Med.* 202–3 τὸ παρὸν ... πλήρωμα, Breitenbach 1934: 246.

συθείς: ptcp. aor. pass. masc. sg. of σεύω 'put in quick motion', here with middle meaning (cf. Smyth §811), an epic word often used in tragedy.

φύλαξ: lit. 'as a guardian', i.e. 'in order to protect them'. Polymestor fears the Trojan women would mangle their corpses (1075–8).

1086 Tit for tat is a crucial concept in Greek ethics and theories of punishment: Aesch. *Ag.* 1529, 1564, *Cho.* 313, Blundell 1989: 28–31.

[1087] The line cannot be authentic: (a) Polymestor is punished by the Trojan women, not by divine agency; (b) at 723 the chorus have stressed their feelings of compassion for Hecuba; it would be strange if they pitied Polymestor's punishment (which he deserves, according to them: 1086), and considered it equivalent to Hecuba's undeserved misfortune; (c) the sentence clumsily mixes a general maxim ('a person who commits immoral actions suffers terrible punishments') and a statement addressed to Polymestor; one would need to supplement σοι in front of δράσαντι (1086); the line erroneously completes the syntax of the previous lines, a well-known type of interpolation ([412n.]); (d) 1087 is almost identical to line 723; this is not by itself a certain sign of spuriousness (279n.), but explains the origin of the interpolation.

1088–98 The second section of the monody is a formal request for help, or βοή, a practice which had legal regulations and implications in real life (177n.). The style is disjointed and emotional, but Polymestor does not forget any of the expected elements: (a) 1088–91b: list of the people who must come to rescue; (b) 1092: shout, or βοή proper; (c) 1093: specific request ('come here'); (d) 1095–8: description of the wrongs suffered, and indication of the culprits. Similar, if less complete, βοαί occur at *Hipp.* 884–6 (elements (a) and (d)), and *Hcld.* 69–72 (elements (a), (c), (d)).

1088–90 'Ah, oh, <I call upon you,> you, spear-bearing, arm-bearing, horse-loving people of Thrace, devoted to Ares.' Thracians are good at using spears (*Il.* 4.533) and fond of horses (9n.). Epic presents Ares as residing in Thrace: *Il.* 13.301, *Od.* 8.361.

1095–6 Repetition of a word at the beginning of successive *cola* (limbs of a sentence) is frequent in dochmii (1063n.) and other lyric metres (170–2n.); for an occurrence in iambs (as here) see *Pho.* 1060–1 γενοίμεθ' ὧδε ματέρες, γενοίμεθ' εὔτεκνοι.

1097: 693n.

1098: 475–8n.

1099 Polymestor's aporetic questions ('Where shall I turn? Where shall I go?' = 'I do not know where I should turn or go') are followed by a deliberative one ('Should I go to heaven or Hades?'): cf. 736–7 and Mastronarde 1979: 9–10.

1100–6 '<Should I move> flying to the high-flying palace of the sky, where Orion or Sirius dart flaming rays of fire from their eyes? Or should I cross in haste the black strait and go to Hades, poor wretch that I am?' After the participle ἀμπτάμενος and the disjunctive ἤ we would expect another participle, but the second section turns into an independent sentence, with a finite verb: *Hel.* 188–90 and 1583, K–G II.100, Smyth §2147 c.

The desire to die or to fly away is frequently expressed in Euripides: see *Ion* 796–7 ἀν' ὑγρὸν ἀμπταίην αἰθέρα πόρσω γαί|ας Ἑλλανίας ἀστέρας ἑσπέρους, *Or.* 1375–7 αἰαῖ· πᾶι φύγω, ξέναι, πολιὸν αἰθέρ' ἀμπτάμενος ἢ | πόντον, Barrett on *Hipp.* 732–4 and 1290–3, Swift 2009. The chorus (1007–8) stress the suicidal aspect of Polymestor's wish, but the desire to fly to the sky may also express the desire of becoming immortal: Collard on *Suppl.* 1140–2, Nagy 1979: 189–210, esp. 201–3 on Orion's myth. The two possibilities are often paired: Eur. *Med.* 1296–7, *Hipp.* 1290–3, Aesch. *Suppl.* 792–7, Soph. *Ai.* 1191–3. Polymestor locates himself at the crossroads between the two endings of Orion's story: as a star in heaven (1100–1) or as hunter in Hades (*Od.* 11.572–5).

1100–1 ἀμπτάμενος: aor. ptcp. from ἀναπέτομαι. For the apocope (ἀν- = ἀνα-) see 1263n.

ὑψιπετὲς ἐς μέλαθρον: the sky is often imagined as a 'palace' or building (*Il.* 5.749, Eur. *Ion* 1–2, *HF* 403–7). The adjective ὑψιπετές is formed from the root of πέτομαι. Heavenly bodies are often described as 'flying': Eur. *El.* 464–7, Ar. *Av.* 576, 698. A derivation from πίπτω (LSJ s.v.) is linguistically possible but gives unsuitable meaning ('falling from high'). On the interpretation and accentuation of compound adjectives in -πετής see Battezzato 2000a.

1102–4 Polymestor's desire to reach Sirius and/or Orion might be astronomically appropriate. A tradition attested in the fifth century BCE dates the fall of Troy to the month Thargelion (May/June), either on the night of day 12 (Hellanicus *FGrHist* 4 F 152 ab) or 23/4 (Damastes of Sigeum *FGrHist* 5 F 7, Ephorus *FGrHist* 70 F 226, Plut. *Cam.* 19): Grafton and Swerdlow 1986. The ancient historians inferred the month of the year from the story about the Pleiads narrated in the *Sack of Ilium* fr. 5 West 2003: 150–1 (= *Little Iliad* fr. 14a West 2013: 209–13), and the date and time of the day from the description of the phase of the moon in the *Little Iliad* fr. 14 West (914n.; Battezzato 2014b). It is possible that Euripides imagined the fall of Troy to have taken place in May/June, following Hellanicus; these astronomical interpretations of the epic cycle do not appear compelling to us, but were part of the 'scholarly' debate in the fifth and fourth centuries BCE.

Ὠαρίων ἢ Σείριος the two stars are listed as alternative possibilities, but they are in fact close to each other. For ἢ 'and/or' cf. 87–9n. Alternatively, read Ὠαρίων καὶ Σείριος. The corruption καί > ἢ is common (Diggle 1981: 27), and, for the sg. verb, cf. West on Hes. *Op.* 609–10 εὖτ' ἂν δ' Ὠρίων καὶ Σείριος ἐς μέσον ἔλθηι | οὐρανόν.

1104–6 ἐς Ἅιδα | μελάγχρωτα πορθμὸν ἄιξω 'should I cross in haste [aor. subj. from ἀίσσω] the black strait and go to Hades?' πορθμός can mean 'travel by sea' (Soph. *Trach.* 571) or 'strait, narrow sea' (Soph. *Ant.* 1145). The accusative here indicates the space traversed, as in Eur. *Alc.*

442–3 γυναῖκ' ἀρίσταν | λίμναν Ἀχεροντίαν πορεύσας, Aesch. *PV* 836–7 τὴν παρακτίαν | κέλευθον ᾖξας πρὸς μέγαν κόλπον Ῥέας: K–G 1.312–13, Diggle 1994: 287. 'To Hades' indicates the final destination.

ἐς Ἅιδα: lit. 'to <the house> of Hades': Smyth §1302. Cf. 1076n.

μελάγχρωτα 'black' is the colour of Hades (*Alc.* 438, *Hipp.* 1388). On adjectives ending in -χρως or -χροος in Euripides see Mastronarde on *Pho.* 138.

1107–8 Many texts of classical Greek state that suicide is justified in order to escape from unbearable psychological or physical suffering (Pl. *Leg.* 873c3–8, Garrison 1995: 11–33 and 100), especially in the cases of blindness and death of children (see Collard on *Suppl.* 980–1113 and 1104–6, van Hooff 1990: 104–5 and 123–6). Several tragic characters however consider suicide unmanly or unwise, even in such circumstances: Bond on *HF* 1248, *Or.* 415. The chorus sarcastically mock Polymestor, instigating him to commit suicide.

συγγνώσθ', ὅταν '<it is> understandable to ... whenever ...' Neuter plural (not only singular) adjectives are often found in reference to an infinitive: see *Med.* 491, 703 συγγνωστά, K–G 1.66–7, Diggle 1994: 507.

κρεῖσσον' ἢ φέρειν 'harder than <what one can> bear'. The usual construction ἢ ὥστε/ἢ ὡς + inf. is avoided in poetry because of the hiatus: cf. Soph. *OT* 1293 τὸ γὰρ νόσημα μεῖζον ἢ φέρειν, K–G II.503.

1109–1295 Dialogue between Hecuba, Agamemnon and Polymestor

1109–13 Agamemnon arrives onstage after hearing the noise and the shouting of Polymestor. Similar scenes can be divided into three main types: (a) a specific character is called; usually the character is inside the *skēnē* (171–8, *IT* 1303–8, *Pho.* 296–303, 1264–71); (b) someone utters a cry for help (βοή: 177n., 1088–98n.); (c) someone arrives after hearing an unusual noise or shouting, e.g. a quarrel (Eur. *IA* 317, Soph. *Ai.* 1318). See Di Benedetto and Medda 1997: 40–3 and 58–65. Polymestor issued a cry for help (1092 βοάν), so we expect situation (b). Agamemnon however behaves as if he simply heard an unusual noise, not a request for help (cf. 'noise': 1111; 'fear': 1113). It is true that people are often unable to hear the details of the cry for help (Mastronarde 1979: 28–30), but, when a βοή is uttered, it is generally recognised as such: Eur. *Hcld.* 69–74, Soph. *OC* 883–90. Agamemnon would have been under great pressure to help Polymestor had he declared that his arrival was motivated by the βοή, whereas his failure to recognise the cry for help allows him to act the impartial judge. Agamemnon does not see Polymestor at first, and his lines are not addressed to any character in particular, but to the 'entire environment' (Mastronarde 1979: 25). It is unusual for the character onstage to start the dialogue: this shows the eagerness of Polymestor to get revenge (Mastronarde 1979: 22 and n. 16).

1109 οὐ ... ἥσυχος 'not quiet', i.e. 'very loud': litotes (1113n., Smyth §3032)

1110–11 πέτρας ὀρείας παῖς ... Ἠχώ 'Echo, daughter of the mountain rock'. Echo is personified already in Pind. *Ol.* 14.21 and figures as a character in Euripides' *Andromeda* (fr. 118; see Ar. *Thesm.* 1059). She is obviously associated with rocks and mountains: *h.hom.* 19.21 (6th/5th cent.), Aesch. *Pers.* 390–1 ἀντηλάλαξε ... πέτρας | ἠχώ.

θόρυβον 'clamour' takes up 872, where Hecuba asked Agamemnon for help in case of θόρυβος or ἐπικουρία *from the Greeks* after the punishment of Polymestor. Events turned out very differently: the Greek army has not come to help Polymestor, and Agamemnon comes to stop the 'clamour' of Polymestor.

1112 ᾔσμεν: pluperfect of οἶδα, corresponding to an imperfect: the condition is counterfactual ('if we did not know').

1113 φόβον 'fear' is the reason given for arriving in response to βοή, as at *Or.* 1324, but also on hearing unusual noises or shoutings: Aesch. *Sept.* 239–41, *PV* 133–5, Eur. *Suppl.* 87–9.

παρέσχ' ἄν 'would have caused'. In a counterfactual apodosis we need ἄν. The elision παρέσχ' is rare but legitimate: Diggle 1994: 109 n. 61 and 197.

οὐ μέσως 'not to a moderate degree', i.e. 'greatly' (litotes: *Andr.* 873).

1114–15 'My dearest – <I call you dearest> because I have recognised you, Agamemnon, on hearing your voice.' It is also possible to interpret the lines as 'I have recognised your voice on hearing it', assuming a strong enjambment between σέθεν and φωνῆς. On this usage of γάρ cf. 688n. For αἰσθάνομαι = 'to understand, to realise' see Eur. *HF* 1312, *Ba.* 178, Soph. *OC* 891 ἔγνων (the blind Oedipus recognises Theseus from his voice). Odysseus too recognises Athena from her voice at Soph. *Ai.* 14–17 and [Eur.] *Rhes.* 608–9. Actors adapted their vocal delivery to fit the characters they played: Pickard-Cambridge 1968: 168–9, Csapo and Slater 1994: 265–7. Polymestor addresses both Hecuba (953–4) and Agamemnon in the same manner, trying to present himself as a friend to both of them, even if in fact he is equally self-centred towards both of them (953–1295n.).

1117 'Who was it that blinded your eyes, making the pupils of your eyes run with blood?' Polymestor's mask showed signs of his blindness. The actor had to change or modify his mask while inside the *skēnē* (1023–55). Euripides repeats the phrase αἱμάξας κόρας in reference to Oedipus, who uses the pins of Jocasta's dress to blind himself (*Pho.* 62, cf. Soph. *OT* 1268–9). Similarly, Hecuba and her helpers use pins to blind Polymestor (1170). Polymestor is a sort of inverted Oedipus, who kills his foster-son and is blinded in retaliation (Battezzato 1999–2000: 361–2, Lee 2015: 131).

1118–19 Agamemnon's use of particles betrays his eagerness to cover up his complicity with Hecuba.

ἦ 'really'.

ὅστις ἦν ἄρα '<and I ask myself> who it was'. On ἄρα 'if one only knew' see Denniston 39–40.

1121 ἀπώλεσ' – οὐκ ἀπώλεσ' ἀλλὰ μειζόνως 'they ruined me – not ruined, but more than that'. Polymestor uses the same language as the Trojan captives to express the misfortune that has fallen upon him: 667n., 948n., 1168–9n.

1122–3 Agamemnon abruptly switches addressee from Polymestor (τί φῄς;) to Hecuba (σύ), signalling her presence to the Thracian king. ὡς λέγει, referring back to φῄς, helps the audience understand that Polymestor cannot be addressed in the second part of 1122. The crucial vocative Ἑκάβη is delayed to the second sentence directed to her (1123); in other cases a vocative immediately signals the change of addressee: *Hcld.* 273 ἄπελθε· καὶ σύ ..., ἄναξ. The vocative can however be omitted, as at *Andr.* 550–1 Μενέλα', ἐπίσχες· μὴ τάχυν' ἄνευ δίκης. | ἡγοῦ σὺ θᾶσσον (in reference to a servant). Stage action and delivery could have helped in identifying the addressee.

τόλμαν ... τήνδ' ἔτλης ἀμήχανον; 'Did you dare to enact such a terrible act? There is no remedy against it.' The word τόλμα 'daring' is on occasion used to mean 'act of daring': Eur. *Andr.* 837 τόλμας (gen. sg.) ... ἂν ῥέξ(α), Soph. *Trach.* 582. The meaning of the verb τλάω 'to suffer/to dare' is made clear by the adjective ἀμήχανον 'against which no remedy is possible'. For the *figura etymologica* τόλμαν ἔτλης see *Ion* 960 τλήμων σὺ τόλμης 'wretched for your daring'.

1124 ὤιμοι, τί λέξεις; 511n.

1125 σήμηνον, εἰπέ: in his impatience, Polymestor doubles the imperatives, like Hecuba at 604 (where the effect is meant to be solemn and authoritative, as appropriate to a queen).

1125–6 ἵν' ἁρπάσας χεροῖν | διασπάσωμαι καὶ καθαιμάξω χρόα 'so that I may grab her and tear her flesh apart with my hands and make it run with blood'. He has already torn to pieces Polydorus (716–18 διεμοιράσω | χρόα) and would like to do the same with his mother. He also wants to retaliate (1117 αἱμάξας). This recalls Achilles' and Hecuba's cannibalistic desires (*Il.* 22.347 'to cut up his flesh and eat it', 24.212–13). He imagines that he will kill his prey with his bare hands, like the bacchants (1034n., *Ba.* 1128). χεροῖν probably refers to both ἁρπάσας (cf. *El.* 819) and διασπάσωμαι (cf. *Ba.* 949). Polymestor does not think it necessary to hide his impulses in front of Agamemnon, expecting him to be on his side against Hecuba.

1127 This *antilabē* (line divided between two speakers) is effectively used at a moment of vivid stage action, when Polymestor begins chasing after Hecuba. He is probably stopped by Agamemnon's attendants (1128 μέθες). Other naturalistically motivated *antilabai* in the early plays of Euripides include such impressive passages as 1283n., *Alc.* 390–1 (death of Alcestis), *Hipp.* 310, 352 (the name 'Hippolytus'), *Andr.* 1077 (Peleus falls to the ground), *Suppl.* 513 (Thesus interrupts Adrastos).

οὗτος, τί πάσχεις; 'Hey, what are you doing?' An identical phrase in *antilabē* occurs at Ar. *Av.* 1044. Agamemnon's tone is quite blunt. On οὗτος 'hey, you', see 1280n. The colloquial τί πάσχεις; (Stevens 1976: 41) is a sign of concern at *Hipp.* 340, *HF* 965; the tone is inquisitive at *Or.* 395. Here it betrays Agamemnon's lack of politeness towards the barbarian Polymestor.

1128 μαργῶσαν χέρα 'my furious hand'. Polymestor would like to present himself as a heroic warrior, 'mad' with warlike fury (cf. *Il.* 5.717 μαίνεσθαι ... Ἄρηα, Graziosi and Haubold on 6.100–1 λίην | μαίνεται), but he imprudently uses a word that has very negative connotations: *Il.* 5. 881–2 ὑπερφίαλον Διομήδεα | μαργαίνειν ... ἐπ᾽ ἀθανάτοισι θεοῖσι, Aesch. *Sept.* 687 δορίμαργος ἄτα, Mastronarde on *Pho.* 1156.

1129 ἐκβαλὼν δὲ καρδίας τὸ βάρβαρον 'after exiling savagery from your heart', 'after purging your heart of savagery', as if τὸ βάρβαρον were an unwelcome person (781, 1284–5n., *Hipp.* 1056, *El.* 61) or a bodily fluid that Polymestor could squeeze out of himself, such as tears (*Hec.* 298) or blood (Soph. *Ant.* 1238). The metaphor is used again at fr. 339.2 ἐκβαλόντ᾽ αὐθαδίαν. The abstract form τὸ βάρβαρον is paralleled by generalisations on the essence of 'Greekness' at *Or.* 486; see τὰ Ἑλληνικά 'all things Greek' Hdt. 4.78.3.

1130–1251 The *agōn* is a set piece in Euripidean tragedy: two characters discuss an issue often in front of a judge, with quasi-legal precision. On this form see 216–443n., Lloyd 1992, Dubischar 2001, Mastronarde on *Med.* 446–626, Mastronarde 2010: 224–45. The peculiarity of this scene is that the focus of the debate shifts from Polymestor's accusation against Hecuba to Hecuba's against Polymestor. The debate turns from a decision on future punishment of Hecuba to the moral justification of a punishment already enacted on Polymestor.

1130 ἐν μέρει 'in turn', a sign of civilised and orderly behaviour: *Cycl.* 253, *Hcld.* 182 (in an *agōn*), Pl. *Smp.* 214b10.

1132–82 Polymestor's speech. His legal case is double. He must defend himself from the accusation of murder, and at the same time he asks Agamemnon to punish Hecuba for the killing of his children and for blinding him. As the plaintiff, Polymestor speaks first (see *Pho.* 465–8), which in Euripidean *agōnes* is a major disadvantage: only in *Medea*,

Andromache and *Phoenician Women* does the first speaker get the upper hand (see Lloyd 1992: 17 for qualifications).

The speech is divided into clearly marked parts, probably following rhetorical models for legal speeches. (a) 1132–44: the killing of Polydorus. Polymestor cleverly admits to self-interest, but claims that it coincided with reasons of state: he wanted to forestall another Trojan war, which would have dire consequences for both Greeks and Thracians. The complex hypothetical period of lines 1138–44 betrays the difficulty of combining these conflicting claims. (b) 1145–75: Hecuba's crime. Polymestor stresses the premeditation (1145–9); he narrates what happened inside the tent (1150–75), in a style that recalls that of tragic messengers (1172n., de Jong 1991: 179–80). (c) 1175–82: Polymestor ends his speech with a final *gnōmē* against the female sex.

Polymestor's speech is weak. He pleads guilty to the killing of Polydorus, arguing that it was morally and politically justified. If these justifications fail to persuade, his case falls. Polymestor in fact does not even know that Agamemnon is aware of his crime, and does not try to take advantage of that circumstance. In his conclusion, Polymestor simply rants about women in general, and fails to argue in particular against Hecuba. For instance, he does not explain the legal or moral reasons why she should be punished for taking justice into her own hands, nor does he suggest what punishment she deserves. Hecuba in her reply simply ignores the accusations levelled against her, and concentrates on Polymestor's crime.

Polymestor chooses not to use an objective tone, suggesting a psychological interpretation of facts (1135 ὕποπτος ὢν δή, 1138 ἔδεισα, 1145 γνοῦσα, 1152 ὡς δή).

1132 λέγοιμ' ἄν 'I shall speak', a formula that marks the beginning of a speech: Fraenkel on Aesch. *Ag.* 838, Barrett on *Hipp.* 336, Battezzato 2001.

ἦν τις 'there was a ...' A traditional way of introducing a narrative, inherited from the Indo-European tradition of poetry: *Il.* 5.9, West 2007: 93–4, Barrett on *Hipp.* 125–8. The indefinite (here τις) can be picked up by a demonstrative or a relative pronoun (slightly less common: see 1133 ὄν).

1133 Πολύδωρος, Ἑκάβης παῖς: identical to the self-presentation of Polydorus at 3. Polymestor gives the precise indication of the name and family of Polydorus, and a short explanation of the nature of their relationship (omitting the *xenia*) and the crime. This sort of introduction to the case is frequent in forensic oratory at the beginning of the *narratio*: Lys. 17.2, Isoc. 1.9, 2.3.

1134 δίδωσι 'he gave'. For the present tense cf. 695–6n.

1135 ὕποπτος ὢν δή 'because of course he was suspecting' (+ gen.). For the active meaning of ὕποπτος see LSJ s.v. II, Thuc. 1.90.2. δή indicates that Polymestor considers Priam's motivations, described by ὕποπτος ὤν, as evident (Drummen 2016: III.2 §79); Polymestor implies that this should elicit contempt from the Greeks (Denniston 205).

1136–7 ἀνθ' ὅτου δ' ἔκτεινά νιν | ἄκουσον, ὡς εὖ καὶ σοφῆι προμηθίαι 'listen for what reason I killed him: how I acted well, and with wise foresight'. For ἄκουσον see 273n. Just like the tyrant Lycus in the *HF*, Polymestor claims that his violence is clever prudence, not wickedness. In Pl. *Resp.* 348d Thrasymachus claims that injustice is in fact εὐβουλία 'prudence' (see Bond on *HF* 165–6). σοφία 'wisdom' characterises Odysseus the demagogue (228n., 399). Hecuba denounces the connection between 'wisdom' and violence (258–9). Polymestor appropriates the language of σοφία (1007), but σοφία thus acquires a negative connotation of 'excessive astuteness', 'cleverness', in the eyes of the audience, who know the hypocrisy of his position: see Soph. *Phil.* 1246, Eur. *Ba.* 395, Guthrie 1969: 27–34.

1138–43 ἔδεισα μή ... ἀθροίσηι καὶ ξυνοικίσηι ... ἄρειαν ... τρίβοιεν ... εἴη: the verbs in the subordinate sentence switch from subjunctive to optative. The subjunctive expresses the immediate fear, whereas the optative (which is the standard mood after secondary tenses) here indicates the consequences of the action of the subjunctive (K–G II.393, Smyth §§2226–7). The participles λειφθείς 'if spared' (1138) and γνόντες 'if they knew' (1140) are in fact the protases of a conditional sentence (Smyth §2344). Polymestor's long and complex sentence is calculated to conceal his true motives and to show him in command of the logic (and the syntax) of the situation. He ends by an appeal to the judge, speciously presenting the Thracians as victims of the war.

1138–41 'I was afraid that, if the son was spared to become your enemy, he would gather the Trojans together, and unite them again; and that if the Greeks knew that one of the sons of Priam was alive, they would muster an army again against the land of the Phrygians'.

1138 λειφθείς: Astyanax is killed for similar reasons (or with similar excuses) at *Tro.* 723. See Bond on *HF* 166ff.

1141 ἄρειαν στόλον 'they would muster an army' (3rd p. pl. aor. opt. of ἀείρω/αἴρω). For the phrase see Aesch. *Pers.* 795 ἀροῦμεν στόλον. The variant δόρυ 'ship' gives a plausible text, 'they would set sail' (*Tro.* 1148 ἀροῦμεν δόρυ), but 'army' fits better with the emphasis on 'plains', 'ravage' and 'plunder' at 1142–3. δόρυ is a gloss of στόλισμα at Σ 1156 in MS V.

1142 τρίβοιεν 'they would ravage' (lit. 'pound'). See Ar. *Pax* 231 τρίβειν ... τὰς πόλεις 'to ravage the cities' (but also 'to grind them, to pound them with a pestle').

1143 λεηλατοῦντες 'plundering <them>'. The fertile plains of Thrace (8n.) would supply food for the army, solving a major logistic problem in a long campaign (Hdt. 7.49.5, Aesch. *Pers.* 792–4).

1143–4 γείτοσιν... ἐκάμνομεν 'and the neighbours of the Trojans [i.e. the Thracians] would suffer the same misery under which we were suffering just now, my lord' (306–8n.). For νῦν 'a little time ago' see *Il.* 3.439, Dem. 29.9, LSJ s.v. 1.2, K–G II.116.

1146–7 λόγωι ... τοιῶιδ'..., ὡς ... φράσουσα 'with the following excuse, <that is> because she was ostensibly going to tell me'. On τοιῶιδ' cf. 576n. On ὡς with causal participle cf. Smyth §2086b. On the hidden treasure see 1002, 1008n.

1148 χρυσοῦ: the enjambment and the separation from 'hidden chests' (κεκρυμμένας | θήκας, also separated by a line boundary) stress the most important word. On emphasis at line beginning, in combination with enjambment, see Dik 2007: 168–224, esp. 197–201 for nouns.

εἰσάγει 'she brought me in', historical present (527–9n., 937n., 1150, 1162, 1171–3).

1149 ἵν' ἄλλος μή τις εἰδείη τάδε 'so that no one else would know these events'. For the optative see 11–12.

1150 κάμψας γόνυ 'bending my knee (in a sitting position)': 1079–81n.

1151–4 'In great number, some on the left-hand side, others on the other side, the Trojan women, taking a seat, as if sitting next to a friend, praised the fabric woven by Thracian weavers.' χειρός (Milton's conjecture) is placed before αἱ μὲν ἐξ ἀριστερᾶς, as if the sentence continued αἱ δ' ἐκ δεξιᾶς ('others from the right-hand side'), but in fact χειρός refers only to the μέν section of the sentence: cf. *HF* 972–4, *Ion* 1621–2, *Or.* 901–2. The subject Τρώων κόραι comes at the end of 1152 as an afterthought. This imitates the 'adding' style of epic: Parry 1971: 251–6, Devine and Stephens 2000: 142–74.

1151–2 χειρὸς αἱ μὲν ἐξ ἀριστερᾶς, | αἱ δ' ἔνθεν elegantly rephrases the expression, common in prose, ἔνθεν καὶ ἔνθεν 'on both sides' (Hdt. 7.36.5).

1153 θάκους ἔχουσαι 'sitting', lit. 'having a seat'. θάκους (Hermann) is acc. pl. from θᾶκος. The MSS read θάκουν 'they were seated', a very unusual unaugmented 3rd p. pl. impf., a form attested only in the *Bacchae*: Rijksbaron 2006: 135–6. The MS text θάκουν presumably arose from an attempt to provide a main verb to the sentence; this mistake occurred because ἔχουσαι was erroneously linked with κερκίδ'.

κερκίδ' 'the weaver's shuttle' = 'the fabric woven with the shuttle', a metonymy (1–2n.), glossed at 1154 with the explanation τούσδε ... πέπλους.

Ἠδωνῆς χερός: lit. 'the Edonian hand'. The Edonians were a population settled in ancient Thrace (see Strabo, Book 7, fr. 7a Radt), in the area of Mount Pangaeus (Aesch. *Pers.* 494–5), where the oracle of Dionysus (1267n.) and the gold mines were located (Eur. fr. 759a.1571–2).

On Thracian greed see 997n.; on their weaving skills see Hall 1989: 137–8. On 'hand' for 'hands' see 65–7n.

1154 ὑπ' αὐγὰς τούσδε λεύσσουσαι πέπλους 'examining the fabric of my robe against the rays' of the sun. For the phrase ὑπ' αὐγάς see Pl. *Phdr.* 268a1 and 269a8. The attention given by the women to typical feminine concerns (weaving, children) is meant to look deceptively reassuring to Polymestor (Jenkins 1985, Battezzato 1999–2000: 353–61). The appearance of his cloak (τούσδε ... πέπλους 'the robe that I wear'), now stained with blood and presumably torn in the fight, stresses the violence of the crime: more skilful speakers, such as Orestes in Aesch. *Cho.* 980–1004, explicitly comment on the bloodstains.

1155–6 Polymestor, like Homeric warriors, has two spears (*Il.* 3.18, *Od.* 1.256) and carries them inside the tent (*Il.* 10.76). Spears are meant for long-distance fighting, and the Trojan women do not use them to kill the children: this would have been highly ironic, but would have turned the women into epic-type warriors (contrast 1034 'you will die by no warrior's hand'). The women use concealed swords, which they obviously prepared in advance (not knowing that Polymestor would have come with his spears). Concealing weapons was of course difficult in a prisoners' camp, and does not sound especially plausible. Deleting 1161 would eliminate the difficulty, but produces a text that is too abrupt. It is clear that the poet could on occasion 'deceive well' (Arist. *Poet.* 1460a19), esp. for events not shown onstage.

κάμακε Θρηικίω 'two Thracian spears'. Hartung's conjecture introduces the necessary dual form, implied by 'twofold' (1156). In using the word κάμαξ 'pole' in the meaning of 'spear' Euripides had the model of Aesch. *Ag.* 66.

διπτύχου 'twofold', just as διπλοῦς, when followed by a singular noun, is often a more elaborate way of saying 'two of X': Eur. *Med.* 1136 δίπτυχος γονή, Aesch. *Cho.* 938 διπλοῦς λέων.

στολίσματος 'equipment', an abstract word probably created by Euripides from the verb στολίζω: *Suppl.* 659 ἐστολισμένον δορί, *IA* 255.

1157 The Trojan women stage an idyllic scene and pose as loving mothers. Their role is suddenly reversed when they kill Polymestor's children. Euripides combines feminine aggressiveness with an 'unnatural' and uncanny imitation of motherly behaviour at *Ba.* 748–64.

1158 τέκν' ἐν χεροῖν ἔπαλλον 'they cradled my children in their arms'. The verb πάλλω is memorably used of Hector tossing the child Astyanax in *Il.* 6.474 αὐτὰρ ὅ γ' ὃν φίλον υἱὸν ἐπεὶ κύσε πῆλέ τε χερσίν, a passage probably echoed here. The verb is normally associated with brandishing spears (*Il.* 16.142, Eur. *Andr.* 697, *HF* 437): the Trojan women ominously toss the children instead of Polymestor's spears, which they have just taken.

1159 διαδοχαῖσ': Euripides, unlike Aeschylus and Sophocles, avoids word-end after the sixth metrical element in recited iambic trimeters if word-end does not occur also after element 5 and/or 7 in the line. He however admits word-end at element 6 if elision follows. This is why we should accept Elsmsley's text διαδοχαῖσ' (elided long dative) instead of διαδοχαῖς (διαδοχαῖσιν gives an impossible split anapaest): Diggle 1994: 82–3, 473–4 n. 151, Garvie on Aesch. *Cho.* 150, West 1982: 83 n. 18.

1160 πῶς δοκεῖς: 'formally a parenthetic question; but in fact merely the lively equivalent of an adverb, "quite remarkably"' (Barrett on *Hipp.* 443–6). However, here its colloquial tone (Stevens 1976: 39) and the formal appeal to the second person are meant to attract the attention of the hearer (esp. that of Agamemnon in his capacity as a judge) to the beginning of the description of the crime.

ἐκ γαληνῶν ... προσφθεγμάτων 'after they addressed me peacefully'. The adjective γαληνός is a faded metaphor, 'not stormy' (of the sea) = 'calm, peaceful' ([531–3n.]): *IT* 345, *Or.* 279, and the verb γαληνίζω in fr. 1079.4.

1161 ἐκ πέπλων ποθέν 'from somewhere inside their clothes'. Indefinite adverbs may combine with prepositional phrases or adverbs expressing the same syntactical function (e.g. motion from a place, etc.): Eur. *Hipp.* 831 πρόσωθεν δέ ποθεν, *Med.* 573, *Ion* 1329 ἀεί ποτε, Soph. *Phil.* 163 πέλας που.

1162–4 αἱ δὲ πολυπόδων δίκην | ξυναρπάσασαι τὰς ἐμὰς εἶχον χέρας | καὶ κῶλα 'the other ones, like octopuses, seized and locked my hands and limbs'. αἱ δέ does not have a preceding αἱ μέν (see *Il.* 22.157, Eur. *HF* 636, *IT* 1350–1, and Denniston 166). The division of the Trojan women into different groups is already mentioned at 1151–2, 1155 and 1157. The tenacious clinging powers of the octopus are proverbial in Greek: *Od.* 5.432–5 and the proverb ἔχεται δ' ὥσπερ πολύπους πέτρας (Macar. 4.26 and 7.21, pp. 169 and 203 Leutsch). The metaphor fits with Polymestor's use of animal imagery (1172–5n.). δίκην here is used adverbially ('like') and governs the preceding genitive: Aesch. *Th.* 85, *Ag.* 3. This construction occurs only here in Euripides (its presence in fr. 1007h.2 is very dubious).

Some scholars defend the MS text πολεμίων δίκην referring to *Ba.* 752–3 ὥστε πολέμιοι | ἐπεσπεσοῦσαι, where Theban women attack villages in the Theban countryside as if they were foreign enemies. Here the women must be compared to something they are not, but here they are enemies (1176); hence the transmitted πολεμίων is impossible.

1165 εἰ μὲν πρόσωπον ἐξανισταίην ἐμόν 'if I tried to raise my head'. εἰ + opt. here describes a repeated action: Smyth §2340, K–G II.476–7.

1166 κόμης κατεῖχον 'they kept me down by the hair'. Prisoners of war were often depicted or described as being *dragged away* (not just held down) by their hair. This humiliation is normally inflicted on *female* prisoners in tragedy: Aesch. *Suppl.* 884 and 909, Eur. *Andr.* 402, *Tro.* 882, *Hel.* 116, *IA* 791–3. This gesture highlights the element of gender reversal in the scene (as in Timotheus 791.144 *PMG*, which implies feminisation of barbarians).

1167 Euripides makes Polymestor confirm the truth of Hecuba's statement about the strength of the πλῆθος 'multitude' of women (884).

1168–9 On the order of events see 1037n.

πῆμα πήματος πλέον 'suffering greater than suffering'. This is standard tragic language, highlighting the last and (for Polymestor) worst act of aggression, the blinding inflicted on him: Aesch. *Ag.* 864–5 κακοῦ | κάκιον ἄλλο πῆμα, Eur. *Med.* 234, *Hcld.* 554–5. For the theme of 'evil surpassing any other (previous or possible) evil' see also 1121n.

1170 πόρπας 'brooches', a typical feminine weapon. See 934n., 1117n., and the story in Hdt. 5.87 and Duris *FGrHist* 76 F 24: the Athenian women used their brooches to kill the messenger who told them of the death of their husbands in a battle against Aegina. Here the Trojan women use both 'male' swords on the children, and 'female' brooches on Polymestor. By removing the brooches, the women would loosen their dress, recalling the self-exposure of Polyxena (558–61n.). At Soph. *Trach.* 923–31 Deianeira removes the brooches from her dress, baring her breast before killing herself with a sword (Battezzato 1999–2000: 362).

1171 κεντοῦσιν αἱμάσσουσιν: on the asyndeton cf. 86n.

1172–5 Polymestor claims that he is both 'like a wild beast' (1173 θήρ ὥς), chasing murderous dogs, and 'like a hunter' (1174 ὡς κυνηγέτης), etymologically, 'he who leads a pack of dogs'). This is in keeping with the mixed imagery of Polymestor's monody, where both he and the Trojan captives are qualified as 'wild animals' (1058 and 1072). Here the shift occurs in a compressed turn of phrase, but the paradox is important: Polymestor is both the animal (and victim) that turns against its hunters, and the hunter who tries to get his revenge. For other mixed images in Euripides see *HF* 860–70. The shift in imagery has prompted emendations and/or excision. Barrett deletes 1173 (writing ἐρευνῶ at 1174), but this eliminates the self-damning comparison to a wild beast (1058). Prinz deletes 1174, but βάλλων 'throwing' is strange when referring to an animal, and 1174 is not in itself objectionable.

1172 ἐκ δὲ πηδήσας 'jumping out'. Tmesis (ἐκ ... πηδήσας: 907–8n., K–G 1.533–5) occurs more frequently in messenger speeches (8x) and lyric (45x) passages of tragedy than in the other, much longer, non-lyric passages (21x). It is used not simply for metrical convenience (Bergson 1959: 34) but also as an echo of the earlier literary tradition, especially epic. It was still in use in fifth-century spoken Attic, in some stock phrases: Barrett on *Hipp.* 256–7, Dunbar on Ar. *Av.* 1506 ἀπὸ γάρ μ' ὀλεῖς.

1175 βάλλων ἀράσσων 'hitting and pounding'. Euripides uses this combination of verbs elsewhere to describe a fight (*Andr.* 1154 and *IT* 310; see also 1044–6n.). Here Polymestor characteristically exaggerates the extent of the damage he caused on his opponents. On the asyndeton cf. 86n.

1175–7 τοιάδε ... Ἀγάμεμνον: this paradox recalls a *topos* of forensic oratory. The speaker often claims that, if convicted, he would be punished for his law-abiding, pious or ethical behaviour, or for benefiting the city: Lys. 1.48–50, esp. 50 'now I stand at risk to lose my life, my property, and everything else, precisely because I abided by the laws of the city', 20.9 and 30, Pl. *Ap.* 36b–e. For this *topos* in tragedy see also Eur. *Or.* 934–7.

τοιάδε ... πέπονθα 'I suffered sufferings of this type', mentioned before. For τοιάδ' referring to what precedes cf. 580n., 1182.

σπεύδων χάριν | ... τὴν σήν 'because I was acting in your favour'. On the interlaced word order cf. 44n., 401n.

1177–82 ὡς δὲ ... ἐπίσταται: Polymestor ends his speech with a misogynistic rant, decrying the 'race of women' (885n.). He alludes to literary and popular misogynistic traditions: 1178 'if someone of the men who lived before us has spoken ill of women', Mastronarde on *Med.* 419–20, Semon. fr. 7 West. In particular Polymestor is adapting and correcting the first stasimon of *Choephori* (585–98), where the chorus claimed that the 'excessively daring attitude of men' and the 'all-daring loves of women' are more dangerous than the monsters that live or are generated on land, in the sea, or in the sky. Polymestor pointedly omits any mention of male guilt: Thalmann 1993: 151–2. Comparing cruel human beings to animals or natural elements is a commonplace: *Il.* 16.33–5, Eur. *Med.* 1342–3. On the final position of the *gnōmē* see 375–8n.

1177 ὡς δὲ μὴ μακροὺς τείνω λόγους 'in order not to extend my speech any longer,' i.e. 'to cut my speech short'. Conciseness, then as today, was appreciated (*Suppl.* 638–9, *Or.* 758). Polymestor's statement implies that he *has* been short, and that he had much more to say. In fact his speech is of normal length in an *agōn* (fifty-one lines, just like Hecuba's following speech). A self-evidently correct claim does not require a long speech (*Med.* 1351) and vice versa ([Eur.] *Rhes.* 837).

1179 ἢ νῦν λέγων ἔστιν τις 'or if someone is now a <harsh> critic' of women (understand κακῶς from the previous line). For the periphrasis see 120–2n., Smyth §§1857 and 1961, Goodwin 1912: §830. Euripides' comic reputation of misogyny is securely attested in plays from 411 BCE (Ar. *Lys.* 283–4, *Thesm.* 372–94, Kannicht 2004: 99–101); if this reputation predated *Hecuba*, this passage could be read as ironically self-referential (R. Hunter, personal communication).

COMMENTARY: 1180–1237

1180 ἅπαντα ταῦτα συντεμών 'expressing all these points concisely'. Similar expressions mark the end of a speech at *IT* 1015–16 and *IA* 1249.

1182 ὁ δ' αἰεὶ ξυντυχών ἐπίσταται 'any man that, on each separate occasion, has something to do <with them>, knows <this>'. For this meaning of αἰεί/ἀεί see *Ion* 323, LSJ s.v. I, K–G 1.595.

1183 μηδὲν θρασύνου 'check your arrogance', another trait of Polymestor's barbarian lack of self-restraint (1286). An accusation of arrogance is a typical reaction to provocative speeches in *agōnes* from the chorus (*Suppl.* 512 ὑβρίζειν) or from a character (*Hipp.* 937, *Or.* 607 θρασύνηι). Arist. *Eth. Eud.* 1234b11–12 noted that θράσος 'rashness' was the negative version of θάρσος 'courage': cf. Diggle on *Phaeth.* 92.

τοῖς σαυτοῦ κακοῖς 'on the basis of your misfortunes'.

1184 In the *Odyssey*, Agamemnon stresses that all women will have shame or bad fame because of the misdeed of a single bad woman, Clytemnestra (*Od.* 11.432–4, 24.200–2), an absurd generalisation (Eur. fr. 657). Polymestor seems to draw the same conclusion on the basis of Hecuba's actions.

τὸ θῆλυ ... πᾶν ... γένος 'the entire race of women' (885n.). English and other modern languages place 'all' before other adjectives modifying the same noun. Greek places first the emphasised adjective: the *female* race, not that of men (contrastive focus): Soph. *Ant.* 1055 τὸ μαντικὸν γὰρ πᾶν φιλάργυρον γένος 'the entire race of soothsayers is fond of money', Eur. *IA* 520. At *Cycl.* 580 the drunken Cyclops feels he is in the company of 'the *entire* sacred and revered community of the gods' (τὸ πᾶν δαιμόνων ἁγνὸν σέβας), and stresses πᾶν.

συνθείς 'including <them> in one group', as in *Med.* 747 and esp. in fr. 657.1.

[1185–6] 'For there are many of us; some of us are odious, whereas others belong by nature to the category of the bad ones.' The lines do not provide the sense required by the context. Conceding that some women are indeed bad is self-damaging for the chorus, and failing to state that many are virtuous is rhetorically disastrous. It is likely that someone added this couplet from a different context or from an anthology, such as those that covered the topic 'censure of women': cf. fr. 657. Various emendations have been advanced (Musgrave: 'many of us are not odious at all'; Porson 'many women <exist>: some are not odious at all'), but only a complete rewriting can eliminate the unwelcome stress on the negative behaviour of women. In an *agōn*, the chorus normally deliver two or three lines (296–8) between the contestants' speeches, rather than four: see *El.* 1051–4, Lloyd 1992: 65.

1187–1237 Hecuba replies to Polymestor in a neatly organised speech, comprising an introduction, addressed to Agamemnon (1187–95), a reply to Polymestor, successfully proving that he acted out of greed, not friendship towards the Greeks (1196–1232), and a final appeal to Agamemnon, stressing that, if he supported Polymestor against her, he would appear not to respect justice or divine law. Her speech contains fifty-one lines, exactly like Polymestor's: for this symmetry in *agōnes* see *Med.* 465–575, Lloyd 1992: 5–6.

The speech develops two of the major themes of the play: the interplay of language and reality and the interaction between ethics and expediency. Hecuba, like many other characters in Euripides, protests against the established order of things in the world, which she finds absurd and unjust (Barrett on *Hipp.* 616–24, Bond on *HF* 655–72). Several characters voice the specific complaint that fine words should not be available to people who want to disguise their evil deeds (Mastronarde on *Med.* 576–83 and *Pho.* 526–7). Hecuba, who had urged the study of Persuasion (816n.), now implies that rhetorical ability is potentially negative, and argues that language should reflect reality, not be stronger than it (1189: cf. fr. 206.5–6). In response to Polymestor, who portrayed himself as *sophos* (1136–7n.), Hecuba claims that rhetoric ultimately fails in disguising reality (1193–4); justice is stronger than *sophia* 'cleverness' (as Neoptolemus argues in Soph. *Phil.* 1246). This ploy implies that the rest of her speech will rely on facts alone, even if this does not necessarily suggest that rhetoric cannot be used to good purposes (Mossman 1995: 133–4, Riedweg 2000: 13–14): Hecuba explicitly calls the first section of her speech a 'proem', using a rhetorically self-conscious term (1195n.). This ambivalent attitude towards rhetoric is found in several Euripidean passages (*Hipp.* 486–9, *Tro.* 966–8; Mastronarde 2010: 211–22, 233–4).

Hecuba's speech demolishes the arguments of Polymestor, who had claimed that his earlier actions were motivated by his relationship of friendly reciprocity with Agamemnon and the Greeks: reciprocity is impossible per se, given the gulf that separates Greeks and barbarians (1199–1204n.), and is ruled out in the specific case by the nature of the killing of Polydorus, which took place only when the Greeks had already conquered Troy (1208–16). This proves that Polymestor is no *philos* of the Greeks. Hecuba views human relationships in terms of the (aristocratic) ethical code of obligation and reciprocity, in which prestige and loyalty come before personal advantage: one is supposed to help friends and harm enemies, even if this is not in one's self-interest. A precise reckoning of benefits is to be avoided: reciprocity is not a commercial relationship (Seaford 1998: 119–23). Polymestor failed to act according to the rules of reciprocity both towards Agamemnon and Polydorus, and is now bereft of friends: Agamemnon will not want to help him, and Polydorus cannot. The very fact that Polymestor values money more than people (1224–32) is something which puts him outside any relationship of reciprocity. Polymestor should have given Polydorus' wealth to the Greeks, because they needed it more than he did: his lack of generosity proves that he was not a real *philos* to them (1218). Respect for the rules of *xenia* would have provided Polymestor with real wealth: Polydorus would have been, literally, a treasure (1229). Thus, avarice brings about the loss of both personal relationships *and* wealth (1230–2). On the ethics of reciprocity see Introduction, section 5.

1187–94 This time Hecuba will succeed in both denouncing the linguistic deception and defeating her opponent (1192–4). Just like other characters in Euripides, Hecuba points out that, even if clever language may disguise the 'facts' (1191n.), the 'facts' have objective value: *Hipp.* 984–5, *Tro.* 285–7, *El.* 1013–17. On *sophia* cf. 1136–7n.

1187 ἀνθρώποισιν 'for human beings', dative of advantage (Smyth §1481).

1189 χρήστ' ἔδρασε '<someone> acted honestly'. The indefinite subject τις, taking up 1187 ἀνθρώποισιν, is omitted, as often: K–G 1.35–6.

1190 εἴτ' αὖ πονηρά 'if on the other hand <he committed> base acts'; to be construed with ἔδρασε at 1189.

τοὺς λόγους εἶναι σαθρούς 'his arguments <should> be unsound', i.e. be clearly unconvincing; to be construed with ἔδει 'should' at 1189. The adjective σαθρός means 'broken, unsound': Beekes 2010 s.v., *Suppl.* 1064 αἴνιγμα σαθρόν, a 'deceitful riddle', [Eur.] *Rhes.* 639 σαθροῖς λόγοισιν 'deceitful words'.

1191 τἄδικ' εὖ λέγειν 'to speak well of unjust deeds', a complaint often made by characters in Euripides: *Hipp.* 503 εὖ λέγεις γὰρ αἰσχρὰ δέ, *Pho.* 526 οὐκ εὖ λέγειν χρὴ μὴ 'πὶ τοῖς ἔργοις καλοῖς, frr. 528 and 583. Contrast 293–4n.

1192 'it is true that those who made a thorough investigation of these matters are clever'. Hecuba concedes that evil-doers like Polymestor may be able to come up with speeches that are not obviously unconvincing, but she argues that these justifications ultimately fail.

μὲν οὖν: 798n.

1193 διὰ τέλους 'until the end', not simply because human fortunes change (*Suppl.* 270, *HF* 103, fr. 273.3) but because, 'with time', evildoers are punished, esp. by Justice: Hes. *Op.* 217–18, Noussia-Fantuzzi 2010 on Solon 13.8 and 4.16 West, Garvie on Aesch. *Cho.* 61–5, Eur. *Hcld.* 941. Hecuba does not state explicitly that justice or the gods acted through her: that would sound presumptuous and would mean encroaching upon Agamemnon's prerogatives as a judge.

1194 ἐξήλυξε 'escaped', aor. from ἐξαλύσκω.

1195 μοι 'from my point of view': dative of person from whose perspective things are viewed ('ethical dative': Smyth §1486).

τὸ μὲν σόν 'what concerns you', Agamemnon: 51–2n.

ὧδε ... ἔχει 'is thus'.

φροιμίοις 'in <my> proem', the first section of a speech, as in 181, Aesch. *Ag.* 829, Eur. *El.* 1060 and, in the poetic plural (265n.) as here, *HF* 538. The term will later become standard in rhetorical theory: [Arist.] *Rh. Al.* 29.

1196 τόνδε 'this man here', i.e. Polymestor, in a contemptuous tone: 674n.

1197 ὃς φῄς 'you who claim'. For the dramatic shift from the third (1196 τόνδε) to the second person ('you', implied by the verb φῄς) see Soph. *OC* 1354, Eur. *HF* 807, Diggle 1994: 98.

1197–8 Ἀχαιῶν ... ἕκατι 'in order to set the Greeks free from the same labour twice over, and for Agamemnon's sake'. The present participle ἀπαλλάσσων expresses purpose (*El.* 1024, Smyth §2965, K–G I.141, II.86). For the syntax see 346–8n.

1199–1204 Hecuba, a barbarian, stresses that Greeks and non-Greeks cannot be friends (1199 φίλον), or related by marriage (1202 κηδεύσων) or by blood (1203 συγγενής). All these relationships are governed by the principle of positive reciprocity, which, Hecuba argues, cannot apply to the interaction between Greeks and barbarians. She is contradicting her previous statements about expectations of positive reciprocity from Odysseus (276n.) and Agamemnon (834n.). Hecuba is using against Polymestor what she has learned through suffering in the very play we have watched so far, and puts Agamemnon in the position of not being able to disagree with her words: see Introduction, section 5.

1199–1201 ἀλλ', ὦ κάκιστε ... οὐδ' ἂν δύναιτο 'But, you vilest scoundrel, first of all, the barbarian race would never be friends with the Greeks, nor could it be.'

πρῶτον: Hecuba does not explicitly list a 'second' point. Her second objection begins at 1206, where she shows that avarice was the main motive driving Polymestor.

οὐδ' 'nor' is the expected form after the negative οὔποτ' (Smyth §2938; K–G II.293–4). The MS text οὔποτε ... οὔτ' is not ungrammatical (K–G II. 288–9, Finglass on Soph. *El.* 1412), but the addition introduced by οὔτε is presented as an 'afterthought' (Denniston 509–10), which would be less appropriate in this tightly constructed speech.

καί: 515–17n.

1201 χάριν 'favour'. Polymestor claimed to have acted out of *charis* in a final passing remark (1175), and Hecuba attacks him with full force on this point, shifting the debate on the question of reciprocity, and away from the question of self-defence (1204–5n.).

1202 κηδεύσων τινά 'with the hope of establishing marriage ties with someone' of the Greeks. Kovacs 1996: 69 conjectures τινί, since the verb κηδεύω normally takes the dative. The accusative is defended by the passive ἐκηδεύθη: Mastronarde on *Pho.* 347–8.

1203 συγγενὴς ὤν: Hecuba mockingly suggests that Polymestor considered himself a blood relative of Agamemnon, which is of course impossible. Greek cities used the language of συγγένεια to indicate a common mythical kinship: Curty 1995: 216–17.

ἢ τίν' αἰτίαν ἔχων 'or what other reason did you have?'

1204–5 ἢ σῆς ἔμελλον γῆς τεμεῖν βλαστήματα | πλεύσαντες αὖθις; 'Or were they [i.e. the Greeks] going to ravage the crops of your land, sailing again [i.e. in the direction of Troy]?' Hecuba does not discuss Polymestor's first and main claim (1138–44) that he acted out of self-interest, a difficult claim to disprove. Instead, she chooses to refute his claims to have acted in accordance with 'friendship', and stresses greed as his main motivation.

1205 τίνα δοκεῖς πείσειν τάδε; 'Who do you think you will persuade of this?' In tragedy, the rhetorical question with δοκεῖς is found esp. in *agōn* speeches: *Alc.* 691, *Hipp.* 958, *Suppl.* 537, Battezzato 2000b: 164–8. Asyndeton is frequent in the passage, both contrastive (1205, 1206) and explanatory (1208) (Smyth §2167).

1207 κέρδη τὰ σά 'your desire for gain', a desire typical of commerce (Kurke 1999: 76–7, 80–9), not of guest-friendship or reciprocity (Seaford 1994: 14–23).

1208 ἐπεί '<I say this> because'. ἐπεί 'introduces a fact which proves the correctness of what has been said' before (Moorhouse 1982: 304); the fact is expressed in the rhetorical question that here follows δίδαξον τοῦτο, as at Soph. *El.* 352 ἐπεὶ δίδαξον, ἢ μάθ' ἐξ ἐμοῦ, τί..., *OC* 969–73.

πῶς 'How come that...?' The interrogative adverb introduces the long question, but is then replaced by τί οὐ at 1211, an interrogative phrase with similar meaning.

1210 Ἕκτορός τ' ἤνθει δόρυ 'and Hector's spear flourished', i.e. his military prowess was at its peak. The verb ἀνθεῖν (lit. 'to blossom'), like θάλλειν ('to sprout, to blossom'), often means 'to prosper': Pind. *Ol.* 13.23 Ἄρης ἀνθεῖ, Eur. *Hipp.* 422. The metaphor paraphrases, in more complex and emotional language, 18 Ἕκτωρ... ηὐτύχει δορί.

1211 τί οὐ 'Why did you not...?' The hiatus is permitted because τί had a special prosodic status, comparable to that of an exclamation: 820, Mastronarde on *Pho.* 878, Garvie on Aesch. *Pers.* 696, K-B 1.196–7. The interpolated δ' would be non-connective ('apodotic'), a usage extremely rare in Euripides: Denniston 177, 182–3.

1211–12 χάριν | θέσθαι 'to do a favour' (1201n.).

1213 ἢ ζῶντ' ἦλθες Ἀργείοις ἄγων; 'or why did you not go to the Greeks bringing him alive?' Polydorus would have been a useful hostage for the Greeks when they besieged Troy.

1214 ἡνίχ' ἡμεῖς οὐκέτ' ἦμεν ἐν φάει 'when we were not safe anymore'. For the metaphorical use of φάος 'light' in reference to 'safety' see Graziosi and Haubold on *Il.* 6.6, Griffith on Soph. *Ant.* 600. The phrase 'to be ἐν φάει' normally means 'to be alive': 248n., 415n.

1215 καπνός δ' ἐσήμην· ἄστυ πολεμίοις ὕπο 'and the smoke made it clear that the city <was> controlled by the enemies', echoing Aesch. *Ag.* 818 'the fallen city is still now easy to recognise (εὔσημος) by the smoke (καπνῶι)'. On the staging see 823n. We must supply a participle ὄν 'being' in reference to ἄστυ: 423, K–G II.66. At the end of the line, the MS reading πολεμίων ὕπο presupposes a rare meaning of ὑπό + gen. 'under the power of' (*Od.* 19.114), not attested in tragedy. For the dative after ὑπό in this meaning see *Hcld.* 231, *Or.* 889.

1216 ξένον ... ἑστίαν: the line is framed by two rhetorically and ideologically charged words: a 'guest' should respect the 'fireplace' of his *xenoi*.

1217 ἄκουσον 'listen', echoing Polymestor at 1137. Hecuba, unlike Polymestor, addresses her opponent, not the judge, as she will do in *Tro.* 923.

ὡς φαίνηι κακός 'how you are shown <to be> wicked', 'how your wickedness is made evident' by what I am going to say. The MS reading φανῆις (2nd p. sg. subj. aor. pass.) gives the wrong meaning ('in order that your wickedness be made evident', as if Polymestor could avoid that outcome by not listening).

1218 χρῆν σ' 'you should have'. In conditional sentences expressing unreal conditions, ἄν may be omitted with the imperfect of verbs expressing obligation (Smyth §2313).

1219 'the gold that you claim to have not as yours but as this man's'.

τοῦδ' 'this man's', lit. 'of him', probably refers to Agamemnon (Meridor 1979–80: 9–10). Polymestor in fact had not said anything of the kind, but Hecuba has some justification in putting these words into his mouth. Polymestor claimed to be a friend of Agamemnon; he had a duty to share his wealth with him at this time. 'The property of friends is a common property', as the proverb said (Eur. *Or.* 735, Arist. *Eth. Nic.* 1159b31). Matthiessen and others refer τοῦδ' to Polydorus, which does not correspond to what Polymestor said or implied; it is also inappropriate for Hecuba to say that Polydorus should have the gold, now that he is dead.

1220–1 πενομένοις τε καὶ ... ἀπεξενωμένοις 'to people who were in a state of deprivation and living for a long time away from their homeland'. A short participle phrase (πενομένοις) is followed by a second, much longer, one, straddling over two lines: the enjambment χρόνον | πολύν and the caesura of πατρώιας : γῆς separate two strictly connected words.

1222–3 'But even now you do not endure [τολμᾶις, as in 323] to let it go from your hand; instead, you still obdurately continue (καρτερεῖς) to keep it in your palace.'

1224 τρέφων is conditional: 'if you had taken care'.

1225 σώσας τε τὸν ἐμόν 'and if you had saved my <son>'. τὸν ἐμόν refers to 1224 παῖδ': 1047n.

1226–7 'Fine people are the best friends in difficult times: prosperous circumstances (τὰ χρηστά) in and of themselves (αὔθ') get friends in every case [ἕκαστα, lit. 'all and severally'].' This commonplace (Mastronarde on *Med.* 561, Bond on *HF* 57–9) once more brands Polymestor as a 'bad friend'.

1229 'my child would have constituted (ὑπῆρχ') a big treasure for you'. On the interlaced word order cf. 44n. *Xenia* is better than money, since it does not fail at crucial moments; so is *philia* (*El.* 565).

1231 χρυσοῦ τ' ὄνησις οἴχεται παῖδές τε σοί 'the possibility of enjoying your gold is gone and your children <are dead>'. In reference to παῖδές τε σοί we must supply the verb οἴχονται ('are gone', i.e. 'are dead') from οἴχεται earlier in the line.

1232 αὐτός τε πράσσεις ὧδε 'and you are in this condition': Hecuba uses a euphemistic expression, avoiding an explicit mention of the blinding.

σοί: Hecuba changes addressee in mid-verse, returning to Agamemnon again (as in 1187–95), and reminding him indirectly of the promise he made at 852–6. She argues that 'defending' (ἀρκέσεις, fut. of ἀρκέω) or 'benefiting' (1235 εὖ δράσεις) is an action which can be directed only towards trustworthy friends or *xenoi*. If Agamemnon helped Polymestor, Agamemnon would be a *kakos* in the ethical, social and religious sense: Polymestor is a 'guest-friend who is disrespectful of divine laws and untrustworthy, unholy, unjust'. εὐσεβής 'pious' and ὅσιος 'holy' overlap in meaning: Pl. *Euthphr.* 12e, Peels 2016: 68–106. Cf. 804n.

1235 οὐχ ... οὐ: after οὔτ' ... οὔτε 'nor ... nor' (1234) we would have expected another οὔτε. Hecuba breaks off with a series in asyndeton, conveying a stronger sense of urgency and indignation: *Hipp.* 1321–2, Denniston 510.

1236–7 αὐτὸν δὲ ... τοιοῦτον ὄντα 'We will say that you are pleased with evil people since you are like them (τοιοῦτον) yourself.'

1237 δεσπότας δ' οὐ λοιδορῶ 'not that I mean to abuse my masters'. Hecuba offers an apology for the potential insult implicit in the previous sentence.

1238–9 The chorus take up Hecuba's initial reflection (1187–94), stressing that good reasons 'always give starting points (ἀφορμάς) for good speeches'. ἀφορμαί is 'a favourite word of Euripides in this quasi-technical rhetorical/legal sense (Dodds on *Ba.* 266–9, Wilamowitz on *HF* 236)': Mastronarde on *Pho.* 199.

φεῦ φεῦ 'ah!', expressing admiration (LSJ s.v. II, *Hcld.* 552).

1240–51 At first Agamemnon adopts an apologetic tone towards Polymestor, stressing that 'it is a burdensome task for me to pronounce judgement on other people's misfortunes' (1240). He claims it is compulsory (1241 ἀνάγκη) for him to do so, since he has taken up the 'matter' (1242) previously (1130–1), and he wants to avoid shame (1241 αἰσχύνην) and blame (1249 ψόγον), a prime concern of his (863n.). Agamemnon's tone changes into harsh generalisations on the moral inferiority of barbarians (1247n.), and his speech ends with an insulting couplet (1250–1n.).

1243–4 οὔτ' ἐμὴν ... χάριν | οὔτ' ... Ἀχαιῶν 'not as a favour towards me or the Greeks': 855n., 1175–7n. Agamemnon ignores Polymestor's point, that he acted out of self interest or in the interests of the Thracians (1138–44), and addresses Hecuba's.

1245 echoes 27.

1247 'Perhaps killing guests is a light matter among you.' Agamemnon manipulates an ethnographer's phrase, παρά + dat. = 'in the usage of', which implies respect for other people's habits (Hdt. 1.10.3, 8.105.2, 9.107.1; see the parody in Ar. *Av.* 755–68), to imply the inferiority of barbarians (1129n.). Cf. the similar phrase at *Andr.* 437, on the moral inferiority of the Spartans. ξενοκτονεῖν is indeed the habit of the barbarian Taurians (*IT* 53) and Egyptians (*Hel.* 155).

1248 δέ γ' 'however' is 'strongly adversative' (Denniston 155), in response to the opinion attributed to the Thracians at 1247.

αἰσχρόν: cf. 311, 1241 αἰσχύνην.

1249 μὴ ἀδικεῖν is scanned – ᴗ –. Eta and alpha coalesce in synecphonesis: West 1982: 13.

1250–1 Agamemnon takes up his earlier (1122–3n.) etymological play on τολμάω ('dare') and τλῆναι ('endure'), and aligns himself with the chorus' tit-for-tat theory of punishment (1086n.), using language reminiscent of Aeschylus (953–1295n.).

τὰ μὴ καλὰ | ... τὰ μὴ φίλα 'what is morally wrong ... what is unpleasant <to you>'. The sound repetition is typical of Agamemnon's quasi-Gorgianic style of speech (850–63n.).

1252–95 Two stichomythic dialogues conclude the *agōn*, one ending in verbal, the other in physical, violence. Polymestor reports a prediction of Hecuba's transformation into a dog and her death by drowning (1259–74). When he also prophesies Cassandra's and Agamemnon's death by the hand of Clytemnestra, the king intervenes in the dialogue, and orders his attendants to seize him and to abandon him on a desert island (1283–5).

Hecuba's transformation into a bitch is not securely attested before Euripides, here and in fr. 62h 'you will become a dog, darling of torch-bearing Hecate', probably from his *Alexander* (415 BCE). Other sources include *PMG* 965, an anonymous, undatable fragment which describes Hecuba as 'a fiery-eyed bitch: Ida and island Tenedos | and the Thracian crags that love the wind | listen to the loud harsh crying | from her grizzled jaws' (trans. Mossman 1995: 35), Lycoph. *Alex.* 1174–88, Cic. *Tusc.* 3.63, Ov. *Met.* 13.565–75 (Introduction, sections 6 and 7).

Playing down the transformation into a bitch and the death by drowning, as many commentators have done, is implausible: Hecuba's end is tinged with negative symbolism and cruel, self-imposed suffering. 'Dog' is a term of abuse in reference to women (Graziosi and Haubold on *Il.* 6.344, Franco 2014). Artemis punished a woman who refused hospitality by transforming her into a dog; 'later, taking pity on her, the goddess transformed her back into a human being' (Call. fr. 461). For human beings, animal metamorphoses in general are a punishment: Forbes Irving 1990: esp. 63 and 140 on Hecuba. Death by drowning is, obviously, an object of special dread, and is inflicted as a terrible punishment by the gods (*Od.* 4. 499–511, Eur. *Tro.* 73–97, Posidippus 89–94 Austin and Bastianini).

Many modern critics see Hecuba's transformation as a symbol of her moral degradation and (with a somewhat post-Enlightenment sensibility) as a condemnation of her excessive and cruel revenge, which included the killing of Polymestor's innocent children (Introduction, section 6, n. 65). Others see the transformation as conferring heroic status (Kovacs 1987: 111–12), argue that 'the dog seems to be emblematic of the maternal impulse' (Gregory 1999: xxxiv), or (Burnett 1998: 173–6) stress that the place of her death will become a landmark ('the tomb of the dog': 1273n.), as if this implied that her fate was not cruel and unusual.

It is true that Hecuba at 1259–74 apparently shows 'no horror or fear' at her fate, and is 'relatively unmoved' by the prophecy (Mossman 1995: 199–200), but, like the audience, she is puzzled by its bizarre details (1263n.) and waits for Polymestor to complete his narration. Her lack of emotion during the stichomythic exchange is parallel to that of Oedipus at the revelation of his identity (Soph. *OT* 1155–81): both characters suppress expression of emotion until the final revelation. Hecuba's response to the prophecy, 'I do not care, now that at least you have paid your just penalty' (1274), implies that, under other circumstances, she would have minded her metamorphosis and manner of death very much. Similarly Orestes claims he accepts death, provided he avenges his father by killing Clytemnestra: see Garvie on Aesch. *Cho.* 438 'may I die after killing her'. Orestes does not imply that death is pleasant or that he actually desires it: the rhetoric of these statements simply suggests that revenge is more important than life.

1252–3 γυναικός ... ἡσσώμενος | δούλης 'defeated by a woman ... who is a slave' (one substantive in apposition to another: 790n.) This enjambment, here reinforced by hyperbaton, emphasises the run-on word (Dik 2007: 178): not just a woman, by a *slave* woman at that. The present ἡσσώμενος has a perfective meaning: see Mastronarde on *Pho.* 1232.

ὡς ἔοιχ' 'as seems clear to me'.

1253 ὑφέξω τοῖς κακίοσιν δίκην 'I will pay the penalty to my social inferiors'. ὑφέξω: fut. from ὑπέχω. For the phrase see Soph. *OT* 552. In a just society, esp. in a democracy, 'the social inferior, if he is right, wins over the powerful' (Eur. *Suppl.* 437; see Soph. *OC* 880). Polymestor, being unaccustomed to the equality of law typical of Greek civilisation (805n.), finds it incredible that a slave woman, whom he judges his inferior because of gender and social status, should be given victory over him.

1254 Hecuba gloats over her victory (as she will also in 1258). This would not work if the line were spoken by Agamemnon, as in most MSS. The structure of the dialogue is also simpler and more effective if Agamemnon does not speak until provoked (1280).

1255 The genitives τέκνων and τῶνδ' ὀμμάτων ... ἐμῶν depend respectively on οἴμοι and τάλας, and express the cause of sorrow (Smyth §1407, K–G 1.388–9).

1256 ἀλγεῖς; τί δ'; ἦ 'μὲ παιδὸς οὐκ ἀλγεῖν δοκεῖς; 'You suffer? What then? Do you think I do not suffer for my child?' The question τί δ'; means 'and what <of this that follows>?' (Denniston 176, Collard 2005: 378). ἦ introduces a question, as often (Denniston 282–3). The text of MS B (corrupted in MO) τί δαί με παιδὸς οὐκ ἀλγεῖν δοκεῖς; 'why then do you not think that I suffer for my child?' gives absurd meaning. δαί is a colloquial expression, rare in tragedy (Kannicht on *Hel.* 1246, Stevens 1976: 45–6).

1257 The indignant question is in line with Polymestor's aggressiveness: 1124, Soph. *Ai.* 1346 σὺ ταῦτ', Ὀδυσσεῦ, τοῦδ' ὑπερμαχεῖς ἐμοί;, Eur. *Ba.* 1032–3. Most editors print the line as a statement, but this makes it sound like a resigned comment, as at *HF* 708 ὕβριν ... ὑβρίζεις, where Amphitryon feigns meekness.

ὑβρίζουσ': in this instance, *hybris* may be defined as 'the committing of acts of intentional insult, of acts which deliberately inflict shame and dishonour on others' (Fisher 1992: 148). In other cases, however, *hybris* is presented as 'a subjective attitude or disposition which can be construed as an implicit affront' (Cairns 1996: 10).

ὦ πανοῦργε σύ 'you rascal', a colloquial insult (Ar. *Ran.* 35, Dionysus speaking to the servant).

1259 'But soon you will not <be happy any more>, when the seawater ...' Polymestor starts reporting the prophecy. The syntax is completed in the next line: Mastronarde 1979: 2–73, esp. 55.

1260 '... perhaps will bring me by ship to the borders of Greece?'

μῶν signals that what follows is a surmise, expressed with apprehension: 752–3n.

ναυστολήσηι is aor. subj., as required after ἡνίκ' ἄν (1259).

1261 'on the contrary [μὲν οὖν: Denniston 475], it will envelop you once you fall from the masthead'. Polymestor corrects Hecuba's surmise. On some types of large ships, 'the mainmast was stout enough to support a main-top [or masthead] (*karchesion* in Greek ...) girdled by a protective railing' (Casson 1971: 233). This implies that Hecuba will be deported on board a large warship.

1262 'Who will force me to jump?', lit. 'At whose command being subjected to forced leaps?' Hecuba expects to be thrown into the sea (*katapontismos*), as a form of capital punishment or human sacrifice: O'Connor-Visser 1987: 217–20, Hughes 1991: 125 and 160–2. Falling into the sea is also a metaphor of rebirth (Nagy 1990: 227–39), but Hecuba's only afterlife is as a geographical landmark, named after the animal she is transformed into, not after her own name (1273n.).

1263 The disconcerting detail that Hecuba, as a dog, will climb up the mast suggests that vestiges of human capabilities will survive in her after the transformation. She climbs like a human being, and commits suicide either as a consequence of mental disturbance or because she refuses life as an animal.

ναός 'of the ship', gen. of ναῦς, a non-Attic form (note the long alpha and the lack of quantitative metathesis), attested alongside Attic νεώς (*IT* 102).

ἀμβήσηι 'you will climb up', fut. from ἀμβαίνω (= ἀναβαίνω). Tragedians occasionally use the shorter form ἀν- instead of ἀνά ('apocope': Smyth §75D). Here the shorter form avoids a resolution in the fourth longum, which is normally avoided with words of this shape in the early plays of Euripides: Devine and Stephens 1981: 51–2, Parker on *Alc.* 526. At this stage of his career, Euripides favours a more poetic form and a metrically stricter style of composition, distancing the language of tragedy from that of everyday speech and comedy. Cf. 1281n.

1264 ὑποπτέροις νώτοισιν 'with wings on my back?' [lit. 'with my winged back']. Hecuba mockingly introduces the theme of metamorphosis, which Polymestor takes up in his reply.

ἢ ποίωι τρόπωι; 'or in what <other> way?' For other instances where a form of ἄλλος is implied see *IT* 511, *Ba.* 1290.

1265 πυρσ' ἔχουσα δέργματα 'having fire-red eyes', 'glancing fire'. Euripides often uses δέργμα 'glance' to mean 'eye' (Mastronarde on *Pho.* 660). Polymestor draws attention to the contrast between his blindness and Hecuba's ferocious glare. In Greek literature, angry people, dangerous beasts and hellish monsters glance fire. Hecuba fits all these categories. Cf. *Il.* 1.104, 13.474, *h.Hom.Merc.* 194 χαροποί δὲ κύνες, Eur. *Ion* 1262–3, and Ar. *Ran.* 292–4 (Empousa is a 'dog' whose 'whole face is lit up with fire'). The link with Empousa is particularly strong, since many sources identify her and Hecate: Ar. fr. 515; Brown 1991: 47–8. Hecuba and Hecate are connected by etymology and geography (1252–95n., 1270n.). Cf. also Charon's fiery eyes in Verg. *Aen.* 6.300 *stant lumina flamma*, Chantraine 1968–80 on χαροπός, χάρων, Χάρων. Polymestor does not explain whether Hecuba will climb up the mast before her metamorphosis, or will have human abilities as a metamorphosed dog. He gives few details about the prophecy, as part of his rhetorical strategy to make it seem more frightening, and to increase his power in controlling the dialogue: the prophecy is the only bargaining tool left to him.

1266 μορφῆς τῆς ἐμῆς μετάστασιν 'the change of my form'. The word μεταμόρφωσις and its cognates are not securely attested until the fourth century (Callisthenes 124 F 56 *FGrHist*).

1267 Thrace hosted an 'oracular shrine of Dionysus', probably on Mount Pangaeum (Diggle 1994: 325, Hdt. 7.111, [Eur.] *Rhes.* 970–3).

1268–9 Polymestor does not specify the circumstances under which he received the prophecy which failed to warn him about his impending fate. One can suppose that he asked the oracle about Hecuba's fate (or Troy's fate) when he planned the murder of Polydorus, or that Dionysus volunteered the prediction. Polymestor wrongly assumed that the god told him everything that mattered. Croesus makes analogous erroneous assumptions at Hdt. 1.47–55 and 85–91. Oracular answers at times only partially match the question: Soph. *OT* 788–93, Hdt. 4.150.3. Oracles at times purposely mislead questioners who plan impious actions, so that they will commit the crime and be rightly punished: Hdt. 1.158–9, T. Harrison 2000: 125 (irrelevant answers) and 146–8 (punishment).

1270 θανοῦσα δ' ἢ ζῶσ' ἐνθάδ' ἐκπλήσω φάτιν; 'Will I fulfil the prophecy by dying or by living here?' Cf. Hdt. 1.43.3 ἐξέπλησε ... τὴν φήμην. The MS text ἐκπλήσω βίον 'will I fulfil, finish my life' is nonsensical in the context: if Hecuba finishes her life here she will die here, and the question becomes pointless.

Euripides is the first author to locate the death of Hecuba near Troy, here and (more vaguely) at *Tro.* 427–30. Nicander (fr. 62 Gow and Schofield 1953) follows this version, whereas Lycoph. *Alex.* 1174–88 mentions Hecuba's metamorphosis, but locates her cenotaph at Pachynos, in Sicily. Stesichorus locates the death of Hecuba in Lycia: his fr. 108 narrates that Apollo was the father of Hector and fr. 109 states that, when Troy was sacked, the god took Hecuba, his former bedmate, to Lycia (Finglass and Davies 2014: 439–40). The very name Hecuba is etymologically linked with ἑκαβόλος, an epithet of Apollo, and with Hecate (1252–95n., 1265n.): Chantraine 1968–80 s.vv. Ἑκάβη, ἐκηβόλος, Ἑκάτη, Janko on *Il.* 16.716–20.

1271 τύμβωι δ' ὄνομα σῶι κεκλήσεται ... 'the name given to your tomb will be ...' The name is given at 1273. Here ὄνομα is the subject and κεκλήσεται takes the dative τύμβωι ... σῶι (Ruijgh 1976: 388); cf. Pl. *Cra.* 385d8–9 καλεῖν ἑκάστωι ὄνομα. The syntax is peculiar: we would expect 'tomb' to be the subject of the sentence, as in other cases where ὄνομα occurs with the passive of καλέω: Hdt. 1.173.3 οἱ δὲ ἐκαλέοντο... οὔνομα... Τερμίλαι, Thuc. 2.37.1, K–G 1.326, Cooper and Krüger 2002: 2006–7. Final prophecies in plays of Euripides often explain the creation of place names in reference to characters in the play: see κεκλήσεται in *El.* 1275, *Hel.* 1674.

1272 μορφῆς ἐπωιδὸν μή τι τῆς ἐμῆς ἐρεῖς; 'I fear that you will say some spell that will change my shape.' A question introduced by μή may express apprehension (Barrett on *Hipp.* 799, Diggle 1981: 120 and 1994: 160).

ἐπωιδόν... τι 'something that casts a spell over': Hecuba suggests that in fact Polymestor will cause her metamorphosis by casting a spell, or simply naming the transformation (on name magic see 1276n.). Thrace is the land of Orpheus (*Alc.* 966–9, *Ba.* 561–4, *Cycl.* 646 ἐπωιδὴν Ὀρφέως).

1273 'the mound of the wretched bitch, a sign for sailors'. This refers to Cynossema, 'the sign/mound of the bitch', a landmark found in the 'narrowest point of the Hellespont' (Hornblower on Thuc. 8.104.5). See also Strabo, Book 7, fr. 21 Radt, Forbes Irving 1990: 207–10, Buxton 2009: 57–9. Hecuba's burial recalls Achilles' tomb by the Hellespont, built to be visible to sailors (37–9n., *Od.* 24.80–4).

1274 'I do not care, now that I have punished you.' Hecuba sees her fate, as predicted by Polymestor, as unpleasant per se: she is willing to accept it only in the context of her defeat of Polymestor (1252–95n.).

1275 Polymestor divulges another shocking detail of the prophecy in order to hurt Hecuba. She cannot claim she does not care, as she did at 1274; she can only wish it does not come true. The death of Cassandra at the hands of Clytemnestra is already attested at *Od.* 11.422; on the traditions on Cassandra see Mazzoldi 2001.

καὶ ... γ᾽ 'and in addition': Denniston 157.

1276 ἀπέπτυσ᾽ 'I avert the bad omen'. The verb literally means 'I spat out': cf. *IT* 1161, *Hipp.* 614. Polymestor, by mentioning death (1275), breaks a taboo (1006n.), and Hecuba attempts to turn the bad luck against him, protecting her daughter Cassandra. Averting bad omens was a crucial speech act: see Cic. *Div.* 1.102–4. Spitting out was considered a way to avert bad luck (Gow on Theoc. 6.39). Hecuba almost certainly does not actually spit onstage, which would be too undignified for tragedy, but uses a 'performative' verb: simply mentioning the act is equivalent to performing it (e.g. 'I swear', 'I promise'). The aorist indicates that the speaker considers the action completed when he or she pronounced the verb; it must be translated as a present in English: Lloyd 1999: 26–8, Bary 2012.

1277 οἰκουρὸς πικρά 'a harmful guardian of the house', a definition echoing Aesch. *Ag.* 155 οἰκονόμος δολία μνάμων μῆνις τεκνόποινος (Thalmann 1993: 154), and 1626 οἰκουρός (in reference to Aegisthus, derogatorily presented as feminine).

1278 μήπω μανείη Τυνδαρὶς τοσόνδε παῖς 'My wish is that the daughter of Tyndareus [= Clytemnestra: 269n.] will never act so crazily.' For μήπω = 'never' (instead of 'not yet') see Dawe 1964: 123, Eur. *Hcld.* 357, Soph. *OT* 105. Hecuba sympathises with Agamemnon, who somehow helped her; she expresses confidence in Clytemnestra's aristocratic breeding, in vain. An attribution to Agamemnon (Weil) is also possible, but it would be strange for Polymestor not to address him in the second person at 1279.

1279 Euripides and Sophocles repeatedly state that Agamemnon was killed with an axe (Soph. *El.* 99, Eur. *El.* 160, 1160, *Tro.* 361–2), not with a sword, as in Aeschylus and Homer (*Od.* 11.424; Prag 1991).

καὐτόν γε τοῦτον 'and <she will kill> this man himself'. The strongly attested variant σε ('and she will kill you ...') implies that Agamemnon speaks 1278. It is better to read γε even if one gives 1278 to Agamemnon: Polymestor speaks of Agamemnon in the third person, contemptuously: 501–2n., 674n., Soph. *OT* 1160.

1280 οὗτος σύ 'hey, you', a colloquialism: 1127n., Stevens 1976: 37–8, Dickey 1996: 154–8. Here the addition of σύ marks more strongly the beginning of dialogic contact between Agamemnon and Polymestor: Eur. *Or.* 1567, Soph. *OT* 1121. However, this usage does not rule out assigning 1278 to Agamemnon: both οὗτος (1127, Ar. *Av.* 57, 1044) and οὗτος σύ (Ar. *Thesm.* 224) can be used in mid-conversation. Agamemnon's colloquial and aggressive language (see also 1282n.) reflects his anger at Polymestor's predictions of future violence, which are a form of verbal retaliation.

κακῶν ἐρᾷς τυχεῖν; 'are you looking for trouble?', another colloquial phrase, as in Ar. *Av.* 135 πραγμάτων ἐρᾷς, 143.

1281 κτεῖν' 'kill me'. For the rhetoric cf. 1274n.

λουτρά: Polymestor has Agamemnon murdered in his bath, as at Aesch. *Ag.* 1109 (a version followed elsewhere by Euripides: *El.* 157, *Or.* 367), not at a banquet, as at *Od.* 11.411 (taken up by Soph. *El.* 193–200: see Finglass *ad loc.*).

ἀμμένει: corresponding to ἀναμένει in standard Attic. See 1263n.

1282 οὐχ ἕλξετ' αὐτόν ... ἐκποδών ...; 'drag him away!' In questions, the future with οὐ expresses an urgent imperative: Barrett on *Hipp.* 212–14, Smyth §1918.

1283 On the *antilabē* see 1127n. Polymestor's pleasure at the suffering of his enemies echoes Hecuba's (1256).

οὐκ ἐφέξετε στόμα; 'shut his mouth!' ἐφέξετε is future from ἐπέχω. For the idiom see *Hipp.* 660, Diggle 1981: 66.

1284 ἐγκλῄετ' 'go ahead and shut me up!' For the spelling cf. 486–7n.

εἴρηται γάρ 'for it has been said', i.e. 'because I finished my speech': in a quasi-metatheatrical remark, Polymestor notes the end of his spoken part (R. Hunter, personal communication). εἴρηται typically marks that a speaker has finished speaking: Mastronarde on *Pho.* 1012, *Or.* 1203.

1284–5 οὐχ ὅσον τάχος | νήσων ἐρήμων αὐτὸν ἐκβαλεῖτέ ποι; 'Banish him as soon as possible somewhere to one of the deserted islands.' The adverb ὅσον τάχος reinforces the imperatival future indicative (*Andr.* 1066–7), just as it reinforces imperatives (*El.* 421). For the genitive with adverbs of place see 1065, *Hipp.* 1153 ποῖ γῆς, Smyth §1439a. The variant που 'where' instead of ποι 'whither' would be acceptable only if the grammar of the sentence stressed the result of the action, as with verbs in the aorist or perfect tense: Soph. *Trach.* 40–1 ὅπου | βέβηκεν 'where he <has gone and> is now' (K–G 1.545). Banishment to a desert island (ἐς νῆσον ἐρήμην) is a punishment in *Od.* 3.270; cf. Soph. *Phil.* 2. We must assume that Agamemnon's attendants carry Polymestor away at this point.

1286 καὶ λίαν: the particle καί intensifies λίαν: *Alc.* 811, Denniston 317.

1287–90 Agamemnon had agreed to postpone the burial of Polyxena in order to allow Hecuba to punish Polymestor (894–7); the concomitant lack of favourable winds from 'the god' could be read as a sign of divine approval (900 and 902). Now Agamemnon urges Hecuba to resume the burial, and notices that favourable winds have started blowing. Explicit divine judgement is lacking, and the return of favourable winds may prompt different interpretations. The audience can assume that Agamemnon and Hecuba think that Hecuba's punishment was after all divinely sanctioned (Heath 1987a: 67); however, this would also imply that the gods now approve the enslavement of the Trojan women, a grim conclusion for Hecuba. In addition, the winds may remind the audience of the storms faced by Agamemnon on his way home (Aesch. *Ag.* 650–74, Kovacs 1987: 110); they certainly bring Agamemnon to his death, which may be seen as another just or divinely sanctioned punishment (cf. Aesch. *Ag.* 1337–42, 1406, 1579).

Many tragedies end with the announcement of a burial (Eur. *Med.* 1378, *Hcld.* 1030, Soph. *Ai.* 1378–1401, Dunn 1996: 55–7) or of a sea voyage (Eur. *Hel.* 1663: πνεῦμα δ' ἕξετ' οὔριον, Soph. *Phil.* 1465), events which suggest a sense of closure. The prophecy of Agamemnon's fate counteracts this, evoking a long chain of future events (Wohl 2015: 58–62). In Euripides' *Trojan Women*, the burial of Astyanax (1246) and the departure of the Trojan slave women by ship (1331–2) close the play.

1289–90 πνοὰς | ... τάσδε ... ὁρῶ 'I see these winds here'. Winds cannot be seen: Hecuba probably means 'I see (the effects caused by) these winds here'. Matthiessen, comparing Aesch. *Sept.* 103 κτύπον δέδορκα 'I saw a noise', interprets this as a synaesthesia.

πρὸς οἶκον ἤδη ... πομπίμους 'that are already sending us home'. For the active meaning of the adjective cf. *Hel.* 1073–4 πόμπιμοι ... πνοαί.

1292 τῶνδ' ἀφειμένοι πόνων 'free from the toils we endured here'. Euripides apparently has Agamemnon echo ironically the word of the watchman at Aesch. *Ag.* 1 'I ask the gods to free me from these toils' (Thalmann 1993: 154–5).

1293–5 The play ends, as often, with an anapaestic section delivered by the chorus (in this case, two anapaestic monometers and a paroemiac: 59–97n. 'Metre'): cf. Barrett on *Hipp.* 1462–6, Mastronarde on *Med.* 1415–19, Roberts 1987.

τῶν δεσποσύνων πειρασόμεναι | μόχθων 'to experience the hardships that our masters will impose on us'. The adjective has this meaning at Aesch. *Pers.* 587 δεσποσύνοισιν ἀνάγκαις 'the coercion imposed by their masters'.

στερρὰ γὰρ ἀνάγκη 'for coercion is painful'. Slavery is assimilated to physical constraints: Aesch. *PV* 1052 ἀνάγκης στερραῖς δίναις, Eur. *Alc.* 965–6 'I found nothing stronger than coercion' (Ἀνάγκας). For 'painful' see *Med.* 1031 στερρὰς ... ἀλγηδόνας. 'Necessity', the last word of the play, evokes one of its major themes (362, 584, 639, 847, 864–9n. and *passim*). The phrasing leaves room for other interpretations, as often with gnomic statements: 'for fate is obdurate' (e.g. Matthiessen). The reference to hardships imposed by the masters in the previous sentence suggests that here, as in 362, ἀνάγκη refers to slavery. Many other plays end on a thematically crucial word: Eur. *Cycl.* 709 Βακχίωι δουλεύσομεν, *Suppl.* 1234 σέβεσθαι, Aesch. *Pers.* 1077 γόοις, *Cho.* 1076 Ἄτης, *PV* 1093 πάσχω, Soph. *Trach.* 1278 Ζεύς.

WORKS CITED

1 EDITIONS AND COMMENTARIES

The following editions and commentaries are referred to by editor's name and, where necessary, reference to the passage of the ancient text. These editions and commentaries are cited by editor's name and year of publication when a reference is made to a passage in the introduction.

Allan, W. 2001: *Euripides: The children of Heracles*, Warminster
  2008: *Euripides: Helen*, Cambridge
Austin, C. and Olson, S. D. 2004: *Aristophanes: Thesmophoriazusae*, Oxford
Barrett, W. S. 1964: *Euripides: Hippolytos*, Oxford
Bond, G. W. 1981: *Euripides: Heracles*, Oxford
Collard, C. 1975: *Euripides: Supplices*, Groningen
Cropp, M. 2000: *Euripides: Iphigenia in Tauris*, Warminster
  2013: *Euripides: Electra*, 2nd edn, Oxford
Denniston, J. D. 1939: *Euripides: Electra*, Oxford
Denniston, J. D. and Page, D. L. 1957: *Aeschylus: Agamemnon*, Oxford
Diggle, J. 1970: *Euripides: Phaethon*, Cambridge
Dodds, E. R. 1959: *Plato: Gorgias*, Oxford
  1960: *Euripides: Bacchae*, 2nd edn, Oxford
Dover, K. J. 1968: *Aristophanes: Clouds*, Oxford
  1993: *Aristophanes: Frogs*, Oxford
Easterling, P. E. 1982: *Sophocles: Trachiniae*, Cambridge
Finglass, P. J. 2007: *Sophocles: Electra*, Cambridge
  2011: *Sophocles: Ajax*, Cambridge
Fraenkel, E. 1950: *Aeschylus: Agamemnon*, Oxford
Friis Johansen, H. and Whittle, E. W. 1980: *Aeschylus: The suppliants*, Copenhagen
Garvie, A. F. 1986: *Aeschylus: Choephori*, Oxford
  2009: *Aeschylus: Persae*, Oxford
Gow, A. S. F. 1950: *Theocritus*, Cambridge
Graziosi, B. and Haubold, J. 2010: *Homer: Iliad 6*, Cambridge.
Griffith, M. 1983: *Aeschylus: Prometheus bound*, Cambridge
  1999: *Sophocles: Antigone*, Cambridge
Hornblower, S. 1991–2008: *A commentary on Thucydides*, 3 vols. Oxford
Hunter, R. L. 1989: *Apollonius of Rhodes: Argonautica, book III*, Cambridge
Hutchinson, G. O. 1985: *Aeschylus: Septem contra Thebas*, Oxford
Janko, R. 1992: *The Iliad: a commentary*, vol. IV: *Books 13–16*, Cambridge
Jebb, R. C. 1887–1900: *Sophocles: the plays and fragments*, Cambridge
Kannicht, R. 1969: *Euripides: Helen*, Heidelberg

Liapis, V. 2012: *A commentary on the Rhesus attributed to Euripides*, Oxford
Mastronarde, D. J. 1994: *Euripides: Phoenissae*, Cambridge
  2002: *Euripides: Medea*, Cambridge
Page, D. L. 1938: *Euripides: Medea*, Oxford
Parker, L. P. E. 2007: *Euripides: Alcestis*, Oxford
Pearson, A. C. 1917: *The fragments of Sophocles*, 3 vols. Cambridge
Richardson, N. J. 1993: *The Iliad: a commentary*, vol. VI: *Books 21–24*, Cambridge
Schein, S. 2013: *Sophocles: Philoctetes*, Cambridge
Seaford, R. 1984: *Euripides: Cyclops*, Oxford
Sommerstein, A. H. 1989: *Aeschylus: Eumenides*, Cambridge
Stevens, P. T. 1971: *Euripides: Andromache*, Oxford
West, M. L. 1978: *Hesiod: Works and days*, Oxford
Wilamowitz-Moellendorff, U. von 1895: *Euripides: Herakles*, 2nd edn, Berlin
Wilkins, J. 1993: *Euripides: Heraclidae*, Oxford
Willink, C. W. 1989: *Euripides: Orestes*, 2nd edn. Oxford

2 MAIN EDITIONS OF *HECUBA*

The following editions of *Hecuba* are referred to by the editor's name only, or by editor's name and year of publication when a reference is made to a passage in the introduction.

Battezzato, L. 2010: *Euripide: Ecuba*, Milan
Biehl, W. 1997: *Textkritik und Formanalyse zur euripideischen Hekabe: ein Beitrag zum Verständnis der Komposition*, Heidelberg
Collard, C. 1991: *Euripides: Hecuba*, Warminster
Daitz, S. G. 1973: *Euripides: Hecuba*, Leipzig
Diggle, J. 1981–94: *Euripidis fabulae*, 3 vols., Oxford
Fix, T. 1855: *Euripidis fabulae*, Paris
Gregory, J. 1999: *Euripides: Hecuba*, Atlanta
Hadley, W. S. 1894: *Euripides: Hecuba*, Cambridge
Hartung, J. A. 1850: *Euripides' Werke*, vol. XI: *Hekabe*, Leipzig
Hermann, G. 1831 [1800]: *Euripidis Hecuba*, Leipzig
Kovacs, D. 1995: *Euripides: Children of Heracles, Hippolytus, Andromache, Hecuba*, Cambridge, Mass.
Matthiessen, K. 2010: *Euripides: Hekabe*, Berlin
Murray, G. 1902–13: *Euripidis fabulae*, 3 vols., Oxford
Nauck, A. 1869–71: *Euripidis tragoediae*, 3rd edn, 2 vols., Leipzig
Paley, F. A. 1872–80: *Euripides*, 2nd edn, 3 vols., London
Porson, R. 1802 [1797]: *Euripidis Hecuba*, 1st edn London, 2nd edn Cambridge

Prinz, R. 1883: *Euripidis fabulae*, vol. I part III: *Hecuba*, Leipzig
Prinz, R. and Wecklein, N. 1902: *Euripidis fabulae*, vol. I part III: *Hecuba*, 2nd edn, Leipzig
Synoudinou, K. 2005: *Euripides: Ekabe*, Athens
Tierney 1946: *Euripides: Hecuba*, Dublin
Weil, H. 1879: *Euripide: sept tragédies*, 2nd edn, Paris

3 WORKS CITED BY AUTHOR'S NAME AND YEAR OF PUBLICATION

Ademollo, F. 2011: *The Cratylus of Plato: a commentary*, Cambridge
Adkins, A. W. H. 1966: 'Basic Greek values in Euripides' *Hecuba* and *Hercules Furens*', *CQ* 16: 193–219
Aland, K. and Aland, B. 1981: *The text of the New Testament*, Grand Rapids and Leiden
Allan, R. J. 2003: *The middle voice in ancient Greek: a study in polysemy*, Amsterdam
Allan, W. 2000: *The Andromache and Euripidean tragedy*, Oxford
  2001: 'Euripides in Megale Hellas: some aspects of the early reception of tragedy', *G&R* 48: 67–86
  2013: 'The ethics of retaliatory violence in Athenian tragedy', *Mnemosyne* 66: 593–615
Allen, D. S. 2000: *The world of Prometheus: the politics of punishing in democratic Athens*, Princeton
  2005: 'Greek tragedy and law', in M. Gagarin and D. J. Cohen (eds.), *The Cambridge companion to ancient Greek law* (Cambridge) 374–93
Archibald, Z. 1998: *The Odrysian kingdom of Thrace: Orpheus unmasked*, Oxford
Asheri, D., Lloyd, A. B. and Corcella, A. 2007: *A commentary on Herodotus books I–IV*, Oxford
Baechle, N. 2007: *Metrical constraint and the interpretation of style in the tragic trimeter*, Lanham
Bain, D. 1977: *Actors and audience: a study of asides and related conventions in Greek drama*, Oxford
Barber, E. J. W. 1992: 'The peplos of Athena', in J. Neils (ed.), *Goddess and the polis: the Panathenaic festival in ancient Athens* (Princeton) 103–17
Barker, E. T. E. 2009: *Entering the agon: dissent and authority in Homer, historiography and tragedy*, Oxford
Barner, W. 1971: 'Die Monodie', in Jens 1971: 277–320
Barrett, J. 2002: *Staged narrative: poetics and the messenger in Greek tragedy*, Berkeley
Barrett, W. S. 1964: *Euripides: Hippolytos*, Oxford
  2007: *Greek lyric, tragedy, and textual criticism: collected papers*, Oxford

Bary, C. 2012: 'The ancient Greek tragic aorist revisited', *Glotta* 88: 31–53
Battezzato, L. 1995: *Il monologo nel teatro di Euripide*, Pisa
  1999–2000: 'Dorian dress in Greek tragedy', *ICS* 24.25: 343–62
  2000a: 'Gli aggettivi in -πετης: senso, accento e teorie bizantine nei vocabolari moderni', *Glotta* 76: 139–61
  2000b: 'Pragmatica e retorica delle frasi interrogative in Euripide', *MD* 44: 141–73
  2000c: Review of Gregory 1999, *CJ* 96: 223–8
  2000d: 'Synizesis in Euripides and the structure of the iambic trimeter: the case of θεός', *BICS* 44: 41–80
  2001: 'Euripides, "Electra" 300–301', *Mnemosyne* 54: 731–3
  2003a: 'I viaggi dei testi', in L. Battezzato (ed.), *Tradizione testuale e ricezione letteraria antica della tragedia greca* (Amsterdam) 7–31
  2003b: 'Ospitalità rituale, amicizia e charis nell'*Ecuba*', in O. Vox (ed.), *Ricerche euripidee* (Lecce) 13–41
  2005: 'Structural elements: lyric', in J. Gregory (ed.), *A companion to Greek tragedy* (Oxford) 149–66
  2008a: 'Colometria antica e pratica editoriale moderna', *QUCC* 89: 133–54
  2008b: *Linguistica e retorica della tragedia greca*, Rome
  2009a: 'Coerenza morfologica e database elettronici: il caso del peso prosodico minimo nel greco antico', in G. Ferrari (ed.), *Atti del convegno della Società di Linguistica Italiana 2006* (Rome) 179–204
  2009b: 'Notes and corrections on papyri of Euripides and Aristophanes (P. Oxy. LXVII 4557 and 4559; PSI VI 720)', *ZPE* 170: 9–15
  2009c: 'Porson e il testo dell'*Ecuba* di Euripide', *Lexis* 27: 155–79
  2009d: 'Textual criticism', in B. Graziosi, G. Boys-Stones and P. Vasunia (eds.), *Oxford handbook of Hellenic studies* (Oxford) 773–87
  2010: *Euripide: Ecuba*, Milan
  2012: 'The language of Sophocles', in A. Markantonatos (ed.), *Brill's companion to Sophocles* (Leiden) 305–24
  2014a: 'Gratitude/ingratitude', in Roisman 2014: 587–90
  2014b: 'La data della caduta di Troia nell'*Ecuba* di Euripide e nel ciclo epico: le Pleiadi, Sirio, Orione e la storiografia greca', *Lexis* 32: 183–95
  2014c: 'Meter and rhythm', in Roisman 2014:: 822–39
  2016: 'Shall I sing with the Delian maidens? Trojan and Greek identities in the songs of Euripides' *Hecuba*', *MD* 76: 139–55
  forthcoming-a: 'Euripides' *Hecuba* and the *Iliad*: ancient commentaries, Virgil and Ovid', in E. Cingano (ed.), *Commentaries on Greek texts: problems, methods and trends of ancient and Byzantine scholarship* (Rome)
  forthcoming-b: 'The language of Euripides', in Markantonatos (forthcoming)

Beekes, R. S. P. 2010: *Etymological dictionary of Greek*, Leiden
Bergson, L. 1959: 'Episches in den ῥήσεις ἀγγελικαί', *RhM* 102: 9–39
Bernabé, A. 1996: *Poetarum epicorum Graecorum: testimonia et fragmenta. Pars 1*, 2nd ed., Stuttgart
Bers, V. 1974: *Enallage and Greek style*, Leiden
    1997: *Speech in speech: studies in incorporated oratio recta in Attic drama and oratory*, Lanham
Bierl, A. 1991: *Dionysos und die griechische Tragödie: politische und 'metatheatralische' Aspekte im Text*, Tübingen
Björck, G. 1950: *Das Alpha impurum und die tragische Kunstsprache: attische Wort- und Stilstudien*, Uppsala
Blondell, R. 2013: *Helen of Troy: beauty, myth, devastation*, Oxford
Blundell, M. W. 1989: *Helping friends and harming enemies: a study in Sophocles and Greek ethics*, Cambridge
Bömer, F. 1982: *P. Ovidius Naso: Metamorphosen. Buch XII–XIII: Kommentar*, Heidelberg
Bonnechère, P. 1994: *Le sacrifice humain en Grèce ancienne*, Athens
Boter, G. 2012: 'The historical present of atelic and durative verbs in Greek tragedy', *Philologus* 156: 207–33
Breitenbach, W. 1934: *Untersuchungen zur Sprache der euripideischen Lyrik*, Stuttgart
Bremer, J. M. 1971: 'Euripides "Hecuba" 59–215: a reconsideration', *Mnemosyne* 24: 232–50
Bremmer, J. N. 2013: 'The Getty hexameters: date, author, and place', in C. A. Faraone and D. Obbink (eds.), *The Getty hexameters: poetry, magic, and mystery in ancient Selinous* (Oxford) 21–9
Brillante, C. 1988: 'Sul prologo dell'"Ecuba" di Euripide', *RFIC* 116: 429–47
    1991: *Studi sulla rappresentazione del sogno nella Grecia antica*, Palermo
Brown, C. G. 1991: 'Empousa, Dionysus and the Mysteries: Aristophanes, *Frogs* 285ff.', *CQ* 41: 41–50
Bruhn, E. 1899: *Sophokles, erklärt von F.W. Schneidewin und A. Nauck*, vol. VIII: *Anhang*, Berlin
Burgess, J. S. 2009: *The death and afterlife of Achilles*, Baltimore
Burkert, W. 1966: 'Greek tragedy and sacrificial ritual', *GRBS* 7: 87–121
    1983: *Homo necans: the anthropology of ancient Greek sacrificial ritual and myth*, Berkeley
    1985: *Greek religion: archaic and classical*, Oxford
Burnett, A. P. 1998: *Revenge in Attic and later tragedy*, Berkeley
Buxton, R. G. A. 1982: *Persuasion in Greek tragedy: a study of peitho*, Cambridge
    2009: *Forms of astonishment: Greek myths of metamorphosis*, Oxford

Cairns, D. L. 1993: *Aidōs: the psychology and ethics of honour and shame in ancient Greek literature*, Oxford
  1996: 'Hybris, dishonour, and thinking big', *JHS* 116: 1–32
  2005: 'Bullish looks and sidelong glances: social interaction and the eyes in ancient Greek culture', in D. L. Cairns (ed.), *Body language in the Greek and Roman worlds* (Swansea) 123–55
  2011: 'Veiling grief on the tragic stage', in D. Munteanu (ed.), *Emotion, gender, and genre in classical antiquity* (London) 15–33
  2012: 'Divine and human action in the *Oedipus Tyrannus*', in D. L. Cairns (ed.), *Tragedy and archaic Greek thought* (Swansea) 119–72
Carrara, P. 2005: 'I papiri dell'*Ecuba*', in G. Bastianini and A. Casanova (eds.), *Euripide e i papiri. Atti del convegno internazionale di studi, Firenze, 10–11 giugno 2004* (Florence) 145–55
Carter, D. M. 2011: *Why Athens? A reappraisal of tragic politics*, Oxford
Casali, S. 2007: 'Correcting Aeneas's voyage: Ovid's commentary on *Aeneid* 3', *TAPhA* 137: 181–210
Casson, L. 1971: *Ships and seamanship in the ancient world*, Princeton
Cavallo, G. 2002: *Dalla parte del libro: storie di trasmissione dei classici*, Urbino
Chantraine, P. 1933: *La formation des noms en grec ancien*, Paris
  1968–80: *Dictionnaire étymologique de la langue grecque: histoire des mots*, Paris
Cingano, E. 2007: 'Teseo e i Teseidi tra Troia e Atene', in P. Angeli Bernardini (ed.), *L'epos minore, le tradizioni locali e la poesia arcaica* (Pisa) 91–102
Clarke, M. 2004: 'The semantics of colour in the early Greek word-hoard', in L. Cleland, K. Stears and G. Davies (eds.), *Colours in the ancient Mediterranean world* (Oxford) 131–9
Cohen, B. 1997: 'Divesting the female breast of clothes in classical sculpture', in A. O. Koloski-Ostrow and C. Lyons (eds.), *Naked truths: women, sexuality, and gender in classical art and archaeology* (London and New York) 66–92
Cohen, D. J. 1995: *Law, violence, and community in classical Athens*, Cambridge
  2005: 'Theories of punishment', in M. Gagarin and D. J. Cohen (eds.), *The Cambridge companion to ancient Greek law* (Cambridge) 170–90
Collard, C. 1991: *Euripides: Hecuba*, Warminster
  2005: 'Colloquial language in tragedy: a supplement to the work of P. T. Stevens', *CQ* 55: 350–86
Collard, C. and Cropp, M. 2008a: *Euripides: fragments. Aegeus–Meleager*, Cambridge, Mass.
  2008b: *Euripides: fragments. Oedipus–Chrysippus. Other fragments*, Cambridge, Mass.

Collard, C., Cropp, M. and Gibert, J. 2004: *Selected fragmentary plays*, vol. II, Warminster
Connor, W. R. 1971: *The new politicians of fifth-century Athens*, Princeton
Conomis, N. C. 1964: 'The dochmiacs of Greek drama', *Hermes* 92: 23–50
Conte, G. B. 2013: *Ope ingenii: experiences of textual criticism*, Berlin
Coo, L. 2006: 'Four off-stage characters in Euripides' *Hecuba*', *Ramus* 35: 103–28
  2007: 'Polydorus and the *Georgics*: Virgil *Aeneid* 3.13–68', *MD* 59: 193–9
Cook, J. M. 1973: *The Troad: an archaeological and topographical study*, Oxford
Cooper, G. L. and Krüger, K. W. 1998: *Attic Greek prose syntax*, Ann Arbor
  2002: *Greek syntax: early Greek poetic and Herodotean syntax*, Ann Arbor
Coray, M. 2009: *Homers Ilias: Gesamtkommentar*, vol. VI: *19. Gesang, fasc. 2: Kommentar*, Berlin and New York
Craik, E. M. 2001: 'Medical reference in Euripides', *BICS* 45: 81–95
Cropp, M. 2000: *Euripides: Iphigenia in Tauris*, Warminster
  (forthcoming) 'The tactful chorus: Euripides, Hecuba 846–9', *Mouseion*
Cropp, M. and Fick, G. 1985: *Resolutions and chronology in Euripides: the fragmentary tragedies*, London
  2005: 'On the date of the extant "Hippolytus"', *ZPE* 154: 43–5
Csapo, E. 1999: 'Later Euripidean music', *ICS* 24–5: 399–426
Csapo, E., Goette, H. R., Green, J. R. and Wilson, P. 2014: *Greek theatre in the fourth century BC*, Berlin
Csapo, E. and Slater, W. J. 1994: *The context of ancient drama*, Ann Arbor
Curley, D. 2013: *Tragedy in Ovid: theater, metatheater, and the transformation of a genre*, Cambridge
Curty, O. 1995: *Les parentés légendaires entre cités grecques*, Geneva
Cuzzotti, C. 2017: *Buonarroti il giovane: Ecuba. Traduzione della tragedia di Euripide*, Lucca
Dale, A. M. 1968: *The lyric metres of Greek drama*, Cambridge
  1969: *Collected papers*, Cambridge
Damen, M. 1989: 'Actor and character in Greek tragedy', *Theatre Journal* 41: 316–40
Dangel, J. 1995: *Accius: œuvres (fragments)*, Paris
Dawe, R. D. 1964: *The collation and investigation of manuscripts of Aeschylus*, Cambridge
de Faveri, L. 2002: *Die metrischen Trikliniusscholien zur byzantinischen Trias des Euripides*, Stuttgart
de Jong, I. J. F. 1991: *Narrative in drama: the art of the Euripidean messenger-speech*, Leiden
  2001: *A narratological commentary on the Odyssey*, Cambridge
  2012: *Homer: Iliad, book XXII*, Cambridge
Dearden, C. 1999: 'Plays for export', *Phoenix* 53: 222–48
Debiasi, A. 2004: *L'epica perduta: Eumelo, il Ciclo, l'occidente*, Rome

Demargne, P. 1984: 'Athena', in L. Kahil (ed.), *LIMC* II.1: *Aphrodisias–Athena* (Zurich and Munich) 954–1044
Denniston, J. D. 1952: *Greek prose style*, Oxford
Derow, P. 1995: 'Herodotus readings', *Classics Ireland* 2: 29–51
Devine, A. M. and Stephens, L. D. 1981: 'Tribrach-shaped words in the tragic trimeter', *Phoenix* 35: 22–41
   1984: *Language and metre: resolution, Porson's bridge, and their prosodic basis*, Chico, Calif.
   1994: *The prosody of Greek speech*, New York
   2000: *Discontinuous syntax: hyperbaton in Greek*, New York
Di Benedetto, V. 1965: *La tradizione manoscritta euripidea*, Padua
Di Benedetto, V. and Medda, E. 1997: *La tragedia sulla scena: la tragedia greca in quanto spettacolo teatrale*, Turin
Dickey, E. 1996: *Greek forms of address: from Herodotus to Lucian*, Oxford
   2007: *Ancient Greek scholarship*, Oxford
Diggle, J. 1981: *Studies on the text of Euripides*, Oxford
   1984: *Euripidis fabulae*, vol. I, Oxford
   1991: *The textual tradition of Euripides' Orestes*, Oxford
   1994: *Euripidea: collected essays*, Oxford
Dik, H. 2007: *Word order in Greek tragic dialogue*, Oxford
Dindorf, W. 1863: *Scholia graeca in Euripidis tragoedias ex codicibus aucta et emendata*, vol. I, Oxford
Dodds, E. R. 1951: *The Greeks and the irrational*, Berkeley
   1960: *Euripides: Bacchae*, Oxford
Dover, K. J. 1968: *Aristophanes: Clouds*, Oxford
   1974: *Greek popular morality in the time of Plato and Aristotle*, Oxford
Drummen, A. 2016: *Particles in ancient Greek discourse: five volumes exploring particle use across genres*, vol. III: *Particle use in Aeschylus, Sophocles, Euripides, and Aristophanes*. Washington, DC
Dubischar, M. 2001: *Die Agonszenen bei Euripides*, Stuttgart
Dugale, E. 2015: 'Hecuba', in R. Lauriola and K. N. Demetriou (eds.), *Brill's companion to the reception of Euripides* (Leiden) 100–42
Dunn, F. M. 1996: *Tragedy's end: closure and innovation in Euripidean drama*, New York
Durand, J.-L. and Lissarrague, F. 1999: 'Mourir à l'autel: remarques sur l'imagerie du "sacrifice humain" dans la céramique attique', *ARG* 1: 83–106
Easterling, P. E. 1987: 'Women in tragic space', *BICS* 34: 15–26
   1993: 'The end of an era? Tragedy in the early fourth century', in A. H. Sommerstein, S. Halliwell, J. Henderson and B. Zimmermann (eds.), *Tragedy, comedy and the polis* (Bari) 559–69
   1994: 'Euripides outside Athens: a speculative note', *ICS* 19: 73–80

Edwards, M. W. 1991: *The Iliad: a commentary*, vol. v: *Books 17–20*, Cambridge
Fantham, E. 1982: *Seneca's Troades*, Princeton
Fantuzzi, M. 1996: 'Odisseo mendicante a Troia e a Itaca: su [Eur.] *Rh.* 498–507; 710–719 e Hom. *Od.* 4, 244–258', *MD* 36: 175–85
2007: 'La *mousa* del lamento in Euripide, e il lamento della Musa nel *Reso* ascritto a Euripide', *Eikasmos* 18: 173–99
2012: *Achilles in love: intertextual studies*, Oxford
Faraone, C. A. 1992: *Talismans and Trojan horses: guardian statues in ancient Greek myth and ritual*, Oxford
Fehling, D. 1968: 'ΝΥΚΤΟΣ ΠΑΙΔΕΣ ΑΠΑΙΔΕΣ: A. *Eum.* 1034 und das sogenannte Oxymoron in der Tragödie', *Hermes* 96: 142–55
1969: *Die Wiederholungsfiguren und ihr Gebrauch bei den Griechen vor Gorgias*, Berlin
Ferrari, F. 1985: 'In margine all'*Ecuba*', *ASNP* 15: 45–9
Finglass, P. J. 2006: 'The interpolated curse', *Hermes* 134: 257–68
2009a: 'Orthographica Sophoclea', *Philologus* 153: 206–28
2009b: 'Sophocles' Tecmessa: characterisation and textual criticism', *Eikasmos* 20: 85–96
forthcoming: 'The textual transmission of Euripides' dramas', in Markantonatos (forthcoming)
Finglass, P. J. and Davies, M. 2014: *Stesichorus: the poems*, Cambridge
Finkelberg, M. 1991: 'Royal succession in heroic Greece', *CQ* 41: 303–16
Fisher, N. R. E. 1992: *Hybris: a study in the values of honour and shame in ancient Greece*, Warminster
Flower, M. A. and Marincola, J. 2002: *Herodotus: Histories, book* IX, Cambridge
Foley, H. P. 2015: *Euripides: Hecuba*, London
Forbes Irving, P. M. C. 1990: *Metamorphosis in Greek myths*, Oxford
Foucault, M. 2001: *Fearless speech*, Los Angeles
Fowler, R. L. 1987: 'The rhetoric of desperation', *HSPh* 91: 5–38
Fraenkel, E. 2007: *Plautine elements in Plautus*, Oxford
Franco, C. 2014: *Shameless: the canine and the feminine in ancient Greece*, Berkeley
Fränkel, H. 1946: 'Man's "ephemeros" nature according to Pindar and others', *TAPhA* 77: 131–45
Fries, A. 2014: *Pseudo-Euripides: Rhesus*, Berlin
Furley, W. D. 2000: '"Fearless, bloodless... like the gods": Sappho 31 and the rhetoric of "godlike"', *CQ* 50: 7–15
Gagarin, M. 1997: *Antiphon: the speeches*, Cambridge
Gagné, R. 2013: *Ancestral fault in ancient Greece*, Cambridge
Gall, D. 1997: 'Menschen, die zu Tieren werden: die Metamorphose in der "Hekabe" des Euripides', *Hermes* 125: 396–412

Gammacurta, T. 2006: *Papyrologica scaenica: i copioni teatrali nella tradizione papiracea*, Alessandria

Garnier, B. 1999: *Pour une poétique de la traduction: l'Hécube d'Euripide en France de la traduction humaniste à la tragédie classique*, Paris

Garrison, E. P. 1995: *Groaning tears: ethical and dramatic aspects of suicide in Greek tragedy*, Leiden

Garvie, A. F. 1969: *Aeschylus' 'Supplices': play and trilogy*, London

George, C. H. 2005: *Expressions of agency in ancient Greek*, Cambridge

Gibert, J. 2011: 'Hellenicity in later Euripidean tragedy', in Carter 2011: 383–401

Gill, C., Postlethwaite, N. and Seaford, R. 1998: *Reciprocity in ancient Greece*, Oxford

Gödde, S. 2000: *Das Drama der Hikesie: Ritual und Rhetorik in Aischylos' Hiketiden*, Münster

Goldhill, S. 1986: *Reading Greek tragedy*, Cambridge

Goldstein, D. M. 2016: *Classical Greek syntax: Wackernagel's law in Herodotus*, Leiden

Gomme, A. W. and Sandbach, F. H. 1973: *Menander: a commentary*, Oxford

Gonda, J. 1959: 'A remark on "periphrastic" constructions in Greek', *Mnemosyne* 12: 97–112

Goodwin, W. W. 1912: *Syntax of the moods and tenses of the Greek verb*, London

Gould, J. 1973: 'HIKETEIA', *JHS* 93: 74–103

2001: *Myth, ritual, memory, and exchange: essays in Greek literature and culture*, Oxford

Gow, A. S. F. and Schofield, A. F. 1953: *Nicander: the poems and poetical fragments*, Cambridge

Grafton, A. J. and Swerdlow, N. M. 1986: 'Greek chronography in Roman epic: the calendrical date of the fall of Troy in the Aeneid', *CQ* 36: 212–18

Gray, V. 2007: *Xenophon on government*, Cambridge

Gregor, D. B. 1957: "Ὦ φίλτατ'", *CR* 7: 14–15

Gregory, J. 1995: 'Genealogy and intertextuality in *Hecuba*', *AJPh* 116: 389–97

1999: *Euripides: Hecuba*, Atlanta

Griffith, M. 1977: *The authenticity of Prometheus bound*, Cambridge

Gundel, J. K. and Fretheim, T. 2004: 'Topic and focus', in L. R. Horn and G. Ward (eds.), *The handbook of pragmatics* (Malden) 174–96

Günther, H.-C. 1995: *The manuscripts and the transmission of the Paleologan scholia on the Euripidean triad*, Stuttgart

Guthrie, W. K. C. 1969: *A history of Greek philosophy*, vol. III: *The fifth-century enlightenment*, Cambridge

Hall, E. 1989: *Inventing the barbarian: Greek self-definition through tragedy*, Oxford

1999: 'Actor's song in tragedy', in S. Goldhill and R. Osborne (eds.), *Performance culture and Athenian democracy* (Cambridge) 96–112
2002: 'The singing actors of antiquity', in P. E. Easterling and E. Hall (eds.), *Greek and Roman actors: aspects of an ancient profession* (Cambridge) 3–38
2006: *The theatrical cast of Athens: interactions between ancient Greek drama and society*, Oxford
Hall, E. and Macintosh, F. 2005: *Greek tragedy and the British theatre, 1660–1914*, Oxford
Hamilton, R. 1978: 'Announced entrances in Greek tragedy', *HSPh* 82: 63–82
Hanink, J. 2014: *Lycurgan Athens and the making of classical tragedy*, Cambridge
Hardie, P. 1997: 'Virgil and tragedy', in C. Martindale (ed.), *The Cambridge companion to Virgil* (Cambridge) 312–26
2015: *Ovidio: Metamorfosi*, vol. VI: *Libri* XIII–XIV, Milan
Harris, E. M. 2013: *The rule of law in action in democratic Athens*, Oxford
2015: 'The family, the community and murder: the role of pollution in Athenian homicide law', in C. Ando and J. Rüpke (eds.), *Public and private in ancient Mediterranean law and religion* (Berlin) 11–36
Harris, W. V. 2001: *Restraining rage: the ideology of anger control in classical antiquity*, Cambridge, Mass.
2009: *Dreams and experience in classical antiquity*, Cambridge, Mass.
Harrison, A. R. W. 1968: *The law of Athens: the family and property*, Oxford
Harrison, T. 2000: *Divinity and history: the religion of Herodotus*, Oxford
Heath, M. 1987a: '"Jure principem locum tenet": Euripides' *Hecuba*', *BICS* 34: 40–68
1987b: *The poetics of Greek tragedy*, London
Heinimann, F. 1945: *Nomos und Physis: Herkunft und Bedeutung einer Antithese im griechischen Denken des 5. Jahrhunderts*, Basel
Henrichs, A. 1975: 'Two doxographical notes: Democritus and Prodicus on religion', *HSPh* 79: 93–123
1981: 'Human sacrifice in Greek religion: three case studies', in J. Rudhard and O. Reverdin (eds.), *Le sacrifice dans l'antiquité* (Vandoeuvres-Geneva) 195–235
1994: '"Why should I dance?" Choral self-referentiality in Greek tragedy', *Arion* 3: 56–111
1996: 'Dancing in Athens, dancing on Delos: some patterns of choral projection in Euripides', *Philologus* 140: 48–62
Herman, G. 1987: *Ritualised friendship and the Greek city*, Cambridge
1990: 'Patterns of name diffusion within the Greek world and beyond', *CQ* 40: 349–63

2006: *Morality and behaviour in democratic Athens: a social history*, Cambridge
Hermann, G. 1831: *Euripidis Hecuba*, Leipzig
Herzog-Hauser, G. 1948: 'Tyche', in K. Ziegler (ed.), *Realencyclopädie der classischen Altertumswissenschaft*, vol. VII.A.2 (Munich and Stuttgart) 1643–89
Heubeck, A., West, S. and Hainsworth, J. B. 1988: *A commentary on Homer's Odyssey*, vol. I: *Introduction and books I–VIII*, Oxford
Hopkinson, N. 2000: *Ovid: Metamorphoses XIII*, Cambridge
Hornblower, S. 1983: *The Greek world, 479–323 BC*, London
2003: 'Panionios of Chios and Hermotimos of Pedasa (Hdt. 8. 104–6)', in P. Derow and R. Parker (eds.), *Herodotus and his world: essays from a conference in memory of George Forrest* (Oxford) 37–57
2008: *A commentary on Thucydides*, vol. III: *Books 5.25–8.109*, Oxford
Horsfall, N. 2006: *Virgil, Aeneid 3: a commentary*, Leiden
Hughes, D. D. 1991: *Human sacrifice in ancient Greece*, London and New York
Itsumi, K. 1982: 'The "choriambic dimeter" of Euripides', *CQ* 32: 59–74
1984: 'The glyconic in tragedy', *CQ* 34: 66–82
1991–3: 'Enoplian in tragedy', *BICS* 38: 243–61
Jacquinod, B. 1989: *Le double accusatif en grec*, Louvain-la-Neuve
Jenkins, I. D. 1985: 'The ambiguity of Greek textiles', *Arethusa* 18: 109–32
Jens, W. 1971: *Die Bauformen der griechischen Tragödie*, Munich
Jocelyn, H. D. 1967: *The tragedies of Ennius*, Cambridge
Johnstone, H. W. 1980: 'Pankoinon as a rhetorical figure in Greek tragedy', *Glotta* 58: 49–62
Jordan, D. R. and Kotansky, R. D. 2011: 'Ritual hexameters in the Getty Museum: preliminary edition', *ZPE* 178: 54–62
Jouan, F. 1966: *Euripide et les légendes des Chants Cypriens*, Paris
Jouanna, J. 1982: 'Réalité et théâtralité du rêve: le rêve dans l'*Hécube* d'Euripide', *Ktèma* 7: 43–52
Kannicht, R. 2004: *Tragicorum Graecorum fragmenta*, vol. V: *Euripides*, Göttingen
Keulen, A. J. 2001: *L. Annaeus Seneca: Troades*, Leiden
King, K. C. 1985: 'The politics of imitation: Euripides' *Hekabe* and the Homeric Achilles', *Arethusa* 18: 47–66
Kirkwood, G. M. 1947: 'Hecuba and nomos', *TAPhA* 78: 61–8
Konstan, D. 1997: *Friendship in the classical world*, Cambridge
2001: *Pity transformed*, London
2006: *The emotions of the ancient Greeks: studies in Aristotle and classical literature*, Toronto
Kopff, E. C. 1990: 'The date of Aristophanes' *Nubes* II', *AJPh* 111: 318–29

Koster, W. J. W. 1974: *Scholia in Aristophanem*, part 1, fasc. 3.2: *Scholia recentiora in Nubes*, Groningen

Kovacs, D. 1987: *The heroic muse: studies in the Hippolytus and Hecuba of Euripides*, Baltimore

1996: *Euripidea altera*, Leiden

Kranz, W. 1933: *Stasimon: Untersuchungen zu Form und Gehalt der griechischen Tragödie*, Berlin

Kron, U. 1981: 'Akamas et Demophon', in L. Kahil (ed.), *LIMC* 1.1: *Aara–Aphlad* (Zurich and Munich) 435–46

Kurke, L. 1991: *The traffic in praise: Pindar and the poetics of social economy*, Ithaca

1999: *Coins, bodies, games, and gold: the politics of meaning in archaic Greece*, Princeton

Lamb, W. R. M. 1967: *Plato in twelve volumes*, vol. III, Cambridge, Mass.

Lane, N. 2007: 'Staging Polydorus' ghost in the prologue of Euripides' *Hecuba*', *CQ* 57: 290–4

Lanza, D. 1963: 'ΝΟΜΟΣ e ΙΣΟΝ in Euripide', *RFIC* 91: 416

Lateiner, D. 1995: *Sardonic smile: nonverbal behavior in Homeric epic*, Ann Arbor

Lauriola, R. and Demetriou, K. N. 2015: *Brill's companion to the reception of Euripides*, Leiden

Lausberg, H. 1998: *Handbook of literary rhetoric: a foundation for literary study*, Leiden

Lee, M. M. 2015: *Body, dress, and identity in ancient Greece*, Cambridge

Ley, G. 1987: 'The date of *Hecuba*', *Eranos* 85: 136–7

Liapis, V. 2012: *A commentary on the Rhesus attributed to Euripides*, Oxford

Lloyd, M. 1992: *The agon in Euripides*, Oxford

1999: 'The tragic aorist', *CQ* 49: 24–45

Lloyd-Jones, H. 1952: 'The robes of Iphigeneia', *CR* 2: 132–5

1972: 'Pindar Fr. 169', *HSPh* 76: 45–56

1990: *Greek epic, lyric, and tragedy: the academic papers of Sir Hugh Lloyd-Jones*, Oxford

Long, A. A. 1968: *Language and thought in Sophocles*, London

2005: 'Law and nature in Greek thought', in M. Gagarin and D. Cohen (eds.), *The Cambridge companion to ancient Greek law* (Cambridge) 412–30

Loraux, N. 1993: *The children of Athena*, Princeton

Lourenço, F. 2011: *The lyric metres of Euripidean drama*, Coimbra

Maas, P. 1951: 'Aeschylus, *Agam*. 231 ff., illustrated', *CQ* 1: 94

MacDowell, D. M. 1963: *Athenian homicide law in the age of the orators*, Manchester

MacLachlan, B. 1993: *The age of grace: charis in early Greek poetry*, Princeton

Macleod, C. 1983: *Collected essays*, Oxford

Manuwald, G. 2000: 'Pacuvius' *Iliona*: eine römische Version des Polydorus-Mythos', in G. Manuwald (ed.), *Identität und Alterität in der frührömischen Tragödie* (Würzburg) 301–14
2012: *Tragicorum Romanorum fragmenta*, vol. II: *Ennius*, Göttingen
Marcovich, M. 1984: *Three-word trimeter in Greek tragedy*, Königstein
Markantonatos, A. (ed.) forthcoming: *Brill's companion to Euripides* (Leiden)
Marr, J. L. and Rhodes, P. J. 2008: *The 'Old Oligarch': the constitution of the Athenians attributed to Xenophon*, Oxford
Marshall, C. W. 1994: 'The rule of three actors in practice', *Text and Presentation* 15: 53–61
2001: 'The consequences of dating the *Cyclops*', in M. Joyal (ed.), *In altum: seventy-five years of classical studies in Newfoundland* (St. Johns) 225–41
2003: 'Casting the *Oresteia*', *CJ* 98: 257–74
2004: '*Alcestis* and the ancient rehearsal process (*P. Oxy.* 4546)', *Arion* 11.3: 27–45
Martindale, C. and Martindale, M. 1990: *Shakespeare and the uses of antiquity*, London
Martinelli, M. C. 1997: *Gli strumenti del poeta: elementi di metrica greca*, Bologna
Mastronarde, D. J. 1979: *Contact and discontinuity: some conventions of speech and action on the Greek tragic stage*, Berkeley
1988: Review of Diggle 1984, *CPh* 83: 151–60
1989: 'Lautensach's law and the augment of compound verbs in EY', *Glotta* 67: 101–5
1990: 'Actors on high: the skene roof, the crane, and the gods in Attic drama', *CA* 9: 247–94
1994: *Euripides: Phoenissae*, Cambridge
2002: *Euripides: Medea*, Cambridge
2010: *The art of Euripides: dramatic technique and social context*, Cambridge
Mastronarde, D. J. and Bremer, J. M. 1982: *The textual tradition of Euripides' Phoinissai*, Berkeley
Matthiae, A. 1821: *Euripidis tragoediae et fragmenta*, vol. VI, Leipzig
Matthiessen, K. 1974: *Studien zur Textüberlieferung der Hekabe des Euripides*, Heidelberg
2010: *Euripides: Hekabe*, Berlin
Matzner, S. 2016: *Rethinking metonymy: literary theory and poetic practice from Pindar to Jakobson*, Oxford
Mazzoldi, S. 2001: *Cassandra, la vergine e l'indovina*, Pisa and Rome
McCabe, M. M. 2008: 'Plato's way of writing', in G. Fine (ed.), *The Oxford handbook of Plato* (Oxford) 88–113

Medda, E. 2012: 'Ifigenia all'altare: il sacrificio di Aulide fra testo e iconografia (Aesch. *Ag.* 231–242)', *Eikasmos* 23: 87–114

Meltzer, G. S. 2006: *Euripides and the poetics of nostalgia*, Cambridge

Mercier, C. E. 1993: 'Hekabe's extended supplication (*Hec.* 752–888)', *TAPhA* 123: 149–60

 1994: '*Hecuba* 154', *Mnemosyne* 47: 217–20

Meridor, R. 1975: 'Eur. *Hec.* 1035–38', *AJPh* 96: 5–6

 1978: 'Hecuba's revenge: some observations on Euripides' *Hecuba*', *AJPh* 99: 28–35

 1979–80: 'Misquotations of Euripides' pleaders', *SCI* 5: 8–15

Michelini, A. N. 1982: *Tradition and dramatic form in the Persians of Aeschylus*, Leiden

Mikalson, J. D. 1991: *Honor thy Gods: popular religion in Greek tragedy*, Chapel Hill

Mitchell, L. G. 1997: *Greeks bearing gifts: the public use of private relationships in the Greek world, 435–323 BC*, Cambridge

Montana, F. and Porro, A. 2014: *The birth of scholiography: from types to texts*, Berlin

Montanari, F., Matthaios, S. and Rengakos, A. 2015: *Brill's companion to ancient scholarship*, Leiden

Moore, T. 2008: 'Parakataloge: another look', *Philomusica online* 7: 143–52

Moorhouse, A. C. 1982: *The syntax of Sophocles*, Leiden

Morenilla Talens, C. 2014: 'Ecos ovidianos en una adaptación de Eurípides: *Hécuba triste* de Pérez de Oliva', *Synthesis* 21: 65–82

Morris, S. P. 1992: *Daidalos and the origins of Greek art*, Princeton

Morrow, G. R. 1937: 'The murder of slaves in Attic law', *CPh* 32: 210–27

Morwood, J. 2009: 'Euripides and the demagogues', *CQ* 59: 353–63

 2014: 'Hecuba and the democrats: political polarities in Euripides' play', *G&R* 61: 194–203

Mossman, J. 1995: *Wild justice: a study in Euripides' Hecuba*, Oxford

Mueller, M. 2001: 'The language of reciprocity in Euripides' *Medea*', *AJPh* 122: 471–504

 2011: 'The politics of gesture in Sophocles' *Antigone*', *CQ* 61: 412–25

Müller, K. O. 1840: *History of the literature of ancient Greece*, London

Murray, G. 1913: *Euripides and his age*, London

Näf, B. 2004: *Traum und Traumdeutung im Altertum*, Darmstadt

Nagy, G. 1979: *The best of the Achaeans: concepts of the hero in archaic Greek poetry*, Baltimore and London

 1990: *Greek mythology and poetics*, Ithaca and London

 2015: *Masterpieces of metonymy: from ancient Greek times to now*, Washington, DC

Naiden, F. S. 2006: *Ancient supplication*, New York and Oxford
Nooter, S. 2012: *When heroes sing: Sophocles and the shifting soundscape of tragedy*, Cambridge
Noussia-Fantuzzi, M. 2010: *Solon the Athenian: the poetic fragments*, Leiden
Nussbaum, M. C. 1986: *The fragility of goodness: luck and ethics in Greek tragedy and philosophy*, Cambridge
O'Connor-Visser, E. A. M. E. 1987: *Aspects of human sacrifice in the tragedies of Euripides*, Amsterdam
O'Sullivan, P. 2008: 'Aeschylus, Euripides, and tragic painting: two scenes from "Agamemnon" and "Hecuba"', *AJPh* 129: 173–98
Ober, J. 1989: *Mass and elite in democratic Athens: rhetoric, ideology, and the power of the people*, Princeton
  1998: *Political dissent in democratic Athens: intellectual critics of popular rule*, Princeton
Ostwald, M. 1969: *Nomos and the beginnings of the Athenian democracy*, Oxford
  1986: *From popular sovereignty to the sovereignty of law: law, society, and politics in fifth-century Athens*, Berkeley
Paduano, G. and Galasso, L. 1999: *Ovidio: opere*, vol. II: *Le metamorfosi*, Turin
Panagl, O. 1971: *Die 'dithyrambischen Stasima' des Euripides: Untersuchungen zur Komposition und Erzähltechnik*, Vienna
Panoussi, V. 2009: *Greek tragedy in Vergil's Aeneid: ritual, empire, and intertext*, Cambridge
Parker, L. P. E. 1958: 'Some observations on the incidence of word-end in anapaestic paroemiacs and its application to textual questions', *CQ* 8: 82–9
  1976: 'Catalexis', *CQ* 26: 14–28
  1997: *The songs of Aristophanes*, Oxford
Parry, M. 1971: *The making of Homeric verse: the collected papers of Milman Parry*, Oxford
Pasquali, G. 1952: *Storia della tradizione e critica del testo*, Florence
Pattoni, M. P. 1989: 'La *sympatheia* del Coro nella parodo dei tragici greci: motivi e forme di un modello drammatico', *SCO* 39: 33–82
  2007: 'L'ingresso del falso *philos*: la scena di Ferete nell'Alcesti di Euripide e i suoi modelli drammatici', *Dioniso* 6: 60–81
Peels, S. 2016: *Hosios: a semantic study of Greek piety*, Leiden
Pertusi, A. 1960: 'La scoperta di Euripide nel primo Umanesimo', *Italia Medievale e Umanistica* 3: 101–52
Pfeiffer, R. 1968: *History of classical scholarship from the beginnings to the end of the Hellenistic age*, Oxford
Pickard-Cambridge, A. W. 1968: *The dramatic festivals of Athens*, Oxford
Pickering, P. E. 2003: 'Did the Greek ear detect "careless" verbal repetitions?', *CQ* 53: 490–9

Platnauer, M. 1960: 'Prodelision in Greek drama', *CQ* 10: 140–4
Pollard, T. 2012: 'What's Hecuba to Shakespeare?', *Renaissance Quarterly* 65: 1060–93
Popp, H. 1971: 'Das Amoibaion', in Jens 1971: 221–75
Porro, A. 1992: 'La versione latina dell'*Ecuba* euripidea attribuita a Pietro da Montagnana', in M. Cortesi and E. V. Maltese (eds.), *Dotti bizantini e libri greci nell'Italia del sec.* xv (Naples) 343–61
Powell, J. U. 1925: *Collectanea Alexandrina*, Oxford
Prag, A. J. N. W. 1991: 'Clytemnestra's weapon yet once more', *CQ* 41: 242–6
Pretagostini, R. 1995: 'L'esametro nel dramma attico del v secolo: problemi di "resa" e di "riconoscimento"', in R. Pretagostini and M. Fantuzzi (eds.), *Struttura e storia dell'esametro greco* (Rome) 163–91
Pritchett, W. K. 1991: *The Greek state at war*, part v, Berkeley
Probert, P. 2003: *A new short guide to the accentuation of ancient Greek*, Bristol
Raaflaub, K. A. 1997: 'Homeric society', in I. Morris and B. Powell (eds.), *A new companion to Homer* (Leiden) 624–48
    2004: *The discovery of freedom in ancient Greece*, Chicago
Race, W. H. 1982: *The classical priamel from Homer to Boethius*, Leiden
Reckford, K. J. 1985: 'Concepts of demoralization in the *Hecuba*', in P. Burian (ed.), *Directions in Euripidean criticism* (Durham, NC) 112–28, 209–13
Redfield, J. M. 2003: *The Locrian maidens: love and death in Greek Italy*, Princeton
Reid, J. D. and Rohmann, C. 1993: *The Oxford guide to classical mythology in the arts, 1300–1990s*, Oxford
Revermann, M. 1999: 'Euripides, tragedy and Macedon: some conditions of reception', *ICS* 24.25: 451–67
Rhodes, P. J. 1986: 'Political activity in classical Athens', *JHS* 106: 132–44
Richardson, N. J. 2010: *Three Homeric hymns: to Apollo, Hermes, and Aphrodite. Hymns 3, 4, and 5*, Cambridge
Riedweg, C. 1990: 'The "atheistic" fragment from Euripides' *Bellerophontes* (286 N^2)', *ICS* 15: 39–53
    2000: 'Der Tragödiendichter als Rhetor? Redestrategien in Euripides' *Hekabe* und ihr Verhältnis zur zeitgenössischen Rhetoriktheorie', *RhM* 143: 1–32
Rijksbaron, A. 2006: 'On false historic presents in Sophocles (and Euripides)', in I. J. F. de Jong and A. Rijksbaron (eds.), *Sophocles and the Greek language: aspects of diction, syntax and pragmatics* (Leiden) 127–49
    2015: 'Stative historical presents in Greek tragedy: are they real?', *Philologus* 159: 224–50

Roberts, D. H. 1987: 'Parting words: final lines in Sophocles and Euripides', *CQ* 37: 51–64
Rode, J. 1971: 'Das Chorlied', in Jens 1971: 85–115
Roisman, H. M. 2014: *The encyclopedia of Greek tragedy*, Chichester
Rose, C. B. 2014: *The archaeology of Greek and Roman Troy*, Cambridge
Rosivach, V. J. 1975: 'The first stasimon of the *Hecuba* 444ff.', *AJPh* 96: 349–62
Ruijgh, C. J. 1976: 'Observations sur l'emploi onomastique de κεκλῆσθαι vis-à-vis de celui de καλεῖσθαι, notamment dans la tragédie attique', in J. M. Bremer, S. L. Radt and C. J. Ruijgh (eds.), *Miscellanea tragica in honorem J.C. Kamerbeek* (Amsterdam) 333–95
Rusten, J. S. 1989: *Thucydides: the Peloponnesian war, book II*, Cambridge
Rutherford, R. B. 2012: *Greek tragic style: form, language, and interpretation*, Cambridge
Sansone, D. 1984: 'On hendiadys in Greek', *Glotta* 62: 16–25
Schibli, H. S. 1990: *Pherekydes of Syros*, Oxford
Schierl, P. 2006: *Die Tragödien des Pacuvius*, Berlin
Schlesier, R. 1988: 'Die Bakchen des Hades: Dionysische Aspekte von Euripides' *Hekabe*', *Métis* 3: 111–35
Schofield, M. 1986: 'Euboulia in the *Iliad*', *CQ* 36: 6–31
Schwartz, E. 1887: *Scholia in Euripidem*, vol. I: *Scholia in Hecubam Orestem Phoenissas*, Berlin
Schwarz, G. 2001: 'Der Tod und das Mädchen: frühe Polyxena-Bilder', *MDAI(A)* 116: 35–50
Schwyzer, E. 1939: *Griechische Grammatik*, vol. I: *Allgemeiner Teil, Lautlehre, Wortbildung, Flexion*, Munich
Scodel, R. 1996: 'Δόμων ἄγαλμα: virgin sacrifice and aesthetic object', *TAPhA* 126: 111–28
  1998: 'The captive's dilemma: sexual acquiescence in Euripides' *Hecuba* and *Troades*', *HSPh* 98: 137–54
  1999: *Credible impossibilities: conventions and strategies of verisimilitude in Homer and Greek tragedy*, Stuttgart
Scullion, S. 2003: 'Euripides and Macedon, or the silence of the *Frogs*', *CQ* 53: 389–400
Seaford, R. 1982: 'The date of Euripides' *Cyclops*', *JHS* 102: 161–72
  1994: *Reciprocity and ritual: Homer and tragedy in the developing city-state*, Oxford
  1998: 'Tragic money', *JHS* 118: 119–39
Sears, M. A. 2013: *Athens, Thrace, and the shaping of Athenian leadership*, Cambridge
Sedley, D. N. 2013: 'The atheist underground', in V. Harte (ed.), *Politeia in Greek and Roman philosophy* (Cambridge) 329–48

Segal, C. 1993: *Euripides and the poetics of sorrow: art, gender, and commemoration in Alcestis, Hippolytus, and Hecuba*, Durham, NC

Seidensticker, B. 1971: 'Die Stychomythie', in Jens 1971: 183–220

Seidensticker, B. and Vöhler, M. 2006: *Gewalt und Ästhetik: zur Gewalt und ihrer Darstellung in der griechischen Klassik*, Berlin and New York

Sewell-Rutter, N. J. 2007: *Guilt by descent: moral inheritance and decision making in Greek tragedy*, Oxford

Sider, D. 1997: *The epigrams of Philodemos*, New York and Oxford

Silk, M. S. 1983: 'LSJ and the problem of poetic archaism: from meanings to iconyms', *CQ* 33: 303–30

Simon, E. 2004: '2.b. Libation', in V. Lambrinoudakis and J. C. Balty (eds.), *Thesaurus cultus et rituum antiquorum*, vol. 1 (Los Angeles) 237–53

Singleton, C. S. 1977: *Dante Alighieri: The divine comedy. Inferno*, vol. 1: *Italian text and translation*, Princeton

Slings, S. R. 1992: 'Written and spoken language: an exercise in the pragmatics of the Greek sentence', *CPh* 87: 95–109

— 1997: 'Figures of speech and their lookalikes: two further exercises in the pragmatics of the Greek sentence', in E. J. Bakker (ed.), *Grammar as interpretation: Greek literature in its linguistic context* (Leiden) 169–214

Sluiter, I. and Rosen, R. M. 2004: *Free speech in classical antiquity*, Leiden

Snell, B. 1966: 'Zu den Urkunden dramatischer Aufführungen', *Nachrichten der Akademie der Wissenschaften in Göttingen: Philol.-hist. Klasse.* 11–37

Sommerstein, A. H. 1982: *Aristophanes: Clouds*, Warminster
2010a: *Aeschylean tragedy*, London
2010b: *The tangled ways of Zeus*, Oxford

Sommerstein, A. H., Fitzpatrick, D. and Talboy, T. 2006: *Sophocles: selected fragmentary plays*, vol. 1, Oxford

Sonnino, M. 2010: *Euripidis Erechthei quae exstant*, Florence

Stamatopoulou, Z. 2012: 'Weaving Titans for Athena: Euripides and the Panathenaic peplos (*Hec.* 466–74 and *IT* 218–24)', *CQ* 62: 72–80

Stanton, G. R. 1995: 'Aristocratic obligation in Euripides' *Hekabe*', *Mnemosyne* 48: 11–33

Steiner, D. 2010: *Homer: Odyssey. Books XVII–XVIII*, Cambridge

Sternberg, R. H. 2005: *Pity and power in ancient Athens*, Cambridge

Stevens, P. T. 1976: *Colloquial expressions in Euripides*, Wiesbaden

Stieber, M. C. 2011: *Euripides and the language of craft*, Leiden

Stinton, T. C. W. 1990: *Collected papers on Greek tragedy*, Oxford

Storey, I. C. 1993: 'The dates of Aristophanes' *Clouds* II and Eupolis' *Baptai*: a reply to E. C. Kopff', *AJPh* 114: 71–84

Sullivan, S. D. 1997: *Aeschylus' use of psychological terminology: traditional and new*, Montreal, Kingston, London and Buffalo

Sutton, D. F. 1980: *The Greek satyr play*, Meisenheim

Swift, L. A. 2009: 'The symbolism of space in Euripidean choral fantasy (*Hipp.* 732–75, *Med.* 824–65, *Bacch.* 370–433)', *CQ* 59: 364–82

Taplin, O. 1977: *The stagecraft of Aeschylus: the dramatic use of exits and entrances in Greek tragedy*, Oxford

   1992: *Comic angels*, Oxford

   1999: 'Spreading the word through performance', in R. Osborne and S. Goldhill (eds.), *Performance culture and Athenian democracy* (Cambridge) 33–57

Tarrant, R. J. 2016: *Texts, editors, and readers: methods and problems in Latin textual criticism*, Cambridge

Telò, M. 2002: 'Per una grammatica dei gesti nella tragedia greca (I): cadere a terra, alzarsi; coprirsi, scoprirsi il volto', *MD* 48: 9–75

Thalmann, W. G. 1993: 'Euripides and Aeschylus: the case of the *Hekabe*', *CA* 12: 126–59

Thompson, W. E. 1971: 'Attic kinship terminology', *JHS* 91: 110–13

Threatte, L. 1980: *The grammar of Attic inscriptions*, vol. I: *Phonology*, Berlin and New York

   1996: *The grammar of Attic inscriptions*, vol. II: *Morphology*, Berlin and New York

Todd, S. C. 2007: *A commentary on Lysias, speeches 1–11*, Oxford

Touchefeu-Meynier, O. 1994: 'Polyxene', in L. Kahil (ed.), *LIMC* VII.1: *Oidipous–Theseus* 431–35

Tuna-Nörling, Y. 2001: 'Polyxena bei Hektors Lösung: zu einem attisch-rotfigurigen Krater aus Tekirdag (Bisanthe/Rhaidestos)', *AA* 1: 27–44

Turyn, A. 1957: *The Byzantine manuscript tradition of the tragedies of Euripides*, Urbana

Ussher, R. G. 1978: *Euripides: Cyclops*, Rome

van Hooff, A. J. L. 1990: *From autothanasia to suicide: self-killing in classical antiquity*, London and New York

Versnel, H. S. 2011: *Coping with the gods: wayward readings in Greek theology*, Leiden

Vian, F. 1952: *La guerre des géants: le mythe avant l'époque hellénistique*, Paris

Visvardi, E. 2011: 'Pity and panhellenic politics: choral emotion in Euripides' *Hecuba* and *Trojan Women*', in Carter 2011: 269–91

Vlassopoulos, K. 2013: *Greeks and barbarians*, Cambridge

Vlastos, G. 1953: 'Isonomia', *AJPh* 74: 337–66

von Reden, S. 1995: *Exchange in ancient Greece*, London

Vossius, G. J. 1647: *De artis poeticae natura ac constitutione liber*, Amsterdam
Wackernagel, J. 2009: *Lectures on syntax with special reference to Greek, Latin, and Germanic*, ed. D. Langslow, Oxford
Wakker, G. 1994: *Conditions and conditionals: an investigation of ancient Greek*, Amsterdam
Walde, C. 2001: *Die Traumdarstellungen in der griechisch-römischen Dichtung*, Munich and Leipzig
Watkins, C. 1967: 'An Indo-European construction in Greek and Latin', *HSPh* 71: 115–19
Weiss, M. 1998: 'Erotica: on the prehistory of Greek desire', *HSPh* 98: 31–61
West, M. L. 1973: *Textual criticism and editorial technique applicable to Greek and Latin texts*, Stuttgart
    1982: *Greek metre*, Oxford
    1984: 'Tragica VII', *BICS* 31: 171–92
    1987: *Introduction to Greek metre*, Oxford
    1990: *Aeschyli tragoediae cum incerti poetae Prometheo*, Stuttgart
    1997: *The East face of Helicon: West Asiatic elements in Greek poetry and myth*, Oxford
    2001: *Studies in the text and transmission of the Iliad*, Munich
    2003: *Greek epic fragments: from the seventh to the fifth centuries BC*, Cambridge, Mass.
    2007: *Indo-European poetry and myth*, Oxford
    2013: *The epic cycle: a commentary on the lost Troy epics*, Oxford
Whitmarsh, T. 2015: *Battling the gods: atheism in the ancient world*, New York
Wilamowitz-Moellendorff, U. v. 1895: *Euripides: Herakles*, Berlin
    1909: 'Lesefrüchte', *Hermes* 44: 445–76
    1926: *Euripides: Ion*, Berlin
    1962: *Kleine Schriften: Lesefrüchte und Verwandtes*, Berlin
Wildberg, C. 2002: *Hyperesie und Epiphanie: ein Versuch über die Bedeutung der Götter in den Dramen des Euripides*, Munich
Williams, B. 1993: *Shame and necessity*, Berkeley
Willink, C. W. 2005: 'Euripides, *Hecuba* 444–6/455–7, *Helen* 1465–77, *Bacchae* 565–75', *Mnemosyne* 58: 499–509
Winiarczyk, M. 1990: 'Methodisches zum antiken Atheismus', *RhM* 133: 1–15
Wohl, V. 1998: *Intimate commerce: exchange, gender, and subjectivity in Greek tragedy*, Austin
    2015: *Euripides and the politics of form*, Princeton
Worman, N. 2002: *The cast of character: style in Greek literature*, Austin

Yunis, H. 1988: *A new creed: fundamental religious beliefs in the Athenian polis and Euripidean drama*, Göttingen

Zeitlin, F. I. 1996: *Playing the other: gender and society in classical Greek literature*, Chicago

Zuntz, G. 1955: *The political plays of Euripides*, Manchester
  1965: *An inquiry into the transmission of the plays of Euripides*, Cambridge

SUBJECT INDEX

Italic numbers refer to the pages of the Introduction; all other references are to line numbers as they are recorded at the beginning of each note in the Commentary. There are no entries for characters in the play.

Acamas 122
accusative 1065, 1073–4; absolute 118–19; cognate 282; depending on passive verb 910–11; double 644–6, 812; internal 271, 911–12; of direction 162–3, 209, 1059–60; of duration 33–4; of respect 359, 989, 1035; of space traversed 1104–6; with verbs of exchanging 1059–60
Achilles 3, 37–9, 40–1, 113–15, 134–5, 188–90, 263, 305, 306–8, 388, 523, 534–41, 536, 551–2, 612, 1125–6; spear 127–9; pyre 436–7; tomb 37–9, [93], 109–10, 150; worshipped as hero 538–41
actors 4–5
address, shift from third to second person 1197; to a part of the body 170–2
adjective, attributive 606–8; coined by Euripides 448–9; compound 151–3, 208, 470–2, 473–4, 478–9, 581, 651–2, 686–7, 708, 933; compound in -πετής 1100–1; ending in -ησιος 831–2; ending in -τος 651–2; order of adjectives modifying the same noun 1184; predicative 606–8, 824, 1032–3; proleptic 499–500, 782; used substantively 880–2; with alpha privative 416, (*see also* alpha privative)
Aeolic cola 444–83, 'Metre', 629–57'Metre', 905–52'Metre'
Aeschylus, *Ag.*: 518–82; 1: 953–1295, 1292; 155: 1277; 231–43: 526; 231–4: 544–5; 232: 524; 233: 150; 239: 558–61; 242: 560; 1035–46: 359; 1343–5: 953–1295; 1343: 1035; 1353: 1042–3; *Cho.* 585–98: 1177–82
agōn 216–443, 271, 1130–1251, 1132–82, 1183, [1185–6], 1187–1237, 1205, 1252–95
Aithiopis 388
alastōr 686–7, 948–9
Alcman 77 *PMG*: 945

allusive language 1023–34
alpha privative 30, 612, 669, 714
altar 150
ambiguity 1021–2, 1054–5
amoibaion 684–721
anacoluthon 971
anadiplosis 167–8, 909, 930, 1028–31, 1063, 1095–6, (*see also* repetition)
anapaests 26, 59–97, 'Metre', [62–3], 98–153, 146–7, 154–215'Metre'; colometry 98–153; sung: 26; symmetry of syntax and metre in anapaests 155
anaphora 629–30
anastrophe 207–8, 292, 354–5, [504], 749
anceps 26
ancient scholarship on the play 568–70, 847
anger 299–300
animal imagery 12, 90–1, 142, 177–9, 205, 206, 1054–5, 1058–9, 1162–4, 1172–5, 1252–95
antidemocratic sentiments 606–8, 864–9
antilabē 1127, 1283
antithesis 860, 902–3
aorist, gnomic 597–8, 847; passive used in a middle sense 546
Aphrodite 825
Apidanus 453–4
apocope 1100–1, 1263
Apollo 458–61, 827, 1270
apostrophe 905
apposition 19, 37–9, 131–3, 303–5, 644–6, 771, 790, 921, 1252–3; internal 460–1; partitive 623–5; to the sentence 1028–31
Ares 1088–90
aristocracy, aristocratic 11, 216–95, 299–331, 375–8, 379–80, 592–8, 600–2, 623–5, 866–7, 1187–1237
Aristophanes, *Nub.* 718–19: 2–3; 1165–6: 2

arrival, at the same time 966; onstage after a cry for help 1109–13
arrogance 1183
arrows 603
Artemis 444–83, 458–61, 935–6
article, repeated 156–8
aside 736–51
assembly 107
astrophic monody 1056–1108
asymmetric syntax 346–8, 623–5, 642–3, 916–18, 1017, 1197–8
asyndeton 70, 86, 278, 387, 507, 840, 847, 997, 1056–7, 1171, 1175, 1205; contrastive 265; explanatory 394–5
atheism 798–805
Athena 444–83; *peplos* for Athena 444–83, 467–70, 472; temple at Troy 1008
Athenian legal practices 291
Attic chauvinism 444–83
audience expectations 1023–34
augment in ηὐ- 18, 301
Augustus 65–7

bacchants 1076
banishment to a desert island 1284–5
barathron 1077–8
barbarians and Greeks *13*, 299–331, 328–31, 1056–1108, 1129, 1187–1237, 1199–1204, 1247
bay tree 458–61
blindness 1066–8, 1107–8, 1265
blood 23–4, 536–7
breastfeeding 424
breuis in longo 27
bride of Hades 210
Briseis 127–9
brooches 1170
burial 484–628, 781, [793–7], 896–7, 1287–90, (*see also* funeral)

cannibalism 1071, 1125–6
Cassandra *12*, 127–9, 827, 830, 1275
castration *16*
Catullus 64.362–70: 518–82
causative verb 53–4
change of addressee 1232
charis 10–14, 131–3, 137, 216–95, 254, 276, 299–331, 384, 830, 855, 1201
chiasm 1079–81
choral 'tag' 296–8, 332–3
chorus 98–153, 444–83, 629–57, 905–52; fail to intervene 1035–41
Cicero, *Tusc.* 3.63: *20*

circle of human affairs 639
Cleanthes 346–8, 369
Cleon 216–95
Clytemnestra 1278
cognitio metrorum 27
colloquialism 613–14, 976, 977, 989, 997, 1257, 1280
colon 27
commentaries, ancient *24*
comparative, reinforced 377
concubinage 834
contact: dialogic 1019–22; physical 245, 334–5, 548–9, 752–3; verbal 736–51; visual 501–2, 684–721, 1044–6
contamination *23*
contrary-to-fact wish 394–5
convention 798–805
correption 64
counterfactual [796–7], 1112
cries from within 1035–41, 1037
Critias *TrGF* 43 F 19.25–6: 798–805
Croesus 623–5, 1268–9
cry for help 1088–98
Cynossema *9*, 1273

dactylo-epitrite 905–52, 'Metre'
dactyls 154–215, 'Metre'
Daedalus 470–2, 836–40
Danaids 886–7
Dante, *Inferno 20*
dative, ethical 426–8, 1195; instrumental 271, 432, 586–8; of advantage 1187; of agent 255, 448–9; of interest 255, 535, 605–6
daylight 32, 68, 167–9, 248, 367–8, 707
deception scenes 1019–22
Delian maidens 462–3
Delos 2, 444–83
demagogue 131–3, 299–331
democracy, democratic *12*, 98–153, 288, 293–4, 864–9, 1253
demonstrative 8, 325; refers to the speaker 202–4, 519–20; used of a character present onstage 674, 778, 966, 1196, 1219
Demophon 122
dialogue, three-way 216–443
Didymus of Alexandria *24*, 847
Dionysus 685–6, 716–21; oracle of 1267
Dioscuri 943–52
direct speech 929–30
dismemberment 716–21

SUBJECT INDEX

dithyrambic style 905–52
dochmius 1023–34, 'Metre', 1056–1108, 'Metre'
dog *9*, *12*, 1252–95, 1265
Dorian women 629–57, 934
'Doric' genitive plural of first declension 482–3
dream 59–97, 71, 703–4, 704–5

Earth 79
Echo 1110–11
Edonians 1153
eisodos 5–7
ekkyklēma 1051–3
ellipsis 843, 876–8
emotion, lack of in stichomythia 1252–95
enallage 467
enclitic pronoun 13, 136–7
enjambment 389–90, 620–1, 731–2, 1114–15, 1148, 1220–1
Ennius *18*
enoplian 629–57, 'Metre', 905–52, 'Metre'
entrance onstage 87–9; announced 724–5; 'at the right moment' 666
ephemeral nature of human beings 285, 317–18, 623–5, 627–8
Epicharmus 472
epimonē 281
Erasmus *21*
erotic gaze 560
escape ode 444–83
ethnicity: *see* barbarians and Greeks; Thrace
etymology [441–3], 631, 649–50, 1250–1
euphemism 252, 473–4, 731–2, 826, 863, 873, 875, 1232
Euripides, life and works *1–2*; *Cycl.*: *3*; 663: 1035; 663–701: 953–1295; *Hcld.* 530–1, 550–1: 548–9; *Or.* 512–17: *15*; *Pho.*: 444–83; *Tro.* 176–229: 444–83; fr. 175: 548–9
Europe 482–3
Eurotas 649–50
eye 1035, 1265; eye contact 342–5, 972, (*see also* blindness)

fire 608
focus of the sentence *28*
freedom *11*, 367–8, 864–75; of speech 234–7

friendship see *philia*
funeral 578, 611; *ekphora* 613–18; *prothesis*: 613, (see also burial)
fury 1128

gender 568–70, 573–4, 879, 885, 1132–82, 1154, 1155–6, 1157, 1166, 1170, 1184, 1252–3
general reflection 283, 328–31, 375–8, 379–80, 848–9, 903–4, 953–60
genitals 568–70
genitive 65–7, 961, 970, 1076; objective 1072; of cause 156–8, 182, 425, 475–8, 661, 1255; of direction 760; of explanation 296–8; of person from whom it is heard 237; of quality 198; of separation 605–6; of what is taken in exchange 482–3; partitive 192–3, 605–6, 609–10; referring to the first element of a compound adjective 478–9
Getty hexameters from Selinus 151–3
ghost *3*, *18*, 1–58, 37–9, 993
gods *14*, 163–4, 787–845, 791, 798–805, 1028–31; divine cruelty 956–61; divine intervention 47–50, 900, 902, 953–1295
gold 109–10, 151–3, 463–5, 543–4, 636, 1148
Gorgias 262–70, 850–63, 1250–1
gratitude 831–2, (see also *charis*)

Hades 2, 79, 1032–3, 1076, 1104–6
hair 837
happiness 627–8
haste 98
Hector 21–2, 356, 1210, 1270
Helen 269, [441–3]
Helenus 87–9
Hellanicus 1102–4
hendiadys 436–7
Heracles 905–52, 906
heralds 484, (*see also* messenger)
Hermotimos *16*
hero cult 527–9, 536, 538–41 (*see also* Achilles)
Herodotus 59–97; 1.30–2: 623–5; 1.207.2: 639; 3.38.4: 798–805; 5.87: 1170; 8.104–6: *16*; 9.120: *17*
hexameter 59–97, 'Metre'
hiatus 27; after τί 1211
hiding 1013
hierodouloi 462–3

Homer, language 205, 356, 394–5, 473–4, 649–50, 907–8, 922, 1061, 1081–4; phrases 117–18, 123, 131–3, 172–3, 246, 322–3, 438, [555–6], 566, 631–5, 857, 915, 976, 1023–34, 1024–7, 1028–9; scenes 553, 736–51, (see also *Iliad, Odyssey*)
Homeric technique 891–94
homicide 292; homicide law 291
hope, deceitful 1032–3
human sacrifice 260, 305, 342–78, 518–82, 548–9
hunting imagery *12*, 1172–5
hybris 1257
Hymn.Hom.Ap. 156–76: 462–3
hymnic style 444–6
hyperbaton 136–7, 292, 299–300, 325, 401, 455–7, 467–70, 690, 749, 1081–4, 1175–7, 1229, 1252–3
Hyperbolus *3*
hyperonym 143
hyponym 716–21
hysteron proteron 266, 762

iambic cola 629–57, 'Metre'
iambic trimeter 25; chanted 684–721; resolution 2, 26
Ibycus 307 *PMG 8*
Iliad 1: 127–9; 1.4–5: 1077–8; 1.118–19: 113–15; 1.118–87: 40–1; 1.163–8: 306–8; 1.176: 231–3; 1.363: 183; 5.62–3: 631–5; 6.269–310: 3; 6.288–95: 444–83; 6.356: 640; 6.474: 1158; 9.316–20: 306–8; 18.74: 183; 23: 1–58, 518–82; 23.218–21: 527–9; 24.28: 640; 24.253–62: 620–1
Iliona *18*
Ilium 922
Iliupersis 8, 23–4, 122, 905–52, 909, 1102–4
impersonal construction 108–9, 195–6, 854, 957
inconsistency 1016
interlaced word order 44, (*see also* hyperbaton)
interpolation 22–3, 59–97, [62–3], [73–8], 90–1, [92–7], [145], 199–200, [211–15], 402–4, [412], [441–3], [490], [504], [531–3], [599], 600–2, [756–9], [793–7], 973–5, [1087], [1185–6], 1211
interrogative, placed late in the sentence 829–30, 876–8

intransitive verb, used transitively 1070; with passive meaning 301, 494
Iphigenia 260, 560
irony 670, 962–7, 990, 992, 1004, 1023
isonomia 291

justice 798–805, 801, 1023–34, 1028–31, 1136–7, 1191

katapontismos 1262
kinship 1203
Kisses *8*
Kisseus *8*, *3*

lament 296–8, 684–721, 685
language 1187–94; cannot match reality 667
law 787–845, 798–805, 802, 847, 1253
left dislocation 109–10
left periphery 595
Lemnian women 886–7
Leto 458–61
libations 527–9, 535
line attribution 1041
litotes 1109, 1113
Little Iliad 122, 239, 914
Locrian Maidens 444–83
Lycophron 1252–95, 1270
Lycurgus (king of Thrace) 716–21
Lysias 2.19: 798–805; 2.18: 613–18; 12.24: 972

magic 72, 836–40
mantic 743
manuscripts 23–24, 25, 29; open manuscript tradition 23
marriage 351–3, 416, (*see also* wedding)
mask 1117
mēchanē 1–58
medical language 567
Menelaus 510
messenger *3*, 98–153, 104–6, 108–9, 484–628, 658–83, 684–721, 953–1295, 1035–41; emotionally involved 518–82; general reflections 581; name of 484; trustworthy 524
metamorphosis *9*, 1252–95, 1264, 1272
metaphor 65–7, 80, 125–6, 142, 246, 568, 583–4, 603, 623–5, 662, 734–5, 831–2, 907–8, 910–11, 1023–34, 1024–7, 1054–5, 1076, 1129, 1160, 1162–4, 1210, 1214
metonymy 1–2, 120–2, 460–1, 567, 1153
metrical dovetailing 1023–34, 'Metre'

metrical pause 27
middle voice 720–1, 1058–9; 'mental process' middle 801
mind, imagined as a board 589–90
mirror 923–6
misdirection 1021–2
misogyny 885, 1177–82, 1179, (*see also* gender)
mitra 923–6
mixed emotions 382–3, 518–82
mocking 1264
moderation 996, 997
monologue 1–58, 229–33, 736–51, 743
Mount Ida 325, 631
mourning 653–7
mutability of fortune 283, 956–61

narrative technique 905–52; in stichomythia 998–1000
nautical imagery 1079–81
necrophilia 558–61, 605–6
negative, position of 866–7; with verb of saying 127–9
Neoptolemus *8*, 566
Nicander *20*, 1270
nightingale 337–8
nominative 971; with imperative 328–31
nomos 798–805, 799–800
Nostoi 8, 37–9, 87–9
nostos 932
noun, abstract 606–8; abstract, explained by defining adjective 362, 1015; used as an adjective 117–18, 274–5
nudity 558–61, 934, 1170

Odyssey 4.242–58: 239; 9.12–13: 518; 9.293: 1071; 11: 518–82; 19.204–9: 433–4; 19.228: 90–1
Oedipus 1117
omen 1276
ominous words 1006, 1019–22, 1021–2
optative 713, 836, 1149; in consecutive clauses 852–5; present, expressing a wish referring to the future 255
oracle 1268–9
Orion 1066–8, 1100–6, 1102–4
Ovid, *Met.* 13: *19–20*; 13.449–82: 518–82; 13.464: [213–14]; 13.466–9: 548–9; 13.475–6: 566; 13.547–71: 22
oxymoron 194, 566

Pacuvius *18*
palm 458–61

Panionios *16*
papyri 23, 29
paradosis 25, 243
paradox 617–18, 659–60, 668, 785, 786, 1066–8, 1172–5
parallelism 850–63
parenthesis 824, 875, 1160
Paris 387, 488–91, 629–57, 905–52, 945; Judgement of 631–5, 640, 644–6
parodos 98–153
paroemiac 26, 154–215, 'Metre'
partial vision of a character entering onstage 733–4
participle, coupled with noun phrase 623–5; coupled with prepositional phrase 346–8, 916–18, 1197–8; governing a relative 994; governing an interrogative 177–9, 448–9; neuter used as abstract noun 299–300; participles in asyndeton, describing successive actions 609–10; present, referring to the past 620–1, 821
particles 1118–19
Peloponnesian War 629–57
performative verb 1276
Pericles 293–4, 299–331
periphrasis 362, 619, 676–7, 724–5, [795], 812, 929–30, 939–40, 963, 965, 977, 1179
periphrastic forms of verb 120–2
Persian wars 906
personal pronoun reinforced by μόνος 243
persuasion 787–845, 816, 1187–1237
philia 10–14, 216–95, 311–12, 848–9, 859–60; untrustworthy friend 953–1295
phyllobolia 11, 573–4
Pindar, fr. 169a: 798–805
Pindaric construction 998–1000
pity 286–7, 806–8
plants 20, 592–8; oak 398
Plato, *Grg.* 482c4–483c6: 798–805; *Prt.* 324a6–b4: *15*; *Resp.* 348d: 1136–7
pleasure in lamentations and suffering 518
pledge 1028–31
plural, alternating with singular 998–1000; distributive 130–1; first person plural 244, 693; first person plural, alternating with singular 370–1, 806–8; masculine

SUBJECT INDEX

generalising 237, 670; neuter plural in reference to an infinitive 1107–8; poetic 11–12, 134–5, 265, 339–41, 402–4, 455–7, 619, 750, 880–2, 1195
polar expressions 146–7, 659
political language 219
pollution 972
Polygnotus 558–61
Polyphemus 953–1295
polyptoton 137–40, 850–63
Porson's law 729, 1006
posthumous honours 313–16
prayer 534–41; not completely fulfilled 541
present tense, historical 10, 21–2, 527–9, 937, 966, 1148; for an action that began in the past and continues in the present 85–6; for an action that will continue in the future 302; for an impending action 184–5; present effect of a past action 266, 695–6, 1134 (*see also* optative)
preverb 167–8
Priam 61, 496; children of 361, 421, 620–1
Priamel 798–805
Procne 337–8
prodelision 387, 901
propemptikon 943–52
prophecy 1252–95, 1270, 1271, 1275
prosaic words and phrases 141
Protagoras *15*
public and private 640
punishment, theories of *15*
Pylos 2
pyre 527–9

question 238; aporetic 736–7, 1099; direct/indirect 984; double 1075; implying a negative answer 829–30; indignant 715, 1257; indirect 351–3; information-seeking 984; question-and-answer patterns 760; rhetorical 154, 785, with deliberative subjunctives 1056–7

rage 1054–5
reciprocity *9–14*, 272, 1187–1237, 1199–1204, 1207
redundancy 26, 37–9, 65–7, 102–3, 334–5, 414, 470–2, 473–4, [490], 525, 701, 827, 922, 927, 938

relative, antecedent implied from an adjective 709–12; attraction 1021–2; singular, after plural antecedent 360
repetition 59–60, 526–8, [531–3], 655–7, 1024–7; of lines 279, [1087], (*see also* anadiplosis)
resolution *see* iambic trimeter
revenge *14–18*, 864–75
rhetoric 147–53, 250, 262–70, 340, 349, 518–82, 787–845, 798–805, 816, 817–18, 836–40, 984, 1132–82, 1175–7, 1238–9
riddle 734–5
road imagery 744, 961

sarcasm 743
Schadenfreude 629–57
scholia *24*
seething 583–4, 1054–5
self-address 736–7
Seneca, *Tro. 20–21*; 1118–64: 518–82; 1154: 566
servant, in stage action 609
sex 825, 831–2, 933
Shakespeare, *Hamlet* 22; *Titus Andronicus* 22
shame 432, 968–75, 970, 1240–51
shortening in hiatus 59–97, 'Metre', 1056–1108, 'Metre'
sigmatism 247
silence [531–3]
Simois 641
singular 1058–9; generalising 575; representative 65–7; singular predicate with two subjects 606–8; singular verb with two subjects 21–2, 458–61
Sirius 1100–6, 1102–4
skēnē 5–7, 53–4; *skēnē* door 5, 1044–6
slavery 234–7, 291, 332–3, 362, 397, 864–75, 864–9, 1252–3
smoke 823, 1215
social constraints 864–75
Solon 623–5
sophia 228, 399, 1007, 1136–7, 1187–1237
sophists 238, 798–805, 817–18
Sophocles, *El.* 59–97, 1035–41, 1279; *Phil.* 953–1295; *Polyxena 3*, 1–2, 37–9
Sparta 2, 629–57, 905–52, 934
speaker names 693
spears 1155–6
speediness 98
stage movements 5–7, 904

Stesichorus, frr. 98–164 Finglass: 905–52
subject, logical 971
subjunctive, deliberative 162–3, 1042, 1056–7; subjunctive and optative after verbs of fearing 1138–43
subversion of linguistic and moral standards 608
suicide 1100–6, 1107–8
superlative, reinforced 620–1; 'rhetorical' 799–800
supplication 216–443, 245, 274–5, 334–5, 342–5, 345, 736–51, 752–3, 787–845, 787, 836–40, 837; through touching the chin 286
synecdoche 16–17, 37–9, 386, 1066–8
synecphonesis 1056–1108, 'Metre', 1249
synizesis 59–97, 'Metre', 110, 551
synonym 156–8
syntax, completed
in stichomythia 1259; running over from antistrophe to epode 647–8; ἀπὸ κοινοῦ construction 28–9, 370–1, 467–8

tact 674
tautology 998–1000
Telemachus 339–41
tetracolon 669
textiles 1154
Theano 8, 3
theologeion 1–58
Thrace 3, 81, 963, 1143–4
three-word trimeters 669
Thucydides 2, 15, 216–95, 260, 293–4
tit for tat 1086, 1250–1
Titans 472
tmesis [504], 907–8, 1172
tomb 221, 726, 1271
topic of the sentence 27, 120–2, 231–3, 332–3, 595, 986
Troy 906, 922; date of the fall 1102–4

tychē 488–91, 786
Tyndareus 15

veiling 432
violence 15, *18*, 716–21, 879, 1034, 1252–95, 1280
Virgil, *Aen.* 3: *19*
virtue 592–8, 600–2
visual arts 523, 524, 558–61, 806–8, 836–40
visual revelation of dead bodies 678–80
vocative, position of 1122–3
voice of actors 1114–15
vox media 786

walking on all fours 1058–9
weakness 798
weaving 363
wedding 523, 611, 612
wind 37–9, 111–12, 444–6, [531–3], 901, 902, 1287–90, 1289–90
women *see* gender
word end (caesura) in iambic trimeters 1159
word or concept supplied from the context 23–4, 155, [211–12], 240, 284, 451, 492, 541, 605–6, 950–2, 957, 961, 970, 976, 1189, 1231
word order 642–3, 1047, (*see also* hyperbaton, left dislocation, topic of sentence)
wordplay with numbers 45, 896–7
written laws 866–7

Xanthippos *17*
xenia 9, 10–14, 781, [794], 1187–1237, 1229

Zenodotus 1077–8
zeugma 409–11
Zeus 345, 488–91, 707; thunderbolt 473–4

GREEK INDEX

αἵμων 90–1
ἀλίαστον 85–6
ἄλλως 'mistakenly' 488–9
ἀμαθία 327
ἄμιλλα . . . λόγων 271
ἀμφί + acc. 706
ἀνάγκη 362, 1293–5; ἀνάγκαι 'obligations' 847
ἀνθρωποσφαγέω 260
ἄντλος 1024–7
ἀνύω + ptcp. 935–6
ἀξίωμα 293–4
ἄρα 231–3
ἆρα 469
ἀράσσω 1044–6

βοή 177

γάρ after a voc. 736–7
γε + 'epexegetic' participial clause 615
γέρας 113–15
γνώμη 188–90

δαίμων 163–4
δαῖτα 1077–8
δέ γ' 'however' 1248
δεινός 379–80; δεινόν introducing a general reflection 846
δή 1135
δίκην 'like' 1162–4
Δῖος 460–1
διοτρεφής 231–3
δόξαι 108–9
δουλόσυνος 448–9
δύναι 253

ἔα 733–4
ἐδάην [73–8]
εἶέν 313
εἰσοράω 'I see, I realise' 954–5
ἐκπίπτω + gen. 'to fall out of' 1024–7
ἐκποδών 52–3
ἐπεί '<I say this> because' 1208
ἐπί + dat. 642–3
ἔχω governing abstract nouns 672–3

ἤ introducing a surmise question 829–30, 1013
ἦ γάρ 765
ἡγέομαι θεούς 799–800

ἠδέ 322–3
ἥσυχος 35–6
ἠχώ 155

θεόδμητος 'built for the gods, sacred' 23–4

ἰδού 'look, here it is' 1041
ἰσόθεος 356
ἴσον 'what is equitable' 805
ἰώ 177

καί 294–5; καί . . . μέν δή 'in any case' 603; καὶ μήν 216; καὶ μήν . . . μέν 824; καί + relative clause 13
κάμνω + ἐν with dative 306–8
κατάρατος 716
κηδεστήν 'male affine' 834
κηδεύω + acc. 1202
κῆρυξ 104–6
κλυών aorist (accent) 743

λαγόνας 'waist, flanks' 559
λέγω 'I reckon, estimate' 828
λιάζομαι 98

μᾶλλον 'too much' 745–6
μάτην 'falsely' 488–9
μέμφομαι 'I have little consideration for' 885
μὲν οὖν 16–17
μεταξύ 436–7
μήπω 'never' 1278
μόσχον 206

νήνεμον [531–3]
νιν 265
νόμωι 'because of the law' 799–800; 'by convention' 798–805

ὅ 'wherefore' 13
ὄζος 123
οἶσθ' οὖν ὃ δρᾶσον 225
οἶσθα-questions 760, 1008
ὅμοια 398
ὅμως 'all the same' 497–8
ὄνομα/ἔργον 357
ὅσιον 'sanctioned by divine law' 804
οὐ μή + aor. subj. 1039

οὐδέν τι μᾶλλον 817–18
οὔκουν 251
οὖν + imperatives 369
οὗτος 'hey, you' 1127, 1280
ὄχλος 'the populace' 868; in reference to objects 1014

πανόδυρτος [212]
πεῖσμα 'mooring cable' 1079–81
πεπρωμένη 43
πέστημα 'corpse' 699–700
πλήν 596
πόθεν; 'no way!' 613–14
προπετής 150
πρός + acc. 188–90
πρόφασις 340

ῥιφθέντες 334–5

σαθρός 'unsound' 1190
σθένος 49
σόφισμα 258
συγκεκλῃμένη 486–7
συμπίπτω 846, 1028–31
σφαγή 1037
σφε 260
σχῆμα 619

τ'... δ' indicating contrast 606–8
τε placed after prepositional phrase 831–2; τε... τε 'just as' 519–20
τί λέξεις; 511
τί... πάθω; 'what else am I to do?' 613–14

τίθημι ἐν + abstract noun 806
τις + def. article 623–5; τις in reference to the speaker 820
τοιαῦτα 'exactly' 776
τόλμα 'act of daring' 1122–3
τολμάω 326

ὑπό + gen. 146–7

φάντασμα 'vision in a dream' 53–4, 704–5
φεῦ φεῦ 'ah!', expressing admiration 1238–9
φοῖνιξ 458–61
φροίμια 181
φροῦδος 160–1
φύσει 'by nature' 798–805

χαίρουσιν 426–8
χαρακτήρ 379–80
χηλῆι 90–1
χλωρῶι 125–6
χρή 260
χωρίς 860

ψυχή 21–2

ὦ repeated, linking connected words 414
ὦ φίλτατ' 505
ὤιμοι 201
ὡς at sentence beginning 400; 'because' 662; exclamatory 662
ὥς for οὕτως [441–3]
ὥστε 205